MW00799204

A TREATISE

May 27
117

ON

THE LAW OF MORTGAGES

AND

DEEDS OF TRUST

FOUNDED ON

The Laws and Judicial Decisions of
the State of Illinois

BY

HENRY CAMPBELL BLACK, M. A.

AUTHOR OF "BLACK'S LAW DICTIONARY" AND OF TREATISES ON "JUDGMENTS,"
"TAX TITLES," "CONSTITUTIONAL LAW," "STATUTORY
CONSTRUCTION," "BANKRUPTCY," ETC.

———

CHICAGO
CALLAGHAN & COMPANY
1903

e/ʌ 12m

JUN 5 1934

Walter T Fisher

BROWN-COOPER TYPESETTING CO.
CHICAGO

PREFACE.

The following pages contain a complete and systematic discussion of the law of mortgages of real estate, including mortgages with power of sale and trust deeds in the nature of mortgages, as the same is regulated by the statutes of the State of Illinois and formulated and applied by the courts of that jurisdiction. Citations will be found to all the reported decisions of the courts of Illinois, including those contained in volume 200 of the reports of the Supreme Court and volume 105 of the Appellate Court reports, so far as they are applicable to the general subject. References have also been incorporated to the decisions of the United States Supreme Court in cases appealed from Illinois, and to the rulings of the inferior federal courts sitting within the State. In addition, numerous decisions of other states have been cited, not as cumulative to the Illinois cases, nor in relation to rules or principles already well settled by the courts of Illinois, but in reference to those details of the law of mortgages as to which the home tribunals have not yet fully expressed themselves. With a view to promote the utility of the work, as a manual of the law of mortgages for use in all the courts where the Illinois practitioner may have occasion to plead, a chapter has been added on Mortgage Foreclosure in the Federal Courts, having reference particularly to the jurisdiction of those courts in cases of this character and to the extent to which their proceedings and decrees are governed by the local laws or practice.

H. C. B.

Washington, D. C., September 1, 1903.

TABLE OF CONTENTS.

CHAPTER I.

THE NATURE OF MORTGAGES.

CHAPTER II.

ABSOLUTE DEEDS TREATED AS MORTGAGES.

CONTENTS.

CHAPTER III.
EQUITABLE MORTGAGES.

- Equitable Mortgages in General.
- Mortgages Defectively Executed.
- Informal Writings Creating a Lien.
- Agreement to Give a Mortgage.
- Advance of Purchase Money.
- Vendor's Lien.
- Deposit of Title Deeds.

CHAPTER IV.
TRUST DEEDS AND POWER-OF-SALE MORTGAGES.

- Trust Deed in the Nature of a Mortgage.
- Trust Deeds Not Contrary to Public Policy.
- Holder of Obligation Secured.
- Legal Title Vested in Trustee.
- Estate Remaining in Grantor.
- What Persons Competent as Trustees.
- Removal and Substitution of Trustees.
- Powers and Duties of Trustees.
- Release on Payment.
- Mortgages with Power of Sale.

CHAPTER V.
MORTGAGES BY CORPORATIONS.

- Power of Corporation to Execute Mortgage.
- Mortgage of Corporate Franchises.
- Authority of Board of Directors.
- Mortgage made by Officers of Corporation.
- Defense of Ultra Vires and Invalidity.
- Mortgages by Railroad Companies.
- Religious Corporations.
- Loan Associations.
- Municipal Corporations.
- Consolidated Corporations.

CHAPTER VI.
FORM AND CONTENTS OF MORTGAGES.

- Formal Requisites of a Mortgage.
- Description of Parties.
- Description of Property Mortgaged.
- Statement of Debt Secured.
- Anticipation of Time of Payment.
- Covenant for Payment of Debt.
- Habendum.
- Covenants of Title and Warranty.

CHAPTER VII.

EXECUTION, ACKNOWLEDGMENT AND DELIVERY OF MORTGAGES.

CHAPTER VIII.

PARTIES TO MORTGAGES.

CHAPTER IX.

MORTGAGEABLE INTERESTS IN REALTY.

CHAPTER X.

PROPERTY COVERED BY A MORTGAGE.

CHAPTER XI.

THE CONSIDERATION OF MORTGAGES.

CHAPTER XII.

FRAUDULENT AND INVALID MORTGAGES.

CHAPTER XVI.

ASSIGNMENT OF MORTGAGES.

CHAPTER XVII.

INSURANCE OF MORTGAGED PROPERTY.

CHAPTER XVIII.

TAXATION OF MORTGAGES AND OF MORTGAGED LANDS.

CHAPTER XIX.

DOWER IN MORTGAGED ESTATES.

CHAPTER XX.

RELATIVE RIGHTS OF PARTIES BEFORE BREACH OF CONDITION.

CHAPTER XXI.

SALE OR TRANSFER OF MORTGAGED PREMISES.

CHAPTER XXII.

RELEASE AND RENEWAL OF MORTGAGES.

CHAPTER XXIII.

RELEASE OF EQUITY OF REDEMPTION TO MORTGAGEE AND MERGER.

CHAPTER XXIV.

PAYMENT AND SATISFACTION OF MORTGAGES.

CHAPTER XXV.

REDEMPTION OF MORTGAGES.

CHAPTER XXVI.

CONTRIBUTION TO REDEMPTION.

CHAPTER XXVII.

ACCOUNTING BY MORTGAGEE.

CHAPTER XXVIII.

REMEDIES OF MORTGAGEE ON BREACH OF CONDITION.

CHAPTER XXIX.

FORECLOSURE BY SCIRE FACIAS.

CHAPTER XXX.

FORECLOSURE BY SUIT IN EQUITY.

PART. I. JURISDICTION.

PART II. COMPLAINANT'S RIGHT OF ACTION.

PART III. LIMITATION OF ACTIONS.

PART IV. PARTIES IN FORECLOSURE.

CONTENTS.

PART. V. PLEADINGS AND EVIDENCE.

Requisites of Bill.
Allegations as to Claims of Third Persons.
Defendant's Plea and Answer.
Cross-Bills.
Evidence in General.
Proof of Debt.

PART VI. DEFENSES.

Defenses Available to Defendant.
Defect or Failure of Title.
Set-Off.

PART VII. APPOINTMENT OF RECEIVER.

Grounds for Appointing Receiver.
Where Mortgage Covers Rents and Profits.
Appointing Receiver after Foreclosure Sale.
Appointment on Application of Junior Mortgagee.
Rights and Duties of Receiver.
Discharge of Receiver.

PART VIII. DECREE OF FORECLOSURE.

Decree of Strict Foreclosure.
Same; When not Proper.
Same; Cases Excepted by Statute.
Frame of Decree of Strict Foreclosure.
Decree of Foreclosure and Sale.
Adjudication as to Amount Due.
Terms as to Payment and Redemption.
Personal Judgment not Proper
Validity and Effect of Decree.
Review and Vacation of Decree.
Conclusiveness of Decree
Lien of Decree.
Decree for Deficiency.
Same; Jurisdiction.
Same; What Persons Liable.

PART IX. SALE ON FORECLOSURE.

Formalities of Sale.
Notice of Sale.
Adjournment of Sale.
Order of Sale.
Sale in Separate Parcels.
Setting Off Homestead.
Who May Purchase.
Combinations Among Bidders.
Rights and Liabilities of Bidders.
Report and Confirmation of Sale.

CHAPTER XXXI.

FORECLOSURE OF TRUST DEEDS AND MORTGAGES WITH POWER OF SALE.

CHAPTER XXXII.

MORTGAGE FORECLOSURE IN THE FEDERAL COURTS.

TABLE OF CASES CITED.

THE LAW OF MORTGAGES

AND

DEEDS OF TRUST

CHAPTER I.

THE NATURE OF MORTGAGES.

§ 1. Ancient History of Mortgages.—The practice of pledging landed property as security for the payment of a debt was familiar to many of the nations of antiquity. Various attempts have been made to trace the legal conception of mortgages to a primitive source, but never with any marked success. It has been plausibly suggested that the Greeks and Romans may have derived their notion of this species of pledge from the Jews, and the Jews in turn from the Egyptians. But no certain knowledge on this point is now possible. Nor is it at all necessary to assume that this idea of extrinsic security was in any given case derivative. It may very well have been of spontaneous origin at different periods of history and among va-

1

rious peoples. Two fixed ideas must become established in the legal history of any people before the evolution of mortgages may be looked for; first, that of borrowing and lending, and second, that of individual ownership of property. But when civilization has advanced so far as to include these two concepts, it is inevitable that men should proceed to the further idea of pledging property, as a security collateral to that of the promise of the debtor, for the repayment of the debt or the discharge of the obligation. "Pledges or pawns," says Coote, "were probably known to the earliest nations. As soon as men recognize the rights of property, their necessities will suggest the idea of pledging that property as the ready means of supplying their wants without parting with their absolute ownership. Their immediate personal property may be the first objects of pledge, afterwards articles of merchandise and barter, and ultimately land."[1]

But the question of the historical origin of the law of mortgages is of interest only to the antiquarian; and, with a single exception, no practical advantage is to be derived from studying either the history or the learning of the nations of the ancient world on this subject. There is, however, one elder system of law which, in this particular, has exercised a profound influence upon the English jurisprudence, insomuch that it is impossible, at the present day, to form an accurate and complete conception of the nature and legal incidents of a mortgage without an understanding of the corresponding features of that earlier system. There are indeed writers who have not hesitated to affirm that the English law of mortgages, in its most essential characteristics, was directly borrowed from the civil law of Rome.[2] While this is perhaps too broad

---

[1] Coote, Mortgages, 2.

[2] Thus, in Gilman v. Illinois & Miss. Tel. Co., 91 U. S. 603, the question being upon the effect of certain mortgages, it was remarked by Judge Swayne that "the civil law is the spring-head of the English jurisprudence upon the subject of these securities." So, in Longwith v. Butler, 8 Ill. 32, Judge Koerner observed: "It will be conceded by all who have any knowledge of the Roman law that the equitable doctrines now prevailing in regard to mortgages have been derived from that source. The civil law, in this as in many other instances, has been the great armory from which the courts of equity in England have supplied themselves with the most efficient weapons to ward off the severities of the stern and unrelenting common law." "The system of mortgages was much affected by the doctrines of the civil law, acting through the

a statement, it is at all events well established that our present system of jurisprudence, so far as it relates to securities
of this kind, was very materially colored, in its early stages
of growth, by the infusion of elements derived from that
source. We deem it important, therefore, to invite the reader's
attention to a brief review of the leading principles of the
Roman law of mortgages.

§ 2. **Roman Law of Mortgages.**—The earliest form of property security in the Roman law (in use as late as the time of
Gaius, but obsolete before Justinian) was called "fiducia." In
this species of contract, both the title and the possession of the
property pledged were passed to the creditor by a formal act
of sale, there being at the same time an express or implied
agreement on the part of the creditor to reconvey the property
by a similar act of sale provided the debt was duly paid. The
fiducia, however, was found to operate very much to the dis-
advantage of debtors. For the creditor, being the legal owner
of the property, could sell or pledge it, or otherwise deal with
it at his discretion, subject only to his obligation to reconvey
upon payment of the debt, for the breach of which obligation
the debtor had only an imperfect remedy. Again, in consequence of the passing of title to the creditor, the particular
article of property could be subjected to but one incumbrance
at a time. Moreover, upon default in the payment of the debt,
the property became absolutely vested in the creditor without
any form of foreclosure and without any right of redemption
in the debtor.[3] The analogies between the fiducia and the
strict common-law form of mortgage before the intervention
of equity cannot fail to suggest themselves to the reader. In
course of time, this form of security gave place to that known
as "hypotheca," while the contemporary contract of "pignus"
or pawn underwent a corresponding development.

In the later period of the imperial Roman law, the two dis-

court of chancery; and a mortgage
is now a security founded on the
common law and perfected by a
judicious and wise application of
the principles of redemption of the
civil law." Scrutton, Influence of
Roman Law, etc., 157. As to the
influence of the Roman law on the
development of the equitable doctrine of mortgages, see, further,
2 Story, Eq. Jur. §§ 1005, 1011, 1013;
4 Kent, Comm. 136, note; 1
Browne, Civil Law, 200-210.

[3] Mackeld. Rom. Law, § 334;
Thomp. & J. Mod. Rom. Law, 182;
Hadley, Rom. Law, 201-203; Poth.
Pand. tit. "Fiducia."

tinct forms of security known respectively as "pignus" and "hypotheca" were in general use. The former was a contract by which a lien was created upon specific property as security for the payment of a debt or the performance of some other obligation and the possession of the property pledged was delivered to the creditor, to be retained until he should receive satisfaction. In the contract of hypotheca, on the other hand, the possession remained with the owner, and the lien was created by the mere agreement of the parties without tradition of the property.[4] The latter form of mortgage was supposed to be derived from the "jus gentium," that is, not from any legal conceptions peculiar to the Roman people, but from the general juristic notions which were assumed to be common to all peoples. But as is shown by the etymology of the name, it was probably borrowed, in whole or in part, from Grecian sources.[5] Although, in a certain general sense, the "pignus" of the Roman law may be said to correspond with our pledge or pawn, and the "hypotheca" with a real-estate mortgage, it must not be supposed that the difference between these two forms of security depended in any degree upon the character of the property upon which the security was given. It is probable that personal property was more usually subjected to the contract of pignus than immovable property; but lands as well as chattels might be impignorated, and, on the other hand, personal effects as well as landed estates might be hypothecated. The true distinction was founded upon the question of the delivery of possession to the creditor or its retention by the debtor.

As to the subject-matter of the contract, any kind of property which possessed value, so as to furnish security to the creditor, and which was susceptible of alienation, whether it was real or personal, corporeal or incorporeal, might be pledged or hypothecated, including not only landed estates, but also servitudes, choses in action, and property already held in pledge.[6] Nor was the mortgaging of after-acquired property unknown to the Roman law. It was held that one who was not the owner of a particular property at the time might give a valid mortgage upon it, if this was done with the consent of the real owner, or if the mortgagor gave the security on the

[4] Dig. 13, 7, 9, § 2; Inst. 4, 6, § 7 in fin.; Dig. 13, 7, 35, § 1.

[5] Thomp. & J. Mod. Rom. Law, 184.

[6] Mackeld. Rom. Law, § 336.

condition that he would become the owner of the property. The pledging or hypothecating of another's property gave an "actio utilis" when the pledgor subsequently became the owner.[7] Also, if the mortgagor, at the time of giving the mortgage, had not a perfect title to the property pledged, but was merely a possessor by an incomplete title of prescription, he might continue and complete the prescription while the property remained under the pledge, and of course his title thus acquired would inure to the benefit of the mortgagee.[8]

The contract of pignus or of hypotheca was always regarded as an accessory and not a principal obligation. It was based upon a claim or consideration which it was designed to secure, and which might be either such a claim as would be enforceable by the strict law or such as rested only upon a moral obligation; but the validity of the claim generally determined that of the security. In other words, the mortgage must be based upon a valid consideration. It was not necessary, however, that there should be a pre-existing or contemporaneous obligation on the part of the mortgagor. For a pledge or hypotheca could be given for an anticipated claim or one to be thereafter created.[9] The consideration might also be collateral; as where a mortgage was given by way of indemnity to one who had become liable as surety or guarantor for the mortgagor.[10] When a pledge or hypotheca was given it secured not only the principal of the debt, but also the interest, costs of suit, if any, and any expenses incurred by the mortgagee in relation to the property pledged, and also a penalty for non-payment if any were agreed upon between the parties at the time of the contract. But if the pledge was expressly given for securing only the principal or the interest, or a part of the debt, it was liable only for that for which it was given.[11] And it appears that if the creditor was in possession of the property, he could not be compelled to surrender it until he should have received satisfaction, not only for the particular debt, but also for any other unsecured claims which he might have against the debtor. But this was allowed only as between the parties, and not as against subsequent creditors.[12]

The mortgagor continued to be the owner of the property.

[7] Dig. 20, 1, 16, § 7; Dig. 13, 7, 41.
[8] Dig. 47, 2, 19, § 6.
[9] Dig. 20, 1, 5, prin., § 2; Dig. 13, 7, 9, § 1.
[10] Dig. 13, 7, 9, § 1.
[11] Dig. 13, 7, 8, prin., § 5; Dig. 13, 7, 11, § 3.
[12] Code, 8, 27, 1.

In the case of an hypotheca, he was entitled to retain the possession of the property and use it as his own and take the issues and profits. In the case of a pledge, as already stated, the possession passed to the creditor, but he was required to account for the profits or products received by him, unless there was a special agreement by which he was given the right to take the issues and profits instead of interest, in which case the contract was called "antichresis."[13] And the mortgagor, unless there was a special agreement to the contrary, retained the right to alienate the property pledged or hypothecated, but subject to the lien of the mortgage.[14]

The nature of the mortgagee's right or title may be briefly described as follows: He had a real right (specific lien) in the property pledged, and, in the case of a pignus, also the right of possession, and this latter right he was entitled to protect by interdict, that is, by an appropriate action either to recover the possession or to enjoin all parties from depriving him of it. But in the case of hypothecation—which most nearly corresponds to our mortgages of realty—the creditor had no right to the possession and could not gain the possession by aid of the law save for the purpose of having a sale of the property for satisfaction of his debt. He might indeed otherwise come into possession of the property, and would then become a "detentor" of it, but this would not entitle him to the interdicts nor would it turn the original contract into a pignus. His claim, however, being a lien on the property itself, would follow it into all hands, and might be enforced against every possessor. Moreover, he had the right to pawn or hypothecate his claim to the property pledged to him, whence arose a species of sub-pledge. Upon default in the payment of the debt at the appointed time, the creditor had the right to sell the property and reimburse himself, and this right he retained until his claim was fully satisfied. It might be restricted by agreement, but he could not be wholly deprived of it.[15]

One of the most characteristic features of the Roman law of mortgages, and one which has had a most pronounced and beneficial influence upon our own law, was the debtor's right of redemption. In the older Roman law, it was permissible for the parties to agree in advance that if the debtor should

---

[13] Mackeld. Rom. Law, § 346.

[14] Code, 8, 28, 12; Dig. 13, 7, 18, § 2.

[15] Mackeld. Rom. Law, § 347; Thomp. & J. Mod. Rom. Law, 185. See, also, Gaius, ii, § 64.

fail to 'pay at the appointed time, the property pledged or hypothecated should ipso facto, without appraisement or sale, become vested in the creditor; or, in other words, that the debtor should forfeit his right of redemption.[16] But this was regarded as a source of great hardship and imposition, and was peremptorily forbidden by a law of the Emperor Constantine.[17] Thereafter it was settled law that even when default was made (or even "after breach of condition," to use the modern phraseology) the debtor still had a right to redeem the pledge upon equitable terms, and that he could not by any contract or stipulation in advance strip himself of this right.

The lien of a pignus or hypotheca was extinguished when the debt for which the lien was created was wholly discharged, and also by a merger of the claim and the property in the same person, as when the creditor became heir to the debtor.[18]

When default had been made in the payment of the loan, the creditor might proceed to sell the pledge for the satisfaction of his claim. It was not necessary that the contract between the parties should give him the right to distrain and sell. In the absence of any stipulation in this regard, his right to exercise this remedy was recognized as a matter of law. Even if there was an explicit agreement that there should be no distraint, the creditor was not absolutely deprived of this remedy; but in that case it was necessary for him to give notice to the debtor three several times of his intention to proceed to foreclose.[19] When the creditor was himself in possession of the property mortgaged, no judicial authorization was necessary to enable him to make sale of the pledge. He might sell on his own motion and without order of court; but he was required to give the debtor due notice, and the sale must be public and fair and conducted in entire good faith. Moreover, if the parties, in making the contract of hypotheca-

---

[16] This was called the "lex commissoria," as to which see 2 Kent, Comm. 583.

[17] Code, 8, 35, 3. This reform in the law so closely resembles the work of the English chancellors in allowing an equity of redemption after default at the law-day, and in creating and enforcing the rule of "once a mortgage always a mortgage," that we cannot but think their inspiration for the innovation upon the strict doctrine of the common law was directly derived from the elder system of jurisprudence.

[18] Dig. 46, 3, 75; Dig. 46, 3, 107.

[19] Dig. 13, 7, 4; Mackeld. Rom. Law, § 348.

tion, had agreed upon the time, terms, or other conditions of the sale, these must be duly observed by the creditor.[20] But if there had been no agreement as to the sale, the creditor might proceed to sell, upon demand and notice or judicial decree, after the lapse of two years, reckoned from the time when the notice was given or the decree pronounced.[21] The method of foreclosing a mortgage when the creditor was not in possession was by the action called "actio hypothecaria." "This action was originally given only to the lessor of a predium rusticum on account of the invecta et illata (lessee's farming effects), by agreement hypothecated to him to secure the payment of rent, and was termed 'actio Serviana.' It was subsequently given by way of analogy to every pawnee and hypothecatee as a 'quasi Serviana' action for the enforcement of their liens, and was extended by Justinian to the praetorian rights of pledge and hypotheca.[22] This action may be instituted against every possessor of the thing pledged or hypothecated, whether it be the debtor himself or a third party. When the action is instituted by the creditor against him who pledged or hypothecated the thing, or against his heirs, or against a third party possessing it who derives his right from him, such creditor need only prove the debt and the pledging or hypothecation; but if he institutes the action against a possessor who does not derive his right from the plaintiff's pledgor or hypothecator, then he must prove that his pledgor or hypothecator was the owner of the thing at the time he burdened it or else that he had a right so to do. The object of the hypothecarial action is for the enforcement of the rights of pawn and hypotheca, and consequently for the surrender of the thing pledged or hypothecated to satisfy the plaintiff's claims.'[23] Out of the proceeds of the sale of the property mortgaged the selling creditor was first entitled to satisfaction in full. The surplus went next to the discharge of junior liens in their order, and the balance, if any, belonged to the debtor. But if the purchase price was not sufficient to satisfy the creditor, the debtor remained liable for the deficiency.[24] If the sale was duly and lawfully made, the purchaser took an absolute title

---

[20] Code, 8, 28, 4 and 9; Code, 8, 34, 3, § 1.

[21] Code. 8. 34, 3, § 1.

[22] Inst. 4. 6. 7.

[23] Mackeld. Rom. Law, § 356.

[24] Dig. 20, 4, 12, 5; Dig. 20, 5, 9, prin.; Code, 8, 34, 3, § 4; Mackeld. Rom. Law, § 348.

to the property, and took the same free from all liens and incumbrances. If the property hypothecated was duly and properly offered for sale by the creditor, for the satisfaction of his claim, but no responsible purchaser was found, then a process was provided by which the creditor, after due notice to the debtor, could have the value of the property judicially ascertained and have it adjudged to him in satisfaction of his claim. But in this case there was reserved to the debtor, for the space of two years, a right to redeem the property on payment of debt, interest, and costs. If, however, he failed to redeem, it became absolutely and irrevocably the property of the creditor.[25]

The same property might be successively mortgaged to several persons, and their right to satisfaction was determined in the order of their priority. A junior incumbrancer could not distrain and sell the property without the consent of the elder lienor. But he might acquire the right of foreclosure by placing himself in the position of the senior mortgagee. This right was called "jus offerendi et succedendi," and in it is to be found the source of the modern equity doctrine of subrogation. When the prior mortgage was due, the junior mortgagee had the right to pay it off and thereby to succeed to all the rights of the senior creditor. Moreover, any person was entitled to the same right of succession who lent money to the debtor for the purpose of paying off the elder lien and with the understanding that he should take the place of the mortgagee. So, a junior creditor might purchase the claim of the senior incumbrancer, with the latter's consent, and succeed to his rank and rights. Again, when the mortgage creditor brought his action against a third person in possession of the property pledged, and the latter satisfied the claim of the creditor, he might demand an assignment of the mortgage.[26]

§ 3. **Influence of Roman Law on English Law of Mortgages.**—Without attempting an exhaustive examination of this very interesting question, it may be profitable, at this point, to mention some of the most important particulars in which the civil law has exercised a modifying influence upon the common law in respect to the character and incidents of mortgages. And first, in regard to the nature of the contract. The

[25] Code. 8, 34, 3, §§ 2-6. Thomp. & J. Mod. Rom. Law, 197,
[26] Mackeld. Rom. Law, § 355; 198.

common law regarded a mortgage as creating an estate in the mortgagee and held him to be the legal owner of the property. The Roman law held a mortgage to be a mere lien or security. Equity so far adopted the civil-law conception as to establish the doctrine that, as to all persons except the creditor, the mortgagor remained the true and beneficial owner oı the property, and that, as between the parties, the title was vested in the mortgagee only for the purpose of making good his security, and only so far as might be necessary for that purpose. Secondly, the doctrine of an "equity of redemption" was wholly a creation of the courts of chancery, and they derived it unquestionably from the Roman law. The chancellors of the Stuart kings, who were familiar with the rules and maxims of the law of Rome, were not slow to perceive the inequity of allowing the mortgagee to acquire an absolute title by mere default in payment, and they established the rule that the debtor should have the right to redeem his estate, after breach of condition, until he was foreclosed. Also, imitating the just and wise legislation of Constantine, they determined that what was "once a mortgage" should be "always a mortgage;" that is, that if the alienation of an estate was originally intended as a security for the payment of a debt, the right of redemption should always follow it, even though the debtor, by an agreement in advance, had attempted to divest himself of it. Thirdly, the doctrine of subrogation, which plays an important part in the law of mortgages, is wholly a creation of equity, and is wholly derived from the civil law.

§ 4. Strict Common-Law Doctrine of Mortgages.—"A mortgage at common law may be defined to be an estate created by a conveyance, absolute in its form, but intended to secure the performance of some act, such as the payment of money and the like, by the grantor or some other person, and to become void if the act is performed agreeably to the terms prescribed at the time of making such conveyance. It is therefore an estate defeasible by the performance of a condition subsequent."[27] By the strict doctrines of the common law, unmod-

---

[27] 2 Washb. Real Prop. (4th edn.) 34. The same learned author observes: "Though conditional in its character, a mortgage differs essentially from an estate upon condition at common law both in its purposes and in many of its incidents. In respect to estates upon condition, the estate vests in the grantee, subject to be defeated; but until defeated by act of the grantor, the estate, with the pos-

ified by the intervention of equity for the protection of the debtor, a mortgage was regarded as passing the whole legal title to the estate pledged to the mortgagee, who became the owner of it, though his title was liable to be defeated on a condition subsequent. He was also entitled at all times to the possession of the estate; and unless he had expressly agreed that the mortgagor might remain in possession, he could maintain ejectment against him, as well before as after default. The time fixed for the payment of the debt or other performance of the condition was called the "law day," and if the debtor punctually performed his part of the contract at the appointed time, the estate of the mortgagee, by performance of the condition, determined and ceased. But as the legal title was in him, the estate was not conveyed or revested in the mortgagor by the mere act in pais of payment or other performance, but it was necessary that the mortgagee should reconvey to him by deed.[28] On the other hand, if the debtor failed to pay or perform at the stipulated time—if there was a breach of the condition—the title of the mortgagee became absolute and indefeasible, and the mortgagor ceased to have any right or interest in the estate.

§ 5. **Origin and Establishment of the Equity of Redemption.**—By the rules of the civil law, as we have already seen, the mortgage debtor had the right to redeem his estate on payment of the debt secured at any time before a sale of the property, and, in some cases, even for a certain length of time after sale. The English chancellors, being much impressed with the equitable principles of the Roman law, and having already begun to mitigate the severity of the common law in many particulars by the exercise of their peculiar powers, were led, at an early day, to look with great disfavor upon the strict common-law doctrine of the absolute forfeiture of the estate upon non-payment of the mortgage debt. "In the eye of equity, the absolute forfeiture of the estate, whatever might be its value, on the breach of the condition, was regarded as a flagrant injustice and hardship, although perfectly accordant with the system on which the mortgage itself was grounded. The courts

---

session and the ordinary incidents of ownership, is in the grantee; whereas a mortgage only becomes effectually an estate in the grantee, called the mortgagee, by the grantor or mortgagor failing to perform the condition." Id. 35.

[28] Harrison v. Owen, 1 Atk. 520.

of equity therefore stepped in to moderate the severity with which the common law followed the breach of the condition. Leaving the forfeiture to its legal consequences, they operated on the conscience of the mortgagee, and, acting in personam and not in rem, they declared it unreasonable that he should retain for his own benefit what was intended as a mere pledge; and they adjudged that the breach of the condition was in the nature of a penalty which ought to be relieved against, and that the mortgagor had an equity to redeem on payment of principal and interest and costs, notwithstanding the forfeiture at law."[29] This right to save the estate in equity after the forfeiture at law was called the "equity of redemption," and the same designation came to be applied to the interest or estate retained by the debtor after conveying the legal title to the mortgagee by the mortgage deed. From the recognition of this equity sprang the jurisdiction of the chancery courts to entertain bills for redemption, and also the doctrine that the mortgagee could not acquire an absolute and indefeasible estate in the land until he had "foreclosed" the debtor's equity of redemption by an appropriate proceeding.

The period at which this doctrine became fully established in equity can be only approximately fixed. It is said that parliament in 1391 refused to admit a redemption after forfeiture; and such estates continued irredeemable during the reign of Edward IV., who died in 1483. There was a struggle, however, on the part of chancery to extend relief in such cases, and to some effect, under a provision in Magna Charta in favor of sureties. It is stated that an equity of redemption is not so much as mentioned in all the writings of Lord Coke.[30] "In the cases of Wade[31] and Goodall,[32] which were decided towards the end of the reign of Queen Elizabeth, the parties do not seem to have entertained the idea of any remedy existing for the mortgagor's relief if the forfeiture was established at law; although Tothill mentions a case in the 37th year of Elizabeth[33] in which the equity was decreed; and it must soon after this time have been generally in practice, for there is a case decided in the first year of Charles I. in which the

[29] Kortright v. Cady, 21 N. Y. 343.

[30] 2 Washb. Real Prop. (4th edn.) 39.

[31] Foxcroft v. Wade, 5 Coke, 114a.

[32] Goodall v. Wyat, 5 Coke, 95b.

[33] Langford v. Barnard, Tothill (edn. of 1820), 134.

doctrine seems fully admitted.''[34] The case here referred to
was a case in which a lease for five hundred years of a manor
had been made by way of mortgage to secure the payment of
debts. The money was paid, but not till after the day appointed. The court of chancery held that the lease was thereby
avoided. The report says: "This court conceived, the said
lease being but a security and the money paid, the said lease
had been void, as well against the said college [a purchaser]
as against any other; and though the money was not paid at
the day but afterwards, the said lease ought to be void in
equity, as well as, on a legal payment, it had been void in law
against them.''[35] It was during the intervening reign, that
of James I., that the court of chancery became fully established in its powers and jurisdiction, and from these indications
it is safe to assume that the doctrine of the equity of redemption was settled and developed during the same period. But
"no sooner was this equitable principle established than the
cupidity of creditors induced them to attempt its evasion,
and it was a bold but necessary decision of equity that the
debtor could not, even by the most solemn engagements entered into at the time of the loan, preclude himself from his
right to redeem; for in every other instance, probably, the rule
of law, 'modus et conventio vincunt legem,' is allowed to prevail. In truth it required all the firmness and wisdom of the
eminent judges who successively presided in the courts of
equity to prevent this equitable jurisdiction being nullified by
the artifice of the parties.''[36] One of the first cases in which
this new rule was applied was that of Newcomb v. Bonham.[37]
In this case the mortgage contained a covenant that it should
be redeemable at any time during the life of the mortgagor;
but in case the lands should not be redeemed in his lifetime,
then he covenanted that the same should never be redeemed.
But the Lord Chancellor said it was a general rule "once a
mortgage and always a mortgage," and since the estate was
expressly redeemable in the mortgagor's lifetime it must continue so afterwards, and he decreed an account and redemption. To this day it has continued to be a fixed rule of equity
that no agreement in advance to waive the equity of redemp-

[34] Coote, Mortg. 15.

[35] Emmanuel College v. Evans, 1 Rep. in Chanc. 18 (1625).

[36] Coote, Mortg. 15.

[37] 1 Vern. 7 (1681). And see Howard v. Harris, Id. 190; Willett v. Winnell, Id. 488; Price v. Perrie, Freem. Ch. 258.

tion can be valid; and that, when once the relation of mortgagor and mortgagee is established, the right of redemption will continue until the mortgage is redeemed and discharged, or the right of redemption is cut off by a foreclosure, or by the running of the statute of limitations, or by a release of the equity of redemption to the mortgagee upon an adequate consideration and by a transaction which is absolutely free from fraud or overreaching.[38]

§ 6. **Common-Law and Equitable Doctrines Concurrent.**—In course of time, a mortgage came to be regarded in equity as something very different from what it was at law. The courts of chancery, "looking at the substance of the transaction rather than its form, and with a view of giving effect to the real intention of the parties, held that the mortgage was a mere security for the payment of the debt; that the mortgagor was the real beneficial owner of the land, subject to the incumbrance of the mortgage; that the interest of the mortgagee was simply a lien and incumbrance upon the land, rather than an estate in it. In short, the positions of mortgagor and mortgagee were substantially reversed in the view taken by courts of equity."[39] Nevertheless the equitable doctrine was not an endeavor to reverse or destroy the theory of the common-law courts. There was no encroachment of either jurisdiction upon the other. Though differing widely in their views of the nature and incidents of the mortgage relation, the two doctrines were always regarded as mutually consistent and equally authoritative. The courts of equity "did not make the attempt of altering the legal effect of the forfeiture at common law; they could not, as they might have wished, in conformity to the principles of the civil law, declare that the conveyance should, notwithstanding forfeiture committed, cease at any time before sentence of foreclosure on payment of the mortgage money."[40] Nor, on the other hand, did the courts of law oppose themselves to the jurisdiction of equity to grant relief after forfeiture. In short, "these two systems grew up side by side, and were maintained for centuries without conflict or even friction between the law and equity tribunals by which they were respectively administered. The

[38] See Quartermous v. Kennedy, 29 Ark. 544; Reed v. Reed, 75 Me. 264; McPherson v. Hayward, 81 Me. 329, 17 Atl. Rep. 164.

[39] Barrett v. Hinckley, 124 Ill. 32, 14 N. E. Rep. 863.

[40] Coote, Mortg. 14.

equity courts did not attempt to control the law courts, or even question the legal doctrines which they announced. On the contrary, their force and validity were often recognized in the relief granted. Thus, equity courts, in allowing a redemption after forfeiture of the legal estate, uniformly required the mortgagee to reconvey to the mortgagor, which was of course necessary to make his title available in a court of law."[41]

The development of the equitable doctrine was gradual. It was not till long after the first conception of an equity of redemption that the idea became fully established that that equity was really the true and beneficial ownership of the estate and the mortgage itself a mere security. And in the early days we find that some of the chancellors themselves were disposed to look upon the new equitable doctrine with considerable doubt, or even apprehension, as to its possible results. Thus, in a case which arose in 1671, it was urged (and the judges agreed) that although an equity of redemption in mortgaged lands was such a right or interest as would pass by a voluntary conveyance, yet where, as in this case, the plaintiff claimed an equity by way of an entail, it ought not to be countenanced in equity, for the consequence would be to make an equity of redemption perpetual. And Chief Justice Hale said: "An equity of redemption is transferable from one to another now, and yet at common law if he that had the equity made a feoffment or levied a fine, he had extinguished his equity at law; and it hath gone far enough already, and we will go no further than precedents in the matter of equity of redemption, which hath too much favor already."[42] Yet by the time of Lord Hardwicke it could be said that "an equity of redemption has always been considered as an estate in the land, for it may be devised, granted, or entailed with remainders, and such entail and remainders may be barred by fine and recovery, and therefore cannot be considered as a mere right only, but such an estate whereof there may be a seisin. The person therefore entitled to the equity of redemption is considered as the owner of the land, and a mortgage in fee is considered as personal assets."[43] And Lord Mansfield, who indeed went further than

[41] Barrett v. Hinckley, 124 Ill. 32, 14 N. E. Rep. 863.

[42] Roscarrick v. Barton, 1 Cas. in Chanc. 217.

[43] Casborne v. Scarfe, 1 Atk. 603. Hence, in this case, it was held that a husband might have an estate by the curtesy in an equity

any other in forcing the equitable doctrine of mortgages, is reported to have said: "A mortgage is a charge upon the land, and whatever would give the money will carry the estate in the land along with it, to every purpose. The estate in the land is the same thing as the money due upon it."[44] And again: "If the estate on which a pauper resides is substantially his property, that is sufficient [to give him a settlement] whatever forms of conveyance there may be; and therefore a mortgagor in possession gains a settlement, because the mortgagee, notwithstanding the form, has but a chattel and the mortgage is only a security. It is an affront to common sense to say the mortgagor is not the real owner. * * * A mortgagor has the right to the possession till the mortgagee brings an ejectment. After the mortgagee has got into possession, he [the mortgagee] might gain a settlement."[45]

§ 7. Mortgages in Illinois.—The common-law doctrine of mortgages, as modified by equitable principles, is in force in this state. A mortgage is regarded as a conveyance of the estate to the creditor, who acquires thereby the legal title to the property, with its usual incidents. Upon breach of condition, this title becomes absolute at law, and there remains in the debtor only an equity of redemption. Expressions used in some of the earlier decisions warranted the inference that a conveyance by way of mortgage was considered as entitling the creditor to immediate possession of the property, unless it had been agreed that the debtor should remain in possession, and that, to secure such possession, the mortgagee might at any time maintain ejectment against the mortgagor.[46] But it is now settled that the mortgagee cannot (under ordinary circumstances) oust the mortgagor from possession of the estate conveyed until there has been a breach of the condition of the mortgage.[47] In equity, on the other hand, the mortgagee has an interest in the mortgaged premises of a personal character, similar to the interest which he has in the debt secured. It is a mere chattel interest.[48] On the equity side,

of redemption belonging to his deceased wife.

[44] Martin v. Mowlin, 2 Burr. 969.

[45] King v. Inhabitants of St. Michael's, 2 Dougl. 630.

[46] Hall v. Byrne, 2 Ill. 140; Nelson v. Pinegar, 30 Ill. 473; Moore v. Titman, 44 Ill. 367; Oldham v. Pfleger, 84 Ill. 102; Taylor v. Adams, 115 Ill. 570.

[47] Kransz v. Uedelhofen, 193 Ill. 477, 62 N. E. Rep. 239.

[48] Dayton v. Dayton, 7 Ill. App. 136.

therefore, the mortgage is regarded as a mere security and as no more than an incident to the debt or principal obligation; yet it confers the right to reduce the premises to possession as a means of obtaining satisfaction of the debt, and to render this right effective, ejectment will lie against the mortgagor at any time when a recovery may be had on the debt.[49] After breach of the condition, if the mortgagor remains in possession, the mortgagee may consider him as his tenant for some purposes, and if he elects so to consider him, it is as a tenant at sufferance.[50] Consequently, if the debt secured is not paid at maturity, it is permissible for the mortgagee to proceed against the mortgagor by ejectment to recover the possession of the estate, and it is not necessary for him to give previous notice of his intention to do so or notice to quit.[51] And when the mortgagee is in possession for condition broken, he will have the right to retain the possession until his debt is fully paid.[52] When the mortgage debt is due and unpaid, the creditor has various remedies, among which he may make his election, or he may pursue one or more of them concurrently, although of course he can have but one satisfaction. He may, as just stated, bring ejectment and recover possession of the premises; he may sue at law on the bond, note, or other evidence of the debt; he may proceed by scire facias to have the amount of the indebtedness fixed and the mortgaged property levied on and sold for its satisfaction; he may bring his bill in equity, either for a strict foreclosure of the mortgage (under certain circumstances to be more fully explained hereafter) or for the more usual remedy of a foreclosure by decree and judicial sale.[53]

But in this state, as in others, the doctrines of equity have encroached more and more upon the strict legal notion of a mortgage, and the composite result differs in some important particulars from that fixed in England at the time of the separation. Thus, in the case of Barrett v. Hinckley,[54] it was

49 Pollock v. Maison, 41 Ill. 516. If a party holding the legal title to land as a security for the repayment of money advanced for the benefit of the beneficial owner devises the land, the devise will carry whatever right the devisor had therein to his devisee. Stew-art v. Fellows, 128 Ill. 480, 17 N. E. Rep. 476.

50 Jackson v. Warren, 32 Ill. 331.
51 Carroll v. Ballance, 26 Ill. 9; Johnson v. Watson, 87 Ill. 535.
52 Harper v. Ely, 70 Ill. 581.
53 Delahay v. Clement, 4 Ill. 201; Vansant v. Allmon, 23 Ill. 30.
54 124 Ill. 32, 14 N. E. Rep. 863.

said: "It must not be concluded, from what we have said,
that the dual system respecting mortgages, as above explained,
exists in this state precisely as it did in England prior to its
adoption in this country, for such is not the case. It is a conceded fact that the equitable theory of a mortgage has in
process of time made in this state, as in others, material encroachments upon the legal theory, which are now fully recognized in courts of law. Thus, it is now the settled law that
the mortgagor or his assignee is the legal owner of the mortgaged estate as against all persons except the mortgagee or his
assigns. Hall v. Lance, 25 Ill. 277; Emory v. Keighan, 88 Ill.
482. As a result of this doctrine it follows that, in ejectment
by the mortgagor against a third party, the defendant cannot
defeat the action by showing an outstanding title in the mortgagee. Hall v. Lance, supra. So, too, courts of law now
regard the title of a mortgagee in fee in the nature of a base
or determinable fee. The term of its existence is measured by
that of the mortgage debt. When the latter is paid off, or becomes barred by the statute of limitations, the mortgagee's
title is extinguished by operation of law. Pollock v. Maison,
41 Ill. 516; Harris v. Mills, 28 Ill. 44; Gibson v. Rees, 50 Ill.
383. Hence the rule is well established at law, as it is in
equity, that the debt is the principal thing and the mortgage
an incident. So, also, while it is indispensable in all cases to
a recovery in ejectment that the plaintiff show in himself
the legal title to the property as set forth in the declaration,
except where the defendant is estopped from denying it, yet
it does not follow that because one has such title he may under
all circumstances maintain the action; and this is particularly
so in respect to a mortgage title. Such title exists for the benefit of the holder of the mortgage indebtedness, and it can only
be enforced by an action in furtherance of his interests; that
is, as a means of coercing payment. If the mortgagee, therefore, should, for a valuable consideration, assign the mortgage
indebtedness to a third party, and the latter, after default in
payment, should take possession of the mortgaged premises,
ejectment would not lie against him at the suit of the mortgagee, although the legal title would be in the latter, for the
reason that it would not be in the interest of the owner of
the indebtedness. In short, it is a well-settled principle that
one having a mere naked legal title to land in which he has
no interest, and in respect to which he has no duty to perform,

cannot maintain ejectment against the equitable owner or any
one having an equitable interest therein with a present right
of possession.''

In a later case it was said: "In many of the states, a mortgage confers no title or estate upon the mortgagee, and it is
nothing but a mere security for a debt or obligation. This
state has adhered to the rule that at law a title vests in the
mortgagee, but only for the protection of his interests. For
the purpose of protecting and enforcing his security, the mortgagee may enter and hold possession by virtue of his title and
take the rents and profits in payment of his mortgage debt.
He may maintain the possessory action of ejectment on the
strength of such title, but the purpose and effect of the action
are not to establish or confirm title in him, but, on the contrary, to give him the rents and profits which undermine and
destroy his title. When the rents and profits have paid the
mortgage debt, both the title and right of possession of the
mortgagee are at an end. The mortgagor's interest in the land
may be sold upon execution; his widow is entitled to dower in
it; it passes as real estate by devise; it descends to his heirs at
his death as real estate; he is a freeholder by virtue of it;
he may maintain an action for the land against a stranger and
the mortgage cannot be set up as a defense. The mortgagee
has no such estate as can be sold on execution; his widow has
no right to dower in it; upon his death the mortgage passes
to his personal representatives as personal estate, and it passes
by his will as personal property. The title of the mortgagee,
even after condition broken, is not an outstanding title of
which a stranger can take advantage, but it is available only
to the mortgagee or one claiming under him. The mortgagor
may sell and convey his title or mortgage it to successive mortgagees, and his grantee or mortgagee will succeed to his estate
and occupy his position subject to the incumbrance. * * *
The mortgagee is the legal owner for only one purpose, while,
at the same time, the mortgagor is the owner for every other
purpose and against every other person. The title of the mortgagee is anomalous, and exists only between him and the
mortgagor and for a limited purpose. * * * The title is
never out of the mortgagor, except as between him and the
mortgagee and as an incident of the mortgage debt, for the
purpose of obtaining satisfaction. When the debt is barred by
the statute of limitations, the title of the mortgagee or trustee

ceases at law as well as in equity. When the debt, the principal thing, is gone, the incident, the mortgage, is also gone. The mortgagor's title is then freed from the title of the mortgagee, and he is the owner of the premises, not by any new title, but by the title which he always had. Statutes of limitation do not transfer title from one to another, and a statute of limitations which would have the effect of transferring the legal title back from the mortgagee to the mortgagor would be unconstitutional. The title of the mortgagor becomes perfect because the title of the mortgagee is measured by the existence of the mortgage debt or obligation and terminates with it.''[55]

It is also to be observed that the common-law rule that an equity of redemption can be cut off only by a foreclosure in equity does not prevail in Illinois. If the creditor sues at law for the amount of the debt secured, obtains judgment, has the property sold on execution, bids it in, and takes a sheriff's deed, he will thus acquire the equity of redemption, which, united with his estate under the mortgage, will give him the absolute title.[56] In fact, ''the law courts, following the rule first set up in equity, have come to recognize mortgages of all kinds to be exactly what they are—mere securities. The title may be differently regarded and treated in different forums, but the actual fact that, until foreclosure has been in some way had, the mortgagor has an interest in the property, is recognized at law as well as in equity. While courts have [spoken] and do frequently speak of the title of the mortgagee being, after forfeiture, that is, after default, absolute, they do not mean that the ownership of the mortgagee is absolute. Nowhere is it now held that, upon forfeiture, the mortgagee may sell the property, give it away, or destroy it, without reference to or consideration for any right or interest of the mortgagor.''[57] As already intimated in the opinions from which we have quoted, a mortgage with which the defendant fails to connect himself is no defense in an action of ejectment. As to strangers, the mortgagor is regarded as the owner of the property; and a mortgage made by the plaintiff in ejectment does not show an outstanding title which will defeat the action.[58]

[55] Lightcap v. Bradley, 186 Ill. 510, 58 N. E. Rep. 221.

[56] Cottingham v. Springer, 88 Ill. 90.

[57] Frankenthal v. Mayer, 54 Ill. App. 160.

[58] Emory v. Keighan, 88 Ill. 482.

§ 8. Once a Mortgage Always a Mortgage.—The saying, "once a mortgage always a mortgage," is very familiar in the courts of equity. It means that no agreement in advance to waive the equity of redemption can be valid, and that, when once a conveyance of land is established in the character of a mortgage, the right to redeem will continue until the debt is paid or barred by limitations or otherwise discharged, or until the equity of redemption is foreclosed, barred, or released by the subsequent act or agreement of the parties.[59] "The right of redemption is so firmly engrafted upon the law of mortgages and so fully protected and enforced that the mortgagor's solemn agreement that, upon non-payment, the estate shall be forfeited is held utterly void in equity."[60] On the same principle, it is not competent for parties to make a conveyance of land, absolute in form, a security for the payment of money by a given day, with the further agreement that, if payment is not then made, the instrument shall be treated as an absolute sale and conveyance. Every deed takes effect from its delivery, and its character thereby becomes at once fixed; and if the instrument is a mortgage when delivered, it will so continue until the right of redemption is cut off in some of the modes recognized by law.[61] Although it may have been the very purpose and intention of the parties, in giving and taking a deed absolute in form, instead of the usual form of a mortgage, to create a security which would eliminate the right of redemption and save the expense of foreclosure, yet the courts rule that, if it appears to have been intended as a mortgage, the right of redemption cannot be thus relinquished.[62] But of course a deed, intended as a security by way of mortgage, may be converted into an unconditional conveyance of the title in fee by the subsequent voluntary agreement of the parties, if it is fair and free from fraud or oppression and founded on a good consideration.[63]

§ 9. Termination of Mortgagee's Title.—Although the mortgagee is spoken of as holding the "legal" title to the land

[59] Newcomb v. Bonham, 1 Vern. 7; Wyncoop v. Cowing, 21 Ill. 570; Tillson v. Moulton, 23 Ill. 648.

[60] Essley v. Sloan, 16 Ill. App. 63; Willets v. Burgess, 34 Ill. 494.

[61] Bearss v. Ford, 108 Ill. 16; Tennery v. Nicholson, 87 Ill. 464.

[62] Johnson v. Prosperity Loan & Bldg. Ass'n, 94 Ill. App. 260.

[63] Richmond v. Richmond, 4 Chicago Leg. News, 41, Fed. Cas. No. 11,801; Carpenter v. Carpenter, 70 Ill. 457.

pledged, yet his ownership is not of such a character as to require a deed of conveyance from him to the mortgagor, in order to restore to the latter the full title in fee, upon the payment or satisfaction of the debt secured. A release of the mortgagee's claims may indeed be made by a separate written instrument, but an entry of satisfaction upon the margin of the record is equally effective.[64] Moreover, the title of the mortgagee may be divested, without any act on his part, by the running of the statute of limitations against the debt secured by the mortgage. When that debt has become barred by the statute, the mortgage is no longer a muniment of title in the mortgagee, and hence his deed purporting to convey the title in fee simple furnishes no basis for an action of ejectment by his grantee against parties in possession of the premises.[65]

§ 10. **Mortgage Distinguished from Assignment for Creditors.**—When property is conveyed to a trustee, to provide a fund for paying the debts of the grantor, it is sometimes a question whether the transaction is to be regarded as a mortgage or as an assignment for the benefit of the creditors. The general rule is that the conveyance is no more than a mortgage or pledge, if the debtor retains an equity of redemption in the property, but if his title is irrevocably passed from him, and the property wholly withdrawn from his control, it is an assignment. Thus, it is said: "A fundamental distinction between a mortgage and an assignment is that a mortgage is a mere security for a debt, the equity of redemption remaining in the mortgagor, while an assignment is more than a security for a debt, and is an absolute appropriation of the property to its payment. It does not create a lien in favor of creditors upon property which in equity is still regarded as the assignor's; but it passes both the legal and equitable title to the property absolutely beyond the control of the assignor. In cases of assignment, therefore, there remains no equity of redemption in the assignor."[66] To the same effect is a decision of the supreme court of Texas, wherein it was said: "A mortgage being the security for a debt, and giving merely a lien on the property, leaves in the grantor an equity of redemp-

[64] Rev. Stat. Ill. c. 95, § 8.   [66] Weber v. Mick, 131 Ill. 520, 23
[65] Schumann v. Sprague, 189 Ill.   N. E. Rep. 646.
425, 59 N. E. Rep. 945.

tion, and any surplus or residue after the payment of the debt
would be subject to the claims of his creditors seeking to
enforce their rights. In the case of a mortgage, the property
does not pass beyond the grantor's control. He may satisfy
the debt it is executed to secure, and the property reverts
to him. Not so in the case of an assignment, which disposes of
the entire property. In the case under consideration, the instrument conveys all of the property, first to be paid to preferred creditors, and the residue to be applied pro rata to those
creditors not before named. This certainly places the property
beyond the grantors' reach, and makes it an assignment.''[67]
On the other hand, where an insolvent debtor conveys property
by deed to a second party, in trust for the benefit of certain
named creditors of the grantor, and empowers the grantee to
apply the rents of the property on the indebtedness, or to sell
the property if necessary, but the deed also provides that the

[67] Preston v. Carter, 80 Tex. 388,
16 S. W. Rep. 17. So, in the case
of Robson v. Tomlinson, 54 Ark.
229, 15 S. W. Rep. 456, it was said:
"The instrument relied on by the
interpleader is in form a mortgage,
and not an assignment for the
benefit of creditors. The presumption, until overcome by proof,
is that the parties intended it to
have the effect the law gives to a
mortgage; that is, that it should
stand as security for a debt. The
fact that it provides that the mortgagor should surrender immediate
possession to the trustee for the
mortgagee does not convert it into
an assignment. To accomplish
that result, it must be shown that
it was the intention of the parties
that the debtor should be divested
not only of his control over the
property but also of his title. The
controlling guide, according to the
previous decisions of the court, is,
was it the intention of the parties,
at the time the instrument was
executed, to divest the debtor of
the title, and so make an appropriation of the property to raise
a fund to pay debts? If the equity
of redemption remains in the
debtor, his title is not divested, and
an absolute appropriation of the
property is not made. In arriving at
the intent of the parties, therefore, the question is not whether
the debtor intended to avail himself of the equity of redemption
by payment of the debt, but, was
it the intention to reserve the
equity? If so, the instrument is
a mortgage, and not an assignment." See, further, on the general subject, Johnson v. Robinson,
68 Tex. 400, 4 S. W. Rep. 625; Box
v. Goodbar, 54 Ark. 6, 14 S. W.
Rep. 925; Low v. Wyman, 8 N. H.
536; Barker v. Hall, 13 N. H. 298;
Danforth v. Denny, 25 N. H. 155;
Peck v. Merrill, 26 Vt. 686; Mc-
Gregor v. Chase, 37 Vt. 225; Dun-
ham v. Whitehead, 21 N. Y. 131;
Gage v. Chesebro, 49 Wis. 486, 5
N. W. Rep. 831; Briggs v. Davis,
21 N. Y. 574; McClelland v. Rem-
sen, 3 Abb. Dec. (N. Y.) 74; Van-
Buskirk v. Warren, 4 Abb. Dec.
(N. Y.) 457.

conveyance shall be void if the grantor shall pay the specified indebtedness on demand, it is a trust deed or mortgage securing the designated creditors, and not a deed of assignment for creditors generally.[68]

§ 11. **Conditional Sales Distinguished.**—Courts are frequently called upon to decide whether a conveyance of land, with a contemporaneous agreement giving the grantor the right to repurchase the property, is to be treated as a mortgage or a conditional sale. "A mortgage, when in form a deed absolute, and a conditional sale are frequently so nearly allied to each other that it is sometimes difficult to say whether a particular transaction is the one or the other. The distinctive difference, however, appears to be this: The former is a security for a debt; the latter a purchase of land for a price paid or to be paid, to become absolute on the occurrence of a particular event, or a purchase accompanied by an agreement to resell in a given time for a given price. It is this latter kind that traverse so nearly the boundary line of being a mortgage. Courts of equity, having a tender regard for the equity of redemption, lean slightly toward declaring them mortgages in doubtful cases. Yet there is no rule in law or equity why sales of land, when fairly made, should not assume the conditional form. It may at times, on a given state of facts, be difficult to ascertain the true character of the transaction, but when once determined to be a conditional sale, the transaction should be carried out between the parties as such."[69]

§ 12. **Same; Intention of Parties to Govern.**—Whether a deed of land, executed with an agreement to reconvey on stipulated terms, shall be construed as a sale or as a mortgage depends upon the actual intention of the parties at the time; and this intention is to be gathered from the facts and circumstances attending the transaction and the situation of the parties at the time, as well as from the written evidences of the contract between them.[70] In other words, the form which

[68] Morriss v. Blackman, 179 Ill. 103, 53 N. E. Rep. 547, affirming Blackman v. Metropolitan Dairy Co., 77 Ill. App. 609. Compare Charles F. Penzel Co. v. Jett, 54 Ark. 428, 16 S. W. Rep. 120.

[69] Slutz v. Desenberg, 28 Ohio St. 371. See, also, Chapman v. Ogden, 30 Ill. 515; Hyman v. Bogue, 135 Ill. 9, 26 N. E. Rep. 40.

[70] Jeffery v. Robbins, 167 Ill. 375, 47 N. E. 725; Horbach v. Hill, 112 U. S. 144, 5 Sup. Ct. Rep. 81; King v. McCarthy, (Minn.) 52 N. W. Rep. 648; Smith v. Crosby, 47 Wis. 160, 2 N. W. Rep. 104.

they have chosen to give to the writings passing between them is not conclusive, but their intention must govern. Contracts for repurchase, made contemporaneously with conveyances of real estate, are sometimes strong evidence tending to show that the conveyances are intended to be mortgages; but when it appears that the parties really intended an absolute sale and a contract allowing the vendor to repurchase the property, such intention must control.[71]

§ 13. **Same; Presumption from Face of Papers.**—There is always a presumption that a deed conveying land was intended by the parties to have just the legal effect which appears on its face. Hence, where the papers show on their face a purchase of land, and an agreement for resale, it is necessary, in order to change the effect of the transaction to that of a mortgage, that the evidence afforded by the face of the papers should be overcome by testimony showing that it was not designed to be a sale. In case of conflict, a preponderance of the evidence will determine this question. But testimony which is loose, indefinite, or unsatisfactory in its character, and which at most only creates a doubt as to the true character of the transaction, will not suffice.[72]

§ 14. **Same; Tests for Determining Character of Transaction.**—In the leading case on this subject in the supreme court of the United States, it was said that it is competent for parties to make a contract for the purchase and sale of lands defeasible by the payment of money at a future day, or, in other words, to make a sale with a reservation to the vendor of a right to repurchase the same land at a fixed price and at a specified time. Such contracts are not prohibited by the letter or the policy of the law. But "as lenders of money are less under the pressure of circumstances which control the perfect and free exercise of the judgment than borrowers, the effort is frequently made by persons of this description to avail themselves of the advantage of this superiority in order to obtain inequitable advantages. For this reason the leaning of courts has been against them, and doubtful cases have generally been held to be mortgages. But as a conditional sale, if really intended, is valid, the inquiry in every case must be whether the contract in the specified case is a security for the repayment of money or an actual sale. In this case, the form of

71 Hanford v. Blessing, 80 Ill.   72 Silsbe v. Lucas, 36 Ill. 462.
188.

the deed is not in itself conclusive either way. The want of a covenant to repay the money is not complete evidence that a conditional sale was intended, but is a circumstance of no inconsiderable importance. If the vendee must be restrained to his principal and interest, that principal and interest ought to be secure. It is therefore a necessary ingredient in a mortgage that the mortgagee should have a remedy against the person of the debtor. If this remedy really exists, its not being reserved in terms will not affect the case. But it must exist in order to justify a construction which overrules the express words of the instrument. * * * That the conveyance is made to trustees is not a circumstance of much weight. It manifests an intention in the drawer of the instrument to avoid the usual forms of a mortgage.'' The court also remarked that circumstances bearing on the question and having weight in determining the character of the transaction were also to be found in the fact that the deed was not given to secure any pre-existing debt, and that there was no negotiation between the parties respecting a loan of money, or any proposition made regarding a mortgage. On the other hand, the fact that the debtor was in jail at the time, and was much pressed for money, should have some influence on the decision of the question, as also the circumstance that the price of the property bore no relation to its real value.[73]

§ 15. **Same; Existence of Debt or Loan.**—There can be no mortgage without a debt or some other obligation to be secured by it; and if there was no pre-existing debt to be secured by the conveyance, nor any loan or advance of money made at the time, this is a circumstance which is practically decisive in showing the transaction to have been a conditional sale rather than a mortgage.[74] Thus, where a person advances money, and at the same time receives a deed and gives a bond to the

[73] Conway v. Alexander, 7 Cranch, 218.

[74] See Crane v. Chandler, 190 Ill. 584, 60 N. E. Rep. 826; Rue v. Dole, 107 Ill. 275; Dwen v. Blake, 44 Ill. 135; Eames v. Hardin, 111 Ill. 634; Conway v. Alexander, 7 Cranch, 218. If the conveyance pays off and discharges an existing debt, instead of merely securing its future payment, it is a sale of the property. If this be accompanied by an agreement to reconvey upon receiving a certain sum at or within a certain time, this makes the sale conditional, but does not create a mortgage. Bridges v. Linder, 60 Iowa, 190, 14 N. W. Rep. 217.

grantor for a reconveyance, the transaction is regarded as a loan and a security in the nature of a mortgage; but when the conveyance is made by the person to whom the consideration is paid, and the obligation is given to another, the transaction is to be regarded as a sale.[75] In a case where property, sold on foreclosure of a mortgage, had been bid in by the mortgagee, and he agreed with the mortgagor to extend the time for redemption, holding the land still as security, and in pursuance of this agreement the mortgagee took a quit-claim deed of the land from the mortgagor and gave him a bond for a reconveyance upon the payment, at a certain time beyond the statutory time for redemption, of a sum which was made up of the amount of the foreclosure decree, with heavy usurious interest, the bond providing that the time of payment of the money should be of the essence of the contract, it was held that the transaction constituted a new mortgage, and not a sale and resale.[76] On the other hand, a contract made after the expiration of the time for redemption from a foreclosure sale, whereby one party agrees to advance money to take up the certificate of sale and to hold it for his own benefit, unless the other parties, the heirs of the original mortgagor, should repay the amount advanced within a certain time, is not a mortgage, but a contract of purchase and resale.[77] So, a conveyance by quit-claim deed from the owner of an equity of redemption in land to the holder of a mortgage thereon, with a bond executed by the latter to the former, by which he agrees to reconvey on the payment of a specified sum at a certain date, do not constitute a mortgage.[78] In another case, it appeared that, after a sale of property under a power-of-sale mortgage, the mortgagor and the stranger who had bought at the sale, being doubtful of their rights, in consequence of an alleged defect in the sale, made an arrangement by which the mortgagor gave a quit-claim deed to the purchaser, and received in return a written instrument giving him the option to repurchase within a given time at a fixed price. It was held that this did not constitute a mortgage, there being no debt or loan of money between the parties, and therefore the mortgagor could not claim a right to redeem after the expira-

[75] Carr v. Rising, 62 Ill. 14.

[76] Harbison v. Houghton, 41 Ill. 522.

[77] Carpenter v. Plagge, 192 Ill. 82, 61 N. E. Rep. 530.

[78] Carroll v. Tomlinson, 192 Ill. 398, 61 N. E. Rep. 484.

tion of his option.[79] So, where the purchaser of a mortgagor's equity of redemption, desiring to cut out a judgment-lien on the premises, made an arrangement with the mortgagee to the effect that the latter should foreclose, buy in the property at the sale, and afterwards allow him to redeem within a limited time, and, on payment of the amount due under the trust deed, make him a deed, it was held to be tantamount to an agreement for a sale with right of repurchase, but not to a mortgage.[80]

§ 16. Same; Previous Negotiations of the Parties.—If it is shown that the negotiations between the parties which culminated in the giving of a deed, with an agreement for reconveyance, contemplated the creation of a mere security for a debt, and especially if the grantee explicitly consented to take a mortgage on the property, this will be strong evidence that the transaction was not intended as a conditional sale.[81] On the other hand, if it appears that there was no negotiation between the parties respecting a loan of money and no proposition made with regard to a mortgage, this helps to establish the character of the conveyance as a conditional sale.[82] For even stronger reasons, evidence that the grantee in the deed positively refused to take a mortgage on the property, when approached on the subject, shows that the deed to him and his agreement to resell were not intended by him merely as a mortgage.[83]

§ 17. Same; Inadequacy of Price.—Where property is conveyed by a deed, absolute on its face, accompanied by an agreement that the grantor may repurchase the same within a limited time on the payment of a specified sum, it will sometimes appear that the consideration passing between the parties, or the amount to be paid by the grantor on exercising his option to repurchase, would be fairly proportioned to the value of the property, if considered as a debt or loan secured by a mortgage thereon, but grossly inadequate if regarded as the price of the land on an outright sale. When this is the case, the circumstance is to be taken into consideration as tending

---

[79] Ranstead v. Otis, 52 Ill. 30.

[80] Gibbs v. Union Mut. Life Ins. Co., 123 Ill. 136, 13 N. E. Rep. 842.

[81] See Ewart v. Walling, 42 Ill. 453.

[82] Conway v. Alexander, 7 Cranch, 218.

[83] Bacon v. National German-American Bank, 191 Ill. 205, 60 N. E. Rep. 846.

to show that a conditional sale could not have been intended, but that the transaction should rather be treated as a mortgage. But it is not conclusive by itself, and is not alone sufficient to justify a court in disregarding the presumption arising from the deed itself.[84]

§ 18. Same; The Rule in Cases of Doubt.—When the court, after considering the facts and circumstances of the case, and giving due weight to all the items of evidence tending to show what was the actual intention of the parties, is still substantially in doubt as to whether they meant the transaction to be a conditional sale or a mortgage, it will generally be held to be a mortgage.[85] This is said to be "from a tender regard for the equity of redemption." In other words, the law favors allowing a debtor to redeem his property, in order that advantage may not be taken of his supposed necessitous condition, and in order also that his property may be made to go as far as possible in paying his debts. But this leaning toward the debtor will not be allowed to influence the court when it would result in giving him an unfair advantage and would work injustice to the other party.[86]

[84] Conway v. Alexander, 7 Cranch, 218; Bridges v. Linder, 60 Iowa, 190, 14 N. W. Rep. 217.

[85] Keithley v. Wood, 151 Ill. 566, 38 N. E. Rep. 149, affirming 47 Ill. App. 102; Jeffery v. Robbins, 167 Ill. 375, 47 N. E. Rep. 725, affirming 62 Ill. App. 190; Landreth v. Massey, 61 Ill. App. 147. Where there is room to doubt whether the contract in question is a mortgage or a conditional sale, but, under the statutes of the state, it would be considered a mortgage, a federal court, in carrying the contract into effect, will be guided by the decisions of the supreme court of the state. Pioneer Gold Mining Co. v. Baker, 23 Fed. Rep. 258.

[86] See Vincent v. Walker, 86 Ala. 333, 5 South. Rep. 465. In this case it was said: "Where the instrument, if construed to be a mortgage, will become void, and operate to promote injustice by losing the grantee his money paid for the land, and restoring to the grantor property without an honest return of the money actually received by him, and for the security of which such property was attempted to be conveyed, the inclination of a court of equity, in case of doubt, will be to regard the transaction as a conditional sale, and not as a mortgage. That construction will be adopted, on well-settled principles, which will uphold the instrument and not destroy it, and which will work equity between the parties and not injustice."

CHAPTER II.

ABSOLUTE DEEDS TREATED AS MORTGAGES.

§ 19. Absolute Deed with Separate Written Defeasance.— A deed conveying the title to real estate, which is absolute and unconditional in form, but is intended as security for the payment of a debt or loan, and which is accompanied by a separate written instrument of defeasance conditioned on such payment, is regarded and treated as a mortgage of the land and nothing more.[1] "A deed, otherwise absolute in its terms as a conveyance in fee simple, becomes, through a defeasance provision, a mere mortgage, and it does not matter whether the defeasance provision is incorporated in the same instrument or in a separate instrument contemporaneously executed."[2] And although the one instrument does not refer to the other, the connection between a deed absolute on its face, and a defeasance on a separate paper, may be shown by parol, so as to establish the transaction as a mortgage.[3] But parol evidence is not admissible to vary the terms of such defeasance when once established.[4]

---

[1] Snyder v. Griswold, 37 Ill. 216; Lanahan v. Sears, 102 U. S. 318. "There is no difference in law whether the condition in a mortgage deed, upon which it is to become inoperative, is written in the body of the deed itself, or in a separate instrument executed at the same time, as a part of the same transaction, by the parties to the deed." Lynch v. Jackson, 123 Ill. 360, 14 N. E. 697.

[2] Johnson v. Prosperity Loan & Bldg. Ass'n, 94 Ill. App. 260.

[3] Preschbaker v. Feaman, 32 Ill. 475.

[4] Snyder v. Griswold, 37 Ill. 216.

30

It is not necessary that the defeasance should be in any particular form, provided it clearly shows the intention of the parties to defeat and terminate the mortgagee's title upon the payment of the debt or performance of the other conditions secured by the deed.[5] But when the parties resort to this form of security, they commonly put the defeasance in the form of a covenant on the part of the grantee to reconvey the estate to the grantor upon performance of the conditions. Where a debtor thus executes an absolute conveyance of land to his creditor, and at the same time receives from the latter a contract to reconvey upon payment of the debt, the two instruments together constitute a mortgage.[6] But the mere execution of a deed absolute on its face and a bond or contract for the reconveyance of the premises, upon certain conditions, does not of itself stamp the transaction as a mortgage. To accomplish this result, it is necessary, first, that the agreement of the grantee should purport to defeat and destroy the estate conveyed to him, upon the performance of conditions by the grantor. Thus, where a grantor conveyed the property by deed absolute, and received back a paper in which the grantee agreed, in consideration of the deed, to endeavor to sell the property within one year, and, after deducting a debt due to himself, and paying a debt of the grantor to a third person, to repay to the grantor all the surplus arising from the sale, together with any rent received by the grantee during the year, it was held that this writing did not constitute a defeasance, for the reason stated, and because it was not under seal.[7] Second, it is necessary that there should be some debt

[5] In a case in New York, where the grantor in a deed absolute in form took back an instrument which was designated as a "declaration of trust," but which would have been invalid as such, imposing on the grantee an obligation to reconvey the property on the payment of a certain sum, it was held that equity would treat the transaction as a mortgage. Connor v. Atwood, 4 N. Y. Supp. 561. In the case of Johnson v. Prosperity Loan & Bldg. Ass'n, 94 Ill. App. 260, it was said: "An agreement to reconvey upon stipulated terms may not suffice of itself to make a deed absolute in terms in effect a mortgage, but a limitation which permits the absolute title to vest only upon the happening of a contingency of a failure to pay could hardly be construed to be other than a mortgage."

[6] Jackson v. Lynch, 129 Ill. 72, 21 N. E. Rep. 580, affirming Lynch v. Jackson, 28 Ill. App. 160; Preschbaker v. Feaman, 32 Ill. 475; Clark v. Finlon, 90 Ill. 245; Bearss v. Ford, 108 Ill. 16; Tedens v. Clark, 24 Ill. App. 510.

[7] Walsh v. Brennan, 52 Ill. 193.

or obligation to be secured by the deed. It may be a pre-existing debt from the grantor to the grantee, or a debt created at the time of the conveyance by a loan or advance of money, or a guaranty or contract of indemnification, or some other condition to be performed by the grantor; but there can be no mortgage without a debt or promise to be secured by it.[8] Third, the transaction does not amount to a mortgage unless the parties so understood and intended it. If the proof shows that they intended an absolute sale of the land, with a right simply to repurchase, that intention must govern; and the transaction cannot be treated as a mortgage merely because the grantor changes his mind and desires to redeem as from a mortgage.[9] It is true that what was originally a conditional sale may be converted into a mortgage by subsequent arrangement between the parties; but this requires a clear understanding on both sides, and a common intention and mutual agreement.[10]

It is said that, when a deed, absolute in form, with a clause for repurchase, is given in consideration of an existing mortgage indebtedness, the court is more inclined to treat it as a mortgage than when given upon an original advance; and when so treated, the new mortgage will not be regarded as a substitute for the former security, unless the intention to that effect is manifest; and in such cases, the original mortgage may be foreclosed notwithstanding the giving of the new one.[11] It is also to be observed that a conveyance of land by a deed absolute on its face together with an agreement for the reconveyance of the land on the payment of an existing debt due from the grantor to the grantee, is none the less a mortgage because the bond for the reconveyance is given to a third person, and the obligation is to convey the land to him when the debt is paid, when the latter has no interest in the transaction and is simply to receive the equitable title in trust for the debtor.[12] When land is conveyed by an absolute deed to secure a loan, and a contract entered into between the parties that the property shall be reconveyed on payment of the loan, the entire legal title vests in the grantee, and no action is required on his part to divest the grantor of his equitable right to

[8] Magnusson v. Johnson, 73 Ill. 156. And see cases cited, infra, § 28.

[9] Pitts v. Cable, 44 Ill. 103;

Bishop v. Williams, 18 Ill. 101.

[10] Heald v. Wright, 75 Ill. 17.

[11] Bearss v. Ford, 108 Ill. 16.

[12] Hunter v. Hatch, 45 Ill. 178.

redeem.[13] But it seems that, the relation between the parties not being that of vendor and vendee, but that of mortgagor and mortgagee, the creditor cannot maintain an action of forcible entry and detainer to recover possession of the premises upon default of payment by the party in possession.[14]

§ 20. **Absolute Conveyance with Parol Defeasance.**—An absolute deed of land with a parol defeasance may be treated as a mortgage. That is, where a conveyance of realty, though absolute and unconditional in its terms, was understood and intended by the parties to be a mere security for the payment of a debt, it will be considered as a mortgage, with a consequent right in the grantor to redeem, although the provision for defeasance was not reduced to writing, but rests wholly in their mere verbal agreement.[15] In Illinois, this general rule of chancery jurisprudence has been enacted in the form of a statute, as follows: "Every deed conveying real estate, which shall appear to have been intended only as a security in the nature of a mortgage, though it be an absolute conveyance in terms, shall be considered as a mortgage."[16] This is in affirmance of a well-settled doctrine in equity that the courts of chancery will not regard the form of a transaction, but the intention of the parties must control; and if in fact the transaction was a loan or security for money owing, although the conveyance be absolute on its face, still it will be treated as a mortgage.[17] It is said: "Courts will look behind, and outside of, deeds, to ascertain whether they were intended as mortgages, though absolute upon their face; and when that character is established, it will ever be treated as a mortgage."[18] The important result of this doctrine is that the debtor's right to recover his property will not be cut off by his failure to pay the debt when it is due. In other words, the effect of treating the conveyance as a mortgage is to prevent a forfeiture for breach of condition. No lapse of time, short of that fixed by the statute of limitations, unless so protracted as to amount to gross laches, will bar or forfeit the right of

---

[13] Fitch v. Miller, 200 Ill. 170, 65 N. E. Rep. 650.

[14] West v. Frederick, 62 Ill. 191.

[15] Whitcomb v. Sutherland, 18 Ill. 578; Tillson v. Moulton, 23 Ill. 648; Hallesy v. Jackson, 66 Ill. 139; Pearson v. Pearson, 131 Ill. 464, 23 N. E. Rep. 418; Keithley v. Wood, 47 Ill. App. 102 (affirmed, 151 Ill. 566); Angell v. Jewett, 58 Ill. App. 596.

[16] Rev. Stat. Ill. c. 95, § 12.

[17] Taintor v. Keyes, 43 Ill. 332.

[18] Smith v. Sackett, 15 Ill. 528.

redemption in the debtor or defeat his interest in the premises.[19] Even although it may have been the very purpose and
intention of the parties, in giving and taking a deed absolute
in form instead of the usual form of a mortgage, to create a
security which would cut off the right of redemption and save
the expense of foreclosure, yet the courts rule that, if it appears
to have been intended as a mortgage, the right of redemption
cannot be thus relinquished.[20]

Again, not merely a deed voluntarily made by the grantor
may thus be considered and treated as a mortgage, but also,
in certain circumstances, the deed received by the purchaser
at a judicial sale of the property, even at a mortgage foreclosure sale. Thus, where land was advertised for sale under
a senior mortgage, and, by an arrangement between the owner,
the junior mortgagee, and a third party, the latter bid off the
land for the amount of both mortgages, and paid the amount
due on the elder mortgage, with money furnished by the
junior mortgagee, with the understanding that the owner might
have further time in which to sell the land, and pay off the
amount due on both mortgages, it was held that this transaction
amounted to a mortgage; and that, upon payment of the
amount due on the two mortgages, the owner was entitled to
a conveyance.[21] So, where a debtor, whose land has been sold
on execution for a debt, confesses judgment in favor of another
creditor, who redeems from the sale and takes a deed from the
sheriff, and subsequently a deed from the debtor, releasing
dower and homestead in the premises, the transaction will be
deemed a loan, and the debtor let in to redeem, if extrinsic
evidence shows this to have been the understanding and intention of the parties.[22] Again, where land is sold on execution
and bought in by the debtor in the name of another, who pays
the money and takes the certificate of purchase to himself to
secure the repayment, and afterwards takes out a deed, but
only claims to hold it as security for the money advanced by
him, a purchaser from him, with notice of the fact, will hold
only as a mortgagee, and the land may be redeemed from

[19] Coates v. Woodworth, 13 Ill.
654.

[20] Johnson v. Prosperity Loan &
Bldg. Ass'n, 94 Ill. App. 260.

[21] Klock v. Walter, 70 Ill. 416.

And see Union Mut. Life Ins. Co.
v. Slee, 110 Ill. 35.

[22] Smith v. Doyle, 46 Ill. 451;
Trogdon v. Trogdon, 164 Ill. 144,
45 N. E. Rep. 575.

him.[23] Also, without special reference to judicial sales, a deed
of land taken by a third party who advances the money to pay
for the property, or to complete a purchase thereof, may, by
agreement of the parties, be treated as a mortgage for the
purpose of a redemption by the original purchaser. Thus,
where a purchaser of land assigned his contract to a third
party, to secure a loan of money to make a payment, and the
assignee, on completing the payments, took from the original
vendor an absolute deed of conveyance to himself, it was held
that this deed should stand in the same condition as the contract; it was a mere security for the money advanced by
him.[24]

Further, a conveyance which was originally an absolute
deed may be transformed into a mortgage by the subsequent
dealings and agreement of the parties. For instance, where
land is sold and conveyed, and the parties afterwards rescind
the sale, or the grantor agrees with the grantee to repurchase
at the price for which the property was sold, and the notes
and mortgage taken for a portion of the price are cancelled,
and the grantee is allowed to hold the title as security for the
repayment of the purchase money paid by him, with interest,
the deed for the land becomes thenceforth a mortgage only.[25]

But here, as in the case of a deed with separate written
defeasance, it is necessary to show that the parties agreed and
understood that the transaction should be a mortgage and not a
sale, that there was a debt or obligation to be secured, and that
the agreement contemplated an absolute termination of the
grantee's right and interest in the premises upon payment of
the debt or performance of the condition, and not a mere
option in the grantor to repurchase. Lacking these essentials,
the transaction cannot be considered as a mortgage, whatever
else it may amount to.[26] It remains to be added that a freehold is not involved in a proceeding in equity to have an absolute deed of real estate declared a mortgage.[27]

§ 21. Same; In Actions at Law.—The rule stated in the
preceding section is not confined to equity. Even in a court

[23] Smith v. Knoebel, 82 Ill. 392.

[24] Smith v. Cremer, 71 Ill. 185.

[25] Heald v. Wright, 75 Ill. 17.

[26] See Caprez v. Trover, 96 Ill.
456; Chicago, B. & Q. R. Co. v.
Watson, 113 Ill. 195; Strong v.
Strong, 126 Ill. 301, 18 N. E. Rep.
665.

[27] Hoover v. Ekdahl, 59 Ill. App.
312.

of law, under proper circumstances, a deed which is absolute
on its face may be shown by parol evidence to be a mortgage,
if such was the intention of the parties.[28] It is true, it is held
that, in an action of ejectment, in which the plaintiff relies on
a deed, evidence in avoidance, that the deed is an equitable
mortgage, is not admissible. "A court of law, upon the trial
of an action of ejectment, will not stop to hear evidence as to
whether a conveyance, absolute on its face, was or was not
intended by the parties to be a mere mortgage security. The
remedy of the grantee [grantor] in such a deed is in equity.
He may there file a bill and enjoin the ejectment suit and show
the true character of the instrument."[29] But this decision is
to be understood as applying only to ejectment and similar
actions. In all proceedings at law where the title is not directly in issue, the rule applies that a deed absolute in form
may be shown to have been intended merely as a security.
"No good reason can be offered for holding such testimony
competent in equity and not in an action at law like this. The
reason such testimony is not competent in an action of ejectment is that there the title is directly in issue, and the legal
title prevails."[30]

§ 22. Grounds of Equitable Jurisdiction.—While it is now
generally admitted that parol evidence is admissible, in equity,
to show that an instrument appearing on its face to be an
absolute deed of lands was in fact intended as a mortgage,
yet different theories obtain in different states as to the exact
grounds on which this jurisdiction of equity should be rested,
and different rules as to the precise extent to which it should
be applied. The English doctrine appears to be that when
a party applies to chancery for the relief implied in turning an
absolute deed into a mortgage, he must bring his application
under some already recognized head of equity jurisdiction.
Thus, he must show fraud or deceit, or that a separate defeasance was intended to be executed but was omitted through
accident, mistake, or fraud, or that there was a verbal agreement for a defeasance, which, for similar reasons, was not
carried into effect. And in the earlier jurisprudence of this

[28] Gillespie v. Hughes, 86 Ill.
App. 202.
[29] Finlon v. Clark, 118 Ill. 32, 7
N. E. Rep. 475.

[30] German Ins. Co. v. Gibe, 162
Ill. 251, 44 N. E. Rep. 490; Northern Assurance Co. v. Chicago Mutual B. & L. Ass'n, 98 Ill. App. 152.

country, the same principle was generally adopted, the courts manifesting a marked indisposition to exercise their powers on this class of cases except on the well-known grounds of fraud, accident, or mistake.[31]   But of late years the tendency has been the other way; and it may now be said that, in a majority of the American states, courts having equity powers will treat a deed absolute on its face as a mortgage, upon being convinced by proper evidence that such was the real intention of the parties, and that it would be contrary to equity to refuse to carry into effect such intention of the parties concerned. And this they will do without requiring the applicant to show fraud, accident, or mistake, or deceit, and without feeling obliged to assume an intended instrument of defeasance, and even where such defeasance was intentionally omitted on an understanding between the parties.   This is the doctrine prevailing in Illinois.[32]   In one of the decisions of the supreme court it was said: ''It will be perceived that in none of these cases (earlier Illinois decisions) did the court attempt to range the jurisdiction to turn an absolute deed into a mortgage, by parol evidence, under any specific head of equity, such as fraud, accident, or mistake, but the rule seems to have grown into recognition as an independent head of equity.   Still, it must have its foundation in this, that where the transaction is shown to have been meant as a security for a loan, the deed will have the character of a mortgage, without other proof of fraud than is implied in showing that a conveyance, taken for the mutual benefit of both parties, has been appropriated solely to the use of the grantee.''[33]   And later decisions have felt it to be unnecessary to connect the authority of the courts in this particular with the general bases of equity jurisdiction even by the slender thread of this implication of fraud.   For it is said that the statute in force in this state permits the courts to hold an absolute deed to be a mortgage upon another and different ground than that of fraud, accident, or mistake, namely, the mere intention of the parties that the conveyance shall operate only as a security.[34]

[31] See Story, Eq. Jur. § 1018; 4 Kent, Comm. 142.

[32] Metropolitan Bank v. Godfrey, 23 Ill. 579, 604; Sutphen v. Cushman, 35 Ill. 186; Tillson v. Moulton, 23 Ill. 648.

[33] Ruckman v. Alwood, 71 Ill. 155.

[34] Gillespie v. Hughes, 86 Ill. App. 202; Rev. Stat. Ill. c. 95, § 12.

§ 23. Parol Evidence Admissible.—The rule which forbids the reception of parol evidence to vary or explain a written contract is subject to the well-established exception in the law of mortgages which permits parties to show by parol that a deed, plain and unambiguous in its terms and absolute on its face, is in reality a mortgage, or mere security for the payment of money or the performance of some other act or duty; and so an instrument, substantially in the form of a mortgage, may in like manner be explained, with a view of discerning the real intention of the parties.[35] Accordingly, we have the settled rule that, where the action concerns the legal effect of a deed, which is on its face an absolute conveyance in fee, but which is alleged to have been understood and intended by the parties only as a mortgage, it is competent to establish this fact not only by written evidence dehors the instrument itself, such as collateral writings between the parties, but also by oral testimony as to the relations between the parties, their previous negotiations, their conduct and declarations, and, in short, whatever will tend to elucidate the real character of the transaction and disclose their actual intention in the matter.[36] The application of this rule is not confined to the courts of the state; it is also the settled doctrine of the federal courts.[37] And even though there may be a written defeasance,

---

[35] Bearss v. Ford, 108 Ill. 16. The rule which excludes parol testimony to contradict or vary a written instrument has reference to the language used by the parties; it does not forbid an inquiry into the object of the parties in executing and receiving the instrument. Brick v. Brick, 98 U. S. 514. In the case of Sutphen v. Cushman, 35 Ill. 186, the rule is thus stated: To determine whether a deed absolute upon its face should be regarded in equity as a mortgage, parol evidence is admissible so far as it conduces to show the relations between the parties, or to show any other fact or circumstance of a nature to control the deed, and establish such an equity as would give a right to redemption, and no further.

[36] Delahay v. McConnel, 5 Ill. 156; Ferguson v. Sutphen, 8 Ill. 547; Purviance v. Holt, Id. 394; Hovey v. Holcomb, 11 Ill. 660; Shaver v Woodward, 28 Ill. 277; Sutphen v. Cushman, 35 Ill. 186; Reighard v. McNeil, 38 Ill. 400; Klock v. Walter, 70 Ill. 416; Ruckman v. Alwood, 71 Ill. 155; Low v. Graff, 80 Ill. 360; Sharp v. Smitherman, 85 Ill. 153; Knowles v. Knowles, 86 Ill. 1; Hancock v. Harper, Id. 445; Wright v. Gay, 101 Ill. 233; Helm v. Boyd, 124 Ill. 370, 16 N. E. Rep. 85; Moffett v. Hanner, 154 Ill. 649, 39 N. E. Rep. 474; Bernhard v. Bruner, 65 Ill. App. 641; Mann v. Jobusch, 70 Ill. App. 440.

[37] Amory v. Lawrence, 3 Cliff. 523, Fed. Cas. No. 336; Andrews v. Hyde. 3 Cliff. 516, Fed. Cas. No.

the fact that a deed of land was intended as a security only may be proved by parol evidence.[38]

It is necessary also to remark that the statute of frauds does not stand in the way of treating an absolute deed as a mortgage, when such was the intention of the parties, though the defeasance or agreement for redemption rests wholly in parol. The statute, it is said, was not intended to facilitate the perpetration of fraud, or to protect fraud, but to prevent it, and the courts will not permit the statute to be used as an engine of fraud.[39]

§ 24. Presumption and Burden of Proof.—While a deed of land, absolute and unconditional in form, may be shown by parol evidence to have been intended as a mortgage, yet (1) the law raises a presumption from the face of the conveyance that the instrument is just what it purports to be, (2) this presumption can be overcome only by clear and convincing proof of the different character of the paper, and (3) the burden of adducing such proof rests upon the party seeking to have the instrument declared a mortgage.[40] "When a deed for land appears on its face to be an absolute and unconditional conveyance, and is acknowledged and delivered, the law will presume, in the absence of proof showing the contrary, that it is what it purports to be, an absolute conveyance. When a warranty deed for land, absolute in form, is claimed to be a mortgage only, the party alleging such a character must sustain his claim by evidence sufficiently clear and satisfactory to overcome this presumption of the law. Loose, indefinite, and unsatisfactory evidence will not suffice."[41] Moreover, the presumption that the intended effect of the conveyance is not different from its apparent legal effect is one which is strengthened by the lapse of time; so that if a very long period elapses before the grantor brings forward his claim that the instrument should be considered as a mortgage, the clearness and weight of the

377; Bentley v. Phelps, 2 Woodb. & Min. 426, Fed. Cas. No. 1,331; Brick v. Brick, 98 U. S. 514.

[38] Tillson v. Moulton, 23 Ill. 648.

[39] Union Mut. Life Ins. Co. v. White, 106 Ill. 67.

[40] Burgett v. Osborne, 172 Ill. 227, 50 N. E. Rep. 206; Williams v. Williams, 180 Ill. 361, 54 N. E. Rep.

229; Heaton v. Gaines, 198 Ill. 479, 64 N. E. Rep. 1081; Workman v. Greening, 115 Ill. 477, 4 N. E. Rep. 385; Bailey v. Bailey, 115 Ill. 551, 4 N. E. Rep. 394; Knowles v. Knowles, 86 Ill. 1; Mann v. Jobusch, 70 Ill. App. 440.

[41] Bentley v. O'Bryan, 111 Ill. 53; Eames v. Hardin, Id. 634.

evidence which is required of him will be correspondingly in-creased.[42] If the bill charges that a deed, absolute on its face, was in fact a security for a loan of money, and the answer, under oath, clearly and distinctly denies the allegation, and insists that it was a sale, the answer is evidence, and must be overcome by preponderating evidence before relief will be granted.[43]

§ 25. Quantum of Evidence Required.—"Where land is con-veyed in fee by a deed with covenants of warranty, and there is no condition or defeasance either in the deed or in a col-lateral paper, and parol evidence is resorted to for the purpose of establishing that the deed was given as a mortgage, such evidence must be clear and convincing, otherwise the presump-tion that the deed is what it purports to be upon its face must always prevail."[44] Or, as the rule is commonly stated, in order to convert a deed, absolute on its face, into a mortgage or mere security, the understanding and intention of the parties in that behalf must be established by "clear, convincing, and satisfac-tory" proof.[45] "Where parties have deliberately given to a transaction all the forms of a sale, slight, indefinite, or unsatis-factory evidence will not be permitted to change its character, but that can be done only by proof which clearly shows that the intention of the parties was that it should be a mortgage and not a sale."[46] A court therefore will not be justified in making a decree declaring such a conveyance to be a mortgage, where the testimony produced in favor of that contention is loose, indefinite, and inconclusive, or where the evidence is contradictory, with a preponderance in support of the absolute

[42] Hancock v. Harper, 86 Ill. 445.
[43] Taintor v. Keys, 43 Ill. 332.
[44] Keithley v. Wood, 151 Ill. 566, 38 N. E. Rep. 149.
[45] Dwen v. Blake, 44 Ill. 135; Price v. Karnes, 59 Ill. 276; Al-wood v. Mansfield, Id. 496; Rem-ington v. Campbell, 60 Ill. 516; Smith v. Cremer, 71 Ill. 185; Mag-nusson v. Johnson, 73 Ill. 156; Purington v. Akhurst, 74 Ill. 490; Low v. Graff, 80 Ill. 360; Hancock v. Harper, 86 Ill. 445; Clark v. Fin-lon, 90 Ill. 245; Maher v. Farwell, 97 Ill. 56; Bartling v. Brasuhn, 102

Ill. 441; Helm v. Boyd, 124 Ill. 370, 16 N. E. Rep. 85; Conant v. Rise-borough, 139 Ill. 383, 28 N. E. Rep. 789; Strong v. Strong, 27 Ill. App. 148. The rule which allows parol evidence to be introduced to show that a deed absolute on its face is a mortgage should not be en-larged, but should be strictly con-strued, and the evidence should be very strong. Howland v. Blake, 7 Biss. 40, Fed. Cas. No. 6,792.

[46] Whittemore v. Fisher, 132 Ill. 243, 24 N. E. Rep. 636.

character of the deed.[47] Thus, a deed will not be declared a
mortgage where the grantee testifies positively that it was an
absolute conveyance, and the evidence for the complainant is
conflicting and unconvincing.[48] Nor should a deed absolute on
its face be decreed to be a mortgage upon the unsupported
testimony of the complainant, contradicted by the defendant.[49]
On the other hand, a decree declaring an absolute deed to be a
mortgage, upon evidence heard in open court, will not be set
aside on appeal as contrary to the evidence, where the testimony is conflicting, and the evidence of defendant's witnesses,
while tending to show a purchase of the land, states a different
consideration therefor from that alleged in the answer.[50]

§ 26. What Evidence Admissible.—In determining the question whether a deed, absolute on its face, was in reality intended as a mortgage, extraneous evidence being admitted, the
court is not restricted to any particular kind of evidence, but
may take into consideration almost any pertinent matters
which tend to prove the real intention and understanding of
the parties and the true nature of the transaction in question.[51]
The one determining factor—the ultimate test—is always the
actual intention of the parties. It is this which must be sought,
and which, when ascertained, will govern the question. But
in the search for this intention, the court may look into the
whole transaction and consider all the attending circumstances.[52] Written documents which illustrate the relation of
the parties and their understanding of the dealings between

[47] May v. May, 158 Ill. 209, 42 N.
E. Rep. 56; Shays v. Norton, 48
Ill. 100; Bentley v. O'Bryan, 111
Ill. 53; Miller v. Green, 138 Ill.
565, 28 N. E. Rep. 837.

[48] Strong v. Strong, 126 Ill. 301,
18 N. E. Rep. 665.

[49] Blake v. Taylor, 142 Ill. 482,
32 N. E. Rep. 401.

[50] Hanks v. Rhodes, 128 Ill. 404,
21 N. E. Rep. 774.

[51] In a case in West Virginia, it
is said that the following facts
and circumstances should have
great weight in determining the
question in favor of the theory
that the conveyance was meant as
a mortgage, rather than as a sale:

(1) that the grantor was hard
pressed for money; (2) that the
conveyance was preceded by negotiations for a loan by the grantee
to the grantor; (3) that the parties
did not apparently consider either
the quantity or the value of the
land conveyed; (4) that the price
was grossly inadequate; (5) that
the possession remained in the
grantor after the conveyance. Gilchrist v. Beswick, 33 W. Va. 168,
10 S. E. Rep. 371.

[52] Mann v. Jobusch, 70 Ill. App.
440; Reece v. Allen, 5 Gilm. (10
Ill.) 236; Williams v. Bishop, 15
Ill. 553.

them will of course be pertinent and admissible. Thus, the conveyance may be considered in connection with a lease accompanying it, from the grantee to the grantor, where both are parts of the same transaction. In such a case, the documents will be construed as though they were different parts of the same instrument.[53] And testimony of matters in pais will be received, so far as it throws light on the disputed issue and helps to disclose the true character of the conveyance. For example, the fact that the grantor in the deed remained in the possession of the estate is a pertinent circumstance which may be shown and considered in determining whether the conveyance is to be treated as a deed or as a mortgage.[54] On the other hand, the transfer of possession to the grantee, and his long continued enjoyment of the estate, without any claim on the part of the grantor to treat the deed as a mortgage and redeem from it, will influence the court in deciding against the theory that the conveyance was intended as a mortgage. In one case it appeared that, shortly after the making of a mortgage on land, the mortgagor gave to the mortgagee a quit-claim deed of the premises and put him in possession. The latter retained possession for over twenty years, claiming and treating the land as his own, making improvements from time to time, and paying the taxes. The grantor lived twelve years after the date of the deed, and in the immediate vicinity, and never claimed the property nor called the grantee to account for it, and his widow and heirs made no such claim until about eight years after the grantor's death. It was held that these facts afforded strong evidence that the quit-claim deed was an absolute conveyance made in satisfaction of the debt, and not a mortgage.[55]

Again, on this question, it may be shown that the consideration named in the conveyance would be entirely inadequate as a price for the realty conveyed, though not too inconsiderable to be secured by a mortgage on the premises.[56] This considera-

[53] Bearss v. Ford, 108 Ill. 16.

[54] Strong v. Shea, 83 Ill. 575.

[55] Hart v. Randolph, 142 Ill. 521, 32 N. E. Rep. 517.

[56] Rubo v. Bennett, 85 Ill. App. 473. And see Huscheon v. Huscheon, 71 Cal. 407, 12 Pac. Rep. 410. To establish the inadequacy of the consideration as a price for the land, the value of the property may be shown by either party; but the grantor's own estimate of its value is not admissible. "He could not give character to his deed by showing what he had thought or said as to the worth of his land."

tion is of course not absolutely conclusive; its force may be
neutralized by other facts tending in the opposite direction.
But still it is a circumstance entitled to great weight in the
decision of the question, being very strong evidence to show
that an absolute sale of the land could not have been intended.
As remarked by the supreme court of the United States, "in
examining this question, it is of great importance to inquire
whether the consideration was adequate to induce a sale. When
no fraud is practised, and no inequitable advantages taken of
pressing wants, owners of property do not sell it for a consideration manifestly inadequate; and therefore, in the cases
on this subject, great stress is justly laid upon the fact that
what is alleged to have been the price bore no proportion to the
value of the thing said to have been sold."[57]   But the presumption that a deed, absolute on its face, was intended as a
mortgage, arising from a gross inadequacy of consideration,
will not control, where the accompanying circumstances warrant the inference that it was intended that the grantor should
have a share in the profits expected to be realized from a subsequent sale of the premises.[58]

§ 27. Same; Declarations of Parties.—The declarations and
statements of the parties made pending the negotiations, and
at the time of the final execution of a deed and contract, are
admissible to show that the deed, though absolute in form, was
taken and intended as a mortgage or security for a debt or
loan of money; and the rule that the terms and conditions of
a written contract cannot be varied by parol evidence does not
here apply.[59]   Also it is held that declarations made by a
party to a deed, after its execution, are competent against him
to show that the deed was intended as a mortgage notwithstanding its form.[60]   But no great reliance should be placed on
this kind of evidence, unless the declarations or statements
shown were very explicit and positive. A word of warning was
spoken in this connection in one of the earlier decisions of the

Pope v. Marshall, 78 Ga. 635, 4 S.
E. Rep. 116.
[57] Russell v. Southard, 12 How.
139.
[58] Story v. Springer, 155 Ill. 25,
39 N. E. Rep. 570.
[59] Helbreg v. Schumann, 150 Ill.
12, 37 N. E. Rep. 99; Darst v. Murphy, 119 Ill. 343, 9 N. E. Rep. 887;
Purviance v. Holt, 8 Ill. 394; Williams v. Bishop, 15 Ill. 553; Whitcomb v. Sutherland, 18 Ill. 578;
Reigard v. McNeil, 38 Ill. 400;
Bartling v. Brasuhn, 102 Ill. 441.
[60] Ross v. Brusie, 64 Cal. 245, 30
Pac. Rep. 811.

supreme court of Illinois, where the evidence offered to show that a deed absolute on its face was intended as a mortgage consisted of certain loose declarations of the grantee in regard to his intentions in the matter. The court, per Sheldon, J., said: "This is a dangerous species of evidence on which to disturb the title to land; it is extremely liable to be misunderstood or perverted, and the allowance of it, for that purpose, does not accord with the policy of the law requiring written evidence to attest the ownership of real property. The kind of parol evidence which is properly receivable to show an absolute deed to be a mortgage is that of facts and circumstances of such a nature as, in a court of equity, will control the operation of the deed, and not of loose declarations of parties touching their intentions or understanding. It has been held that evidence of such declarations alone is insufficient proof to show an absolute deed to be a mortgage."[61]

§ 28. Same; As to Existence of Debt.—On the question whether a deed absolute in form was intended as a mortgage, it may be shown that the relation of debtor and creditor existed between the grantor and the grantee in the conveyance at the time of its execution; and indeed it is indispensable, in order to convert the instrument into a mortgage, to show that there was an existing debt which they may have intended to secure, or a contemporaneous loan or advance of money, or some obligation or duty assumed by the grantor, or existing against him, and enforceable at the instance of the grantee; since there can be no mortgage without something to be secured by it.[62] Thus, evidence that a creditor took a deed of land in payment of his debt, and acknowledged that the debt was paid, and that afterwards the debtor gave the creditor another conveyance, absolute in form, for the purpose of securing him from loss arising in case the land should prove to be worth less than the debt, is not sufficient to show that the second conveyance was a mortgage, since, at the time it was given, there was no existing debt to be secured by it. "The burden was upon appellants," said the court, "to prove that this agreement was in fact a security for a subsisting

[61] Lindauer v. Cummings, 57 Ill. 195.

[62] Westlake v. Horton, 85 Ill. 228; Ennor v. Thompson, 46 Ill.

214; Sutphen v. Cushman, 35 Ill. 186; Crane v. Chandler, 190 Ill. 584, 60 N. E. Rep. 826.

indebtedness. It is not enough that the proof shall merely show a parol agreement to reconvey. There must be a continuing, valid indebtedness secured by it, which may be enforced by appellee in an action at law, or it is not a mortgage, whatever else it may be.''[63]

But it is very necessary to remark that the mere fact of a pre-existing debt between the parties does not prove conclusively that the conveyance was intended as a mortgage; for this fact does not exclude the hypothesis that the grantor intended to convey the land in satisfaction of the debt, and without intending to reserve any right of redemption; and this clearly may be shown by the grantee. Therefore, when the fact of an existing debt is admitted or established by proof, the next inquiry will be as to the effect of the conveyance on such debt. The test by which to determine whether the deed (made in consideration of the grantor's indebtedness to the grantee) was to operate as a sale or a mortgage, is to be found in the question whether the debt was discharged by the conveyance or not.[64] If the conveyance leaves the debt still due and owing, the grantor being bound to pay it at some future time, and being entitled to receive back his property when he does pay it, then the whole transaction amounts to a mortgage, whatever form the parties may have given to it.[65] But evidence merely that the parties to the deed agreed that the land might be redeemed is not sufficient to prove that the deed was a mortgage, where there is no evidence of the existence of any mortgage debt.[66] On the other hand, where it is entirely clear that no debt continues to exist, or is created, between the parties, a conveyance absolute on its face cannot be shown

---

[63] Batcheller v. Batcheller, 144 Ill. 471, 33 N. E. Rep. 24. So, in the case of Knaus v. Dreher, 84 Ala. 319, 4 South. Rep. 287, it was said: "To establish the proposition that a conveyance, absolute in form, was in intention and fact only a mortgage security, there must be a continuing, binding debt from the mortgagor to the mortgagee to uphold it,—a debt in its fullest sense; not a mere privilege reserved in the grantor to pay or not at his election, but a debt which the grantee can enforce as a debt, and for its collection may foreclose the conveyance as a mortgage. Where there is no debt, there can be no mortgage; for if there is nothing to secure, there can be no security."

[64] Glass v. Doane, 15 Ill. App. 66.

[65] Keithley v. Wood, 151 Ill. 566, 38 N. E. Rep. 149; Helm v. Boyd, 124 Ill. 370, 16 N. E. Rep. 85.

[66] Fisher v. Green, 142 Ill. 80, 31 N. E. Rep. 172.

to be a mortgage.[67] Thus, an absolute deed cannot be held to be a mortgage if it is shown that a previously existing debt between the parties was cancelled and discharged by the conveyance, leaving no consideration to support the instrument in the character of a mortgage.[68] But the fact that the grantor's notes, cancelled, and exhibited to him as cancelled and paid, were not delivered to him at the time he executed a deed in payment thereof, does not make the deed a mere mortgage.[69]

§ 29. **Rights of Grantor.**—The grantor in a deed absolute in form, but intended only as a security in the nature of a mortgage, has all the rights of a mortgagor with respect to redemption of the estate. That is, on paying the debt, or performing the other conditions secured by the conveyance, he will have the right to require a reconveyance of the premises from the grantee.[70] And conversely, the grantee in such a deed will have the right to foreclose it as a mortgage. He may file a bill in equity for the sale of the grantor's equity in the premises, notwithstanding the agreement between the parties provides that he himself may make sale and account for the proceeds.[71] If the grantee refuses to recognize the instrument as a mortgage, claiming it as an absolute sale and conveyance to himself, and therefore declines to receive payment of the debt, or performance of the other conditions, by way of redemption, the remedy of the grantor is in equity. He may there file a bill praying that the conveyance shall be decreed to be a mortgage only, and that he may be allowed to redeem from the same, and the grantee ordered to reconvey to him on such redemption being made.[72] But since it is only by the aid of a court of

[67] Kerting v. Hilton, 152 Ill. 658, 38 N. E. Rep. 941; Freer v. Lake, 115 Ill. 662, 4 N. E. Rep. 512.

[68] Mann v. Jobusch, 70 Ill. App. 440; Johnson v. Prosperity Loan & Bldg. Ass'n, 94 Ill. App. 260.

[69] Miller v. Green, 37 Ill. App. 631, affirmed, 138 Ill. 565, 28 N. E. Rep. 837.

[70] Roberts v. Richards, 36 Ill. 339.

[71] Reid v. McMillan, 189 Ill. 411, 59 N. E. Rep. 948.

[72] A court of equity, after ascertaining that a transfer by absolute deed with a contract for reconveyance is a mortgage, will allow the mortgagor to redeem after the time agreed upon, although the parties have attempted to make time of the essence of the contract. Jackson v. Lynch, 129 Ill. 72, 22 N. E. Rep. 246. But a bill to have a deed absolute on its face declared a mortgage will not lie after the right to foreclose is barred by the statute of limitations, since the right to redeem and the right to foreclose are reciprocal. Green v. Capps, 142 Ill. 286, 31 N. E. Rep. 597.

equity that the grantor in such an instrument can show that it was intended as a mortgage, he becomes subject to the rule that "he who seeks equity must do equity." Hence he must fulfill, or offer to fulfill, all the obligations which would rest upon him as a mortgagor.[73] But it appears that the fact that one of the motives in executing a deed absolute in terms, but in intention and legal effect a mortgage, was to hinder the grantor's creditors, is not a defense to a suit for redemption.[74]

As to the possession of the premises conveyed, it is usually a matter of agreement between the parties. If possession is surrendered to the grantee, or if he otherwise acquires it by lawful means, he will have the rights of a mortgagee in possession, and consequently cannot be dispossessed by the grantor except upon payment of the debt or other obligation secured. The holder of an ordinary mortgage, as will appear more fully in another place, is not entitled to maintain ejectment against the mortgagor, to recover possession of the mortgaged estate, until there has been a breach of condition. But it is said that a deed absolute in form, intended as a security, differs from an ordinary mortgage in this particular, and must be regarded as vesting the legal title and the right of possession in the grantee, so that the latter (in the absence of an agreement on the subject) will be entitled to recover possession of the property at any time, whether before or after breach of condition, unless the grantor interposes his equitable defense, by an offer to redeem.[75]

But the fact that the conveyance has been made in the form supposed does not vest the grantee with such absolute ownership of the estate as will release him from the ordinary liability of a mortgagee in possession, with respect to accounting for the rents and profits. In other words, the fact that an instrument intended only to pledge land as security for the payment of a debt was put in the form of an absolute deed, instead of the form of a mortgage, will not deprive the grantor of the right to recover for rents and profits of the land accruing or

[73] Heacock v. Swartwout, 28 Ill. 291.

[74] Livingston v. Ives, 35 Minn. 55, 27 N. W. Rep. 74. But compare Kitts v. Wilson (Ind.), 29 N. E. Rep. 401.

[75] Burdick v. Wentworth, 42 Ia. 440; Richards v. Crawford, 50 Ia. 494; Bennett v. Robinson, 27 Mich. 26; Jeffrey v. Hursh, 42 Mich. 563, 4 N. W. Rep. 303. Compare Connolly v. Giddings, 24 Nebr. 131, 37 N. W. Rep. 939.

received by the grantee between the time of the making of such deed and a reconveyance to the grantor.[76] Finally, it is said that a conveyance of a homestead by a deed absolute on its face, but in fact intended as a mortgage, does not destroy its character as a homestead.[77]

§ 30. **Loss or Relinquishment of Equity of Redemption.**— Very long delay, amount to gross laches, will defeat the right to redeem from an equitable or constructive mortgage.[78] Hence a party who has a right to treat a deed absolute on its face as a mortgage and make redemption from it must exercise such right in apt time, and a failure to do so will constitute laches and bar his right. If there is such a change in the relations of the parties or in the subject-matter of the suit as to make it inequitable to grant the relief, or if the delay is so great in asserting the right as to justify the presumption that the right had been abandoned, relief will be denied in equity without reference to any statutory period.[79] Thus, in one case, where a bill to redeem from a deed, absolute on its face, but claimed to have been intended as a mortgage, was not filed until thirteen years after the date of the transaction, and more than seven years after the grantee had distinctly refused to recognize the rights claimed by the complainant, and no sufficient excuse for the delay was offered, it was held that complainant's right to relief was barred by his laches.[80]

Furthermore, although a deed absolute on its face may be made under such circumstances and with such an understanding between the parties as to amount in equity to a mere mortgage, yet afterwards, if the parties both agree thereto, it may lose its character as an equitable mortgage, and become what it purports to be, an unconditional conveyance.[81] And it is not essential to the proper extinguishment of the right of redemption, by an arrangement between the parties themselves, that it should be done by an instrument which will operate as a technical conveyance of the mortgagor's estate in the land. If such transactions have occurred between the parties as would render it inequitable that the grantor should be

[76] Haworth v. Taylor, 108 Ill. 275.

[77] McClure v. Braniff, 75 Iowa, 38, 39 N. W. Rep. 171.

[78] King v. Wilder, 75 Ill. 275.

[79] Turner v. Littlefield, 46 Ill.

App. 169, affirmed, 142 Ill. 630.

[80] Maher v. Farwell, 97 Ill. 56.

[81] Richmond v. Richmond, 4 Chicago Leg. News, 41, Fed. Cas. No. 11,801; Carpenter v. Carpenter, 70 Ill. 457.

permitted to redeem, that, of itself, without a technical release, will operate as a cancellation of the agreement for defeasance, or instrument of defeasance, and give to the deed the effect of an original, absolute conveyance as between the parties.[82]

§ 31. **Rights of Creditors of Grantor.**—It is said that, where there is an absolute conveyance of land intended as a mortgage, and a separate covenant by the grantee to reconvey to the grantor on payment of a sum of money, this is an equitable mortgage; but it is a mortgage only in equity. At law, it leaves the mortgagor without any interest in the land; he has nothing but an equity to demand a reconveyance on complying with the conditions. This equity is not an estate in the land to which the lien of a judgment can attach, and it cannot be sold on an execution at law against him.[83] While this may be conceded, it is also true that the right to show that a deed absolute on its face was in fact intended as a mortgage is not always confined to the grantor therein. A creditor of such grantor may establish this fact, and thereby render the equity of redemption available as assets for the satisfaction of his claim.[84] And it has been said that a party who takes a mortgage in the form of an absolute deed must, if questioned by a creditor of the mortgagor, or other person having an interest in knowing the fact, carefully and truly disclose the true nature of his security. An untruthful statement touching a material fact in relation to such security, or a failure to make a full and true disclosure when required, will postpone such security to that of a subsequent attaching creditor.[85] Again, a conveyance of property which is absolute on its face, but which is in reality intended as a mortgage or security, though valid between the parties, may work such a fraud upon other creditors of the grantor as to be voidable at their instance: as, when the grantor is insolvent, and the purpose of the transaction is to put the property beyond the reach of the other creditors or to hinder and delay them in collecting their claims.[86] Thus, where a person conveyed all his real estate

[82] West v. Reed, 55 Ill. 242.

[83] Baird v. Kirtland, 8 Ohio, 21; Loring v. Melendy, 11 Ohio, 355.

[84] DeWolf v. Strader, 26 Ill. 225; Macauley v. Smith, 132 N. Y. 524, 30 N. E. Rep. 997.

[85] Geary v. Porter, 17 Oreg. 465, 21 Pac. Rep. 442.

[86] Fuller & Fuller Co. v. Gaul, 85 Ill. App. 500, affirmed, 185 Ill. 43.

to his legal adviser, for the purpose of preventing his creditors
from reaching it, as well as to secure a debt due to the grantee,
and was induced to do so by the advice and artifice of the
grantee, it was held that equity should treat the deed as a mortgage and allow a redemption, notwithstanding the fraud
attending the transaction, the parties not being in pari
delicto.[87]

§ 32. **Rights of Purchaser from Grantee.**—If a person holding the legal title to land under a deed which was absolute
and unconditional in form, but which was in reality intended
as a mortgage, makes a sale of the property to a third person,
who buys in good faith and for a valuable consideration, the
rights of the purchaser will depend upon his notice, or want
of notice, of the true character of the conveyance to his vendor.
On the one hand, where an absolute conveyance of lands is
designed as a mortgage, it will retain its character as a mortgage in the hands of each subsequent purchaser who takes it
with notice of the rights of the parties; and therefore if the
subsequent grantee had actual knowledge of the nature of the
original transaction, or knowledge of facts which would put
him upon inquiry, he cannot claim to be the unconditional
owner of the estate. He will occupy exactly the position of an
assignee of the mortgage; and the mortgagor will have the
same right to redeem the estate from him as from the original
grantee.[88] And the fact that the original owner of the property makes an assignment for the benefit of his creditors, and
fails to schedule therein the equity of redemption as assets,
will not preclude him from asserting such equity as against
a subsequent purchaser with notice, even though his purpose
was to defraud creditors.[89]

But on the other hand, if the purchaser relies on the apparently perfect legal title of his vendor, and has no knowledge of any agreement or understanding as to the character
of the original deed, nor any notice, actual or constructive, of
the facts which are alleged to convert that deed into a mort-

[87] Herrick v. Lynch, 150 Ill. 283, 37 N. E. Rep. 221.

[88] Brown v. Gaffney, 28 Ill. 149; Shaver v. Woodward, Id. 277; Smith v. Knoebel, 82 Ill. 392; De Clerq v. Jackson, 103 Ill. 658; Union Mut. Life Ins. Co. v. Slee,

123 Ill. 57, 13 N. E. Rep. 222; Howat v. Howat, 101 Ill. App. 158; Eisaman v. Gallagher, 24 Nebr. 79, 37 N. W. Rep. 941.

[89] Over v. Carolus, 171 Ill. 552, 49 N. E. Rep. 514.

gage, then it would be grossly unjust to deprive him of the fruits of his purchase on a claim by the original owner that he had a right to redeem. It is true, one of the earlier decisions in Illinois holds that if the property has been sold to a bona fide purchaser, who makes valuable improvements thereon, on the supposition and belief that he has a good title, and not with a view of enhancing the redemption money, a court of equity, on an application to redeem, will allow him for such improvements.[90] But later decisions, in accordance with the rule elsewhere, fully recognize the rule that the original owner has no right of redemption as against such a purchaser taking without notice; the latter's title is indefeasible.[91] More especially is this the case where the grantor in the original deed has estopped himself from claiming a right to redeem by declarations admitting his conveyance of the absolute title to the grantee and by permitting the latter to deal with it as an absolute owner.[92]

When the title to the property is thus irrevocably lost to the original owner, in consequence of its transfer to an innocent purchaser without notice, he has his remedy against his grantee, who has violated his legal duty by dealing as absolute owner with property which was only conveyed to him by way of pledge. As to this proposition there is no dissent. But the authorities are not agreed as to the proper measure of damages in such an action. In Illinois, it appears to be the doctrine that, if no actual fraud on the part of the grantee is shown, he is chargeable only with the value of the lands at the time he sold the same.[93] The supreme court of the United States adheres to the rule that the defendant, in such an action, must account to the owner of the equity of redemption for all that he actually received over and above the amount of the debt originally secured by the deed.[94] And in some other states, the courts have decided that the measure of the grantor's recovery should be the value of the land at the time of the trial of the action, less the debt, with interest.[95]

90 Miller v. Thomas, 14 Ill. 428.

91 Maxfield v. Patchen, 29 Ill. 39; Gruber v. Baker, 20 Nevad. 453, 23 Pac. Rep. 858.

92 Jenkins v. Rosenberg, 105 Ill. 157.

93 Gibbs v. Meserve, 12 Ill. App. 613.

94 Shillaber v. Robinson, 97 U. S. 68.

95 Boothe v. Feist (Tex.), 15 S. W. Rep. 799.

CHAPTER III.

EQUITABLE MORTGAGES.

§ 33. **Equitable Mortgages in General.**—In the preceding chapter we considered the effect of an absolute deed with a separate written defeasance, or with a parol agreement for defeasance, as an equitable mortgage. Summarizing some of the conclusions there reached, it may be stated that, in equity, in determining whether or not a given transaction is to be treated as a mortgage, the form of the transaction is not regarded, but the substance must control; that the intention of the parties, to be determined in the light of surrounding circumstances, must give character to the contract in that regard; that it is not necessary, in order to constitute a mortgage, that it should be so expressed in the conveyance, but it may appear by a separate instrument, in the nature of a defeasance; that it is not necessary that the deed and the defeasance should refer to each other, but their connection may be shown by parol; and that it is not even necessary that the defeasance should be in writing.[1] In the course of the present chapter it will be shown that almost any instrument in writing, intended by the parties to pledge land as security for the payment of a debt, will be considered and treated in equity as a mortgage, although it may lack the formal requisites of a mortgage, and be insufficient to constitute a mortgage either at common law or under the statute, or though it be so defectively executed as to be invalid as a legal instrument, or though it amount to no more than an unexecuted agreement to give a mortgage. Thus, where the equitable owner of land consents in writing that the holder of the legal title to the same may hold the title as security for the payment of money

---

[1] Preschbaker v. Feaman, 32 Ill. 475.

borrowed by such owner from a third person, this will be sufficient to create an equitable lien on the land for the benefit of the creditor.[2] But a mere promise to pay an existing debt out of the proceeds of the sale of property, transferred to the creditor for the purpose of making such sale, is not sufficient to create an equitable mortgage upon the property itself. "The intention must be to create a lien upon the property, as distinguished from an agreement to apply the proceeds of a sale of it to the payment of a debt."[3]

Further, a court of equity may raise a mortgage where the parties did not intend anything of the kind, if justice and the peculiar circumstances of the case require it. For example, where the grantee of land purchases the same without any actual notice of an intention on the part of the grantor to defraud his creditors, but for a consideration so inadequate that it would be inequitable to allow the deed to stand as a conveyance, equity may set it aside, so far as it purports to be an absolute conveyance, but permit it to stand as security for the money actually advanced.[4] Where an equitable mortgagee covenants to reconvey, free from incumbrances and by good and sufficient deed, he must be understood as referring to the same title that he has received from the mortgagor, and is not bound to convert an imperfect title received into an estate in fee simple.[5]

§ 34. **Mortgages Defectively Executed.**—A written instrument intended by the parties to be a mortgage of realty, but which fails of that effect at law on account of its defective execution, though otherwise sufficient, will be considered in equity as a contract or agreement to give a mortgage, or as a memorandum of such agreement, and will, in equity, be accorded the force and the lien of a mortgage. This rule is applied where the instrument lacks a seal, or is not properly acknowledged, as required by the statute.[6] Even the lack of

[2] Chadwick v. Clapp, 69 Ill. 119.

[3] Vaniman v. Gardner, 99 Ill. App. 345. And see Mix v. White, 36 Ill. 484.

[4] Shepherd v. Fish, 78 Ill. App. 193.

[5] Parmelee v. Lawrence, 44 Ill. 405.

[6] Peckham v. Haddock, 36 Ill. 38; Vaniman v. Gardner, 99 Ill. App.

345; Atkinson v. Miller, 34 W. Va. 115, 11 S. E. Rep. 1007; Watkins v. Vrooman, 51 Hun, 175, 5 N. Y. Supp. 172; Abbott v. Godfroy, 1 Mich. 178; Westerly Sav. Bank v. Stillman Mfg. Co., 16 R. I. 497, 17 Atl. Rep. 918; Bryce v. Massey, 35 S. Car. 127, 14 S. E. Rep. 768; Martin v. Halley, 61 Mo. 196.

the mortgagor's signature may not invalidate the instrument in equity. In a case in Missouri, where the deed of trust was regular in all respects, except that the grantor had by mistake omitted to sign it, but he had acknowledged it before a proper officer as his act and deed, it was held that equity would regard and enforce it as a mortgage, the court saying: "The doctrine seems to be well established that an agreement in writing to give a mortgage, or a mortgage defectively executed, or an imperfect attempt to create a mortgage, or to appropriate specific property to the discharge of a particular debt, will create a mortgage in equity or a specific lien on the property so intended to be mortgaged.'"[7]

§ 35. Informal Writings Creating a Lien.—"As a general rule, any written contract entered into for the purpose of pledging property or some interest therein as security for a debt, which is informal or insufficient as a common-law or statutory mortgage, but which shows that it was the intention of the parties that it should operate as a charge upon the property, will constitute an equitable mortgage, and may be enforced as such in a court of equity.''[8] This applies not merely to cases where the instrument in question is defective in not employing the formal language or appropriate words of a mortgage, but also to cases where its different provisions are inconsistent, and to instances where the parties have attempted to incorporate provisions in the nature of a mortgage in some instrument originally of an entirely different character. Thus, in one of the earlier cases before the supreme court of the United States, the defeasance in the mortgage in question was for the payment of the debt according to the condition of a bond which was recited in the mortgage; but the day on which the bond was made payable had already passed at the time of the execution of the mortgage. It was held that the mortgage would not be avoided in equity for this reason, but would be considered as intended as a security, and would be treated in equity as an ordinary mortgage, though it would be absolute at law.[9] So, a clause in a lease giving to the lessor a

---

[7] Martin v. Nixon, 92 Mo. 26, 4 S. W. Rep. 503.

[8] Vaniman v. Gardner, 99 Ill. App. 345. And see Edwards v. Hall, 93 Ill. 326.

[9] Hughes v. Edwards, 9 Wheat. 489. It will be perceived that, the condition being impossible, the defeasance was void at law, but the grant good. Hence the transac-

lien for rent on the buildings and machinery to be erected by
the lessee on the demised premises will constitute an equitable
mortgage on such property when erected and in place.[10]

§ 36. **Agreement to Give a Mortgage.**—When parties enter
into a written agreement by which the one promises to execute
a mortgage on specific property in favor of the other, to secure
the payment of a debt, the instrument may fail to take effect
at law as a mortgage, by reason of its merely executory character, or because it lacks the formal words of a mortgage, or
because it is not executed or acknowledged according to the
statutory requirements for mortgages. But equity treats that
as done which was promised and which ought to have been
done; and therefore a court of equity will give effect to such
a contract as an equitable mortgage, and will enforce it as
such against all parties to the agreement and against any
strangers having notice, and will, on a proper case being made,
order its foreclosure and decree a sale of the property intended
to be pledged.[11] Thus, an instrument which is intended to
revive a mortgage previously existing but afterwards discharged, but which fails to accomplish this purpose at law, by
reason of its defective or insufficient execution, or for other
causes, may be considered as an agreement to give a mortgage
on the lands in question, and hence may be enforced as an
equitable mortgage.[12] But it is only in plain cases that equity
will take this course. A bill in equity to enforce an agreement
for a mortgage or lien on lands will not be sustained in a case
where the terms of the agreement are not sufficiently clear
and specific to enable the court to give effect to the understanding and intention of the parties.[13]

§ 37. **Advance of Purchase Money.**—Where one person advances money to enable another to make a purchase of lands,
the former taking the title in his own name, he will hold the

tion resolved itself into the case of
a deed, absolute in form, but intended as a security.

[10] First Nat. Bank v. Adam, 138
Ill. 483, 25 N. E. Rep. 576. And
see Russel v. Russel, 1 Brown Ch.
269.

[11] Gest v. Packwood, 39 Fed.
Rep. 525; Wright v. Shumway, 1
Biss. 23, Fed. Cas. No. 18,093;

Richardson v. Hamlett, 33 Ark.
237; McQuie v. Peay, 58 Mo. 56;
Daggett v. Rankin, 31 Cal. 821;
Racouillat v. Sansevain, 32 Cal.
376.

[12] Peckham v. Haddock, 36 Ill.
38.

[13] McClintock v. Laing, 22 Mich.
212; Nelson v. Hagerstown Bank,
27 Md. 51.

property only as security for his repayment, and equity will regard him as in effect a mortgagee, and consequently will allow a redemption of the lands on payment of the advance. Thus, where one party agrees by parol with another to purchase property at a public sale, for the latter, advancing the necessary money, on which interest is to be paid, and taking title in his own name, the transaction is a loan; and, upon payment of the debt and interest, equity will compel the creditor to convey the property to the debtor.[14] So, where one person has a contract for a conveyance of land to him, and procures another to complete the payments for him, and such other person does so and takes the deed in his own name as security for his advances, the transaction, as between the parties, constitutes an equitable mortgage of the property.[15] In an interesting case in a federal court it appeared that a settler on public lands, entitled to a pre-emption, procured a capitalist to pay the purchase money of the land into the United States land office, and allowed him to hold the receipt and certificate of location as security for repayment, receiving back the bond of the capitalist to give a deed upon repayment, on a certain day, of the purchase money with interest. It was held that these facts constituted, in equity, a mortgage of the land, redeemable by the settler, or his alienee, at or before the time of payment, according to the contract.[16] In fact, courts of equity strongly incline to treat all securities for money, or for indemnification, as mortgages. And by an extension of the principles above stated, it is held that, when a promise is made by a purchaser, at or before a judicial sale, to extend the time for redemption beyond the period allowed by law, those courts will treat the transaction as a mortgage on the lands sold, the real right of the creditor extending no further than to receive full satisfaction of his debt.[17]

§ 38. **Vendor's Lien.**—The lien which arises by implication of law in favor of the vendor of land, for unpaid purchase money, is regarded in Illinois as personal, and not assignable

---

[14] Davis v. Hopkins, 15 Ill. 519; Smith v. Sackett, Id. 528; Smith v. Cramer, 71 Ill. 185. And see Holle v. Bailey, 58 Wis. 434, 17 N. W. Rep. 822. Compare Stephenson v. Thompson, 13 Ill. 186.

[15] Stewart v. Fellows. 128 Ill. 480,

[17] N. E. Rep. 476; McPherson v. Hayward, 81 Me. 329, 17 Atl. Rep. 164.

[16] Wright v. Shumway, 1 Biss. 23, Fed. Cas. No. 18,093.

[17] Pensoneau v. Pulliam, 47 Ill. 58.

nor transmissible even by contract. It can be enforced only
by the vendor. The assignment of the note given for the
purchase money does not carry with it to the assignee the
vendor's lien, so as to make it enforceable by the assignee in
his own name. But a lien for the purchase money expressly
reserved in the vendor's conveyance, being created by contract and not by implication of law, constitutes a mortgage,
and, in equity at least, will pass with an assignment of the note
or bond. Accordingly, it is held that such an express vendor's
lien may be foreclosed by a bill in equity by the vendor himself, or by his assignee, or by his executor if he is dead, the
lien surviving his decease; and the decree of foreclosure in
such a case must reserve a right of redemption.[18] So where a
bond is given for a deed to land to be made upon payment of
the notes given for the unpaid purchase price, the bond and
notes will constitute one contract, and they will be treated in
equity as a security in the nature of a mortgage, and a sale
and assignment of the notes will pass the security, which may
be enforced in the name of the assignee.[19] And where a vendor
of land, after the sale, loans the vendee money, taking back an
assignment of the contract to secure its repayment, with an
agreement that it shall be forfeited if the money is not repaid
when due, the transaction will be regarded as an equitable
mortgage.[20] But a mere agreement to purchase land does not
constitute a mortgage.[21]

§ 39. Deposit of Title-Deeds.—In England, and according
to the doctrines of the common law, a deposit of the title-deeds
of an estate in the hands of a creditor, as security for a debt,
creates a lien which is considered and enforced as an equitable
mortgage of the property.[22] But in this country, generally, it
is held that such a doctrine is inconsistent with the theory of
our registration laws; and that the mere deposit of title-deeds,
without more, will not create an equitable lien against the
debtor, or against a judgment creditor of his, although there
may be special equities attending the transaction which would

[18] Markoe v. Andras, 67 Ill. 34,
Kimble v. Esworthy, 6 Ill. App.
517; Robinson v. Appleton, 22 Ill.
App. 351; Ober v. Gallagher, 93 U.
S. 199; Bell v. Pelt, 51 Ark. 433,
11 S. W. Rep. 684.

[19] Hutchinson v. Crane, 100 Ill.
269; Wright v. Troutman, 81 Ill.
374.

[20] Fitzhugh v. Smith, 62 Ill. 486.
[21] Greene v. Cook, 29 Ill. 186.
[22] Mandeville v. Welch, 5 Wheat.
277.

suffice to raise a mortgage out of the holding of deeds as
securities.[23]   In some of the states, however, the authorities
appear to recognize the possibility of an equitable mortgage
grounded on such mere deposit of deeds. But it is said that
such a mortgage can exist only where the deposit of the deeds
is the matter solely relied upon, without anything further being
done. Thus, in a case in South Carolina, where the title-deeds
were deposited with an attorney for the purpose of having a
mortgage drawn, and the mortgage was actually drawn, and
sent with the title-deeds to the intended mortgagor for formal
execution, which was prevented by his sickness and death, it
was held that no equitable mortgage was created or could be
claimed.[24]   In the single case in Illinois in which this question
has been touched on, it appeared that a person who had just
acquired certain real estate by purchase placed the deed which
he received for the same in the hands of one of his creditors,
and at the same time executed a written instrument, under
seal, stating in substance that he had borrowed a certain sum
of money from that creditor and that he delivered the deed to
the creditor to be held by the latter in escrow, and that it was
not to be recorded until the sum due should be repaid, which
was to be done within three years. To this the debtor bound
himself, his heirs and assigns. It was held that this constituted
an equitable mortgage of the land.[25]

[23] First Nat. Bank v. Caldwell,
4 Dill. 314, Fed. Cas. No. 4,798;
Davis v. Davis, 83 Ga. 191, 14 S. E.
Rep. 194.

[24] Hutzler v. Phillips, 26 S. Car.
136, 1 S. E. Rep. 502.
[25] Mallory v. Mallory, 86 Ill. App.
193.

CHAPTER IV.

TRUST DEEDS AND POWER-OF-SALE MORTGAGES.

§ 40. Trust Deed in the Nature of a Mortgage.—This form of pledging real property as security for a debt or loan possesses certain advantages of convenience over the common form of mortgage, and has come into very general use in late years. It is, in brief, a conveyance of the property intended to be pledged, in fee simple, to one or more trustees, who are to hold the same for the benefit of the lawful holder of the note, bond, or other obligation secured, permitting the grantor to retain the possession and enjoy the rents and profits of the estate until default shall be made in the payment of the obligation secured, and with a power in the trustee or trustees, upon such default, to make a sale of the premises and satisfy the holder of the debt out of the net proceeds, returning the surplus, if any, to the grantor.[1] A deed of trust of this description is in legal effect nothing more than a mortgage, and is identical with it in almost every respect. Like a mortgage, it is a mere security for a debt or for the performance of certain undertakings by the grantor. It is a mere incident to the debt which it secures, upon which it depends, and which it follows.[2] But

---

[1] But in Illinois, since 1879, property conveyed by a trust deed cannot be sold by virtue of the power of sale contained in the deed itself; such a security can be foreclosed only by a proper proceeding in the courts, and the sale made only in pursuance of the judgment or decree of a court of competent jurisdiction. Act of May 7, 1879; Myers' Rev. Stat. Ill. c. 95, § 22; 2 Starr & C. Stat. c. 95, § 17.

[2] Union Mut. Life Ins. Co. v. White, 106 Ill. 67; Thompson v. Marshall, 21 Oreg. 171, 27 Pac. Rep. 957; Central Trust Co. v. Burton, 74 Wis. 329, 43 N. W. Rep. 141.

the distinction must be noted between an absolute deed of trust and a deed of trust in the nature of a mortgage. The latter is conditional and defeasible upon performance of the stipulated conditions; the former, for the purposes of the trust, is unconditional and indefeasible.[3]

The principal reason for preferring the deed of trust, as a form of security, to the common mortgage, is that the interposition of a third person, in the character of trustee, to hold the legal title, permits the security to inure to the benefit of any lawful holder of the debt or obligation secured, without the necessity of an assignment of the instrument of conveyance. The deed of trust, being but an incident to the debt which it secures, will pass with an assignment of the debt to the holder thereof.[4] So that the note or bond secured may pass through the hands of any number of successive holders without any change in the status of the legal title to the estate, which always remains in the trustee. This consideration is especially operative when the mortgage debt is represented by a group or series of notes or bonds, which may be negotiated many times, and may, when the powers of the trustee are finally to be exercised, be lodged in the hands of many different holders. No matter who those holders may ultimately be, nor what transfers of ownership may have taken place with respect to the notes or bonds, the benefit of the security inures to each and all of them in turn, without any formal assignment or transfer of the instrument of conveyance. With regard to the validity of the trustee's title to the property, and the necessity of a consideration to support it, it is held that the deed of trust, being under seal and reciting a consideration, is presumed to have been given for a valuable consideration; and the obligation of the trustee therein, being based on the transfer

---

3 Hoffman v. Mackall, 5 Ohio St. 124. There is no right of redemption from a sale under a trust deed, when the deed conveys the absolute title to the trustees on a declared trust. Gillespie v. Smith, 29 Ill. 473. "When a deed of trust is executed with the understanding between the parties that the title is to be transferred forever from the grantor to the grantee and his heirs or grantees, then such deed of trust is not a mortgage; but when the deed of trust is executed with the understanding between the parties that it is a mere security for a debt, and that when the debt is paid the title shall be again placed in the grantor, such deed of trust is a mere mortgage." McDonald v. Kellogg, 30 Kans. 170, 2 Pac. Rep. 507.

4 Stiger v. Bent, 111 Ill. 328.

to him of the property described, rests upon a sufficient consideration.[5]

§ 41. **Trust Deeds Not Contrary to Public Policy.**—Deeds of trust in the nature of mortgages, and intended as securities, are not prohibited by law, nor are they contrary to any sound principles of public policy.[6] In an instructive case in another state, it was observed that securities of this character are for the best interests of both parties. They encourage the loaning of money by providing a form of security which is more effectual, more convenient, and more prompt and easy of enforcement; and, in return, they have a tendency to lower the rate of interest. The courts should see to it that no unfair advantage is taken of the debtor, that there is a proper notice of sale, and that the sale is fairly conducted. But in reviewing transactions of this character, it is their duty to afford facilities for the accomplishment of the intention of the parties, rather than to oppose or obstruct that intention by dilatory precautions and impediments.[7] In Illinois, the necessity of resorting to the courts for the foreclosure of trust deeds has probably rendered them less attractive as a form of security to creditors; but in other respects, the foregoing observations are pertinent and noteworthy.

§ 42. **Holder of Obligation Secured.**—As already stated, the security afforded by a trust deed in the nature of a mortgage inures to the benefit of the legal holder, for the time being, of the debt secured; and he may be identified by his lawful possession and ownership of the note or bond. The deed of trust usually names the creditor to whom the debt is originally due and for whose benefit, in the first instance, the security is given. But if it is silent on this point, evidence is admissible to show who furnished the money secured by the deed, and for whom the trustee was acting at the time.[8] Nor is a trust deed, which is perfect in other respects, rendered void by the omission of the name of the beneficiary,[9] nor by an uncertainty or indefiniteness in the description of the person or

[5] Jones v. Shepley, 90 Mo. 307, 2 S. W. Rep. 400.

[6] Weld v. Rees, 48 Ill. 428.

[7] First Nat. Bank v. Bell Silver & Copper Min. Co., 8 Mont. 32, 19 Pac. Rep. 403.

[8] Charter Oak Life Ins. Co. v. Stephens, 5 Utah, 319, 15 Pac. Rep. 253.

[9] Sleeper v. Iselin, 62 Iowa, 583, 17 N. W. Rep. 922.

persons to be secured;[10] but it may be enforced by the real
beneficial owner of the debt, identified as above described, or
his name being supplied by the trustee, as against the original
grantor or his alienee. But where a deed of trust is given by
the maker of a promissory note, which is payable to his own
order, to secure its payment, he cannot be treated as being in
his own person a mortgagee. The note being operative and
binding only after he has indorsed it, the indorsee becomes the
mortgagee, the same as if the note had been made payable to
him in the first instance.[11]

§ 43. **Legal Title Vested in Trustee.**—A deed of trust in the
nature of a mortgage vests the legal title to the estate conveyed in the trustee; the equitable title or equity of redemption remains in the grantor or mortgagor.[12] In fact, the relation between the grantor in such a deed and the trustee is
that of mortgagor and mortgagee, and as against the grantor
the trustee is the owner of the fee, and may, after condition
broken, maintain ejectment for the possession of the premises.[13] Several important consequences flow from the recognition of the fact that the legal title is in the trustee. In the
first place, if the trustee executes a deed of release without
payment or satisfaction of the debt secured, it is a breach of
trust, but nevertheless it will restore the legal title to the
grantor or mortgagor. This will not discharge the lien as
between the original parties, nor as to any subsequent purchasers who are chargeable with notice of the breach of trust;
but as to one who had no notice and relied on the record title,
whether as a purchaser from the mortgagor or as a subsequent
incumbrancer, the trustee's release will be effective both at
law and in equity.[14]

Again, a conveyance of the land by the trustee to a stranger,

---

[10] First Nat. Bank v. Kilbourne, 127 Ill. 573, 20 N. E. Rep. 681.

[11] Hosmer v. Campbell, 98 Ill. 572.

[12] Stephens v. Clay, 17 Colo. 489, 30 Pac. Rep. 43. The fact that a trust deed fails to show when the notes thereby secured will mature will not affect the title acquired under it, as in favor of a purchaser of the equity of redemp-tion, for he could ascertain the date of maturity of the notes by inquiry of the holder. Farrar v. Payne, 73 Ill. 82.

[13] Ware v. Schintz, 190 Ill. 189, 60 N. E. Rep. 67.

[14] Lennartz v. Quilty, 191 Ill. 174, 60 N. E. Rep. 913; Stiger v. Bent, 111 Ill. 328; Williams v. Jackson, 107 U. S. 478.

with or even without notice, as required in the deed of trust, will pass the legal title to his grantee, and until a redemption is effected, the latter will hold the legal title, and may set it up in defense to an action of ejectment, no equities being triable in that form of action.[15] If the trustee aliens the property otherwise than as provided in the deed, the equity reserved to the grantor will not be divested, but still the legal title will pass. To illustrate this doctrine, we quote the following language from an opinion of the supreme court of Colorado: "The legal title of the trustee is supplemented by a power which authorizes him, upon default in payment of the mortgage debt, to advertise and sell the property, the right to exercise this power being dependent upon his possession of such legal title. The object of the power of sale is not to enable him to convey the legal title vested in himself, but to clothe him with authority to sell and convey the equitable title remaining in the trustor. He may divest himself of the legal title without compliance with the conditions of the trust. But a sale and deed, except in strict compliance with the power specified, are of no effect whatever, so far as the trustor's equitable estate is concerned. If the trustee, in disobedience of the trust conditions, by deed transfers the legal title, his grantee takes only the trustee's interest. He steps into the trustee's shoes, so to speak, and holds subject to all reserved rights of the trustor. Neither courts of law nor courts of equity regard the trustee's deed as absolutely void. Both recognize the fact that it conveys the legal title. The difference is that the grantee's title or ownership cannot be challenged at law, while equity treats him as a successor to the trust, and protects the trustor's estate. Equity does not vacate the trustee's deed and regard the legal title as remaining in him. Appropriate equitable relief is usually obtained in one of the following modes: The cumulative remedy of a regular judicial foreclosure and sale is allowed; or a decree is entered requiring the grantee to execute the power in accordance with the terms of the trust deed, as the trustee should have done; or the execution of the power is, by decree, devolved upon a new trustee appointed for the purpose."[16]

Finally, a conveyance by warranty deed, by the grantor in

---

[15] Wilson v. South Park Commissioners, 70 Ill. 46.

[16] Stephens v. Clay, 17 Colo. 489, 30 Pac. Rep. 43.

a deed of trust to the party whose debt is secured by the same, of a part of the trust property, will pass nothing but the equity of redemption, and invests the grantee with the entire equitable title, but not with the legal title, which remains in the trustee. The grantee in such a case no doubt has a right to require a conveyance of the legal title from the trustee, but if the grantee does not require such conveyance, it will not relieve the trustee of the duties assumed by him, and the grantee may still require the trustee to execute the trust.[17]

§ 44. **Estate Remaining in Grantor.**—The equitable title to property conveyed by a trust deed in the nature of a mortgage, or the equity of redemption, remains in the grantor, together with the right to the possession and enjoyment of the premises, unless, as to the latter, there is a different provision in the deed. Indeed it has been decided that a clause in such a deed permitting the grantor to enjoy the rents, issues, and profits of the land until default in payment of the debt, is merely declaratory, such being the legal effect of the deed independent of such a clause; but upon default the permission ends.[18] Judgments will attach as liens upon the residuary interest of a party who executes a deed of trust to secure a creditor; but to make the liens available they should be enforced against the trust property by a levy and sale subject to the incumbrance of the trust deed. A sale of the property under the trust deed converts the estate into money, on which the judgments are not liens, and consequently the liens of the judgments will be cut off by such a sale.[19]

§ 45. **What Persons Competent as Trustees.**—In general, it may be said that any responsible person, competent to hold and convey the title to real estate, may be selected to act as the trustee in a deed of trust. The appointment of an insolvent or untrustworthy person as trustee, though done with a fraudulent purpose on the part of the grantor, will not render the deed void, and will not affect the rights of bona fide creditors secured by the deed, at least in the absence of any actual notice on their part of the intended fraud. In such a case, it is said, a court of equity, on a proper showing, may take charge of the trust property, and put it in the hands of

---

[17] Meacham v. Steele, 93 Ill. 135.   [19] Pahlman v. Shumway, 24 Ill.
[18] Anderson v. Strauss, 98 Ill. 127.
485.

a receiver, and thus administer the trust according to the provisions of the deed.[20] There is no legal reason why the holder of the notes secured by a deed of trust should not be constituted the trustee therein, and act in that capacity.[21] And the fact that the trustee, at the date of the deed to him and when the sale was made, was an officer of the corporation whose claim it was given to secure, does not invalidate a sale made under it to the corporation, which was in conformity to the deed and free from fraud.[22]

There is no legal necessity that the trustee should be a resident of the state where the land lies, provided he is not an alien.[23] But in respect to corporations chartered in other states, the laws of Illinois have imposed certain duties upon them as conditions prerequisite to their capacity to act as trustees. And it is held that a foreign corporation cannot act in Illinois as the trustee in a deed of trust to secure corporate bonds, where it has any active duties to perform in the capacity of trustee, such as to certify the bonds and superintend their sale and application, without complying with the statutes regulating trust companies and requiring the deposit of securities with the Auditor of Public Accounts.[24] But it is also ruled that the failure of a foreign trust company to make such deposit, as required by the act, does not invalidate a decree foreclosing a trust deed executed to it as trustee, to secure the

[20] Cohn v. Ward, 32 W. Va. 34, 9 S. E. Rep. 41.

[21] Foster v. Latham, 21 Ill. App. 165; Longwith v. Butler, 3 Gilm. 38; Darst v. Bates, 95 Ill. 513.

[22] Clark v. Trust Co., 100 U. S. 149.

[23] A statute of Indiana, which provided that it should not be lawful to nominate or appoint any person as trustee in a deed or mortgage, nor for any person to act in that capacity, unless he was a bona fide resident of the state, was held unconstitutional and void, because in conflict with that provision of the constitution of the United States which declares that "the citizens of each state shall be entitled to all the privileges and immunities of citizens in the several states." Robey v. Smith, 131 Ind. 342, 30 N. E. Rep. 1093. But it is settled by the court of last appeal on such questions, that *corporations* are not "citizens," within the meaning of this clause. Black, Const. Law (2d edn.) 247. Hence the statute of Illinois would not be open to constitutional objection, even if it altogether prohibited foreign corporations from acting as trustees, instead of merely imposing conditions upon their right to act in that capacity.

[24] Farmers' Loan & Trust Co. v. Lake Street El. R. Co., 173 Ill. 439, 51 N. E. Rep. 55, affirming 68 Ill. App. 666.

payment of bonds, where the only duties performed by the company were certifying the bonds (which was done outside the state) and joining with the bondholders in filing the bill for foreclosure. A bill filed by such a company for the foreclosure of the trust deed is but a prayer to the court to divest it of title by decree and sale, and even though the company is not qualified to execute active powers as a trustee, it is not necessary for the court to remove it or to appoint a new trustee before decreeing foreclosure.[25]

§ 46. Removal and Substitution of Trustees.—Deeds of trust usually provide for the substitution of a new trustee in case the one originally appointed resigns or refuses to act, or becomes disabled from executing the powers conferred upon him. Thus, it is not uncommon to provide for the exercise of the power by a substituted trustee in the event of the original trustee's "absence from the state." But this is held to mean a permanent removal from the state, not a mere temporary absence.[26] So, where the trustee in a deed of trust is temporarily imprisoned in the penitentiary, this is not a "removal" on his part, within the meaning of a clause in the deed providing for the vesting of the legal title in his successor in the trust in case of the trustee's "death, removal from the county, permanent inability, or refusal to act."[27] A written resignation by the trustee in a deed of trust (which provides for the appointment of a successor on the trustee's refusal to act), duly signed and acknowledged, and the written appointment of a successor, also signed and acknowledged, constitute such appointee the lawful successor in the trust, and clothe him with the same power and authority as were possessed by the original trustee.[28] In the event of the death of the sole trustee named in the deed, equity would undoubtedly have power to appoint a new trustee on application of the parties in interest; though it is usual to insert a provision in the deed itself for the substitution of a new trustee in that contingency; and where this is done, the substituted trustee may execute the power of sale as the original trustee could have

[25] Morse v. Holland Trust Co., 184 Ill. 255, 56 N. E. Rep. 369, affirming 84 Ill. App. 84.

[26] Equitable Trust Co. v. Fisher, 106 Ill. 189.

[27] Ware v. Schintz, 190 Ill. 189, 60 N. E. Rep. 67.

[28] Lake v. Brown, 116 Ill. 83, 4 N. E. Rep. 773. And see Irish v. Antioch College, 126 Ill. 474, 18 N. E. Rep. 768.

done.[29] And where the deed provides that, upon the death of the trustees therein named, the same title and powers vested in them shall vest in their successors, it is not necessary that there should be any additional written conveyance of the property to new trustees, lawfully appointed to fill the place of the original trustees, since deceased, in order to enable them to execute the power of sale contained in the deed.[30] But the power cannot be executed after the death of the trustee, without the appointment of a new trustee, although the deed might be foreclosed in equity without such appointment.[31]

Where the deed vests the legal title and the power of sale in joint trustees, and one or more of them is dead at the time when the power is to be executed, it is a question whether the surviving trustees are competent to act alone. There are intimations in the books that the power may be well exercised by the survivor or survivors;[32] and this view gains some corroboration from the rule announced by the United States supreme court that a sale made under the power contained in a deed of trust will not be void, nor liable to be set aside, merely because one of the joint trustees was not personally present at the sale.[33] Still, it is more prudent to insert in the trust deed a provision that the powers therein granted to joint trustees may be exercised by "the survivor or survivors of them." And if the deed contains no such provision, it will be the safer course to apply to the court of equity to appoint a new trustee in the place of the one deceased.

If the trustee named in a deed of trust unwarrantably refuses to perform the duties with which he is charged (as, to sell the property upon default, or to execute a release to the grantor upon payment of the debt), a court of equity may compel him, by decree, to discharge his duty, provided he is within the jurisdiction of the court, or he may be removed from his office and a new trustee appointed, with directions to execute the trust. It is said that the mere absence of the trustee from the state, though it may cause inconvenience to the parties, will not of itself constitute sufficient ground for his removal;

[29] Lake v. Brown, 116 Ill. 83, 4 N. E. Rep. 773.

[30] Craft v. Indiana, D. & W. Ry. Co., 166 Ill. 580, 46 N. E. Rep. 1132.

[31] Waughop v. Bartlett, 165 Ill. 124, 46 N. E. Rep. 197.

[32] See Franklin v. Osgood, 14 Johns. (N. Y.) 527; Hannah v. Carrington, 18 Ark. 85.

[33] Smith v. Black, 115 U. S. 308.

but when, in addition to his absence, it is shown that he neglects to give attention to his duties as trustee, a court is fully warranted in removing him, and appointing a suitable person to carry the trust into effect.[34] So, also, if the trustee becomes mentally or otherwise incapacitated for performing his duties, or proves himself an unfit or unsafe person to exercise the power, as by manifesting personal hostility to either of the parties, in place of the absolute impartiality which it is his duty to maintain, it is competent and proper for a court of equity to remove him and appoint another in the place.[35] But where the deed gives the power to appoint a substituted trustee in case the original trustee refuses or fails to act, the appointment of a new trustee while the original trustee is advertising the property for sale under the deed confers no title on the substituted trustee.[36] And it has been held that, where the debt secured by the deed of trust is barred by the statute of limitations, and the trustee refuses to execute his power of sale, a plea of limitation is a good defense to a suit for the appointment of a substitute trustee.[37]

§ 47. Powers and Duties of Trustees.—It is necessary that the trustee named in a deed of trust given to secure the payment of a debt should accept the trusteeship; but if he acts under the deed, by advertising the property for sale on default in payment, this will constitute an acceptance of the trust by him, although he may not have the deed in his possession.[38] He is the representative and trustee of both parties to the instrument, not merely of the debtor nor merely of the creditor; and his relations must be absolutely impartial as between them; he must act with entire fairness towards both parties and not exclusively in the interest of either.[39] But when he is spoken of as "representing" either or both of the parties, it must be understood that his power and duty in that regard are restricted to the uses and purposes of the trust. For example, in a suit for the enforcement of a mechanic's lien on property incumbered by a deed of trust, both the trustee and the holder of the obligation secured should be joined as parties.

[34] Lill v. Neafie, 31 Ill. 101.

[35] McPherson v. Cox, 96 U. S. 404.

[36] Chesnutt v. Gann, 76 Tex. 150, 13 S. W. Rep. 274.

[37] Fuller v. O'Neal (Tex.), 18 S. W. Rep. 479.

[38] Crocker v. Lowenthal, 83 Ill. 579.

[39] Gray v. Robertson, 174 Ill. 242, 51 N. E. Rep. 248; Williamson v. Stone, 128 Ill. 129, 22 N. E. Rep. 1005; Ventres v. Cobb, 105 Ill. 33.

"While the trustee is a necessary party because of the legal title being vested in him, his trust is not of that nature that can make him a proper representative of his cestui que trust. Until default in the payment of the note, his is a mere passive trust. His duties are defined and limited by the terms of the power in the deed, and he is not charged with the responsibility of protecting the interests of the holder of the note in matters foreign to the proper execution of his power. He is neither bound nor authorized to appear and answer for the party secured, nor would a decree against him alone, assuming to determine the priority of the respective liens, be binding upon the rights of the cestui que trust."[40] Again, the fact that a person is made the trustee in a deed of trust gives him no right or authority to receive payment of the debt secured by such deed.[41] But if the legal holder of the note secured intrusts the note to the possession of the trustee after its maturity, he is bound by the trustee's extension of the time of payment, especially when the agreement for extension was acted upon by the parties.[42]

The peculiar circumstances of individual cases sometimes cause serious doubts as to the duties, or the extent of the powers, of a trustee. But he need not, for that reason, run any great risk of personal liability. It is laid down as a fixed rule that trustees who are in doubt as to the proper performance of their duties under the deed of trust, or as to the manner of exercising the powers thereby conferred upon them, may apply to a court of general equity jurisdiction for its aid and direction.[43] But for any actual misconduct on the part of the trustee the law provides ample remedies. If, for instance, he makes

[40] Clark v. Manning, 4 Ill. App. 649.

[41] Leon v. McIntyre, 88 Ill. App. 349.

[42] Kranz v. Uedelhofen, 193 Ill. 477, 62 N. E. Rep. 239.

[43] Craft v. Indiana, D. & W. Ry. Co., 166 Ill. 580, 46 N. E. Rep. 1132. "That a trustee is considered as the agent of both parties, and bound to act impartially between them; that it is his duty to use every reasonable effort to sell the estate to the best advantage; and that it is his duty to apply to a court of equity where there is a cloud upon the title, or where there is doubt or uncertainty as to the amount to be raised, or as to the relative amounts or priorities of the liens on the trust subject, or where there is a conflict between the lienors, or in any case in which the aid of a court of equity is necessary to remove impediments in the way of a fair execution of the trust,—are propositions which none will deny, and which have been repeatedly affirmed by this court." Muller's Adm'r v. Stone, 84 Va. 834, 6 S. E. Rep. 223.

an entry of satisfaction of the debt secured, without authority
from the holder of the debt, or without its actual payment,
such entry may be set aside, or a suit to foreclose the trust deed
may be maintained without any regard to such entry.[44] If,
on the other hand, he wrongfully neglects or refuses to release
the deed of trust, upon request thereto, and knowing the debt
to have been paid, he is liable to a statutory penalty.[45] If he
acts corruptly or unfairly in making a sale under the power,
as, by selling the property before the debt is due, or otherwise in disregard of the limitations or conditions of the deed,
the remedy is in equity, a court of chancery having power, in
such circumstances, to set aside the sale or to allow the debtor
to redeem from it.[46]

It is also a well-settled rule that the trust reposed in one selected by the parties to a trust deed in the nature of a mortgage is personal. The trustee cannot lawfully delegate to
any other person the powers granted to him by the deed. He
is chosen and confidence is reposed in him by the parties, and
he must execute the trust. It is true he may employ an agent
to perform the mechanical parts of a sale, to act as auctioneer,
or to advertise and sell the lands held in trust, and such an
employment is not a delegation of the trust. But the trustee
must be present in person at the sale, and supervise and control it for the best interests of the parties, and should, so far
as he may be able, prevent the sacrifice of the interests of either
party.[47]

§ 48. **Release on Payment.**—When the debt secured by a
deed of trust is paid, it is the duty of the trustee to release the
deed, so as to restore the legal title to the grantor. If he
neglects or refuses to execute a release, upon request and the
tender of his reasonable charges, the statute makes him liable to a penalty, to be recovered at the suit of the party aggrieved.[48] But before releasing the trust he should be satisfied
that the debt has really been discharged. Evidence of this fact
is commonly furnished to him by the surrender of the note or
other obligation secured, and its exhibition to the trustee cancelled or indorsed as paid. But it is ruled that when the debtor
and creditor, or those representing them, both agree to a re-

[44] Stiger v. Bent, 111 Ill. 328.
[45] Rev. Stat. Ill. c. 95, § 10.
[46] See infra, § 481.

[47] Taylor v. Hopkins, 40 Ill. 442;
Gillespie v. Smith, 29 Ill. 473.
[48] Rev. Stat. Ill. c. 95, § 10

lease of a deed of trust executed to secure the indebtedness, the fact that the evidences of the debt are not surrendered affords no reason for the refusal of the trustee to execute a release. Thus, when the deed secures the payment of certain bonds, and every person interested in both the debt and the property incumbered requests the trustee to make a release, such request being indorsed on the bonds, it is his duty to comply, although the bonds are not cancelled.[49] After such a trustee has released his power of sale by a formal deed of release, the party named as his successor, to exercise the power in case of his death or absence, has no authority to make a sale of the land conveyed by the trust deed; and where such release is recorded before such a sale, a purchaser of the land from the owner will not be bound to search the records to see if a conveyance has been made under the power after its release.[50]

§ 49. **Mortgages with Power of Sale.**—It is said that there is no substantial difference in legal effect between a mortgage with a power of sale vested in the mortgagee himself, to be exercised on default of payment of the debt, and a deed of trust executed to secure a debt, where the power of sale is placed in a third person. "Both are securities for a debt; both create specific liens on the property; and in both the equitable title or right of redemption remains in the debtor, and is an estate or interest in the property that the debtor may sell, or that may be seized and sold under judicial process by his other creditors, subject to the lien created by the mortgage or deed of trust."[51] And there is no doubt that the mortgagee, under a mortgage containing such a power of sale, may sell the mortgaged premises, and convey a good title to the purchaser.[52] It is also competent for a married woman to join her husband in the execution of a mortgage on land owned by him, which shall confer upon the mortgagee and his assigns the power to make sale of the premises in case of default in

[49] Pearce v. Bryant Coal Co., 121 Ill. 590, 13 N. E. Rep. 561, affirming 25 Ill. App. 51.

[50] Porter v. McNabney, 77 Ill. 235.

[51] Bartlett v. Teah, 1 Fed. Rep. 768; Levy v. Burkle, (Cal.) 14 Pac. Rep. 564.

[52] Longwith v. Butler, 3 Gilm. 32. Of course this statement is to be taken subject to the limitation established by the act of May 7, 1879; Myers' Rev. Stat. Ill. c. 95, § 22; 2 Starr & C. Stat. c. 95, § 17.

payment, without a decree for that purpose, so that a sale under such power shall operate to bar the equity of redemption, not only of the husband, but also of the wife, in case she survives him.[53]

In Illinois, it is the rule that such a power of sale contained in a mortgage, authorizing the mortgagee or his assigns to make sale on breach of condition and to convey to the purchaser, is a power coupled with an interest, and therefore is not revoked by the death of the mortgagor. On this point it has been said:—"It is true that a mere simple power, or naked power, as it is generally termed, to do a thing in the name of and for the benefit of another ceases at the death of the grantor. Such is a letter of attorney. But if the power is coupled with an interest in an estate on which the power is to be exercised, and is to be executed in the name of the grantee, then such power is deemed a part of the estate, and is not dependent upon the life of the grantor. And of this nature is a power to sell contained in a mortgage deed, on default of payment. Such power is there coupled with an interest in the estate itself, and does not become inoperative by reason of the death of the mortgagor."[54] But the statute provides that such a power of sale cannot be exercised after the death of the owner of the equity of redemption; in such case, the mortgage must be foreclosed by suit, as if it contained no such provision.[55]

---

[53] Strother v. Law, 54 Ill. 413.

[54] Strother v. Law, 54 Ill. 413. And see Hudgens v. Morrow, 47 Ark. 515, 2 S. W. Rep. 104; More v. Calkins, (Cal.) 30 Pac. Rep. 583. A contrary rule prevails in several of the states. See, for instance, Johnson v. Johnson, 27 S. Car. 309, 3 S. E. Rep. 606; Lockett v. Hill, 1 Woods, 552, Fed. Cas. No. 8,443.

[55] Rev. Stat. Ill. c. 95, § 13.

CHAPTER V.

MORTGAGES BY CORPORATIONS.

§ 50. **Power of Corporation to Execute Mortgage.**—Every private corporation, in virtue of the general grants to it of corporate power, has the right to borrow money, to aid it in carrying forward the legitimate objects of its incorporation, unless this is expressly forbidden to it, or unless it is impliedly prohibited in consequence of the nature and character of the business for the prosecution of which the corporation was created. And having the power to borrow money, it may exercise this power like any natural person; and, without any statutory authority other than such as is implied in the grant of power to make contracts and to acquire and dispose of real property, it may evidence and secure the debts which it contracts by notes or bonds and mortgages on its property securing the payment of the same.[1] In addition to this general principle of law, we have, in Illinois, a statutory provision that corporations organized under the general corporation act (which, however, does not include those formed for the business of banking, insurance, real estate brokerage, the operation of railroads, and the loaning of money) "may borrow money at legal rates of interest, and pledge their property, both real and personal, to secure the payment thereof."[2] Also, as to corporations formed not for purposes of pecuniary profit, the

---

[1] West v. Madison County Agricultural Board, 82 Ill. 205; Wood v. Whelen, 93 Ill. 153; Reichwald v. Commercial Hotel Co., 106 Ill. 439. And see White Water Valley Canal Co. v. Vallette, 21 How. (U. S.) 414; Jones v. New York Guaranty Co., 101 U. S. 622; Gaytes v. Lewis, 2 Biss. 136, Fed. Cas. No. 5,288; Lord v. Yonkers Fuel Gas Co., 99 N. Y. 547, 2 N. E. Rep. 909; Wright v. Hughes, 119 Ind. 324, 21 N. E. Rep. 907.

[2] Rev. Stat. Ill. c. 32, § 5.

statute provides that the "trustees, managers, or directors may, upon consent of the corporation, society, or association, expressed by the vote of a majority of the members thereof, borrow money, to be used solely for the purposes of their organization, and may pledge their property therefor."[3] Further, there are special statutory provisions relating to railroads, religious organizations, and some other species of corporations, which will be noticed in the sections dealing specifically with those bodies.

It has been ruled that the mere insolvency of a corporation does not deprive it of power to mortgage its corporate property in good faith to secure its debts, even though the result may be to give one creditor a preference or advantage over another.[4] And it appears from a decision in another state that, when all the stock of a private corporation is owned by one person, a mortgage executed by him creates a valid equitable lien on the property of the corporation, enforceable against him and his representatives, and it is not necessary for the corporation, as such, to unite with him in the mortgage.[5]

§ 51. Mortgage of Corporate Franchises.—Although the question is not entirely free from doubt, the weight of authority inclines to the doctrine that a corporation cannot lawfully mortgage its franchises without authority from the power which created it and bestowed its franchises upon it.[6] A study of the decisions, however, will show that this doctrine is mainly, if not exclusively, applied to those corporations which, on account of the nature of their business, are regarded as public or quasi-public bodies, and are under the obligation of discharging certain duties to the public. It is not lawful for such corporations to dispose of their property in such a manner as to incapacitate themselves for the performance of these duties; and since their franchises are conferred in consideration of the assumption of duties and responsibilities on their part, such rights should not be transferable without the con-

[3] Rev. Stat. Ill. c. 32, § 32.

[4] State Nat. Bank v. Union Nat. Bank, 168 Ill. 519, 48 N. E. Rep. 82, affirming 68 Ill. App. 25.

[5] Swift v. Smith, 65 Md. 428, 5 Atl. Rep. 534.

[6] Pullan v. Cincinnati, etc., R. Co., 4 Biss. 35 Fed. Cas. No. 11,461;

Commonwealth v. Smith, 10 Allen (Mass.), 448; Coe v. Columbus, P. & I. R. Co., 10 Ohio St. 372; Atkinson v. Marietta & C. R. Co., 15 Ohio St. 21; Gloninger v. Pittsburgh & C. R. Co., 139 Pa. St. 13, 21 Atl. Rep. 211.

sent of the incorporating power. As to corporations of other
kinds, it is almost universally the case that their franchises,
as such, have little or no pecuniary value, and therefore the
application of the doctrine to them is not important.

In Illinois, it is provided by statute that any railroad corporation organized under the laws of the state shall have power
"to borrow such sums of money as may be necessary for completing, finishing, improving, or operating any such railway,
and to issue and dispose of its bonds for any amount so borrowed, and to mortgage its corporate property *and franchises*
to secure the payment of any debt contracted by such corporation for the purposes aforesaid," provided the holders of two-
thirds of the stock of the corporation shall consent.[7] Under
a provision of this character the franchises are not only subject to be mortgaged, but will also pass to and vest in the
purchaser at foreclosure sale. "Authority to mortgage the
franchises of a railroad company necessarily implies the power
to bring the franchises so mortgaged to sale, and to transfer
them, with the corporeal property of the company, to the purchaser."[8] Hence, where a corporation has power by charter
or statute to mortgage its property and franchises, it cannot
allege, as against a purchaser at the foreclosure sale, that a
conveyance of its franchise is prohibited by law. In one of the
cases, it appeared that the franchise in question consisted of
the right to construct and operate an elevated railroad, with
a right in the company to use the streets of a city for its
tracks, but the city ordinance granting this right provided that
the consent therein given should never authorize another person or corporation to use the franchise. It was held that this
did not preclude the mortgaging of the company's property
and franchise for the purpose of raising money to build the
road, and that such a mortgage would not be ultra vires, although a purchaser at a sale on foreclosure of the mortgage
would, as to such franchise, acquire no right to operate the
road without the consent of the city. It was said: "The conveyance of its own right to use the franchise may have given
no right thereto to the purchaser as against the city. It did,
however, as against the mortgagor. The conveyance was good
as between the parties. The city could exercise its discretion

7 Rev. Stat. Ill. c. 114, § 20, cl.   8 New Orleans, S. F. & L. R. Co.
10.   v. Delamore, 114 U. S. 501.

about giving its consent to the purchaser to use the franchise.
As to this, the purchasers at the foreclosure sale took the
chances. But the sale of even a worthless thing, all parties
knowing the facts and taking the risks as to its thereafter becoming valuable, is not invalid. The refusal of the city to
authorize the purchaser to use the franchise might affect its
value perhaps, but would not avoid the sale as between the
parties."[9] A similar decision in another state instructs us that
a provision in a municipal ordinance forbidding a gas company to sell its property, franchises, or privileges to another
gas company does not prevent the mortgaging of its franchises
and a sale under foreclosure to a new company.[10] And the
supreme court of the United States has also decided that,
where the charter of a corporation, giving the exclusive right
to use certain water power, gives it authority to sell all its
rights under its charter, it may mortgage the same; and the
franchises granted are not of so personal and exclusive a character that the mortgage would be void as far as it included
them.[11]

§ 52. Authority of Board of Directors.—Except in certain
instances to be presently mentioned, it is within the powers
of the board of directors of a business corporation to execute a
mortgage upon its property, for the purpose of securing a debt
of the corporation, without the authorization or consent of the
stockholders. "It is undeniably the law," says the supreme
court of Illinois, "that all business relating to the legitimate
objects of the corporation, authorized by its charter, may be
transacted by the directors without the sanction of the stockholders. The act under which the gas company [the mortgagor in this case] was incorporated provides that such companies shall have power to borrow money and secure the same
by deed or lien on their real or personal property or both. As
borrowing money for the purpose of forwarding the objects
of the corporation is among the ordinary duties of the board
of directors, it follows that the directors may secure the same
by deed or other lien. It is a part of the business transactions

[9] Chicago & South Side Rapid
Transit R. Co. v. Northern Trust
Co., 90 Ill. App. 460, affirmed on
appeal, Wells v. Northern Trust
Co., 195 Ill. 288, 63 N. E. Rep. 136.
[10] City of Detroit v. Mutual Gas

Co., 43 Mich. 594, 5 N. W. Rep.
1039.
[11] Willamette Woolen Mfg. Co.
v. Bank of British Columbia, 119
U. S. 191.

of the corporation which has always been regarded as within the province of the directors to perform."[12]

Exceptions to this rule are found in the case of corporations not formed for purposes of pecuniary profit—such as religious, charitable, scientific, literary, or social organizations—and in the case of railroad companies. In regard to the former class, the statute provides that the trustees, managers, or directors may borrow money, to be used solely for the purposes of their organization, and mortgage the corporate property therefor, but only "upon consent of the corporation, society, or association, expressed by the vote of a majority of the members thereof."[13] In regard to railroad companies, there is a positive provision that the consent of the holders of two-thirds of the stock of the corporation shall be necessary to the validity of a mortgage on its corporate property and franchises.[14] But while these requirements were meant to be complied with, and their neglect may destroy the validity of the mortgage, yet it must be remembered that the stockholders who could have authorized an act in advance may give it validity by their subsequent ratification. In Illinois, the decisions do not appear as yet to have dealt with the effect of such ratification on the part of stockholders. But in other states, this rule is fully recognized. It is laid down as a general rule that, where the statute requires the authorization, by vote or otherwise, of a certain proportion of the stockholders of a corporation, in order to enable the directors to mortgage its property, the directors cannot make a valid mortgage without such authority. Yet, though the mortgage may not be valid at its inception, it will become binding and effective if not repudiated by the stockholders. The latter have the power and capacity to ratify the act of the directors; and when there are no intervening rights, the ratification will relate back to the date of the act ratified. Nor is it necessary that there should be a direct proceeding with an express intent to ratify. It may be done indirectly, and by acts of recognition and acquiescence, such as accepting and enjoying the fruits of the mortgage, or by acts which are inconsistent with disapproval and repudiation.[15]

[12] Wood v. Whelen, 93 Ill. 153. And see Hodder v. Kentucky & G. E. R. Co., 7 Fed. Rep. 793; Thompson v. Natchez Water Co., 68 Miss. 423, 9 South. Rep. 821.

[13] Rev. Stat. Ill. c. 32, §§ 32, 43.

[14] Rev. Stat. Ill. c. 114, § 20, cl. 10.

[15] Scott v. First Methodist Church, 50 Mich. 528, 15 N. W.

In regard to the action of the directors of a corporation in mortgaging its property, in cases where the assent of the stockholders is not required by law, it is held that irregularities in the meeting of the directors of the corporation at which the mortgage is executed do not affect the mortgagee dealing in good faith with the company, but such mortgagee has the right to assume that the provisions of the by-laws have been complied with. Thus, the defense that a meeting of the board of directors, at which a mortgage of its property was made, was held under an irregular notice and at an unauthorized place, is not available in a suit to foreclose the mortgage, where no action has been taken in disaffirmance of the proceedings at the meeting or in repudiation of the note or mortgage.[16]

§ 53. Mortgage Made by Officers of Corporation.—The officers of a business corporation have generally no power to incumber its property by a mortgage, unless authorized by the board of directors. At the same time, where a mortgage, which is regular on its face, has been executed in the name of the corporation, signed by the properly constituted officers, and sealed with the corporate seal, it is prima facie evidence that the mortgage was made by the authority of the corporation, and parties objecting must assume the burden of proving that it was not so executed.[17] And in the case cited it was also held that, though the mortgage may have been executed originally without competent authority, yet the board of directors may adopt the instrument, giving it the full force of a deed of the corporation, by a simple resolution to that effect, without the form of again attaching the seal of the corporation to the paper. But a mortgage executed by the president of an Illinois corporation, upon corporate property in Illinois, is invalid when executed in pursuance of a resolution of the directors at a meeting held outside the state, not authorized by a

Rep. 891; Beecher v. Marquette & Pacific Rolling Mill Co., 45 Mich. 103, 7 N. W. Rep. 695; Rochester Sav. Bank v. Averell, 96 N. Y. 467; Texas W. Ry. Co. v. Gentry, 69 Tex. 625, 8 S. W. Rep. 98. The case last cited was ruled under a statute of Texas which enacts that no mortgage of a railroad company shall be valid unless authorized by resolution adopted by a vote of two-thirds of all the stock,—a requirement exactly similar to that in Illinois. Compare, however, Duke v. Markham, 105 N. Car. 131, 10 S. E. Rep. 1017.

[16] Ashley Wire Co. v. Illinois Steel Co., 164 Ill. 149, 45 N. E. Rep. 410, affirming 60 Ill. App. 179.

[17] Wood v. Whelen, 93 Ill. 153.

two-thirds vote of the directors as required by the act on corporations; and it is not cured by the fact that it might have been valid if it had been executed by the president under his general powers, where it appears that the president, in executing the mortgage, acted in pursuance of the resolution and not on his own authority. But even such a mortgage may be subsequently ratified and confirmed by the directors, by due and appropriate action, though not to the prejudice of intervening liens.[18] In another state, we find a decision to the effect that a mortgage executed by the president and secretary of a corporation, instead of by its directors, and without any formal authorization, is nevertheless valid where there were only three directors, and two of them were the officers mentioned, and the money secured by the mortgage was received by the corporation and used for its benefit.[19]

§ 54. Defense of Ultra Vires and Invalidity.—If a mortgage given by a corporation is ultra vires, no one but the state can take advantage of the defect of power involved; that is to say, where a person dealing in good faith with a corporation, has loaned money to it, on the security of a mortgage given by the company, which money has actually been received and used by the corporation for its own purposes, the corporation will not be allowed to plead the defense of ultra vires in a suit to foreclose the mortgage, or in a proceeding on its own part to have the instrument cancelled or its foreclosure enjoined.[20] This applies not only to cases where the corporation was restrained by its charter or by general law from raising money by mortgage on its property, and to cases where the mortgage was executed without due authority from the corporation mortgagor; but it is also laid down that the illegality of the purpose for which a corporation was originally organized cannot become a material inquiry in a suit to foreclose a mortgage upon the property of the concern, if the mortgage was made while the corporation had power to create it, and the illegality was wholly extrinsic to the mortgage.[21]

[18] State Nat. Bank v. Union Nat. Bank, 168 Ill. 519, 48 N. E. Rep. 82, affirming 68 Ill. App. 25.

[19] Dexter v. Long, 2 Wash. St. 435, 27 Pac. Rep. 271.

[20] Jones v. New York Guaranty Co., 101 U. S. 622; Bradley v. Ballard, 55 Ill. 413; Darst v. Gale, 83 Ill. 137; Ward v. Johnson, 95 Ill. 215; Wright v. Hughes, 119 Ind. 324, 21 N. E. Rep. 907.

[21] Dickerman v. Northern Trust Co., 176 U. S. 181.

While the mortgage of a corporation, like that of a private individual, must be supported by a valid consideration, and will be invalidated by a fraudulent or illegal purpose, it is the rule that a corporation may prefer one creditor to another; and a mortgage made by a solvent corporation will not be rendered invalid by the mere fact that the mortgagee was an officer, director, or stockholder of the company, provided the debt to be secured was a genuine obligation of the company.[22] But if the officers or directors of a corporation, in violation of their duty and in betrayal of their trust, secure their own claims by mortgage, to the injury of stockholders and creditors, the mortgage is not valid.[23] And where, on the organization of a corporation, one of the subscribers advances more money than the amount he has subscribed, the excess being in payment for stock issued to another subscriber, the corporation is not liable for such excess, and a note and mortgage given by it therefor are invalid.[24]

§ 55. Mortgages by Railroad Companies.—In the absence of some special statute to the contrary (or in respect to matters not expressly regulated by statute), railroad mortgages are subject to the same laws as all others.[25] In Illinois, however, there are several important particulars in which securi-

---

[22] Mullanphy Bank v. Schott, 135 Ill. 655, 26 N. E. Rep. 640; affirming 34 Ill. App. 500; Omaha Hotel Co. v. Wade, 97 U. S. 13. "Corporations can make contracts and transfer property, possessing the same powers in such respects as private individuals. Such is the rule in the absence of a statute and therefore it has the right to prefer one creditor to another. The fact that the preference is exercised in favor of directors or shareholders of the corporation is immaterial, although the director or shareholder may have voted for the proposition, and the security given was to secure an indebtedness to himself." Warfield v. Marshall County Canning Co., 72 Iowa, 666, 34 N. W. Rep. 467.

[23] Koehler v. Black River Falls Iron Co., 2 Black (U. S.) 715. Thus, where the directors of a railroad company voted to issue bonds of the company to be used or sold to aid in the construction and equipment of the company's road, and the president issued them in payment of indebtedness of a land company, of which he was also president, to persons who knew for what purposes they had been voted, it was held that the bonds, being without consideration to the railroad company, were ultra vires and void, and that the persons to whom they were issued were not bona fide holders. City of Chicago v. Cameron, 22 Ill. App. 91.

[24] Hodson v. Eugene Glass Co., 156 Ill. 397, 40 N. E. Rep. 971, affirming 54 Ill. App. 248.

[25] Palmer v. Forbes, 23 Ill. 301.

ties of this kind have been made the subject of legislation. In the first place, the constitution provides that no railroad company shall issue any stock or bonds except for money, labor, or property actually received and applied to the purpose for which such corporation was created.[26] In the next place, the statutes give such corporations power to borrow money, and to mortgage their property and franchises for its repayment, but only for "such sums of money as may be necessary for completing, finishing, improving, or operating any such railway;" and the consent of the holders of two-thirds of the stock of the corporation shall be necessary to the validity of a mortgage so given.[27] But it is held that the act relating to chattel mortgages was never intended to apply to railroad mortgages. And hence a mortgage or deed of trust made by a railroad company, embracing all its real and personal property, with its franchise, made in pursuance of express authority in its charter and recorded in each county through which the road passes, will create a valid and binding lien on its personal as well as its real property, notwithstanding it has not been acknowledged in accordance with the requirements of the chattel mortgage act.[28] A mortgage given by a railroad company to secure the payment of its bonds, which declares that it shall include all property owned or to be acquired by the company, will operate upon after-acquired property as soon as it is obtained by the mortgagor.[29]

§ 56. **Religious Corporations.**—By statute in Illinois, the trustees of a religious corporation, when so directed by the congregation, church, or society, may "mortgage, incumber, sell and convey any real or personal estate of such corporation, provided that no mortgage, incumbrance, sale, or conveyance shall be made of any such estate so as to defeat or destroy the effect of any gift, grant, devise, or bequest which may be made to such corporation."[30] The limitation contained

[26] Const. Ill. art. 11, § 12. A plan of reorganization of a railroad company upon foreclosure of its mortgage, by which it is agreed that the property shall be bought in by a trustee for the bondholders, to whom new bonds for a larger amount than the old shall be issued, is not void for conflict with this constitutional provision.

Cushman v. Bonfield, 36 Ill. App. 436.

[27] Rev. Stat. Ill. c. 114, § 20, cl. 10. And see, supra, § 52.

[28] Cooper v. Corbin, 105 Ill. 224.

[29] Frost v. Galesburg, E. & E. R. Co., 167 Ill. 161, 47 N. E. Rep. 357; Coopers v. Wolf, 15 Ohio St. 523.

[30] Rev. Stat. Ill. c. 32, § 43.

6

in the last sentence is the only restriction upon the power of such an organization to pledge its property as security for its debts. Subject to this one condition, a religious society has full power to borrow money for the legitimate purposes of its incorporation, and to mortgage its real estate as security for the same.[31] As to the authority of the trustees in this regard, and the necessity of the consent and direction of the society or church, we are to read the specific direction of the statute in connection with a general clause in the same act, relating to all corporations formed not for purposes of pecuniary profit, which declares that the trustees or directors of such bodies may incumber the property by mortgage "upon consent of the corporation, society, or association, expressed by the vote of a majority of the members thereof."[32] As to the power of the congregation or members of the church to validate, by subsequent ratification, a mortgage made by the trustees without their previous consent or direction, the reader is referred to section 52, above, where this subject is discussed in general terms.

§ 57. **Loan Associations.**—A loan association, organized under the act of 1879, has no authority to acquire and hold real estate except such as has been mortgaged to it or in which it has an interest; and therefore such an association has no power, in exchanging properties, to acquire a lot in which it had no interest and assume a mortgage thereon, and no deficiency decree can be rendered against it on foreclosure of the mortgage.[33]

§ 58. **Municipal Corporations.**—Whatever may be the rule in other states, it appears to be well settled in Illinois that a municipal corporation cannot mortgage its property unless directly authorized thereto by statute. It is said: "Counties are political subdivisions of a state for governmental purposes, only possessing a low order of corporate existence, and for this reason they are generally designated 'quasi corporations' and are conceded to possess no powers except such as are expressly

[31] Zion Church v. Mensch, 178 Ill. 225, 52 N. E. Rep. 858, affirming 74 Ill. App. 115. And see Scott v. First Methodist Church, 50 Mich. 528, 15 N. W. Rep. 891; Keith & Perry Coal Co. v. Bingham, 97 Mo. 196, 10 S. W. Rep. 32.
[32] Rev. Stat. Ill. c. 32, § 32.
[33] National Home Bldg. & Loan Ass'n v. Home Savings Bank, 181 Ill. 35, 54 N. E. Rep. 619, reversing 79 Ill. App. 303.

or by necessary implication conferred upon them by the legislative department of government. In conformity with this well-recognized principle, it was settled at an early period in our judicial history, and the rule has been steadily adhered to ever since, that a county has no power to give away or otherwise dispose of its funds or property for a purpose not authorized by law.'' That the power of municipal corporations to execute mortgages on their property "is not to be found among their general powers—if indeed they may be said to have any such powers—is too palpable to admit of serious discussion.''[34]

§ 59. Consolidated Corporations.—A mortgage made by an organization assuming without warrant of law to act as a corporation, formed by the consolidation of several railroad companies, is invalid, for the reason that there is no corporation in existence with capacity to act or be bound.[35] But the consolidation of the stock of a railroad company created by the laws of another state with that of one created by the laws of Illinois does not make the consolidated corporations one corporation of both states or of either, but the corporation of each state continues a corporation of the state of its creation, although the same persons, as officers and directors, may manage and control both corporations as one body. And where, after such consolidation, by legislative act, the name of the Illinois corporation is made the same as that of the other corporation, and a mortgage is made in the corporate name by the officers of the company as consolidated, upon the line of railroad of the Illinois corporation, such mortgage is the sole mortgage of the Illinois corporation, and is legal and valid as such.[36]

[34] Scates v. King, 110 Ill. 456.

[35] American Loan & Trust Co. v. Minnesota & N. W. R. Co., 157 Ill. 641, 42 N. E. Rep. 153.

[36] Racine & Miss. R. Co. v. Farmers' Loan & Trust Co., 49 Ill. 331.

CHAPTER VI.

FORM AND CONTENTS OF MORTGAGES.

§ 60. **Formal Requisites of a Mortgage.**—No particular form or language is necessary to constitute a mortgage; if a contract for the conveyance of land is intended as a security for a debt, it is a mortgage, whatever may be its form or the name given to it by the parties.[1] It is only requisite that the instrument should evince a present purpose on the part of the grantor or mortgagor to convey the title to specified real estate (sufficiently described to render it capable of identification) to a designated person as mortgagee, to be held by the latter as security for the payment of a certain sum of money or for the performance of some other act on the part of the mortgagor.[2] It is not essential that an instrument of conveyance should follow any exact or prescribed form of words, provided the intention to convey is expressed; courts will so construe a conveyance as to give effect to the intention of the parties, and if it cannot operate as intended by the letter, it will be held to operate in some other form, to effect that intention.[3] Thus, an instrument which, to secure an indebted-

---

[1] Bredenberg v. Landrum, 32 S. Car. 215, 10 S. E. Rep. 956; Schriber v. Le Clair, 66 Wis. 579, 29 N. W. Rep. 570; Cotterell v. Long, 20 Ohio, 464.

[2] New Orleans Banking Ass'n v. Adams, 109 U. S. 211.

[3] Cross v. Weare Commission Co., 153 Ill. 499, 38 N. E. Rep. 1038.

ness, purports to "grant, sell, convey, and confirm" an elevator attached to realty, describing the same as "the steam elevator on the railroad elevator lot," will operate to convey such elevator as real estate, although the instrument is written upon a chattel mortgage form, and acknowledged as such, and the property is referred to in the instrument as "goods and chattels."[4] So, an instrument executed and acknowledged in due form by the holders of the legal title to real estate, which recites the execution and recording of a mortgage on such property, the destruction of the record of the mortgage by fire, the re-establishment of the record according to law, and which admits a specified sum to be due on the mortgage, which sum the parties thereby agree to pay in installments, is itself a mortgage and may be recorded as such.[5]

It may be remarked in this connection that the date of a mortgage, if material at all, is important only in fixing the time for the payment of the debt secured. Hence post-dating the mortgage does not prevent its becoming operative immediately upon its delivery. It creates a present charge upon the property, of which subsequent purchasers or incumbrancers are bound to take notice if the instrument is recorded.[6]

§ 61. **Description of Parties.**—The parties to a mortgage must be so described in the instrument as to be identified with certainty. The omission of the name of the mortgagee from the granting clause will invalidate the mortgage if nothing else appears to identify the party to whom the conveyance is supposed to be made; but not if the party intended as mortgagee is plainly identified by other parts of the instrument, as, by being explicitly named in the recital of the indebtedness, or in the habendum clause.[7] So, where the name of the mortgagee is by mistake written in the blank left for the name of the mortgagor, and the name of the mortgagor in that left for the mortgagee, but the instrument is signed by the right party, and is acknowledged by the signer, the mistake in the transposition of the names being evident, the mortgage will not be invalidated thereby, and its record will be notice to subse-

[4] Cross v. Weare Commission Co., 153 Ill. 499, 38 N. E. Rep. 1038.

[5] Hunt v. Innis, 2 Woods, 103, Fed. Cas. No. 6,892.

[6] Jacobs v. Denison, 141 Mass. 117, 5 N. E. Rep. 526.

[7] Richey v. Sinclair, 167 Ill. 184, 47 N. E. Rep. 364, reversing 67 Ill. App. 580. And see Shirley v. Burch, 16 Oreg. 83, 18 Pac. Rep. 351.

quent purchasers from the mortgagor.[8] A trifling mistake in
the name or description of either of the parties, arising from
a mere clerical error and apparent at sight, where there is no
mistake as to their identity (such as a slight misnomer of a
corporation, not calculated to mislead or to raise an uncertainty as to the corporation intended), will neither invalidate
the instrument nor require its reformation.[9] So, a mortgage
is not invalidated by the fact that the mortgagor and his wife
are described by Christian names or initials which do not belong to them, in the granting, defeasance, and testatum
clauses, and in the certificate of acknowledgment, if they sign
the instrument in their true and proper names.[10]

While a mortgage purporting to be given to a grantee who
has no real existence is a nullity, it is not so with a conveyance to a real person under an assumed name. As observed
by the court in California: "If there be no grantee, and the
deed is to a mere fictitious name, it is obvious that it is a
nullity. But if there be a person in existence, and identified,
and delivery is made to him, it makes no difference by what
name he is called. He may assume a name for the occasion,
and a conveyance to and by him under such name will pass
the title."[11] But the fact that the grantee in a mortgage is
described by a wrong name will not invest him with the right
to sue for foreclosure in a fictitious name. He must sue in
his proper name, averring in his bill that the defendant made
the mortgage to him by the name mentioned therein. If, on
the other hand, he sues in the name given in the mortgage,
the mortgagor will not be estopped to plead the misnomer in
abatement.[12] It is held that a wife joining in a mortgage is
sufficiently described therein if her first name is given and she
is described as the wife of the other grantor; as in the formula
"John Doe and Jane, wife of said John Doe."[13]

§ 62. Description of Property Mortgaged.—Where the description of the property covered by a mortgage is so indefinite
that it cannot be identified, or if the description calls for premises which have no existence, or which cannot possibly be

[8] Beaver v. Slanker, 94 Ill. 175.
[9] Germantown Farmers Mut. Ins.
Co. v. Dhein, 57 Wis. 521.
[10] Dodd v. Bartholomew, 44 Ohio
St. 171, 5 N. E. Rep. 866.

[11] Wilson v. White, 84 Cal. 239,
24 Pac. Rep. 114.
[12] Pinckard v. Milmine, 76 Ill.
453.
[13] Edgell v. Hagens, 53 Iowa, 223,
5 N. W. Rep. 136.

found, the mortgage must be considered void, and the courts cannot receive extraneous evidence to explain the intention of the parties, nor reform the mortgage.[14] But a latent ambiguity in the description—that is to say, an ambiguity which is not inconsistent with a clear intention on the part of the grantor, but arises from the uncertainty or inaccuracy of the language employed—may be explained and removed by evidence extraneous to the instrument. For example, where the mortgage purports to grant a certain number of acres of land in a particular tract or division (the tract or division being unmistakably described), but it transpires that the grantor did not own land in that tract or division situated in such a part of it as would fit the description in the mortgage, it may be shown that he did own an equal number of acres lying in a different part of the same tract or division, and the mortgage will then attach according to his presumed intention to convey what he owned.[15] So, where the mortgage describes a particular quantity of land, improved in a certain manner, situated in a designated section in a named county, it is not invalidated by the fact that there may be several sections of that number in the same county; for parol evidence is admissible to show that only one of the sections bearing that number included land owned by the mortgagor and improved in the manner described.[16]

[14] Carter v. Barnes, 26 Ill. 454. The record of a mortgage operates as constructive notice to subsequent purchasers or incumbrancers only so far as the property is correctly described in the mortgage and record, unless it is apparent from the record itself that there is a misdescription. Slocum v. O'Day, 174 Ill. 215, 51 N. E. Rep. 243. The equity of a mortgagee in a tract of land intended to be mortgaged to him, but which is misdescribed in the mortgage, is superior to the lien of a general judgment against the mortgagor, rendered before the mistake in the description had been corrected, but not to the lien of an attachment judgment against the particular land, rendered before correction of the faulty description, and before the plaintiff in attachment had notice of the mortgagee's equity therein. Yarnell v. Brown, 170 Ill. 362, 48 N. E. Rep. 909.

[15] Denison v. Gambill, 81 Ill. App. 170. And see Sharp v. Thompson, 100 Ill. 447.

[16] Bybee v. Hageman, 66 Ill. 519. In this case, the mortgage described the property as "one acre and a half in the northwest corner of section 5, together with the brewery contained therein," situated in a designated county in the state of Illinois, but without giving any township and range. There being several sections in that county bearing the same number, the am-

Again, where the description of the property mortgaged contains enough to identify it with certainty and without ambiguity, but there is a clause added which is subordinate and incorrect, the latter part may be rejected as surplusage; and evidence is admissible to show that, striking out the incorrect part of the description, that which remains corresponds to the property actually owned by the mortgagor and intended to be covered by the mortgage.[17] And it is held that where the land is described by the numbers of the section, township, range, and meridian, and also by the name of the county in which it is supposed to lie, the former description will prevail over the latter, if the two are inconsistent.[18]

In explaining an ambiguous or imperfect description of property in a mortgage, recourse may be had to the record of the deed under which the mortgagor claims; and it is held that the description in the mortgage, aided by that in a deed referred to in the mortgage for greater certainty, even if defective, sufficiently describes the premises to put all persons upon inquiry and to charge them with notice.[19] But while parol testimony is admissible to aid in locating the land by the description contained in the mortgage, such evidence as to what the records show as to land owned by the mortgagor at the time of executing the mortgage is not to be received; for the reason that the original deed, or the record of it, if the original cannot be produced, would be the best evidence.[20]

biguity was held to be a latent one, and to be susceptible of explanation by evidence outside the mortgage, to show in what township and range the land was situated, and therefore the mortgage was not void for uncertainty. The ambiguity was removed by evidence showing that, at the time the mortgage was made, the mortgagor was living on a tract of land in the northwest quarter of section 5, township 6 north, range 1 west, and had a dwelling-house and brewery there, and had no brewery anywhere else. In Myers v. Perry, 72 Ill. App. 450, it was held that a mortgage of lands properly on file in the recorder's office, from the description of the lands in which the word "township" was inadvertently omitted by the scrivener who drew it, is nevertheless sufficient to put judgment creditors of the mortgagor upon inquiry as to what particular lands the parties to the mortgage in question intended to incumber.

[17] Myers v. Ladd, 26 Ill. 415. And see Kruse v. Scripps, 11 Ill. 98.

[18] Sickmon v. Wood, 69 Ill. 329.

[19] Clark v. Wallick, 56 Ill. App. 30. And see Bent v. Coleman, 89 Ill. 364.

[20] Cornwell v. Cornwell, 91 Ill. 414; Chicago Dock & Canal Co. v. Kinzie, 93 Ill. 415.

Where the mortgage purports to convey "one acre of land" (or a designated number of acres) lying in a certain corner of a tract or division of land which is accurately described, it will not be void for the want of a more particular description of the shape of the parcel conveyed, but will be taken as passing the designated quantity of land in the form of a square.[21] Finally, it has been pointed out by the supreme court of the United States that generality in the language employed in the description will not necessarily render it void for uncertainty; for a mortgage or deed purporting to convey "all my estate," or "all my lands wherever situated," or "all my property," will be sufficient to pass the title.[22]

§ 63. Statement of Debt Secured.—A mortgage should set forth with certainty and precision the nature and amount of the obligation it is intended to secure. If given to secure an ascertained debt, the amount thereof should be stated; if to secure a debt not ascertained, such data should be given respecting it as will put persons interested in the inquiry upon the track leading to a discovery; if meant to secure an existing or future liability, the foundation of such liability should be set forth. Failing this requirement, the record of the mortgage will not furnish constructive notice to subsequent purchasers or incumbrancers.[23] But not every trifling error or uncertainty will have this effect. Thus, the record is sufficiently certain to be constructive notice even though the amount of the note secured is not expressly stated, when the note is in other respects identified, and the rate of interest is specified, together with the number and amount of each interest coupon and the respective dates for their payment.[24] So, where a promissory note secured by a mortgage provided for interest at a specified rate per annum after date, payable annually, but the mortgage described the note as bearing interest "from due until paid," but from subsequent recitals in the mortgage it might be inferred that the note bore interest from its date, it was held that the note was not so misdescribed as to prevent a foreclosure of the mortgage when default was made in the payment

[21] Bybee v. Hageman, 66 Ill. 519; Richey v. Sinclair, 167 Ill. 184, 47 N. E. Rep. 364, reversing 67 Ill. App. 580.

[22] Wilson v. Boyce, 92 U. S. 320.

[23] Metropolitan Bank v. Godfrey, 23 Ill. 579, 603; Bergman v. Bogda, 46 Ill. App. 351; Bullock v. Battenhausen, 108 Ill. 28.

[24] Gardner v. Cohn, 191 Ill. 553, 61 N. E. Rep. 492, affirming 95 Ill. App. 26.

of the first year's interest.[25] And the omission from the description of a note in a mortgage of a nugatory clause therein does not constitute a variance.[26]

It is also held that the recital in a mortgage of a larger amount to be secured than is really due to the mortgagee will not of itself avoid the mortgage, the same being duly recorded, as against a subsequent purchaser without actual notice.[27] In fact, what is required by the law in regard to the statement of the consideration or indebtedness in a mortgage is not so much truth as certainty or definiteness. A false statement or overstatement of the amount due will not per se make the mortgage void. It is a proper subject of inquiry at the instance of any one whose rights are liable to be affected, and may be evidence of fraud between the original parties. But if no actual fraud appears, mere inaccuracy of the statement as to the consideration will not avoid the security. But at the same time it must be remarked that, where a mortgage does not purport to secure an existing indebtedness, but merely the payment of a certain note, and there was no such note in existence at the time the mortgage was made, it cannot be foreclosed as drawn, to the prejudice of the intervening rights of third persons, although an indebtedness actually existed and a note corresponding to that described in the mortgage was afterwards drawn.[28]

§ 64. Anticipation of Time of Payment.—A stipulation in a mortgage to the effect that the entire principal sum shall become due and payable,—or that the mortgagee may, at his option, declare it to be due and payable,—if the mortgagor shall fail to make due and prompt payment of any part of the principal or interest as it falls due, is legal and valid, and will be enforced by courts of equity as well as of law. Such a provision is not properly a penalty or forfeiture, but merely an acceleration of the time of payment. And at any rate, where the penalty or forfeiture created by the agreement of the parties amounts to no more than a mere pecuniary obligation, equity will not grant relief against it when the default arises

[25] Merrill v. Elliott, 55 Ill. App. 34.

[26] Hoskins v. Cole, 34 Ill. App. 541.

[27] Miller v. Rouser, 25 Ill. App. 88.

[28] Ogden v. Ogden, 180 Ill. 543, 54 N. E. Rep. 750, affirming 79 Ill. App. 488; Whiting Paper Co. v. Busse, 95 Ill. App. 288.

from negligence or a wilful and persistent refusal to pay what is due. Stipulations of this kind in a mortgage are not to be regarded with disfavor by the courts, but are to be construed and enforced, and the intentions of the parties ascertained, in accordance with the same rules which are applicable to other contracts.[29] But such a provision is permissive only, and it does not of itself cause the notes secured by the mortgage to mature, upon such a default, so as to start the statute of limitations running against the debt.[30] Nor will the negotiability of a note secured by mortgage be affected by a provision in the mortgage that the note may be declared due before the day fixed for its payment, upon the happening of some contingency.[31]

§ 65. **Covenant for Payment of Debt.**—It is not essential to constitute an instrument a mortgage that it should contain a personal covenant on the part of the mortgagor to pay the debt or obligation secured.[32] It is said: "In Great Britain, it is usual to insert in the mortgage itself a covenant for the payment of the money. When such a covenant is found in the mortgage, it being under seal, and the debt to secure which it was given is not [under seal], a bar to the recovery of the debt, if of a shorter period than a bar to a sealed instrument, could not affect the remedy on the covenant in the mortgage. If the statutory period necessary to bar an unsealed instrument be of shorter duration than a sealed instrument, a mortgage containing such a covenant given to secure the payment of a debt evidenced by an unsealed note would be governed by the longer period required to bar a recovery on sealed instruments."[33] At the same time, it appears to be the accepted doctrine that a mortgage, unless it contains some express contract to that effect, is not of itself an instrument which imports personal liability; and the remedy on such mortgage is con-

---

[29] Houston v. Curran, 101 Ill. App. 203; Hoodless v. Reed, 112 Ill. 105, 1 N. E. Rep. 118; Ottawa Plank-Road Co. v. Murray, 15 Ill. 336; Ruggles v. Southern Minn. R. Co., 5 Chicago Leg. News, 110, Fed. Cas. No. 12,121. And see, infra, § 372.

[30] Watts v. Hoffman, 77 Ill. App. 411.

[31] Hunter v. Clarke, 184 Ill. 158, 56 N. E. Rep. 297, affirming Clarke v. Hunter, 83 Ill. App. 100.

[32] Flagg v. Mann, 2 Sumn. 486, Fed. Cas. No. 4,847; Niggeler v. Maurin, 34 Minn. 118, 24 N. W. Rep. 369.

[33] Harris v. Mills, 28 Ill. 44.

fined to the land put in pledge, unless it is accompanied by
some cause of action which of itself creates a personal liability, in which case the mortgage is merely a collateral security,
and does not merge the claim.[34] Hence, if the mortgage contains a covenant for payment, it imposes a personal liability on
the mortgagor, in addition to the security furnished by the
land pledged, and although there may be no accompanying
note or bond; but if there is no such covenant in the mortgage,
and no collateral obligation in the way of a note, bond, or other
separate evidence of the debt, the property alone is charged
with the lien and must be looked to by the mortgagee as the
sole source out of which he is to make good his claim,[35] unless,
indeed, he can prove by parol, as he is permitted to do, that
the mortgagor verbally promised to pay the mortgage debt.[36]
Where the mortgage is given to secure the payment of a third
person's notes, and contains no covenant to pay the debt, it
is erroneous to enter a personal decree against the mortgagor
for the balance of the debt that may remain after the sale of
the mortgaged premises on foreclosure.[37] And a recital, in a
mortgage given to secure purchase money, that the debt is not
payable until, by the vendor's conveyance of a certain homestead interest to the mortgagor, and certain other acts, "the
title is fixed up," embraces the perfecting of the defective
title.[38]

§ 66. **Habendum.**—It is a well-established general rule that
the use of the word "heirs," or other appropriate words of
perpetuity, in the habendum clause of a mortgage or other
deed of conveyance of lands, is essential to pass an estate in
fee simple. But this is not an inflexible rule admitting of no
exception or qualification. On the contrary, the manifest intention of the parties will prevail against the presumption arising from the use or omission of technical terms. Thus, a mortgage may be deemed to pass the fee, although the word "heirs"
is not used, if this is evidently the intention of the grantor;
as where the words employed, "mortgage and warrant," are
sufficient to convey the fee in the state where the deed was

[34] Baum v. Tomkin, 110 Pa. St.
569, 1 Atl. Rep. 535.
[35] Pioneer Gold Mining Co. v.
Baker, 10 Sawy. 539, 23 Fed. Rep.
258.

[36] Tonkin v. Baum, 114 Pa. St.
414, 7 Atl. Rep. 185.
[37] Hoag v. Starr, 69 Ill. 362.
[38] Weaver v. Wilson, 48 Ill. 125.

made, though not in the state where the land lies.[39] In regard
to what may be called the quantity of the estate conveyed, it
is held that, where the habendum clause of a mortgage, containing a power of sale in the mortgagee, purports to pass "all
the right, title, interest, claim, demand, and equity" of the
mortgagor in the premises, this will embrace all possible interest the mortgagor could have, including his equity of redemption, so that a sale under the power would operate to cut off
his right to redeem.[40]

§ 67. **Covenants of Title and Warranty.**—The defendant in
a bill to foreclose a mortgage containing covenants of seisin
and special warranty cannot set up a prior and paramount
equitable title in himself.[41]   And in Illinois, under the conveyance act of 1874,[42] the use of the words "grant, bargain, and
sell," in a mortgage, operates as a covenant to the mortgagee
and his heirs that the mortgagor was seised in fee simple of
the land mortgaged, free from all incumbrances, etc., and a
title subsequently acquired by the mortgagor, whether legal
or equitable, will inure to the benefit of the mortgagee.[43]   But
a deed not purporting to convey an estate in fee simple absolute in the lands (as, where it merely quitclaims all the right,
estate, title, and demand which the grantor has or ought to
have in the property) is not such a conveyance as that an after-
acquired title of the grantor will inure to the grantee under the
statute.   If one conveys lands with a general covenant of warranty against all lawful claims and demands, he cannot be allowed to set up as against his grantee, or those claiming under
him, any title subsequently acquired, either by purchase or
otherwise, but such new title will inure by way of estoppel to
the use and benefit of the grantee and his heirs and assigns.
But where the deed, on its face, does not purport to convey
an indefeasible estate, but only the right, title, and interest of
the grantor, although the deed may contain a covenant of general warranty, the doctrine of estoppel will not apply so as to
pass an after-acquired estate to the grantee.   The covenants
of warranty in a deed are limited and restrained by the estate

---

[39] Brown v. First Nat. Bank, 44
Ohio St. 269, 6 N. E. Rep. 648.
[40] Strother v. Law, 54 Ill. 413.
[41] McManness v. Paxson, 37 Fed.
Rep. 296.

[42] Rev. Stat. Ill. c. 30, § 8.
[43] Pratt v. Pratt, 96 Ill. 184; Elder v. Derby, 93 Ill. 228.   And see
Gochenour v. Mowry, 33 Ill. 331;
Wells v. Somers, 4 Ill. App. 297.

conveyed on the face of the deed. These principles apply to mortgages and deeds of trust.[44] By force of the statute, if A. conveys land to B., and B., in a mortgage of the same land to C., uses the words "has granted, bargained, sold, and conveyed" to C., "his heirs and assigns, forever," any subsequent interest that B. may acquire thereto by a deed to A. which inures to B.'s benefit, will pass by the mortgage to C., or by any sale made pursuant to its terms.[45]

§ 68. Tax and Insurance Clauses.—Mortgages and deeds of trust usually contain a covenant on the part of the mortgagor or grantor to pay all taxes which may be assessed against the property during the life of the mortgage, and also (if the property is improved) to keep it insured for the benefit of the mortgagee in some good and responsible insurance company. And it is commonly provided that the mortgagee shall be reimbursed for any money expended by him, for his own protection, in consequence of the mortgagor's failure to comply with this undertaking. But the parties may go further than this, and make the neglect or refusal of the mortgagor to pay taxes, or to insure the property, a breach of the condition of the mortgage, entitling the mortgagee to an immediate foreclosure. The supreme court of another state has held that a stipulation in a mortgage that, upon failure to pay taxes levied on the mortgaged premises, the principal debt secured thereby shall immediately become due and payable, is valid. It was said: "There is nothing to vitiate such a contract. It is not prohibited by statute, nor against public policy. Nor is it a hard contract, which it would be unconscionable to enforce. The lender of money may well insist that the security be kept intact or the loan mature. This is but parallel to the case of a stipulation that, upon a failure to pay interest promptly, the principal shall become due. Such stipulations have almost invariably been sustained."[46]

§ 69. Provision for Solicitor's Fee.—A mortgage may contain a stipulation to pay a reasonable sum for the fee of the complainant's solicitor, in case of a foreclosure or bill filed for that purpose, to be included in the decree. Such an agreement on the part of the mortgagor is not contrary to public

[44] Holbrook v. Debo, 99 Ill. 373; Bowen v. McCarthy, 127 Ill. 17, 18 N. E. Rep. 757.

[45] Gibbons v. Hoag, 95 Ill. 45.

[46] Stanclift v. Norton, 11 Kans. 218, per Brewer, J.

policy, nor is it prohibited by any law, nor will it, by itself, render the mortgage usurious.[47]   But if the fee so promised to be paid is intended as a mere gratuity, it is without consideration; and if it is intended as a cover for usurious interest, it is prohibited by the statute and for that reason cannot be enforced. If it is intended to indemnify the mortgagee against the expense of a foreclosure, it will be allowed to the extent of the attorney's proper and necessary services, but will not embrace useless and superfluous services on the part of the solicitor, however extensive or laborious they may have been.[48]

§ 70. Clause of Defeasance.—The "defeasance" clause in a common-law mortgage is that which provides that, upon payment of the debt secured or performance of the other conditions of the mortgage, the instrument shall become void and of no effect, or that the estate thereby granted shall cease and determine, or shall revest in the mortgagor. It is not necessary that this provision should be inserted in the mortgage itself. In equity, a deed of land, absolute and unconditional on its face, but accompanied by a separate written instrument having the legal effect of a defeasance, will be held to be a mortgage; and in the same forum it is considered that even a parol defeasance, if clearly ascertained and established, will be sufficient to give the character of a mortgage to the transaction between the parties, in whatever form they may have chosen to cast it.[49] If the defeasance is incorporated in the mortgage itself, according to the more usual and regular form, its language is not deemed very important, in the sense that it must follow any established form of words; it is sufficient if the clause plainly shows the intention of the parties to terminate the estate of the mortgagee, upon performance of the conditions, and reinvest the mortgagor with the full legal title. Thus, a deed which is otherwise absolute on its face, but which contains the words "subject, nevertheless, to the right of redemption of the property by the grantor," will be held to operate as a mortgage.[50] But the defeasance clause is of importance

[47] Halderman v. Massachusetts Mut. Life Ins. Co., 120 Ill. 390, 11 N. E. Rep. 526; Soles v. Sheppard, 99 Ill. 616; Fowler v. Equitable Trust Co., 141 U. S. 411.

[48] Soles v. Sheppard, 99 Ill. 616.

[49] Supra, §§ 19, 20. And see Jeffery v. Hursh, 58 Mich. 246, 25 N. W. Rep. 176; McMillan v. Bissell, 63 Mich. 66, 29 N. W. Rep. 737; Pearce v. Wilson, 111 Pa. St. 14, 2 Atl. Rep. 99; Marshall v. Stewart. 17 Ohio, 356; Cosby v. Buchanan, 81 Ala. 574, 1 South. Rep. 898.

[50] Mellon v. Lemmon, 111 Pa. St. 56, 2 Atl. Rep. 56.

in the construction of the instrument, when there is any doubt or ambiguity as to its meaning; for this is considered as the part which furnishes the plainest indications of the intention of the parties. The purpose of a mortgage, it is said, is most certainly manifested by the condition on which it is to become void, although other parts of the mortgage may be considered in connection with the clause of defeasance, if necessary, in the ascertainment of its meaning.[51]

§ 71. **Statutory Form of Mortgage.**—The statutes of Illinois provide that "mortgages of lands may be in the following form, substantially:

The mortgagor (here insert name or names) mortgages and warrants to (here insert name or names of mortgagee or mortgagees) to secure the payment of (here recite the nature and amount of indebtedness, showing when due and the rate of interest, and whether secured by note or otherwise) the following described real estate (here insert description thereof) situated in the county of ————, in the State of Illinois. Dated this —— day of ————— A. D. 18—.

A. B. [L. S.]''

And it is also provided that "every such mortgage [in the statutory form], when otherwise properly executed, shall be deemed and held a good and sufficient mortgage in fee to secure the payment of the moneys therein specified; and if the same contains the words 'and warrants,' the same shall be construed the same as if full covenants of seisin, good right to convey, against incumbrances, of quiet enjoyment, and general warranty, as expressed in section 9 of this act, were fully written therein; but if the words 'and warrants' are omitted, no such covenants shall be implied.''[52] A mortgage, therefore, in the statutory form, with the addition of the words mentioned, carries with it all covenants of title, and is a conveyance of the fee. It does not differ materially from the common-law form of mortgage in respect to the rights of the mortgagee, and it enables him to maintain an action of ejectment, after breach of condition, against the mortgagor or any other person who may be in possession of the mortgaged property.[53] It also

[51] Chambers v. Prewitt, 172 Ill. 615, 50 N. E. Rep. 145.

[52] Rev. Stat. Ill. c. 30, § 11 (Starr & C. § 12).

[53] Esker v. Heffernan, 159 Ill. 38, 41 N. E. Rep. 1113.

results from the statutory declaration that the words "and
warrants" shall import an effect equivalent to the insertion of
all the common-law covenants of warranty, that, where such a
mortgage is given, a title subsequently acquired by the mortgagor will inure to the benefit of the mortgagee. An estoppel
arises against the mortgagor out of the covenants of title, so
that he cannot deny his title or claim adversely to the mortgage.[54]

§ 72. **Erasures and Alterations.**—An alteration in a mortgage, made by the mortgagee or by any one acting in his
interest and behalf, after the execution of the instrument, will
avoid it and prevent its foreclosure when (1) it is done with a
fraudulent intent, (2) and without the consent or acquiescence
of the mortgagor, and (3) when it changes the effect of the
mortgage in some particular materially affecting the rights
and obligations of the parties.[55] All these elements are essential. First, if there was no fraudulent or dishonest intention
on the part of the person making the alteration, it will not
avoid the instrument, although the effect may be to confer an
additional advantage upon him. Thus, if the alteration is made
in good faith and in the honest effort to correct a real mistake
and to make the instrument conform to the actual intention of
the parties at the time of its execution, it will not invalidate
the mortgage, though done by the mortgagee without the
privity of the mortgagor, or by the mortgagee and one of the
mortgagors acting in concert but without the consent of the
other mortgagor.[56] Secondly, whatever may have been the
motive or purpose of the mortgagee in making the alteration,
his act may be validated by the consent of the mortgagor
thereto, by his authorization of it, or by his acquiescence in
the effect of the instrument as altered. More especially is this
the case, where the change is only intended to correct an error,
and the instrument is reacknowledged after the alteration.[57]
Thirdly, the alteration must have been material. On this point
it is said: "While the general rule is that the unauthorized

[54] Lagger v. Mutual Union L. &
B. Ass'n, 146 Ill. 283, 33 N. E. Rep.
946.

[55] Daub v. Englebach, 9 Ill. App.
99; McIntyre v. Velte, 153 Pa. St.
350, 25 Atl. Rep. 739; Johnson v.

Moore, 33 Kans. 90, 5 Pac. Rep.
406.

[56] Foote v. Hambrick, 70 Miss.
157, 11 South. Rep. 567.

[57] Casler v. Byers, 28 Ill. App.
123, affirmed, 129 Ill. 657, 22 N. E.
Rep. 507.

alteration of a contract by a party to it renders it void, the rule has been so far relaxed, at least in this country, that such an alteration, though made by a party to the contract, will not destroy its validity unless the alteration is found to be material. * * * The effect of an alteration in a written instrument depends upon its nature, the person by whom, and the intention with which, it was made. If neither the rights or interests, duties or obligations, of either of the parties are in any manner changed, an alteration may be considered as immaterial.''[58] But an alteration which increases the stated consideration of the mortgage must be regarded as material, and if fraudulently made by the mortgagee without the knowledge or consent of the mortgagor, will prevent the enforcement of the mortgage as security for any portion of the debt described.[59] And the same is true of an alteration which gives the mortgagee a more speedy remedy upon the security, or authorizes a foreclosure upon a default not originally intended to make the mortgage fall due.[60]

Most of the cases have been concerned with the effect of alterations made by the mortgagee alone. But it must also be observed that, in the case of joint mortgagors, an alteration made by one of them alone, in collusion with the mortgagee, will avoid the mortgage as against the other mortgagor, not joining in the act or consenting to it. Thus, in a case in Minnesota, it appeared that a husband and wife joined in the execution of a mortgage, and after it had been signed and acknowledged by the husband, and had been signed by the wife, and had gone out of her possession for the purpose of being delivered to the mortgagee, a clause providing for the allowance of attorneys' fees in case of foreclosure was inserted in the mortgage by the husband, with the knowledge and consent of the mortgagee and in his presence, but without the knowledge of the wife, and without her assenting thereto at any time. It was held that such insertion was, as to her, a material alteration of the mortgage, and that it would avoid the instrument as to her.[61] But on the other hand, if an alter-

[58] Ryan v. First Nat. Bank, 148 Ill. 349. And see Elliott v. Blair, 47 Ill. 342; Rodriguez v. Hayes, 76 Tex. 225, 13 S. W. Rep. 296.

[59] Johnson v. Moore, 33 Kans. 90, 5 Pac. Rep. 406.

[60] McIntyre v. Velte, 153 Pa. St. 350, 25 Atl. Rep. 739.

[61] Coles v. Yorks, 28 Minn. 464, 10 N. W. Rep. 775.

ation in a mortgage is made by a mere stranger to it, not acting in privity with the mortgagee, nor under his direction nor
at his instance, it is what is technically termed a "spoliation"
of the instrument. It does not destroy its legal effect nor
invalidate it; but it then becomes the right of the mortgagee
to have the instrument restored and enforced as originally
executed.[62] But the officer who takes the acknowledgment
of a mortgage cannot, after its execution, change it in a material particular (as, in the description of the premises mortgaged) without the assent of the mortgagor, even to make the
document conform to the contract of the parties as he under-
stands it.[63] An alteration so made might not invalidate the
mortgage, if made without the consent or direction of the mortgagee, but he would not be able to enforce it as changed,
but only according to its original tenor. There is also authority for the statement that, where a fraudulent alteration of a
mortgage, being detected, is itself altered, so as to make the
instrument read as it read at the time of its execution, the
mortgagee, who had no hand in the falsification of the paper,
will not be precluded from enforcing it according to its proper
and original terms.[64]

Where the alteration is made, not in the mortgage itself,
but in the note or other obligation which it secures, the effect
on the enforcibility of the mortgage will depend on the
presence or absence of a fraudulent intention. "In a court
of equity a mortgage is regarded as an incident of the debt;
and where a mortgagee has released or discharged the debt
by a fraudulent alteration or destruction of the written evidence of it, he ought not to be permitted to sustain a suit for
its recovery; but where the alteration was not fraudulent,
although the identity of the instrument may be destroyed, we
think it should not cancel a debt of which the instrument was
merely evidence. If there was no attempt to defraud, there
is no reason why a court should not assist the creditor as far
as it can consistently."[65] Finally, it is to be remarked that
erasures or alterations made in a note secured by mortgage
do not avoid it when made before the execution of the note;

[62] Russell v. Reed, 36 Minn. 376,
81 N. W. Rep. 452.

[63] Pereau v. Frederick, 17 Nebr.
117, 22 N. W. Rep. 235.

[64] See Osborn v. Andrees, 37
Kans. 301, 15 Pac. Rep. 153.

[65] Vogle v. Ripper, 34 Ill. 100.
And see Heath v. Blake, 28 S. Car.
406, 5 S. E. Rep. 842.

because its subsequent execution amounts to an acceptance and approval of the paper as altered. And it is competent for parties interested to explain such erasures or alterations and to show the time when they were made, with reference to the execution of the note; and for this purpose reference may be made to the conditions of the mortgage, and to such pertinent considerations as the handwriting of the note and the alterations in it and the ink with which they were written.[66]

§ 73. **Filling Blanks.**—A mortgage or deed of trust, which does not disclose the name of any mortgagee or grantee, or which lacks a description of property conveyed, being blank in respect to these particulars, is void and of no effect so long as such blanks remain unfilled. But where an instrument, otherwise perfect and complete, is filled up, in respect to such omissions, in accordance with the written or verbal instructions of the mortgagor or grantor, whether in his presence or not, and whether before or after its delivery, and under it the property, then or afterwards, comes to the hands of some innocent and bona fide holder for value, the instrument will be held to be valid. But on the other hand, if the blank instrument is filled up contrary to the directions of the maker and to his prejudice, and with full knowledge on the part of the party who takes and holds under it, it will be entirely null and void as against the maker.[67] In the case of Wilson v. South Park Commissioners,[68] it was held that if a deed of trust has no description of any land, nor the name of any grantee, but is in blank as to these particulars, and the blanks are afterwards filled, without authority, so as to show a grantee and a description of land, the deed will be void; and further, that the delivery of a deed of trust in blank, by which to obtain money from one not informed of the fact that it is in blank, affords strong evidence that a gross and palpable fraud was intended, which will make all the parties to the fraud liable in an action for the damages resulting.

§ 74. **Rules for Construction of Mortgages.**—The elementary rule in the construction or interpretation of a mortgage is to

[66] Cook v. Moulton, 59 Ill. App. 428.

[67] State v. Matthews, 44 Kans. 596, 25 Pac. Rep. 36. And see Whitaker v. Miller, 83 Ill. 381; Harding v. Des Moines Nat. Bank, 81 Iowa, 499, 46 N. W. Rep. 1071; Shirley v. Burch, 16 Oreg. 83, 18 Pac. Rep. 351.

[68] 70 Ill. 46.

ascertain from the instrument the actual intention of the parties, giving meaning and effect to all the words and clauses used, if possible, and then to give effect to the intention thus ascertained.[69] In this process, the whole of the mortgage, and all its parts, must be construed together; and a reservation or waiver in favor of the grantor or mortgagor must be interpreted in the light of the other provisions of the instrument; and if the mortgage is equally susceptible of two interpretations, that meaning will be adopted which is adverse to the interests of the mortgagor and favorable to those of the mortgagee.[70] Again, when the mortgage is given to secure the payment of a note or bond, the two instruments being made at the same time, they are to be construed together, as if they were parts of one and the same document and in relation to the same subject, as parts of the same transaction, together constituting one contract. The mortgage may, as well as the note or bond, describe the debt or some other particular of the transaction, and may thus qualify the terms of the note or bond.[71] Parol evidence cannot be considered to vary or contradict a mortgage, but is competent to identify the subject-matter thereof referred to in general terms, or to show the situation, condition, and mutual relations of the parties, to make clear the meaning of language used which would otherwise be uncertain.[72] But when a contract is reduced to writing, the presumption is that the entire actual agreement of the parties is contained in it, and parol evidence as to conversations between them prior to its execution is not admissible to vary or explain it. Consequently, the terms and conditions of a mortgage or deed of trust cannot be varied by evidence of what the parties said to each other during the negotiations leading up to its execution.[73]

§ 75. **Reformation of a Mortgage in Equity.**—Equity has power to reform and correct a mortgage which, in consequence of a mistake, fails to embody the contract actually intended by the parties to be made; and this relief may be granted in an action for the foreclosure of the mortgage; that is, the bill

[69] Clark v. Brenneman, 86 Ill. App. 416.

[70] United States Mortgage Co. v. Gross, 93 Ill. 483.

[71] Boley v. Lake Street El. R. Co., 64 Ill. App. 305.

[72] Chambers v. Prewitt, 172 Ill. 615, 50 N. E. Rep. 145.

[73] Morris v. Calumet & Chicago Canal Co., 91 Ill. App. 437.

may pray for reformation of the mortgage and for its foreclosure as reformed, and the court, in a proper case, may decree accordingly.[74] The circumstances necessary to make a proper case for the action of a court of equity in this behalf have been well stated by the court in another state, as follows: "In order that a written instrument may be reformed in equity for mistake, it must appear that the parties agreed upon a certain contract; that they executed a contract, the one sought to be reformed; that the contract executed was not the one agreed upon; that the variance between the contract agreed upon and the one executed occurred by mistake; in what the mistake consisted; and that the mistake was mutual."[75] Thus, if the draftsman, in preparing a mortgage, made a mistake and omitted some portion of the contract of the parties, or if by mistake he inserted into it some matter which was not a part of the agreement as made by the parties, and rendered the agreement variant from the contract they designed and supposed they had executed, then a court of equity, on a proper showing of the facts, has power to reform the contract, and then enforce it as it was designed to have been executed.[76] If the evidence shows that a mistake was made in the description of the property intended to be covered by the mortgage, the instrument may be reformed so as to carry out the intention of the parties.[77] And a court of equity may correct a mistake which consists merely in the use of repugnant terms, after a sufficiently accurate description of the property.[78] So also, where the mortgage is defective for the want of a seal, the mortgagee, as against the mortgagor, may have it reformed by affixing the seal.[79]

§ 76. Same; As to Mistakes of Law.—The earlier decisions in Illinois were quite positive in laying down the rule that a deed or mortgage cannot be reformed where the mistake com-

[74] Citizens' Nat. Bank v. Dayton, 116 Ill. 257, 4 N. E. Rep. 492.

[75] Gassert v. Black, 11 Mont. 185, 27 Pac. Rep. 791.

[76] Carter v. Barnes, 26 Ill. 454. But the giving of a construction to a mortgage, as to which of two inconsistent descriptions of the premises conveyed shall prevail, is not to be regarded as a reformation of the mortgage, in any such sense that the question could arise as to the power of the court to reform the mortgage in case it was made by a married woman. Sharp v. Thompson, 100 Ill. 447.

[77] Fisher v. Porter, 23 Fed. Rep. 162.

[78] Post v. First Nat. Bank, 138 Ill. 559, 28 N. E. Rep. 978.

[79] Bullock v. Whipp, 15 R. I. 195, 2 Atl. Rep. 309.

plained of was a mistake of law. But a late case relaxes the severity of this rule so far as to hold that, while equity will not generally correct a mistake of law in a deed or mortgage, yet relief will not be denied where the error arises from the act of the scrivener, who ignorantly inserted in the deed words which gave it an entirely different legal effect from that intended and desired by the parties, and where the parties, upon discovering the consequences, attempted to correct the mistake by a second deed before any rights of third persons had intervened.[80]

§ 77. **Equity Will Not Create New Contract.**—While equity has power to reform and correct a conveyance which, by mistake, does not truly set forth the contract made by the parties, it will not, under guise of granting relief of this character, make a contract for the parties where they themselves entirely failed to make any contract, nor create a contract different from that which they intended and supposed themselves to have made.[81] Thus, the court will not consent, under the pretext of correcting a mistake, to make that a conveyance which is not in itself a conveyance; a court of equity cannot give life to an instrument which has no vitality in itself.[82] Where, for example, the description of the property supposed to be covered by a mortgage is so indefinite that it cannot be identified, or if the description calls for premises which have no

[80] Kyner v. Boll, 182 Ill. 171, 54 N. E. Rep. 925. And see Horst v. Dague, 34 Ohio St. 371.

[81] "The principle upon which courts of equity interpose to afford relief in this class of cases is one of great strictness, and is never applied except where the case is made out to the entire and complete satisfaction of the court. Where the proof is of such a character as to leave no doubt whatever in the mind of the court that mistake has intervened, and the instrument sought to be rectified is variant from the actual contract of the parties, there can be no doubt, at this day, of the competency of a court of equity so to amend the instrument as to make it conform to the real intention of the parties. But in such cases, it is not enough to show the intention of one of the parties to the instrument only; the proof must establish, incontrovertibly, that the error or mistake alleged was common to both parties; in other words, it must be conclusively established that both parties understood the contract as it is alleged it ought to have been expressed, and as in fact it was, but for the mistake alleged in reducing it to writing. The court will never, by assuming to rectify an instrument, add to it a term or provision which had not been agreed upon, though it may afterwards appear very expedient or proper that it should have been incorporated." Stiles v. Willis, 66 Md. 552, 8 Atl. Rep. 353.

[82] Lindley v. Smith, 58 Ill. 250.

existence, or which cannot possibly be located, the mortgage must be considered void, and the court cannot receive extraneous evidence to explain the intention of the parties, nor reform the mortgage in this particular.[83] Nor will equity create a contract between the parties which was not intended by either of them. Hence a mortgage executed by a debtor to his creditor to indemnify the latter for signing a note as surety, cannot, upon failure of the debtor to sign the note as agreed, be enforced in equity as security for the original debt, although the creditor was to receive the money raised by his suretyship.[84]

§ 78. **Reforming Mortgage of Married Woman.**—In Illinois, in earlier times, it was held that a court of equity had no power or jurisdiction to reform or correct mistakes in deeds or mortgages made by married women, though it might decree such reformation as against the husband, if he joined in the execution of the instrument, in which case the decree would affect only his interest in the lands.[55] But since the passage of the statute giving to married women the right to convey and mortgage their property as if sole, the courts may decree reformation of a mortgage given by a feme covert, as, by correcting a mistake in the description of the property conveyed, under the same conditions as if no coverture existed.[86]

§ 79. **Intervening Rights of Third Persons.**—On an application to reform or correct a mortgage of lands, a court of equity will refuse to grant the relief asked, where the consequences of the correction prayed for would be prejudicial to the intervening rights of a third person who has acquired an interest in the property, or a lien upon it, without any notice of the mistake sought to be rectified, such as a purchaser of the estate taking title in good faith and for a valuable consideration, either by private purchase from the mortgagor or at judicial sale, or a judgment creditor whose lien attaches subsequent to the execution of the mortgage, under like circumstances.[87] But as to parties claiming under the mortgagor in the char-

[83] Carter v. Barnes, 26 Ill. 454. And see Turner v. Hart, 1 Fed. Rep. 295.

[84] Stone v. Palmer, 166 Ill. 463, 46 N. E. Rep. 1080.

[85] Board of Trustees v. Davison, 65 Ill. 124; Martin v. Hargardine,

46 Ill. 322; Moulton v. Hurd, 20 Ill. 137.

[86] Edwards v. Schoeneman, 104 Ill. 278; Snell v. Snell, 123 Ill. 403, 14 N. E. Rep. 684.

[87] Sickmon v. Wood, 69 Ill. 329; Bent v. Coleman, 89 Ill. 364; Sny-

acter of an heir, legatee, devisee, assignee, or voluntary
grantee, and as to any subsequent purchasers or incumbrancers,
who had notice of the mistake or misdescription in the mortgage, the rule is different. Persons thus in privity with the
mortgagor, or thus chargeable with knowledge of the facts,
can have no better right or higher claim than the mortgagor
himself would be permitted to assert; and as against them, the
superior equity of the mortgagee to have the mistake corrected
must prevail.[88] Thus, where a mistake was made in the
description of land in a conveyance and in a mortgage given
to secure the purchase money, and the grantee took possession
of the land intended to have been conveyed, and the grantor,
upon discovering the mistake, made a conveyance of the land
actually sold, it was held that the mortgagee, on a bill to have
his mortgage corrected, had a superior equity to a judgment
creditor who had notice of the mistake before the making of
the second deed, and who, after such notice, caused his execution to be levied on the land.[89] And so, a mortgage executed
under the belief, on the part of both mortgagor and mortgagee,
that a certain building which was the principal security stood
on the mortgaged land, but which by mistake had been built
upon adjoining lots not owned by the mortgagor, will be corrected so as to cover the lots on which the building stands,
as against a grantee through mesne conveyances of the property, who, sharing the common mistake of all the parties interested, purchased subject to the mortgage, and who, to protect
himself, and with full knowledge of the original mistake,
bought the lots under the building at their mere ground value.
But in such case, the mortgage, when corrected, should be
made to cover only the after-acquired lots on which the building is situated, and cannot be made to cover both those and
the original lots described in the mortgage.[90] An assignee in
bankruptcy occupies the position of the mortgagor (the bankrupt) in this particular. Thus, a mortgage to secure future
advances is good as against the assignee in bankruptcy for the

der v. Partridge, 138 Ill. 173, 29
N. E. Rep. 851. And see Morgan
v. Meuth, 60 Mich. 238; White v.
Denman, 16 Ohio, 59; Clements v.
Doerner, 40 Ohio St. 632.

[88] Strang v. Beach, 11 Ohio St.
283.

[89] Milmine v. Burnham, 76 Ill.
362.

[90] Way v. Roth, 159 Ill. 162, 42
N. E. Rep. 321, reversing 58 Ill.
App. 198.

amount of advances actually made thereon, and a mistake in
the description of the premises in such mortgage may be corrected as against the assignee, to the same extent as would
have been allowed against the mortgagor.[91]

§ 80. Cancellation of Mortgages.—It is fully within the
jurisdiction of a court of equity to decree the cancellation of
a mortgage (or to order it to be delivered up for cancellation)
when it appears that the debt secured thereby has been fully
paid, or the other conditions of the mortgage completely complied with, or that the instrument was obtained from the mortgagor by means of fraud, or that it is otherwise invalid.[92]
But relief of this kind will not be granted without requiring
the applicant to do all that justice and fair dealing requires
of him. If any sum of money remains due to the mortgagee,
or has been received from him and enjoyed and not returned,
its repayment will be made a condition precedent to the granting of the relief asked. Thus, where a husband, after voluntarily conveying property to his wife, makes a deed of the
same in trust to secure the repayment of money advanced at
his request to discharge a lien existing upon the property at
the time of such transfer, equity will not set aside the trust
deed as a cloud on the wife's title without requiring repayment
of the money so advanced.[93]

[91] Schulze v. Bolting, 8 Biss. 174,
Fed. Cas. No. 12,439.

[92] Valentine v. Fish, 45 Ill. 462;
Black v. Purnell (N. J. Ch.) 24 Atl.
Rep. 548; Kingman v. Sinclair, 80
Mich. 427, 45 N. W. Rep. 187;
Travelers' Ins. Co. v. Jones, 16
Colo. 515, 27 Pac. Rep. 807; Wool-
sey v. Bohn, 41 Minn. 235, 42 N.
W. Rep. 1022.

[93] Martin v. Martin, 164 Ill. 640,
45 N. E. Rep. 1007, reversing 62
Ill. App. 378. And see Horman v.
Hartmets, 128 Ind. 353, 27 N. E.
Rep. 731.

CHAPTER VII.

EXECUTION, ACKNOWLEDGMENT AND DELIVERY OF MORT-GAGES.

§ 81. Execution of a Mortgage.—It is generally essential to the validity of a mortgage that it should be signed by the mortgagor. But there is authority for the statement that a mortgage, regular in form, and acknowledged by the grantor before a competent officer as his act and deed, but lacking the grantor's signature, which was omitted by mistake, will be regarded in equity as a mortgage, and enforced as such as against the lien of a subsequent judgment creditor.[1] If the grantor is unable to write his name, it may be done for him by another person, the grantor then making his mark, and the whole being attested by a disinterested witness; and there is no reason why the mortgagee may not thus assist the mortgagor, as well as any other person.[2] A discrepancy between the name of the mortgagor as signed at the foot of the instrument and that signed to the acknowledgment is not fatal to the validity of the mortgage, when the difference is not irreconcilable (as, where the mortgagor's first name appears in the one place in full, and in the other is contracted to a mere initial), but may be obviated by testimony that the two signatures were made by the same person.[3] And when a person signs a mortgage in a certain style, and it is acknowledged by him in the same style, and the certificate of acknowledgment

[1] Martin v. Nixon, 92 Mo. 26, 4 S. W. Rep. 503.
[2] Johnson v. Davis, 95 Ala. 293, 10 South. Rep. 911.
[3] Hill v. Banks, 61 Conn. 25, 23 Atl. Rep. 712.

repeats the signature and declares the identity of the mortgagor, he will not be permitted to take advantage of the fact
that the name so signed by him was not his true name.[4] It is
also a rule that, when a deed or mortgage is signed by several
persons, and the names of some of them are not set forth in
the body of the instrument or granting clause, it is not the
deed or mortgage of those whose names are omitted from the
corpus of the instrument and whose names appear only among
the signatures. But it seems that this does not apply to a case
where two persons (as, husband and wife) jointly sign a mortgage, but no names of grantors appear at all in the body of
the instrument.[5]

At law, it is also necessary that a mortgage, to be a valid
and enforceable instrument, should be under seal.[6] But in
equity, the instrument may still be enforced in the character of
a mortgage, though it lacks a seal, on the principle that it
amounts at least to an agreement to give a mortgage, and such
an agreement is recognized as an equitable mortgage.[7] A
mortgage given by a corporation must be executed under the
seal of the company; and it is necessary that the seal should
be affixed by some one having lawful authority to do so.[8] In
the case cited it was also said that, when a mortgage purporting to be given by a corporation has the corporate seal
attached, the presumption is that the seal is there rightfully;
but this presumption is not conclusive, and parol evidence is
admissible to rebut it. When neither of the officers who signed
the mortgage, nor the secretary of the company, who was the
proper custodian of the seal, had any knowledge of the way
in which the seal became attached to the mortgage, then the
burden of proof is thrown on the party offering it to show the
circumstances under which the mortgage was sealed and that
it was rightfully and properly done. But a mortgage of a
corporation made by its attorney in fact is sufficient if executed in the name of the corporation under the attorney's own
hand and seal; and it is no objection that the seal of the corporation was not affixed thereto, when it appears that the
power of attorney was under seal.[9]

[4] Shelton v. Aultman & Taylor
Co., 82 Ala. 315, 8 South. Rep. 232.
[5] Sheldon v. Carter, 90 Ala. 380,
8 South. Rep. 63.
[6] Butler v. Meyer, 49 Ill. App.
176; Rev. Stat. Ill. c. 30, § 1.

[7] See supra, § 34.
[8] Koehler v. Black River Falls
Iron Co., 2 Black (U. S.) 715.
[9] First Nat. Bank v. Salem Capital Flour-Mills Co., 39 Fed. Rep.
89.

§ 82. Necessity of Acknowledgment.—In Illinois, a deed or mortgage is valid, as between the parties to it, without being acknowledged. And hence where a deed of land and a mortgage securing the purchase money are executed on the same day, and each instrument is handed to its proper owner at the same time, the delivery is perfected so as to preserve the lien of the mortgage, even though it is not acknowledged by the mortgagor until several months after the delivery and recording of the deed.[10] Generally speaking, acknowledgment of a conveyance is required to entitle it to be recorded, and thereby to furnish constructive notice to persons afterwards dealing with the property. But in Illinois, a statute provides that "deeds, mortgages, and other instruments of writing relating to real estate, shall be deemed, from the time of being filed for record, notice to subsequent purchasers and creditors, though not acknowledged or proven according to law; but the same shall not be read as evidence, unless their execution be proved in the manner required by the rules of evidence applicable to such instruments, so as to supply the defects of such acknowledgment or proof."[11]

§ 83. Who May Take Acknowledgment.—In Illinois, the acknowledgment of a mortgage, if taken within the state, may be taken by a master in chancery, a notary public, a United States commissioner, a circuit or county clerk, a justice of the peace, or any court of record having a seal, or any judge, justice, or clerk of any such court. If taken before a notary public or United States commissioner, the acknowledgment shall be attested by his official seal; if before a court or the clerk thereof, by the seal of such court. When it is taken before a justice of the peace, there shall be added the certificate of the county clerk, under his official seal, that the person taking such acknowledgment was a justice of the peace in said county at the time of taking the same. But if the justice resides in the county where the land lies, no such certificate shall be required.[12] A mortgage acknowledged before a jus-

---

[10] Roane v. Baker, 120 Ill. 308, 11 N. E. Rep. 246. But see Parrott v. Kumpf, 102 Ill. 423.

[11] Rev. Stat. Ill. c. 30, § 31 (Starr & C. § 32).

[12] Rev. Stat. Ill. c. 30, § 20 (Starr & C. § 21). A mortgage may be acknowledged before a police magistrate of a village, by a resident of the township in which the village is situated, although he is not a resident or voter in the village. Ticknor v. McClelland, 84 Ill. 471.

tice of the peace of a county other than that in which the land
lies, but recorded in the county where the premises are situated, shall be adjudged and treated by all courts as legally
executed and recorded, notwithstanding the lack of a certificate to the official character of the justice; provided that such
record (or a certified transcript thereof) shall not be read in
evidence unless the certificate of the proper county clerk, under
his official seal, is produced, or other competent evidence presented, showing that the person purporting to take the
acknowledgment was a justice of the peace at the date thereof,
and for this purpose, the certificate of the proper county clerk
shall be prima facie evidence.[18]

§ 84. Disqualification of Officer Taking Acknowledgment.—

If the notary or other officer purporting to take the acknowledgment of a mortgage or deed of trust is himself the mortgagee or the sole trustee named in the deed of trust, his interest
will disqualify him, and his action will be null and void.[14] Nor
is this rule at all affected by the fact that the mortgagee or
trustee was the only officer in the township or other district,
or accessible to the parties, who was qualified to take acknowledgments. As to third persons, the acknowledgment will be
void, and the parties will be remitted to their rights at common
law.[15] But if the disqualifying interest of the officer who took
the acknowledgment of a mortgage is not apparent on the face
of the mortgage or of the certificate, the recording of the
mortgage will furnish constructive notice of the same to the
extent of the lien created thereby.[16] In the case of a deed of
trust made to two or more trustees, it is held that if the
acknowledgment is taken before one of such trustees, in his
character as an officer, it will render the deed void as to that
trustee, but this will not affect the validity of the deed as to
the other trustees, as they have no community of interest, and

---

[18] Rev. Stat. Ill. c. 30, § 21 (Starr
& C. § 22).

[14] West v. Krebaum, 88 Ill. 263;
Rothschild v. Dougher (Tex.) 20 S.
W. Rep. 142. The acknowledgment of the grantor in a deed of
trust, taken before the trustee as
a notary public, is void, though
the latter has not expressly accepted the trust; for, the deed being for his benefit, his acceptance

will be presumed until his dissent
is shown, and such dissent will
not be implied from the fact of
his taking the acknowledgment.
Bowden v. Parrish, 86 Va. 67, 9
S. E. Rep. 616.

[15] Hammers v. Dole, 61 Ill. 307.

[16] Ogden Bldg. & Loan Ass'n v.
Mensch, 196 Ill. 554, 63 N. E. Rep.
1049.

the disqualification of one will not render the others incompetent; and if the execution of the deed is sufficiently proved, by evidence aliunde the acknowledgment, this will cure the defect.[17] As to mortgages given to corporations, the rule is that the acknowledgment cannot be taken by any officer who is the owner of stock in the company. Thus, where the notary public who took the acknowledgment of such a mortgage was a stockholder in the corporation to which the mortgage was given, it was held that the acknowledgment was void because of his financial interest in the debt secured, and that the mortgage would not pass the homestead estate of the mortgagor in the premises; but as to land covered by it other than the homestead, it would be binding and effectual if its execution was proved by competent evidence independently of the acknowledgment.[18] But a notary public is not disqualified to take the acknowledgment of a mortgage given to a private corporation by the fact that he is a director, officer, or agent of the corporation, provided he is not a stockholder.[19]

An acknowledgment of a mortgage is valid if taken by a de facto officer; as where the person taking it had been duly commissioned as a notary public, and had given bond, and was acting as such officer, although he was not eligible to the office by reason of his being an alien.[20] In another case, the sufficiency of the acknowledgment of a mortgage was assailed on the ground that the deputy clerk of court who took it had not been legally appointed. The law required deputy clerks to take an oath for the faithful discharge of the duties of their offices; and it appeared that, in this instance, the deputy was only verbally appointed as such, that he was never sworn into office, and that he had not executed any official bond, but he was acting as a deputy clerk and had taken acknowledgments of other conveyances in the same manner. It was held that he was at least an officer de facto, and his act in taking the acknowledgment was valid.[21]

§ 85. **Acknowledgment Taken in Another State.**—A statute in Illinois makes provision for the acknowledgment of deeds and mortgages, affecting lands in Illinois, in other states or

[17] Darst v. Gale, 83 Ill. 136.

[18] Ogden Bldg. & Loan Ass'n v. Mensch, 196 Ill. 554, 63 N. E. Rep. 1049.

[19] Idem.

[20] Wilson v. Kimmel (Mo.), 19 S. W. Rep. 24.

[21] Sharp v. Thompson, 100 Ill. 447.

territories of the Union, or the District of Columbia, before a justice of the peace, notary public, United States commissioner, commissioner of deeds, mayor of a city, clerk of a county, judge, justice, or clerk of a federal or state court, and provides for the attestation and certification of acknowledgments so taken. It also enacts that such an acknowledgment may be made in conformity with the laws of the state, territory, or district where taken, and certified as being so made by the clerk of a court of record under his hand and the seal of the court; and when so certified, or where it appears from the laws of such state or territory that the acknowledgment conforms to the laws thereof, duly proved and certified copies of the record of the deed or mortgage may be read in evidence in the courts of Illinois.[22] On the other hand, when a mortgage or deed of trust on lands in Illinois is executed and acknowledged in another state, it is immaterial whether or not the acknowledgment is taken in conformity with the laws of the state where taken, if it conforms to the laws of Illinois; that is sufficient to make it admissible in evidence in the courts of Illinois.[23]

§ 86. **Requisites of Certificate.**—Although the certificate of the officer taking the acknowledgment of a mortgage of real estate may not be in the precise form given by the statute, yet if it contains all the substantial requirements of the statute, it will be sufficient.[24] The fact that the name of the county is omitted from the caption to an acknowledgment taken by a justice of the peace of a town will not invalidate the acknowledgment, as the courts will take judicial notice of the incorporated towns of the state and also of the names of the justices of the peace in the county where the court sits.[25] But that part of the certificate which establishes the identity of the person making the acknowledgment is absolutely essential and cannot be omitted. In respect to this it is enacted that "no judge or other officer shall take the acknowledgment of any person to any deed or instrument of writing, unless the person offering to make such acknowledgment shall be personally known

[22] Rev. Stat. Ill. c. 30, § 20 (Starr & C. § 21) par. 2. As to acknowledgments taken in foreign countries, see Id., par. 3, and § 22.

[23] Dawson v. Hayden, 67 Ill. 52.

[24] Edwards v. Schoeneman, 104 Ill. 278; Livingston v. Ketelle, 6 Ill. (1 Gilm.) 116.

[25] Gilbert v. National Cash Register Co., 176 Ill. 288, 52 N. E. Rep. 22.

to him to be the real person who and in whose name such
acknowledgment is proposed to be made, or shall be proved
to be such by a credible witness, and the judge or officer taking
such acknowledgment shall, in his certificate thereof, state that
such person was personally known to him to be the person
whose name is subscribed to such deed or writing, as having
executed the same, or that he was proved to be such by a
credible witness, naming him.''[26] Where the grantor or mortgagor is a married woman, her acknowledgment may now be
taken in the same manner as that of any other party to a deed
or mortgage. "The acknowledgment or proof of any deed,
mortgage, conveyance, release of dower, power of attorney,
or other writing of or relating to the sale, conveyance, or other
disposition of lands or real estate, or any interest therein, by
a married woman, may be made and certified the same as if
she were a feme sole, and shall have the same effect.''[27]

§ 87. **Impeaching Certificate of Acknowledgment.**—The certificate of an officer authorized by law to take acknowledgments of deeds and mortgages imports verity. It is not, indeed, conclusive. It may be impeached and contradicted for
fraud, collusion, or imposition.[28] But when the certificate is
in due form and apparently regular, it is prima facie evidence
of the acknowledgment of the instrument by the person purporting to be the maker thereof, and is to be regarded as having great and controlling weight until it is overcome by clear,
convincing, and satisfactory proof. And for this purpose, the
uncorroborated testimony of the grantor or mortgagor, however positive and explicit, denying the acknowledgment of the
instrument, is not sufficient.[29] The doctrine is even more
strongly stated in a recent case, as follows: "It is a rule that
the acknowledgment of a deed cannot be impeached for anything but fraud, and in such cases the evidence must be clear

[26] Rev. Stat. Ill. c. 30, § 24 (Starr
& C. § 25). See Wheeler v. Gage,
28 Ill. App. 427, affirmed, 129 Ill.
197, 21 N. E. Rep. 1075.

[27] Rev. Stat. Ill. c. 30, § 19 (Starr
& C. § 20).

[28] Monroe v. Poorman, 62 Ill.
523; Brady v. Cole, 164 Ill. 116,
45 N. E. Rep. 438; Foster v.
Latham. 21 Ill. App. 165; Fisher
v. Stiefel, 62 Ill. App. 580.

[29] Graham v. Anderson, 42 Ill.
514; Monroe v. Poorman, 62 Ill.
523; Marston v. Brittenham, 76 Ill.
611; McPherson v. Sanborn, 88 Ill.
150; Warrick v. Hull, 102 Ill. 280;
Fitzgerald v. Fitzgerald, 100 Ill.
385; Post v. First Nat. Bank, 138
Ill. 559, 28 N. E. Rep. 978; Wash-
burn v. Roesch, 13 Ill. App. 268;
Foster v. Latham, 21 Ill. App. 165;
Fisher v. Stiefel, 62 Ill. App. 580.

and convincing, beyond a reasonable doubt. The mere evidence of the party purporting to have made the acknowledgment cannot overcome the officer's certificate, nor will it with slight corroboration."[30] As to the nature of the evidence admissible for this purpose, it may be remarked that the testimony of the officer who took an acknowledgment of a mortgage is competent for the purpose of impeaching his own official certificate.[31]

§ 88. **Damages for False Certificate.**—An action for damages will lie against an officer who gives a false certificate of acknowledgment of a mortgage or deed of trust. Thus, under the statute in force in Illinois, providing that the party executing an instrument must be personally known to the officer taking the acknowledgment thereof, or must be proved to be such by a credible witness, a clerk of court who takes the acknowledgment of a mortgage and certifies that the mortgagor therein is personally known to him performs a ministerial act (not a judicial act), and is liable to the mortgagee if the certificate is false, as where a stranger, falsely personating the mortgagor, imposed upon the clerk, the latter neglecting to protect himself in the manner pointed out in the statute.[32] But where a justice of the peace gives a mortgage to one of his creditors, and attempts to take his own acknowledgment thereto and certify it, the creditor's consequent loss of his debt is caused by an act done by the justice in his individual capacity, not as a justice, and therefore no action will lie on his official bond.[33]

§ 89. **Delivery of a Mortgage.**—A statute of Illinois enacts that "livery of seisin shall in no case be necessary for the conveyance of real property; but every mortgage not procured by duress, signed and sealed by the party making the same, the maker or makers being of full age, sound mind, and discovert, shall be sufficient, without livery of seisin, for the mortgaging of any lands, tenements, or hereditaments in this state, so as, to all intents and purposes, absolutely and fully to vest in every mortgagee all such estate or estates as shall be specified in any such mortgage."[34] But "a delivery is an essential part of the execution of a deed, and it will only

[30] Brady v. Cole, 164 Ill. 116, 45 N. E. Rep. 438.

[31] McCurley v. Pitner, 65 Ill. App. 17.

[32] People v. Bartels, 138 Ill. 322,

27 N. E. Rep. 1091. And see Bartels v. People, 45 Ill. App. 306, affirmed 152 Ill. 557.

[33] People v. Scott, 45 Ill. 182.

[34] Rev. Stat. Ill. c. 30, § 1.

become operative by and take effect from its delivery. Without delivery it is void. No special form or ceremony is necessary to constitute a sufficient delivery. It may be by acts or
words, or both, but something must be said or done showing an
intention that the deed shall become operative to pass the title,
and that the grantor loses all right of control over it. The
delivery need not necessarily be made to the grantee, but may
be made to another in his behalf and for his use; but it is
indispensable that the grantor shall part with control over the
deed and shall not retain a right to reclaim it."[35] The delivery
of a mortgage, proved to have been signed and acknowledged,
is not established by proof of statements made by the mortgagor that he had bought the land from the mortgagee and
had a long time to pay for it, in which statements no reference
was made to a mortgage.[36] But it seems that proof of the
mortgagor's previous anxiety as to the delivery of the mortgage (there being difficulties in the way of its reaching the
party for whom it was intended) and subsequent expressions
of satisfaction at the accomplishment of the act, is admissible.[37]

It is not always essential that delivery should be made to
the very person named in the instrument as the mortgagee or
grantee. Thus, an actual delivery of a deed of trust to the
trustee therein named, who has no interest in the trust, is not
required, but a delivery to the cestui que trust, together with
the notes secured by it, will fully answer the requirements of
the law.[38] So where, on the dissolution of a partnership, one
of the partners assumes the payment of a note of the firm,
and executes a mortgage to the payee of the note to secure it,
which is also conditioned to indemnify his co-partner against
the payment of the note, a delivery of the mortgage to such

[35] Hawes v. Hawes, 177 Ill. 409,
53 N. E. Rep. 78. In the case of
Nazro v. Ware, 38 Minn. 443, 38
N. W. Rep. 359, it was said: "No
particular ceremony is necessary
to the delivery of a deed. It may
consist in an act without words,
or in words without any act; and
if in words, it is immaterial
whether they are spoken or written. Manual possession of a deed
by the grantee is not essential.
Whether there has been a delivery
is rather a question of fact than
of law, depending upon the intent
of the grantor to vest an estate
in the grantee. If a deed be so
disposed of as to evince clearly
the intention of the parties that
it should take effect as such, it is
sufficient."

[36] Baker v. Updike, 155 Ill. 54,
39 N. E. Rep. 587.

[37] Gunnell v. Cockerill, 84 Ill.
319.

[38] Crocker v. Lowenthal, 83 Ill.
579.

other partner is sufficient.[39]   Again, where a mortgage runs to
several creditors of the mortgagor, and it has been delivered
to one of them for the benefit of all, and none of the creditors
is shown ever to have repudiated it, it will not be necessary
to prove an acceptance by each of them.[40]

§ 90. **Constructive Delivery.**—Actual manual delivery of a
mortgage from the hands of the mortgagor to those of the
mortgagee is not essential; other acts, if accompanied by a
clear intention to pass the title from the one to the other, are
equally efficacious in establishing a delivery.[41]   But the mere
execution of a mortgage,—and even the recording of it, if not
done in pursuance of the directions of the mortgagee or in pursuance of a previous agreement,—does not constitute a delivery
of the instrument to the mortgagee, where it is not actually
placed in his hands, or in the possession of some one authorized
to receive it for him, and where the money loaned is not paid
over by such mortgagee.   There can be no legal delivery of
the mortgage until the mortgagee is willing to accept it, and
does accept it, and pay over the consideration.[42]   Thus, where
a party executed a mortgage on real estate to a person who
was not personally present nor represented by an agent, and
left the same for record, with directions that it should be sent
to the mortgagee by mail when recorded, which was done, it
was held that there was no delivery until the mortgage was
deposited in the mail.[43]   But where a deed of real estate is
executed and placed on record, and the grantee subsequently
conveys the estate to another, he will be held to have accepted
the delivery of the deed by ratification and will be bound by
its covenants.[44]   Moreover, it is a good and sufficient delivery
of a mortgage or deed of trust if the grantor or mortgagor
files it for record in pursuance of the mortgagee's directions
to that effect, and with the intention of passing the title.[45]

[39] Conwell v. McCowan, 81 Ill.
285.

[40] Shelden v. Erskine, 78 Mich.
627, 44 N. W. Rep. 146.

[41] Knapstein v. Tinnette, 156 Ill.
322, 40 N. E. Rep. 947, affirming
57 Ill. App. 570.

[42] Houfes v. Schultze, 2 Ill. App.
196; Stiles v. Probst, 69 Ill. 385;
Kingsbury v. Burnside, 58 Ill. 310;
Lanphier v. Desmond, 187 Ill. 370,

58 N. E. Rep. 343, affirming Desmond v. Lanphier, 86 Ill. App. 101.

[43] Partridge v. Chapman, 81 Ill.
137.

[44] Kinncy v. Wells, 59 Ill. App.
271.

[45] Lawrence v. Lawrence, 181 Ill.
248, 54 N. E. Rep. 918; Capital
City Bank v. Hodgin, 24 Fed. Rep.
1; In re Guyer, 69 Iowa, 585, 29 N.
W. Rep. 826.

CHAPTER VIII.

PARTIES TO MORTGAGES.

§ 91. Married Women.—The earlier enabling statute in Illinois provided that "any married woman, being above the age of eighteen years, joining with her husband in the execution of any deed, mortgage, conveyance, power of attorney, or other writing of or relating to the sale, conveyance, or other disposition of her lands or real estate, or any interest therein, shall be bound and concluded by the same, in respect to her right, title, claim, or interest in such estate, as if she were sole."[1] But a later statute has removed the last vestige of disability arising out of coverture, in respect to the wife's free power to mortgage and sell her own lands. It is enacted that "a married woman may, in all cases, sue and be sued without joining her husband with her, to the same extent as if she were unmarried, and an attachment or judgment in such action may be enforced by or against her as if she were a single woman. * * * Contracts may be made and liabilities incurred by a wife, and the same enforced against her, to the same extent and in the same manner as if she were unmarried. * * * A married woman may own, in her own right, real and personal property obtained by descent, gift, or purchase, and manage, sell, and convey the same to the same extent and in the same manner that the husband can property belonging to him."[2] This places a married woman upon a perfect equal-

---

[1] Rev. Stat. Ill. c. 30, § 18. On the construction of this statute, and particularly with reference to the necessity of the husband's joining in the conveyance, see Bressler v. Kent, 61 Ill. 426; Barnes v. Ehrman, 74 Ill. 402; Herdman v. Pace, 85 Ill. 345; Elder v. Jones, Id. 384; Wilhelm v. Schmidt, 84 Ill. 183.

[2] Rev. Stat. Ill. c. 68; §§ 1, 6, 9.

117

ity with her husband, so far as concerns the mortgaging or conveyance of her land, and renders it unnecessary to the validity of the deed or mortgage that the husband should join in the conveyance.[3] Moreover, under the laws now in force, it is held that a married woman may lawfully mortgage her property for the purpose of securing her husband's debts.[4]

§ 92. **Infants.**—Although a statute in Illinois makes it essential to the validity of a mortgage that it should be made by a person "of full age,"[5] it is undoubtedly a general rule that the mortgage of an infant is not absolutely void, but voidable at his election, and that it may be ratified or confirmed by him when he attains his majority.[6] And where an infant buys land and gives back a purchase-money mortgage thereon, the mortgage, though it may be voidable, is not void; and if, on reaching his majority, he sells and conveys the land, he thereby affirms the mortgage. The law which protects infants "is to be used as a shield, as a means by which he may be protected against inequitable bargains. It is not designed as a means of enabling him to rob others by procuring and retaining their property without paying for it. Therefore if he purchases real estate and receives a deed therefor, and, to secure the consideration, he executes a mortgage upon such land, and after coming of age sells the real estate as his own, his plea of invalidity of the mortgage will be unavailing; that is, he cannot confirm that part of the transaction which is beneficial to him and repudiate that which imposes an obligation."[7] It is also said that the capacity of a party to make a mortgage, so far as it depends on age, is fixed by the law of the jurisdiction wherein the property is situated, and not by that of the owner's domicile. Hence if the mortgage is made in a state where the owner is domiciled, and where it would be invalid on account of his infancy, yet if the age of the mortgagor would be sufficient by the law of the state where the premises are situated, it is a good and valid mortgage.[8]

§ 93. **Guardians.**—A statute in Illinois provides that "the

[3] Edward v. Schoeneman, 104 Ill. 278.

[4] Post v. First Nat. Bank, 38 Ill. App. 259; Field v. Brokaw, 148 Ill. 654, 37 N. E. Rep. 80; Stone v. Billings, 167 Ill. 170, 47 N. E. Rep. 372.

[5] Rev. Stat. Ill. c. 30, § 1.

[6] See 3 Washb. Real Prop. 559; Burnham v. Kidwell, 113 Ill. 425.

[7] Uecker v. Koehn, 21 Nebr. 559, 32 N. W. Rep. 583.

[8] Sell v. Miller, 11 Ohio St. 331.

guardian may, by leave of the county court, mortgage the real
estate of the ward for a term of years not exceeding the
minority of the ward or in fee; but the time of the maturity
of the indebtedness secured by such mortgage shall not be
extended beyond the time of minority of the ward. Before
any mortgage shall be made, the guardian shall petition the
county court for an order authorizing such mortgage to be
made, in which petition shall be set out the condition of the
estate, and the facts and circumstances on which the petition
is founded, and a description of the premises sought to be
mortgaged. Foreclosures of mortgages authorized by this act
shall only be made by petition to the county court of the
county where letters of guardianship were granted, or, in case
of non-resident minors, in the county in which the premises,
or some part thereof, are situated, in which proceeding the
guardian and ward shall be made defendants; and any sale
made by virtue of any order or decree of foreclosure of such
mortgage may, at any time before confirmation, be set aside
by the court for inadequacy of price, or other good cause, and
shall not be binding upon the guardian or ward until confirmed
by the court." And it is also enacted that "no decree of
strict foreclosure shall be made upon any such mortgage, but
redemption shall be allowed as is now provided by law in cases
of sales under executions upon common-law judgments."[9]
Under this statute, the county court has jurisdiction to authorize a guardian to borrow money on mortgage to pay off prior
incumbrances, and to replace buildings on the land of his ward
which have been destroyed by fire.[10] And a mortgage executed
under the decree of the county court will warrant the guardian
in paying the debts to satisfy which the mortgage was ordered,
and also the interest on the mortgage debt, so long as the
decree, though possibly erroneous, remains unreversed.[11] But
the court has no authority to order a mortgage to be given
where the wards take under a will by which the testator directs
that his land "be reserved for his children and be equally
divided among them when the youngest attains the age of
twenty-one years," and devises the land to his executors in
trust during the minority of the children.[12]

[9] Rev. Stat. Ill. c. 64, §§ 24, 25,
26, 27.

[10] United States Mortgage Co. v.
Sperry, 138 U. S. 313.

[11] Kingsbury v. Powers, 131 Ill.
182, 22 N. E. Rep. 479.

[12] Kingman v. Harmon, 131 Ill.
171, 23 N. E. Rep. 430.

In proceedings to foreclose a mortgage executed under the authorization of the county court, conveying the property of minor heirs, it is open to them to question its validity.[13] And in such an action both the guardian and the ward are necessary parties; and any sale made on a decree of foreclosure may, at any time before confirmation, be set aside for cause, and will not be binding on either the guardian or the ward until confirmed. And in such a suit, the ward may have the entire proceeding reviewed by the court, including the authority to give the mortgage.[14]

In so far as the statute under consideration directs that proceedings for the foreclosure of such mortgages shall be brought only in the county courts, it is binding solely upon the courts of the state, and does not limit the jurisdiction of the courts of the United States sitting within the state; and therefore a suit for the foreclosure of such a mortgage may be maintained in the proper federal court, notwithstanding the statute, if the diverse citizenship of the parties, and the amount in controversy, are sufficient to confer jurisdiction.[15]

In regard to mortgages as investments for guardians,—or mortgages taken by guardians as security on making loans of their wards' money,—it has been remarked by the supreme court of a neighboring state that a guardian is not an insurer of the safety of investments made of his ward's funds, nor is he to be held to an extraordinary degree of care and diligence, but he is required to exercise ordinary care and prudence. Thus, ordinary care requires that a guardian should not accept a second mortgage. But if he exercises care and diligence in endeavoring to secure a first mortgage, but is induced by false representations to accept a mortgage believing in good faith that it is a senior lien, he is not personally liable though it proves to be a junior lien. And again, as a general rule, the guardian should require the wife of the mortgagor to join in executing the mortgage; and if she does not, the burden is upon the guardian to show that the husband's interest in the land furnished ample security for the loan.[16]

§ 94. Lunatics and Spendthrifts.—By force of a statute in

[13] Kingman v. Harmon, 32 Ill. App. 529.

[14] Kingsbury v. Sperry, 119 Ill. 279, 10 N. E. Rep. 8.

[15] United States Mortgage Co. v. Sperry, 138 U. S. 313; Davis v. James, 10 Biss. 51, 2 Fed. Rep. 618.

[16] Slanter v. Favorite, 107 Ind. 291, 4 N. E. Rep. 880.

Illinois, any note or bill, bond, or other contract made by an idiot or lunatic, distracted person, or spendthrift, after the finding of a jury on a judicial inquisition as to his mental capacity, shall be void as against him and his estate, but binding upon the other party to the transaction. Any contract made before such finding may be avoided, except in favor of the person fraudulently making the same.[17] Hence a deed or mortgage made by a person of unsound mind, but before he has been legally adjudged insane and placed under the care of a conservator, is not absolutely void. Like the deed of an infant, it is only voidable. And where money is loaned in good faith to a person who is actually insane, but not yet so adjudged, and he gives a mortgage on his lands to secure its repayment, and the proceeds of the loan are expended in and about his care and support, the mortgage cannot be avoided or set aside until the money so received and expended by the insane mortgagor has been returned or tendered.[18] The conservator of a lunatic, idiot, or spendthrift may, by leave of the county court, mortgage the real estate of the ward for a term of years or in fee. But "before any mortgage shall be made, the conservator shall petition the county court for an order authorizing such mortgage to be made, in which petition shall be set out the condition of the estate and the facts and circumstances on which the petition is founded, and a description of the premises sought to be mortgaged." And "no decree of strict foreclosure shall be made upon any such mortgage, but redemption shall be allowed as is now provided by law in cases of sales under executions upon common-law judgments."[19] It is held that where a court having jurisdiction has authorized and ordered the conservator of an insane person to execute a mortgage on his lands to secure a debt, the regularity and validity of the proceedings in which the conservator was appointed cannot be attacked on a bill for the foreclosure of the mortgage.[20]

§ 95. **Executors and Administrators.**—Power to mortgage

---

[17] Rev. Stat. Ill. c. 86, §§ 14, 15.

[18] Burnham v. Kidwell, 113 Ill. 425. As to the degree of mental incapacity or unsoundness of mind which will render a mortgage voidable, see Edwards v. Davenport, 20 Fed. Rep. 756; Baldrick v. Garvey, 66 Iowa, 14, 23 N. W. Rep. 156; White v. Farley, 81 Ala. 563, 8 South. Rep. 215.

[19] Rev. Stat. Ill. c. 86, §§ 20-22.

[20] Schmidt v. Pierce, 17 Ill. App. 523.

the real property of their decedents is accorded to executors
by a statute in Illinois, which enacts that "real estate may be
mortgaged in fee or for a term of years, or leased, by executors,
provided that the term of such lease, or the time of the
maturity of the indebtedness secured by such mortgage, shall
not be extended beyond the time when the heirs entitled to
such estate shall attain the age of twenty-one years, or
eighteen years if a female; and provided also that, before any
mortgage or lease shall be made, the executors shall petition
the county court for an order authorizing such mortgage or
lease to be made, and which the court may grant if the interests
of the estate may require it; provided further that the executor
making application as aforesaid, upon obtaining such order,
shall enter into bond, with good security, faithfully to apply
the moneys to be raised upon such mortgage or lease to the
payment of the debts of the testator; and all money so raised
shall be assets in the hands of such executor for the payment
of debts, and shall be subject to the order of the court in the
same manner as other assets. Foreclosures of such mortgages
shall only be made by petition to the county court of the
county in which the premises, or a major part thereof, are
situated; and any sale made by virtue of any order or decree
of foreclosure may, at any time before confirmation, be set
aside by the court for inadequacy of price or other good cause,
and shall not be binding upon the executor until confirmed by
the court." It is also provided that no decree of strict foreclosure can be made upon any mortgage so given by an executor under authority of the court, but redemption shall be
allowed as is provided by law in cases of sales under executions issued upon judgments at law.[21]

It is here necessary to note the difference between the powers
of an executor and those of an administrator. "The statute
has not conferred authority on an administrator to mortgage
the lands belonging to an estate of which he is the administrator, and in the absence of such authority, a mortgage made
by an administrator would be void. An administrator may

[21] Rev. Stat. Ill. c. 3, §§ 120-122.
So much of the statute as vests in
the county courts exclusive jurisdiction of petitions for the foreclosure of such mortgages must be
understood as restricted to the
courts of the state; it does not,
and could not, abridge the proper
jurisdiction of the United States
courts in such cases. See, supra,
§ 93.

obtain a decree to sell the lands belonging to the estate to pay debts, but as a general rule this is all the power or control that he can exercise over the lands of the estate.''[22] A court of equity, therefore, will not sustain a title derived under a mortgage made by an administrator, to raise money to pay off debts of the estate, even though the money borrowed is honestly applied in the payment of such debts.[23]

§ 96. **Partners.**—It is generally necessary to the validity of a mortgage given by a partnership on property of the firm that all the partners should join in its execution, or, at least, that those not joining should have given formal authority for the making of the mortgage, or should subsequently ratify it by some formal action. More especially is it the rule that one partner cannot mortgage the real property of the firm to secure his individual debt. This would be a fraud upon the creditors of the firm, and such a mortgage, therefore, cannot abridge their rights nor the rights of the other partners.[24] Even a surviving partner has no right, as against the heirs of the deceased partner, to mortgage the interest of the latter in the partnership lands for his own individual debts, or for any other purpose except to close up the business and pay debts of the firm.[25] But when the legal title to lands which really belong to a firm is in one of the partners only, a mortgage executed by the one holding the legal title to secure his individual debt, to one who has no notice of the equitable rights of the other partners, will vest a lien in the mortgagee discharged of any equity in their favor or in favor of creditors of the firm. But if the mortgagee takes the mortgage with notice that the lands belonged to the firm, and the other partners did not consent to the mortgage, he will hold subject to their superior lien upon their proportionate interest in the lands for the payment of the firm debts, and an equity will attach to that superior lien in favor of the creditors of the firm.[26]

---

[22] Smith v. Hutchinson, 108 Ill. 662.

[23] Johnson v. Davidson, 162 Ill. 232, 44 N. E. Rep. 499. And see Jones v. Lamar, 34 Fed. Rep. 454.

[24] Moline Wagon Co. v. Rummell, 12 Fed. Rep. 658; Deeters v. Sellers, 102 Ind. 458, 1 N. E. Rep. 854. But one of the partners may give a chattel mortgage on the partnership stock in trade, and deliver possession thereof, to secure a firm creditor. Nelson v. Wheelock, 46 Ill. 25.

[25] Brown v. Watson, 66 Mich. 223, 33 N. W. Rep. 493.

[26] Reeves v. Ayers, 38 Ill. 418; Robinson Bank v. Miller, 153 Ill.

In regard to mortgages made to partners as mortgagees, it has been held that, in an action for the foreclosure of such a mortgage, it is no defense that the mortgage runs to the partnership in the firm name only, and not to any individual name; since, to maintain the action, it is only necessary that a lien should exist, and not that the mortgage should convey a good title.[27]

§ 97. **Agents and Attorneys.**—The owner of real estate may invest an agent or attorney with power and authority to incumber the same by mortgage, by giving him a power of attorney sufficiently explicit in its terms to warrant the placing of a mortgage on the property. And if the principal ratifies a mortgage executed by his attorney in fact, by accepting and enjoying the money raised by means thereof, he cannot afterwards deny its validity by repudiating the power of attorney.[28] But an attorney in fact cannot give a mortgage on his principal's lands to secure his own debt, even though he had authority to borrow money for the principal and mortgage the lands as security for the sums so borrowed; and a mortgage so given is not binding on the principal if the mortgagee knew that the agent intended to use the money borrowed for his individual purposes.[29] And an ordinary power of attorney to sell land does not embrace any implied authority to mortgage such land, although, in some cases, a power to sell for the

244, 38 N. E. Rep. 1078; Chittenden v. German-American Bank, 27 Minn. 143, 6 N. W. Rep. 773. Where land belonging to a firm is mortgaged by one of the partners to secure a firm debt, and the other partner tells the mortgagee that he has no interest in the land, he and the judgment-creditors of the firm with notice are estopped to deny that the mortgage passed the entire title of the firm. Cross v. Weare Commission Co., 153 Ill. 499, 38 N. E. Rep. 1038, affirming 45 Ill. App. 255.

[27] Foster v. Trowbridge, 39 Minn. 373, 40 N. W. Rep. 255. Herein the court said: "In this respect there is a difference between a foreclosure under a power of sale and a foreclosure by action. In the former case, the title must pass by virtue of the mortgage, and the mortgage must be sufficient to operate as a conveyance as soon as the equity of redemption is barred by the sale. But in the latter case the title passes by virtue of the decree and sale under it. There is no going behind the decree to ascertain if the mortgage was sufficient to operate as a conveyance."

[28] McAdow v. Black, 4 Mont. 475, 1 Pac. Rep. 751. And see Alta Silver Min. Co. v. Alta Placer Min. Co., 78 Cal. 629, 21 Pac. Rep. 373.

[29] Hibernia Savings & Loan Society v. Moore, 68 Cal. 156, 8 Pac. Rep. 824.

purpose of raising money may imply a power to mortgage.[30] It remains to be stated that the rule requiring a mortgagee dealing with a trustee, under some circumstances, to see to the application of the money loaned, does not apply to a case of agency, where the owner of the property has executed a mortgage and placed it in the hands of his agent to negotiate the loan and receive the money, nor where, in the case of a trust, the trustee must apply the money in a manner requiring deliberation, time, and discretion on his part.[31]

§ 98. **Trustees.**—The authority of a trustee to incumber the trust estate by a mortgage depends entirely upon the scope of the powers vested in him by the deed or will under which he holds. Thus, a trustee who merely holds the legal title to land for the separate use of a married woman cannot incumber it without express or implied authority in the deed creating the trust.[32] A power in the trustee to sell the property and reinvest the proceeds will not authorize him to mortgage it, even to secure the payment of the purchase price of lands bought by him for the cestui que trust.[33] In one of the cases dealing with this subject, it appeared that the deed under which property was conveyed in trust for certain infants provided that the trustee should not incumber the property. The record of the deed having been burnt, it was restored by a decree in which the deed was declared to authorize the trustee to mortgage the property. Afterwards, in another suit, a new trustee was appointed, and authorized to borrow money by a mortgage on the trust property. It was held that, as against the mortgagee, making the loan in good faith, the infants had no right to have the decree authorizing the mortgage declared void by bill of review, since a decree against infants cannot be attacked for mere mistake as against third persons who have, in good faith, acquired rights under it.[34] On the other hand, a mortgage of trust property, executed jointly by the trustee and the cestui que trust, to secure a debt due from the latter, will

[30] Salem Nat. Bank v. White, 159 Ill. 136, 42 N. E. Rep. 312; Reed v. Kimsey, 98 Ill. App. 364.

[31] Seaverns v. Presbyterian Hospital, 173 Ill. 414, 50 N. E. Rep. 1079, affirming 64 Ill. App. 463.

[32] Seborn v. Beckwith, 30 W. Va. 774, 5 S. E. Rep. 450.

[33] Green v. Claiborne, 83 Va. 386, 5 S. E. Rep. 376.

[34] Franklin Savings Bank v. Taylor, 4 C. C. A. 55, 53 Fed. Rep. 854, following Lloyd v. Kirkwood, 112 Ill. 338.

be valid.[35] And it is even held that a mortgage made by the cestui que trust alone will be sustained in equity as if he were the legal owner.[36]

§ 99. Receivers.—Although it is unusual for a receiver to give a mortgage on the property in his charge to secure money loaned to him, yet this may be authorized or directed by the court having jurisdiction of the receivership, in a proper case. It is said that the power to mortgage is in principle the same as the power to issue receiver's certificates and make them a first lien on the property.[37] And in a case arising in another state, it appeared that real property which had been devised in trust had been sold for delinquent taxes, that the period for redemption from such sale was nearly expired, and that there were no funds in hand with which to redeem the land, so that there was danger that the trust property would be lost and the trust destroyed. In these circumstances, it was held that a court of equity, having previously appointed receivers to take charge of the trust property, had authority to empower them to raise money to redeem the lands from the tax sale, and to secure the repayment of the loan by placing a mortgage on the property.[38]

§ 100. Joint Mortgagors and Joint Mortgagees.—Joint owners of land may pledge the estate, as an entirety, by their joint mortgage upon it. Thus, where three persons, being tenants in common of land, make a joint and several obligation for the payment of money and secure the same by their joint mortgage on the land, and one of them pays to the mortgagee one-third of the amount due on the mortgage, and thereafter the mortgagee brings his bill to foreclose as to the remainder, the mortgagor who made the payment has no equity to compel him to resort first to the undivided two-thirds interest of his co-tenants for satisfaction of the balance of the debt; but the mortgagee may proceed to subject the entire estate covered by the mortgage to its payment. The proper rule in such cases is to require payment from all or either of the mortgagors, according to their undertaking, and if, as between themselves, either is compelled to pay more than his equitable

[35] Brokaw v. Field, 33 Ill. App. 138.

[36] Tillson v. Moulton, 23 Ill. 648.

[37] Brown v. Schintz, 98 Ill. App. 452.

[38] Burroughs v. Gaither, 66 Md. 171, 7 Atl. Rep. 243.

share, he may be subrogated to the rights of the mortgagee to
enforce contribution from those jointly liable with him.[39] So,
conversely, where a mortgage is given to mortgagees jointly,
but to secure the amount of the separate indebtedness of the
mortgagor to each of them, they do not take as joint tenants,
but as tenants in common, each having an undivided interest
in proportion to his claim; and therefore the fact that the
mortgage may be void, as to one of the mortgagees, as against
creditors of the mortgagor, will not affect its validity as to
the others.[40] So where an absolute deed was made to the
president of a bank, who thereupon gave back a defeasance
undertaking to reconvey upon the payment of what the debtor
owed to the bank and to another creditor, the presumption is
that the bank and the other creditor were to share pro rata
in the proceeds of the security.[41]

§ 101. **Foreign Corporations as Mortgagees.**—It is stated to
have been the policy of the legislature of Illinois, for many
years, to invest corporations with the power to loan money and
take mortgages on real estate as security therefor; and that
foreign corporations of like character were not prohibited by
any existing legislation from exercising like powers within the
state.[42] The act of April 9, 1875, provided that "any corporation formed under the laws of any other state or country, and
authorized by its charter to invest or loan money, may invest
or loan money in this state; and any such corporation that
may have invested or lent money as aforesaid may have the
same rights and powers for the recovery thereof, subject to
the same penalties for usury, as private persons, citizens of this
state," and may purchase at foreclosure sale.[43] But important
restrictions were imposed by the act of May 26, 1897 (Laws
1897, p. 174). This statute requires that every foreign corpora-

---

[39] Schoenewald v. Dieden, 8 Ill.
App. 389.

[40] Farwell v. Warren, 76 Wis.
527, 45 N. W. Rep. 217. And see
Burnett v. Pratt, 22 Pick. 556; Gilson v. Gilson, 2 Allen (Mass.) 115.

[41] Adams v. Robertson, 37 Ill. 45.

[42] Commercial Union Assur. Co.
v. Scammon, 102 Ill. 46; Stevens
v. Pratt, 101 Ill. 206; Hards v. Connecticut Mut. Life Ins. Co., 8 Biss.
234, Fed. Cas. No. 6,055.

[43] The retrospective feature of
this statute, validating loans or investments previously made in Illinois by foreign corporations, is not
in conflict with the provisions of
the federal constitution prohibiting laws impairing the obligation
of contracts or depriving persons
of property without due process of
law. Gross v. United States Mortgage Co., 108 U. S. 477.

tion, before it shall be permitted to do business in Illinois or to maintain any suit or action at law or in equity, shall have and maintain a public office within the state for the transaction of its business, where legal service may be had upon it, and where proper books shall be kept to enable it to comply with the laws of the state applicable to it; that it shall file in the office of the Secretary of State a duly certified and authenticated copy of its charter or articles or certificate of incorporation, and a sworn statement showing how much of its capital is represented by its property located and business transacted in Illinois; and that it shall pay, upon the proportion of its capital stock represented by its property and business in Illinois, incorporating taxes and fees equal to those required of similar corporations organized under the laws of Illinois. In one of the recent cases, the supreme court, after remarking that the legislature may enlarge, limit, or alter modes of procedure to enforce a contract, but cannot deny a remedy altogether, nor so embarrass a remedy with restrictions as seriously to impair the value of the right conferred by the contract, held that the act of 1897 could not be given a retrospective operation, even if the language employed had indicated an intention to make it apply retroactively, which, in the opinion of the court, was not the case. And consequently it was decided that a foreign corporation, which had loaned money in Illinois, and taken a mortgage as security, prior to the time when the act of 1897 went into operation and effect, might maintain a bill to foreclose its mortgage, without showing that it had complied with that statute.[44] It has also been held that the statute providing that every trust company shall deposit a designated large sum of money with the Auditor of Public Accounts, as a condition prerequisite to its right to accept any trust, does not apply to a mortgage made to such a corporation to secure a debt; that if the mortgage provides for the execution of

[44] Richardson v. United States Mortgage & Trust Co., 194 Ill. 259, 62 N. E. Rep. 606, affirming 89 Ill. App. 670. In other states, it is held that, in an action by a purchaser at a sale under foreclosure of a mortgage, to obtain possession, the defendant, the mortgagor, is estopped to plead that the mortgage is void because the mortgagee, a foreign corporation, had not complied with the statute regulating foreign corporations doing business within the state. Sherwood v. Alvis, 83 Ala. 115, 3 South. Rep. 307; Craddock v. American Freehold Land & Mortgage Co., 88 Ala. 281, 7 South. Rep. 196.

trusts which are within the prohibition of the statute, the trusts may be void for failure of the corporation to comply with the law, but the mortgage will not be invalidated; and that both the grantor in such a mortgage and a purchaser who has assumed the mortgage debt are estopped to assert that the corporation has no power to take as mortgagee.[45]

It may be observed in this connection that, notwithstanding any laws prohibiting aliens from holding real estate, an alien mortgagee has a right to come into a court of equity and have the property which has been pledged for the payment of his debt sold for the purpose of raising the money. His demand is merely a personal one, the debt being considered as the principal thing and the security on the land as an incident.[46]

§ 102. **National Banks as Mortgagees.**—The national banking act provides that banks organized under it may "purchase, hold, and convey real estate for the following purposes, and for no others: * * * Second, such as shall be mortgaged to it in good faith by way of security for debts previously contracted."[47] On the face of the statute, therefore, a national bank has no power or authority to take a mortgage on lands as security for a loan of money made at the same time with the mortgage, or as security for future advances to be made. Still, the statute does not declare that contracts made in excess of the permission which it grants shall be void. Disregard of the law in this respect will simply lay the bank open to proceedings against it at the instance of the United States; it will not release the mortgagor from his liability, nor avoid the mortgage as against subsequent purchasers or lienors. Hence it may be stated, as the general rule, that a mortgage taken by a national bank on real estate, to secure a contemporary loan or as security for future advances, if voidable at all, is so only at the suit of the general government. A state court of equity, having jurisdiction in an otherwise proper case, should not

[45] Farmers' Loan & Trust Co. v. Chicago & N. P. R. Co., (U. S. Circt. Ct., N. D. Ill.) 68 Fed. Rep. 412.

[46] Hughes v. Edwards, 9 Wheat. 489.

[47] Rev. Stat. U. S. § 5137. See Shinkle v. First Nat. Bank, 22 Ohio St. 516; Allen v. First Nat. Bank, 23 Ohio St. 97; Kansas Val-

ley Bank v. Rowell, 2 Dill. 371, Fed. Cas. No. 7,611. A national bank does not transcend its powers in taking from a customer, as collateral security for a loan to him, the note and mortgage of a third person together with certain personal securities; and if the borrower becomes insolvent and the personal securities prove insuf-

refuse its aid to such a bank as complainant in a bill to foreclose such a mortgage.[48]

ficient, the bank can maintain a bill to foreclose the mortgage. Merchants' Nat. Bank v. Mears, 8 Biss. 158, Fed. Cas. No. 9,450.

[48] Warner v. DeWitt County Nat. Bank, 4 Ill. App. 305. Herein it was said: "It is true our supreme court, in Fridley v. Bowen, 87 Ill. 151, has decided such securities void, and refuses relief thereon when sought in equity; yet since that decision was made, the supreme court of the United States, in Union Nat. Bank v. Matthews, 98 U. S. 621, has decided that such securities are not void, but only voidable, and the sovereign alone can object." And see National Bank of Genesee v. Whitney, 103 U. S. 99; Fortier v. New Orleans Nat. Bank, 112 U. S. 439; Waterloo Bank v. Elmore, 52 Iowa, 541, 3 N. W. Rep. 547.

CHAPTER IX.

MORTGAGEABLE INTERESTS IN REALTY.

§ 103. **Mortgageable Interests in General.**—"The doctrine is understood to be that everything which may be considered as property, whether in the technical language of the law denominated real or personal property, may be the subject of mortgage, as advowsons, rectories, tithes. Reversions and remainders, being capable of grant from man to man, and possibilities also, being assignable, are mortgageable, a mortgage of them being only a conditionable assignment. Rents, also, and franchises may be made the subject of mortgages."[1] Again, it is said: "In equity, whatever property, real or personal, is capable of an absolute sale may be the subject of a mortgage. Therefore rights in remainder and reversions, possibilities coupled with an interest, rents, franchises, and choses in action are capable of being mortgaged; and courts of equity support assignments of, or contracts pledging, property, or contingent interests therein, and also things which have no present, actual, potential existence, but rest in mere possibility."[2] But whatever may be the subject of the mortgage, the mortgagor must have a real and appreciable interest in the land affected. For instance, a trust deed duly recorded, executed by a party claiming an interest in the premises pledged under a tax deed conveying to him so small a part thereof

---

[1] Curtis v. Root, 20 Ill. 518. "Also, as a man may make a feoffment in fee in mortgage, so a man may make a gift in tail in mortgage, and a lease for term of life, or for term of years, in mortgage. And all such tenants are called 'tenants in mortgage,' according to the estates which they have in the land." Littleton, Tenures, bk. 3, c. 5, § 333.

[2] Wright v. Shumway, 1 Biss. 23, Fed. Cas. No. 18,093.

as to have no practical existence (as, "the vigintillionth of a vigintillionth of the east sixty-fourth of an inch" of a certain lot), which purports to convey "all interest" in the entire lot as security for a large sum, may be set aside in equity as a cloud on the true owner's title. In making this decision, the court observed that, if the tax purchaser had contented himself with making a mortgage on his interest in the property, according to the description in the tax deed, and the complainant had then filed a bill to remove the cloud on his title, they would have had no hesitation in applying the maxim "de minimis non curat lex" and dismissing the bill on the ground that a conveyance of such an infinitesimal portion of the premises cast no cloud on the title.[3]

§ 104. **Estates in Remainder.**—As stated in the preceding section, an estate in remainder in real property is capable of being made the subject of a mortgage.[4] In one of the cases, where a father, by his will, devoted certain land to be a home for his children so long as they should remain unmarried, and with remainder to such children, it was considered that the right of present possession and occupancy and the estate in remainder constituted interests in the children which were entirely distinct and independent of each other, and a mortgage on the estate in remainder would not, of itself alone, affect the right of present possession and enjoyment of the premises.[5]

§ 105. **Estates for Life.**—A vested equitable life estate is such an interest in land as will pass by a mortgage of the same; and where such estate is conveyed or incumbered by the cestui que trust, without the concurrence of the trustee holding the legal title, it will become the duty of the trustee to recognize the rights of the grantee or mortgagee. But the purchaser under such a mortgage will take only such right as the mortgagor had, that is, an estate for the life of the mortgagor.[6] So, where a deed was made to a married woman and "her body heirs," it was held that, as the legal effect of the deed was to give her a life estate, and as there was no restriction of alienation, it was competent for her, by uniting with her husband (as the law then required), to mortgage her estate

---

[3] Glos v. Furman, 66 Ill. App. 127, affirmed, 164 Ill. 585.

[4] Curtis v. Root, 20 Ill. 518; Wright v. Shumway, 1 Biss. 23, Fed. Cas. No. 18,093.

[5] Springer v. Savage, 143 Ill. 301, 32 N. E. Rep. 520.

[6] Bryan v. Howland, 98 Ill. 625.

and release her homestead, and that such a mortgage created
a valid lien upon her interest in the land.[7]

§ 106. Leasehold Interests.—A mere term of years, or leasehold interest in land, is also mortgageable as realty. But the
lien created by such a mortgage will be coextensive with the
term, and will be extinguished by mere lapse of time whenever
the term ends; and it cannot, upon the expiration of the term,
be foreclosed as against the reversioner, although the bill for
foreclosure may have been filed before the term expired.[8] On
the other hand, where the lease is accompanied by special advantages or privileges to the lessee, such as an option to purchase the property at a fixed price within a limited time, the
act of the lessee, after mortgaging his interest, in surrendering
and conveying all rights remaining in him to the lessor, will
in no manner affect the rights of the mortgagee.[9]

§ 107. Titles Under Executory Contract for Sale of Land.—
Where the owner of lands in fee has executed a valid and
binding agreement for their sale and conveyance to another,
and the contract remains executory and no deed has passed,
each of the parties has an interest in the premises which may
be made the subject of a mortgage. A mortgage by the vendor,
in such circumstances, will pass to his mortgagee exactly the
rights which remained in the vendor, and no others; that is,
the right to require execution of the contract of purchase on
the part of the vendee, and to receive from him any unpaid
balance of the purchase money until the debt secured by the
mortgage is discharged.[10] In one of the Illinois cases on this
point, where the owner of land sold it to another person, giving
him a bond for a deed, and the purchaser took possession, and
the vendor then executed a mortgage on the same premises
to secure a debt to a third person, but still retained the purchaser's notes given for the unpaid balance of the purchase
money, it was held that the mortgagee would have the right
to enjoin the payment of the notes to the vendor, until the
mortgage debt should be satisfied, or, if that debt was already
due, he could have the notes paid to him. But the purchaser

[7] Hosmer v. Carter, 68 Ill. 98.

[8] Griffin v. Marine Co., 52 Ill.
130; Rogers v. Herron, 92 Ill. 583.

[9] McCauley v. Coe, 150 Ill. 311,
37 N. E. Rep. 232.

[10] Wright v. Kentucky & G. E.
Ry. Co., 117 U. S. 72; Ranney v.
Hardy, 43 Ohio St. 157, 1 N. E. Rep.
523.

of the premises could not protect the mortgagee's rights on his own initiative. In the absence of any proceedings to enjoin him, he would be bound to pay the notes to the legal holder of them, at maturity and on demand. Further, if the notes in such a case, not falling due until after the maturity of the mortgage debt, had been assigned to a bona fide purchaser on a precedent debt, without notice of the mortgagee's equitable claim to them, the purchaser of the land, not having any defense and being unable to resist their collection, would be protected in paying them and would not be liable to the mortgagee, even if he had notice of his rights, and also the assignee of the notes would be protected against the mortgagee; and after the notes had been paid and title had fully passed, the purchaser would be entitled to have the mortgage cancelled as a cloud on his title.[11] On the same principle, where a party acquires the legal title to lots from one who had previously made contracts for their sale and conveyance, together with an assignment of the contracts, he has such an interest in the lots as may be the subject of a transfer by mortgage. In such case he does not hold the title in trust for the purchasers.[12]

Conversely, the purchaser under an executory contract for the sale of land has an interest therein which is mortgageable.[13] But his mortgagee will take no greater or other rights than the vendee had; that is, he will acquire simply a right to purchase the property for the consideration stipulated in the contract of purchase, or to require a conveyance of the estate from the vendor according to the terms of the agreement, on completing the payment of the purchase price.[14] And although a bond for a deed to land may provide for a forfeiture for non-payment, yet if the vendor does not declare a forfeiture, the holder under the bond has such an equitable estate as may be mortgaged by him.[15]

§ 108. **Undivided Interests in Land.**—An undivided interest in land, such as that held by a joint tenant or tenant in common, may be made the subject of a mortgage. And a mortgage given by one tenant in common will carry with it, on the prin-

[11] Doolittle v. Cook, 75 Ill. 354.

[12] Chickering v. Fullerton, 90 Ill. 520.

[13] Curtis v. Root, 20 Ill. 518; Baker v. Bishop Hill Colony, 45 Ill. 264; McCauley v. Coe, 51 Ill. App. 284, and same case on appeal, 150 Ill. 311, 37 N. E. Rep. 232.

[14] Alden v. Garver, 32 Ill. 32.

[15] Irish v. Sharp, 89 Ill. 261; Sheen v. Hogan, 86 Ill. 16.

ciple of subrogation, any lien which the mortgagor had upon
the shares of his co-tenants for improvements made upon the
common mortgaged property.[16] Where the undivided interest
of a tenant in common of land is mortgaged, and the mortgage
foreclosed, the purchaser at the foreclosure sale becomes himself a tenant in common in the place of the mortgagor, and
takes subject to the same duties and relations to the co-tenants; and consequently his possession of the land and payment
of taxes thereon will not, in the absence of actual notice that
it is adverse, give title as against his co-tenants, where the
record disclosed the state of the title.[17] It will be observed
that a mortgage given by one tenant in common on the property is binding only on the interest of the party making the
same, and, after a decree of sale in a proceeding for partition,
will follow his interest only in the proceeds. Such an incumbrance will in no wise adversely affect the interest of the other
tenants in the premises, or their interests in the proceeds of the
sale.[18] As remarked in one of the cases, ''the effect of a partition, in which a mortgagee is joined as a party, is to substitute for an undivided interest in the whole land the portion
set off to the mortgagor in severalty; and the lien of the mortgage, which was theretofore upon an undivided interest, falls
upon the particular portion so set off and aparted to the mortgagor.''[19]

§ 109. **Inchoate Title to Public Lands.**—An Act of Congress
provides that ''before any person claiming the benefit of this
chapter [relating to the pre-emption of public lands] is allowed
to enter lands, he shall make oath that he has not directly or
indirectly made any agreement or contract, in any way or manner, with any person whatsoever, by which the title which he
might acquire from the government of the United States should
inure in whole or in part to the benefit of any person except
himself; and if any person taking such oath swears falsely in
the premises, any grant or conveyance which he may have
made, except in the hands of bona fide purchasers for a valuable consideration, shall be null and void.''[20] There has been

[16] Salem Nat. Bank v. White, 159
Ill. 136, 42 N. E. Rep. 312.

[17] McMahill v. Torrence, 163 Ill.
277, 45 N. E. Rep. 269.

[18] Speck v. Pullman Palace Car
Co., 121 Ill. 33, 12 N. E. Rep. 213.

[19] Rochester Loan & Banking Co.
v. Morse, 181 Ill. 64, 54 N. E. Rep.
628, reversing 74 Ill. App. 326;
Loomis v. Riley, 24 Ill. 307.

[20] Rev. Stat. U. S. § 2262.

much doubt as to whether this provision would prevent the giving of a valid mortgage on his claim by a pre-emptioner. But the preponderance of authority is to the effect that such a claimant may lawfully mortgage his interest after his right to a patent has become fully fixed, by his complete compliance with the law in all respects, so that nothing remains but the mere issuance of the patent to invest him with the complete legal title to the land; but that a mortgage given before his right to a patent becomes vested in this manner is prohibited by the statute.[21]

As to homestead entries on the public lands, it is enacted that "no lands acquired under the provisions of this chapter shall in any event become liable to the satisfaction of any debt contracted prior to the issuing of a patent therefor."[22] But it has been said that this provision "was manifestly intended for the protection of the party entering the land, to prevent its appropriation in invitum to the satisfaction of his debts, and not for the purpose of disabling him from dealing with it as his own [as by mortgaging it] after he has acquired a right to it by complying with the terms of the law. The only restraint which the statute seems to impose on the party's power of disposition applies only to a time before he makes his final proofs."[23]

§ 110. Buildings Considered as Realty.—A law in Illinois declares that the term "real estate," as used in the statutes regulating conveyances, shall include chattels real. In one of the cases before the supreme court, the question concerned a grain elevator, permanent in its structure, which had been built on the right of way of a railroad, under a lease which provided that the lessor might terminate the lease on sixty days' notice, and that the lessee should have the right to remove buildings erected by him on the leased ground at any time before the expiration of the lease. It was held that the elevator, together with the leasehold estate, was a chattel real, and therefore to be classed as real estate within the meaning

[21] See Myers v. Croft, 13 Wall. 291; Quinby v. Conlan, 104 U. S. 420; Warren v. Van Brunt, 19 Wall. 646; Webster v. Bowman, 25 Fed. Rep. 889; Brewster v. Madden, 15 Kans. 249; Mellison v. Allen, 30 Kans. 382. Compare Jones v. Tainter, 15 Minn. 512; Norris v. Heald (Mont.), 29 Pac. Rep. 1121.

[22] Rev. Stat. U. S. § 2296.

[23] Lewis v. Wetherell, 36 Minn. 386, 31 N. W. Rep. 356. And see Seymour v. Sanders, 3 Dill. 437, Fed. Cas. No. 12,690.

of the statute, so that the holder of a recorded mortgage thereon would have priority over a subsequent execution creditor, even though he had not taken possession within two years after the date of the mortgage, as would be necessary in the case of a chattel mortgage. It was also considered that the fact that the mortgage described the property as "the grain elevator and the leased ground the same stands upon," and the fact that it was acknowledged before a justice of the peace, and entered on his docket in the form required for chattel mortgages, would not estop the mortgagor from claiming that the property was real estate.[24]

[24] Knapp v. Jones, 143 Ill. 375, 32 N. E. Rep. 382.

CHAPTER X.

PROPERTY COVERED BY A MORTGAGE.

§ 111. Homestead Estate of Mortgagor.—A statute in Illinois provides that "every householder having a family shall be entitled to an estate of homestead, to the extent in value of $1,000, in the farm or lot of land and buildings thereon, owned or rightly possessed, by lease or otherwise, and occupied by him or her as a residence; and such homestead, and all right and title therein, shall be exempt from attachment, judgment, levy or execution, sale for the payment of his debts, or other purposes, and from the laws of conveyance, descent, and devise, except as hereinafter provided."[1] Hence it appears that, to entitle a mortgagor to a homestead in the mortgaged premises, he must not only be the head of a family, but, at the time of making the mortgage, he must reside with his family on the mortgaged premises, and so continue to reside.[2] These conditions being fulfilled, a homestead may be claimed as against a mortgage on the premises (not containing a release of the homestead right) provided the value of the whole does not exceed the statutory exemption; but a mortgage or deed of trust on property occupied by the mortgagor as a homestead will create a lien which may be enforced against the premises to the extent to which their value exceeds one thousand dollars.[3] The manner of working out the respective rights of the homestead claimant and the mortgagee, on foreclosure, is thus regulated by statute: "In the enforcement of a lien

[1] Rev. Stat. Ill. c. 52, § 1.

[2] Fergus v. Woodworth, 44 Ill. 374.

[3] Young v. Morgan, 89 Ill. 199; Boyd v. Cudderback, 31 Ill. 118.

in a court of equity upon premises, including the homestead, if such right is not waived or released as provided in this act, the court may set off the homestead and decree the sale of the balance of the premises; or, if the value of the premises exceeds the exemption, and the premises cannot be divided, may order the sale of the whole and the payment of the amount of the exemption to the person entitled thereto.''[4] To entitle the mortgagee to have his lien enforced in this manner and to this extent, it is necessary—when the homestead exemption is claimed in the answer to the bill for foreclosure—that the bill and the proofs should show that the premises are worth more than a thousand dollars; in the absence of any such averment and proof, or any averment denying the homestead right set up, no decree of sale can be made.[5] Even if the right to a homestead is not put in issue, and the decree of foreclosure simply orders the sale of the mortgaged premises, the purchaser at such sale will only acquire an interest in the property over and above the value of the homestead exemption; he will not be entitled to immediate possession of the land, and if he brings ejectment, the mortgagor may then avail himself of his homestead right.[6]

But no homestead right can be set up against a mortgage which did not exist at the time the mortgage was made. That is, no such exemption can attach to premises in consequence of the mortgagor's taking up his residence thereon, and claiming a homestead, after the execution of the mortgage.[7] And, moreover, this right depends upon the continued occupancy of the premises by the mortgagor and his family as a place of residence. Where the owner of land on which his homestead is established conveys the same by an absolute mortgage, legally executed, the fee in the premises conveyed, no matter what their value, passes to the mortgagee, subject only to the right of occupancy on the part of the mortgagor, in case the homestead has not been relinquished; and when such occupancy terminates, the homestead right is annihilated, it not being an estate in the premises which can be transferred as against a former conveyance that has passed the fee.[8] Hence, where the owner of land, which he occupied as a homestead, executed a

[4] Rev. Stat. Ill. c. 52, § 8.
[5] Black v. Lusk, 69 Ill. 70.
[6] Parrott v. Kumpf, 102 Ill. 423; Asher v. Mitchell, 92 Ill. 480.

[7] McCormick v. Wilcox, 25 Ill. 275.
[8] McDonald v. Crandall, 43 Ill. 231; Hewitt v. Templeton, 48 Ill.

mortgage thereon, but without releasing the homestead right formally in writing, and afterwards abandoned the premises without intending to return to them, this was held to be such a waiver of the homestead in favor of the mortgagee that a subsequent conveyance of the premises by the mortgagor, with a formal written release of the homestead right, would not operate to pass any right to his grantee, in respect to the homestead, which could be asserted against the mortgage.[9] And a first mortgage, without release of homestead, upon the abandonment of the homestead, will take precedence of a subsequent mortgage waiving the homestead exemption.[10] Where a man and his wife executed a mortgage on their homestead without the statutory waiver, and afterwards conveyed it to a third person, subject to the mortgage lien, such lien forming a part of the purchase price, and the mortgagee brought suit to foreclose, it was held that the vendee, having obtained the premises by admitting the lien and assuming its payment, was estopped from setting up as a defense the omission of the mortgagors to release their homestead right in the mortgage.[11]

§ 112. Same; Release of Homestead.—A grantor or mortgagor of land may waive or release his right of homestead therein. But "no deed or other instrument shall be construed as releasing or waiving the right of homestead unless the same shall contain a clause expressly releasing or waiving such right. And in such case, the certificate of acknowledgment shall contain a clause substantially as follows: 'Including the release and waiver of the right of homestead,' or other words which shall expressly show that the parties executing the deed or other instrument intended to release such right. And no release or waiver of the right of homestead by the husband shall bind the wife unless she join in such release or waiver."[12]

367; Hartwell v. McDonald, 69 Ill. 293.

[9] Vasey v. Board of Trustees, 59 Ill. 188.

[10] Asher v. Mitchell, 9 Ill. App. 335.

[11] Pidgeon v. Trustees of Schools, 44 Ill. 501.

[12] Rev. Stat. Ill. c. 30, § 27 (Starr & C. § 28). When the mortgagor, using the statutory form of mortgage (as to which see, supra, § 71), desires to release or waive his homestead right in the land conveyed, it may be done by inserting in the statutory form, after the words "State of Illinois," the following words, in substance: "Hereby releasing and waiving all rights under and by virtue of the homestead exemption laws of this State." See Rev. Stat. Ill. c. 30, § 11 (Starr & C. § 12).

Mortgages and deeds of trust, it is said, being conveyances upon condition, are clearly within both the letter and the spirit of the act relating to homesteads, and must be executed and acknowledged in accordance with the requirements of the laws respecting the alienation of homesteads.[13] Hence, where a husband and wife execute a mortgage on lands to which a homestead right has attached, it is not enough, to pass such right, that it is expressly released in the body of the deed; it must appear from the certificate of acknowledgment that the wife acknowledged that she released this particular right freely and voluntarily and without compulsion.[14] But where a mortgage was executed and acknowledged in a manner sufficient to release the homestead, and afterwards, by consent of all parties, the description of the property conveyed was altered so as to correct a clerical error, and the mortgage was then reacknowledged without release of homestead, it was held on a bill to foreclose, that, the original description having been sufficient to pass the lands intended by the parties, the correction did not affect the waiver of homestead.[15]

It is also provided by statute that, when a mortgage containing a release or waiver of homestead "includes different pieces of land, or the homestead is of greater value than $1,000, said other lands shall first be sold before resorting to the homestead, and in case of the sale of such homestead, if any balance shall remain after the payment of the debt and costs, such balance shall, to the extent of $1,000, be exempt, and be applied upon such homestead exemption in the manner provided by law."[16] Consequently, as against subsequent judgment creditors, the mortgagor is entitled to his homestead exemption out of the surplus proceeds of a sale under a mortgage containing a waiver of the homestead.[17]

§ 113. Same; Purchase-Money Mortgage.—It is enacted that no property shall, by virtue of the act granting homestead exemptions, be "exempt from sale for non-payment of taxes or assessments, or for a debt or liability incurred for the purchase or improvement thereof."[18] Consequently, a homestead exemption cannot be claimed in mortgaged premises, by the

13 Eldridge v. Pierce, 90 Ill. 474.   16 Rev. Stat. Ill. c. 52, § 4.
14 Boyd v. Cudderback, 31 Ill. 113.   17 First Nat. Bank v. Briggs, 22
15 Casler v. Byers, 129 Ill. 657,   Ill. App. 228.
22 N. E. Rep. 507.   18 Rev. Stat. Ill. c. 52, § 3.

mortgagor or his wife, as against the mortgagee in a mortgage given to secure the purchase money of the same premises, or a part thereof.[19]

§ 114. After-Acquired Title.—The conveyance act in Illinois provides that "if any person shall sell and convey to another, by deed or conveyance, purporting to convey an estate in fee simple absolute in any tract of land or real estate, lying and being in this State, not then being possessed of the legal estate or interest therein at the time of the sale and conveyance, but after such sale and conveyance the vendor shall become possessed of and confirmed in the legal estate to the land or real estate so sold and conveyed, it shall be taken and held to be in trust for the use of the grantee or vendee; and the conveyance aforesaid shall be held and taken, and shall be, as valid as if the grantor or vendor had the legal estate or interest at the time of said sale or conveyance."[20] And by the succeeding section of the same act it is provided that the use of the words "grant, bargain, and sell," in a mortgage, shall operate as a covenant to the mortgagee and his heirs that the mortgagor was seised in fee simple of the land mortgaged, free from all incumbrances, etc. Further, a mortgage in the statutory form, which contains the words "and warrants" is equivalent to a mortgage containing all the formal covenants of warranty. It follows, therefore, that when a mortgage of realty embraces the covenants of title or warranty, either in the full or the abbreviated form, or the words which, under the statute, import such covenants, any title to the premises subsequently acquired by the mortgagor, or accruing to him after the execution of the mortgage, whether legal or equitable, will inure to the benefit of the mortgagee, and will be subject to the mortgage, and cannot be set up in hostility to it.[21] It has been said that courts of equity extend the lien of a mortgage to after-acquired property or titles on the theory

[19] Austin v. Underwood, 37 Ill. 438; Magee v. Magee, 51 Ill. 500; Kimble v. Esworthy, 6 Ill. App. 517; Allen v. Hawley, 66 Ill. 164; Gaither v. Wilson, 164 Ill. 544, 46 N. E. Rep. 58; Campbell v. Maginnis, 70 Iowa, 589, 31 N. W. Rep. 946.

[20] Rev. Stat. Ill. c. 30, § 7.

[21] Pratt v. Pratt, 96 Ill. 184; Elder v. Derby, 98 Ill. 228; Gochenour v. Mowry, 33 Ill. 331; Gibbons v. Hoag, 95 Ill. 45; Lagger v. Mutual Union L. & B. Ass'n, 146 Ill. 283, 33 N. E. Rep. 946; Bybee v. Hageman, 66 Ill. 519; Taylor v. Kearn, 68 Ill. 339; Wells v. Somers, 4 Ill. App. 297.

that, though ineffective as a conveyance, it operates as an executory agreement attaching to the property or title when acquired.[22] But the rule finds a sufficient support in the doctrine of estoppel. At law, one can neither convey nor incumber that which he does not own. But in equity, an estoppel arises against the mortgagor out of the covenants of title, so that he cannot deny his title nor claim adversely to the mortgage under any title newly acquired.[23]

But it must be noted that a deed not purporting to convey an estate in fee simple absolute in the lands (as, where it merely quitclaims all the right, estate, title, and demand which the grantor has or ought to have in the property) is not such a conveyance as that an after-acquired title of the grantor will inure to the grantee under the statute. If one conveys lands with a general covenant of warranty against all lawful claims and demands, he cannot be allowed to set up as against his grantee or those claiming under him, any title subsequently acquired, either by purchase or otherwise, but such new title will inure by way of estoppel to the use and benefit of the grantee and his heirs and assigns. But where the deed, on its face, does not purport to convey an indefeasible estate, but only the right, title, and interest of the grantor, although the deed may contain a covenant of general warranty, the doctrine of estoppel will not apply so as to pass an after-acquired estate to the grantee. The covenants of warranty in a deed are limited and restrained by the estate conveyed on the face of the deed; and these principles apply to mortgages and deeds of trust.[24]

As a corollary to the main proposition, it may be stated that if the mortgagee buys in an outstanding title to the mortgaged premises, under an arrangement with the mortgagor that it is to be held, like the mortgage, subject to redemption, he will not be allowed, when the title is acquired, to insist that he purchased as a stranger; but he must permit the mortgagor to redeem.[25]

§ 115. Fixtures.—When a fixture, permanent in its char-

[22] Grape Creek Coal Co. v. Farmers' Loan & Trust Co. (U. S. Circt. Ct. of App., 7th Circuit), 12 C. C. A. 350, 63 Fed. Rep. 891.

[23] Lagger v. Mutual Union L. & B. Ass'n, 146 Ill. 283, 33 N. E. Rep. 946; Campbell v. Texas & N. O. R.

Co., 2 Woods, 263, Fed. Cas. No. 2,369.

[24] Holbrook v. Debo, 99 Ill. 373; Bowen v. McCarthy, 127 Ill. 17, 18 N. E. Rep. 757.

[25] Moore v. Titman, 44 Ill. 367.

acter, is erected or placed upon mortgaged premises, and so annexed to the freehold as to evince an intention that it shall remain there, it becomes subject to the lien of the mortgage, and cannot be removed unless with the consent of the mortgagee. As it enhances the value of the property and increases the security of the mortgage, it is regarded as inuring to the benefit of the mortgagee.[26] Contentions in regard to the character of fixtures, and the claims of mortgagees upon them, chiefly arise in the case of machinery. But it may be stated as a general rule that, when machinery is placed in a mill or factory by the owner of the land, and either actually or constructively attached to the building, and is of such a character that it is suitable only for use in that connection, and is necessary for the prosecution of the business for which the mill or factory was erected, so that the plant could not be operated as a mill or factory without such machinery, then such machinery must be regarded as a fixture which will pass with the realty under a mortgage thereon.[27] For example, machinery fastened to the floor, or to a plank nailed to the floor, of a building erected for use as a shoe factory, by large screws, and belted to the shafting overhead, or fastened to benches by wooden screws and belted to the shafting, the benches being nailed to the floor, intended to form a part of the plant, where such machinery was placed in the building for the purpose of manufacturing shoes, and is essential to the plant, is a fixture and as such will pass by a mortgage of the land on which the building is erected.[28] So, where the owner of land erected a slaughterhouse thereon, and sold the property to another, to be used as a slaughterhouse, taking back a mortgage to secure the purchase money, and the latter erected machinery thereon and operated the premises as a slaughterhouse, and the property was sold under the mortgage, and the mortgagee rented it from the purchaser, it was held that the machinery passed to the purchaser as a part of the realty.[29] On the other hand, a bar counter and shelf placed in a building by a tenant for the purpose of conducting a drinking saloon, and attached

[26] Williams v. Chicago Exhibition Co., 188 Ill. 19, 58 N. E. Rep. 611; Kelly v. Austin, 46 Ill. 156.

[27] Hill v. National Bank, 97 U. S. 450; Calumet Iron & Steel Co. v. Lathrop, 36 Ill. App. 249; Roddy v. Brick, 42 N. J. Eq. 218, 6 Atl. Rep. 806.

[28] Fifield v. Farmers' Nat. Bank, 148 Ill. 163, 35 N. E. Rep. 802.

[29] Kloess v. Katt, 40 Ill. App. 99.

to the realty in such a manner that they can be removed without injury to the premises, are "trade fixtures" and do not pass with the real estate.[30]

We must also note that articles personal in their nature may retain the character of personalty, by the agreement of the parties, although they are attached to the realty in such a manner that, without such agreement, they would lose that character, provided they are so attached that they may be removed without material injury to the article itself or to the freehold. Where chattels are sold to the owner of the soil on an agreement that their character as personalty is not to be changed, and a chattel mortgage is taken thereon to secure the purchase money, a prior mortgagee of the land cannot claim them, although they are subsequently annexed to the freehold.[31] But the fact that a creditor of a person owning a factory may have taken a chattel mortgage on the fixtures of the factory building will not affect his rights under a mortgage of the realty subsequently taken to secure the same debt. In such a case, if the property is a fixture it will pass under the mortgage as a part of the realty.[32]

§ 116. **Rules for Determining Fixtures.**—The tests for determining whether given property is to be regarded as a fixture are stated to be as follows: First, real or constructive annexation of the thing in question to the realty; second, appropriation or adaptation to the use or purpose of that part of the realty with which it is connected; and third, the intention of the party making the annexation to make it a permanent accession to the freehold, this intention being inferred from the nature of the article affixed, the relation and situation of the party making the annexation, and the policy of the law in relation thereto, the structure and mode of the annexation, and the purpose or use for which the annexation has been made. Of these tests, the clear tendency of the authorities seems to be to give the pre-eminence to the question of intention to make the article a permanent accession to the freehold, and the others seem to derive their chief value as evidence of such intention. It is in the power of the owner of the freehold

[30] Berger v. Hoerner, 36 Ill. App. 360.

[31] Ellison v. Salem Coal & Mining Co., 43 Ill. App. 120.

[32] Fifield v. Farmers' Nat. Bank, 148 Ill. 163, 35 N. E. Rep. 802.

to affix to it any property he pleases, and when he does so, it becomes a fixture in the general sense of the term, and goes with the freehold under a deed or mortgage.[33] In another case it is said that, although the question whether structures are real or personal estate cannot always be determined by the known intention of the party erecting them, yet in cases of doubt it will have a controlling influence.[34] And in another it is remarked: "In determining whether chattels such as are involved in this controversy [machinery] pass with the realty and become a part of the realty, so as to be covered by a mortgage or deed, reference is to be had as well to the intention of the parties as to the uses and purposes for which the building and the machinery are to be used. It is not necessary that the chattel should always be fastened or attached to the realty so as to make it a part of it."[35] But it is clear that there must be some sort of annexation or attachment, constructive if not actual. In an instructive case from another state we find the doctrine stated that the various tests proposed for determining whether the thing in question remains a chattel or has become a fixture, such as the intention of the parties, and the like, "while having an important bearing upon the question whether there has been an annexation, and, if so, its effect, do not do away with the necessity of annexation, either actual or constructive, to constitute a fixture. This would involve a contradiction of terms, and wipe out the fundamental distinction between real and personal property. * * * While physical annexation is not indispensable, the adjudicated cases are almost universally opposed to the idea of mere loose machinery or utensils, even where it is the main agent or principal thing in prosecuting the business to which the realty is adapted, being considered a part of the freehold for any purpose. To make it a fixture, it must not merely be essential to the business of the structure, but it must be attached to it in some way, or at least it must be mechanically fitted, so as, in the ordinary understanding, to constitute a part of the structure itself. It must be permanently attached to, or the component part of, some erection, structure, or machine which is attached to the freehold, and without which the erection, structure, or machine would be imperfect or incomplete."[36] Where

---

[33] Fifield v. Farmers' Nat. Bank, 148 Ill. 163, 35 N. E. Rep. 802, citing Ewell on Fixtures, 21; Arnold v. Crowder, 81 Ill. 56.

[34] Kelly v. Austin, 46 Ill. 156.

[35] Otis v. May, 30 Ill. App. 581.

[36] Wolford v. Baxter, 33 Minn. 12, 21 N. W. Rep. 744.

a mortgage covers land, buildings, and machinery, it must speak for itself as to what it does or does not include, viewed in the light of the status of the property and the surrounding circumstances.[37] But if it does not distinguish between fixtures and personal property, nor specifically declare the character of any item therein mentioned, it leaves the character of each item to be determined by proof aliunde.[38]

§ 117. **Improvements on the Land.**—All improvements or betterments placed on real estate by the owner of it, while the property is incumbered by a mortgage, are regarded as a part of the mortgaged estate. Their cost or value cannot be claimed by the mortgagor as against the mortgage. On the contrary, they inure to the benefit of the mortgagee, become subject at once to the lien of the mortgage, go to increase the security, and may be sold as a part of the mortgaged premises on foreclosure of the mortgage.[39] Thus, where a mortgagor, while owning the equity of redemption, erects a house upon the mortgaged premises, without any agreement with the mortgagee, it becomes a part of the realty, and passes with it to a purchaser under the foreclosure of the mortgage.[40] So, where the holder of a mechanic's lien, on land which was incumbered by a mortgage subordinate to his lien, foreclosed and bought in the property at the sale, and afterwards placed valuable improvements upon the premises, and after this was done, the decree in the lien proceedings was reversed on writ of error, and the mortgagee then claimed the benefit of the improvements made subsequent to the mortgage, it was held that he was entitled thereto.[41] On the other hand, where a mortgagor, after the execution of the mortgage, proceeded, jointly with his partner in business, to erect a building on the mortgaged land for the purposes of their trade, and the structure was built with money of the firm, and was in no manner permanently fixed to the freehold, but was merely a temporary erection designed and used for business purposes, it was held that the mortgagee obtained no interest therein and could not

---

[37] Jones v. Ramsey, 3 Ill. App. 303.

[38] McKinley v. Smith, 29 Ill. App. 106.

[39] Baird v. Jackson. 98 Ill. 78; Wood v. Whelen, 93 Ill. 153; Mar-

tin v. Beatty, 54 Ill. 100; Asher v. Mitchell, 9 Ill. App. 335; Mann v. Mann, 49 Ill. App. 472.

[40] Matzon v. Griffin, 78 Ill. 477.

[41] Powell v. Rogers, 11 Ill. App. 98.

prevent the removal of the building.[42] In a case where money was advanced upon a mortgage, and it turned out that another than the mortgagor was the beneficial owner of the property, of which the mortgagee was notified at the time of taking the mortgage, it was held, upon a bill to quiet title, that the one claiming the beneficial ownership should pay for the improvements which had been made upon the property by the expenditure of the money which the mortgage was given to secure.[43]

§ 118. **Products of the Soil.**—"It is a well-settled rule of law that crops growing on mortgaged land are covered by the mortgage, whether planted before or after its execution, and until they are severed the mortgage attaches as well to the crops as to the land; and if the land be sold for condition broken before severance, the purchaser is entitled to the growing crops, not only as against the mortgagor, but against all persons claiming in any manner through or under him, subsequent to the recording of the mortgage."[44] But until foreclosure of the mortgage, or possession taken by the mortgagee for breach of condition, the mortgagor is entitled to the emblements, and may harvest the crop; and when the products of the soil are severed, he has an absolute right to them without any liability to account for them. Hence, before the foreclosure of a mortgage on the land, the crops may be pledged as security by a chattel mortgage, and may be severed and taken for the satisfaction of such a mortgage, or sold on execution against the mortgagor. But a chattel mortgage on crops, given after the recording of a general mortgage on the land, will be subordinate thereto, in so far as that a foreclosure and sale under the general mortgage will cut off the right of the chattel mortgagee to take the crop (not already severed) in satisfaction of his mortgage.[45] Also, where the mortgagor remains in possession of the land after a decree of foreclosure and a sale thereunder, and pending the period allowed for redemption, and produces a crop, one who in good faith buys

[42] Kelly v. Austin, 46 Ill. 156.

[43] Union Mut. Ins. Co. v. Campbell, 95 Ill. 267.

[44] Yates v. Smith, 11 Ill. App. 459; Sugden v. Beasley, 9 Ill. App. 71; Harmon v. Fisher. Id. 22. But where, by a defect in the acknowledgment, the mortgage deed does not convey the homestead right, a purchaser at foreclosure sale is not entitled to that portion of the growing crop sown upon the homestead. Brock v. Leighton, 11 Ill. App. 361.

[45] Rankin v. Kinsey, 7 Ill. App. 215.

such crop, before the appointment of a receiver to take charge
of the issues and profits of the estate, will be protected.[46] A
severance of the crop, to be effectual as against the rights of
the mortgagee of the land, must be actual. Thus, as between
the parties to a judgment, the seizure and sale of growing
crops on execution issued on the judgment will constitute a
severance of the crops from the realty. But as to a mortgagee
or grantee in a deed of trust given by the execution debtor
before the execution became a lien, such seizure and sale will
not work a severance. The purchaser at the sheriff's sale takes
subject to the rights of the mortgagee, which will not be cut
off or affected by such sale.[47]

These rules apply as well to the natural growth of the soil
as to the products of agricultural cultivation. Thus, timber
growing upon land mortgaged is a portion of the realty and is
embraced in the mortgage as part of the security. The mortgagor has no right to cut it after default made in any of the
payments of the mortgage. His cutting of timber may be restrained by injunction, upon proper application, by a court of
equity. And if the mortgagor sells the timber which he has
cut, this does not divest the lien of the mortgage, but the purchaser takes subject to the paramount rights of the mortgagee.
But when the amount due according to the stipulations of the
mortgage is paid, the lien of the mortgage upon the timber
which may have been cut down, and so severed from the realty,
is discharged, and the timber reverts to the mortgagor, or any
vendee of his.[48]

§ 119. Accretions.—Where land is conveyed by a mortgage,
which is bounded on one side by a lake or stream, the line
between the land and the water will form a boundary, and
such line will follow the receding water. And since accretions
thus formed belong to the littoral owner, and since whatever is
added to mortgaged land inures to the benefit of the mortgagee, it follows that the accretion thus formed will pass to
the mortgagee, not as appurtenant to the land granted, but as
a part of it; and the rule is the same where a lot is described
by reference to a recorded map or plat which shows a boundary
by the lake or stream on one side.[49]

[46] Knox v. Oswald, 21 Ill. App.
105.

[47] Anderson v. Strauss, 98 Ill.
485. Compare White v. Pulley, 27
Fed. Rep. 436.

[48] Hutchins v. King, 1 Wall. 53.

[49] Chicago Dock & Canal Co. v.
Kinzie, 93 Ill. 415.

§ 120. **Rents and Profits.**—The rents and profits of property may be the subject of a mortgage; and while a mortgage of real estate does not ordinarily include the income of the property, yet it may provide that, in case of foreclosure, a receiver shall be appointed to collect the rents and profits from the institution of the suit to the end of the period allowed for redemption, and this will create a valid lien on such rents and profits which equity will enforce, without regard to the mortgagor's insolvency, upon the application of the mortgagee.[50] We also find decisions (in other states) to the effect that, although the mortgage is expressly declared to be upon the "rents, issues, and profits" only, yet if these prove insufficient to satisfy the mortgage debt, recourse may be had to the corpus of the estate. It is said: "The meaning of the words 'rents, issues, and profits' has often been before the courts, and by a long line of decisions the courts of chancery have declared that, unless these words be connected with other words which restrain the meaning of the term to the rents, issues, and profits as they arise (as if the trust is to pay debts out of the annual rents), the courts will give the words a meaning broad enough to include the sale of the property itself. The strict meaning of the words, as opposed to land, is the annual rents, issues, and profits; yet the courts hold that they should not be confined thereto, but should be taken, in a more enlarged sense, to include every mode by which land may be made to yield profits, out of which money so charged upon it may be taken, and, consequently, to include the sale of the property itself. The doctrine is thus laid down broadly by Judge Story in his work on Equity Jurisprudence. It is likewise laid down in Perry on Trusts, in Hawkins on Wills, Powell on Mortgages, and in other works, citing an array of authorities."[51]

§ 121. **Mortgage of Both Realty and Personalty.**—A mortgage may be made to cover both real and personal property; but in order to be effective as a security upon chattels described and pledged in it (other than chattels real), it is necessary that it should be executed, acknowledged, and recorded in accordance with the statute in reference to chattel mortgages.[52]

[50] First Nat. Bank v. Illinois Steel Co., 174 Ill. 140, 51 N. E. Rep. 200, affirming 72 Ill. App. 640.

[51] Charter Oak Life Ins. Co. v. Stephens, 5 Utah, 319, 15 Pac. Rep. 253.

[52] Long v. Cockern, 29 Ill. App. 304.

CHAPTER XI.

THE CONSIDERATION OF MORTGAGES.

§ 122. Necessity of a Consideration.—A mortgage being a conditional conveyance of property as a security for the payment of money or the performance of some act or duty, it is essential to its creation and existence that there should be a subsisting indebtedness or obligation to pay money or to perform some duty or act. When the debt or obligation is released or extinguished, the conveyance becomes null and void. Land cannot be conveyed as a security for a debt (that is, conveyed by way of mortgage), when no debt exists.[1] A mortgage, therefore, given without any consideration to support it, is void and cannot be enforced against the mortgagor, either by the original mortgagee or by his assignee.[2] Nor has it any effect as a lien; it can take effect in that character only from the time when some debt or liability secured by it is created.[3] But the consideration of a mortgage need not pass at the time of the execution of the instrument, but may be given prior or subsequent thereto.[4] It has been ruled that a deed of trust

---

[1] Rue v. Dole, 107 Ill. 275; Bacon v. National German-American Bk., 191 Ill. 205, 60 N. E. Rep. 846; Gaines v. Heaton, 100 Ill. App. 26, affirmed, 198 Ill. 479. Compare Fitzgerald v. Forristal, 48 Ill. 228.

[2] Stone v. Palmer, 68 Ill. App. 338, affirmed, 166 Ill. 463.

[3] Schaeppi v. Glade, 195 Ill. 62, 62 N. E. Rep. 874.

[4] Duncan v. Miller, 64 Iowa, 223, 20 N. W. Rep. 161.

given by a corporation to trustees, conveying its real property, to secure the performance of an undertaking which the company has made to pay dividends or interest on its guarantied preferred stock issued and sold, and ultimately to pay for the stock itself, is in the strictest sense a mortgage, resting upon a consideration.[5]

§ 123. Sufficiency of Consideration.—A pre-existing debt between the parties, whether past due or not yet payable, will serve as a sufficient consideration for a mortgage on the debtor's property; it is not necessary that there should be a new consideration created contemporaneously with the mortgage.[6] But doubt arises in cases where there is no debt or obligation, but a consideration to support the mortgage is attempted to be deduced from the mere relationship of the parties or the mutual interest of members of the same family. It has been ruled that a deed of trust, executed as security for notes which were given merely in consideration of natural love and affection, is invalid for want of consideration, and cannot be enforced against the grantee of the maker, unless such grantee has in some way assumed and agreed to pay the notes.[7] On the other hand, there is a decision that the relationship existing between father and daughter is sufficient to uphold a mortgage given by her to him as security for her deceased husband's debts, though they could not have been enforced as against her.[8] And in Illinois, it is settled that the husband's indebtedness is a sufficient consideration for a mortgage given by him and his wife jointly, on her separate property, to secure his debt.[9]

Indulgence given to the debtor is universally recognized as a good and sufficient consideration. Hence, where the creditor grants to the debtor an extension of the time for the payment of an antecedent debt, or for the payment of interest thereon, though it be for so short a time as a single day, it is a sufficient consideration to support a mortgage executed as security for the debt.[10] And more especially is this the case

---

[5] Fitch v. Wetherbee, 110 Ill. 475.

[6] Laubenheimer v. McDermott, 5 Mont. 512, 6 Pac. Rep. 344.

[7] Brooks v. Owen, 112 Mo. 251, 19 S. W. Rep. 723.

[8] Ray v. Hallenbeck, 42 Fed. Rep. 381.

[9] Edwards v. Schoeneman, 104 Ill. 278.

[10] Sullivan Savings Institution v. Young, 55 Iowa, 132; Martin v. Nixon, 92 Mo. 26, 4 S. W. Rep. 503.

where the extension of the time of payment of the debt is coupled with a further detriment to the creditor in the form of a reduction of the rate of interest.[11] In a case where a married woman executed a mortgage upon her property and delivered it to her husband, who used it as collateral security to obtain an extension on certain notes given by a firm of which he was a member, it was held that such extension was a sufficient consideration and the mortgage was valid, although the mortgagor had no knowledge at the time of its execution of the purpose for which it was to be used.[12]

Accord and satisfaction is also always a good consideration. Hence a mortgage executed in settlement of a controversy between the parties which was in litigation is founded upon a consideration sufficient to support it.[13] And a sufficient consideration is not lacking where a creditor surrenders a mortgage, with the accrued interest thereon, and takes a new mortgage in its place.[14] And again, where the claim of the creditor is for a considerable sum of money, but is not secured in any way, and he agrees with the debtor to accept the latter's note for a smaller sum with a mortgage on real property to secure it, this is a good accord and satisfaction, and it cannot be alleged that the mortgage does not rest upon a sufficient consideration.[15]

§ 124. Effect of Description of Debt in the Mortgage.—A mortgage expressed to be given as security for a particular debt, either present or prospective, cannot be enforced as security for another and different debt.[16] At the same time,

[11] Farmers' & Merchants' Nat. Bank v. Wallace, 45 Ohio St. 152.

[12] Maclaren v. Percival, 102 N. Y. 675. And see Burkle v. Levy, 70 Cal. 250, 11 Pac. Rep. 643. Compare Kansas Mfg. Co. v. Gandy, 11 Nebr. 448, 38 Am. Rep. 370.

[13] Commercial Exchange Bank v. McLeod, 67 Iowa, 718, 25 N. W. Rep. 894.

[14] Constant v. University of Rochester, 111 N. Y. 604.

[15] Post v. First Nat. Bank, 138 Ill. 559, 28 N. E. Rep. 978.

[16] Stone v. Palmer, 68 Ill. App. 338, affirmed, 166 Ill. 463. And see Lewter v. Price (Fla.), 6 South. Rep. 439; Morris v. Alston, 92 Ala. 502, 9 South. Rep. 315. Where the mortgage is expressed to secure the joint debt of two named parties and any individual debt of either of them, this will not cover a partnership obligation of a firm composed of such parties and a third person. In re Shevill, 11 Fed. Rep. 858. Where mortgagees agreed in writing with one purchasing the mortgaged property, consisting of a mill and machinery, from the mortgagor, that when they should receive all moneys due to them from the mortgagor and the firms of which

the validity of a mortgage does not depend upon the description of the debt, nor upon the form of the indebtedness; it depends rather upon the existence of the debt it was given to secure. It may be valid without a note or bond, although it purports to secure, and substantially describes, a note or bond. The true state of the indebtedness need not be disclosed by the instrument, but, in cases free from fraud, may be shown by parol.[17] Thus, where a mortgage purported on its face to have been executed to secure the payment of a designated sum according to the condition of a certain bond, and it appeared that no such bond was ever executed, it was held that that fact was not of itself fatal to the claims of the mortgagee, and that parol evidence might be received to sustain the mortgage.[18] In this connection it has been said: "While it is quite true that a written contract cannot be contradicted or varied by parol evidence, yet such evidence is competent to apply a written contract to its proper subject-matter; as, for example, in the case of a mortgage, to the debt really intended to be secured thereby." Hence such evidence is competent to show that a mortgage purporting to secure a note of an amount certain, therein described, was in fact security for future advances not to exceed the sum specified as the amount of the note.[19] It has even been held that parol evidence is admissible to show that a mortgage, apparently given to secure the debt of an individual, was really given as security for a debt due from a corporation.[20] And although the defeasance contained in the mortgage itself provides that the instrument shall be discharged upon the payment of a certain fixed sum, it may be shown, by a separate written agreement between the parties, that the mortgage was to stand as security for whatever sum should be found to be due on a future accounting and settlement between them; and if the sum so ascertained as due is less than the amount named in the mortgage, it is only for

---

he was a member they would assign and transfer to such purchaser their mortgage and all their claims upon the property, it was held that this estopped them from claiming, under their mortgage, any more than such indebtedness due to them from the mortgagor and his firms. Preble v. Conger, 66 Ill. 370.

[17] Lee v. Fletcher, 46 Minn. 49, 48 N. W. Rep. 456.

[18] Baldwin v. Raplee, 4 Bened. 433, Fed. Cas. No. 801.

[19] Moses v. Hatfield, 27 S. Car. 324, 3 S. E. Rep. 538.

[20] Jones v. New York Guaranty Co., 101 U. S. 622.

the smaller sum that the mortgagee can foreclose.[21] Again,
where the mortgage was given to secure the payment of a
certain note "and also in consideration of the further sum of
$500," it was held that parol evidence was admissible to show
the nature of the indebtedness and the true amount of the
consideration, and that the mention of the sum of $500 was suf-
ficient to put a subsequent purchaser of the premises on inquiry
as to the true amount due under the mortgage.[22] But where
a deed of trust specified that it was given to secure all indebtedness of the grantor as maker and indorser of notes and drafts
held by the beneficiary, a bank, or negotiated with it, through
the trustee, it was held that parol evidence was not admissible
to prove that, at the time of making the deed of trust, the
grantor verbally agreed that it should be held as security for
any debts due by him to the trustee individually,[23] for the very
obvious reason that this would not be applying the description
in the mortgage to its proper subject-matter, but applying the
mortgage to an entirely different debt from that mentioned and
described. A mortgage note or bond bearing interest at a given
rate continues to bear that rate of interest so long as the
principal remains unpaid.[24] In this connection, it may be
mentioned that, by a statute in Illinois, a penalty of twenty
per cent. is imposed for omitting prompt repayment of school
moneys loaned; but it is imposed only on the borrower, and is
not secured by the bond or mortgage.[25]

§ 125. Future Advances.—A mortgage may be made as well
to secure future advances of money to be made by the mortgagee to the mortgagor as for a present debt or liability, and
if executed in good faith, it will be a valid security.[26] And a
mortgage taken to secure future advances will be valid although it does not show upon its face the real character of the
transaction, except as against the rights of a person who has

[21] Stacey v. Randall, 17 Ill. 467.
Compare Moffitt v. Maness, 102 N.
Car. 457, 9 S. E. Rep. 399.

[22] Babcock v. Lisk, 57 Ill. 327.

[23] Union Nat. Bank v. International Bank, 22 Ill. App. 652, affirmed, 123 Ill. 510, 14 N. E. Rep.
859.

[24] United States Mortgage Co. v.
Sperry, 26 Fed. Rep. 727.

[25] Bradley v. Snyder, 14 Ill. 263.

[26] Lawrence v. Tucker, 23 How.
(U. S.) 14; Frye v. Bank of Illinois, 11 Ill. 367; Preble v. Conger,
66 Ill. 370. "A mortgage for future
advances was recognized as valid
by the common law. It is believed
they are held valid throughout the
United States, except where forbidden by the local law." Jones v.
New York Guaranty Co., 101 U. S.
622.

been prejudiced by the misrepresentation. But upon such a mortgage, the mortgagee can recover only the amount actually due at the date of the sale of the equity of redemption.[27] It is also settled that a mortgage to secure future advances may become a prior lien for the amount actually loaned, although the advancements are not made until after subsequent mortgages or other liens have come into force.[28] On this point the rule for determining questions of priority as between a mortgage for future advances and a subsequent mortgage securing a present debt depends upon the question whether the agreement of the parties left it optional with the first mortgagee to make the advances, or absolutely bound him to do so. It is stated as a settled rule that, "where the mortgagee has the option to make the advances or not, each advance is as upon a new mortgage [and will therefore be subordinated to intervening liens]; but where the mortgagee is bound to make the advances, the lien relates back to the date of the mortgage and is superior to any subsequent lien or conveyance."[29] But where a first mortgage is given to secure future advances, and a second mortgage attaches, the first mortgagee must have notice of the existence of the second, in order that the second mortgagee can claim to have priority over advances made by the first after the attaching of the second and which it was optional with the first to make. But constructive notice to the first mortgagee is sufficient; and the recording of the junior mortgage will charge him with such notice.[30]

Even after breach of condition of the mortgage, the mortgagee may make further advances under an oral agreement that the mortgage shall stand as security for them; and a court of equity will not aid the mortgagor to redeem without requiring repayment of such advances in addition to the amount due on the original debt. Equity will impose this condition on the mortgagor to avoid circuity of action, and also on the principle that he who seeks equity must do equity. But "this doctrine is limited to cases where the mortgagee is invested with the legal title to the property, and makes further advances, in addition to the original debt secured, upon the credit of the

[27] Collins v. Carlile, 13 Ill. 254; Brant v. Hutchinson, 40 Ill. App. 576.

[28] Schimberg v. Waite, 93 Ill. App. 130.

[29] Tompkins v. Little Rock & F. S. Ry. Co., 15 Fed. Rep. 6.

[30] Frye v. Bank of Illinois, 11 Ill. 367.

land to which the title is held, and where the title held is made available to secure the further advances by a legal contract between the parties, and where the rights of subsequent incumbrancers or persons who have acquired junior liens are not prejudiced thereby. Debts created or advances made to a mortgagor subsequent to the mortgage cannot be tacked to the mortgage debt to the prejudice of third persons who have acquired junior liens upon the mortgaged property."[31]

§ 126. **Mortgage by Surety or Guarantor.**—A mortgage may be given to secure a debt or liability by a person who is secondarily liable therefor, in the character of a surety or guarantor for the principal debtor; and the contingent liability of the mortgagor will constitute a sufficient consideration for the instrument. But in order to create an enforceable liability upon a mortgage executed by one as surety or guarantor for another, the actual debt must correspond with that recited in the mortgage, and any particular limitations set forth in the mortgage must be strictly followed.[32] But these conditions being met, the courts have no hesitation in enforcing mortgages of this kind. In one of the cases, it appeared that two parties were liable on a promissory note held by a bank, the one as principal and the other as surety. On its maturity, the surety made a new note for the same amount to the principal debtor, which the latter indorsed, and the bank took the new note, secured by a mortgage on the surety's land, in payment of the old. On bill to foreclose the mortgage, the surety contended that, as he owed nothing to the principal debtor, the bank could not enforce the note and mortgage. But it was held that, the note being intended as a payment to the bank, it might be considered as given directly to the bank, and therefore the mortgage could be foreclosed by the bank.[33] In another case, pending an appeal from a judgment against certain joint obligors, one of the defendants gave a deed of trust to secure the payment of such judgment, or any judgment rendered in any other suit on the same cause of action. The judgment was reversed and the suit abandoned. After the death of the mortgagor defendant and one of the plaintiffs, the surviving plaintiffs sued the surviving defendants on the

[31] Carpenter v. Plagge, 192 Ill.   Ryan v. Shawneetown, 14 Ill. 20.
82, 61 N. E. Rep. 530.   [33] First Nat. Bank v. Davis, 108
[32] Thomas v. Olney, 16 Ill. 53;   Ill. 633.

same cause of action, and recovered a judgment. It was held that the deed of trust might be enforced as security for the payment of such second judgment, notwithstanding the change in the parties.[34]

§ 127. **Indemnity Mortgages.**—It is well settled that a mortgage given by way of indemnity, that is, to secure the mortgagee against loss or damage in consequence of his liability as surety for the mortgagor, is valid and enforceable, the contingent responsibility of the surety being a sufficient consideration to support it.[35] The kind of liability assumed by the mortgagee is not very material, provided only that it is a responsibility which may involve him in the payment of money on the default of the mortgagor. For instance, a mortgage executed by parties living in Illinois, to be used in another state, to indemnify any person who might become bail for a person who had been indicted in the latter state for a criminal offense, which mortgage is assigned to the person who became bail, is valid, and may be enforced to the extent of the loss suffered by the bail on the recognizance.[36] So a deed by a defaulting state officer, in trust to indemnify the sureties on his official bond, is good, and will take precedence of any lien the state may subsequently acquire by judgment against him.[37] The liability of the surety need not even be a present one; the mortgage may cover a liability which he has agreed to assume in the future. Thus, a mortgage given to indemnify a person against loss or damage growing out of indorsements thereafter to be made by the mortgagee for the mortgagor is valid, and will create a lien superior to the lien of a judgment recovered after such indorsements have been made.[38]

Where a debtor gives a mortgage to his surety to indemnify the latter against loss, the mortgage cannot be enforced until the liability of the mortgagee has become absolutely fixed. The property mortgaged can be applied to the indemnification of the mortgagee only when the latter has actually paid the debt for which he was surety or has become immediately and

[34] Walker v. Rand, 131 Ill. 27, 22 N. E. Rep. 1006.

[35] Duncan v. Miller, 64 Iowa, 223, 20 N. W. Rep. 161; Williams v. Silliman, 74 Tex. 626, 12 S. W. Rep. 534.

[36] Stevens v. Hay, 61 Ill. 399.

[37] State v. Hemingway, (Miss.), 10 South Rep. 575.

[38] Kramer v. Farmers' & Mechanics' Bank, 15 Ohio, 253.

certainly liable for its payment; until then a court of equity will not interfere.[39] So, also, where mortgages are given by co-sureties, each to the other to indemnify him for an over-payment, unless one of them has been compelled to pay and has in fact paid an excess beyond his agreed share of the debt, there can have been no breach of the condition of the mortgage and consequently no right to a foreclosure and sale of the mortgaged premises.[40] And for the same reason, when a surety holds a note and mortgage for purposes of indemnity and assigns the same, his assignee cannot enforce the mortgage until the mortgagee has paid the debt for which he was surety or in some way has been damnified.[41]

If the principal debtor duly pays or discharges the debt or obligation, thus releasing the surety from liability, the consideration of the mortgage will of course fail and the instrument will lose its vitality. And so it is held that, when there has been no breach of the condition of an indemnity mortgage, and when it is certain that there never can be such breach, because of the illegality of the claim against which the mortgagee was to be indemnified, a subsequent purchaser of the mortgaged premises may maintain a bill to have the mortgage cancelled as a cloud upon his title.[42] But if a breach of condition has occurred, it is said that costs of collection, as being an incident of the debt, are embraced in and secured by the indemnity mortgage.[43]

In regard to the interest which the creditor may have in such a mortgage, it is ruled that, when the purpose of a mortgage given by a debtor to his surety is personal, and it is intended solely to indemnify the surety, the creditor can avail himself of such mortgage only by subrogation, claiming through the surety, and therefore he cannot proceed until a remedy accrues to the surety by his being actually damnified or becoming liable for the debt. But when the mortgage is given for the

[39] Constant v. Matteson, 22 Ill. 546. But the sale of land under a trust deed given to indemnify a surety will not be enjoined where the debt is past due, and the parties have agreed that the trustee may advertise in time to sell by a certain day, although the surety has not yet paid the debt. Brower v. Buxton, 101 N. Car. 419, 8 S. E. Rep. 116.

[40] Hampton v. Phipps, 108 U. S. 260.

[41] Stevens v. Hurlburt, 25 Ill. App. 124.

[42] Hopple v. Hipple, 33 Ohio St. 116.

[43] Williams v. Silliman, 74 Tex. 626, 12 S. W. Rep. 534.

better security of the debt, or to provide the surety with means
to pay it in case of the principal's default, then, although the
purpose is to indemnify the surety, a trust also attaches to the
mortgage for the benefit of the creditor which the courts will
enforce.[44]

§ 128. **Usury.**—In Illinois, the legal rate of interest is five
per cent. Parties may contract for seven per cent., but no
more, under penalty of forfeiture of the entire interest contracted for, provided the usury is pleaded.[45] The usury laws
apply to mortgages given by private individuals and corporations (and to the obligations they are given to secure), but not,
as it would appear, to mortgages executed under the authority
and direction of a court. On this point we find a decision in
another state to the effect that, where a court of equity has
charge of a trust estate by receivers appointed by it, and
through them executes a mortgage on the lands of the estate,
the cestuis que trustent cannot raise the question of usury as
a defense to an action for the foreclosure of the mortgage.
The court, it was said, is amply able to protect itself against
extortion, and is not in the position of a needy individual
forced by his necessities to submit to unconscionable charges.[46]

The exaction of usury does not commonly appear on the face
of the mortgage. And when the contract on its face is for
legal interest only, then, in order to constitute usury, it must
be proved that there was some corrupt agreement, device, or
shift to cover usury, and that it was intended by the parties.[47]
The form of the transaction is of little consequence, the inquiry being in all cases as to the real intention of the parties.
Thus, where a principal note contained a promise to pay interest, and notes for the amount of the interest were also given,
this fact being recited in the principal note, it was held that
this did not render the transaction usurious, only one payment
of interest being in fact intended.[48] So, where the borrower

---

[44] Chambers v. Prewitt, 172 Ill.
615, 50 N. E. Rep. 145. But mortgages given by co-sureties, each to
the other as security to indemnify
him against any claim against his
proportion assumed, are not in
equity securities for the payment
of the principal debt which inure
to the benefit of creditors upon the
principle of subrogation. Hampton v. Phipps, 108 U. S. 260.

[45] Rev. Stat. Ill. c. 74, §§ 1-7.

[46] Burroughs v. Gaither, 66 Md.
171, 7 Atl. Rep. 243.

[47] Omaha Hotel Co. v. Wade, 97
U. S. 13.

[48] Abbott v. Stone, 70 Ill. App.
671, affirmed, 172 Ill. 634.

agreed to pay interest at the rate of six per cent., but in case payments were not made promptly, then the principal was to draw ten per cent., it was held that the agreement to pay increased interest in case of default was in the nature of a penalty, and did not taint the original transaction with usury.[49] And where one of two loans is usurious, the other is not affected merely because they were made at about the same time and are secured by the same mortgage. If the loans are in fact separate and independent, they will be so treated in regard to usury.[50]

The right to insist upon a forfeiture of interest on account of usury may also be waived by the debtor. Thus, a mortgagor who has conveyed the mortgaged land to the mortgagee, in consideration of a release from personal liability on the debt secured, cannot afterwards attack the mortgage on the ground of usury, since the conveyance constitutes a voluntary payment of the entire debt.[51] And the grantor in a deed of trust which authorizes a sale on the non-payment of interest, for the entire debt, cannot show, in an action of forcible detainer against him by the purchaser at foreclosure sale, that there was no interest due, on account of usury in the transaction; the purchaser's title cannot be questioned for such cause in this form of action, the grantor's remedy, if any, being in equity.[52]

§ 129. Same; Commissions of Broker or Agent.—It is a well-established rule in Illinois that brokers, in negotiating loans of the money of others, may charge the borrower commissions, without thereby making the loan usurious, although it already bears the full legal rate of interest. If the broker acts as the agent of the mortgagor, his commission may be regarded as compensation for his services in procuring the loan, and is not a part of the consideration of the mortgage. If he represents

[49] Upton v. O'Donahue (Nebr.), 49 N. W. Rep. 267.

[50] Jackson v. May, 28 Ill. App. 305.

[51] Mason v. Pierce, 142 Ill. 331, 31 N. E. Rep. 503. In another case, a debtor, as security for a usurious loan, executed a trust deed of land. On default in payments, the land was sold under the deed of trust to the creditor. Afterwards an arrangement was entered into between the parties as a final adjustment of all matters between them, by which a portion of the land was conveyed back to the debtor, and the latter gave his note, secured by deed of trust, for the purchase money. It was held that the usury of the former transaction did not affect the new note given. Ryan v. Newcomb, 125 Ill. 91, 16 N. E. Rep. 878.

[52] Chapin v. Billings, 91 Ill. 539.

11

the lender, his commission cannot be considered as usury, unless it is shown that his principal received the benefit of it, or authorized such a charge to be made in excess of the legal interest, or at any rate had knowledge of it.[53] So, where a principal makes a loan through his agent, who is not authorized to charge more than the legal rate of interest, and the principal does not know that the agent has so charged excessive interest, and does not receive the excess, the transaction is not usurious as to the principal.[54] But where the agent who makes an usurious loan is a general agent, his principal is held to notice of the usury.[55] Thus, where a principal deposits money to the credit of his agent, with the privilege of loaning it, stipulating that it shall net the owner ten per cent., the agent becomes the general agent of the owner; and if the agent exacts usury from his loans, the principal is presumed to have known and authorized it; and unless this presumption is rebutted, the transaction will be usurious.[56] And where a person agrees with a trust company to procure and forward applications for loans, with the understanding that he shall receive no compensation from the company, but is to obtain his remuneration from borrowers, and he thereafter, in communications to the company and to others, styles himself as "agent" for it, he must be so considered; and a payment to him of a commission by the borrower for securing a loan from the company at the highest legal rate makes the transaction usurious.[57] But, on the other hand, the fact that a loan agent, who is in the habit of sending applications to and obtaining loans from an insurance company, as well as other parties, is the agent of said company for the purpose of procuring insurance does not constitute him its agent in respect to loans procured by him from it, and so render it liable on a charge of usury for commissions deducted by him.[58]

It is also permissible for the parties to agree that the mort-

---

[53] Haldeman v. Massachusetts Mut. Life Ins. Co., 21 Ill. App. 146; Goodwin v. Bishop, 145 Ill. 421, 34 N. E. Rep. 47; Ballinger v. Bourland, 87 Ill. 513; Cox. v. Insurance Co., 113 Ill. 385; Haldeman v. Massachusetts Mut. Life Ins. Co., 120 Ill. 390, 11 N. E. Rep. 526; Jennings v. Hunt, 6 Ill. App. 523; Phillips v. Roberts, 90 Ill. 492.

[54] Telford v. Garrells, 31 Ill. App. 441.

[55] Matzenbaugh v. Troup, 36 Ill. App. 261.

[56] Stevens v. Meers, 11 Ill. App. 133.

[57] Fowler v. Equitable Trust Co., 141 U. S. 384, following Payne v. Newcomb, 100 Ill. 611.

[58] Massachusetts Mut. Life Ins.

gagor shall pay a reasonable fee to the attorney or the broker who negotiates the loan, to cover the cost of abstracting or examining the title to the mortgaged property, or for the expense of preparing and recording the mortgage. This may be by a direct payment, or by a proportionate deduction from the money loaned. In either case, if it is done in good faith and not as a mere cloak for the exaction of excessive interest, it does not render the transaction obnoxious to the laws against usury, although the loan bears the highest legal rate of interest.[59] But where a charge for expense and trouble on the part of the lender himself, in securing money with which to make the loan, is included in the note, the transaction is usurious if the total of such charge and the interest reserved exceed the legal rate.[60]

§ 130. **Same; Interest on Overdue Interest.**—Where the debt secured by a mortgage is evidenced by a promissory note, and separate coupons or interest notes are given for the successive installments of interest on the debt, it is lawful to make such interest notes or coupons bear interest, each from the date of its maturity until it is paid; and although the rate of interest stipulated for on the principal debt is already as high as the law allows, this reservation of interest on overdue installments of interest will not make the loan usurious.[61] But compound interest reserved directly on the debt itself is not lawful. An agreement to make interest, as it matures, become principal, so as to bear interest, when such interest is not evidenced by separate negotiable instruments, and the rate of interest charged is the highest legal rate, constitutes usury.[62]

§ 131. **Same; Stipulation for Attorney's Fee, Taxes, and Insurance.**—A provision in a mortgage for the payment by the mortgagor of a reasonable fee for the mortgagee's attorney in case of foreclosure, as a part of the expenses of the foreclos-

Co. v. Boggs, 121 Ill. 119, 13 N. E. Rep. 550.

[59] Goodwin v. Bishop, 145 Ill. 421, 34 N. E. Rep. 47; Ammondson v. Ryan, 111 Ill. 506; Goodwin v. Bishop, 50 Ill. App. 145; Ellenbogen v. Griffey, 55 Ark. 268, 18 S. W. Rep. 126.

[60] Jackson v. May, 28 Ill. App. 305.

[61] Telford v. Garrels, 132 Ill. 550, 24 N. E. Rep. 573; Abbott v. Stone, 172 Ill. 634, 50 N. E. Rep. 328, affirming 70 Ill. App. 671. And see Hawley v. Howell, 60 Iowa, 79, 14 N. W. Rep. 199; Taylor v. Hiestand, 46 Ohio St. 345, 20 N. E. Rep. 345.

[62] Drury v. Wolfe, 134 Ill. 294, 25 N. E. Rep. 626.

ure, does not render the mortgage usurious, although such fee is described in the mortgage as a certain percentage upon the principal, interest, and costs, and although the addition of such fee to the interest reserved would raise the rate of interest above the legal limit.[63] It is true, such arrangements may be resorted to as a cloak to cover up a transaction really usurious in its nature; and when this is clearly shown to be the case, the courts will visit the mortgagee with the penalties of usury. But in an action on a note or mortgage containing a provision for attorney's fees, not on its face usurious, the defendant has the burden of proving that such provision was intended as a cover for usury.[64]

A covenant on the part of the mortgagor to pay all the taxes assessed upon the land, in addition to interest at the highest legal rate, does not make the contract usurious; for it is his duty in any event to pay the taxes, and the amount expended for this purpose does not swell the profits of the mortgagee, nor inure to his benefit, except indirectly.[65] And for similar reasons, a stipulation in the mortgage that the borrower shall keep the buildings on the mortgaged land insured in some responsible company, and shall pay the premiums on such insurance, does not make the transaction obnoxious to the laws against usury, although the interest reserved on the debt is at the highest rate allowed by the law.[66]

§ 132. Same; Contracts of Loan Associations.—Under the laws in force in Illinois, contracts of a building and loan association with its members are not usurious, although the borrower may be required to pay a higher price for the use of the money advanced to him than is allowable under the general law regulating the rate of interest; and consequently, usury is no defense to a proceeding to foreclose a mortgage given by him to secure such loan.[67] But to enjoy this immunity from the operation of the laws against usury, it is necessary that the money of the association available for loans should be

---

[63] Clawson v. Munson, 55 Ill. 394; Barton v. Farmers' & Merchants' Nat. Bank, 122 Ill. 352, 13 N. E. Rep. 503; Abbott v. Stone, 172 Ill. 634, 50 N. E. Rep. 328, affirming 70 Ill. App 671; Matzenbaugh v. Troup, 36 Ill. App. 261.

[64] Mumford v. Tolman, 157 Ill. 258, 41 N. E. Rep. 617.

[65] Kidder v. Vandersloot, 114 Ill. 133.

[66] New England Mortgage Security Co. v. Gay, 33 Fed. Rep. 636.

[67] Hedley v. Geissler, 90 Ill. App. 565; Rhodes v. Missouri Sav. & Loan Co., 63 Ill. App. 77.

offered at a public meeting of the directors of the association to the highest bidder. If the interest reserved in a mortgage made to the association is not thus fixed by competitive bidding, and exceeds the legal rate, the contract is usurious, and the usual consequences follow.[68]

§ 133. Same; Conflict of Laws.—In a contract for the loan of money, the law of the place where the contract is made is to govern; and it is immaterial that the loan was to be secured by a mortgage on lands in another state. In such a case, the statutes of usury of the state where the contract was made, and not those of the state where the mortgaged lands lie, are to govern it, unless there be some other circumstance to show that the parties had in view the laws of the latter state.[69] Consequently, when a mortgage conveys lands situated in Illinois, but the note, bond, or contract which it secures is made in another state, the question whether the rate of interest reserved is usurious, so as to invalidate the security, is to be determined with reference to the laws of such other state, not the laws of Illinois.[70] And where notes are executed and made payable in one state, and the maker resides and intends to use the money borrowed in another state, where also the property mortgaged to secure the payment of the notes is situated, the *locus contractus* is the state in which the notes were executed and made payable.[71] And if the contract is made in Illinois, and the mortgaged lands also lie in the same state, the rate of interest which the parties may agree upon is determined by the laws of Illinois, notwithstanding the fact that the repayment is expressly stipulated to be made in some other state; so that, if the interest exacted is lawful in Illinois, it is entirely immaterial that the rate may be greater than would be allowed by the laws of the state where payment is to be made.[72]

§ 134. Same; Relief in Equity on Bill to Redeem.—Where a debtor applies to a court of equity for relief against an usurious contract, the court will grant the relief asked only on

[68] Jurgens v. Jamieson, 97 Ill. App. 557; Trainor v. German-American Sav., L. & B. Ass'n, 102 Ill. App. 604.

[69] DeWolf v. Johnson, 10 Wheat. 367; Lockwood v. Mitchell, 7 Ohio St. 387.

[70] Adams v. Robertson, 37 Ill. 45.

[71] Central Trust Co. v. Burton, 74 Wis. 329, 43 N. W. Rep. 141.

[72] Fowler v. Equitable Trust Co., 141 U. S. 384. And see Joslin v. Miller, 14 Nebr. 91, 15 N. W. Rep. 214; Fitch v. Remer, 1 Biss. 337, s. c., 1 Flip. 15, Fed. Cas. No. 4,836.

condition that he shall pay the principal of the debt with legal
interest. That is, it will relieve him from the necessity of
paying more than the legal rate of interest, but will not decree
a forfeiture of all interest; and this, on the principle that he
who seeks equity must do equity.[73] Hence a mortgagor, seeking to redeem, cannot, in equity, insist upon a forfeiture of all
interest because usury has been agreed upon or reserved. He
will be required to pay interest at the legal rate, whether an
agreement for usurious interest is established or not.[74] And in
an action to foreclose a mortgage, a cross bill for relief, on the
ground of usury, should be dismissed, if the defendant does
not offer to pay the mortgage debt with legal interest.[75]

§ 135. Same; On Bill for Foreclosure.—Where the aid of a
court of equity is invoked by the mortgagee, as on a bill to
foreclose the mortgage, if it is shown that the mortgage is
tainted with usury, a forfeiture of all interest follows as a necessary consequence under the statute, and it would be erroneous
to allow the mortgagee interest at the legal rate.[76] In some
states, the rule is strictly applied that a defendant who desires
to avail himself of the defense of usury to a bill to foreclose
a mortgage must set up the usury specifically and particularly,
stating the terms of the agreement and the amount of the
usurious interest.[77] But in Illinois, the courts are unwilling to
apply too rigid a rule. It is held, for instance, that where the
answer to a bill to foreclose a mortgage, praying an account
on the notes secured, simply claims, without itemizing, that
the usurious interest paid in excess of the legal rate should be
applied as a credit on the debt, it will avail for such payments,
either on the notes or in the transactions upon which they were
based.[78] And where the bill on its face discloses the fact that
a higher rate of interest has been reserved in the contract than
the law allows, and the master computes the interest on that
basis, the question of usury may be presented by exceptions to
the master's report, without having been raised by answer or

[73] Clark v. Finlon, 90 Ill. 245.
[74] Sutphen v. Cushman, 35 Ill.
186; Snyder v. Griswold, 37 Ill.
216; Cushman v. Sutphen, 42 Ill.
256.
[75] Stevens v. Meers, 11 Ill. App.
138.
[76] Snyder v. Griswold, 37 Ill. 216;

Cushman v. Sutphen, 42 Ill. 256;
Clark v. Finlon, 90 Ill. 245; Harbison v. Houghton, 41 Ill. 522.
[77] Kilpatrick v. Henson, 81 Ala.
482, 1 South. Rep. 188.
[78] Jenkins v. Greenbaum, 95 Ill.
11.

plea.[79] Where the defense of usury is set up in the answer, the complainant may remit all claims for interest, and have a decree for the amount of money actually advanced and other legal charges.[80] And, on the other hand, where a bill is filed to foreclose an usurious mortgage, in which the usurious interest is claimed, if the mortgagor pays into court all that the mortgagee is legally entitled to, the bill should be dismissed at the cost of the complainant.[81] Where, by an oversight in not erasing the rate of interest printed in an old blank form of mortgage, advances for taxes and insurance are made to draw usurious interest, but the principal sum loaned draws legal interest only, it is proper for the court, on foreclosure, to confine the effect of the usurious agreement to advances for the purposes mentioned.[82]

§ 136. Right of Mortgagor's Grantee to Plead Usury.—In one of the earlier cases in Illinois it was said: "There is some discrepancy in the authorities as to how far other persons beside the debtor may raise the question of usury. We hold the better rule to be that if, in a sale of land subject to a mortgage tainted with usury, the purchaser is informed of the fact of the usury by the vendor, and authorized by him to set it up as against the mortgage, the abatement to which the mortgage would be subject on account of usury thus constituting an element in the price of the land, the purchaser in such circumstances would be at liberty to raise the question. But if the mortgage on its face draws only legal interest, and the purchaser buys from the mortgagor subject to the mortgage as it stands, no reference being had in the price to any hidden taint of usury, the presumption is that the vendor desires the mortgage paid according to its terms, and it is not for the purchaser, who has bought the land expressly subject to the mortgage, and who has probably been allowed for it in the purchase money, to undertake to evade its full payment by setting up usury."[83] In a later case, the principles which should govern this question, in its various possible phases, were fully discussed and settled on lines which have not since been departed from.

[79] Drake v. Latham, 50 Ill. 270.

[80] Stanley v. Chicago Trust & Sav. Bank, 61 Ill. App. 257, affirmed, 165 Ill. 295.

[81] Blythe v. Small, 67 Ill. App. 319.

[82] Lurton v. Jacksonville Loan & Bldg. Ass'n, 187 Ill. 141, 58 N. E. Rep. 218, affirming 87 Ill. App. 395.

[83] Henderson v. Bellew, 45 Ill. 322.

The court said: "It seems to be the doctrine generally recognized that if a party purchases from a mortgagor without any deduction from the price on account of the incumbrance, the grantee thereby becomes invested with the right to interpose the same defenses as might have been made by the mortgagor. In such a case, the conveyance amounts to an authority to the purchaser to interpose the defense of usury. In another class of cases it is held that, where the mortgagor only sells the equity of redemption, or the amount of the incumbrance is deducted from the purchase money, the grantee or junior mortgagee will not be permitted to make the defense of usury. In some of the cases referred to the mortgagor made default or had failed in his defense of usury, but the grantee or subsequent mortgagee was nevertheless permitted to set up and rely upon the defense. The principle announced is that a person purchasing the title, or receiving a junior mortgage, without receiving any deduction from the price because of the usury, is such a privy of the mortgagor as may urge this defense. It is true that in some cases it is said that the grantee or a subsequent mortgagee cannot interpose the defense without the permission of the mortgagor. But it is not held that such authority must be express, either written or verbal. We apprehend that an implied authority is all that is required, and we hold that when it is not agreed or understood that the grantee or subsequent mortgagee shall pay the incumbrance with the usury, the authority to make the defense will be implied. The cases in this court do not announce a rule in conflict with this conclusion. It is true they do say there must be express authority, but in that the expression is inaccurate, as implied authority only is required. Equity and good conscience demand that when the mortgagor conceals, fraudulently or otherwise, the existence of the incumbrance, and his grantee purchases without actual notice, he should be permitted to set up and rely upon the usury. On the other hand, where the grantee contracts with a view to the incumbrance, or is informed of its existence and fails to obtain permission to urge the defense, or fails to take covenants against the incumbrance, the presumption is that the incumbrance, as it appears on its face, formed a part of the consideration he was to pay for the property, and it would be inequitable to permit him to escape its burden. The party holding an usurious agreement has no legal right to its enforcement. It is only when the defense is

not interposed that he may recover his usurious interest; and
he will not be permitted to do so when it will operate unjustly
against others who are in no fault. He has knowingly violated
the statute, whilst a grantee who purchases without examining a record simply omits a precaution usually employed by
prudent persons, the omission of which may subject him to
loss.''[84] It is also held that if a party sells land subject to a
mortgage thereon, which is given to secure a debt, with usury
reserved, and the purchaser assumes the payment of the debt
as a part of the purchase money, he cannot interpose the
defense of usury to a bill to foreclose the mortgage, nor can
any one claiming under him.[85] But where the mortgagor
inserts in the deed a clause to the effect that it is subject to the
prior mortgage "which the grantee assumes and agrees to
pay, except as to any usurious and illegal interest in the
same,'' the effect of the provision is that the right of the
mortgagor to an abatement of the usury will be understood
to have entered into the consideration of the purchase as an
element of the price, and the grantee will have the right to
question the validity of the mortgage in respect to usury.[86]
On the other hand, where a conveyance was made subject to a
mortgage, and the purchaser expressly covenanted to pay the
indebtedness secured thereby, and the amount of the incumbrance, provisionally at least, was deducted from the price,
but it was claimed that there was an oral contemporaneous
agreement by which the purchaser was to endeavor to reduce
the amount of the incumbrance by setting up the usury, and
in case of success, to pay to the grantor the amount of the
reduction out of the purchase money retained by him, it was
held that the rights of the parties must be controlled exclusively by the terms and covenants of the deed, the oral agreement being incompetent to contradict the terms of the written
agreement.[87]

§ 137. Right of Junior Mortgagee to Allege Usury.—Notwithstanding some dicta in the cases cited in the preceding

[84] Maher v. Lanfrom, 86 Ill. 513.
And see Essley v. Sloan, 116 Ill.
391, 6 N. E. Rep. 449; Crawford v.
Nimmons, 180 Ill. 143, 54 N. E.
Rep. 209, reversing 80 Ill. App.
543; Essley v. Sloan, 16 Ill. App.
63; Flanders v. Doyle, Id. 508;

Cleaver v. Burcky, 17 Ill. App. 92;
Wightman v. Suddard, 93 Ill. App.
142.
[85] Stiger v. Bent, 111 Ill. 328.
[86] Pike v. Crist, 62 Ill. 461.
[87] Cleaver v. Burcky, 17 Ill. App.
92.

section, which would appear to place a junior mortgagee of land in the same position with a purchaser of the equity of redemption, in respect to the right to plead usury as against the senior mortgage, it must not be inferred that their rights are identical. On the contrary, a second mortgagee, whose mortgage has not been foreclosed, and who has not been let into possession under his mortgage, cannot set up the defense of usury to a bill to foreclose the first mortgage. On this point it has been said: "It would seem to be self-evident that the same right to elect to plead usury to a mortgage, or to waive the usury, and affirm the entire validity of the mortgage, cannot be in different and distinct parties in interest at the same time; for if this were not so, one party might elect to do one thing, and the other party might elect to do directly the opposite, and thus one election would nullify the other. The equity of redemption of the mortgagor is the right to redeem from the first and senior mortgage, either by paying the amount of the principal debt only, or by paying that amount and the amount of interest usuriously contracted to be paid, as he shall elect. The junior mortgage, conveying a lien only on that right, does not cut it off, but leaves it still to be exercised by the mortgagor until he shall terminate it by grant or it shall be terminated by foreclosure. The junior mortgagee does not, therefore, occupy the same relation toward the property that the mortgagor did before he executed that mortgage; and since the mortgagor has not parted with his right of election to plead or to waive the defense of usury, it is impossible that the junior mortgagee can have acquired it."[88] So also, where a mortgage secures the payment of separate debts to two different persons, and a contest arises between them as to the division of the proceeds of the mortgaged property, one creditor cannot raise against the other the question of usury in behalf of the debtor; the latter must assert his own rights.[89] Finally, usury in a mortgage cannot be taken advantage of by a judgment creditor of the mortgagor.[90]

[88] Union Nat. Bank of Chicago v. International Bank of Chicago, 123 Ill. 510, 14 N. E. Rep. 859. And see Tyler v. Massachusetts Mut. Life Ins. Co., 108 Ill. 58.

[89] Adams v. Robertson, 37 Ill. 45.
[90] Mason v. Pierce, 142 Ill. 331, 31 N. E. Rep. 503.

CHAPTER XII

FRAUDULENT AND INVALID MORTGAGES.

§ 138. Fraud as to Creditors of Mortgagor.—Where the owner of real property gives a mortgage on the same with the purpose and intention of hindering, delaying, or defrauding his creditors, and such purpose is known to and participated in by the mortgagee, the conveyance is invalid by reason of the fraud, and may be avoided, or its foreclosure as a lien prevented, at the instance of the creditors to whose prejudice it operates. Equity will not lend its aid to the consummation of a dishonest scheme of this kind.[1] The same rule applies without regard to the form given to the transaction. Deeds of trust, equally with mortgages, are invalid when made to defraud creditors; and it is held that a conveyance which is absolute and unconditional on its face, but which is really intended as a mere security and is therefore to be regarded in equity as a mortgage, is constructively fraudulent as to the other creditors of the grantor; it is a secret trust and is therefore fraudulent in law.[2] And subsequent creditors, as well as those whose claims existed at the time the mortgage was made, may attack it for fraud. But a mortgage made by one indebted at the time, though without consideration, cannot be avoided by subsequent creditors without showing actual fraud or a secret trust for the benefit of the grantor.[3]

But though a note is executed without any consideration,

[1] Scott v. Magloughlin, 33 Ill. App. 162; Griffin v. Haskins, 22 Ill. App. 264; Kirkpatrick v. Clark, 132 Ill. 342, 24 N. E. Rep. 71.

[2] Beidler v. Crane, 135 Ill. 92, 25 N. E. Rep. 655; Watkins v. Arms, 64 N. H. 99, 6 Atl. Rep. 92.

[3] Webb v. Roff, 9 Ohio St. 430.

and a mortgage given to secure it, with the intent to defraud a third person, the mortgage may be valid and binding as between the mortgagor and mortgagee, under the statute of frauds. Assuming the mortgagee to be innocent of any participation in the fraudulent purpose of the mortgagor, the conveyance will be voidable only as to the party or parties intended to be hindered or defrauded.[4] But where a mortgage is given, not for any consideration received by the mortgagor at the time of its execution, or any detriment then suffered by the mortgagee, but to secure a debt that has long existed, the mortgagor is not the recipient of such benefits under the mortgage that he will be estopped to deny its validity.[5] And notwithstanding the intended fraud upon third persons, the mortgagor is not without remedy against the mortgagee if he has satisfied the obligation meant to be secured, or otherwise fulfilled the terms of the agreement. Thus, if the conveyance took the form of an absolute deed with a parol defeasance, he may maintain a bill for redemption, or, if he has paid the debt, he may invoke the aid of a court of equity to have the deed declared a satisfied mortgage and cancelled.[6] It was said by the court in the case cited: "It is doubtless the rule that where parties are concerned in illegal agreements, they are left without remedy against each other, provided they are in pari delicto. The law in such cases refuses to lend its aid to either party, but leaves them where it finds them, to suffer the consequences of their illegal or immoral acts. This rule is applied to executed transactions as well as those which are executory, and is enforced by courts of law as well as courts of equity. But the fraudulent grantor, though unable to assert or maintain any rights or remedies founded on the unlawful thing done or intended to be done, does not forfeit any right or privilege beyond that, or with respect to any other matter or thing not within the purpose of the wrongful act, and not affected by the corrupt intent, or caused or produced in consequence of it. To the extent of his intended wrong he is without remedy, but in all other respects his rights and remedies are the same as if no such wrong had been done or intended. Though guilty of a wrong or transgression of the law

---

[4] Fitzgerald v. Forristal, 48 Ill. 228. See Ellwood v. Walter, 103 Ill. App. 219.

[5] State Nat. Bank v. Union Nat. Bank, 68 Ill. App. 25, affirmed, 168 Ill. 519, 48 N. E. Rep. 82.

[6] Halloran v. Halloran, 137 Ill. 100, 27 N. E. Rep. 82.

in one particular, he does not become an outlaw or forfeit his rights to legal protection in all others, nor lay himself open to the frauds and machinations of others to be practised against him with impunity. It must be clearly shown that the debtor seeks relief from the fruit of his own wrong, or from the consequences of his own unlawful act, before his action can be dismissed. If it be not these, but something outside and independent of his unlawful act or purpose, and not necessarily resulting from it, he is entitled to favorable consideration, and his action should be retained.''

§ 139. **Preferences not Necessarily Fraudulent.**—A mortgage is not necessarily fraudulent simply because it gives to one creditor an advantage over others. A debtor, even though insolvent, may in good faith secure a particular bona fide creditor, by mortgage, to the exclusion of all others.[7] ''A creditor has unquestionably the right to pursue his legal remedies against his debtor, so long as he does so in good faith, and if he thus succeeds in obtaining priority, either by suit or by the voluntary act of his debtor, he is entitled to hold the advantage gained, even though the result may be to postpone or even defeat other creditors. This court has long adhered to the doctrine that even an insolvent debtor may prefer one creditor to another, and that his motives for so doing, provided the preferred creditor has done nothing improper, cannot be inquired into. To render a preference fraudulent, both parties must concur in the intent to commit the wrong.''[8] It must also be added that the statute regarding assignments for the benefit of creditors, and avoiding preferences thereunder, is not intended to regulate the action of the creditor. Notwithstanding the statute, he may, if he does not know that his debtor contemplates making an assignment, take a mortgage or other security for his debt, in good faith, and enforce the same; and if he obtains a preference over those creditors whose claims are to participate in the assignment, by his own diligence and without collusion with the debtor, the subsequent assignment will not affect his security.[9]

[7] Sidener v. Kiler, 4 Biss. 391, Fed. Cas. No. 12,843; McIntire v. Yates, 104 Ill. 491; Moriss v. Blackman, 179 Ill. 103, 53 N. E. Rep. 547; Ross v. Walker, 52 Ill. App. 137, affirmed, 150 Ill. 50.

[8] Union Nat. Bank v. State Bank, 168 Ill. 256, 48 N. E. Rep. 169, affirming 68 Ill. App. 43.

[9] Grafe v. Peter Schoenhofen Brewing Co., 78 Ill. App. 570; Weber v. Mick, 131 Ill. 520, 23 N. E. Rep. 646.

§ 140. **Mortgagee's Participation in Fraudulent Purpose.**—
To avoid a mortgage given to secure fair and honest claims
against the mortgagor, on the ground that it was made with
the intent to hinder or defraud his other creditors, it must
be shown that both the mortgagor and the mortgagee participated in the fraudulent intention.[10] A creditor who obtains from an insolvent debtor a conveyance of property as
security for his debt may know that the debtor is acting with
a design to delay or defraud other creditors, but he will not
lose his preference by reason of such knowledge, if he takes the
conveyance in good faith, and without any view of aiding in
the consummation of the debtor's purpose, further than necessarily results from the securing of a preference to himself.[11]
But it is erroneous to decree the foreclosure of a mortgage,
alleged to have been given in fraud of creditors, where it was
not executed to secure an actual debt and where no consideration was advanced by the mortgagee.[12]

§ 141. **Proof of Fraud.**—The party who seeks to impeach
the validity of a mortgage, fair and regular on its face, on
the ground of its being fraudulent as against creditors, must
assume the burden of establishing his contention, and must
show the fraud by clear and convincing evidence. "The notes
and mortgage being fair on their face, the presumption is that
they are valid and binding until that presumption is overcome by satisfactory proof. To create a mere suspicion of
fraud is not sufficient, but if it exists it must be satisfactorily
shown. The policy of the law is opposed to overturning solemn
written instruments and deeds and conveyances on slight evidence. The law designs that such instruments shall stand until
overcome by evidence that convinces the understanding that
they have been entered into for a purpose that is prohibited
by the law. Whilst courts are vigilant in relieving against
fraud, they are careful to protect fair and honest transactions.
On the mere production, then, of the notes and mortgage, the
presumption is that they are valid, and it devolves upon those
challenging their validity to impeach their fairness."[13] The
mere fact that the mortgage recites a greater indebtedness

[10] Herkelrath v. Stookey, 63 Ill.
486; Webber v. Mackey, 31 Ill.
App. 369.

[11] Ball v. Callahan, 95 Ill. App.
615.

[12] Miller v. Marckle, 21 Ill. 152.

[13] Pratt v. Pratt, 96 Ill. 184;
Union Nat. Bank v. State Nat.
Bank, 168 Ill. 256, 48 N. E. Rep.
169.

than actually existed at the time of its execution is not conclusive evidence of fraud; that must be determined from all
the circumstances. On this point it is said: "The fraud must
be determined by the jury from all the circumstances,—the
intent and agreement of the parties, if any existed, as to the
purpose of the mortgage. If the design was to shield the
property, and to hinder and delay creditors by the insertion
of the large amount in the mortgage, then it was fraudulent
and void. The transaction must be real, and entered into in
good faith, to secure against present or future liability."[14]
But it is said that a chattel mortgage to secure a note for a
large sum on short time, and a note for a merely nominal sum
on much longer time, is not bona fide, but may be taken as
intended to prevent a seizure by creditors.[15]

§ 142. **Fraud or Deception Practised on Mortgagor.**—When
the owner of real property is induced by means of fraud,
deception, or false representations to execute a mortgage on
his estate, he may procure its cancellation or defend against
its foreclosure. Thus, in one of the cases, a party subscribed
for stock in a corporation and gave his note, secured by mortgage, in payment for the same. It was shown that he was
induced to take this action by false and fraudulent representations made by the officers of the company, and by others on
its behalf, in regard to its financial condition and as to the
value of the stock and the probable dividends. It was adjudged that the fraud so practised upon him was a good
defense to a bill for the foreclosure of the mortgage.[16] So,
where a party fraudulently obtains a deed of conveyance,
without consideration, from the owner of lands, and surrep-
titiously places it on the record, and afterwards mortgages
the land to a third person, the owner in the mean time being
in the open and visible possession of the land, such possession
will be notice to the mortgagee of the fraud perpetrated upon
the owner and of his rights, and the mortgage will not be a

---

[14] Bell v. Prewitt, 62 Ill. 361;
Sawyer v. Bradshaw, 125 Ill. 440,
17 N. E. Rep. 812. A contemporaneous parol agreement, not included in the mortgage, may be
shown by evidence, where such an
agreement would render the mortgage void as against third parties,
under the statute. Aleshire v. Lee
County Savings Bank, 105 Ill. App.
32.

[15] Hixon v. Mullikin, 18 Ill. App.
232.

[16] Melendy v. Keen, 89 Ill. 395.

valid lien on the property.[17] If the signature of the pretended
mortgagor to the instrument is forged, it will of course be
invalid; but here it is held that the mortgagor may so far
approve and adopt the spurious document as that it will be
fully binding upon him, as though he had in fact originally
executed it himself. This is the case if, with full knowledge
of the mortgage and of the circumstances attending its execution, he receives and appropriates the proceeds.[18] Ignorance
of his rights in the premises or of the legal effect of the mortgage may also be ground for impeaching its validity, if taken
advantage of by the mortgagee. Thus, if a wife is induced to
join with her husband in the execution of a mortgage, but is
ignorant of the fact that she is thereby releasing her homestead rights in the premises, the purport of the instrument
not being made known to her at the time of its execution, she
may maintain a bill in chancery to avoid the mortgage so far
as regards such release.[19] But in the absence of fraud, the
mere fact that a mortgage, drawn by the agent of the mortgagor, contained an unauthorized stipulation, would not avail
as a defense to its foreclosure, although the mortgagor could
not read the instrument, not understanding the English language, and the same was not read to him before its execution.[20] And it seems that the declarations of a mortgagor,
as to his intention in executing the mortgage, are not admissible in evidence to impeach the title of the mortgagee, by
showing fraud, unless they were brought to his knowledge
prior to the execution of the mortgage.[21] And where one in
good faith and without fraud takes a mortgage from a husband and wife to secure a just debt, a court will hesitate long
before ordering that it be cancelled or set aside, even on proof
that the husband procured the wife's execution thereof by
false and fraudulent representations, and that she was not
guilty of negligence in failing to ascertain its contents.[22]

§ 143. Same; Undue Influence.—Undue influence exerted
upon a mortgagor by the mortgagee may be sufficient to

[17] Rea v. Croessman, 95 Ill. App. 70.

[18] Livings v. Wiler, 32 Ill. 387.

[19] Eyster v. Hatheway, 50 Ill. 521.

[20] Wilson v. Winter, 6 Fed. Rep. 16.

[21] Prior v. White, 12 Ill. 261.

[22] Spurgin v. Traub, 65 Ill. 170. And see Paxton v. Marshall (U. S. Circ. Ct., N. D. Ill.), 18 Fed. Rep. 361.

invalidate the instrument, where it amounts to that kind of persuasion—equivalent to a sort of moral coercion—which may be exercised by one having authority and control over another, or by a superior intelligence and masterful will playing upon a feeble mind and pliant disposition, the free agency and choice of the mortgagor, in either case, being dominated and controlled to his prejudice. This will be the case, for example, where it appears that the party executing the mortgage was rendered imbecile by habitual drunkenness, and reduced to a condition verging upon insanity by the mortgagee, who had obtained complete power over him, the mortgagee not being able to show that he had given any valid consideration for the mortgage.[23] But the mere fact that the mortgage was executed while the grantor was in the last stages of a mortal illness does not show that the execution was procured by fraud or undue influence, especially where the instrument was executed in his own house and in the absence of the mortgagee.[24] The relation of husband and wife offers frequent opportunities for this unlawful kind of influence to be exerted. But it is said that mere importunity on the part of a husband, urging his wife to mortgage her property as a means of extricating him from difficulties, is not sufficient to avoid a mortgage made by her in compliance with such urging, when it does not amount to either duress, threats, coercion, oppression, or fraud.[25] So where the wife and children of an aged person procured him to convey his real estate to a son, so as to enable the latter to raise money by his mortgage, from an innocent party, to be invested in a homestead for the father, which the children

[23] Van Horn v. Keenan, 28 Ill. 445. In the case of Willcox v. Jackson, 51 Iowa, 208, 1 N. W. Rep. 513, it is said that, to set aside a contract or conveyance on account of intoxication, it is not sufficient that the party was under undue excitement from liquor. It must rise to that degree which may be called excessive drunkenness, where the party is utterly deprived of his reason and understanding. But where one of the parties to the transaction so manages and contrives that the other becomes intoxicated, and does this for the purpose of procuring an unconscionable advantage over him in the settlement of their accounts, and thereby succeeds in getting from him a note for an amount too large, and a mortgage to secure it, both the note and mortgage are to be treated as fraudulent and void.

[24] Johnston v. Derr, 110 N. Car. 1, 14 S. E. Rep. 641.

[25] Lefebvre v. Dutruit, 51 Wis. 326, 8 N. W. Rep. 149.

inherited after his death, it was held that the widow and heirs were estopped from defeating the mortgagee's lien by insisting that the father was non compos mentis, and did not under-stand the arrangement by which the money was obtained.[26] And in this connection, it is well to remember the remark made by a learned judge to the effect that "it is not unlawful to influence a weak-minded person to do that which is just and for the best good of such person. Such influence is not undue, —in other words, is not fraudulent,—and does not necessarily vitiate the act produced by it."[27]

The relation between a lawyer and his client is such that any transaction between them involving the transfer of the latter's property to the former will be scrutinized jealously by the courts. It is said that, where the parties to a mortgage occupied the position of attorney and client, at the time it was given, the client executing the mortgage and the attorney receiving it, and fraud is set up as a defense to its foreclosure, the burden of proof rests upon the attorney to show that the transaction was fair and consistent with equity and founded on an adequate consideration; and if he fails to make satisfactory proof in this regard, equity will treat the case as one of constructive fraud.[28]

§ 144. **Mortgages Obtained by Duress.**—The validity of a mortgage may be impeached, and its foreclosure prevented, when it was extorted from the mortgagor by means of duress practised upon him by the mortgagee.[29] Thus, where the execution of the mortgage was procured under a threat of arrest on an outstanding warrant, the instrument may be held void, not only as having been procured under duress, but because it is contrary to public policy to permit such an abuse of legal process, and no person should have the aid of a court to profit by it.[30] In one of the cases, it appeared that the mortgagor, who was an aged woman with little property except her homestead, was induced to execute the mortgage as a means of saving her grandson from imprisonment, the latter being charged by the mortgagee, his employer, with forgery and embezzlement, causing a loss to the latter of a sum of

[26] Jeneson v. Jeneson, 66 Ill. 259.
[27] Dailey v. Kastell, 56 Wis. 444, 14 N. W. Rep. 635.
[28] Faris v. Briscoe, 78 Ill. App. 242. And see Morrison v. Smith,

130 Ill. 304; Ross v. Payson, 160 Ill. 349.
[29] Eyster v. Hatheway, 50 Ill. 521.
[30] Bane v. Detrick, 52 Ill. 19.

money equal to the debt set forth in the mortgage. A warrant for the arrest of the young man was actually issued, but not formally served, the deputy sheriff being instructed to hold the person of the defaulter until the matter should be fixed up. The mortgagee, then, accompanied by the deputy sheriff and his pretended prisoner, went to the house of the mortgagor, and so worked upon her fears and her affections as to extort from her the mortgage in question. It was held that a court of equity would make a decree declaring the mortgage to be null and void, as obtained by duress, and setting it aside as a cloud on title, and perpetually enjoining the mortgagee from attempting to enforce it.[31]

But menaces do not constitute duress where the only threat is to take some civil action, or seek some redress in the civil courts, which is the fair legal right and privilege of the mortgagee. Thus, a threat to foreclose a trust deed already due, and which the party had a legal right to foreclose, does not constitute duress as to the execution of another note and trust deed given to prevent foreclosure.[32] And "it cannot be regarded as duress when a husband and wife of more than ordinary intelligence and information, under no restraint, at perfect liberty to obtain legal advice as to their rights, execute a mortgage under the mistaken idea that the husband is to be arrested upon a criminal charge, when in fact the only threats used were that attachment proceedings would be instituted to enforce a claim."[33]

Again, it is necessary, to constitute duress, that the threats or pressure should have proceeded in some way from the party to be benefited by the resulting action. For instance, a mortgage given by a husband and wife upon their homestead cannot be said to have been obtained by duress, although the desperate state of the husband's financial affairs was known to the wife, as also the fact that he was in danger of being arrested for embezzlement, and these circumstances may have influenced her decision to sign the mortgage, where it does not appear that the mortgagee was in any way connected with the proceedings for the arrest (although he had been defrauded

---

[31] Bradley v. Irish, 42 Ill. App. 85. And see (a very similar case), McCormick Harvesting Machine Co. v. Hamilton, 73 Wis. 486, 41 N. W. Rep. 727.

[32] Hart v. Strong, 183 Ill. 349, 55 N. E. Rep. 629, reversing Strong v. Hart. 83 Ill. App. 213.

[33] Post v. First Nat. Bank, 38 Ill. App. 259.

by the husband) and he did not seek to influence the wife's action.[34] In another case, a married woman executed a deed of trust upon her separate property to secure a debt of her husband, acting with great reluctance, and after much importunity from the latter and many threats on his part to desert her if she did not sign it, and for the purpose of preserving her relations with her husband. But on the other hand, neither the trustee nor the creditor whose debt was thus secured was a party to such coercion, or had any knowledge of it, and it appeared that the woman admitted to the officer taking the acknowledgment, separate and apart from her husband, that she executed the same freely, and it was shown that she was well acquainted with the contents of the deed, and never made known the facts until after the property was sold. On this state of facts, it was held that, while it could not be said that she had executed the deed freely and voluntarily, yet the court could not then annul it and set aside the sale, since that would have the effect of allowing her to perpetrate wrong and injustice to other innocent parties.[35]

§ 145. **Illegality of Consideration.**—Where the consideration given for a note or bond which is secured by a mortgage or deed of trust was illegal, in the sense of being prohibited by statute, immoral, or contrary to public policy, the obligation is void and the mortgage cannot be enforced as a security. Thus, where the original contract or bargain between the parties was illegal because of champerty, a deed in the nature of a mortgage, given to secure its performance, will not be enforced in a court of equity.[36] So, where the consideration for a note was the price of intoxicating liquors sold in violation of the laws of the state, the illegality of the transaction may be set up in defense to an action to foreclose a mortgage given for securing the payment of the note.[37] On the same principle, it is said that it is a sufficient defense to a suit to foreclose a trust deed that the note which it secures was given without consideration, for the purpose of defrauding the maker's divorced wife of her claim for alimony, since equity will not enforce a fraudulent agreement.[38]

[34] Bogue v. Franks, 199 Ill. 411.
[35] Marston v. Brittenham, 76 Ill. 611.
[36] Gilbert v. Holmes, 64 Ill. 548.
[37] Ressegieu v. Van Wagenen, 77 Iowa, 351, 42 N. W. Rep. 318.
[38] Scott v. Maglouglin, 133 Ill. 33, 24 N. E. Rep. 1030.

§ **146. Agreement to Stop Criminal Prosecution.**—It is universally agreed that, where the consideration for a note or other obligation for the payment of money was an agreement on the part of the payee to compound a felony, or to stifle, settle, or abandon a criminal prosecution begun by him against the maker, or a relative of the latter, the obligation is void, as being illegal and contrary to public policy; and if a mortgage is given to secure the payment of the same, a court of equity will not permit its foreclosure, but the illegality of the consideration is a complete defense.[39] And it is immaterial that other and valid considerations may have existed between the parties and may have entered to some extent into the foundation for the note. Neither the mortgage nor the consideration therefor is divisible, and if any part of either is illegal the whole is so tainted as to be void.[40] Some doubt arises, however, in cases where the action is not one brought by the mortgagee to enforce such a mortgage, but one brought by the mortgagor to have it cancelled or adjudged void as a cloud on his title, or to have its foreclosure enjoined, or to set aside a sale which has been made under it. In some jurisdictions, the courts are disposed to refuse any relief on an application of this kind. Their reasoning is that the parties are equally guilty of an attempt to violate the law, and that, as they are thus in pari delicto, the courts will not aid either of them, but will leave them where they stand,—that if a judicial tribunal should not assist the mortgagee in foreclosing his lien, neither should it give any aid to the mortgagor seeking to avoid the consequences of his illegal conduct.[41] But the better reason appears to be with the cases holding that the parties, in the circumstances supposed, are not precisely in pari delicto, and that more consideration should be shown to the one who has been made the victim of an unconscionable advantage; and that, even if they must be held equally in fault, still the highest considerations of public policy require that the vicious bargain

[39] Bane v. Detrick, 52 Ill. 19; Henderson v. Palmer, 71 Ill. 579; Maxfield v. Hoecker, 49 Hun. (N. Y.), 605; Pearce v. Wilson, 111 Pa. St. 14, 2 Atl. Rep. 99; Raguet v. Roll, 7 Ohio, 76; Smith v. Steely, 80 Iowa, 738, 45 N. W. Rep. 912; Small v. Williams, 87 Ga. 681, 13 S. E. Rep. 589.

[40] Pearce v. Wilson, 111 Pa. St. 14, 2 Atl. Rep. 99; Small v. Williams, 87 Ga. 681, 13 S. E. Rep. 589.

[41] See Williams v. Englebrecht, 37 Ohio St. 383.

should not be allowed to stand, but that relief should be granted to the party upon whom coercion has been exercised.[42] Thus, in one of the Illinois cases, a note was given in consideration of a promise by the payee to stop a prosecution for a felony which was then pending against a son of the maker of the note, and a mortgage was given to secure the payment of the note. This mortgage was foreclosed by scire facias, and thereafter the mortgagor brought his bill in equity to set aside the mortgage and the proceedings by scire facias as a cloud upon his title. It was held that, as the mortgagor would not have been permitted to plead the illegality of the consideration in the scire facias proceedings, he was not guilty of laches in failing to do so, and that the bill should be entertained and the relief granted as prayed for.[43] More especially is this principle applicable where the prosecution against the mortgagor has no real foundation, but is merely set on foot for the purpose of working on his fears and extorting money from him.[44] In Illinois, we also find a decision that a person prosecuting another upon a charge of crime may receive from the accused private satisfaction for his private injury, and the fact that he receives this while the prisoner is in confinement, and forbears further prosecution, does not of itself render the transaction illegal. But if the prosecutor detains his debtor in prison unlawfully, by covin with the jailer, refusing the prisoner's demand to be taken before a magistrate or court for a hearing, this constitutes such duress as will invalidate a mortgage extorted from the debtor under such circumstances.[45]

§ 147. **Gambling Contracts.**—It is provided by statute in Illinois that where the whole or any part of the consideration for any mortgage shall be for any money, property, or other thing of value won by gambling or betting, or for paying back any money or property knowingly lent or advanced at the time or place of such gambling or betting to any person engaged in the game or wager, the mortgage shall be void and of no effect. A mortgage given upon such consideration may be set aside and vacated by any court of equity, upon bill filed for

---

[42] Meech v. Lee, 82 Mich. 274, 46 N. W. Rep. 383; Bradley v. Irish, 42 Ill. App. 85.

[43] Henderson v. Palmer, 71 Ill. 579.

[44] James v. Roberts, 18 Ohio, 548.

[45] Schommer v. Farwell, 56 Ill. 542.

that purpose by the mortgagor, or his executor or administrator, or by any creditor, heir, devisee, purchaser, or other
person interested therein; and no assignment of the mortgage, or the note or other evidence of debt which it secures,
shall in any manner affect the right of the mortgagor to defend
against it on this ground, or the remedies of any person interested therein.[46] In regard to this statute it is to be observed,
in the first place, that a mortgage will not be saved, even pro
tanto, by the fact that other good and valid considerations
may enter into the note or other obligation secured. If any
part of the consideration is a gambling debt, the whole is
invalid. Secondly, the remedy against it is given to any person
interested in the property affected, including not only the
personal representatives of the mortgagor and those deriving
title from him, whether by way of devise, intestacy, or purchase, but also creditors and junior incumbrancers. Thirdly,
obligations founded upon gambling transactions are void in the
hands of all persons, even when they take the form of negotiable paper and are passed before maturity to innocent and
unsuspecting purchasers. Such obligations cannot be made
valid by any renewals or transfers to bona fide holders. Therefore a deed of trust, executed to secure a note given in payment of a gambling debt, is void, although it has been renewed
and transferred to the hands of an innocent purchaser.[47] But
on a bill filed by a party to set aside a sale of his land under
decree of foreclosure of a mortgage, on the ground that the
mortgage was given to secure money won by gambling, the
burden of proof is on him to establish, by a preponderance of
evidence, not only that he lost money while gambling with the
defendant, but that all or some part of the money so lost by
gambling was money for which the note and mortgage were
given, either in whole or in part.[48]

§ 148. **Conflict of Laws.**—The validity of a mortgage of real
estate is to be tested and determined by the laws of the state
wherein the mortgaged property is situated; and although
the mortgage itself is executed, and the mortgagor is domiciled, in another state, and although, by the laws of the latter

[46] Criminal Code Ill., §§ 131, 135, 136.

[47] International Bank of Chicago v. Vankirk, 39 Ill. App. 23.

[48] Patterson v. Scott, 142 Ill. 138, 31 N. E. Rep. 433.

state, it would not be competent for him to make such a mortgage, or other reasons would exist to render it invalid or ineffective as a security, yet this will not affect the right to enforce the mortgage in the state where the land lies, if it is not invalid under the laws of the last-named jurisdiction.[49] And conversely, although the mortgage may be good and valid by the laws of the state where it is executed, yet if it does not comply with the laws of the state where the mortgaged land is situated, it cannot be enforced there.[50]

[49] Dawson v. Hayden, 67 Ill. 52; Post v. First Nat. Bank, 138 Ill. 559, 28 N. E. Rep. 978, affirming 38 Ill. App. 259; Fessenden v. Taft, 65 N. H. 39, 17 Atl. Rep. 713.

[50] Swank v. Hufnagle, 111 Ind. 453, 12 N. E. Rep. 303.

CHAPTER XIII.

THE RECORDING OF MORTGAGES.

§ 149. **Requisites of Record.**—It is held in some of the states that, if a mortgage is not entitled to be recorded, because not in proper form or not properly executed or acknowledged, the actual record of it is a mere nullity and cannot serve the purpose of imparting notice to persons subsequently dealing with the property.[1] But in Illinois a statute declares that "deeds, mortgages, and other instruments of writing relating to real estate shall be deemed, from the time of being filed for record, notice to subsequent purchasers and creditors, though not acknowledged or proven according to law; but the same shall not be read in evidence, unless their execution be proved in the manner required by the rules of evidence applicable to such writings, so as to supply the defects of such acknowledgment or proof."[2] Although the laws of this state provide that mortgages shall take effect, as against subsequent purchasers and creditors, from the time of their being filed for record, this serves only to fix the date or time of their attaching as liens, and does not dispense with the necessity for their being duly and fully recorded. Hence where a mortgage has been withdrawn from the files by the mortgagee, or by the mortgagor with the former's consent, before it has been spread upon the records, it will not affect the rights of subsequent purchasers or incumbrancers in good faith giving a valuable consideration.[3]

[1] Irwin v. Welch, 10 Nebr. 479, 6 N. W. Rep. 753.

[2] Rev. Stat. Ill. c. 30, § 31 (Starr & C. § 32).

[3] Kiser v. Heuston, 38 Ill. 252; Yerger v. Barz, 56 Iowa, 77, 8 N. W. Rep. 769.

It is a question how far the mortgagee is responsible for mistakes or omissions made in the transcription of the mortgage upon the record. On the one hand, the highest degree of prudence would require the mortgagee to examine the record for the purpose of verifying its accuracy. On the other hand, records made by public officers regarding real property are presumed to be correct. It has been held that the rights of the mortgagee will not be affected, nor the efficacy of the instrument as a means of giving notice to interested parties impaired, by errors or omissions, however material, made by the recorder in transcribing the mortgage. The mortgagee, it is said, has done all that is required of him when he has deposited the mortgage, properly executed, in the proper office, with directions to record it; he is not bound to oversee the work of the transcriber nor to verify it afterwards.[4] Subject to the qualifications mentioned in the succeeding sections (as to the necessity of a proper description of the property and a proper statement of the amount secured), this rule would probably be everywhere accepted as correct. And in Illinois it is ruled that actual notice of a mortgage covering the whole premises to be conveyed puts a purchaser on inquiry, which is not satisfied by mere inspection of the record of the mortgage, in which there is a clerical error.[5] But an index to the record of a mortgage forms no part of the record, and is not essential to make the record effective to charge subsequent purchasers with notice.[6] As to deeds which are absolute in form, though intended to operate only as securities, in the nature of mortgages, it is held that they are properly recorded in a book kept for the record of deeds, and will be valid against purchasers and creditors, though the statute may require the recording of mortgages in a separate book. The reason given is that every person is presumed to know that a conveyance absolute on its face may have the legal effect of a mortgage, and that an intending purchaser or subsequent lienor would not be satisfied (if he was duly prudent and careful) with merely searching the records of mortgages, but would also examine the records of deeds, for the purpose of ascertaining

[4] Meherin v. Oaks, 67 Cal. 57, 7 Pac. Rep. 47.

[5] Hoopeston Building Ass'n v. Green, 16 Ill. App. 204.

[6] Green v. Garrington, 16 Ohio St. 548; Semon v. Terhune, 40 N. J. Eq. 364, 2 Atl. Rep. 18.

whether his proposed grantor had not parted with the title, either absolutely or conditionally.[7]

§ 150. **Contents of Record; Description of Property.**—The record of a mortgage operates as constructive notice to subsequent purchasers, incumbrancers, or creditors, only so far as the property covered is correctly described in the mortgage and in the record of it, unless it is apparent from the record itself that there is a mistake or misdescription, in which case such persons would be put upon inquiry as to the real condition of the title.[8] Thus, in a case where a mortgage describing the property conveyed as 2,000 acres of land, more or less, was incorrectly recorded as conveying "200 acres, more or less," but the boundaries were correctly described in the mortgage and correctly copied into the record, it was held that the record, notwithstanding the mistake of quantity, was sufficient to affect a subsequent mortgagee with notice.[9]

§ 151. **Same; Statement of Amount of Debt.**—The record of a mortgage or deed of trust to secure a debt must state the amount of such debt, or it will not be sufficient to charge subsequent bona fide purchasers or incumbrancers of the land with notice of the security. On this point it has been said: "A statement upon the record of the amount claimed to be due informs all what lien is claimed. They know what they must contest, or subject to what they must take, in subsequently dealing with the property. It prevents secret conspiracies between mortgagors and mortgagees as to the fact and amount of indebtedness to the prejudice of subsequent purchasers and creditors, by compelling them at once to make known the real claim. In some instances, subsequent dealers with mortgaged property could not have information from the holders of indebtedness secured by mortgage, because they could not be found, as in the case of negotiable securities running for a long time and negotiated many times before maturity; and it might often be, as in the instance before us, perilous to rely on the word of the mortgagor. Undoubtedly, as between mortgagor and mortgagee, and as to persons having

[7] Haseltine v. Espy, 13 Oreg. 301, 10 Pac. Rep. 423; Kennard v. Mabry, 78 Tex. 151, 14 S. W. Rep. 272.

[8] Slocum v. O'Day, 174 Ill. 215, 51 N. E. Rep. 243; Harms v. Coryell, 177 Ill. 496, 53 N. E. Rep. 87; supra, § 62.

[9] Kennedy v. Boykin, 35 S. Car. 61, 14 S. E. Rep. 809.

actual notice of the facts, both at common law and under our statute, a deed absolute on its face may be held to be a mortgage; but such cases are totally unaffected by our registry laws, and cannot therefore have the slightest analogy to the present case. It may also be well to observe that the present case is in no wise analogous to cases wherein the debt is described by reference to another instrument. In those cases there is only the labor of going to the other instrument, where full and reliable information can be obtained. It is fixed, and beyond evasion or perversion. But that is not the case where the reference is to an individual whose interest may be to misrepresent the truth, or who may not with reasonable efforts be found. A note for one amount as well as another will answer the description here, and this note might have been lawfully negotiated and transferred many times before maturity, and its holder then not have been traceable except at a labor and expense beyond any benefit derived from the knowledge he could impart. To hold this sufficient would, in cases that may readily and not unreasonably be conceived, practically prohibit subsequent parties from having anything to do with the property."[10] Hence if a mortgage is given to secure an ascertained debt, the amount of that debt should be stated in the record, and if it is intended to secure a debt not liquidated, such data should be given respecting it as will put any one interested in the inquiry upon the track leading to a discovery. If it is given to secure an existing or future liability, the foundation of that liability should be set forth.[11]

§ 152. Place of Record.—The statute in Illinois provides that mortgages shall be recorded in the county in which the mortgaged land is situated; "but if such county is not organized, then in the county to which such unorganized county is attached for judicial purposes." If the mortgage covers land lying in several counties, it may be recorded in one of them, and then certified copies may be recorded in the other counties.[12] But a mortgage becomes a matter of record by being registered in the county in which the mortgaged premises are situated, and a scire facias may properly issue from the circuit

[10] Bullock v. Battenhousen, 108 Ill. 28. And see Bergman v. Bogda, 46 Ill. App. 351.

[11] Metropolitan Bank v. Godfrey, 23 Ill. 579, 603.

[12] Rev. Stat. Ill. c. 30, §§ 28, 29 (Starr & C. §§ 29, 30).

court of that county, although lands in other counties may also be included in the mortgage, and the instrument may not have been recorded in those other counties.[13] But placing a mortgage on record in a county where no part of the mortgaged premises lies will not furnish constructive notice to subsequent purchasers or creditors in the county where the land is actually situated.[14] Where a mortgage is given by a railroad company on its road, which passes through several counties, and is recorded in one of those counties before the recovery of a judgment against the mortgagor by a third person, but is not recorded in the other counties, it will have a priority of lien over the judgment upon the part of the road lying in that particular county, but not upon such portions of it as lie in the other counties.[15]

§ 153. **Effect of Unrecorded Mortgage.**—It is enacted by statute in Illinois that "all deeds, mortgages, and other instruments of writing which are authorized to be recorded, shall take effect and be in force from and after the time of filing the same for record, and not before, as to all creditors and subsequent purchasers without notice; and all such deeds and title papers shall be adjudged void as to all such creditors and subsequent purchasers without notice, until the same shall be filed for record."[16] The effect of this statute, in its modification of the common law, is to leave a mortgage good and valid as between the parties to it although it is not recorded. Where no conflicting rights of third persons intervene, the instrument will create a lien on the property affected and may be foreclosed by proper proceedings, without proof of its having been placed on the record; and the rule is the same as against subsequent purchasers or incumbrancers who take with actual notice of the unrecorded mortgage. It is only as against persons subsequently dealing with the land without actual notice that the recording of the mortgage is necessary to make it effective.[17] Even though the mortgage is made by a person

---

[13] Woodbury v. Manlove, 14 Ill. 213.

[14] Oberholtzer's Appeal, 124 Pa. St. 583, 17 Atl. Rep. 143; Van Meter v. Knight, 32 Minn. 205, 20 N. W. Rep. 142.

[15] Ludlow v. Clinton Line R. Co., 1 Flip. C. C. 25, Fed. Cas. No. 8,600.

[16] Rev. Stat. Ill. c. 30, § 30 (Starr & C. § 31).

[17] Alvis v. Morrison, 63 Ill. 181. And see Stewart v. Hopkins, 30 Ohio St. 502; Northwestern Forwarding Co. v. Mahaffey, 36 Kans.

in failing circumstances and for the purpose of preferring one of his creditors, and is not recorded, still, if no actual fraud is involved, it will be valid as against other creditors who have notice of it before they acquire liens on the property.[18] And the mere withholding of a mortgage from the record, though done at the instance and request of the mortgagor, though it may be evidence of fraud, will not of itself make the mortgage fraudulent as to subsequent creditors or purchasers with notice of its existence.[19] But still it must be remembered that an unrecorded mortgage is a secret lien, and is not favored either at law or in equity.[20] And the fact that a mortgage withheld from record was given for the purchase money of the land will not validate it as against interested parties without notice, nor give it priority over a later mortgage duly recorded.[21]

Although, as above stated, an unrecorded mortgage may be good as between the parties, yet a person claiming as assignee or trustee under an assignment made by the mortgagor for the benefit of his creditors does not stand in the place of the mortgagor, but of the creditors; and as to him the mortgage will not be a valid security if the creditors could have avoided it.[22] So also, under the present United States bankruptcy law, it is provided that "claims which, for want of record or for other reasons, would not have been valid liens as against the claims of the creditors of the bankrupt, shall not be liens against his estate" in bankruptcy.[23]

§ 154. Record as Constructive Notice.—Under the recording laws, the placing of a mortgage on the record has the effect, from the time it is filed for record, of charging all persons subsequently becoming interested in the property with notice of what the record discloses. But it is constructive notice only to subsequent purchasers, incumbrancers, or creditors of the mortgagor. It affords no notice whatever to a prior pur-

152, 12 Pac. Rep. 705; Downing v. Le Du, 82 Cal. 471, 23 Pac. Rep. 202.

[18] Sternbach v. Leopold, 50 Ill. App. 476, affirmed, 156 Ill. 44.

[19] Haas v. Sternbach, 156 Ill. 44, 41 N. E. Rep. 51, affirming Sternbach v. Leopold, 50 Ill. App. 476. And see Hutchinson v. First Nat. Bank (Ind.), 30 N. E. Rep. 952.

[20] Heathman v. Rogers, 54 Ill. App. 592, affirmed, 153 Ill. 143.

[21] Jackson v. Reid, 30 Kans. 10, 1 Pac. Rep. 308.

[22] Bank of Alexandria v. Herbert, 8 Cranch, 36.

[23] Bankruptcy Act 1898, § 67a. And see Moore v. Young, 4 Biss. 128, Fed. Cas. No. 9,782.

chaser from the grantor, and without actual notice he may lawfully complete his payments to his vendor, without becoming liable to the subsequent mortgagee.[24] And where a party presents a mortgage to the recorder, who indorses it as "filed for record," and the party immediately and before any entry is made in relation thereto, withdraws it for the alleged purpose of having a revenue stamp put upon it, and it is not returned for record for more than a month afterwards, the first filing is not sufficient to give constructive notice of the existence of the mortgage.[25]

§ 155. Effect of Destruction of Record.—When a mortgagee places his mortgage on record, his rights under it are fixed, and it serves the purpose of giving notice thereof for all time, and the destruction of the record books does not extinguish or revoke such notice, nor affect the rights of the mortgagee injuriously. The fact that the records have been burned, and an act of the legislature passed to restore them, imposes no obligation upon a mortgagee, whose mortgage was duly recorded before such destruction of the books, to incur the trouble and expense of having his mortgage restored. As against a subsequent grantee of the mortgagor, taking in good faith and without any knowledge of the mortgage, the mortgagee has the superior equity, both because he has performed his whole duty in recording his mortgage originally, and because the purchaser should have inquired of the mortgagor with reference to incumbrances on the property, and if he buys without making any such inquiry, it is his own fault or folly if he finds the land liable to a mortgage.[26] And it is even held that the fact that the mortgagor, when selling the property, informed the purchaser that the title was perfect and subject to no incumbrance, will not change the rule or affect the rights of the mortgagee, the latter having no knowledge of such representations, nor will the fact that the mortgagor remained in possession of the premises, and paid the taxes thereon, as that would not be inconsistent with the lien created by the mortgage.[27]

§ 156. Registration Under Land Titles Act.—The statute in Illinois concerning the registration of land titles (the so-called

[24] Doolittle v. Cook, 75 Ill. 354.
[25] Worcester Nat. Bank v. Cheeney, 87 Ill. 602.
[26] Shannon v. Hall, 72 Ill. 354.
[27] Hall v. Shannon, 85 Ill. 473.

"Torrens" act) provides that "every mortgage and other instrument intended to create a lien, incumbrance, or charge upon registered land, or any interest therein, shall be deemed to be a charge thereon, and may be registered." "A trust deed in the nature of a mortgage shall be deemed to be a mortgage, and be subject to the same rules as a mortgage." Assignments of a mortgage may also be registered. But "no mortgage, lien, charge, or lesser estate than a fee simple shall be registered, unless the fee simple to the same land is first registered."[28] This act has been sustained by the supreme court and held valid and constitutional.[29]

[28] Act of May 1, 1897; Laws 1897, p. 141; 4 Starr & C. Ann. Stat. c. 30, § 21; Myer's Stat. c. 30a.

[29] People v. Simon, 176 Ill. 165, 52 N. E. Rep. 910.

§ 157. Extent and Duration of Lien.—A mortgage of real property does not attach as a lien upon the estate of the debtor generally, but only upon the particular parcel of land described in it and intended to be conveyed by it; and it stands as security only for the specific indebtedness or obligation set forth as the consideration for it, and not for any and all debts due from the mortgagor to the mortgagee, however fair and just they may be.[1] But the mortgage, if it contains proper covenants, will bind a title subsequently acquired by the mortgagor, whether it be by the purchase or release of an outstanding title, or by the extinguishment of an elder lien.[2] It is also a rule that the lien of a mortgage is not divested or disturbed by a mere change in the form of the security, if it is not intended to operate as a payment of the debt or a release of the mortgage.[3] Thus, where a creditor to whom land has been conveyed in trust, to secure a debt, by a deed absolute in form,

[1] See Hardin v. Eames, 5 Ill. App. 153.

[2] See, supra, § 114. If the assignee of an equity of redemption acquires a title obtained under a judgment prior in time to the mortgage. and has refunded to him by the mortgagor the amount which he paid for the judgment, the title acquired under the judgment will be held subject to the mortgage. White v. Butler, 13 Ill. 109.

[3] Rogers v. School Trustees, 46 Ill. 428; Bond v. Liverpool, L. & G. Ins. Co., 106 Ill. 654; Salem Nat. Bank v. White, 159 Ill. 136, 42 N. E. Rep. 312.

reconveys to his grantor and simultaneously takes back a mortgage to secure the same debt, he does not lose his lien in equity as against a judgment subsequent to the original conveyance.[4]

The lien of a mortgage is liable to be extinguished or terminated in several different ways. In the first place, it may come to an end by merger. If the mortgagor conveys the mortgaged premises to the mortgagee in payment and satisfaction of the debt secured, the lien of the mortgage will be merged in the fee; and the same result may follow (and will follow unless there are equitable reasons for keeping the mortgage alive) when the mortgagee acquires the title in fee to the mortgaged property in any other manner.[5] Again, the lien of the mortgage may be divested by a release. A release given by a mortgagee, under no circumstances of fraud or undue influence, but solely to enable the mortgagor to sell the land with a clear title, will be valid and effective to discharge the lien of the mortgage, the same as if it had been given upon payment of the debt.[6] Payment of the debt or obligation secured will of course extinguish the lien of the mortgage, unless, for special reasons, the parties are allowed to keep the mortgage alive. Upon such payment, the mortgagee may be compelled to enter satisfaction upon the record, which will operate as a formal release of the lien. Even after default in payment of the debt according to the terms of the mortgage, the mortgagor may exercise his right of redemption, until the same is cut off by foreclosure or in some other proper manner. And if the circumstances are such that he cannot

[4] Christie v. Hale, 46 Ill. 117. And see Jeneson v. Jeneson, 66 Ill. 259. Where a mortgagor moves a house from the mortgaged premises to another tract of land belonging to him, but not covered by the mortgage, the lien on the house is not thereby impaired. Turner v. Mebane, 110 N. Car. 413, 14 S. E. Rep. 974.

[5] Gage v. McDermid, 150 Ill. 598, 37 N. E. Rep. 1026; Lyman v. Gedney, 114 Ill. 388, 29 N. E. Rep. 282; Shinn v. Fredericks, 56 Ill. 439.

[6] McMillan v. McMillan, 184 Ill. 230, 56 N. E. Rep. 302. And a mortgagee may release part of the premises and retain his lien for the whole indebtedness on the remainder, in the absence of notice that third persons have become interested in other parts of the premises than that released. Hazle v. Bondy, 173 Ill. 302, 50 N. E. Rep. 671. A formal release of the mortgage of record should be under seal; but a release or discharge of the debt may be verbal; and when the debt is released, the mortgage falls. Mutual Mill Ins. Co. v. Gordon, 20 Ill. App. 559.

otherwise obtain relief, he may file his bill in equity to obtain
redemption and have a decree to that effect. In either case,
the result is to divest the lien of the mortgage. Again, the
lien may be annihilated by the running of the statute of limitations. No action can be maintained for the foreclosure of
any mortgage or deed of trust after ten years from the time
when the right of action therefor accrued, or after the debt
secured has become barred by the operation of the statute.[7]
And of course the removal of the only means of enforcing the
lien practically extinguishes the lien itself. But a mortgage
thus barred by the statute of limitations may be revived by
the mortgagor, as, by partial payments on the debt or by a
new promise in writing; and when this is done, it will take
precedence of subsequent liens, attaching before the mortgage
became barred and not foreclosed until after its revival.[8]

On the other hand, the lien of a mortgage is not divested
by the death of the mortgagor. When this happens, the mortgagee cannot be compelled to relinquish his lien and share in
the general assets of the estate. If he desires to rely wholly
on his security, he need not probate his claim, but may foreclose on default against the property covered by the lien.
But if he wishes to guard against a deficiency, and to have
the right to come upon inventoried assets in case the land
does not sell for enough to cover his demands, then he must
prove his claim in the probate proceedings.[9]

The holder of a mortgage may proceed in several different
ways, concurrently, to recover his money. And if he reduces
the claim to a judgment, and the lien of the judgment as a
judgment expires by lapse of time, still the lien of the mortgage will not be divested until it, in turn, becomes barred by
the statute.[10] But if he proceeds to enforce his judgment by
means of an execution levied on the same property covered by
the mortgage, and buys it in and takes a sheriff's deed, he

[7] Rev. Stat. Ill. c. 83, § 11; Pollock v. Maison, 41 Ill. 516; Murray
v. Emery, 187 Ill. 408, 58 .N. E.
Rep. 327; Jones v. Lander, 21 Ill.
App. 510.

[8] Kerndt v. Porterfield, 56 Iowa,
412, 9 N. W. Rep. 322; Aetna Life
Ins. Co. v. McNeely, 166 Ill. 540,
46 N. E. Rep. 1130.

[9] Waughop v. Bartlett, 165 Ill.

124, 46 N. E. Rep. 197; Jones v.
Null, 9 Nebr. 57, 1 N. W. Rep. 867.

[10] Priest v. Wheelock, 58 Ill. 114.
But where notes secured by mortgage are reduced to judgment
after their maturity, the statute of
limitations begins to run against
the right to foreclose at the date
of such judgment. Litch v. Clinch,
136 Ill. 410, 26 N. E. Rep. 579.

acquires the equity of redemption, which, united with his estate under the mortgage, will give him an absolute title, and so extinguish the lien of the mortgage on the principle of merger of estates.[11] Foreclosure of the mortgage will of course cancel the lien. But the lien of a mortgage is not merged merely in a decree for its foreclosure. If the mortgagee fails or neglects to avail himself of the remedy and advantage given by such decree, it does not release the land from the lien, nor prevent him from taking other means for obtaining satisfaction. The mortgage still remains a record, and will support a scire facias.[12] The case is clearly different, however, when the decree of foreclosure is enforced by a sale of the premises. On this point it has been said: "By virtue of the lien created, the mortgagee or cestui que trust had the right to have the security foreclosed and the property sold and the proceeds applied in payment of the secured debt. But when this has been done, and the lien enforced by a sale of the property and the proceeds applied, the mortgage or trust deed has expended its force, and the property is no longer subject to its provisions. Nor does it in any way affect the result that the holder of the secured indebtedness becomes the purchaser at the sale, whether he be the mortgagee or cestui que trust or not. By becoming the purchaser, a new relation created by the statute exists, in no wise dependent upon any privity of contract between the purchaser and the mortgagor."[13]

§ 158. **Subsequent Conveyance Subject to Lien.**—The sale and conveyance of land which is already incumbered by a mortgage passes only the equity of redemption; that is, the lien of the mortgage adheres to the property, and is not divested by one or any number of alienations, provided the mortgagee has not released to the purchaser, nor estopped himself from asserting his lien, nor otherwise placed himself in a position where, on the principles of equity, his claims must be subordinated to the rights of such purchaser.[14] As a general

---

[11] Cottingham v. Springer, 88 Ill. 90.

[12] Roberts v. Lawrence, 16 Ill. App. 453.

[13] Davis v. Dale, 150 Ill. 239, 37 N. E. Rep. 215.

[14] One who holds a junior conveyance of real estate and claims to be a bona fide purchaser, and to be entitled to protection against a senior conveyance, must show that he has truly paid his money, independently of the recitals in the deed or mortgage. Houfes v. Schultze, 2 Ill. App. 196.

rule, a purchaser of land on which there is a mortgage duly
recorded at the time he buys and takes his deed is chargeable
with notice of the same; and the fact that the mortgagor told
him that the mortgage was satisfied will not relieve him from
the consequences of such notice in the event that the mortgage was not in fact satisfied; he should have applied to the
holder of the mortgage to learn the truth of the statement.[15]
The case is different where such inquiries are addressed to the
mortgagee in the first instance. Where a party holding notes
secured by mortgage on real estate makes a declaration to a
purchaser of the same land, at the time of the sale, that the
notes have been paid, and that the land is free of the incumbrance of his mortgage, he will be estopped from claiming
afterwards that his mortgage was not satisfied, as against such
purchaser, provided the latter acted on the faith of such
assurance and paid his money in reliance upon it.[16] And the
same .result follows if the purchaser, on searching the records,
finds a release of the mortgage, in due form and duly recorded,
although the release afterwards turns out to have been invalid.[17] What is true of a sale of the premises by private
negotiation between the mortgagor and the purchaser is also
true of a judicial sale of the land, on a lien which is not
superior to that of the mortgage. Thus, a sheriff's sale of
land, by virtue of a judgment and execution subsequent to a
mortgage on the same land, does not divest the lien of the
mortgage.[18]

§ 159. Lien of Mortgage as Against Equities of Third Persons.—A person who loans money and takes a mortgage or
deed of trust on real estate, to secure the repayment of the
loan, the record showing a clear title in the mortgagor, will
be protected against any equities in the premises claimed by
third persons, of which he had no notice actual or constructive.
Thus, the lien of the mortgage will prevail against the right of
a stranger to have the mortgagor's title set aside as having
been obtained by fraud or false representations;[19] or against
the rights of one who afterwards establishes a claim that the
patent under which the mortgagor claims by mesne convey-

[15] Pratt v. Pratt, 96 Ill. 184.
[16] Tucker v. Conwell, 67 Ill. 552.
[17] Battenhausen v. Bullock, 11
Ill. App. 665.

[18] Febeiger's Lessee v. Craig-
head, 4 Dall. 151.
[19] Bradley v. Luce, 99 Ill. 234.

ances should be set aside and the land patented to him, on account of his prior entry;[20] or against an equitable claim made by the wife of the mortgagor to the effect that it was her money which paid for the land and that the deed for the same ought to have been made to her.[21] So where a debtor purchases real estate, and causes it to be conveyed to his wife, in fraud of his creditors, a person taking a mortgage in good faith from the husband and wife will not be affected by the fraud.[22] Again, the lien of a mortgagee, who has no notice of the non-payment of the purchase money of the land, will be superior to that of the vendor of the mortgaged premises.[23] And a resulting trust cannot be set up to defeat the right of a mortgagee without notice of the trust.[24] In illustration of the same principle, we may cite a case in which it was held that a contractor, who builds a railroad, and thereby gives value to the property, does not acquire an equitable lien superior to that of a mortgage given before his contract was made.[25]   .

On the other hand, if the mortgagee of land takes with notice, either actual or constructive, of rights or equities claimed by third persons, his lien will be subordinated to the same when that is necessary to make those equities effective. Thus, a mortgage taken with knowledge of the rights of a lessee of the premises will be subject to the lease, although the latter was not acknowledged and not recorded.[26] Again, a mortgage executed by a father upon land which he had previously given to his daughter (not being indebted at the time), and upon which she resided, is subject to her title, where the mortgagee knew of her occupancy under claim of title.[27] So, where a deed operates to convey a life-estate to one and the fee to another, and a purchase-money mortgage is executed by the grantee of the life-estate, the record of the deed is notice to an assignee of the mortgage that the mortgagor had a life-estate only, to which alone the mortgage could attach; and he has no equity entitling him to relief against the grantee of the fee, although

---

[20] Robbins v. Moore, 129 Ill. 30, 21 N. E. Rep. 934.

[21] Whelchel v. Lucky, 41 Fed. Rep. 114.

[22] Shorten v. Drake, 38 Ohio St. 76.

[23] Patterson v. Johnston, 7 Ohio, 225.

[24] Fessenden v. Taft, 65 N. H. 39, 17 Atl. Rep. 713.

[25] Appeal of Reed, 122 Pa. St. 565, 16 Atl. Rep. 100.

[26] Arnold v. Whitcomb, 83 Mich. 19, 46 N. W. Rep. 1029.

[27] Sanford v. Davis, 131 Ill. 570, 54 N. E. Rep. 977.

the latter is not a purchaser for value.[28] On the same principle, the actual possession of land, by a purchaser holding a
bond for a deed from his vendor, is notice of his rights to one
taking a mortgage on the land from the vendor, and the mortgagee will take a lien only on the vendor's right.[29] Conversely,
the record of a mortgage given by one having only an equitable
title under a bond for a deed which is not recorded, is not
notice to a subsequent purchaser of the legal title from one in
possession of the land, as such purchaser's title is not derived
through the title of the mortgagor, and he will not take subject
to the mortgage although it is recorded.[30]

§ 160. **Priority as Against Judgment Liens.**—A mortgage
executed before the rendition of a judgment against the mortgagor, and in good faith and for a valuable consideration,
is a superior incumbrance to the lien of the judgment. That
is, the lien of the judgment will attach only to the debtor's
equity of redemption; and the recording of the mortgage is
deemed notice in law to all subsequent incumbrancers, by judgment or otherwise.[31] The lien of a prior mortgage upon property is not postponed to that of a subsequent judgment recovered under the provisions of the dram-shop act (Rev. Stat. Ill.
c. 43, § 10) for damages arising in consequence of the sale of
intoxicating liquors on the mortgaged premises by or with the
permission of the owner. The provisions of that act, making
the building and premises where liquors are sold with the permission of the owner liable to sale under a judgment against
the occupant for damages from the sale of such liquors, apply
only to such owners as have a rentable interest in the property, and not to a contingent interest such as that of a mortgagee.[32] But on the other hand, judgments recovered against
a railroad company by owners of abutting property, for damages to their land caused by the construction and operation of
the road, are entitled to priority of payment over mortgage
bonds out of the fund produced by a sale of the road on foreclosure of the mortgage; because the right of the owners of
private property, taken or damaged for public use, to receive
compensation therefor, as guarantied by the constitution, can-

---

[28] Lehndorf v. Cope, 122 Ill. 317,
13 N. E. Rep. 505.

[29] Doolittle v. Cook, 75 Ill. 354.

[30] Irish v. Sharp, 89 Ill. 261.

[31] Warner v. Helm, 6 Ill. 220.

[32] Bell v. Cassem, 158 Ill. 45, 41
N. E. Rep. 1089, affirming 56 Ill.
App. 260.

not be defeated by mortgaging the property of the corporation which appropriates or damages the property.[33]

§ 161. Priority as Between Mortgage and Mechanic's Lien.

—A mechanic's lien for labor and material to be expended in the erection of improvements on land is fixed by the contract with the owner and attaches from the date thereof; and it is superior to the lien of a mortgage given subsequently, though before the labor and material are so expended; nor will the priority of the mechanic's lien be forfeited by an extension of the time for completing the work, and of the time of payment, beyond the time stipulated in the contract.[34] On the other hand, where land is already incumbered by a mortgage at the time when labor is performed or material furnished for the erection of a building thereon, the lien of the mechanic or material-man is prior to that of the mortgagee as to the building, but subject to it as to the land; and when a sale of the premises becomes necessary, the proportion of the value of the building to that of the whole estate should first be ascertained, and that amount applied to the satisfaction of the claims of the mechanic or material-man.[35] From the rule which establishes the priority of the mortgage as to the land, it follows that if the improvements are destroyed by fire, the lien of the mechanic has nothing on which to attach except the equity of redemption, and the subsequent sale of the premises under the prior mortgage or deed of trust will have the effect to cut off such lien entirely.[36] The mechanic's lien may indeed, in some circumstances, attach to the insurance money recovered for the loss of the buildings on which the lien originally attached, but not, it would appear, as against the lien of a purchase-money mortgage executed before the contract with the mechanic was made, though filed on the same day, where the mortgagee took out the insurance on the buildings, and caused the same to be made payable to himself, though the policy stood in the name of the mortgagor.[37]

§ 162. Priority as Fixed by Date of Record.—Under ordinary circumstances, the question of priority as between two

[33] Penn Mut. Life Ins. Co. v. Heiss, 141 Ill. 35, 31 N. E. Rep. 138.

[34] Stout v. Sower, 22 Ill. App. 65.

[35] Langford v. Mackay, 12 Ill. App. 223; Edler v. Clark (U. S. Circ. Ct. N. D. Ill.), 51 Fed. Rep. 117.

[36] Condict v. Flower, 106 Ill. 105.

[37] Elgin Lumber Co. v. Langman, 23 Ill. App. 250.

mortgages on the same land, or between a mortgage and a conveyance, will be determined by the respective dates when they were filed for record. Thus, where a deed of trust on real estate given to secure an indebtedness of the grantor is recorded before any other deed made by him is filed for record, a regular foreclosure of the trust deed, by a sale which would bar the debtor's equity of redemption, will cut off and bar all claim of title by parties claiming under a deed from the grantor which was recorded after the trust deed.[38] Conversely, a junior mortgage which is first put on the record will take precedence of a senior mortgage, and give a first lien on the premises, unless the junior mortgagee, at the time of taking his security, had notice of the existence of the prior mortgage.[39] And in this connection it is to be remembered that the relative rank or priority of a mortgage as a lien on the property does not depend solely on the date when the mortgage was executed or when it was recorded. It is also necessary to take into account any knowledge which the mortgagee may have had as to the true state of the title, aside from the record, or of the rights or equities of third persons having claims or liens against the property, but whose evidences of title have not been recorded.[40] And it is said that one who receives a deed of trust from the grantor therein is bound by the record of conveyances in such grantor's apparent chain of title, and hence takes subject to a conveyance of the property by warranty deed which was recorded before the delivery of the deed of trust, though after the actual recording of the latter conveyance.[41]

§ 163. Same; Mortgages Filed the Same Day.—As between two mortgages made by the same mortgagor on the same premises, and filed for record on the same day, that one which

---

[38] Miller v. Shaw, 103 Ill. 277.

[39] Huebsch v. Scheel, 81 Ill. 281.

[40] Inter-State Bldg. & Loan Ass'n v. Ayers, 177 Ill. 9, 52 N. E. Rep. 342, affirming 71 Ill. App. 529. An agreement to give a mortgage at a future date, which shall be a first lien on the property, may be enforced, not only as against the mortgagor, but also as against any incumbrancer who took with notice or without consideration, after the agreement but before its execution, but not as against a mortgage given to a stranger, without notice and for value. Dye v. Forbes, 34 Minn. 13, 24 N. W. Rep. 309.

[41] Lanphier v. Desmond, 187 Ill. 370, 58 N. E. Rep. 343, affirming Desmond v. Lanphier, 86 Ill. App. 101.

was filed at the earlier hour will have the priority.[42] But if both the mortgages are handed to the recorder, not only on the same day but at the same moment and by one and the same act, neither will be entitled to precedence over the other, unless some extrinsic circumstance can be found which will give one of the lienors a stronger claim to priority than can be set up by the other. Such a claim, however, must be supported by some substantial equity, and cannot be rested on grounds which are merely trifling or technical. Thus, neither of the instruments can be given the advantage of prior recording on the ground that, in giving them consecutive numbers, the recorder assigned a lower number to one than to the· other,[43] nor on the ground of an undisclosed wish or intention on the part of the mortgagor to give precedence to one over the other.[44] But an actual understanding and agreement of the parties that one of the mortgages shall outrank the other will justify a court in giving it priority.[45] And so, where two mortgages covering the same property, to secure two notes made payable to the same nominal payee for convenience in negotiating them, were filed for record on the same day and at the same hour, but one of them was numbered and entered by the recorder for record before the other, and it also secured the note bearing the earlier date, and was the first to be transferred for value, it was held that it had priority of lien over the other.[46] Likewise, where the holder of a mortgage covering two lots seeks foreclosure, claiming priority over two other mortgages, each of which covers one of the lots separately, and it appears that all three were filed for record simultaneously it may be shown by extrinsic evidence, on the question of priority, that the money secured by the two mortgages on the separate lots was to be advanced for building purposes at all events, while complainant's mortgage was not to become effective unless it became necessary to draw the money thereunder to pay the interest on the other two, and that the money was not so drawn until the funds had been advanced under the two separate mortgages.[47]

[42] Fischer v. Tuohy, 87 Ill. App. 574.

[43] Schaeppi v. Glade, 195 Ill. 62, 62 N. E. Rep. 874.

[44] Koevenig v. Schmitz, 71 Iowa, 175, 82 N. W. Rep. 320.

[45] Corbin v. Kincaid, 33 Kans. 649, 7 Pac. Rep. 145.

[46] Fischer v. Tuohy, 186 Ill. 143, 57 N. E. Rep. 801.

[47] Schaeppi v. Glade, 195 Ill. 62, 62 N. E. Rep. 874.

§ 164. Priority of Taxes and Other Statutory Liens.—
Statutory provisions in force at the time of the execution of
a mortgage enter into and become part of the contract; and
where they provide that liens of a certain class shall be paramount and have priority over all others, the mortgagee takes
his lien subject to such liens of the kind specified as may be
afterwards acquired under the statute.[48] Thus, it is competent for the legislature of a state to enact that the taxes
assessed upon particular parcels of real estate shall constitute
a lien on the land superior and paramount to every existing
lien created by the act of the parties, and when this is done, a
sale of the land for non-payment of the taxes so assessed will
cut out the lien of a mortgage on the same property, even
though the mortgage was executed before the lien for taxes
attached.[49] But as the tax lien does not exist at all except by
statute, neither does it possess this paramount rank and priority unless the law so declares. An enactment merely that a
certain tax shall be a lien upon land is not enough to make it a
first lien. If the legislature has manifested no intention of
giving it peculiar or extraordinary force, or of defining its
rank as a lien, such questions must be determined by the general law on the subject of liens.[50]

[48] Warren v. Sohn, 112 Ind. 213, 13 N. E. Rep. 863.

[49] Dunlap v. Gallatin Co., 15 Ill. 7; Mix v. Ross, 57 Ill. 121; Cooper v. Corbin, 105 Ill. 234; People v. Weber, 164 Ill. 412, 45 N. E. Rep. 723. But the rule making the lien of taxes paramount to all other liens applies only in the case of taxes on realty; it is not true of taxes on personalty, which do not become a lien until delivery of the tax books to the collector, and then are subject to any prior valid incumbrances. Cooper v. Corbin, supra. In a case where a mort-gage was given to secure money furnished to purchase an outstand-ing tax title, the validity of which was not questioned, upon property previously owned by the mort-gagor, such mortgage was held to take precedence of mortgages exe-cuted by the same party on the property prior to the existence of the tax title; because the prior mortgages were divested by- the tax sale, and when the property came back to the mortgagor by the extinguishment of the tax title, their lien attached again as of that date, but that was the same date when the purchase-money mortgage attached. Kaiser v. Lembeck, 55 Iowa, 244, 7 N. W. Rep. 519.

[50] Black, Tax Titles (2d edn.) § 185; State v. Aetna Life Ins. Co., 117 Ind. 251, 20 N. E. Rep. 144. It is not only competent for the legislature to provide that taxes shall be a paramount lien upon the lands assessed, but it is with-in its constitutional power to enact that such lien shall 'have the pre-cedence over all mortgages and

§ 165. **Displacement of Mortgage Lien by Receiver's Certificates.**—When a court of equity takes charge of business property, through its receiver, and authorizes the continuance of the business or the expenditure of money on the property, as a means of preserving the corpus of the estate for those entitled, it is undoubtedly within its competence to make the expenses of the receivership, or certificates authorized to be issued by the receiver as security for money borrowed by him, a charge upon the property superior and paramount to the lien of a mortgage already existing. But this is not done as a matter of course. It is a power which may become very dangerous in the exercise, and is to be used sparingly and with great caution.[51] Indeed, there is good authority for saying that

other incumbrances made or given before the enactment of the law creating the tax lien and existing at the date of its passage. But such retrospective operation is not favored, and the legislative intention must be plainly manifested. Black, Tax Titles, § 186; Lydecker v. Palisade Land Co., 33 N. J. Eq. 415; Finn v. Haynes, 37 Mich. 63. See Yeatman v. King (N. Dak.), 51 N. W. Rep. 721.

[51] Makeel v. Hotchkiss, 190 Ill. 311, 60 N. E. Rep. 524, affirming Hotchkiss v. Makeel, 87 Ill. App. 623. In the opinion of the appellate court it was said: "The power to subordinate the lien of a mortgage to the charges of a receiver has been frequently exercised by equity courts in recent years, in the case of mortgages of railroads and other properties impressed with a public duty. But, wherever exercised, it has been because of the peculiar character of the property. A mortgage is a contract obligation, and is as sacred as any other contract; and anything that destroys or impairs its lien destroys or impairs a contract. The reason that supports the excepted cases of railroads and

some other business properties is that, they being charged with a duty to the public that is superior to any private obligation, the mortgage owner has knowledge, when he invests, that his security is liable to be displaced in favor of that first obligation. In no well-considered case that we know of has the power been exercised to the subversion of the rights of a prior mortgagee of purely private property, unless for very peculiar reasons. But it is contended in this case that the mortgagee stood by, encouraged, and saw his security protected and perhaps enhanced by the receiver. There is no evidence that the mortgagee did anything except of a permissive character, and it would be a hazardous equitable doctrine to hold that a mortgagee of private property who stands by and sees the owners thereof, or a receiver appointed in a suit to which he is not a party, between contending and rival owners, subject to his mortgage, care for and improve the security, does so at the peril of having his lien displaced in favor of the cost of such care and improvement. We cannot assent

such a power should not be exercised at all in the case of purely private corporations, not charged with a public duty, but should be resorted to only in cases of receiverships of railroad corporations and possibly of some other similar companies. "Extensive as are the powers of courts of equity, they do not authorize a chancellor thus to impair the force of solemn obligations and destroy vested rights. Instead of displacing mortgages and other liens upon the property of private corporations and natural persons, it is the duty of courts to uphold and enforce them against all subsequent incumbrances. It would be dangerous to extend the power which has been recently exercised over railroad mortgages (sometimes with unwarranted freedom), on account of their peculiar nature, to all mortgages."[52]

§ 166. Postponement of Elder to Junior Lien.—Regularly, and in the absence of special equities, a second mortgage is an incumbrance only on the remnant of the property which may be left after satisfying the first mortgage; and if a judgment creditor of the mortgagor succeeds in having the first mortgage set aside, as against himself, this will not put the second mortgage in the place of the first, but the judgment creditor will come in before the second mortgage, up to the amount of the first mortgage.[53] But a junior mortgage may be given the precedence over a senior mortgage either in consequence of an agreement to that effect, or on the ground of a superior equity in the junior lienor.[54] Thus, where two mortgages stand on an equal footing, and are to be paid out of the same fund, the written promise of one mortgagee that he will see the other paid will postpone the mortgage of the former and give priority to the latter.[55] And a release of mortgaged premises by a prior to a subsequent mortgagee, without an assignment of the debt secured, will operate as an extinguishment of the prior mortgage.[56] So also, there will be a reversal of the order of priority when the first mortgagee agrees with the mortgagor to allow his security to be subordinated to the

to such a doctrine." And see also Humphreys v. Allen, 101 Ill. 490.

[53] Farmers' Loan & Trust Co. v. Grape Creek Coal Co. (U. S. Circ. Ct. S. D. Ill.), 50 Fed. Rep. 481.

[53] Simon v. Openheimer, 20 Fed. Rep. 553.

[54] Brown v. Baker, 22 Nebr. 708, 36 N. W. Rep. 273.

[55] Sanders v. Barlow, 21 Fed. Rep. 836.

[56] Hill v. West, 8 Ohio, 222.

lien of a second mortgage to be given to another person.[57] Again, the conduct of the senior mortgagee may be such as to estop or prevent him, in equity, from asserting the precedence of his lien. This is the case if he denies that he has any lien on the premises, when interrogated by a person proposing to take another mortgage, or if he fraudulently conceals the existence of his mortgage, when the circumstances are such as to require him, in fairness and honest dealing, to disclose it. But the holder of a mortgage duly recorded cannot be charged with fraudulent conduct merely because he acts as counsel in the preparation of a second mortgage and remains silent as to his own.[58] And it must be remembered that the record of a subsequent deed or mortgage is not notice to the prior mortgagee, nor is he required to search the records for subsequent incumbrances; and a junior incumbrancer, desiring to protect himself, must bring home to the prior mortgagee actual notice of his equities.[59] And where the first and second mortgagees receive notice, each of the other's equities, concurrently, the equities being of equal merit, the lien which is elder in point of time will prevail.[60]

§ 167. Purchase-Money Mortgages.—It is well settled that a mortgage given for the unpaid balance of purchase money on a sale of land, simultaneously with a deed of the same and as a part of the same transaction, takes precedence of all existing and subsequent claims and liens of every kind against the mortgagor, to the extent of the land sold.[61] This rule is

[57] Beasley v. Henry, 6 Ill. App. 485; Beasley v. McGhee, Id. 489. But an agreement by a director of a corporation that the proceeds of a second mortgage loan should be applied in payment of a prior mortgage to him before the same was due, does not constitute a waiver of his prior lien, where such proceeds are not in fact paid over to him. Mullanphy Bank v. Schott, 135 Ill. 655, 26 N. E. Rep. 640.

[58] Paine v. French, 4 Ohio, 318. An implied covenant against incumbrances contained in a second mortgage by a corporation does not amount to a fraudulent representation that there is no previous mortgage, so as to preclude the holder of the first mortgage, who was a director of the corporation but who did not in fact sign the second mortgage, from insisting upon the priority of his lien. Mullanphy Bank v. Schott, 135 Ill. 655, 26 N. E. Rep. 640.

[59] Boone v. Clark, 129 Ill. 466, 21 N. E. Rep. 850.

[60] Houfes v. Schultze, 2 Ill. App. 196.

[61] Curtis v. Root, 20 Ill. 53; Austin v. Underwood, 37 Ill. 438; Christie v. Hale, 46 Ill. 117; Elder v. Derby, 98 Ill. 228.

based upon the doctrine of law that the deed for the land and
the purchase-money mortgage constitute simultaneous parts of
one and the same transaction, and hence, in contemplation of
law, there is no interval of time between the execution of the
deed and the execution of the mortgage during which any
lien or claim against the mortgagor could attach upon the
property. In other words, in the same instant of time in which
he acquires the title by the conveyance he also subjects the
title to the lien of the mortgage. But to bring the rule into
operation, it is necessary that the mortgage should be made
contemporaneously with the deed to the mortgagor.[62] This
does not mean, however, that the two instruments should be
executed at the same moment or even on the same day, provided the execution of the deed and of the mortgage constituted part of one continuous transaction, and was so intended,
so that both should in equity be given a contemporaneous
operation in order to promote the intention of the parties.[63]
It is even held that a purchase-money mortgage, executed
when the title to the land passes, will take precedence of one
previously given to secure money borrowed by the purchaser
to make the cash payment on the land, though the latter was
recorded first, at least where the vendor of the land had no
knowledge of the previous mortgage.[64] And where the lien of
a purchase-money mortgage has thus attached, it will not be
affected by a change in the form of the security. Thus, where
promissory notes with personal security are given for the deferred payments on a purchase of real estate, and afterwards
these notes are surrendered, and new notes are given in their
stead, with a mortgage on the land purchased, the substitution
will not deprive the mortgage of the character of a purchase-
money mortgage; for the debt being for purchase money, no
change in the form of the instrument by which it is evidenced
or secured will change its character.[65] And the same rule
applies where an original purchase-money mortgage is given
up and a deed of trust on the same premises substituted for
it.[66] So, where land is sold and a written contract is executed

[62] Roane v. Baker, 120 Ill. 308, 2 N. E. Rep. 501.

[63] Stewart v. Smith, 36 Minn. 82, 30 N. W. Rep. 430.

[64] Brower v. Witmeyer, 121 Ind. 83, 22 N. E. Rep. 975; Schoch v. Birdsall, 48 Minn. 441, 51 N. W.
Rep. 382; Tolman v. Smith, 85 Cal. 280, 24 Pac. Rep. 743.

[65] Kimble v. Esworthy, 6 Ill. App. 517.

[66] Spitzer v. Williams, 98 Ill. App. 146.

by the parties, whereby it is agreed that the vendor shall retain the title to the land as security for the unpaid purchase money, and the vendee executes his notes for such balance, the notes and the contract will be considered as one instrument, and regarded as a security in the nature of a mortgage, which may be sold and assigned, and enforced in the name of the assignee by decree in equity.[67] It should be added that it is not only as against other mortgages that a mortgage for the purchase money has the priority, but it will also take precedence over the lien of judgments recovered against the mortgagor (purchaser) prior to the conveyance.[68]

While a purchase-money mortgage, like any other, must be put on record, and proper diligence is required of the mortgagee in doing this, yet it is held that the priority of such a mortgage is not lost by the mere fact that the owner of it allows a junior mortgage to be first recorded, if there are no other circumstances to show his agreement or acquiescence in the postponing of his security.[69] Especially is this rule applied where the junior incumbrancer had notice of the elder mortgage. Thus, a mortgage executed by a vendee of land to a third person, and recorded by the latter before the vendee's deed or the mortgage given back by him for the purchase money had been acknowledged and recorded, but of the existence of which deed and mortgage such third person had notice, will not take precedence over the purchase-money mortgage.[70] And knowledge of the vendor's rights in the premises may be inferred from the fact of his continued possession of the land.[71]

Where the purchaser of land executes a mortgage thereon

---

[67] Wright v. Troutman, 81 Ill. 374. The written agreement in this case is the feature which distinguishes it from the case of a vendor's lien arising by implication of law. The law does not authorise the assignment or transfer of a vendor's lien to the purchaser of notes given for the purchase money. Such a lien is not assignable, but is personal, and to be enforced by the vendor only. He cannot enforce it by suit in his own name for the benefit of another who is the purchaser of the notes. Elder v. Jones, 85 Ill. 384.

[68] Curtis v. Root, 20 Ill. 53; Fitts v. Davis, 42 Ill. 391; Roane v. Baker, 120 Ill. 308, 2 N. E. Rep. 501; 1 Black on Judgm. § 447.

[69] Elder v. Derby, 98 Ill. 228; Roane v. Baker, 120 Ill. 308, 2 N. E. Rep. 246.

[70] Continental Investment & Loan Society v. Wood, 168 Ill. 421, 48 N. E. Rep. 221, affirming 66 Ill. App. 491.

[71] Brainard v. Hudson, 103 Ill. 218.

to a third person, who advances the purchase money for him, such mortgage is entitled to the same preference and priority which it would have had if made to the vendor himself.[72] But in order that a mortgage so given should have the rank and priority of a purchase-money mortgage, it is necessary that the third person should deal directly with the vendor of the land. And if a purchaser of land is already indebted to the vendor for the price of the same, and then borrows money from a third person for the purpose of discharging this debt, and gives a mortgage on the land to such third person, this mortgage is not entitled to the standing of a purchase-money mortgage.[73]

§ 168. Lien of Unrecorded Mortgage.—As was shown in an earlier section, the lien of a mortgage is valid and enforceable, although the instrument is not recorded, as against the mortgagor and against any subsequent purchasers or creditors who had actual notice of it.[74] In order to charge the person acquiring a title with notice of an unrecorded mortgage, the proof of the same should be clear and convincing, but the fact of notice may be proved either by direct evidence or by other facts from which it may be clearly inferred, but in the latter case, the inference must be not only probable but necessary and unquestionable.[75] And the burden of proving that a party in interest had knowledge of an unrecorded mortgage is upon the one who asserts that such knowledge existed.[76] It is said, however, that any fact or circumstance which tends to give notice or informs a party that there is an incumbrance on land, is sufficient to charge him with notice of its existence. When such information comes to the knowledge of a purchaser or subsequent incumbrancer, the law requires him to pursue it until it leads to notice.[77] Further, the mere recording of a mortgage or deed of trust to secure a loan of money does not create a lien upon the property where the money has not in fact been received by the borrower. It becomes a lien, as against the rights and equities of a third person under a prior unrecorded mortgage or trust deed only from the time the money is in fact received.[78]

[72] Curtis v. Root, 20 Ill. 53; Magee v. Magee, 51 Ill. 500.

[73] Small v. Stagg, 95 Ill. 39; Eyster v. Hatheway, 50 Ill. 521; Austin v. Underwood, 37 Ill. 438.

[74] Supra, § 153. And see Williams v. Tatnall, 29 Ill. 553.

[75] Aurora Nat. Loan Ass'n v. Spencer, 81 Ill. App. 622.

[76] Lindley v. English, 89 Ill. App. 538.

[77] Aetna Life Ins. Co. v. Ford, 89 Ill. 252.

[78] Schultze v. Houfes, 96 Ill. 335.

14

CHAPTER XV

RELATIVE RIGHTS OF SENIOR AND JUNIOR MORTGAGEES.

§ 169. **Equities Entitling Junior Lien to Priority.**—As we have stated in an earlier section, to give a junior mortgagee the right of priority over a senior one, there must be either an agreement to that effect or a superior equity in the junior mortgagee; but such an equity may grow out of the conduct of the elder lienor, when it is of such a nature as to estop him from claiming the precedence to which he would ordinarily be entitled.[1] It is also a rule that a senior mortgagee will be postponed to a junior lien to the extent of rents and profits improperly paid to the owner of the equity of redemption and not applied on the debt.[2] But a second mortgagee cannot take any advantage of a delay by the first mortgagee in foreclosing, though it lasts for several months, if his own security has not matured.[3] Where the owner of a prior incumbrance buys any part of the indebtedness secured by a junior mortgage, it must, as between the two incumbrancers, be held to be so much in the nature of a partial redemption as to leave to the holder of the residue priority of right to the satisfaction of that residue before satisfying that part of the debt so sold.[4] In this connection must also be mentioned the rule that, where a first mortgage is given to secure future advances (it being left optional with the mortgagee to make the advances or not), and a

[1] Supra, § 166. And see Brown v. Baker, 22 Nebr. 708, 36 N. W. Rep. 273.

[2] Hitchcock v. Fortier, 65 Ill. 239.

[3] Cunningham v. Nelson Mfg. Co., 17 Ill. App. 510.

[4] Magloughlin v. Clark, 35 Ill. App. 251.

second mortgage on the same premises to secure an existing debt, the junior lien is entitled to priority over the senior to the extent of any advances made by the first mortgagee after the attaching of the second, providing the first mortgagee had notice of the existence of the second.[5]

§ 170. **Duty of Senior Mortgagee as to Protecting Security.**—A senior mortgagee is not bound to respect the equitable rights of a junior incumbrancer in the property unless he has notice, either actual or constructive, of such rights; and since he is not bound to search the records for conveyances subsequent to his own, the recording of the junior mortgage is not sufficient to charge the senior mortgagee with notice of its existence or of the equitable rights of the junior mortgagee. But when the elder lienor has the requisite notice, any dealing on his part with the mortgaged property which would operate to the prejudice of the security of the junior mortgagee, will be at the peril of having his own lien subordinated pro tanto. Thus, the junior mortgagee has a right to insist that the senior mortgagee shall not release from the lien of his mortgage any property upon which the second incumbrancer has no lien, to the prejudice of the latter.[6] So a junior mortgagee may set up a claim against the senior mortgagee for acts of waste upon the property in which they are both interested, detrimental to the security of the junior lienor; and such a claim may be asserted either in a direct proceeding for the purpose or in a suit brought by the senior mortgagee to foreclose his lien.[7]

§ 171. **Right to Impeach Validity of Senior Mortgage.**—It is the right of a junior mortgagee to maintain an action to have a senior mortgage on the same property set aside or adjudged void, for fraud, want or illegality of consideration, or other adequate cause.[8] A second mortgagee who has foreclosed under a power of sale and purchased the land may sue to have the first mortgage adjudged paid, although no steps have been taken to foreclose it, and although the time for redemption from his own foreclosure has not expired.[9] And so, a junior

[5] Frye v. Bank of Illinois, 11 Ill. 367; supra, § 125.

[6] Sarles v. McGee, 1 N. Dak. 365, 48 N. W. Rep. 231.

[7] Whorton v. Webster. 56 Wis. 356, 14 N. W. Rep. 280.

[8] Leopold v. Silverman, 7 Mont: 266, 16 Pac. Rep. 580.

[9] Redin v. Branhan, 43 Minn. 283, 45 N. W. Rep. 445.

mortgagee, out of possession, may maintain a suit in equity against the senior mortgagee, also out of possession, and the mortgagor, in possession, to have the first mortgage cancelled, after the senior mortgagee has lost all right to proceed on his mortgage by the running of the statute of limitations applicable thereto.[10] But it is said that when a party accepts a junior mortgage which recites the first mortgage and provides for its payment, he thereby estops himself to deny the existence of the senior mortgage or the validity of its lien.[11]

§ 172. **Rights of Junior Mortgagee Paying Off Senior Mortgage.**—A junior mortgagee of land has the right, as a measure necessary for the protection of his own interests, to pay off the senior mortgage when there has been default in the payment of the same and steps are taken for its foreclosure. It is true he cannot compel the senior mortgagee to make him a formal assignment of the mortgage and the debt which it secures;[12] he can only require him to accept the amount due and release the mortgage of record. But a common-law assignment is not necessary to his due protection, for the courts, in proper circumstances, will recognize the junior mortgagee who has paid off the elder lien as an equitable assignee thereof, or an assignee by operation of law, and accord him the rights appertaining to that position. It is also well settled that a junior mortgagee who pays off the senior mortgage for his own protection is entitled in equity to be subrogated to the rights of the senior mortgagee,[13] provided he has paid the entire amount of the elder lien.[14] The payment of the elder incumbrance in this manner will not necessarily extinguish it. For the junior mortgagee, having paid the amount, may elect to treat the elder mortgage as being paid and satisfied, cancel the note secured, and have satisfaction entered on the record; but he may also, if he chooses, take an assignment of the note and mortgage, thereby electing to give the transaction the form of a purchase and assignment, rather than a payment, and may so keep the elder mortgage alive.[15] And he will be treated as a purchaser or assignee of the senior incumbrance, unless

[10] Fox v. Blossom, 17 Blatchf. 352, Fed. Cas. No. 5,008.

[11] Clapp v. Halliday, 48 Ark. 258, 2 S. W. Rep. 853.

[12] Handly v. Munsell, 109 Ill. 362.

[13] Tyrrell v. Ward, 102 Ill. 29; Ball v. Callahan, 95 Ill. App. 615.

[14] Loeb v. Fleming, 15 Ill. App. 503.

[15] Pursley v. Forth, 82 Ill. 327.

the facts show that he intended an absolute payment; and if, for example, the senior mortgage contains a waiver of homestead, while the junior mortgage does not, the junior incumbrancer, after thus acquiring the senior mortgage, may foreclose as against the homestead.[16] Further, it is his right to deal with his original (second) mortgage without reference to his purchase of the first. He is not obliged to bring the senior mortgage forward and include it in a decree foreclosing the second. And the foreclosure of the second mortgage, after the holder thereof has become the owner of the first mortgage by purchase and assignment, does not merge the latter in the one foreclosed so as to give the purchaser at the sale a superior title.[17]

§ 173. **Doctrine of Tacking.**—It was a rule of the common law (or rather of the earlier equity law of mortgages) that the holder of a third mortgage on land, who acquired the first mortgage by purchase, might "tack" or attach his third mortgage to the first, and take satisfaction of both out of the proceeds of a foreclosure, thus cutting out the rights of the second mortgagee, or at least postponing him to the third as well as to the first mortgage. But this doctrine was recognized as harsh and unreasonable and founded on very doubtful principles; and it is not in force at all in the United States, being contrary to the purpose and spirit of the recording laws. But the holder of the youngest lien may tack to his mortgage the amount which he has paid for the purchase of the senior lien, not, however, to the prejudice of the intervening second incumbrancer, but in subordination to the rights of the latter.[18] Or he may, as stated in the preceding section, keep the first mortgage alive, and even foreclose it without reference to his own junior lien, though this will not in any way affect the relative priority of the three incumbrances. Where a second mortgagee in possession under the foreclosure of his mortgage, also becomes the owner by purchase of judgments obtained against the mortgagor subsequent to the execution of the first mortgage, of which he had full notice, it is said that he cannot complain of a decree foreclosing the first mortgage, which charges

---

[16] Ebert v. Gerding, 116 Ill. 216, 5 N. E. Rep. 591.

[17] Wahl v. Zoelck, 178 Ill. 158, 52 N. E. Rep. 870, affirming 77 Ill. App. 226.

[18] Mosier v. Norton, 83 Ill. 519; Magilton v. Holbert, 52 Hun, 444, 5 N. Y. Supp. 507.

him with rent for the property while it remained in his possession, and credits him only with the sum paid for the judgments.[19]

§ 174. **Redemption from Elder Mortgage.**—A junior mortgagee of real property may, at his option, redeem from the senior mortgage, though he is under no obligation to do so.[20] And if his mortgage covers several different lots or tracts, some of which are subject to the prior mortgage and others not, he may redeem from the senior incumbrance without showing that it is necessary to protect the security of his mortgage debt, or that the other tracts in his mortgage are not of sufficient value to pay his debt; he is not bound to take any risks as to the adequacy of his security.[21] Further, this right of redemption in the junior mortgagee is a right to redeem from the prior mortgage by paying the amount due according to its terms as recorded. As against him, no new terms can be incorporated into the prior mortgage, and no additional indebtedness can be secured by it. For instance, his right of redemption cannot be affected by an agreement between the parties to the first mortgage for a higher rate of interest than that specified in the mortgage.[22] And he may enforce his right of redemption, on a bill properly framed, without regard to a conveyance of the mortgagor's equity of redemption, made to the first mortgagee, after the execution of the junior mortgage.[23] Further, this right of redemption may be exercised by the junior incumbrancer after a foreclosure of the prior mortgage, as well as before, provided he was not made a party to the foreclosure suit.[24] When the land has been sold on foreclosure of the senior mortgage, the junior mortgagee will have the right, under the statute, to redeem from that sale at any time within twelve months; but if he has obtained a personal judgment or decree for the debt secured by his mortgage, and a sale of the mortgaged premises, his right of redemption will be that of a judgment creditor, that is, he will have the right to redeem from the foreclosure sale after the expiration of twelve months and within the three months following.[25] It is also to

[19] Crawford v. Munford, 29 Ill. App. 445.

[20] Rogers v. Herron, 92 Ill. 583.
[21] Morse v. Smith, 83 Ill. 396.
[22] Gardner v. Emerson, 40 Ill. 296.

[23] Rogers v. Herron, 92 Ill. 583.
[24] Strang v. Allen, 44 Ill. 428; Hodgen v. Guttery, 58 Ill. 431; Hurd v. Case, 32 Ill. 45.
[25] Whitehead v. Hall, 148 Ill. 253. 35 . . . . . .

be remarked that the right of the successive holders of a series of notes, maturing at different times, and secured by the same mortgage, to redeem from a foreclosure and sale in favor of the holder of the note first maturing, is the same as that of separate junior incumbrancers to redeem from a foreclosure of a prior mortgage.[26]

§ 175. **Compelling Foreclosure of Senior Mortgage.**—While a junior mortgagee has the right, as already stated, to redeem from a senior mortgage on the same property, and, if necessary, to maintain this right by means of a bill in equity filed for the purpose, he cannot in any way foreclose a prior mortgage; that is, he cannot compel the senior mortgagee to take steps for foreclosure, nor can he, on any bill filed by himself, obtain a decree foreclosing the elder mortgage. It is the privilege of the holder of the prior incumbrance to foreclose it or not as he may see fit.[27]

§ 176. **Effect of Foreclosure of Senior Mortgage.**—The rights of a junior mortgagee upon the foreclosure of the senior mortgage will depend, in the first instance, upon the question whether or not he was made a party to the foreclosure proceedings. It is said to be "one of the cherished objects of a court of equity to avoid a multiplicity of actions concerning the same subject-matter, by bringing all of the parties interested before it, and making a full and complete settlement between them of their respective rights. Hence the general rule that all persons ought to be made parties whose rights or interests may be affected by the decree. This rule is especially applicable to the case of a foreclosure, where a sale of the mortgaged premises is sought. All persons having an interest in the equity of redemption, and in the distribution of the surplus, are highly proper if not indispensable parties. Such are subsequent purchasers and incumbrancers."[28] Now if the junior mortgagee is made a party to the suit for the foreclosure of the senior mortgage, his lien on the premises will be entirely cut off by the decree and sale. The equity of redemption of the mortgagor will of course be extinguished. and therefore nothing will remain upon which the junior

---

[26] Preston v. Hodgen, 50 Ill. 56.

[27] Rose v. Chandler, 50 Ill. App. 421; Garrett v. Peirce, 74 Ill. App. 285.

[28] Montgomery v. Brown, 2 Gilm. (7 Ill.) 581.

mortgage could attach as a lien, or which could be sold on its foreclosure. The legal title to the mortgaged premises will vest in the purchaser at the foreclosure sale, and nothing will remain to the junior mortgagee but the right to redeem in equity. If, however, he does exercise this right of redemption, he may then foreclose his own mortgage and have the land sold in satisfaction of his claims, including the sum advanced to make the redemption from the senior mortgage.[29] If the proceeds of the sale on the foreclosure of the senior mortgage are more than sufficient to discharge the debt secured thereby, the junior mortgagee will have a claim on the surplus, and the same may be applied for his benefit; but if he was not a party to the foreclosure suit, he must, in order to entitle himself to the surplus, either file a cross bill or establish his claim by proof at the trial or before the master.[30] If the junior mortgagee is not joined as a party in the suit for foreclosure of the elder lien, it is said that his rights will depend upon the form of the action. Where the proceeding is by scire facias, subsequent incumbrancers are cut off though not made direct parties to the proceeding. But if the foreclosure is by bill in chancery, they are not absolutely barred unless made parties, but they cannot be permitted to assert their equity of redemption against an equity still stronger.[31] And a junior incumbrancer not made a party to the foreclosure of the senior lien must resort to a court of equity to establish whatever equitable rights he may have. Thus, in ejectment, where both parties are mortgagees, claiming from a common source, the party having the elder mortgage from the common mortgagor, and who first forecloses and acquires a deed, must prevail, as having the paramount legal title.[32] It remains to consider the rights of a junior mortgagee where the senior incumbrancer, instead of foreclosing, takes a conveyance of the debtor's equity of redemption. This will not extinguish or in any way disturb the junior liens on the property; but they will still

[29] Rose v. Walk, 149 Ill. 60, 36 N. E. Rep. 555. Where a senior mortgagee, at his foreclosure sale, bought in the mortgaged premises for less than the debt, and after receiving his certificate of purchase, procured an award for a special execution to make the residue, it was held that a junior mortgagee, redeeming under the statute from the sale, took the land free from any lien of the first mortgage. Seligman v. Laubheimer, 58 Ill. 124.

[30] Ellis v. Southwell, 29 Ill. 549; Hart v. Wingart, 83 Ill. 282.

[31] Kenyon v. Shreck, 52 Ill. 382.

[32] Aholtz v. Zellar, 88 Ill. 24.

remain subordinate to the senior mortgage, and the same may be enforced as against them, if there was no intention on the part of the senior mortgagee to release or discharge his mortgage as against them.[33]

§ 177. **Marshalling Securities.**—The general rule in regard to the marshalling of securities is that, where there are two funds or properties, to both of which a prior lien holder may resort, while a junior lien holder can resort to but one of them, the former will be required first to enforce his claim out of the fund to which the latter cannot have recourse.[34]   Thus, where a person takes a mortgage on property which is already subject to an elder mortgage, which also covers additional property, the junior mortgagee will have the right, in equity, to compel the senior incumbrancer to satisfy his debt out of such additional property, so far as it will go, before coming upon the land which is subject to both the liens.[35] And as an extension of the same rule it is held that the lien of a senior mortgagee who fraudulently releases property on which his mortgage is the exclusive lien, the same being adequate security, will be postponed to that of the junior mortgagee.[36] So, if one holding a first mortgage upon land has additional security upon personal property, which he releases or loses by his own negligence, one holding a junior mortgage on the land only may compel the first mortgagee, on foreclosure, to deduct the value of the security so released or lost, provided the first mortgagee had actual or constructive notice of the subsequent mortgage.[37] But where the first mortgage covers the homestead and other land, and the second mortgage covers the other land only and not the homestead, the usual rule of marshalling does not apply, and the junior mortgagee cannot require that ·

[33] See Powell v. Jeffries, 5 Ill. 387; Stimpson v. Pease, 53 Iowa, 572, 5 N. W. Rep. 760.

[34] Merchants' Nat. Bank v. Mc-Laughlin, 1 McCrary, 258, 2 Fed. Rep. 128; Russell v. Howard, 2 McLean, 489, Fed. Cas. No. 12,156.

[35] Dodds v. Snyder, 44 Ill. 53; Orr v. Blackwell, 93 Ala. 212, 8 South. Rep. 413.

[36] Jordan v. Hamilton County Bank, 11 Nebr. 499, 9 N. W. Rep. 654.

[37] Alexander v. Welch, 10 Ill. App. 181. And it is not necessary that the junior mortgagee should have known, at the time he took his mortgage, that the senior incumbrancer had additional or collateral security, or that the former should have taken his mortgage in reliance on the equitable right to compel the marshalling of the assets. Sherron v. Acton, (N. J.) 18 Atl. Rep. 978.

the homestead shall be first sold.[38] And further, this rule cannot be stretched so far as to compel a first mortgagee holding
a lien on a single tract of land to resort, at the instance of the
junior mortgagee, to other property of the mortgagor not embraced in his mortgage.[39]

It is doubtful whether the doctrine of marshalling should be
applied as between several successive junior incumbrancers,
their equities being so nearly equal. At any rate, it cannot be
invoked where the result of its application would work injustice to any person interested. Thus, where A. has a mortgage
upon two lots, and B. has a subsequent mortgage upon one, and
C. has a mortgage junior to B.'s upon the other of the two lots,
A. cannot be compelled, at the instance of B., to exhaust first
the lot on which C. has his mortgage; but he will be required
to take his debt out of the proceeds of both lots, in proportion
to the amount which each may produce.[40] So, on an application by a second mortgagee for surplus moneys arising from
a sale on foreclosure of the first mortgage, he will not be compelled to release his lien in favor of subsequent mortgagees, on
proof merely that his debt is amply secured by other property
on which his mortgage is a lien.[41]

§ 178. Foreclosure of Junior Mortgage.—When no foreclosure has yet been made under the senior mortgage, a junior

[38] Dodds v. Snyder, 44 Ill. 53;
Armitage v. Davenport, 64 Mich.
412, 31 N. W. Rep. 408; Equitable
Life Ins. Co. v. Gleason, 62 Iowa,
277, 17 N. W. Rep. 524. Compare
Abbott v. Powell, 6 Sawy. 91, Fed.
Cas. No. 13.

[39] State v. Aetna Life Ins. Co.,
117 Ind. 251, 20 N. E. Rep. 144.

[40] Green v. Ramage, 18 Ohio, 428.
Marshalling is a pure equity and
does not at all rest upon contract,
and it will not be enforced to the
prejudice of either the dominant
creditor, or third persons, or even
so as to do an injustice to the
debtor. It is not an equity that
fastens itself upon the situation
at the time the successive securities are taken; but on the contrary it is one to be determined at
the time the marshalling is asked

for. The equity can become a
fixed right only by taking proper
steps to have it enforced, and until
this is done it is subject to displacement and defeat by subsequently acquired liens upon the
funds. Hence the rule will not be
applied where there are a large
number of mortgage creditors,
none of whom has an exclusive
lien on any particular fund, and
where the application of the rule
would necessarily work injustice
to some of the creditors. In such
a case, the several mortgage debts
should be paid pro rata, in the order of priority, out of the proceeds
of the funds covered by each.
Gilliam v. McCormack, 85 Tenn.
597, 4 S. W. Rep. 521.

[41] Quackenbush v. O'Hare, 129
N. Y. 485, 29 N. E. Rep. 958.

mortgagee will have the right to foreclose his mortgage upon the equity of redemption, the sale, of course, passing the estate subject to the lien of the elder mortgage.[42] The purchaser at the junior mortgagee's foreclosure sale will take the property subject to the incumbrance of the senior mortgage, and is bound to know that the mortgagor or owner of the equity of redemption will be entitled to the possession and rents of the premises during the running of the period allowed for redemption. He acquires an interest in the equity of redemption only, and presumably bids no more than the premises are worth in excess of the amount secured by the senior mortgage. He has no right of recovery, either at law or in equity, against a grantee of the equity of redemption who has assumed to pay the amount secured by the prior mortgage.[43] As a general rule, the senior mortgagee is not a necessary party to the junior mortgagee's bill for foreclosure, since his rights will not be affected by the decree. But if he is joined as a party, the proper decree to be entered is for a sale of the premises subject to the senior mortgage.[44] As to the application of the income of the property, it is said that "where the first mortgagee is not made a party defendant to a bill to foreclose filed by a second mortgagee, such second mortgagee, procuring the appointment of a receiver to collect the rents and profits, is entitled to have such rents and profits applied upon his mortgage to the exclusion of the prior mortgagee; and in such case the prior mortgagee will not be entitled to payment out of the rents until he files a bill to foreclose his mortgage and procures the receivership to be extended to his security. * * * It must appear that the first mortgagee is not a party to the foreclosure suit begun by the second mortgagee, or that the receiver was appointed for the benefit of the second mortgagee alone, and not for the benefit of all the parties to the suit, in order to secure to the second mortgagee the exclusive right to

---

[42] Rose v. Walk, 149 Ill. 60, 36 N. E. Rep. 555. A junior mortgagee is not bound to see that an amount sufficient to satisfy prior liens is realized from a sale under his mortgage, nor is the prior mortgagee bound to take notice of the sale and bid. Herrick v. Tallman, 75 Iowa, 441, 39 N. W. Rep. 699.

[43] Eggleston v. Hadfield, 90 Ill. App. 11; Dodds v. Snyder, 44 Ill. 53.

[44] Galford v. Gillett, 55 Ill. App. 576; Hibernian Banking Ass'n v. Law, 88 Ill. App. 18.

the rents of the mortgaged property."[45]   Further, the junior mortgagee, seeking foreclosure, may impeach the validity of the senior mortgage, and have a decree adjudging it void and excluding it from participation in the proceeds of the sale; but for this purpose it is not sufficient to allege merely that the present holder of the senior lien, a corporation, which acquired it by assignment, was incapable under its charter of taking such assignment.[46]

[45] Cross v. Will County Nat. Bank, 177 Ill. 33, 52 N. E. Rep. 322, affirming 71 Ill. App. 404.

[46] Daniels v. Belvidere Cemetery Ass'n, 193 Ill. 181, 61 N. E. Rep. 1031, affirming 96 Ill. App. 387.

CHAPTER XVI.

ASSIGNMENT OF MORTGAGES.

§ 179. Who May Make Assignment.—A valid assignment of a mortgage can be made only by the person who has the real and beneficial ownership of the debt which it secures at the time of the transfer;[1] and it is the duty of the assignee to satisfy himself as to the title of the assignor. If the latter is not the original mortgagee, and if the papers do not show any transfer of the mortgage to him, or any indorsement to him of the note secured, the purchaser will be put upon inquiry, and will take the security at the risk of the assertion of their rights by the parties legally entitled thereto.[2] So, if the holder of a note and mortgage has authority to dispose of them for the maker, but only for cash, a purchaser who knows this fact and who takes the securities in part payment of a debt due to himself, and without paying any money or parting with any rights, does not take a title freed from the equities between

---

[1] Bonham v. Galloway, 13 Ill. 68.　　[2] McConnell v. Hodson, 7 Ill. 640.

the maker of the note and the party having it for sale.[3] So, if
a trustee, having no title to a trust deed and note, fraudulently
transfers them to another person, as collateral, it devolves
upon that person to show that he took the paper in good faith,
without notice, for value, before maturity, and in the usual
course of business; and if the indorsements on the note show
that another person than the trustee is the legal holder of it,
the assignee has no right to rely on his explanation of the indorsements, instead of making inquiry as to the real ownership
of the note.[4] In regard particularly to deeds of trust given as
securities, it is the rule that an assignment thereof can be made
only by the beneficiary or holder of the debt secured, not by
the trustee; a transfer attempted to be made by the latter
(not having an interest in the trust) will not have the effect of
a sale or conveyance made pursuant to the terms of the deed.[5]

Any person having the legal right to sell and assign a mortgage may of course empower another to do it for him; and it
is held that an authority to assign a mortgage as agent or
attorney for the owner need not be in writing.[6] In case of the
death of the mortgagee, or holder of the security, the right to
sell and assign the mortgage devolves upon his executor or
administrator,[7] and if there are two joint executors, one alone
may make a valid assignment of a mortgage belonging to the
estate.[8] The interest of a mortgagee, though technically an
estate in the land, is not real property, such as descends to an
heir to the exclusion of the personal representative. On the
contrary, the debt secured is regarded as the principal thing
and the mortgage as only an incident. Hence the heir of a
deceased mortgagee cannot make an effective transfer of the
debt and mortgage, whether by an ordinary assignment or by
a deed of the land, unless, indeed, it is shown that the estate
has been fully administered and settled and the debts paid,
and that the mortgage, upon a final distribution, has been

[3] Brueggestradt v. Ludwig, 184
Ill. 24, 56 N. E. Rep. 419, affirming
82 Ill. App. 435.

[4] Chicago Title & Trust Co. v.
Brugger, 196 Ill. 96, 63 N. E. Rep.
637, affirming 95 Ill. App. 405.

[5] McFarland v. Dey, 69 Ill. 419.

[6] Moreland v. Houghton, 94
Mich. 548, 54 N. W. Rep. 285.

[7] Pierce v. Brown, 24 Vt. 165;

Collamer v. Langdon, 29 Vt. 32;
Crooker v. Jewell, 31 Me. 306;
Libby v. Mayberry, 80 Me. 137, 13
Atl. Rep. 577; Smith v. Dyer, 16
Mass. 18; Johnson v. Bartlett, 17
Pick. 477; Richardson v. Hildreth,
8 Cush. 225.

[8] George v. Baker, 3 Allen
(Mass.) 326.

passed to such heir.[9] There was at one time some question
as to the authority of an executor or administrator to make an
assignment of a mortgage covering land in a state other than
that in which he was appointed. But the modern doctrine is
that, if such a representative, by virtue of his appointment, has
acquired title to the debt evidenced by the mortgage, he may
make a valid assignment of it, though the land lies in another
state, and that his authority in that behalf will be presumed
in the absence of evidence to the contrary.[10]

In case of a mortgage given to, or held by, a partnership,
it is now decided that either one of the partners may validly
transfer the same by signing the firm name to the assignment,
unless there is some restrictive provision in the articles of co-
partnership which would require the concurrence of all the
members of the firm.[11] When the owner of the mortgage is a
corporation, authority to assign the debt and security should
regularly emanate from the board of directors. But if a principal officer of the company (such as the president, treasurer,
or secretary) makes the assignment, with the knowledge of
the directors and their subsequent acquiescence in the act, this
will be equivalent to a prior authorization, and the transfer
will be binding, in the absence of proof of fraud.[12] It is not
necessary that an assignment of a mortgage executed to a corporation should be made by an attorney of the corporation,
appointed specially for that purpose; and the assignment will
not be avoided by reason of the omission of a part of the corporate name of the assignor, when the full name appears in
the mortgage, and the assignment is attested by the corporate
seal, and the identification of the corporation as the assignor
is otherwise sufficient.[13] Where a mortgage is made to certain
persons, described as the trustees of an unincorporated association, the legal title under the mortgage vests in the named
persons as individuals, and an assignment of the mortgage

[9] McConnell v. Hodson, 7 Ill.
640; Albright v. Cobb, 30 Mich.
355; Taft v. Stevens, 3 Gray, 504.

[10] Gove v. Gove, 64 N. H. 503,
15 Atl. Rep. 121; Clark v. Black-
ington, 110 Mass. 369. Compare
Cutter v. Davenport, 1 Pick. 81, 11
Am. Dec. 149.

[11] Moses v. Hatfield, 27 S. Car.
324; Morrison v. Mendenhall, 18
Minn. 232.

[12] Darst v. Gale, 83 Ill. 136; Irwin v. Bailey, 8 Biss. 523, Fed. Cas.
No. 7,079.

[13] Chilton v. Brooks, 71 Md. 445,
18 Atl. Rep. 868.

purporting to be made by the association, or made by only one of the mortgagees, will not be valid.[14]

§ 180. Capacity of Assignee.—The right and capacity of a person to take an assignment of a mortgage will in general be tested by the same rules which determine his capacity to hold the estate as original mortgagee.[15] Thus, as to national banks, while the act of congress grants them the right to hold mortgages as security for debts previously contracted, and impliedly forbids them to receive such security for loans contemporaneously made, yet it is settled that the risk of ouster and dissolution, to be invoked only at the instance of the United States, is the sole penalty contemplated by congress for the violation of this prohibition; and consequently a national bank taking an assignment of a mortgage, as security for a loan made at the same time, will not be disabled from enforcing its security at the plea of the debtor.[16]

The original mortgagor himself may take a valid assignment of the mortgage, after his equity of redemption in the premises has been passed to another, whether by his voluntary conveyance subject to the lien of the mortgage or by a seizure and sale on execution against him. If, under such circumstances, he buys the debt and mortgage from the holder thereof, it will not operate as a discharge and satisfaction of the incumbrance, but he will be entitled to be subrogated to the rights of the mortgagee, and may transfer the security unimpaired to another purchaser, or enforce it against the land, in the absence of any intervening rights of third persons.[17] Where a note secured by mortgage is indorsed to two persons by name, each will be entitled to one-half the value of the note and its proceeds, as well as the security, and neither can transfer any other or greater interest.[18] And so, the assignment of a mortgage to two persons as trustees of an unincorporated society

---

[14] Austin v. Shaw, 10 Allen (Mass.) 552.

[15] As to the right of foreign corporations to take and hold mortgages, see, supra, § 101.

[16] Supra, § 102. And see State Nat. Bank v. Flathers, 45 La. Ann. 75, 12 South. Rep. 243; Worcester Nat. Bank v. Cheeney, 87 Ill. 602; Rev. Stat. U. S. § 5137.

[17] Bullard v. Hinckley, 5 Me. 272; Kinnear v. Lowell, 34 Me. 299; Barker v. Parker, 4 Pick. 505; Gerdine v. Menage, 41 Minn. 417, 43 N. W. Rep. 91; Baker v. Northwestern Guaranty Loan Co., 36 Minn. 185, 30 N. W. Rep. 464.

[18] Herring v. Woodhull, 29 Ill. 92.

vests the title in them as joint tenants, and not as tenants in common.[19]

§ 181. **Consideration for Assignment.**—An assignment of a mortgage, like any other contract, must, as between the parties to it, be supported by a good and sufficient consideration. The assignee of a mortgage who has given no other consideration therefor than his own promissory note, on which he has paid nothing, is not a bona fide holder for value.[20] But here it is necessary to discriminate carefully between the consideration for the assignment and the consideration of the mortgage itself. Though the consideration passing from the assignee to the assignor may have been illegal, contrary to public policy, or within the express prohibition of a statute, this will not invalidate the mortgage, with which it has no connection, and therefore will be no objection to the enforcement of the mortgage by the assignee.[21] And as a general rule, it is not open to the mortgagor, when made defendant in foreclosure proceedings by the assignee of the mortgage, to inquire into or impeach the consideration upon which the assignment of the mortgage was made.[22] Although the amount which the assignee paid for the mortgage may have been much less than the face value of the mortgage debt, still it may be a valid security, in the hands of the assignee, for the full amount of the debt; and the mortgagor will not be permitted, on this ground alone, to resist a foreclosure or to have the amount of the decree correspondingly reduced; nor will he be permitted to redeem without payment of the full amount due upon the mortgage.[23] In fact, it is said that the sale by one person of a bond and mortgage made by another, if made in good faith, is not illegal nor impeachable by the mortgagor, no matter how exorbitant may have been the rate of discount.[24]

[19] Webster v. Vandeventer, 6 Gray, 428.

[20] Chancellor v. Bell, 45 N. J. Eq. 538, 17 Atl. Rep. 684. Marriage is a good consideration for an assignment of a mortgage; it is such consideration as will give the assignee the rights of a purchaser for value. Mellick v. Mellick, 47 N. J. Eq. 86, 19 Atl. Rep. 870.

[21] Rowan v. Adams, 1 Smedes &

M. Ch. (Miss.) 45; Smith v. Kammerer, 152 Pa. St. 98, 25 Atl. Rep. 165.

[22] Croft v. Bunster, 9 Wis. 503; Johnson v. Beard, 93 Ala. 96, 9 South. Rep. 535.

[23] Knox v. Galligan, 21 Wis. 470; Pease v. Benson, 28 Me. 336.

[24] Donnington v. Meeker, 11 N. J. Eq. 362.

§ 182. **Mode of Making Assignment.**—To pass a good title at law to the securities intended to be transferred, it is necessary that the assignment of a mortgage should be in writing and under seal.[25] And further, if the debt secured is evidenced by a promissory note, it must be properly indorsed to the assignee. If the owner assigns the note and mortgage upon a separate paper, but without indorsing the note, the legal title will not pass, but only an equitable title, which will be subject to all infirmities and equities.[26] But since the statutes of Illinois do not provide for the acknowledgment of assignments of mortgages, a written assignment, duly recorded, is none the less a record, and entitled to the effect of a record, because it was not acknowledged. Unless the statutes so require, it is not necessary that an instrument should be acknowledged in order to entitle it to be recorded.[27]

It is held that, as a mortgage is a mere incident of the debt which it is intended to secure, a deed of conveyance executed by the mortgagee, purporting to transfer his interest, without a foreclosure, and without an assignment of the debt, is considered in law a nullity and passes no title.[28] But the decisions in some other states hold that a conveyance of the premises by the mortgagee to a third person may be shown to have been intended to operate as an assignment of the mortgage and debt, and may be so treated in equity when that intention is made to appear.[29] And there are also authorities to the effect that if the mortgagee is in possession of the mortgaged estate, or even has a right of immediate possession for breach of condition, his deed of the premises to a third person will be effectual to pass at least the right of possession, so that the mortgagor could not oust the grantee without redemption from the mortgage.[30] An absolute deed with a defeasance back amounts to a mortgage, and an absolute conveyance made by the grantee in such a deed will be equivalent to an assignment of the mortgage.[31] Also a specific bequest of a mortgage

[25] Barrett v. Hinckley, 124 Ill. 32, 14 N. E. Rep. 863; Morrison v. Mendenhall, 18 Minn. 232.

[26] Fortier v. Darst, 31 Ill. 212. Compare Miller v. Hicken, 92 Cal. 229, 28 Pac. Rep. 339.

[27] Honore v. Wilshire, 109 Ill. 103.

[28] Delano v. Bennett, 90 Ill. 533; Devlin v. Collier, 53 N. J. Law, 422, 22 Atl. Rep. 201.

[29] Greve v. Coffin, 14 Minn. 345, 100 Am. Dec. 229.

[30] Pickett v. Jones, 63 Mo. 195; Ruggles v. Barton, 13 Gray, 506.

[31] Halsey v. Martin, 22 Cal. 645.

will entitle the legatee to the possession of the securities and
enable him to bring suit upon the same to enforce the collection of the debt.[32]

§ 183. **Assignment of Debt Without Mortgage.**—The owner
of a debt secured by mortgage may assign or transfer the debt
without intending to transfer the mortgage security and without legally doing so. The debt is regarded as the principal
thing, and the mortgage as a mere incident of it. The mortgagee may deal with, and do such acts in respect to, the debt
as may usually be done in relation to money transactions,
verbally or in writing, without regard to the mortgage security.
The necessity of acting under seal in relation to such a debt
depends upon the nature of the act as affecting the mortgage
security or the title to the land, by assignment or release of
the mortgage security. But so far as power and mode of action
are concerned in transferring the debt or the note given for it,
there is no difference between one secured by mortgage and one
not so secured. Its transfer or payment is a mere question of
fact and intention, as if no mortgage existed, and the rules of
law and evidence and the power of the parties are the same.
The existence of a mortgage securing the debt might assist in
ascertaining and explaining the intention of the parties as
evidenced by particular acts, but could not vary or control
their power or mode of dealing with or settling the debt.[33]
But, on the principle that the assignment or transfer of the
principal thing carries with it its incidents or accessories, it
is held, in equity, that if the debt or obligation be assigned
or transferred the mortgage will go with it, unless there is
some agreement to the contrary; and if the mortgage is not
actually assigned or delivered to the assignee of the debt,
still the original mortgagee will have no further interest in it
than to hold it as a trustee for the assignee of the debt.[34] But
when the debt secured is assigned to a third person, without
an assignment of the mortgage, the interest which he acquires

[32] Proctor v. Robinson, 35 Mich.
284.

[33] Ryan v. Dunlop, 17 Ill. 40.

[34] Barrett v. Hinckley, 124 Ill.
32, 14 N. E. Rep. 863; Union Mut.
Life Ins. Co. v. Slee, 123 Ill. 57,
12 N. E. Rep. 543; Miller v.
Larned, 103 Ill. 562; Towner v.
McClelland, 110 Ill. 542; Lucas v.
Harris, 20 Ill. 165; Pardee v. Lind-
ley, 31 Ill. 174; Mapps v. Sharpe,
32 Ill. 13; Vansant v. Allmon, 23
Ill. 30; Harris v. Mills, 28 Ill. 44;
Herring v. Woodhull, 29 Ill. 92;
Mann v. Merchants' Loan & Trust
Co., 100 Ill. App. 224.

is recognized and enforceable only in equity. Hence if he desires to proceed for the enforcement of the security, it must be in the name of the person who holds the legal title. But such person, whether it be the original mortgagee or some one to whom he has conveyed his interest, is treated as trustee for the owner of the debt, and the suit of the equitable assignee, brought in the name of such person, will be sustained.[35] As another consequence of the doctrine that this kind of assignment is recognized only in equity, it follows that the transferree, acquiring only an equity in the mortgage, will take it subject to any defenses which the mortgagor may have as to the note, the same as in the hands of his assignor.[36]

Where the debt secured by a mortgage has been merged in a judgment recovered upon it at law, the mortgage is changed in effect into a security for the payment of the judgment; and hence an assignment of the judgment will be an equitable transfer of both the judgment and the mortgage.[37]

§ 184. Assignment of Mortgage Without Debt.—The debt being the principal thing and the mortgage only an incident of it, it follows that the mortgage cannot be assigned without the debt. The mortgage interest, as distinct from the debt secured, has no determinate value, and is not a fit subject of assignment. Hence an attempt to assign the mortgage without any transfer of the debt will not pass the mortgagee's interest to the assignee, but will merely make him a holder of the mortgage in trust for the owner of the debt.[38] "There can be no effectual assignment of the mortgage that does not pass the debt it is given to secure. An attempt to assign the mortgage severed from the debt would be wholly inoperative. So, when it is said [in order to show the plaintiff's right to foreclose] that the mortgage was duly assigned, it includes an assignment of the debt."[39] It follows from this principle that a mortgage which gives a power of sale to the mortgagee and "his heirs or assigns" does not authorize a sale by one

---

[35] Kilgour v. Gockley, 83 Ill. 109.

[36] Petillon v. Noble, 73 Ill. 567; Olds v. Cummings, 31 Ill. 188.

[37] Wayman v. Cochrane, 35 Ill. 152.

[38] Medley v. Elliott, 62 Ill. 532; Hamilton v. Lubukee, 51 Ill. 415; Carpenter v. Longan, 16 Wall. 271;

Pope v. Jacobus, 10 Iowa, 262; Jackson v. Willard, 4 Johns. 41; Merritt v. Bartholick, 36 N. Y. 44; Bloomingdale v. Bowman, 51 Hun, 639.

[39] Foster v. Trowbridge, 39 Minn. 378, 40 N. W. Rep. 255.

to whom the mortgage, but not the note which it secures, is transferred, a mortgage not being assignable at law.[40] But when the language of the instrument of assignment is sufficient to carry both the debt and the mortgage, it will be sustained as an assignment of both, though not in the usual form; and particularly so where it is admitted on the record, by both the assignor and assignee, as complainants, that both the debt and mortgage were intended to be assigned.[41]

§ 185. **Constructive and Equitable Assignments.**—There are numerous cases in which courts of equity will recognize a third person as entitled to the rights and privileges of an assignee of a mortgage, although there has been no formal transfer of the security to him. Thus, an indorsee of a mortgage note, who has possession of the mortgaged property and also of the mortgage itself, cannot be dispossessed by the mortgagor or his grantee until the mortgage debt is paid, since he is the equitable assignee of the mortgage.[42] So, where a mortgagee in possession sells the property, or a portion of it, subject to the equity of redemption, against which he agrees to indemnify the purchaser to the extent of the purchase money, the mortgage debt being then long past due, the transaction will amount, in equity, to an assignment pro tanto of the mortgage debt.[43] On similar principles, a bond and mortgage executed to the receivers of an insolvent corporation may be sued on in equity by their successors in their own names, as equitable assignees of all their rights under the same.[44]

Again, in many instances, a person who is obliged for his own interest to pay off a mortgage incumbrance may be treated in equity as an assignee of the mortgage debt. That which, in form, is a payment and discharge of a mortgage may be treated in equity as an assignment, where such a construction best accords with justice and the intentions of the parties.[45] Generally speaking, the court will not compel the owner of the mortgage, in circumstances of this kind, to execute a formal assignment of it to the person entitled to stand in his place.[46]

[40] Sanford v. Kane, 133 Ill. 199, 24 N. E. Rep. 414.

[41] Jordan v. Sayre, 24 Fla. 1, 3 South. Rep. 329.

[42] Brown v. Bookstaver, 141 Ill. 461, 31 N. E. Rep. 17.

[43] Union Mut. Life Ins. Co. v. Slee, 123 Ill. 57, 12 N. E. Rep. 543.

[44] Iglehart v. Bierce, 36 Ill. 133.

[45] Gucklan v. Riley, 135 Mass. 71. And see Booker v. Anderson, 35 Ill. 66.

[46] Handley v. Munsell, 109 Ill. 362.

But such a formal transfer would not be essential to the rights of the latter. Equity can easily accomplish the same result by simply treating the person who has made the payment in the same manner as he would be entitled to be treated if he held a formal assignment of the security (which may be called a species of assignment "by operation of law") or by subrogating him to the rights of the holder of the mortgage. This is the course pursued in the case of a junior mortgagee who, for his own protection, pays off the senior incumbrance, not intending to discharge or extinguish the same,[47] or in the case of a purchaser of the mortgagor's equity of redemption, subject to the mortgage, who pays the mortgage note to save the land from foreclosure,[48] or in the case of one of several tenants in common of mortgaged lands, who pays the whole amount of the mortgage debt in order to effect a redemption from a foreclosure, thus becoming an equitable assignee of the mortgage for the purpose of enabling him to enforce contribution from his co-tenants to the extent of their respective interests.[49] Again, where an administrator uses his own money to pay a mortgage given by his intestate, the payment will not generally extinguish the debt, but may be regarded as working an assignment of the security to the administrator.[50] So also, where a stranger intervenes at the request of the mortgagor, and pays a balance due on the mortgage debt, and the mortgage is delivered to him by the mortgagee, he may be treated as an equitable assignee of the security.[51] For similar reasons, when a mortgage is foreclosed and the lands bought by a stranger at the foreclosure sale, but the sale proves to have been invalid and is set aside, or for any reason is ineffectual to convey the title, such purchaser will be treated as an equitable assignee of the mortgage, or will be subrogated to the rights of the mortgagee.[52] Again, it is held that where, in proceedings in attachment, the process of garnishment is served upon one who is indebted to the defendant upon notes secured by mortgage, and judgment is rendered for the plaintiff, the notes and mort-

[47] Ebert v. Gerding, 116 Ill. 216, 5 N. E. Rep. 591.

[48] Stiger v. Bent, 111 Ill. 328.

[49] Hubbard v. Ascutney Mill-Dam Co., 20 Vt., 402.

[50] Goodbody v. Goodbody, 95 Ill. 456

[51] Stelzich v. Weidel, 27 Ill. App. 177.

[52] Bruschke v. Wright, 166 Ill. 183, 46 N. E. Rep. 813. And see Muir v. Berkshire, 52 Ind. 149; Johnson v. Robertson, 34 Md. 165.

gage are, in legal effect, assigned to the plaintiff, and he may maintain an action to foreclose the mortgage.[53] And it appears that the same result may follow from a levy on the notes secured by the mortgage, under process of execution against the mortgagee, and their transfer by the officer to a third person; but not where the notes are seized in a foreign state, without jurisdiction acquired over the person of the defendant.[54]

§ 186. **Assignment of Trust Notes.**—Where a deed of trust is made to secure the payment of promissory notes, and the notes are assigned or transferred by the payee to another person, the assignment of the notes will carry the security with it, as an incident of the debt, and the assignee will succeed to all the rights of the assignor under the deed of trust. In case the notes are not paid at maturity, the assignee will have the right to call upon the trustees to sell the property and apply the proceeds in payment of the debt; and if the trustees neglect or refuse to act, the holder of the notes may obtain the aid of a court of equity to compel them to discharge their duty.[55] But one taking a trust deed as assignee of the notes secured thereby is chargeable with notice of all equities appearing in the chain of title whereby he acquires a lien under the trust deed; he is bound by recitals in a deed to the grantor in the deed of trust showing equities in a third person.[56]

§ 187. **Separate Assignment of Separate Notes.**—When a mortgage is given to secure the payment of several different notes or demands, it is an incumbrance upon the land for the security of all and each of the notes, in whosesoever hands they may legally be, until all are paid.[57] In a case in Illinois it appeared that interest was paid for some years on a part of certain railroad bonds, while on other bonds of the same class held by other parties it remained unpaid. A foreclosure could have been compelled at any time after default in the payment of interest by any holder of the bonds on which interest was not paid. On a distribution of the fund arising from a subsequent foreclosure, it was held that the holders of bonds who

[53] Alsdorf v. Reed, 45 Ohio St. 653, 17 N. E. Rep. 73.

[54] Owen v. Miller, 10 Ohio St. 136.

[55] Sargent v. Howe, 21 Ill. 148.

And see Clark v. Jones, 93 Tenn. 639, 27 S. W. Rep. 1009.

[56] United States Mortgage Co. v. Gross, 93 Ill. 483.

[57] Johnson v. Brown, 31 N. H. 405.

had received no interest were not entitled to any priority over those to whom the interest had been paid.[58] When all the notes secured by a mortgage are assigned, the mortgage goes with them; but when a part only are assigned, it is a question whether the whole mortgage, or a proportionate part of it, or any interest therein, is assigned; and this question depends upon the real contract and actual agreement of the parties.[59] For it is legally possible for the holder of a mortgage to transfer by indorsement one or more of the several notes secured thereby without passing any interest in the mortgage. If such is the actual agreement, understood and acted upon by both parties, he may transfer to his indorsee only the right to recover on the note assigned, reserving to himself the entire mortgage interest as security for the remaining portion of the debt.[60] But such an agreement must be explicit. Where one of several notes secured by a single mortgage is transferred, an equitable interest in the mortgage will pass to the transferee, if nothing to the contrary is said or agreed upon. On the other hand, if it is the intention of the parties that the purchaser of the note shall have the benefit of the mortgage security, to the extent of the note transferred to him, it is not necessary that this agreement should be expressed in writing; it will be sufficient if there is a mere oral understanding to that effect.[61]

§ 188. **Same; Order of Payment.**—It very frequently happens that a mortgage is given to secure the payment of a group or series of notes or bonds, and that these obligations are assigned or transferred to, and held by, a number of different persons. When this is the case, and when the proceeds of a sale on foreclosure of the mortgage are not sufficient to pay all the obligations in full, the question arises whether the fund should be applied upon all the notes, giving to each a pro rata share, or whether a priority, involving payment in full, should be given to the note first maturing or to the one first assigned. On this question, different rules prevail in the different states. But in Illinois, it is well settled that the assignment of one of such notes is an equitable transfer of the mortgage pro tanto,

[58] Humphreys v. Morton, 100 Ill. 592.

[59] Langdon v. Keith, 9 Vt. 299.

[60] Rolston v. Brockway, 23 Wis. 407.

[61] Norton v. Palmer, 142 Mass. 433, 8 N. E. Rep. 346.

and the proceeds of the foreclosure sale, if not sufficient to pay all the obligations, should be applied to the notes in the order of their maturity. That is, the holder of the note which first becomes due is entitled to be satisfied out of the proceeds, in full, and then the others in their order; and this rule, though of course liable to be modified by an express agreement of the parties, or by controlling equities peculiar to the special case, is not affected by the priority of assignment of one of the younger notes.[62] And the United States courts sitting within the state will adopt and follow the same rule of distribution,

---

[62] Herrington v. McCollum, 73 Ill. 476; Humphreys v. Morton, 100 Ill. 592; Koester v. Burke, 81 Ill. 436; Vansant v. Allmon, 23 Ill. 30; Flower v. Elwood, 66 Ill. 438; Gardner v. Diederichs, 41 Ill. 158; Schultz v. Plankinton Bank, 40 Ill. App. 462, s. c., 141 Ill. 116, 30 N. E. Rep. 346; Chandler v. O'Neil, 62 Ill. App. 418. An excellent statement of the grounds which have influenced courts to hold the rule that the notes should be paid in the order of their maturity is found in the case of Penzel v. Brookmire, 51 Ark. 105, 10 S. W. Rep. 15. Herein it was said by Battle, J.: "The courts adhering to the doctrine that the notes should be paid in the order of their maturity say that the debt is the principal thing and the mortgage to secure it is only an incident; that the assignment of the debt passes the mortgage without being referred to in the assignment; that the assignee of the debt takes the security by the assignment in the same condition and to the same extent is was held by the payee at the time of the assignment, as security for the debt assigned, and succeeds under it to all the rights of the assignor; that the assignor, the payee, in the absence of a stipulation to the contrary, had the right to foreclose the mortgage when default should be made in the payment of the notes first falling due, and as each one should fall due, and satisfy them out of the proceeds in the order of their maturity, so far as the proceeds would extend, although there should not be enough to pay all; and that, therefore, inasmuch as the assignee, by the assignment of any one of the notes, succeeds to the rights which his assignor had, he has the right, in the event there is not enough to pay all, to be paid out of the mortgaged property so far as it will extend, according to the order in which his note stands in the line of maturity with the others secured by the mortgage; and that the different installments in a mortgage, when secured by corresponding notes, may be regarded as so many successive mortgages, each having priority according to the time of becoming payable." And so, in Vansant v. Allmon, 23 Ill. 30, it is held that the assignee of the first due of several notes secured by the same mortgage has a priority of claim, and can foreclose and sell on default in the payment of his note; and the holders of the other notes can redeem in succession, according to privilege.

upon the foreclosure of a mortgage on land within the state.
For the question is not one of general commercial law, but
one that pertains to the transfer of property, and therefore
the rule adopted by the courts of the state becomes in effect
a rule of property, and will be regarded as obligatory by the
federal courts.[63]

But this rule of distribution is enforced only in the absence
of an agreement between the parties regulating the order in
which the notes shall be paid. It is entirely competent for
the owner of several notes falling due at different times, which
are all secured by the same mortgage, to stipulate with one to
whom he indorses or assigns one of the earlier notes that it
shall be held subject to the lien of the mortgage for the notes
subsequently becoming due.[64] And conversely, in transferring
the notes last maturing, he may stipulate with the assignee that
the latter shall hold a lien on the mortgaged premises for the
security of the notes so transferred prior to that retained for the
security of the notes first maturing; and such a contract will
be binding as between the parties and upon all persons having
notice thereof. And further, if an assignee of mortgage notes
knows that there are other negotiable notes secured by the
same mortgage, it is his duty to inquire of the maker and the
payee whether the others have been sold with a preferred lien
on the security. To omit such inquiries is negligence on his
part; and if such a preferred lien has been given, it will be
valid against the assignee who fails to take this proper precaution.[65]

If the several notes or other obligations secured by the mortgage are all made to fall due at the same time, so that there is
no priority to be claimed on account of the earlier maturity of
one of them, the rule in Illinois is that the proceeds of a foreclosure sale shall be applied pro rata upon all the notes, each
receiving a share proportioned to its amount as compared with
the amounts of the others. In this case, it makes no difference
that the notes were not all assigned to the present holders
at the same time, but were successively transferred. Priority
of assignment does not affect the equal equities of the holders. Nor can any claim to preference be founded on the fact

[63] New York Security & Trust
Co. v. Lombard Inv. Co., 65 Fed.
Rep. 271.

[64] Romberg v. McCormick, 194
Ill. 205, 62 N. E. Rep. 537.

[65] Walker v. Dement, 42 Ill. 272.

that some of the holders may have received interest on their notes, while others have not.[66]

§ 189. **Assignment as Collateral Security.**—An assignment of a note and mortgage as collateral security for a debt or loan differs from an ordinary sale and assignment of the same only in respect to the right of the assignor to recover the securities on discharging the principal debt. This right may be cut off by proper proceedings. Thus, where a mortgagee pledges the note and mortgage to secure a loan, and the pledgee forecloses the mortgage, making the mortgagee a party defendant, and obtains a decree foreclosing the rights of all the defendants, and proceeds to buy the property at the foreclosure sale, and obtains a deed therefor, he holds the title free from any right of redemption on the part of the mortgagee.[67] So, where a junior mortgage was assigned·by a deed absolute on its face, but in fact as a security for the payment of money, to one who afterwards purchased the equity of redemption from the mortgagor, and also purchased the land at a sale under a senior mortgage, and then sold to a third person, who had no notice of the private agreement between the assignor and assignee of the junior mortgage, it was held that such purchaser took the absolute title, discharged of any claim under either of the mortgages.[68] And one to whom a mortgage has been assigned as collateral security may, as against the mortgagor and those claiming under him, execute a power of sale contained in the mortgage as fully as if the assignment had been absolute.[69] But one to whom guarantied notes, together with a mortgage securing them, are assigned as collateral security for a loan made by him to the payee, must use all proper diligence and care in the management of such notes and mortgage, in order that the guarantor may have the benefit of their avails.[70]

§ 190. **Successive Assignments.**—As between successive

---

[66] Humphreys v. Morton, 100 Ill. 592.

[67] Anderson v. Olin, 145 Ill. 168, 34 N. E. Rep. 55. And the fact that the mortgagee failed to defend the suit because he thought it related to other property does not give him any right to file a bill to redeem, where his mistake was not caused by any acts or representations of the pledgee. Id.

[68] Baldwin v. Sager, 70 Ill. 503.

[69] Holmes v. Turner's Falls Lumber Co., 150 Mass. 535, 23 N. E. Rep. 305.

[70] Holmes v. Williams, 177 Ill. 386, 53 N. E. Rep. 93, reversing 69 Ill. App. 114.

assignees of the same mortgage, both taking in equal good
faith, the assignment which is first recorded will have the
priority.[71] But in the absence of this test, the preference of
one assignee over the other must be determined by the relative
strength of their equities, as fixed by their good or bad faith
with reference to the transfers, the presence or absence of
notice, and the degree of care and diligence which they exercise in the transaction. Thus, where a written assignment of
a bond and mortgage is given to A., but no papers are delivered to him, and the assignment is not indorsed on the bond
or entered on the record, and he gives no notice to the mortgagor, and afterwards the mortgagee makes another assignment of the mortgage to B., who takes the papers, has the
assignment indorsed on the bond, gives notice to the mortgagor, and pays the money in good faith, B. has the superior
equity and claim upon the mortgage. This is not a case for the
application of the maxim that "he who is first in time is first
in right," but rather for the rule that when one of two innocent persons must suffer, the burden or loss must fall upon
him whose act or neglect has made it possible; or, to state it
differently, B.'s conduct gives him the right to take the
security free from the secret equity of A.[72] Conversely, a
prior unrecorded assignment of a note and mortgage is good
as against a subsequent recorded assignment of the same, where
the second assignee, knowing that the note and mortgage are
not, at the time of the assignment to him, in his assignor's possession, makes no inquiry as to the latter's title.[73] And so,
where a mortgagee assigns the securities, the assignment being
recorded, and fraudulently procures a reassignment to himself, which he does not record, and later fraudulently obtains
the mortgage and note, and assigns them to a third person
who is ignorant of the previous assignment and reassignment,
the title to the note and mortgage, as between the two

[71] Oregon & W. Trust Co. v.
Shaw, 5 Sawy. 336, Fed. Cas. No.
10,556.

[72] Porter v. King, 1 Fed. Rep.
755. So, in Harding v. Durand, 36
Ill. App. 238, it was said: "The assignment taken by H. on a separate piece of paper, of a note and
mortgage in the hands of some-
body else, assigned before maturity for a valuable consideration,
could not affect the title of the
real holder of the note and mortgage. Such an assignment, as
against a holder for value before
maturity, was a mere nullity."

[73] O'Mulcahy v. Holley, 28 Minn.
31, 8 N. W. Rep. 906.

assignees is in the former, for the latter is deemed to have constructive notice of the title as it appears of record.[74] Payment of a mortgage note to the legal holder before maturity, without indorsement or surrender of the note and mortgage, while not a defense to an action on the note by a subsequent innocent holder before maturity, is a good defense to an action by the latter to foreclose the mortgage.[75]

In one of the cases it appeared that the holder of a trust deed and the notes secured thereby sold and transferred to one purchaser certain forged notes purporting to be the notes secured, but without transferring to him the deed of trust, the purchaser taking the notes in entire reliance on the good faith of his assignor and without making any inquiries of the grantor in the deed, and afterwards such holder sold and transferred the genuine notes and the deed of trust to another purchaser, who had no notice of the prior transaction. It was held that the latter purchaser, not the former, had the right to a foreclosure of the trust deed for the purpose of realizing the debt. This decision was based on several grounds. First, the assignment of the spurious notes did not carry with it an assignment of the security; that would result only from a transfer of the genuine notes. Second, the rule that the assignee of a chose in action takes it free from latent equities in favor of third persons would protect the purchaser of the genuine notes; for while the assignment of the forged notes as genuine would estop the assignor to deny their validity, such estoppel would operate only in favor of the first purchaser, and would not descend upon the second purchaser, who took the real notes without notice. Third, the equity of the second purchaser was superior to that of the first; for while the latter had only the representations of the assignor, the former had, in addition to such representations, the fact that he had obtained and held the notes actually secured and the deed. And finally, where one of two innocent persons must suffer by a deceit, it is more consonant to reason that he who puts trust and confidence in the deceiver should be the loser than that the other should bear the loss.[76]

---

74 Murphy v. Barnard, 162 Mass. 72, 38 N. E. Rep. 29.

75 Buehler v. McCormick, 169 Ill. 269, 48 N. E. Rep. 287, affirming McCormick v. Buehler, 67 Ill. App. 73.

76 Himrod v. Bolton, 44 Ill. App. 516. This decision was affirmed by the supreme court. Himrod v. Gilman, 147 Ill. 293, 35 N. E. Rep. 373. Compare Kernohan v. Durham, 48 Ohio St. 1.

§ 191. What Passes by Assignment.—A formal and valid assignment of a mortgage and the debt which it secures will generally invest the assignee with all the rights, powers, and equities possessed by the original mortgagee. Thus, when the mortgage contains a power of sale, to be executed by the mortgagee, his heirs or assigns, and the debt secured is of a character assignable at law, an assignee of the debt and mortgage will acquire the right to execute the power of sale,[77] and may make the deed of conveyance to the purchaser,[78] and this power will be divested altogether from the original mortgagee, and can no longer be exercised by him, being, as against him, a power coupled with an interest and therefore irrevocable.[79] But the mere assignment of the mortgage alone by an indorsement thereon, without an assignment of the note or debt, the mortgage not being an instrument assignable by indorsement, either by the common law or under the statute, will not operate to pass the power of sale to the assignee.[80] And the same rule applies where the debt is not evidenced by any of the instruments which are legally assignable, but only by the mortgage itself.[81] Further, the power of sale cannot be thus transferred if the language of the mortgage is such as to make it personal to the mortgagee. If it grants a power of sale to the mortgagee, "his representatives or attorney," a sale of the premises by a person claiming to represent the assignee of the mortgage note, as an agent with discretionary power, will not be valid; for even if the mortgage had given the power of sale to the assignee, the sale could not properly be made by his agent.[82]

In other respects, the assignee will succeed to the exact position filled by his assignor. If, for instance, the mortgage gives the mortgagee the privilege of electing to declare the entire debt due upon default in the payment of any installment of principal or interest when due, the assignee of the mortgage may exercise this option, and his election will bind both the maker of the note and the assignor.[83] Even where

[77] Bush v. Sherman, 80 Ill. 160; Pardee v. Lindley, 31 Ill. 174; Strother v. Law, 54 Ill. 413.

[78] Heath v. Hall, 60 Ill. 344.

[79] Hamilton v. Lubukee, 51 Ill. 415; Pardee v. Lindley, 31 Ill. 174.

[80] Hamilton v. Lubukee, 51 Ill.

415; Sanford v. Kane, 24 Ill. App. 504.

[81] Mason v. Ainsworth, 58 Ill. 163.

[82] Flower v. Elwood, 66 Ill. 438; Wilson v. Spring, 64 Ill. 14.

[83] Stewart v. Ludlow, 68 Ill. App.

the assignee cannot proceed in his own name, he will have the right to use all the remedies necessary for the collection of the mortgage debt, in the name of the mortgagee, for his own use and benefit, including the remedy by ejectment, and also the taking of possession, upon default, in the character of an agent of the mortgagee.[84] The assignee will indeed have no right to maintain an action for waste committed upon the mortgaged property, or for any other injury to it or conversion of it, happening before the assignment to him was made; but he may sue any person who injures the property or does any act diminishing the value of the security, after the assignment.[85] On similar principles, it is held that a tax title acquired by the mortgagor, after the assignment, will inure to the benefit of the assignee of the mortgage,[86] and the same will be true of any collateral undertaking or obligation which constitutes a part of the security. Thus, a house standing on the mortgaged land having been destroyed by fire, the mortgagor executed and delivered to the mortgagee a bond, with sureties, conditioned that he would rebuild the house within a limited time. Afterwards, the mortgagee assigned the mortgage and the debt secured thereby, but did not formally assign the bond. It was held that the bond was a part of the security for the debt, and passed to the assignee with the debt, and further, that such change in the ownership of the debt and security did not release the sureties on the bond.[87] So, the purchaser of a note, secured by a deed of trust, without notice of a mistake therein making it bear interest from maturity instead of from date, acquires all the equities of the original creditor.[88] And one purchasing a mortgage upon the representation that it is a first lien is entitled to the benefit of everything appearing of record which will sustain his rights, whether he examined the records or not.[89] As to the case where a part only of a debt secured by mortgage is assigned, it is held that such a

349; Swett v. Stark, 31 Fed. Rep. 853.

[84] Kilgour v. Gockley, 83 Ill. 109. Compare Williams v. Teachey, 85, N. Car. 402.

[85] Bowers v. Bodley, 4 Ill. App. 279; Gobbert v. Wallace, 66 Miss. 618, 5 South. Rep. 394; Overton v. Williston, 31 Pa. St. 155; Kimball v. Lewiston Steam Mill Co.,

55 Me. 494; Gordon v. Hobart, 2 Story, 243, Fed. Cas. No. 5, 608.

[86] Gardiner v. Gerrish, 23 Me. 46.

[87] Longfellow v. McGregor, 61 Minn. 494, 63 N. W. Rep. 1032.

[88] Frink v. Neal, 37 Ill. App. 621.

[89] Mann v. Jummel, 183 Ill. 523, 56 N. E. Rep. 161, affirming Jummel v. Mann. 80 Ill. App. 288.

partial assignment will carry the benefit and control of the security upon such terms as the relations between the assignee and the holder of the residue of the debt may require.[90]

§ 192. **Right of Assignee to Foreclose.**—Where a note or bond and the mortgage securing its payment have been assigned, a scire facias to foreclose the mortgage may be brought in the name of the mortgagee for the use of the assignee.[91] But when the proceeding for foreclosure is by bill in equity, the action should be instituted in the name of the real owner of the debt secured.[92] Even an equitable assignment of a note secured by mortgage will authorize the assignee to foreclose the mortgage in his own name.[93] The bill, in this case, should not be filed in the name of the original mortgagee for the use of the assignee; but if wrongly brought, it is amendable.[94] The assignor is not even a necessary party to the assignee's suit for foreclosure.[95]

§ 193. **Giving Notice to Mortgagor.**—Neither notice to the mortgagor nor his consent to the transaction is essential to make an assignment of the mortgage valid and effectual.[96] But a person taking a mortgage by assignment must give notice to the mortgagor that he has succeeded to the rights of the original mortgagee; for if he fails to do so, and the mortgagor afterwards in good faith makes a payment to the original mortgagee or his authorized agent, it will be good as against the assignee, and the latter will have no remedy against the mortgagor or on the security.[97] This rule is plainly just in cases where the mortgage is the sole evidence of the debt or where the debt is in the form of a bond. But the matter is not so clear if the debt secured is evidenced by a negotiable promissory note. Here it would seem to be the duty of the mortgagor, on making a payment, to ask to see the note and to have the payment indorsed on it, or, if it is an interest note, to have it delivered up. For he knows that a negotiable note may pass to an indorsee, and that, if it does, the lawful holder

[90] Magloughlin v. Clark, 35 Ill. App. 251.

[91] Bourland v. Kipp, 55 Ill. 376.

[92] Hahn v. Huber, 83 Ill. 243.

[93] Sedgwick v. Johnson, 107 Ill. 385; McNamara v. Clark, 85 Ill. App. 439.

[94] Irish v. Sharp, 89 Ill. 261.

[95] McNamara v. Clark, 85 Ill. App. 439.

[96] Jones v. Gibbons, 9 Vesey, 407.

[97] Towner v. McClelland, 110 Ill. 542; Napieralski v. Simon, 198 Ill. 384, 64 N. E. Rep. 1042; Carey v. Kutten, 98 Ill. App. 197.

is alone authorized to receive payment. Hence, in some of the
states, the courts hold that want of notice, in this case, would
not protect the mortgagor in paying the debt to the original
payee of the note.[98] There is also a question as to whether
the recording of the assignment of the mortgage will be sufficient notice to the mortgagor to protect the assignee against
a bona fide payment by the mortgagor to the mortgagee. In
some states, the doctrine prevails that such a record is notice
only to parties subsequently dealing with the mortgagee, as
subsequent assignees or purchasers; that the mortgagor is
not in the position of one whose duty is to search the record
and inform himself of the state of the title; that he has a right
to presume that the mortgage continues in the person to
whom he originally gave it; and that if any other person has
become entitled to receive the money, it is obligatory on him
to give the mortgagor actual notice of the fact.[1] But such
indications as can be gleaned from the Illinois decisions on this
point appear to sustain the theory that the recording of the
assignment is equivalent to actual notice to the mortgagor.[2]

It is also held that the rule requiring the assignee to give
notice of the assignment to the mortgagor does not extend to
subsequent purchasers of the property who assume and agree
to pay the incumbrance; and notwithstanding the assignee
has not recorded the assignment, nor given notice thereof to
anyone, he is entitled to protection against payments made by
the purchasers to the mortgagee in the belief that he still
owned the indebtedness. "Their equities must be classed with
those mentioned as the latent equities of third persons."[3]

---

[98] Biggerstaff v. Marston, 161
Mass. 101, 36 N. E. Rep. 785; Murphy v. Barnard, 162 Mass. 72, 38
N. E. Rep. 29; Eggert v. Beyer, 43
Nebr. 711, 62 N. W. Rep. 57; Blu-
menthal v. Jassoy, 29 Minn., 177,
12 N. W. Rep. 517.

[1] Foster v. Carson, 159 Pa. St.
477, 28 Atl. Rep. 356; Eggert v.
Beyer, 43 Nebr. 711, 62 N. W. Rep.
57. In New York and several
other states it is expressly provided by statute that "the record
of an assignment of a mortgage
shall not of itself be deemed notice

to the mortgagor, his heirs or personal representatives, so as to invalidate any payment made by
them or either of them to the
mortgagee." 1 Rev. Stat. N. Y. p.
763, § 41; Comp. Stat. Nebr. § 4132;
2 How. Stat. Mich. § 5687; 1 Gen.
Stat. Kans. 1889, § 3887; Gen. Stat.
Minn. 1894; § 4183; 1 Sanb. & B.
Stat. Wis., § 2244.

[2] See Carey v. Kutten, 98 Ill.
App. 197; Schultz v. Sroelowitz, 191
Ill. 249, 61 N. E. Rep. 92; Sheldon
v. McNail, 89 Ill. App. 138.

[3] Schultz v. Sroelowitz, 191 Ill.

§ 194. Recording Assignment.—The registry laws of Illinois contemplate the recording of assignments of mortgages, as well as other instruments relating to real estate; and it is the part of prudence for the assignee of a mortgage to have the assignment placed on the record, in order to protect himself against subsequent mortgagees or purchasers of the premises, as well as against any fraudulent conduct of his assignor in subsequently attempting to sell and assign the same mortgage to another person, or in executing and recording a release of the debt secured.[4] The importance of taking this step is illustrated by a decision in a neighboring state, from which we quote as follows: "It is assumed everywhere that if the recording acts afford the assignee of a mortgage the opportunity of giving notice of his rights by procuring and putting on record an assignment of the mortgage, a neglect on his part to do so will estop him from asserting the invalidity of a duly recorded release executed by his assignor after an innocent purchaser has paid his money on the faith of the public records. It is settled everywhere that unrecorded assignments of mortgages are void as against subsequent purchasers, whose interests may be affected thereby, and whose conveyances are duly recorded, provided such assignments are embraced by the recording acts. It follows that when assignments of mortgages are within the recording acts, a release executed by the person who appears by the records to be the owner of the mortgage is sufficient to protect a purchaser who has in good faith parted with his money on the faith of such a release, and without other notice than that afforded by the record."[5]

§ 195. Assignment Subject to Equities between Original Parties.—In Illinois, the doctrine is settled by a long line of decisions that the assignee of a mortgage takes the same subject to all existing infirmities, and subject to all the defenses or equities which could be set up against it by the mortgagor as against the original mortgagee. A mortgage is not a negotiable instrument, nor is it assignable at law, but only in equity. Hence even where the debt secured is evidenced by a negotiable

249, 61 N. E. Rep. 92, reversing Sroelowitz v. Schultz, 86 Ill. App. 341.

[4] Smith v. Keohane, 6 Ill. App. 585; Williams v. Pelley, 96 Ill. App. 346. Compare Walker v. Dement, 42 Ill. 272.

[5] Connecticut Mut. Life Ins. Co. v. Talbot, 113 Ind. 373, 14 N. E. Rep. 586. And see Peaks v. Dexter, 82 Me. 85, 19 Atl. Rep. 100.

promissory note, and is purchased by one who takes it without notice, for value, and before maturity, still the mortgage (as distinguished from the note) will be subject to the defenses and equities of the mortgagor, as stated.[6] It is said that he who buys that which is not assignable at law, relying upon a court of chancery to protect and enforce his rights, takes it subject to all the infirmities to which it would have been liable in the hands of the assignor. A promissory note, though secured by a mortgage, is still commercial paper, assignable at law; and when the remedy is sought upon it, all the rights incident to commercial paper will be enforced in the courts of law; but when resort is had to a court of equity to foreclose the mortgage, that court will let in any defense which would have been good against the mortgage in the hands of the mortgagee himself; and this, regardless of the fact that the assignee may have purchased the notes in good faith and before their maturity.[7]

In respect to the application of this rule, there is no legal difference between an ordinary mortgage and a deed of trust in the nature of a mortgage.[8] And the fact that a trust deed secured the payment of a promissory note "to the legal holder thereof," which note was made payable to the maker's order and indorsed by him in blank, does not render the trust deed negotiable so as to except it from the rule.[9] Further, the rule

[6] Olds v. Cummings, 31 Ill. 188; Walker v. Dement, 42 Ill. 272; Sumner v. Waugh, 56 Ill. 531; Kleeman v. Frisbie, 63 Ill. 482; White v. Sutherland, 64 Ill. 181; Haskell v. Brown, 65 Ill. 29; Thompson v. Shoemaker, 68 Ill. 256; Bryant v. Vix, 83 Ill. 11; United States Mortgage Co. v. Gross, 93 Ill. 483; Miller v. Larned, 103 Ill. 562; Ellis v. Sisson, 96 Ill. 105; Towner v. McClelland, 110 Ill. 542; Shippen v. Whittier, 117 Ill. 282, 7 N. E. Rep. 642; Hodson v. Eugene Glass Co., 156 Ill. 397, 40 N. E. Rep. 971; McAuliffe v. Reuter, 166 Ill. 491, 46 N. E. Rep. 1087; Buehler v. McCormick, 169 Ill. 269, 48 N. E. Rep. 287; Hazle v. Bondy, 173 Ill. 302, 50 N. E. Rep. 671;

Romberg v. McCormick, 194 Ill. 205, 62 N. E. Rep. 537; Grassley v. Reinback, 4 Ill. App. 341; Jenkins v. Bauer, 8 Ill. App. 634; Belt v. Winsor, 38 Ill. App. 333; Cameron v. Bouton, 72 Ill. App. 264; Faris v. Briscoe, 78 Ill. App. 242; Whiting Paper Co. v. Busse, 95 Ill. App. 288; Hahn v. Geiger, 96 Ill. App. 104; Bouton v. Cameron, 99 Ill. App. 600; Bebber v. Moreland, 100 Ill. App. 198; Elser v. Williams, 104 Ill. App. 238.

[7] Olds v. Cummings, 31 Ill. 188. And see Wright v. Taylor, 8 Ill. 193.

[8] Foster v. Strong, 5 Ill. App. 223. Compare Worcester Nat. Bank v. Cheeney, 87 Ill. 602.

[9] Buehler v. McCormick, 169 Ill.

applies not only to assignees who take the security by purchase and transfer from the original mortgagee, but also to
those who acquire title thereto indirectly or by operation of
law, as, for instance, the heir or legatee of the mortgagee.[10]
But the rule does not embrace equities or defenses springing
from defaults, or even fraud, of the assignor, committed subsequent to the assignment, and which had no existence, and
were simply possibilities, at the time of the assignment.[11]

As to defenses against the note itself, the ordinary rules
governing commercial paper will apply, as stated in the leading
case. But any equities or defenses of which the assignee had
notice, at the time he took the assignment, may be urged
against the note in his hands.[12] And of course, a person who
buys a promissory note secured by mortgage, after its maturity, will take it subject to the defense of payment by the
maker, or to any equitable defense which would be available
against his assignor.[13]

§ 196. Same; Estoppel of Mortgagor to Defend.—Although
a mortgagor may have good defenses at law, or equities, against
the enforcement of the mortgage, he may estop himself, by
his conduct and declarations, from setting them up as against
an assignee of the mortgage. This is the case where the mortgagor, having knowledge of the proposed assignment, or being
interrogated by the proposed assignee, conceals or denies the
fact of his having a defense or equity, or deceives or misleads
the purchaser by false or equivocal representations.[14] It is
therefore prudent and proper for one proposing to take an
assignment of a mortgage to inquire of the mortgagor whether
any reason exists why the debt secured should not be paid, and
he will have a right to rely on the mortgagor's answers.[15] It

269, 48 N. E. Rep. 287, affirming
McCormick v. Buehler, 67 Ill.
App. 73.

[10] Clark v. Clark, 62 N. H. 267.

[11] Bush v. Cushman, 27 N. J. Eq.
131.

[12] Mullanphy Bank v. Schott, 135
Ill. 655, 26 N. E. Rep. 640. After
the filing of a bill by a mortgagor
to set aside and cancel notes and
a mortgage given by him, a party
acquiring such notes and mortgage by assignment will possess

no equities superior to those of the
assignor from whom he took them.
Ellis v. Sisson, 96 Ill. 105.

[13] McLain v. Lohr, 25 Ill. 507;
Scott v. Magloughlin, 133 Ill. 33,
24 N. E. Rep. 1030.

[14] Woodruff v. Morristown Savings Inst., 34 N. J. Eq. 174.

[15] Chicago Title & Trust Co. v.
Aff, 183 Ill. 91, 55 N. E. Rep. 659;
Sheldon v. McNall, 89 Ill. App. 138.
More than a hundred years ago,
Lord Chancellor Rosslyn said

is in fact highly desirable, if it can be obtained, to take from the mortgagor a written statement to the effect that he has no claim or defense against the mortgage debt and that the same is justly due according to the terms of the mortgage.[16] But)

"that persons most conversant in conveyancing hold it extremely unfit and very rash, and a very indifferent security, to take an assignment of a mortgage without the privity of the mortgagor as to the sum really due; that in fact it does happen that assignments of mortgages are taken without calling upon the mortgagor, but that the most usual case where that occurs is where it is the best security that can be got for a debt not otherwise well secured; but no conveyancer of established practice would recommend it as a good title to take an assignment of a mortgage without making the mortgagor a party and being satisfied that the money was really due." Matthews v. Wallwyn, 4 Vesey, 118, 127.

[16] In Pennsylvania (and perhaps some other states) this result is accomplished by means of a written statement called a "declaration of no set-off." A form for such declaration, the terms of which explain themselves, is as follows: "Whereas, I, John Doe (of such a place) am informed that George Goe, of the same place, is about to take an assignment of a certain bond and mortgage given and executed by me, the said John Doe, to Richard Roe, bearing date (of a day designated), to secure the payment of the sum of one thousand dollars, with interest, which said mortgage is recorded (giving date and place of record), the premises described in said mortgage being a certain lot, piece or parcel of land (giving description) with the improvements thereon. Now, therefore, at the request of the said George Goe, I do hereby certify, acknowledge and declare that I have no defense, setoff or claim whatever, in law or in equity, to make against the said bond and mortgage, so to be assigned as aforesaid, but that the whole of the principal sum thereby secured, to-wit, one thousand dollars (with interest from a certain date, or otherwise according to the circumstances) is justly payable according to the provisions of the said bond and mortgage, and I do further declare that I am now seized in fee simple of and in the premises described and granted in and by the said indenture of mortgage." Signed and witnessed. It is said that "in order that a declaration of no set-off may operate as an estoppel, it must be made to him who acts· upon it, who has reason to rely upon it, and who is thereby induced to alter his condition upon the faith of it. By this it is not meant, of course, that the declaration must be renewed at each successive assignment. The protection which it affords is not confined to the immediate assignee to whom or for whose security it was made. Any subsequent assignee claiming under him may avail himself of it. Ashton's Appeal, 73 Pa. St. 153. Such declarations operate in favor of all those whose conduct it may fairly be supposed they were intended to influence; but strangers, casually hearing of them, cannot, by acting upon them,

the courts show a disposition to hold that the assignee will take the security free from equities and defenses on the part of the mortgagor, if the assignment is made with the knowledge and consent of the latter and without objection on his part, even though he does not actually represent it to the assignee as a valid security.[17] Thus, it is ruled that, where a party executes notes, and a mortgage securing them, and delivers them to the payee therein named, to be by him sold upon the market to raise money to be used for a certain purpose, a sale of such notes by the payee in the market must be held to be a sale by the consent and authority of the maker, through his agent, and the maker is estopped from calling in question the validity of the notes and mortgage, even though the payee does not use the money received therefor for the purpose intended.[18] So where a party who was the owner of the equity of redemption in certain mortgaged land encouraged another to purchase the mortgage, saying that the land was not worth any more than the amount due on the mortgage, and that he would never redeem, and thereupon the other bought the mortgage and made extensive improvements on the land, it was held that such owner was not entitled to the aid of a court of equity to enable him to redeem the land.[19]

§ 197. Same; Exceptions to General Rule.—Of late years the courts have shown considerable uneasiness under the burden of the rule announced in Olds v. Cummings (31 Ill. 188), and have rather sought to find exceptions to it than to extend its scope. Thus, it was said: "The rule in that case rests at least in part on technical grounds, which have lost much of their force in more recent times by reason of the manifest tendency of judicial thought to an equitable standard, and while it is not intended to question the authority of that case, yet, for the reasons suggested, we do not think the principle should be extended to cases that are not clearly shown to be within the rule there announced."[20] Accordingly it was ruled in the case cited that the rule in question has no application to deeds

preclude the party from showing the truth." Griffiths v. Sears, 112 Pa. St. 523, 4 Atl. Rep. 492.

[17] Melendy v. Keen, 89 Ill. 395; Matthews v. Warner, 33 Fed. Rep. 369; Purser v. Anderson, 4 Edw.

Ch. 17; Hoy v. Bramhall, 19 N. J. Eq. 563.

[18] McIntire v. Yates, 104 Ill. 491.

[19] Fay v. Valentine, 12 Pick. (Mass.) 40.

[20] Peoria & Springfield R. Co. v. Thompson, 103 Ill. 187.

of trust given to secure railroad coupon bonds intended to be thrown on the market and circulated as commercial paper, and to be used as securities for permanent investments. So where such railroad bonds, secured by deed of trust for the benefit of the holders thereof, had been issued, and delivered to contractors engaged in the construction of the road, and by them disposed of in the market to innocent purchasers, on bill by the trustee to foreclose the deed of trust for the benefit of the bondholders, it was held that the unsettled equities and matters of account between the company and the contractors could not be set up in defense against the bill. Again, it has been decided that the rule that a mortgagor may make the same defenses against an equitable assignee as he could against the original mortgagee has no application to an assignee or holder of accommodation paper secured by mortgage. The maker of such paper cannot set up any defense against one who has taken it in good faith and in the usual course of business.[21] And again, the rule does not extend so far as to permit the mortgagor to set off a debt due to him from the assignor of the mortgage, at least where it arises out of a collateral matter.[22]

§ 198. Same; The Act of 1901.—It is doubtful whether the rule discussed in the preceding sections has or has not been abrogated by statute in Illinois. Among the laws of 1901 we find the following provision: ''Whenever a mortgage, trust deed, or other conveyance in the nature of a mortgage, is executed, conveying real estate for the purpose of securing an indebtedness on the real estate mentioned in said mortgage, trust deed, or other conveyance, such mortgage, trust deed, or other conveyance shall be considered as incident to the indebtedness secured thereby, and shall be exempt from defenses to the same extent as negotiable paper described in said mortgage, trust deed, or other conveyance, if held by a bona fide purchaser for value before the maturity of the indebtedness mentioned in and secured by said mortgage, trust deed, or other conveyance.''[23] This statute appears in the official volume of laws for 1901, printed by authority of the General Assembly and certified by the Secretary of State. It is, however, said

[21] Miller v. Larned, 103 Ill. 562.   [23] Act of May 10, 1901; Laws Ill.
[22] Colehour v. State Savings   1901, p. 248.
Inst., 90 Ill. 152.

to be asserted on good authority (and that the records at
Springfield appear to support the statement) that no such act
was ever passed by the House of Representatives.[24]   And a
letter from the Secretary of State has been printed, in which
he states that the act, as printed, is a copy of Senate Bill No.
229; that the journal of the House of Representatives shows
the defeat of the bill in that branch of the legislature by a
decisive vote; but that the journal of the Senate contains a
message from the clerk of the House reporting the concurrence
of the House in said bill, and the Senate's record of the bill
also shows its passage by the House. The act was signed by the
presiding officers of both houses and approved by the Gov-
ernor.

It is well settled that the journal of a legislative body is
absolutely conclusive and unimpeachable evidence of what took
place in that body.[25]   But it could not be contended that the
journal of the Senate was final evidence of what took place in
the House, especially when flatly contradicted by the House's
own journal. And of course no message or certificate from the
clerk of a legislative body could prevail against the evidence
of its journal. It would therefore appear that the invalidity of
this statute could be conclusively proved by the journal of the
House of Representatives, provided it is permissible in a collateral action (such as a suit for the foreclosure of a mortgage)
to go behind a bill duly signed and certified by the proper
authority, for the purpose of showing that it was never legally
enacted. On this question, there is much conflict among the
authorities. But in Illinois, the decided cases very clearly
appear to permit such inquiries to be made.[26]

§ 199. Same; Rule of the Federal Courts.—In respect to the
right of a mortgagor of realty to set up, as against an assignee
of the mortgage, defenses which would have been available to
him if the security had remained in the hands of the original
mortgagee, the debt being evidenced by a negotiable note, the
courts of the United States do not consider themselves bound

[24] Jones & Addington, Supple-
ment to Starr & Curtis, Ann. Stat.,
vol. 4, p. 891. And see Chicago
Legal News, vol. 33, p. 369, date of
June 22, 1901.

[25] United States v. Ballin, 144
U. S. 1.

[26] See Spangler v. Jacoby, 14 Ill.
297; People v. Starne, 35 Ill. 121;
Grob v. Cushman, 45 Ill. 119;
Leach v. People, 122 Ill. 420; and
other cases cited in the standard
works on Constitutional law.

to follow the decisions of the state courts, the question being one of general commercial law. Consequently, the rule on this subject established by the decisions of the Supreme Court of Illinois is not binding on the federal courts sitting within that state; but the latter will follow the rule laid down by the Supreme Court of the United States, that where a mortgage given to secure a negotiable promissory note is transferred, before the maturity of the note, to a bona fide holder for value, and a suit in equity is brought to foreclose the mortgage, no other defenses can be interposed against the mortgage than would be allowed in an action at law to recover on the note.[27]

§ 200. Same; Latent Equities of Third Persons.—As a general rule, the assignee of a mortgage, taking the same in good faith and without notice, will hold it free from any latent equities in favor of third persons which may have existed against it in the hands of the original mortgagee.[28] As we have already seen, it is the duty of one intending to take an assignment of a mortgage to inquire of the mortgagor whether there is any reason why it should not be paid; but he could not be expected to interrogate the whole world as to possible reasons why the security should not be worth its face value in his hands. "As to equities existing between the mortgagor and the assignor, the assignee has the means of protection by the exercise of ordinary diligence, while, as to latent equities existing in favor of third persons, against the assignor, the most diligent inquiry would not insure such protection. If the rule were otherwise than as stated, no one, however diligent, could deal in such securities with safety."[29] To illustrate this rule we may cite a case where it was held that, where an agent under a power of attorney fraudulently sells and conveys land of his principal to a third person, who gives his notes for the price, payable to the agent, secured by mortgage on the property sold, and the payee transfers the notes to an inno-

[27] Swett v. Stark (U. S. Circ. Ct. N. D. Ill.), 31 Fed. Rep. 858; Carpenter v. Longan, 16 Wall, 271; Myers v. Hazzard, 50 Fed. Rep. 155.

[28] Olds v. Cummings, 31 Ill. 188; Sumner v. Waugh, 56 Ill. 531; Walker v. Dement, 42 Ill. 272; Mullanphy Bank v. Schott, 135 Ill. 655,

26 N. E. Rep. 640; Humble v. Curtis, 160 Ill. 193, 43 N. E. Rep. 749; Schultz v. Sroelowitz, 191 Ill. 249, 61 N. E. Rep. 92; Himrod v. Bolton, 44 Ill. App. 516; Hubbard v. Turner, 2 McLean, 519.

[29] Himrod v. Gilman, 147 Ill. 293, 35 N. E. Rep. 373.

cent purchaser for value, the original owner of the land cannot have the sale of the land set aside, as against the rights of the assignee of the notes, and the latter will have the right to enforce the security for their payment.[30]

But latent equities or secret trusts in favor of third persons of which the assignee of the mortgage had notice may be set up against him; and so also, where he had knowledge of such facts as should have put him upon inquiry, when such inquiries, diligently prosecuted, would have brought those equities to his actual knowledge.[31] Thus, one who takes a mortgage on land pending a suit to foreclose a vendor's lien thereon, is chargeable with notice of the lien, and so are his assignees.[32] Notice sufficient to charge the assignee may be furnished by the record. It is said that "a mortgagee of real estate and his assignees of the secured debt stand in no better position than a purchaser of the land and his assignees. The doctrine of constructive notice imparted by a recorded instrument applies alike to deeds and to mortgages. The assignee of the mortgage takes it subject to all prior liens and mortgages, which are duly recorded, because he has constructive notice of them. If the title of the mortgagor is impressed with a trust in favor of a third person at the date of the mortgage, and this trust is disclosed by the recorded title, it can make no difference whether the note secured by the mortgage is negotiable or non-negotiable. In such case every assignee, as well as the mortgagee, is charged with constructive notice of the trust, and must yield to the trust."[33] Again, the purchaser of a note secured by a mortgage is chargeable with knowledge of all the recitals in any recorded deed forming a link in his chain of title; and he takes it subject to all the equities fastened upon it by stipulations or recitals in any such deed.[34]

§ 201. **Discharge or Release of Mortgage by Assignor.**—In order to protect his rights against the subsequent action of the

---

[30] Silverman v. Bullock, 98 Ill. 11.

[31] Sumner v. Waugh, 56 Ill. 531; Tantum v. Green, 21 N. J. Eq. 364. But it is said that the assignee of a mortgage, having actual notice of a latent equity or secret trust, may nevertheless take advantage of want of notice by the mortgagee. Bartlett v. Varner, 56 Ala. 580.

[32] Montgomery v. Birge, 31 Ark. 491.

[33] Patterson v. Booth, 103 Mo. 402, 15 S. W. Rep. 543. And see Buchanan v. International Bank, 78 Ill. 500.

[34] Orrick v. Durham, 79 Mo. 174.

mortgagee, it is necessary for the assignee of the mortgage
to have his assignment recorded. If the original owner of the
mortgage, after assigning it for value, fraudulently makes a
second sale and assignment of it to another purchaser without
notice, and for value, or enters a discharge or release of the
mortgage on the record, thus enabling the mortgagor to sell the
land with an apparently clear title, or to make a new mortgage
to a stranger, in either case the title of the original assignee
will be subordinated to the intervening rights of the third
person, thus coming in, unless he has duly recorded the assignment to him.[35] On the other hand, after a mortgagee has
assigned the mortgage and the assignment has been recorded,
his power to deal with the security, real or apparent, is at an
end, and his subsequent discharge or release of the mortgage
is of no effect as against the assignee.[36] It may happen, however, that even an unrecorded assignment of a mortgage will
prevail against the rights of one who relies on a release or
discharge by the original mortgagee, when the conduct of the
latter has been so careless or negligent that he cannot claim to
have an equity of equal strength with that of the assignee of
the mortgage. For example, one who advances money to pay
off a prior mortgage on real estate, with the intention that the
mortgage made to secure his advance shall thereby become the
paramount lien, should see to it that the note secured by the
old mortgage is duly taken up and cancelled; and if he neglects this, and is content to rely on a formal release of the
mortgage executed by the mortgagee therein, he cannot claim
a lien prior to that of an assignee of the old mortgage, holding
the same in good faith, although the assignment was not recorded.[37] In a case in New York it was said that if the mort-

[35] Howard v. Ross, 5 Ill. App.
456; Smith v. Keohane, 6 Ill. App.
585; Ogle v. Turpin, 102 Ill. 148.
And see §190, supra. It was at
one time thought that the assignee,
in order to be fully protected,
should take and record a deed
from the mortgagee, conveying his
legal title to the mortgaged premises. Edgerton v. Young, 43 Ill.
464. But the later decisions show
it to be fully sufficient if the assignment is recorded.

[36] Center v. Elgin City Banking
Co., 185 Ill. 534, 57 N. E. Rep. 439,
affirming 83 Ill. App. 405.
[37] Skeele v. Stocker, 11 Ill. App.
143. And see Keohane v. Smith,
97 Ill. 156. The release by the
mortgagee of a mortgage of which
he is not in possession, and which
had been assigned before maturity, does not affect the title of the
real holder of the note and mortgage. Harding v. Durand, 36 Ill.
App. 238.

gagee fraudulently enters upon the record a cancellation or release of a first mortgage, which he has already assigned, this will not take away the priority of lien which that mortgage enjoys as against the holder of a second mortgage, who took it with notice that the first mortgage was still a valid first lien. But if the holder of such second mortgage assigns it for value to an innocent holder without notice, who relies upon the record, the latter will acquire a first lien, his equity being here superior to that of the owner of the first mortgage. If, however, the second mortgage comes again into the hands of the person who assigned it, or of any one having notice of the facts, the equity of the assignee of the first mortgage will be revived, and his lien will again take the precedence.[38] It should also be remarked that an unauthorized release of a mortgage by a mortgagee who has assigned the debt cannot be set up as a defense by the mortgagor, without first paying the debt, where no rights of third persons have intervened.[39]

§ 202. Guaranty of Notes and Mortgage Assigned.—Upon the assignment of a mortgage, the assignor may be understood as impliedly warranting that the securities are genuine, that they represent an actual debt equal to that appearing on their face, and which has not been paid or released, and that he is the lawful owner of them and has good right to assign them. But in the absence of an express contract, or representations equivalent thereto, he cannot be understood as warranting the title of the property, nor the solvency of the mortgagor, nor that the land is worth the amount of the mortgage, nor that the debt is otherwise collectible.[40] And if the debt has in fact already been paid to the assignor, he is liable for the consideration received by him from the assignee, but not on the contract of assignment.[41] But although there may be no express war-

---

[38] Clark v. McNeal, 114 N. Y. 287, 21 N. E. Rep. 405.

[39] Jennings v. Hunt, 6 Ill. App. 523.

[40] French v. Turner, 15 Ind. 59; Dixon v. Clayville, 44 Md. 573; Haber v. Brown, 101 Cal. 445, 35 Pac. Rep. 1035; Nally v. Long, 71 Md. 585, 18 Atl. Rep. 811. But in West Virginia, it is held that, in the absence of an express agree-ment to the contrary, the assign-ment of a bond or non-negotiable note imports a guaranty that the assignee shall receive the full amount of the bond or note as-signed, if he fails to collect the same by the exercise of due dili-gence. Thomas v. Linn (W. Va.), 20 S. E. Rep. 878.

[41] French v. Turner, 15 Ind. 59.

ranty, still representations made by the vendor of the mortgage as to the responsibility of the mortgagor and the value of the securities, which are false in fact, though honestly made in the belief that they are true, if they are relied on and mislead the purchaser, are equivalent in legal effect to fraud and will give a right of action.[42] But equity will not relieve a person who buys a mortgage upon real estate, where the title to the property is defective, as shown by the record, unless the assignor of the mortgage has made some statement respecting the title upon which the purchaser was justified in relying.[43] Where the assignor gives a certificate that he has not received any payment upon the notes described in the mortgage, with certain exceptions, which certificate proves to be false, the assignee has a right of action in deceit, even though it was stated on the transfer of the mortgage that there should be no recourse against the assignor.[44]

It is also held, in New York, that a guaranty given to a person to secure the payment of a mortgage that has been assigned to him, may, in the absence of any express stipulations to the contrary, be assigned by him with the mortgage. "It is true that a guaranty could be so drawn as to be personal, and to have force and effect only as to the party to whom it is given, and so as not to be transferable or assignable to any other person. But in order thus to limit a guaranty, the language should be plain and peculiar and the intention of the parties should not be left in uncertainty. There is nothing personal about the guaranty of the payment of a mortgage, and it can only be made so by very express and plain language."[45] And even where a third person, without consideration, joins with the mortgagee in indorsing a general guaranty on a bond and mortgage, in order to enable the mortgagee to effect a sale of the same to a contemplated purchaser, he will be liable on his guaranty to a different purchaser, to whom the mortgage is sold a year later by the mortgagee, and who takes it relying upon the guaranty.[46]

[42] Webster v. Bailey, 31 Mich. 36.

[43] Vincent v. Berry, 46 Iowa, 571.

[44] Hexter v. Bast, 125 Pa. St. 52, 17 Atl. Rep. 252.

[45] Stillman v. Northrup, 109 N. Y. 473, 17 N. E. Rep. 379. And see

Lemmon v. Strong, 59 Conn. 448, 22 Atl. Rep. 293.

[46] Tucker v. Blaudin, 48 Hun, 439. Compare Briggs v. Lathan, 36 Kans. 205, 13 Pac. Rep. 129.

CHAPTER XVII.

INSURANCE OF MORTGAGED PROPERTY.

§ 203. **Application for Insurance; Representations as to Incumbrance.**—Policies of fire insurance usually provide that if the property to be insured, or any part of it, is incumbered, it must be so represented to the underwriters or the policy will be void, and sometimes it is made the duty of the applicant for insurance to make a full and true disclosure of all facts within his knowledge which are material to the risk. Under either of these conditions it is incumbent upon one applying for insurance on his property, on being interrogated as to the incumbrances thereon, to make a full and substantially accurate statement of the incumbrances which rest upon it. If he falsely represents the title as being free and clear, when in fact the property is subject to a mortgage, this will avoid the policy so that he cannot recover upon it in case of a loss.[1] Even though the mortgage is not recorded, still it is an "incumbrance" within the meaning of this provision and its existence must be disclosed, at the risk of invalidating the

---

[1] Stevens v. Queen Ins. Co., 81 Wis. 335, 51 N. W. Rep. 555; Murphy v. People's Fire Ins. Co., 7 Allen (Mass.) 239; Aetna Ins. Co. v. Resh, 40 Mich. 241.

policy.[2] But the applicant for insurance is not bound to make a statement concerning a mortgage which has been fully paid, nor to give information respecting one which is null and void for fraud practised upon him in its procurement.[3] Nor must this rule be taken to mean that the condition of the property in respect to incumbrances must be stated with the utmost precision and minute accuracy. A trifling error in regard to the amount due on a mortgage will not forfeit the contract of insurance, while, on the other hand, if the variation were of so great an amount in proportion to the value of the property, or if the true amount of the debt would so materially increase the risk, that the underwriter, having full information, would probably have refused it, then the misstatement must be regarded as fatal to the policy.[4] For the purpose of acquiring this information, however, the agent who procures the insurance stands in the place of the company, and his knowledge is imputable to his principal; so that if the agent is truthfully informed by the assured as to the incumbrances on the property, or otherwise has actual knowledge of the same, and either omits to impart his knowledge to the company, or falsely represents the property as being unincumbered, his acts will be deemed a waiver of the provision of the policy and the contract of insurance will not be invalidated by the misrepresentation.[5]

Where the policy contains a provision that the company shall not be liable "for loss of property owned by any other party, unless the interest of such party be stated in the policy," it is not avoided by the fact that the insurance was taken out in the name of a mortgagee of the premises (without a particular statement of his interest), when the mortgagor procured the policy to be written, in pursuance of an agreement to give the mortgagee further security, and paid the premium and after-

[2] Hutchins v. Cleveland Mut. Ins. Co., 11 Ohio St. 477.

[3] Lycoming Fire Ins. Co. v. Jackson, 83 Ill. 302.

[4] McNamara v. Dakota F. & M. Ins. Co., 1 S. Dak. 342, 47 N. W. Rep. 288; Phoenix Ins. Co. v. Fulton, 80 Ga. 224, 4 S. E. Rep. 866; Smith v. Agricultural Ins. Co., 118 N. Y. 518, 23 N. E. Rep. 883; Ryan v. Springfield F. & M. Ins. Co.,

46 Wis. 671; Glade v. Germania Fire Ins. Co., 56 Iowa, 400.

[5] Weed v. London & L. F. Ins. Co., 116 N. Y. 106, 22 N. E. Rep. 229; Bartlett v. Fireman's Fund Ins. Co., 77 Iowa, 155, 41 N. W. Rep. 601; Boetcher v. Hawkeye Ins. Co., 47 Iowa, 253; Gristock v. Royal Ins. Co., 84 Mich. 164, 47 N. W. Rep. 549.

wards paid the mortgage debt.[6] When the policy requires the
assured to make a full and true disclosure of "all facts material
to the risk," the last word is not to be taken in the narrow
sense of the hazard of the destruction of the property by fire,
but as embracing the whole subject-matter of the contract of
insurance; and in this wider sense it clearly includes the
existence of a mortgage on the property.[7]

§ 204. **Mortgaging Insured Premises; Effect on Policy.**—
If real property is conveyed by mortgage or deed of trust, after
the issuance of a policy of fire insurance on the improvements
thereon, contrary to the express provisions of the policy, the
contract of insurance will be avoided and no recovery can be
had on the policy in case of loss.[8] Where the condition of the
policy is that it shall become void in case of an "alienation"
of the property "by sale or otherwise" without the consent
of the insurer, or in case simply of a "sale" of the premises,
or a "sale, alienation, transfer, or conveyance thereof," the
incumbrance of the property by a mortgage or deed of trust
does not come within the terms of the contract and will not
avoid the insurance.[9] And the same rule applies where the

[6] Norwich Fire Ins. Co. v. Boomer, 52 Ill. 442.

[7] Towne v. Fitchburg Mut. F. Ins. Co., 7 Allen (Mass.) 51; Elliott v. Hamilton Ins. Co., 13 Gray (Mass.) 139.

[8] Dwelling House Ins. Co. v. Shaner, 52 Ill. App. 326. The execution of a mortgage on the insured property is of itself an increase of the risk, and a decrease of the security of the insurer, since it lessens the interest of the assured in the property. Lee v. Agricultural Ins. Co., 79 Iowa, 379, 44 N. W. Rep. 683.

[9] Aurora Fire Ins. Co. v. Eddy, 55 Ill. 213; Commercial Ins. Co. v. Spankneble, 52 Ill. 53. This doctrine rests upon the familiar rule of law that any condition in a contract which is intended to operate by way of forfeiture should be construed most strongly against the party for whose benefit it is inserted. This rule requires that the term "alienate" shall be taken in its proper technical sense, as designating only a voluntary conveyance of a man's whole title, legal and equitable. As a mortgage leaves the owner in the possession of at least an equitable estate in the premises, and as he retains an insurable interest, and would suffer loss by the destruction of the property, it is evident that a mortgage cannot be regarded as falling within this meaning of the term. The rule is said to be specially applicable where the assured held only an equity of redemption in the insured premises, the same being mortgaged at the time the policy was written, and he merely executed another mortgage to a different person, and for a different amount, and applied the proceeds to the payment of the prior incumbrance and to other

prohibitory clause of the policy is directed against a "voluntary sale, transfer, or conveyance" of the premises.[10] But the sale and conveyance of the property and taking back a mortgage on the same to secure the purchase money (whereby the interest of the insured is reduced from that of an absolute owner to that of a mortgagee only) is an "alienation" of the property within the meaning of the policy,[11] unless the company consents in writing to a transfer of the policy to the purchaser and makes an indorsement that the loss, if any, shall be payable to the original owner, now the mortgagee.[12] In another case, where the suit was on a policy containing this provision: "If any change takes place in the title or possession of the property, whether by sale, legal process, judicial decree, voluntary transfer or conveyance, then the policy shall be void," it was held that the giving of a mortgage on the property was not embraced in this provision.[13]

On the other hand, policies sometimes contain a clause avoiding the insurance if the assured shall "incumber" the property. This of course includes a mortgage. But it is said that the placing of a mortgage upon a tract of land other than that upon which the insured house stands will not vitiate the policy, a provision therein prohibiting incumbrances without permission of the company, although the policy refers to the house as standing upon the aggregate number of acres.[14] And a mortgage which, as a matter of law, is void constitutes no incumbrance on the property, whatever the parties may have intended, and hence does not avoid the insurance.[15] And a mere renewal or change of incumbrances on the insured property, in connection with the sale of a part of the land, does not necessarily create a breach of this condition. Whether or not there is a breach depends on whether the hazard is increased. If the incumbrance remaining on the property unsold is less in proportion to the quantity than was upon the whole property when the policy was issued, there is no breach.[16]

purposes. Aurora Fire Ins. Co. v. Eddy, 55 Ill. 213.

[10] Friezen v. Allemania Fire Ins. Co., 30 Fed. Rep. 352.

[11] Abbott v. Hampden Mut. F. Ins. Co., 30 Me. 414.

[12] Getman v. Guardian Fire Ins. Co., 46 Ill. App. 489.

[13] Hartford F. Ins. Co. v. Walsh,

54 Ill. 164; Hanover F. Ins. Co. v. Connor, 20 Ill. App. 297.

[14] Phenix Ins. Co. v. Hart, 39 Ill. App. 517.

[15] Watertown Fire Ins. Co. v. Grover & Baker S. M. Co., 41 Mich. 131, 1 N. W. Rep. 931.

[16] Russell v. Cedar Rapids Ins. Co., 71 Iowa, 69, 32 N. W. Rep. 95.

§ 205. Same; Absolute Deed as Mortgage.—A deed of conveyance of real property, which is intended merely as a security for the payment of a debt, although it is in form absolute and unconditional, and which is accompanied by a bond for reconveyance, or by a separate written instrument of defeasance, or even by a mere parol agreement for defeasance, is in legal effect nothing more than a mortgage;[17] and therefore will not invalidate a policy of insurance on the premises, which policy provides that the insurance shall become void if there is an "alienation," or a "sale," or a "voluntary transfer or conveyance" of the property, or if there shall be a "change in the title or possession," without the consent of the insurer; and in an action on such policy, if a defense is made on this ground, parol evidence is admissible to show the real nature of the deed in question, and that it was not such a divestiture of the title out of the assured as contemplated by the restrictive clause of the policy.[18] In one case, the policy prohibited any change in the title, or the mortgaging or incumbering of the property, and required the insured to be "the sole and unconditional owner" of the property. Yet even here it was held that there was no violation of the conditions of the policy by the execution of a deed of the insured property, not followed by a transfer of possession, which was absolute in form, but meant only as a security for money to be advanced, when the money was never in fact advanced.[19]

§ 206. Same; Alienation by Foreclosure.—The entry of a decree of strict foreclosure on a mortgage on the insured property, since it entirely divests all title and equities of the mortgagor, is an "alienation" of the premises, within the meaning of the prohibitive clause of the policy; but the mere entry of a decree on a bill in chancery in ordinary proceedings for the foreclosure of the mortgage does not work this result; no alienation takes place until the decree is consummated by a sale made under it, the expiration of the period allowed for

[17] See supra, §§ 19, 20.

[18] Northern Assurance Co. v. Chicago Mutual B. & L. Ass'n, 98 Ill. App. 152; Barry v. Hamburg-Bremen F. Ins. Co., 110 N. Y. 1, 17 N. E. Rep. 405; Walsh v. Fire Ass'n of Philadelphia, 127 Mass. 383; Bryan v. Traders' Ins. Co., 145 Mass. 389, 14 N. E. Rep. 454; Aetna Ins. Co. v. Jacobson, 105 Ill. App. 283. Compare Western Mass. Ins. Co. v. Riker, 10 Mich. 279.

[19] German Ins. Co. v. Gibe, 162 Ill. 251, 44 N. E. Rep. 490, affirming 59 Ill. App. 614.

redemption, and the vesting of title in the purchaser.[20]   But when the rights and title of the mortgagor are thus completely divested, it is an "alienation," as fully within the meaning of the policy as if the change of title had been accomplished by his voluntary conveyance.[21]   When the property is sold under the power contained in a deed of trust, or a mortgage with power of sale, but the sale is invalid, and the owner continues to occupy and use the property, repudiating and denying the validity of the sale, and is so occupying it at the time of the loss, there is not such an alienation, or loss of interest in the property on his part, as will avoid the policy.[22]   Thus, where the mortgagee sold the land under a power of sale in the mortgage, and bought it in himself, but the mortgagor remained in possession, and afterwards obtained a decree setting aside the sale and allowing him to redeem, it was held that such sale, being illegal, and made without the consent of the assured, did not cause a forfeiture of the policy, even though the policy contained a clause providing that the insurance should cease in case of the "entering or foreclosure of a mortgage."[23]   But when a valid sale on foreclosure, followed by the vesting of title in the purchaser, has caused a forfeiture of the policy, it cannot be revived by the mere entry of an order of court, made by consent of all parties, setting aside the foreclosure decree; so that, where a loss occurs after the foreclosure and sale, there can be no recovery on the policy, though the action for such recovery is not begun until the foreclosure decree has been vacated.[24]

§ 207. Insurable Interest of Mortgagor.—Where real property is subject to a mortgage, each of the parties thereto— mortgagor and mortgagee—has an insurable interest in the buildings on the premises; and the interest of both may be covered by one policy, or each may take out a separate policy

[20] Pearman v. Gould, 42 N. J. Eq. 4; Marts v. Cumberland Mut. F. Ins. Co., 44 N. J. Law, 478; Essex Savings Bank v. Meriden F. Ins. Co., 57 Conn. 335, 17 Atl. Rep. 930; Commercial Union Assur. Co. v. Scammon, 102 Ill. 46.

[21] McIntire v. Norwich F. Ins. Co., 102 Mass., 230; Bishop v. Clay F. & M. Ins. Co., 45 Conn. 430.

[22] Commercial Union Assur. Co. v. Scammon, 126 Ill. 355, 12 N. E. Rep. 324.

[23] Niagara F. Ins. Co. v. Scammon, 144 Ill. 490, 28 N. E. Rep. 919; Scammon v. Commercial Union Assur. Co., 20 Ill. App. 500.

[24] Mount Vernon Mfg. Co. v. Summit County Mut. F. Ins. Co., 10 Ohio St. 347.

for his own benefit.[25] As remarked by the supreme court of Illinois, "we believe no court has ever questioned that a mortgagor has an insurable interest."[26] And this is true notwithstanding the fact that the property may be mortgaged up to its full value.[27] And although a mortgagor has conveyed his equity of redemption to another, he retains an insurable interest in the property if he remains liable for the payment of the mortgage debt; for in that case he has an interest in the preservation of the property charged with the payment of the debt.[28] For the same reason, the grantee of the equity of redemption has an insurable interest in the premises.[29] And generally, the owner of an equity of redemption has an insurable interest equal to the value of the insurable property embraced therein, whether or not he is personally liable for the mortgage debt.[30] It is immaterial whether the mortgagor's equity of redemption has been voluntarily conveyed or taken on judicial process. At least, where the mortgagor's interest in the property, being an equity to redeem from the mortgage, has been seized and sold on execution against him, he retains an insurable interest in the property so long as he has a right to redeem from the execution sale.[31] And even after the entry of a decree for the foreclosure of the mortgage in ordinary proceedings for that purpose (not a decree of strict foreclosure), or after a sale of the property made in pursuance of such decree, the mortgagor retains an insurable interest in the property so long as he has a right to redeem from the foreclosure.[32]

§ 208. Insurance by Mortgagor for his own Benefit.—In the absence of a covenant in the mortgage to keep the property insured for the protection of the mortgagee, the latter has no

[25] Honore v. Lamar F. Ins. Co., 51 Ill. 409; Westchester F. Ins. Co. v. Foster, 90 Ill. 121; Concord Union Mut. F. Ins. Co. v. Woodbury, 45 Me. 447; Jackson v. Massachusetts Mut. F. Ins. Co., 23 Pick. (Mass.) 418.

[26] Lycoming F. Ins. Co. v. Jackson, 83 Ill. 302.

[27] Higginson v. Dall, 13 Mass. 96; Gordon v. Massachusetts F. & M. Ins. Co., 2 Pick. (Mass.) 249.

[28] Buck v. Phoenix Ins. Co., 76 Me. 586; Wilson v. Hill, 3 Metc. (Mass.) 66.

[29] Agricultural Ins. Co. v. Clancey, 9 Ill. App. 137.

[30] Royal Ins. Co. v. Stinson, 103 U. S. 25.

[31] Strong v. Manufacturers' Ins. Co., 10 Pick. (Mass.) 40.

[32] Stephens v. Illinois Mut. F. Ins. Co., 43 Ill. 327; Mechler v. Phoenix Ins. Co., 38 Wis. 665; French v. Rogers, 16 N. H. 177.

interest in a policy of insurance taken out by the mortgagor, or by one standing in the place of the mortgagor, for his own benefit.[33] Policies of insurance against loss by fire are personal contracts with the assured, and do not attach to the property insured, nor in any manner go with the same as an incident to a conveyance or transfer of the title, or the creation of a lien thereon, without express agreement or manifest intention on the part of the assured that the insurance was effected for the benefit of some other person interested in the property. Consequently, a mortgagee has no right to claim the benefit of a policy underwritten for the benefit of the mortgagor on the mortgaged property in case of a loss by fire, unless where the policy has been assigned to him or expressly made payable to him. The contract is strictly a personal contract for the benefit of the mortgagor, to which the mortgagee has no more title than any other creditor.[34] Conversely, a policy of insurance issued to the mortgagor, which provides that it shall be forfeited "if the assured, or any other person or parties interested" shall take out additional insurance, will not be vitiated by a policy taken out by the mortgagee without the consent of the mortgagor, since the mortgagee is not a person interested in the former policy.[35] In another case, it appeared that the mortgagor of property procured a policy of insurance in his own name. Afterwards, a sale was made under a power contained in the mortgage, and thereupon the purchaser at such sale, without the consent of the mortgagor, insured the premises in his own name, and, on the destruction of the building by fire, collected the insurance money under his policy. On a bill by the mortgagor, the sale was set aside, and an accounting had in respect to the money so received. It was held that this was no bar to an action by the mortgagor to recover on his prior policy, for the loss sustained.[36]

§ 209. **Covenant of Mortgagor to Insure.**—A covenant in a mortgage, to the effect that the mortgagor will keep the buildings on the mortgaged premises insured for the benefit of the mortgagee, is as binding as any other condition of the mortgage; and the mortgagor is not excused from its punctual

[33] Ryan v. Adamson, 57 Iowa, 30, 10 N. W. Rep. 287.

[34] Lindley v. Orr, 83 Ill. App. 70.

[35] Niagara F. Ins. Co. v. Scammon, 144 Ill. 490, 28 N. E. Rep. 919.

[36] Commercial Union Assur. Co. v. Scammon, 126 Ill. 355, 18 N. E. Rep. 562.

performance by the fact that, at the time of the execution of
the mortgage, he was informed by the mortgagee's agent that
the latter would insure the premises.[37] But a mortgagor who
has agreed to insure the property in a fixed sum for the benefit
of the mortgagee has the right, nevertheless, to procure additional insurance in favor of himself or of a subsequent incumbrancer, so long as the total insurance does not exceed the
value of the property.[38] And where the mortgagor fulfills his
covenant, by effecting insurance which is acceptable to the
mortgagee, though one of the companies in which the insurance is written afterwards becomes insolvent, the mortgagee
has no claim upon other insurance taken out by the mortgagor
for his own benefit and protection, after the satisfaction of the
covenant to insure.[39]

§ 210. **Same; Charging Mortgagor with Premiums.**—If
there is no provision in the mortgage requiring the mortgagor
to keep the property insured, or authorizing the mortgagee to
do so, the latter cannot charge the mortgagor with premiums
paid by him for insurance taken out for his own interest and
benefit.[40] But if the mortgage contains a covenant to insure,
and the mortgagor fails or refuses to fulfill it, it is proper for
the mortgagee to take out insurance, and he may add to his
mortgage debt the amount paid in premiums, if fair and reasonable.[41] So also, where the mortgage is transferred by the
mortgagee, as collateral security for a debt of his own, the
assignee is entitled, on a bill in equity against him to redeem,
to the allowance of sums paid by him for insurance while the
mortgagor did not insure.[42] If the mortgage provides that the
mortgagor shall keep the property insured, and that any sums
advanced by the mortgagee for that purpose shall be allowed
him out of the proceeds of sale on foreclosure, it is not necessary for the mortgagee to make a demand upon the mortgagor
before renewing the insurance, the policy expiring during the

---

[37] Brant v. Gallup, 111 Ill. 487.

[38] Kirchgraber v. Park, 57 Mo.
App. 35.

[39] Nordyke & Marmon Co. v.
Gery, 112 Ind. 535, 13 N. E. Rep.
683.

[40] Saunders v. Frost, 5 Pick.
(Mass.) 259.

[41] Leland v. Collver, 34 Mich.

418; Carr v. Hodge, 130 Mass. 55;
Robinson v. Sulter, 85 Ga. 875, 11
S. E. Rep. 887; Burgess v. South-
bridge Sav. Bank, 2 Fed. Rep. 500;
Mix v. Hotchkiss, 14 Conn. 32;
Barthell v. Syverson, 54 Iowa, 160,
6 N. W. Rep. 178.

[42] Montague v. Boston & A. R.
Co., 124 Mass. 242.

life of the mortgage.[43] But it has been held that, where the
mortgage authorizes the inclusion in a decree of foreclosure of
all "moneys advanced for taxes and assessments and other
liens," without more, the court cannot properly include the
amount of a premium paid by the mortgagee, for insurance on
the mortgaged premises, although the mortgagor covenanted to
keep up the insurance and failed to do so.[44] As a corollary
to the main rule above stated, it is held that if the mortgagee
charges the mortgagor with the cost of insurance paid for by
him, he should account to the mortgagor for any rebate of
premium obtained by him from the insurance company upon a
cancellation of the policy.[45]

§ 211. Same; Mortgagee's Equitable Lien on Policy.—A
covenant or a contract expressed or implied by the mortgagor
that he will keep the mortgaged premises insured during the
existence of the mortgage, for the benefit of the mortgagee,
will create an equitable lien in favor of the latter, to the extent
of his interest in the property, upon the money due for a loss
under a policy taken out by the mortgagor in his own name
upon the mortgaged property; and this, although the policy
is not assigned to the mortgagee, nor made payable to him,
and there is nothing on its face to show his interest.[46] In this
condition of affairs, when a loss occurs, it is proper for the
mortgagee to give notice of his claims on the policy to the
insurance company, and after receiving such notice, the company cannot pay the loss to the mortgagor or to any other
claimant, except at its peril, until the rights of the mortgagee
shall have been adjusted.[47] This equitable lien also will be
valid as against the assignee in bankruptcy of the mortgagor.[48]
And so, where the mortgagor, in pursuance of his covenant,
takes out policies of insurance to an amount sufficient to cover
the mortgage debt, in favor of the mortgagee, and afterwards

[43] Baker v. Jacobson, 183 Ill. 171,
55 N. E. Rep. 724.
[44] Culver v. Brinkerhoff, 180 Ill.
548, 54 N. E. Rep. 585, reversing
76 Ill. App. 679.
[45] Parker v. Trustees of Smith
Charities, 127 Mass. 499.
[46] Norwich Ins. Co. v. Boomer,
52 Ill. 442; Grange Mill Co. v.
Western Assur. Co., 118 Ill. 396, 9

N. E. Rep. 274; Wheeler v. Factors'
& Traders' Ins. Co., 101 U. S. 439;
Nichols v. Baxter, 5 R. I. 491.
[47] Grange Mill Co. v. Western
Assur. Co., 118 Ill. 396, 9 N. E.
Rep. 274.
[48] In re Sands Ale Brewing Co.
(U. S. Dist. Ct. N. D. Ill.) 3 Biss.
175.

takes out other policies which are made payable to other persons, and upon the occurrence of a loss, all the policies are scaled, so that those payable to the mortgagee do not cover his debt, he is entitled to payment from the balance of the policies before the named beneficiaries receive any sum.[49]

§ 212. **Assignment of Policy to Mortgagee.**—When the mortgagor of property takes out insurance in his own name, and then assigns the policy to the mortgagee as collateral security for the payment of the mortgage debt, with the consent of the insurer, where that is necessary, the assignee takes the policy subject to all the conditions which it contains, and his equities confer no higher right in this respect. Consequently, if the assignor, at the time a loss occurs, has forfeited all right of recovery, by violating the conditions of the policy, his assignee occupies the same position, and cannot recover.[50] The insurance, it will be observed, remains the insurance of the mortgagor, and no new contract between the insurer and the mortgagee is created by the assignment; the right of action on the policy is merely transferred as a security for the debt and as incident thereto. Hence, when the mortgage debt is satisfied in any manner, even by a sale under a decree of foreclosure, the mortgagor is entitled to the return of his policy if it is still in force.[51] Without an actual return or re-assignment of the policy, he will become subrogated in equity to the rights of the mortgagee, so as to be enabled to maintain an action on the policy if a loss takes place.[52] Similar principles govern the case where the mortgagee takes out the insurance and assigns the policy to a third person, to whom he also assigns the mortgage and the debt which it secures. Thus, where the insured held certain notes secured by a mortgage upon a house which he procured to be insured, and he afterwards, before a loss occurred, assigned the notes and mortgage and the policy, with the assent of the insurer, it was held that the ultimate liability of the assured upon his assignment of the notes, and his consequent interest in having the insurance money go to the satisfaction of these notes in the hands of his assignee

[49] Wilson v. Hakes, 36 Ill. App. 539.

[50] Illinois Mut. F. Ins. Co. v. Fix, 53 Ill. 151; Home Mut. F. Ins. Co. v. Hauslein, 60 Ill. 521; Carpenter v. Providence-Washington Ins. Co., 16 Pet. 495. Compare New England F. & M. Ins. Co. v. Wetmore, 32 Ill. 221.

[51] Digby v. National Loan & Bldg. Ass'n, 60 Ill. App. 644.

[52] Billings v. German Ins. Co., 34 Nebr. 502, 52 N. W. Rep. 397.

constituted a sufficient interest to authorize him to sue in his own name for a recovery of the insurance money.[53]

§ 213. Effect of Making Policy Payable to Mortgagee.—
Instead of assigning a policy of insurance as collateral security for the mortgage debt, it is not uncommon to indorse on the policy a provision making the "loss, if any, payable to [the mortgagee by name] as his interest shall appear." The legal effect of such an indorsement, when assented to by the insurer, is an agreement that the latter will pay the loss arising under the policy, if any there be, to the mortgagee to the extent of his lien or charge upon the premises.[54] It operates to give the mortgagee precisely the same rights and interests in the policy which he would have had if, without such words, the policy had been assigned as collateral security to the mortgage debt.[55] "In such a case," it is said, "it is very clear that, in case of loss, the insurers must pay the whole amount of the loss without regard to the fact that the debt has or has not been paid. If the mortgage debt has not been paid, the money received will go to pay it pro tanto, and thus inure to the benefit of the mortgagor, by leaving so much less of his debt for him to pay. If the mortgage debt has been paid, then the loss, when received by the mortgagee, is received from a fund placed in his hands for a special purpose which has been accomplished; it is the proceeds of an insurance of the interest of the mortgagor, by a contract with him, on a consideration made by him; and of course he receives it to the use of the mortgagor, and must account to him for it."[56]

As to the right of action on a policy so indorsed, it was at one time thought that the suit should be brought in the name of the mortgagor for the use of the mortgagee;[57] then that the mortgagee might institute the action, but must use the name of the mortgagor.[58] But now the decisions hold that a policy of insurance indorsed payable to the mortgagee, as his interest may appear, is in effect an independent contract with the mort-

[53] New England F. & M. Ins. Co. v. Wetmore, 32 Ill. 221.

[54] Sias v. Roger Williams Ins. Co., 8 Fed. Rep. 187.

[55] Connecticut Mut. Life Ins. Co. v. Scammon (Circt. Ct. U. S., N. D. Ill.), 4 Fed. Rep. 263, affirmed, 117 U. S. 634.

[56] King v. State Mut. F. Ins. Co., 7 Cush. (Mass.) 1.

[57] Illinois F. Ins. Co. v. Stanton, 57 Ill. 354; Friemansdorf v. Watertown Ins. Co., 1 Fed. Rep. 68.

[58] Peterson v. Hartford F. Ins. Co., 87 Ill. App. 567.

gagee which may be enforced in his own name.[59]   Still, the
insurance remains an insurance of the mortgagor's interest;
and hence, just as in the case of an assignment of the policy
as collateral, the mortgagee takes it subject to all the conditions
contained in the policy, and no recovery can be had, merely in
consequence of the equities of the mortgagee, if the mortgagor
has lost the right to recover by violating the terms of the
contract.[60]   Thus, if the assured has done any act in regard
to the property which would avoid the policy, as, by leaving
the premises vacant and unoccupied contrary to a stipulation in
that regard, this will continue to be a good defense for
the insurance company, notwithstanding the direction with
reference to the payment of the loss to the mortgagee.[61]   So,
where the policy provides that if the insured shall take out any
other insurance without the consent of the insurer the policy
shall be void, it is rendered void by the subsequent act of the
mortgagor in taking out an insurance on his own interest as
mortgagor, although the policy in question was really paid
for by the mortgagee and was made payable to him as his
interest might appear.[62]   But when the policy provides that,
in case an interest shall exist in favor of a mortgagee, "the
conditions hereinbefore contained shall apply in the manner
expressed in such provisions and conditions of insurance relating to such interest as shall be written upon, attached, or
appended thereto," the mortgagee is subjected to those conditions only which are stipulated in the part of the policy evidencing his interest, and unless it is therein stated, he is not
bound to make proof of loss and bring suit according to the
conditions imposed upon the insured in the body of the policy.[63]

§ 214. **Same; Adjustment of Loss.**—A mortgagee, to whom
a policy of fire insurance is made payable in case of loss, is
not bound by an adjustment of such a loss effected without his

[59] Crawford v. Aachen & Munich
F. Ins. Co., 100 Ill. App. 454, affirmed, 199 Ill. 367.

[60] Illinois Mut. F. Ins. Co. v. Fix,
53 Ill. 151; Hale v. Mechanics' Mut.
F. Ins. Co., 6 Gray (Mass.) 169;
Brunswick Sav. Inst. v. Commercial Union Ins. Co., 68 Me. 313;
Loring v. Manufacturers' Ins. Co.,
8 Gray (Mass.) 28.

[61] Franklin Sav. Inst. v. Central

Mut. F. Ins. Co., 119 Mass. 240;
Smith v. Union Ins. Co., 120 Mass.
90; Fitchburg Sav. Bank v. Am-
azon Ins. Co., 125 Mass. 431.

[62] Sias v. Roger Williams Ins.
Co., 8 Fed. Rep. 187; Continental
Ins. Co. v. Hulman, 92 Ill. 145.

[63] Queen Ins. Co. v. Dearborn
Savings, L. & B. Ass'n, 175 Ill. 115,
51 N. E. Rep. 717.

knowledge or consent by the assured, the mortgagor, with the insurance company.[64] So, although the policy provides that, at the request of either party, the loss shall be fixed by arbitrators, and the amount so fixed shall be binding on the parties, the mortgagee to whom the policy has been made payable will not be bound by the result of an arbitration entered into between the insured and the company, without the authority or consent of the mortgagee.[65]

§ 215. Special Mortgage Clause in Policy.—In modern times, policies of insurance written on property which is incumbered by mortgage usually contain a "special mortgage clause." This clause provides that the insurance, as to the interest of the mortgagee therein, shall not be invalidated by any act or neglect of the mortgagor or owner of the property, nor by the occupation of the premises for purposes more hazardous than are permitted by the policy; that the mortgagee shall notify the insurance company of any change of ownership or any increase of hazard coming to his knowledge, and shall pay for any increase of hazard not permitted to the owner; that, whenever the company shall pay to the mortgagee any sum for a loss under the policy, and shall claim that, as to the mortgagor or owner, no liability therefor existed, it shall at once be legally subrogated to all the rights of the mortgagee, under all the securities held as collateral to the mortgage debt, to the extent of such payment, or may, at its option, pay to the mortgagee the whole principal due or accruing on the mortgage, with interest, and shall thereupon receive a full assignment and transfer of the mortgage and other securities; but that no such subrogation shall impair the right of the mortgagee to recover the full amount of his claim. The effect of this clause is to make a new and separate contract between the mortgagee and the insurance company, and to effect a separate insurance of the interest of the mortgagee, which is dependent for its validity solely upon the course of action between those parties, and is not affected by any act or neglect of the mort-

---

[64] Harrington v. Fitchburg Mut. F. Ins. Co., 124 Mass. 126; Hall v. Fire Association of Philadelphia, 64 N. H. 405, 13 Atl. Rep. 648; Hathaway v. Orient Ins. Co., 134 N. Y. 409.

[65] Bergman v. Commercial Union Assur. Co., 92 Ky. 494, 18 S. W. Rep. 122; Brown v. Roger Williams Ins. Co., 5 R. I. 394.

gagor, of which the mortgagee is ignorant, whether occurring or permitted prior or subsequent to the issue of the mortgage clause.[66] Even the voluntary destruction of the insured premises by the owner will not prevent a recovery by the mortgagee.[67] And additional insurance procured by the mortgagor, in which the mortgagee has no interest, will not affect the latter's right to recover the full amount of the policy, although the policy also provides that the insurer shall not be liable for a greater proportion of any loss than the amount thereby insured shall bear to the whole amount of insurance on the property.[68] And since, under this clause, the mortgagee becomes privy to the promise of the insurance company contained in the policy, to pay the loss to him, he may maintain a suit at law on that promise in his own name.[69] But the failure of the mortgagee to comply with the conditions of the clause, imposing particular duties on him, suspends the operation of the same, and leaves in force the stipulations in the policy as to the acts on the part of the owner or mortgagor which will operate to forfeit the policy.[70] And when a question arises as to the mortgagee's right to recover a loss from the insurance company, under this clause, and at the same time an action is brought to foreclose the mortgage, the mortgagor cannot defeat complainant's recovery, nor claim the right to set off the amount of the policies against the amount due on the mortgage, so long as the question between the mortgagee and the insurance company remains undetermined.[71]

A further result of the insertion of this "mortgage clause" is to deprive the mortgagor of all beneficial interest in the policy, though it was originally written in his name, and consequently a payment to the mortgagee, under the policy, will not discharge the mortgage, but merely subrogate the insurer to the mortgagee's rights under it. Hence if the mortgagor desires to redeem, he must pay to the insurance company the full amount of the mortgage debt; he cannot claim to have it

[66] Syndicate Ins. Co. v. Bohn, 12 C. C. A. 531, 65 Fed. Rep. 165.

[67] Hartford Fire Ins. Co. v. Williams, 11 C. C. A. 503, 63 Fed. Rep. 925.

[68] Eddy v. London Assurance Corp., 143 N. Y. 311, 38 N. E. Rep. 307.

[69] Hartford Fire Ins. Co. v. Olcott, 97 Ill. 439; Meriden Savings Bank v. Home Mut. Ins. Co., 50 Conn. 396.

[70] Ormsby v. Phoenix Ins. Co., 5 S. Dak. 72, 58 N. W. Rep. 301.

[71] Detwiler v. Hibbard, 66 Ill. App. 82.

reduced by the amount paid on the loss.[72] But the insurance company, on payment to the mortgagee, will not become subrogated to his rights, unless it was in fact not liable on the policy as against the mortgagor.[73]

§ 216. **Application of Insurance Money Received by Mortgagee.**—If insurance on the mortgaged property is taken out by the mortgagor in his own name, and assigned or made payable to the mortgagee; or if the latter procures insurance upon the interest and in the name of the mortgagor, at the request or by the authority of the mortgagor, or under circumstances which would make him chargeable with the premium; then the mortgagee will have the right to collect the whole amount of a loss, but the mortgagor will be entitled to have the insurance money so collected by the mortgagee go in reduction of the mortgage debt.[74] And if several notes, payable at different times, were secured by the mortgage, and are all overdue, the insurance money so collected is to be applied first to the payment of interest on all the notes, and the surplus to the payment of the principal of the notes in the order of their maturity.[75] But the payment made by the insurance company to the mortgagee cannot be appropriated to the payment of the mortgage debt before it becomes due, without the consent of the mortgagor.[76]

§ 217. **Insurable Interest of Mortgagee.**—Each of the parties to a mortgage of realty—the mortgagee as well as the mortgagor—has an insurable interest in the improvements thereon. The interest of both may be covered in one policy, or each may take out a separate policy on his own interest and for his own benefit.[77] And the fact that the mortgagor has a prior insurance upon his interest will not defeat a policy afterwards taken out on the same property by the mortgagee in his own name or in the names of both, when the loss is made

[72] Allen v. Watertown Fire Ins. Co., 132 Mass. 480.

[73] Traders' Ins. Co. v. Race, 142 Ill. 338, 29 N. E. Rep. 846, and 31 N. E. Rep. 392.

[74] Honore v. Lamar Fire Ins. Co., 51 Ill. 409.

[75] Larrabee v. Lumbert, 32 Me. 97; Concord Union Ins. Co. v. Woodbury, 45 Me. 447.

[76] Gordon v. Ware Savings Bank, 115 Mass. 588.

[77] Honore v. Lamar Fire Ins. Co., 51 Ill. 409; Concord Union Ins. Co. v. Woodbury, 45 Me. 447; Jackson v. Massachusetts Mut. F. Ins. Co., 23 Pick. (Mass.) 418, 34 Am. Dec. 69.

payable to the mortgagee and the mortgagor is not privy to its issue; to constitute a double insurance, within the prohibitions of a policy, the two policies must not only be for the benefit of the same person and on the same subject, but also for the same entire risk.[78] It is also held that different mortgagees of the same property have independent interests which each may insure for his own benefit to the full amount;[79] that a trustee in a deed of trust in the nature of a mortgage has an insurable interest in the mortgaged property distinct from that of the mortgagor;[80] and that, when the original mortgagee has assigned the mortgage to a third person, and indorsed over to him the note secured by the mortgage, he still retains an insurable interest in the mortgaged property, in consequence of his liability on his indorsement.[81]

§ 218. **Mortgagee Insuring His Separate Interest.**—When the mortgagee insures his own interest in the mortgaged property, at his own expense and for his own benefit, and a loss by fire occurs and the amount of the insurance is paid to him, such payment does not operate as a payment pro tanto on the mortgage debt; the mortgagor has no claim upon the proceeds of the policy, and cannot require the mortgagee to apply the insurance money on the debt.[82] But of course, in this case, the mortgagee has no right to charge the mortgagor with the amount of the premium paid.[83] It is said that "the contract of insurance with the mortgagee is not an insurance of the debt or of the payment of the debt; that would be an insurance of the solvency of the debtor."[84] But it must be regarded as so far an insurance of the mortgagee's debt that "if the debt is afterwards paid or extinguished, the policy ceases from that time to have any operation, and even if the premises insured are subsequently destroyed by fire, he has no right to recover

[78] Westchester Fire Ins. Co. v. Foster, 90 Ill. 121; Niagara Fire Ins. Co. v. Scammon, 144 Ill. 490, 28 N. E. Rep. 919.

[79] Fox v. Phenix Fire Ins. Co., 52 Me. 333.

[80] Dick v. Franklin Fire Ins. Co., 10 Mo. App. 376, affirmed in 81 Mo. 103.

[81] Williams v. Roger Williams Ins. Co., 107 Mass. 377.

[82] Honore v. Lamar Fire Ins. Co., 51 Ill. 409; Ely v. Ely, 80 Ill. 532; Russell v. Southard, 12 How. 139, 157; Stinchfield v. Milliken, 71 Me. 567.

[83] Clark v. Washington Ins. Co., 100 Mass. 509.

[84] King v. State Mut. F. Ins. Co., 7 Cush. (Mass.) 1.

for the loss, for he sustains no damage thereby; neither can the mortgagor take advantage of the policy, for he has no interest whatsoever therein. On the other hand, if the premises are destroyed by fire before any payment or extinguishment of the mortgage, the underwriters are bound to pay the amount of the debt to the mortgagee, if it does not exceed the insurance. But then, upon such payment, the underwriters are entitled to an assignment of the debt from the mortgagee, and may recover the same amount from the mortgagor, either at law or in equity according to circumstances; for the payment of the insurance by the underwriters does not in such a case discharge the mortgagor from the debt, but only changes the creditor.''[85] The decisions in Illinois, as in other states, fully recognize the rule that, in such a case, the insurance company is entitled to be subrogated to the rights and remedies of the mortgagee.[86] Or practically the same result may be accomplished by a clause in the policy providing that, upon payment of the loss to the mortgagee, he shall assign the mortgage to the insurance company; and it is held to be a sufficient compliance with such a clause if he assigns so much of the mortgage debt as will cover the amount of the insurance; he is not required to assign the entire debt when it exceeds the amount insured. And it is not an unreasonable condition, upon making such an assignment, to require that the insurance company shall bear the cost of foreclosing the mortgage or otherwise collecting the debt.[87]

Where buildings on a property which is subject to a deed of trust are burned, and the insurance money is collected by the trustee, at a time when the mortgagor is not in default, it is not the duty of the trustee to apply it on the loan, or to pay it over to the mortgagor on a mere promise to rebuild. The insurance money takes the place of the buildings destroyed and becomes a part of the security for the debt. It is to be held until the mortgage falls due, and then applied in part payment. If, in the mean time, the trustee should have wasted it, the mortgagor can compel him to account for the amount received by him, and to reduce the mortgage debt pro tanto.[88]

[85] Carpenter v. Providence-Washington Ins. Co., 16 Pet. 495.

[86] Honore v. Lamar Fire Ins. Co., 51 Ill. 409; Washington Fire Ins. Co. v. Kelly, 32 Md. 421.

[87] New England F. & M. Ins. Co. v. Wetmore, 32 Ill. 221.

[88] Fergus v. Wilmarth, 117 Ill. 542, 7 N. E. Rep. 508.

CHAPTER XVIII.

TAXATION OF MORTGAGES AND OF MORTGAGED LANDS.

§ **219. Taxation of Mortgages.**—Debts secured by mortgage on realty are property within the meaning of the provision in the state constitution authorizing the legislature to provide for levying a tax on every person in proportion to the value of his property.[1] And accordingly, it is provided by statute that "every person of full age and sound mind, being a resident of this state," shall list for the purposes of taxation "all his moneys, credits, bonds * * * moneys loaned or invested. He shall also list all moneys and other personal property invested, loaned, or otherwise controlled by him as the agent or attorney, or on account, of any other person or persons, company, or corporation whatsoever."[2] A debt secured by mortgage is taxable to the person who is the real and beneficial owner of it at the time. But it is said that "when a mortgage is made to a trustee for bondholders, the mortgage interest is taxable to the trustee who represents them, as it would have been to the bondholders themselves if the mortgage had been made to them directly."[3] The provisions of the tax laws apply not only to mortgages in the ordinary form, but also to deeds of trust in

[1] People v. Worthington, 21 Ill. 171.

[2] Rev. Stat. Ill. c. 120, § 6.

[3] Knight v. City of Boston, 159 Mass. 551, 35 N. E. Rep. 86.

the nature of a mortgage, and to absolute deeds held only as
security for a loan. Thus, it is enacted that "where a deed
for real estate is held for the payment of a sum of money,
such sum, so secured, shall be held to be personal property, and
shall be listed and assessed [for taxation] as credits."[4] In
fact if the transaction really amounts to a mortgage, whatever
may be its form, the grantee is taxable as a mortgagee; but
not if it amounts to no more than a sale of the land to the
grantee, with a right in the grantor to repurchase.[5] It is also
held that a certificate of purchase of real estate, issued by a
master in chancery upon a sale made under a decree of foreclosure, which entitles the holder to receive the amount of his
bid with interest in ease the premises shall be redeemed within
a specified time, or to receive a deed of the premises if not so
redeemed, is taxable property, and its value is presumed to be
the amount of the purchaser's bid.[6]

It remains to be stated that a law imposing a tax upon mortgages does not impair the obligation of the contract between
the debtor and the creditor, within the meaning of the constitutional prohibitions, although it applies to mortgage contracts
made before its enactment, and which were not taxable at the
time of their execution.[7]

§ 220. Not Invalid as Double Taxation.—Wherever the question has arisen, it has been held that the constitutional or
statutory provisions against double taxation do not prevent
the legislature from imposing a tax upon mortgages, or rather,
upon debts secured by mortgage, although at the same time
the real property covered by the mortgage may be taxable and
may be taxed to the owner of the equity of redemption at its
full value.[8]

§ 221. Situs of Mortgages for Purposes of Taxation.—It is a
well-settled rule that intangible personal property has its only
situs, for purposes of taxation, at the place of its owner's
domicile; and a mortgage (considered as representing a debt)
follows its owner's person, and is assessable for taxation only

---

[4] Rev. Stat. Ill. c. 102, § 21.

[5] Thomas v. Holmes County, 67
Miss. 754, 7 South. Rep. 552.

[6] Wedgbury v. Cassell, 164 Ill.
622, 45 N. E. Rep. 978.

[7] Mumford v. Sewall, 11 Oreg. 67,

4 Pac. Rep. 585; Dundee Mortgage
Co. v. School District, 19 Fed. Rep.
359.

[8] Appeal Tax Court v. Rice, 50
Md. 302; Lamar v. Palmer, 18 Fla.
147; People v. Board of Super-

at the place where he resides.[9] It is immaterial that the mortgage may be recorded, or the mortgaged premises situated, in another jurisdiction.[10] And it does not affect the operation of this rule that the documents evidencing the debt—the mortgage and the notes or bonds which it secures—may not be physically present at the place of taxation.[11] Taxation is not imposed on the papers, but on the debt; and that is inseparable from the owner's domicile, except in the case of investment securities held by a local agent for a non-resident principal, which will be noticed in a later section. Again, the situs of the land covered by the mortgage is not material in fixing the situs of the mortgage debt for purposes of taxation. It is competent for a state to tax one of its resident citizens for a debt due to him from a citizen of another state, which is evidenced by the note or bond of the debtor secured by mortgage on real estate situated in the state of the debtor's residence.[12] And conversely, although the lands covered by a mortgage may lie in a given state, where also the mortgagor resides and where the mortgage is recorded, so that the realty will be taxable in that state, yet it is not competent for that state to impose a tax on the mortgage debt if it is held and owned by a non-resident.[13] And unless there is some statutory provision to the contrary, a debt for money loaned by a citizen of one state to a citizen of another state is taxable in the state and county where the creditor resides, although the debt may be payable at the place of the debtor's residence to an agent of the creditor.[14]

§ 222. Same; Case of "State Tax on Foreign-Held Bonds."
—In a celebrated case before the Supreme Court of the United States, it was held that bonds issued by a railroad company are property in the hands of the holders, and when they are held by non-residents of the state in which the company was incorporated, they are property which is beyond the jurisdic-

visors, 71 Mich. 16, 38 N. W. Rep. 639; People v. Whartenby, 38 Cal. 461.

[9] Worthington v. Sebastian, 25 Ohio St. 1; Latrobe v. Mayor of Baltimore, 19 Md. 13; Barber v. Farr, 54 Iowa, 57.

[10] Latrobe v. Mayor of Baltimore, 19 Md. 13.

[11] Hunter v. Board of Supervisors, 33 Iowa, 376.

[12] Kirtland v. Hotchkiss, 100 U. S. 491.

[13] Senour v. Ruth, 140 Ind. 318, 39 N. E. Rep. 946.

[14] Scripps v. Board of Review of Fulton County, 183 Ill. 278, 55 N. E. Rep. 700.

tion of that state. And hence a law of the state which requires the treasurer of such a company to deduct and retain a certain percentage of the interest due on the bonds, by way of a state tax, when the bonds are made and payable out of the state to non-residents, being citizens of other states, and held by them, is invalid. It was said: "It is undoubtedly true that the actual situs of personal property which has a visible and tangible existence, and not the domicile of its owner, will, in many cases, determine the state in which it may be taxed. The same is true of public securities consisting of state bonds and bonds of municipal bodies, and circulating notes of banking institutions. The former, by general usage, have acquired the character of, and are treated as, property in the place where they are found, though removed from the domicile of the owner; the latter are treated and pass as money wherever they are. But other personal property, consisting of bonds, mortgages, and debts generally, has no situs independent of the domicile of the owner, and certainly can have none where the instruments, as in the present case, constituting the evidences of debt, are not separated from the possession of the owners."[15]

§ 223. Same; Mortgages Held by Non-Residents.—From the principles stated in the preceding section, and from the rule that a mortgage, considered as security for a debt, is a mere chose in action, and as such attaches to the person of the holder and is taxable at the place of his domicile, the deduction follows inevitably that a mortgage held and owned by a non-resident of the state cannot be taxed by the state, although the land upon which the incumbrance rests is within the jurisdiction of the taxing power.[16]

§ 224. Same; Mortgages in Hands of Local Agents.—Notwithstanding the rule stated in the last section, it is held that, although mortgage securities may be the property of a person who is not a resident of the taxing state, yet if the securities are in fact within the state, being in the hands of an agent of the owner, for renewal or collection, with a view of re-loaning the

---

[15] Case of State Tax on Foreign-Held Bonds, 15 Wall. 300.

[16] Goldgart v. People, 106 Ill. 25; City of Davenport v. Mississippi & M. R. Co., 12 Iowa, 539; Board of Commissioners of Arapahoe County v. Cutter, 3 Colo. 349; State v. Earl, 1 Nevada, 394; City of St. Paul v. Merritt, 7 Minn. 258.

money by the agent as a permanent business, without any
special directions from his principal, such property will have a
situs within the state for the purpose of taxation; but it must
be under the actual and effective control of the agent at the
place of his residence within the state.[17] Thus, it was said in
a neighboring state: "We are of opinion that a business may
be done in buying and selling property, including bonds,
stocks, notes, and mortgages, and in making loans and investments, collecting and reloaning from year to year; and that
if the moneys and securities so used are retained in this state
[by the owner or by a local agent] they should be subject to
taxation here, quite the same as any other kind of property."[18]
And it is to meet cases of this kind that the legislature of
Illinois has enacted that every resident of the state, besides
listing his own property and investments for taxation, "shall
also list all moneys and other personal property invested,
loaned, or otherwise controlled by him as the agent or attorney, or on account, of any other person or persons, company, or
corporation whatsoever."[19]

§ 225. **Assessment of Taxes on Mortgaged Lands.**—In the
absence of some constitutional provision to the contrary, lands
within the state may be assessed for taxation at their full
value, without any deduction for mortgages or other incumbrances thereon.[20] But the assessment must be made to the
mortgagor, or the owner of the equity of redemption at the
time, not to the mortgagee. The latter is not an "owner" of
the property merely in virtue of his conditional and defeasible
title at law. And hence, taxes imposed on the land itself, as
distinguished from a tax on the mortgage debt, cannot lawfully
be assessed to the mortgagee, at least when he is not in possession and has never entered for the purpose of foreclosure;
and if they are so assessed, a sale made by the collector for the
non-payment of such taxes will be invalid and will pass no
title.[21]

§ 226. **Relative Rank of Tax Lien and Mortgage Lien.**—It

[17] Goldgart v. People, 106 Ill. 25;
People v. Davis, 112 Ill. 272; Board
of Supervisors of Tazewell County
v. Davenport, 40 Ill. 197; People v.
Smith, 88 N. Y. 576; Finch v. York
County, 19 Nebr. 50, 26 N. W. Rep.
589.

[18] Buck v. Miller, 147 Ind. 586,
47 N. E. Rep. 8.

[19] Rev. Stat. Ill. c. 120, § 6.

[20] Tax Cases, 12 Gill & J. (Md.)
117; Allen v. Harford County, 74
Md. 294, 22 Atl. Rep. 398.

[21] Coombs v. Warren, 34 Me. 89.

was shown in a preceding section that it is competent for the legislature of a state to enact that the taxes assessed upon particular parcels of real estate shall constitute a lien on the land superior and paramount to every existing lien created by the act of the parties, and when this is done, a sale of the land for the non-payment of the taxes so assessed will cut out the lien of a mortgage on the same property, even though the mortgage was executed before the lien for taxes attached.[22] But the rule making the lien of taxes paramount to all other liens applies (in Illinois) only in the case of taxes on realty; it is not true of taxes on personalty, which do not become a lien until delivery of the tax books to the collector, and then are subject to any prior valid incumbrance. Hence when the property of a corporation has been incumbered by the execution and due recording of a valid mortgage thereon, and afterwards taxes assessed on its capital stock attach as a lien, the tax lien will bind only the company's equity of redemption, and when that equity is cut off by a foreclosure and sale under the mortgage, the purchaser will take the property free from any lien of such taxes.[23] On the other hand, where specific taxes (such as drainage taxes) assessed upon real property are made by statute a paramount lien, outranking all existing incumbrances, a mortgagee of the land is not a necessary party to a bill by the state to foreclose a tax lien, for the superiority of the latter over the mortgage lien could not be contested or made the subject of litigation. There is no reason for making any person a defendant except the owner in possession who is liable for the tax. "Every person interested in the premises must, at his peril, see that the lien for taxes is discharged."[24]

§ 227. **Payment of Taxes by Mortgagor.**—When the mortgagor of land remains in the possession of the premises, it is his duty to pay all the taxes which are assessed and accrue thereon; and if he fails to do so, the mortgagee has the right to advance the amount necessary to discharge the taxes and look to the mortgagor to refund the money.[25] It is clear that payment of the taxes by the mortgagor will not entitle him to a

[22] Supra, § 164.

[23] Cooper v. Corbin, 105 Ill. 224. And see Parsons v. East St. Louis Gas-Light Co., 108 Ill. 380.

[24] People v. Weber, 164 Ill. 412, 45 N. E. Rep. 723.

[25] Wright v. Langley, 36 Ill. 381.

credit for the amount paid on the debt secured by the mortgage.[26] And neither the mortgagor nor his grantee, when in
possession, can acquire any rights hostile to the mortgagee by
paying the taxes on the mortgaged premises. It is their duty
to do so, and the mortgagee may well regard such payment as
a protection of his interest.[27]

§ 228. **Effect of Tax Clause in Mortgage.**—Mortgages and
deeds of trust commonly contain a covenant on the part of
the mortgagor or grantor to pay all the taxes assessed upon
the mortgaged premises during the life of the mortgage, with
a provision that his default in so doing shall authorize the
mortgagee to pay such taxes and add the amount thereof to
the debt secured by the mortgage. Such a provision is perfectly valid and will be enforced by the courts.[28] And where
a deed of trust on property of a corporation provides that the
grantor shall pay the taxes on the premises, any creditor secured by the trust deed may, in the character of a mortgagee,
pay such taxes when the company fails to do so, and in that
event, he will, as to the taxes so paid, have a prior lien in equity
upon the mortgaged premises or upon the fund arising from
their sale on foreclosure.[29] The tax clause in a mortgage sometimes goes further than this, and provides that a failure on

[26] Kilpatrick v. Henson, 81 Ala.
464, 1 South. Rep. 188.

[27] Medley v. Elliott, 62 Ill. 532.

[28] New England Mortgage Security Co. v. Vader, 28 Fed. Rep. 265.
And although the state may subsequently apportion the taxes between the mortgagor and the mortgagee according to the value of
their respective interests, and require each to pay his share thereof
into the state treasury directly, it
cannot annul or modify the contract contained in the mortgage, as
between the parties, and in case
the mortgagee is required to pay
and does pay any of such taxes, he
may enforce the repayment of the
same in the manner provided in
the mortgage. Id.

[29] Humphreys v. Allen, 100 Ill.
511; Sharp v. Thompson, Id. 447.
Where the bill, on foreclosure, alleges that the deed of trust contained a covenant for the payment of taxes, and that such covenant had been broken, and the
property allowed to be sold for
taxes, and the trust deed is attached to the bill, and is found to
provide that on non-payment of
taxes the deed may be foreclosed,
and the taxes paid from the proceeds of the foreclosure sale, the
allegations will warrant the introduction of evidence showing that
the complainant had paid money
to purchase an outstanding tax
title. Cheltenham Imp. Co. v.
Whitehead, 128 Ill. 279, 21 N. E.
Rep. 569. But a purchaser of part
of the lands subject to the deed of
trust cannot obtain the affirmative
relief, after he has defaulted, of
having taxes paid on part of the
land not bought by him appor-

the part of the mortgagor to pay taxes assessed against the property, when due, shall constitute a breach of the condition of the mortgage and shall authorize the mortgagee to proceed to a foreclosure. This provision also is held to be valid and lawful.[30] But there is some doubt as to whether a payment of the delinquent taxes by the mortgagee is not a condition precedent to his right to foreclose. In New York, it is considered that the mere failure of the mortgagor to make the necessary payment of the taxes will not alone give the mortgagee a right to foreclose; but he must found his claim upon his own payment of the taxes in the place and stead of the defaulting mortgagor.[31] But in some other jurisdictions it is held that mere default in the payment of the taxes, though there be no other default, will give the mortgagee the right to foreclose; and it makes no difference that the mortgagee has the right to pay the taxes and charge them to the mortgagor, the same to become part of the debt secured by the mortgage lien. The right to foreclose is not waived or lost, or the default condoned, by the mortgagee, on his paying the taxes and charging the amount thereof to the mortgagor.[32]

§ 229. **Payment of Taxes by Mortgagee.**—Where a mortgagor of realty neglects to pay the taxes assessed and payable thereon during the continuance of the mortgage lien, and the mortgagee pays the same, for his own protection, he is entitled to be reimbursed by the mortgagor for the amount so expended.[33] Thus, if the mortgagee has taken possession of the premises for breach of condition, it will be his duty to pay the accruing taxes, and his right to make the rents a fund for that purpose or for his own reimbursement;[34] and on an accounting by a mortgagee so in possession, he must be credited with the amount properly and lawfully paid by him in the discharge of accruing taxes.[35] So also, a tender of the mort-

tioned to such part. Cheltenham Imp. Co. v. Whitehead, 26 Ill. App. 609.

[30] Stanclift v. Norton, 11 Kans. 218; Condon v. Maynard, 71 Md. 601, 18 Atl. Rep. 957.

[31] Williams v. Townsend, 31 N. Y. 411.

[32] Brickell v. Batchelder, 62 Cal. 623; Northwestern Mut. Life Ins. Co. v. Allis, 23 Minn. 337.

[33] Brown v. Miner, 128 Ill. 148, 21 N. E. Rep. 223; Hicklin v. Marco, 6 C. C. A. 10, 56 Fed. Rep. 549.

[34] Harper v. Ely, 70 Ill. 581; Gorham v. Farson, 119 Ill. 425, 10 N. E. Rep. 1.

[35] McCumber v. Gilman, 15 Ill. 381; Moore v. Titman, 44 Ill. 367; Strang v. Allen, Id. 428.

gage debt, at its maturity, will not be sufficient unless it includes the sums which the mortgagee has been compelled to
pay for taxes. And if the mortgagor brings his bill in equity
to redeem, the mortgagee will be entitled to credit for the
taxes paid by him on the mortgaged premises.[36] And again,
when the mortgagee proceeds in equity for the foreclosure of
the mortgage, the court may properly include in its decree
amounts expended by the mortgagee for taxes, when such
items are authorized by the mortgage and the payments are
shown by the evidence.[37] Where the interest on the mortgage
debt is payable annually, the mortgagee, in foreclosing for
unpaid interest due, may have included in the decree taxes
paid by him to preserve his security, and is not bound to wait
until the principal debt is due.[38] And where the mortgage
stipulates for the payment of ten per cent. interest on any
sums advanced by the mortgagee for taxes, the agreement is
valid, and such interest may also be added to the amount to be
recovered on foreclosure.[39] So, in one of the cases, where the
mortgage provided that the mortgagee, on default of the
mortgagor, should have the right to pay the amount of any
tax or assessment chargeable upon the property, "with any
expenses attending the same," it was held that, under this
clause, the mortgagee could recover the fee paid by him to an
expert tax examiner, who had examined and obtained a reduction of the taxes imposed on the premises which the mortgagor
had failed to pay.[40] Where the mortgage to be foreclosed expressly covenants for the payment of the taxes by the mortgagor, and the bill alleges that the mortgagee had been compelled to pay them to protect the estate, a junior mortgagee
cannot object to the allowance of the amount so paid.[41] It is
also held that, in a suit for the foreclosure of a mortgage, it
is proper to allow the complainant for money advanced for the
payment of taxes, after the filing of the bill, under the prayer

[36] Dooley v. Potter, 146 Mass. 148, 15 N. E. Rep. 499.

[37] Loughridge v. Northwestern Mut. Life Ins. Co., 180 Ill. 267, 54 N. E. Rep. 153; Abbott v. Stone, 172 Ill. 634, 50 N. E. Rep. 328 (affirming 70 Ill. App. 671); De Leuw v. Neely, 71 Ill. 473; McCashland v. Allen, 60 Ill. App. 285; Douglass v. Miller, 102 Ill. App. 345.

[38] Kepley v. Jansen, 107 Ill. 79.

[39] Cleaver v. Burcky, 17 Ill. App. 92.

[40] Equitable Life Assur. Soc. v. Von Glahn, 107 N. Y. 637, 13 N. E. Rep. 793.

[41] Boone v. Clark, 129 Ill. 466, 21 N. E. Rep. 850.

for general relief, the contingencies which would justify such
payment having been set forth in the bill; in such case, it is not
necessary to file a supplemental bill.[42]

It is also provided by statute in Illinois that if taxes or assessments accrue and become a lien on any real estate, after its
sale on foreclosure and during the running of the period allowed for redemption, they may be paid by the holder of the
certificate of purchase, and in that case, if a redemption is
made, he must be reimbursed for the amount so paid, with six
per cent. interest thereon.[43]

But it must be remarked that the mortgagee has a right to
assume, and ought to assume, until the tax is returned as delinquent, that it will be paid by the mortgagor; and he has
no right to intervene and pay the tax himself until it is manifest that the mortgagor will not do so.[44] And a mortgagee cannot add to his claim under the mortgage taxes paid by him on
lands not covered by his mortgage. He may well have an interest in keeping the title to such other lands in the mortgagor;
as, where his lien is junior to that of another mortgage which
covers both the tracts, so that the junior mortgagee would
have a right to invoke the rule of marshalling securities. Still,
if he pays the taxes on such other lands, he must take the
chance of recovering the amount from the mortgagor; he cannot tack it to his mortgage debt.[45]

§ 230. Tax Sale of Mortgaged Lands.—A mortgagor of real
estate cannot set up a tax title to the same against the mortgagee. If he suffers the taxes on the premises to become delinquent, and the land to be sold therefor, and at the sale
buys the lands in, he does not thereby defeat the lien of the
mortgage, but his purchase must be regarded merely as a payment of the taxes by him.[46] So where the mortgagor, colluding
with his son, has the latter buy in the title at the tax sale, and
has the tax deed made in his name, the title so acquired, in the
hands of the son or his grantee pending a suit for foreclosure,

[42] Loewenstein v. Rapp, 67 Ill.
App. 678; Brown v. Miner, 21 Ill.
App. 60 (affirmed, 128 Ill. 148, 21
N. E. Rep. 223); Rhodes v. Mis-
souri Savings & Loan Co., 63 Ill.
App. 77.

[43] Rev. Stat, Ill. c. 77, § 27a.

[44] Pond v. Drake, 50 Mich. 302,
15 N. W. Rep. 466.

[45] Crane v. Cook, 61 Wis. 110, 20
N. W. Rep. 673.

[46] Frye v. Bank of Illinois, 11
Ill. 367; Choteau v. Jones, Id. 300;
Voris v. Thomas, 12 Ill. 442.

will not extinguish the lien of the mortgage.[47] And in regard
to the application of this rule, any person who purchases the
equity of redemption from the mortgagor, with notice of the
mortgage, stands upon the same footing with the mortgagor;
such a grantee cannot acquire a title superior to the lien of
the mortgage by allowing the land to be sold for taxes and
bidding it in.[48] Nor is the case different where the person
who makes the pretended purchase is the owner of only a small
undivided interest in the equity of redemption. Whatever his
interest may be, it will disqualify him from buying the property at a tax sale as against the mortgagee.[49]

The converse of this proposition is equally true. A mortgagee, whether in or out of possession, cannot acquire and set
up a tax title against the mortgagor. His purchase of the
property at a sale for taxes will neither oust the mortgagor nor
affect his right of redemption. When the mortgagee, instead
of paying the mortgagor's delinquent taxes, buys the property at the tax sale, either in his own name or through a third
person, the mortgagor may treat such purchase as a payment,
and have the certificate cancelled on refunding the amount
paid, with interest.[50] The same rule also applies to an assignee
of the mortgage. If such assignee acquires a tax title to the
land, and then transfers the mortgage and the tax title to a
third person, the mortgagor will have the right to redeem
both from the mortgage and from the tax title, the latter being
held to have been acquired only as an additional security to
the mortgage, and not as an adverse title.[51]

[47] McAlpin v. Zitser, 119 Ill. 273,
10 N. E. Rep. 901. And "indeed, it
has been said that whenever,
through the medium of tax proceedings and a sale, a delinquent
tax payer is apparently divested
of title to realty, and then, by a
subsequent conveyance, for a price
of about the same amount as the
taxes paid, he is apparently rein-
stated, with a new title, a fair presumption is raised of the tax debtor's intention to clear the land of
some incumbrance thereon; and in
such cases, the proceedings and
sale have only the effect of a payment of the taxes and an acquit-

tance for the same, and they leave
the title where it was before they
began."   Black, Tax Titles (2d
edn.) § 276.

[48] Hagan v. Parsons, 67 Ill. 170;
Harding v. Durand, 36 Ill. App.
238.

[49] Middletown Savings Bank v.
Bacharach, 46 Conn. 513.

[50] Stinson v. Connecticut Mut.
Life Ins. Co., 174 Ill. 125, 51 N. E.
Rep. 193 (affirming Connecticut
Mut. Life Ins. Co. v. Stinson, 62
Ill. App. 319); Moore v. Titman, 44
Ill. 367; Ragor v. Lomax, 22 Ill.
App. 628.

[51] Ragor v. Lomax, 22 Ill. App.
628.

§ 231. Notice of Redemption from Tax Sale.—The purchaser at a tax sale is not bound to serve notice of the expiration of the time for redemption upon a mortgagee who is not in possession of the premises, and his failure to do so does not in any way affect his right to take out a deed. Nor can the mortgagee, after the time for redeeming from the tax sale has expired, enjoin the purchaser from taking out a deed, on the ground of want of notice to him, even though he relied on a statement by the mortgagor that the tax sale was a mistake and that he would have it cancelled.[52]

§ 232. Redemption or Purchase of Outstanding Tax Title.—A mortgagee of real estate has a right to redeem the same from a sale for delinquent taxes, and to have the amount so paid refunded to him on foreclosure; or he will be regarded as subrogated to the rights of the state, and the amount paid to extinguish the tax lien will constitute a first lien on the land.[53] But a mortgagee in possession who allows the land to be sold for taxes will be allowed only the amount of the tax with interest—not the amount paid by him to redeem.[54] Where the mortgage secures several notes or bonds, which are held by different persons, and one of such persons redeems the land from a tax sale, or procures the sale to be judicially annulled, the consequent liberation of the land from the tax lien will inure to the benefit of all the holders of the notes or bonds; but all must contribute to the expense borne by the one who freed the land.[55] It is also permissible for a mortgagee to buy in an outstanding tax title to the land mortgaged, when the time for redemption from the tax sale has expired; and since in so doing, he acts for the benefit of the mortgagor, no less than for the protection of his own interests, he will be entitled to be reimbursed for the amount paid to secure the tax title, provided such amount was reasonable.[56]

[52] Glos v. Evanston Building & Loan Ass'n, 186 Ill. 586, 58 N. E. Rep. 374 (reversing 86 Ill. App. 651); Smyth v. Neff, 123 Ill. 310, 17 N. E. Rep. 702.

[53] Pratt v. Pratt, 96 Ill. 184; Wright v. Langley, 36 Ill. 381; Ellsworth v. Low, 62 Iowa, 178, 17 N. W. Rep. 450; Chard v. Holt, 136 N. Y. 30, 32 N. E. Rep. 740.

[54] Moshier v. Norton, 100 Ill. 63.

[55] Weaver v. Alter, 3 Woods, 152, Fed. Cas. No. 17,308.

[56] Pratt v. Pratt, 96 Ill. 184; Windett v. Union Mut. Life Ins. Co., 144 U. S. 581 (affirming 36 Fed. Rep. 838); Clark v. Laughlin, 62 Ill. 278.

§ 233. **Suit to Set Aside Tax Sale.**—A mortgagee of lands always has the right to raise the question of the invalidity of tax sales of the land subsequent to his mortgage.[57] And he may sue to set aside an illegal tax sale of a part of the mortgaged land, even though the mortgage debt could be collected by an action against the mortgagor and a sale of the rest of the land.[58] Also, it is held that a tax title obtained by collusion with the owner of mortgaged premises for the purpose of defeating the mortgage lien, is not an independent title, adverse and paramount to the mortgage, and, being subject to the mortgage, it may be inquired into in proceedings for foreclosure, and the tax deed cancelled.[59] Money advanced by a mortgagee for expenses and counsel fees in setting aside tax titles to the mortgaged property may be recovered by him from the mortgagor in a suit to foreclose the mortgage [60]

[57] Cromwell v. MacLean, 123 N. Y. 474, 25 N. E. Rep. 932.

[58] Miller v. Cook, 135 Ill. 190, 25 N. E. Rep. 756.

[59] McAlpin v. Zitser, 119 Ill. 273, 10 N. E. Rep. 901.

[60] Burton v. Perry, 146 Ill. 71, 34 N. E. Rep. 60.

CHAPTER XIX.

DOWER IN MORTGAGED ESTATES.

§ 234. **Mortgagor's Widow Entitled to Dower.**—By the common law, a conveyance of land by mortgage vested the legal title in the mortgagee and left in the mortgagor only an equity of redemption. There could be no dower in equitable estates. And consequently, if the owner of realty died after executing a mortgage on the same, and more especially after breach of the condition of the mortgage, there was no estate in which his widow could have dower.[1] But in Illinois this rule has been abolished by statute;[2] and in that state the widow of a deceased mortgagor (or the surviving husband, when the mortgage was made by the wife on her own estate) is dowable in the lands mortgaged, even after condition broken.[3] And even if the death of the mortgagor occurs after the entry of a decree of foreclosure, if before sale, his interest in the land descends as real estate to his widow and heirs.[4] But a widow

[1] Stelle v. Carroll, 12 Pet. 201; Mayburry v. Brien, 15 Pet. 21, citing Dixon v. Saville, Bro. Ca. Ch. 326; Co. Litt. 3b.

[2] Rev. Stat. Ill. c. 41, § 1, providing that "the surviving husband or wife shall be endowed of the third part of all the lands whereof the deceased husband or wife was seized of an estate of inheritance, at any time during the marriage, unless the same shall have been relinquished in legal form. Equitable estates shall be subject to such dower, and all real estate of every description contracted for by the deceased husband or wife, in his or her lifetime, the title of which may be completed after his or her decease."

[3] Cox v. Garst, 105 Ill. 342. And see Greenbaum v. Austrian, 70 Ill. 591; Davenport v. Farrar, 2 Ill. 314; Owen v. Robbins, 19 Ill. 545; Atkin v. Merrill, 39 Ill. 62; Stow v. Steel, 45 Ill. 328; Carter v. Goodin, 3 Ohio St. 75.

[4] Holden v. Dunn, 144 Ill. 413, 33 N. E. Rep. 413.

is not entitled to dower in land which she and her husband have mortgaged, when the mortgage has been foreclosed, the land bought in by the mortgagee, and the time for redemption has expired before the death of the husband.[5] Further, a widow is not entitled to dower in lands purchased by her husband until he acquires an equitable title thereto, or in other words, is in a position to enforce a specific performance of the contract; and if he sells or incumbers his interest before that time, the purchaser or mortgagee will take free from any claim of dower, and having so taken, no subsequent act of the husband can operate to create a dower right in the premises to his prejudice. Therefore, where a husband buys land, and, before completing his payments or receiving a deed, gives a mortgage on the same, and afterwards completes the payment of the purchase money, and the title passes, under a strict foreclosure, to the mortgagee, the mortgagor's widow will not be entitled to dower in such land.[6]

§ 235. Purchase-Money Mortgage Superior to Dower.— When the husband takes a conveyance in fee, and at the same time mortgages the land back to the grantor or to a third person to secure the purchase money in whole or in part, dower cannot be claimed as against rights under the mortgage. The husband is not deemed sufficiently or beneficially seized by an instantaneous passage of the fee in and out of him to entitle his widow to dower as against the mortgage.[7] This rule is established in Illinois by a statute, which provides that, under such circumstances, the surviving husband or wife shall not be entitled to dower in such lands as against the mortgagee or those claiming under him, though she or he may not have united in the mortgage, but shall be entitled to dower as against all other persons.[8] But it appears that the widow will be dowable in any surplus which may remain after the payment of the purchase-money mortgage.[9]

§ 236. Mortgage Executed Before Marriage.—A statute of Illinois declares that "where a person seized of an estate of

[5] Shape v. Schaffner, 140 Ill. 470, 30 N. E. Rep. 872.

[6] Taylor v. Kearn, 68 Ill. 339.

[7] Mayburry v. Brien, 15 Pet. 21; Sheldon v. Hufnagle, 51 Hun. 478, 4 N. Y. Supp. 287.

[8] Rev. Stat. Ill. c. 41, § 4. And see Frederick v. Emig, 186 Ill. 319, 57 N. E. Rep. 883.

[9] Culver v. Harper, 27 Ohio St. 464; Fox v. Pratt, Id. 512.

inheritance in land shall have executed a mortgage of such estate before marriage, the surviving husband or wife of such person shall, nevertheless, be entitled to dower out of the lands mortgaged, as against every person except the mortgagee and those claiming under him.''[10] Where a husband has mortgaged his land before marriage, the wife, on the marriage, takes an inchoate right to dower only in the excess of the value of the land over the amount of the mortgage, and if the husband pays the mortgage debt, he acquires the title that was in the mortgagee, and the wife's dower attaches to it the same as to any other interest in land acquired by him during the coverture.[11] Or if the husband dies and his heir redeems from the mortgage, the widow may obtain dower by contributing ratably to the redemption; her right of dower will be restored only upon a redemption by her husband or his legal representatives.[12] In one of the cases, it appeared that a deed of trust was dated and acknowledged by the grantor nearly a month before his marriage; and afterwards his wife was made a party, and the deed was executed by her, and acknowledged by both the husband and wife. It was held that the wife's right of dower was from the first subordinate to the trust deed; the presumption being that the deed was delivered on the day of its date.[13] It is also held, under the statute above quoted, that a second wife, who survives her husband, is entitled to dower in lands mortgaged jointly by the husband and his first wife.[14]

§ 237. **Effect of Sale of Equity of Redemption.**—If a mortgagor of land has sold and transferred his equity of redemption, and afterwards dies, it is doubtful whether his widow can compel the grantee of the equity of redemption to redeem from the mortgage. But if such grantee does effect a redemption, the widow may have her dower (if otherwise entitled thereto), but only upon condition that she contributes her share of the redemption money. The owner of the equity of redemption, upon making the redemption, acquires an equitable lien upon the whole estate, which he may hold against the widow

---

[10] Rev. Stat. Ill. c. 41, § 3.

[11] Selb v. Montague, 102 Ill. 446.
See Walker v. Rand, 131 Ill. 27, 22
N. E. Rep. 1006.

[12] Virgin v. Virgin, 91 Ill. App.
188.

[13] Walker v. Rand, 131 Ill. 27, 22
N. E. Rep. 1006.

[14] Shape v. Schaffner, 140 Ill. 470,
30 N. E. Rep. 872.

until she makes contribution according to the value of her interest; and her share of the redemption money will be an amount bearing the same ratio to the whole debt that the computed present value of her dower bears to the whole value of the land.[15]

§ 238. Release of Dower.—"A married woman may relinquish her right of dower in any of the real estate of her husband, or in any real estate, by joining with her husband in a deed, mortgage, conveyance, power of attorney, release, or other writing of or relating to the sale, conveyance, or other disposition thereof."[16] Consequently, where a married woman joins with her husband in the execution of a mortgage on his lands, she waives and releases her right of dower in such lands.[17] But if the wife of the mortgagor does not join in the mortgage, and thereby release her dower right, she will still be entitled to dower in the mortgaged premises upon his death, and a decree of foreclosure rendered thereafter must save her dower right.[18]

§ 239. Redemption by Dowress.—The widow of a deceased mortgagor, in virtue of her dower interest, has the right to redeem the premises from the mortgage, at any time before the equity of redemption is cut off by a foreclosure.[19] And in so doing, she will not be required to pay off the entire incumbrance to protect her dower, but only her ratable share of the redemption money, the heirs contributing their proper proportion.[20]

§ 240. Redemption by Heir; Contribution by Widow.—If the mortgage is paid off by the heir of the mortgagor, after the latter's death, this is equivalent to a purchase by the heir of that interest in the estate which was in the mortgagee; and

---

[15] Cox v. Garst, 105 Ill. 342; Noffts v. Koss, 29 Ill. App. 301; Everson v. McMullen, 113 N. Y. 293, 21 N. E. Rep. 52.

[16] Rev. Stat. Ill. c. 30, § 17 (Starr & C. § 18). It is also provided by the Dower Act that no deed or conveyance of realty made by a husband or wife shall prejudice the right of the other to dower, unless made with the assent of such other, evidenced by an acknowledgment of the conveyance as required by law. Rev. Stat. Ill. c. 41, § 16.

[17] Virgin v. Virgin, 91 Ill. App. 188, affirmed, 189 Ill. 144, 59 N. E. Rep. 986.

[18] Hall v. Harris, 113 Ill. 410.

[19] Leonard v. Villars, 23 Ill. 377; Pope v. North, 33 Ill. 440.

[20] Cox v. Garst, 105 Ill. 342; Jones v. Gilbert, 135 Ill. 27, 25 N. E. Rep. 566.

the widow of the mortgagor will have no dower in such new
estate unless she makes just contribution towards the cost
of removing the incumbrance, or pays her ratable share of the
redemption money.[21] So, the discharge of a mortgage on land
occupied by the widow as a homestead being necessary to the
preservation of the estate of homestead as well as the interest
of the heir of the mortgagor, therefore, when the mortgage is
paid, whether by the widow and dowress or by the heir entitled to the reversion, the widow must contribute her proper
share of the debt.[22] In one of the cases, it appeared that land
belonging to the estate of a deceased person was distributed
between his widow and heirs without reference to a mortgage
covering part of the land assigned to some of the heirs. Afterwards, other land, for the conveyance of which a bond for
deed had been given, was sold, and the proceeds used by the
widow, who was also the administratrix of her deceased husband's estate, in paying off the mortgage on the land which
had been previously divided. It was held that the widow
should be required to contribute to the discharge of such mortgage in the proportion the value of her dower bore to the total
value of the land.[23]

§ 241. Dower in Surplus on Foreclosure.—Where a mortgage is foreclosed after the death of the mortgagor, his widow
will be entitled, by way of dower, to a life interest in the interest or income of one-third of any surplus that may remain
after payment of the mortgage debt and costs.[24] And where
the mortgagor dies after the entry of a decree of foreclosure,
the court may, on petition of the widow, modify the decree
after the mortgagor's death so as to give the widow her dower

[21] Selb v. Montague, 102 Ill. 446.
[22] Jones v. Gilbert, 135 Ill. 27,
25 N. E. Rep. 566.
[23] Zinn v. Hazlett, 67 Ill. App.
410.
[24] "When in either of the cases
specified in the two preceding sections [i. e., whether the mortgaged land was purchased before
or after the marriage] the mortgagee or those claiming under him
shall, after the death of such husband or wife, cause the land mortgaged to be sold, either under a
power contained in the mortgage,
or by virtue of the judgment or
decree of a court, and any surplus
shall remain, after the payment
of the moneys due on such mortgage, and the costs and charges of
sale, such survivor shall be entitled to the interests or income of
one-third part of such surplus, for
life, as dower." Rev. Stat. Ill. c.
41, § 5.

in the surplus, if any.[25] But, under the terms of this statute, the widow is entitled to dower only in the surplus, and not in the gross proceeds of the sale, where the lands are sold on the petition of the administrator to pay a mortgage given by her husband before their marriage.[26] And she cannot make the land itself liable for her claim, in the hands of a bona fide purchaser at the foreclosure sale, as he is not bound to see to the application of the purchase money.[27] And further, the statute gives this right of dower in the surplus only in cases where the foreclosure is made after the death of the mortgagor. Where a mortgage, in which the wife joined, has been foreclosed, and a surplus remains after the satisfaction of the mortgage debt, the court will not decree that one-third of such surplus shall be invested for the wife's benefit, to await the possibility of her surviving her husband. The inchoate dower right attaches to the equity of redemption, and the wife may protect this by satisfying the mortgage debt or by redeeming; but on her failure to do this, equity will not tie up a portion of the surplus to await the possible maturing of such inchoate right. The surplus in the hands of the trustee or officer of the court, after satisfying the mortgage, is personalty and the property of the husband, and may be seized for the payment of his other debts. Dower in the surplus is, by the statute, limited to the survivor, and a claim for dower in the surplus cannot be allowed while both husband and wife are living.[28]

§ 242. **Widow of Mortgagee Not Dowable.**—From the legal doctrine that a mortgage vests the title in fee in the mortgagee, leaving nothing but an equity of redemption in the mortgagor, it might be thought that the widow of the mortgagee would be entitled to dower in the mortgaged lands. This, however, has not been conceded by the authorities; and in Illinois it is expressly provided by statute that "no person shall be endowed of lands conveyed to his or her wife or husband by way of mortgage, unless such wife or husband have acquired an absolute estate during the marriage."[29]

[25] Holden v. Dunn, 144 Ill. 413, 33 N. E. Rep. 413.

[26] Virgin v. Virgin, 189 Ill. 144, 59 N. E. Rep. 986, affirming 91 Ill. App. 188.

[27] Hurst v. Dulaney, 87 Va. 444, 12 S. E. Rep. 800.

[28] Kauffman v. Peacock, 115 Ill. 212, 3 N. E. Rep. 749.

[29] Rev. Stat. Ill. c. 41, § 6.

CHAPTER XX

RELATIVE RIGHTS OF PARTIES BEFORE BREACH OF CON-
DITION.

§ 243. **Nature of Mortgagor's Title.**—According to the well-
settled doctrine in Illinois, "the mortgagor is the legal owner
of the mortgaged premises against all persons except the mortgagee;"[1] and "until some condition of the mortgage is broken,
the control of the mortgagor is as absolute, except in the permitting or committing of waste, as if no mortgage lien existed."[2] As concerns all the rights and privileges, both civil
and political, of which the ownership of a freehold is one of
the conditions, the mortgagor is a freeholder, while the mortgagee, by the mere virtue of his mortgage title, cannot claim
to be such.[3] Further, "the mortgagor's interest in the land
may be sold upon execution; his widow is entitled to dower in
it; it passes as real estate by devise; it descends to his heirs at
his death as real estate; he is a freeholder by virtue of it; he
may maintain an action for the land against a stranger, and
the mortgage cannot be set up as a defense."[4] The mortgagor,
while in possession, may lawfully sell or lease the mortgaged
premises. His grantee succeeds to his estate, occupies his
position, takes subject to the incumbrance, and is subject to
the same equities. His possession is not hostile to, nor inconsistent with, the rights of the mortgagee, and he is not a trespasser. But of course, the mortgagor or his grantee cannot
make a lease of the mortgaged premises which will give any

[1] Seaman v. Bisbee, 163 Ill. 91,
45 N. E. Rep. 208.
[2] Bell v. Cassem, 158 Ill. 45, 41
N. E. Rep. 1089.

[3] Marks v. Robinson, 82 Ala. 69,
2 South. Rep. 292.
[4] Lightcap v. Bradley, 186 Ill.
510, 58 N. E. Rep. 221.

greater right than he possesses, or which will interfere with the right of the mortgagee to enter for breach of condition.[5] And upon such entry by the mortgagee, the latter may, at his option, treat the party in possession, whether it be the mortgagor or his grantee or lessee, either as his (the mortgagee's) tenant or as a trespasser.[6]

Moreover, an equity of redemption in mortgaged land is an interest which may be attached, or levied upon and sold on execution, the purchaser taking subject to the mortgage if the judgment was junior to it.[7]

As against all third persons, the mortgagor is the owner of the property. He may maintain ejectment for the possession of it, and a mortgage with which the defendant fails to connect himself is no defense; it does not show an outstanding title such as would defeat the action.[8] Also the mortgagor will be entitled to maintain actions of trespass for injuries to the freehold; and it is said that such an action may be brought by the mortgagor even against the mortgagee, the latter not being in possession.[9]

§ 244. Duty to Protect Mortgagee's Interests.—It is the duty of the mortgagor of realty to protect the rights and interests of the mortgagee, and not to attempt to overthrow or destroy them. Thus, as we have seen in an earlier section, he cannot divest the title of the mortgagee by allowing the taxes on the property to fall into arrear and buying in the premises at the tax sale.[10] So, the mortgagor will be estopped to deny that the mortgage is a lien on his property to the extent of the title which he had or claimed to have at the time he executed the mortgage.[11] And an agreement which puts an interpretation on the conveyance under which the mortgagor acquired title, will not affect the mortgagee, if he was no party

[5] Taylor v. Adam, 115 Ill. 570, 4 N. E. Rep. 837.

[6] Medley v. Elliott, 62 Ill. 532.

[7] Curtis v. Root, 20 Ill. 53; Fitch v. Pinckard, 5 Ill. 69; Vallette v. Bennett, 69 Ill. 632. It was not so at common law, for nothing was subject to execution unless the debtor had the legal title to it. But in the United States generally the equitable doctrine of mortgages has so far prevailed as to establish the rule that an equity of redemption may be sold as real estate on an execution. Van Ness v. Hyatt, 13 Pet. 294.

[8] Emory v. Keighan, 88 Ill. 482.

[9] Morse v. Whitcher, 64 N. H. 591, 15 Atl. Rep. 207; Chamberlain v. Thompson, 10 Conn. 243, 26 Am. Dec. 390.

[10] Supra, § 230.

[11] Madaris v. Edwarus, 32 Kans. 284, 4 Pac. Rep. 313.

thereto.[12] So again, the possession of the mortgagor, or of those claiming under him, continuing in the occupancy of the mortgaged premises, and acknowledging the existence of the mortgage, is not adverse to the rights of the mortgagee, and will not ripen into a title superior to the mortgage.[13]

§ 245. **Nature of Mortgagee's Title.**—At law, the mortgagee of real property is regarded as the owner of the fee, and is entitled to all the rights and remedies which the law gives to such an owner. After breach of condition, he may recover the possession of the premises by ejectment against the mortgagor. But the legal title is vested in him for the sole purpose of making his security effectual. And in equity, the mortgagor, subject to the mortgage, remains the real and beneficial owner of the estate, the mortgage being regarded as no more than a security for the payment of the debt.[14] Upon the death of the mortgagee, the legal title to the premises becomes separated from the ownership of the debt secured; but his heir, to whom the title descends, will be regarded in equity as the trustee of the executor or administrator until the debt is paid, and will be decreed to convey.[15] Before foreclosure or entry for breach of condition, the interest of the mortgagee in the mortgaged land is not such an interest as can be attached or levied upon and sold under execution.[16] And a mortgagee who has neither the possession nor the right of possession of the mortgaged premises has no interest therein which he can lease.[17] But he may sue to set aside an illegal tax sale of part of the mortgaged land, even though the mortgage debt could be collected by a sale of the rest of the property covered and an action against the mortgagor.[18] In a proceeding to enforce a mechanic's lien against property incumbered by a deed of trust, the trustee, as well as the holder of the debt secured, is a necessary party; but if the latter allows a decree to pass

[12] Maxon v. Lane, 102 Ind. 364, 1 N. E. Rep. 796.

[13] Allen v. Everly, 24 Ohio St. 97.

[14] Oldham v. Pfleger, 84 Ill. 102; Moore v. Titman, 44 Ill. 367; Lightcap v. Bradley, 186 Ill. 510, 58 N. E. Rep. 221.

[15] Dayton v. Dayton, 7 Ill. App. 136.

[16] Nicholson v. Walker, 4 Ill. App. 404; Brown v. Bates, 55 Me. 520, 92 Am. Dec. 613; Courtney v. Carr, 6 Iowa, 238.

[17] Union Mut. Life Ins. Co. v. Lovitt, 10 Nebr. 301.

[18] Miller v. Cook, 135 Ill. 190, 25 N. E. Rep. 756.

upon the merits, without the joinder of the trustee as a party, he and those claiming under him will be bound by the decree.[19]

§ 246. Right of Possession.—By the strict doctrine of the common law, the mortgagee was regarded as invested with the legal estate in the property mortgaged, and this carried with it the right to the immediate possession. Consequently, even before breach of condition, the mortgagee had a legal right to enter upon the possession, and if it was withheld from him, he could maintain ejectment against the mortgagor. The earlier cases in Illinois followed this rule. But the recent decisions hold that the mortgagee will not be entitled to claim the possession of the estate, by an action of ejectment, until there has been a default in the payment of the mortgage debt, or interest thereon, or some other breach of the condition of the mortgage.[20] It is prudent to insert in the mortgage or deed of trust a clause permitting the mortgagor or grantor to retain the possession until breach of condition; but even if this is not done, the courts will easily infer such a permission if there is anything in the mortgage indicating that such was the intention of the parties.[21] If the mortgagee does not take

[19] Bennitt v. Wilmington Star Min. Co., 119 Ill. 9, 7 N. E. Rep. 498; s. c., 18 Ill. App. 17.

[20] Kransz v. Uedelhofen, 193 Ill. 477, 62 N. E. Rep. 239. Herein it was said: "At common law, a mortgage deed conveyed the fee in the land to the mortgagee, and under it the mortgagee could oust the mortgagor immediately on the execution and delivery of the mortgage without waiting for the period fixed for the performance of the condition. In other words, at common law, the mortgagee might maintain ejectment against the mortgagor before condition broken and turn him out of possession, unless the right of the mortgagee to do so was restrained by the terms of the mortgage. It is claimed, on the part of the appellant, that this common-law rule prevails in this state; and the contention is sustained by some of the earlier cases decided by this court. It must be remembered, however, that the equitable theory of a mortgage has, in process of time, made, in this state, material encroachments upon this legal theory. * * * The doctrine is still maintained that the mortgagee can bring ejectment against the mortgagor, but the tendency of the later decisions has been to hold that this right has been so far limited as to confine the bringing of the action to cases where the condition of the mortgage has been broken, or where there has been a failure to make payment of principal or interest according to the terms of the mortgage. The more reasonable rule is that the title exists for the benefit of the holder of the mortgage indebtedness, and as a means of coercing payment of that indebtedness."

[21] Kransz v. Uedelhofen, supra.

or recover the possession of the property when the debt is due and unpaid, but proceeds to a foreclosure and sale, the mortgagor will be entitled to retain the possession, and to receive the rents and income of the property, after the sale on foreclosure and until the expiration of the period allowed by law for redemption.[22]

But it is clearly competent for the parties to stipulate in the mortgage, or by a verbal agreement, that the mortgagee may take and hold possession of the premises before default; and when this is done, and the possession is voluntarily surrendered to the mortgagee, he will be entitled to retain the possession and to collect the rents and other issues of the estate until the mortgage debt is paid.[23] But where the mortgagee receives possession of the property from a grantee of the mortgagor before the mortgage debt is due, under a contract of purchase, he cannot afterwards be allowed to claim that such possession is held under his mortgage. Good faith requires the surrender of possession thus obtained before claiming to hold under the mortgage.[24]

§ 247. **Restraining Commission of Waste.**—A mortgagor of realty may exercise the rights of an owner while he remains in the possession of the mortgaged premises, provided he does nothing to destroy or impair the security of the mortgagee; but a court of equity will grant its writ of injunction, on the application of the mortgagee, to stay the commission of waste by the mortgagor or his tenants, when the acts threatened or complained of are such as may result in annihilating or impairing the security of the mortgage.[25] For instance, the removal of a building or other improvement permanently attached to the freehold is per se an injury to the freehold, and will be regarded as waste; and therefore equity will restrain the same, at the instance of the mortgagee, without regard to the question of the mortgagor's solvency.[26] Again,

[22] Davis v. Dale, 150 Ill. 239, 37 N. E. Rep. 215 (affirming Dale v. Davis, 51 Ill. App. 328); Bartlett v. Amberg, 92 Ill. App. 377; Cohn v. Franks, 96 Ill. App. 206; Carroll v. Haigh, 97 Ill. App. 576.

[23] Edwards v. Wray, 11 Biss. C. C. 251, 12 Fed. Rep. 42.

[24] Cable v. Ellis, 86 Ill. 525.

[25] Williams v. Chicago Exhibition Co., 188 Ill. 19, 58 N. E. Rep. 611 (reversing 86 Ill. App. 167); Minneapolis Trust Co. v. Verhulst, 74 Ill. App. 350; Fairbank v. Cudworth, 33 Wis. 358.

[26] Williams v. Chicago Exhibition Co., 188 Ill. 19, 58 N. E. Rep. 611; Matzon v. Griffin, 78 Ill. 477;

if the chief value of the mortgaged property consists in the value of the timber growing upon it, it is evident that the cutting and removal of such timber, in any considerable quantities, would diminish the security afforded by the mortgage, and perhaps render it entirely inadequate as a source for the satisfaction of the mortgage debt. When this is made to appear, a court of equity will not hesitate to enjoin the mortgagor, or his tenants, as the case may be, from severing and removing the timber.[27] But the right of the mortgagor to deal with the property and its products as his own will not be unnecessarily interfered with. That is, he will not be enjoined unless the acts complained of as waste may so far impair the value of the property as to render it insufficient, or of doubtful sufficiency, as security for the debt.[28]

§ 248. Remedy for Impairment of Security.—Where waste has already been committed upon mortgaged premises (as, by the removal of buildings or of valuable timber), and the mortgagee did not discover it in time to sue out an injunction, he may still have a remedy for the consequent impairment of the value of his security. Though the point does not appear to have been discussed by the courts of Illinois, it is held in other states that the lien of the mortgage may still be enforced against fixtures or other property removed from the mortgaged premises, if they still remain in the possession of the mortgagor, or of any person acting in collusion with him, or of a purchaser with notice of the mortgage.[29] But if the lien of the mortgage is lost, as regards such property, the remedy of the mortgagee is by an action on the case, for damages for the impairment of his security, against the mortgagor or against any third person who has committed the unlawful act, it being necessary for him to show, in such action, that the

Triplett v. Parmlee, 16 Nebr. 649, 21 N. W. Rep. 403.

[27] Nelson v. Pinegar, 30 Ill. 473. And see, supra, § 118. But where the mortgagor of a farm, while in possession, cuts a reasonable quantity of wood for his own use as fuel, he may, on leaving the farm, remove the wood for use elsewhere. Judkins v. Woodman, 81 Me. 351, 17 Atl. Rep. 298.

[28] Moriarty v. Ashworth, 43 Minn. 1, 44 N. W. Rep. 530.

[29] Thus, where the mortgagor, without the knowledge or consent of the mortgagee, removes a building from the premises, leaving the property entirely insufficient as security for the debt, and then disposes of the premises to which the building was removed, the lien of the mortgage on the building is

mortgage security has been in fact impaired and rendered insufficient.[30]

§ 249. **Rights of Mortgagee in Possession.**—A mortgagee who has lawfully gained the possession of the mortgaged premises is entitled to hold the same, receiving the rents and profits and applying them on his debt, until such debt is paid wholly and in full. And it is a well-settled general rule that, so long as any sum remains due to a mortgagee in possession, he will not be deprived of that possession, at the suit of the mortgagor, by the appointment of a receiver. Especially is this the rule when it appears that the mortgagee is of sufficient means to make good to the mortgagor any excess of the rents and profits received by him over and above the amount due on the mortgage, or that he will give security to do so. It is otherwise, however, when it is shown that there is danger that the income from the property may be lost and dissipated, and that the mortgagee is insolvent or not financially responsible, or if it appears that he is committing waste upon the property or injuring it in material respects. In such a state of affairs, it will be proper, as a means of securing justice and fair play. for all parties, to appoint a receiver to take charge of the property until satisfaction of the mortgage debt is made.[31] And the same principles apply where the application for a receiver is made in a creditor's bill filed by a judgment creditor of the mortgagor.[32] So again, the mortgagee in possession cannot be ousted by a purchaser of the premises at a sheriff's sale on execution of the equity of redemption, the judgment being junior to the mortgage.[33] The mortgagee in possession being bound to manage the property prudently and so as to derive an income from it, it is of course competent for him

not impaired as against a purchaser with notice. Betz v. Muench, (N. J.) 13 Atl. Rep. 622.

[30] Chelton v. Green, 65 Md. 272, 4 Atl. Rep. 271; Morgan v. Gilbert, 2 Flip. 645, 2 Fed. Rep. 835; Betz v. Verner, 46 N. J. Eq. 256, 19 Atl. Rep. 206.

[31] Springer v. Lehman, 50 Ill. App. 139; Bolles v. Duff, 35 How. Prac. (N. Y.) 481.

[32] Peterson v. Lindskoog, 93 Ill. App. 276.

[33] Dickason v. Dawson, 85 Ill. 53. And it makes no difference that the mortgagee took possession after the sheriff's sale under an arrangement with the mortgagor to allow rent by way of credits on the mortgage debt; and the fact that he is called a tenant and takes a lease from the mortgagor does not in any way change his rights as a mortgagee. Id.

to lease the premises to a tenant; but such a lease will necessarily be terminated by the redemption of the mortgage, unless there was some express or implied authority from the mortgagor to make leases for a given time extending beyond the time for redemption.[84]

Such being the rights of a mortgagee in possession, the duties and liabilities of the mortgagor, out of possession, are such as may fitly correspond with them. For example, a mortgagor who is out of the possession and control of the property, real or personal, ought not to be held liable for any tortious acts of the mortgagee, who is in possession of the property and who has an independent and adverse control of it. So a railroad company is not liable, at common law, or under the statutes imposing liability for injuries causing death, for the negligence of mortgagees who are operating the road under a possession taken and held adversely.[85] It remains to be remarked that a mortgage is a contract; and if it stipulates that the creditor may take and retain possession of the mortgaged property until the debt is paid, this is a valuable and substantial part of the contract; and hence a law which gives the right of possession to the mortgagor cannot constitutionally apply to mortgages made before its enactment.[86]

§ 250. **Right to Rents and Profits.**—While the mortgagor of realty remains in possession of the mortgaged premises, and before there has been any breach of the condition of the mortgage, he is entitled to receive the rents, issues, profits, and emblements of the estate and to apply the same to his own use, and he is under no obligation to turn over such rents and profits to the mortgagee, or to account to the latter for the same.[87] Thus, where a railroad mortgage provides that, until default, the railroad company may continue to possess and use its road, and receive the rents, profits, and increase arising therefrom, the earnings of the company, derived from the operation of the road, though subject to the mortgage, con-

[84] Holt v. Rees, 46 Ill. 181.

[85] Wisconsin Central R. Co. v. Ross, 142 Ill. 9, 31 N. E. Rep. 412.

[86] Mundy v. Monroe, 1 Mich. 68.

[87] Moore v. Titman, 44 Ill. 367; Mississippi Valley & W. Ry. Co. v. United States Express Co., 81 Ill. 534; Cross v. Will County Nat. Bank, 177 Ill. 33, 52 N. E. Rep. 322; Rooney v. Crary, 11 Ill. App. 213; Young v. Northern Illinois Coal & Iron Co., 9 Biss. C. C. 300, 13 Fed. Rep. 806; Teal v. Walker, 111 U. S. 242; Chelton v. Green, 65 Md. 272, 4 Atl. Rep. 271.

tinue to be the property of the company, before foreclosure of
the mortgage or possession taken by the trustee, in so far as
that they may be reached by other creditors of the company,
and are liable to garnishment.[38]

Upon breach of the condition of the mortgage, the mortgagee
may enter, and render his security productive by the percep-
tion of the rents and profits; but this is allowed only for the
purpose of protecting his security and making it effectual;
and therefore he must apply the income of the property received by him in reduction of the mortgage debt.[39] And his
mere right to enter upon default will not render the mortgagor
liable for the rents and profits. If the mortgagee does not
exercise this right, by actually taking possession, or by causing the mortgagor's tenants to attorn to him, he cannot claim
the rents.[40] Nor does the mere filing of a bill for foreclosure
entitle the mortgagee to receive the income of the estate. For
that purpose he must procure the appointment of a receiver.
Thus, the purchaser of the equity of redemption is not bound to
account for the rents and profits from the time a bill for foreclosure is brought until the decree, unless there is some covenant on the part of the mortgagor that the mortgagee shall be
entitled to receive them.[41] Even after the sale of the property
in pursuance of a decree of foreclosure, the mortgagor is
entitled to receive the rents and profits during the statutory
period allowed for redemption.[42] The only exception to this
rule is in cases where there is a deficiency and a receiver has
been appointed to collect the income of the property. And
even in that case, as against the purchaser at foreclosure, the
mortgagor is entitled to any balance of the rents and profits
collected by the receiver, during the period allowed for redemption, which may remain in the receiver's hands after paying
the deficiency decree and other items allowed by the court.[43]
When the rents and profits of the land, as well as the land

---

[38] Mississippi Valley & W. Ry.
Co. v. United States Express Co.,
81 Ill. 534, citing Gilman v. Illinois & Miss. Tel. Co., 91 U. S. 603,
and distinguishing Galena & C. U.
R. Co. v. Menzies, 26 Ill. 121.

[39] Moore v. Titman, 44 Ill. 367;
Rooney v. Crary, 11 Ill. App. 213.

[40] Teal v. Walker, 111 U. S. 242;

Forlouf v. Bowlin, 29 Ill. App. 471.

[41] Silverman   v.   Northwestern
Mut. Life Ins. Co., 5 Ill. App. 124.

[42] Wilson v. Equitable Trust Co.,
98 Ill. App. 81; Talcott v. Peterson,
63 Ill. App. 421.

[43] Stevens   v.   Hadfield, 178 Ill.
532, 52 N. E. Rep. 875, affirming 76
Ill. App. 420.

itself, are pledged by the mortgage as security for the amount
due to the mortgagee, he acquires, by the appointment of a
receiver, an equitable lien upon such rents and profits during
the statutory period allowed for redemption for the full payment of any deficiency that may arise upon a sale of the
premises to pay the debt.[44]

§ 251. **Purchase of Outstanding Title.**—A mortgagee may
buy in an outstanding title, or the equity of redemption, either
from the mortgagor or from a third person who has acquired
it by grant, directly from him, or by a purchase under a judgment or decree which was a prior lien to his mortgage, and
hold the title absolutely in his own right, provided he has made
no arrangement with the mortgagor, or any promise, or done
any act which would preclude him from so doing. The mere
relation of mortgagor and mortgagee will not prevent the latter
from so acquiring the outstanding title.[45]   And a mortgagee
in possession, before foreclosure, who buys in an outstanding
lien to protect his possession, is entitled to receive the amount
paid, with legal interest.[46]

[44] Oakford v. Robinson, 48 Ill.
App. 270.
[45] Roberts v. Fleming, 53 Ill. 196.

And see Turner v. Littlefield, 142
Ill. 630, 32 N. E. Rep. 522.
[46] Comstock v. Michael, 17 Nebr.
283, 22 N. W. Rep. 549.

CHAPTER XXI.

SALE OR TRANSFER OF MORTGAGED PREMISES.

§ 252. **Sale of Equity of Redemption.**—Notwithstanding the existence of a mortgage on land, the owner thereof may sell and convey his interest—that is, the equity of redemption—to a third person, transferring to the latter all his own rights in the premises.[1] But the lien of the mortgage follows the land into the hands of all successive purchasers having notice. That is, where land is purchased with notice of an outstanding mortgage, it is liable to be charged with its payment in the same manner as it would have been had the legal title remained in the vendor.[2] The purchaser, or his alienees, will of course have the same right of redemption from the mortgage which belonged to the mortgagor; and they can be deprived of that right only by a foreclosure of the mortgage, or by its being barred in some of the modes recognized by the law.[3] More-

[1] Coffing v. Taylor, 16 Ill. 457.

[2] Willis v. Henderson, 5 Ill. 13; Dunlap v. Wilson, 32 Ill. 517.

[3] Dunlap v. Wilson, 32 Ill. 517.
Where a mortgage is executed on an equity held by the mortgagor

301

over, if the purchaser of mortgaged land has notice, actual or constructive, of the mortgage, he is to be charged with full notice of its legal effects, and will acquire no other rights than those of the mortgagor. The construction of the mortgage must be the same whether the mortgagor has conveyed the equity of redemption or not.[4] Again, the lien of the mortgage cannot be discharged or affected by any agreement entered into between the mortgagor and the purchaser; though the mortgagee may restrict or apportion his lien, in accordance with such an agreement, if all interested parties consent.[5] And the mortgagee is in no wise concerned with the question whether the mortgagor has conveyed the equity of redemption to a third person for a full consideration or gratuitously, or for the purpose of hindering or defrauding his creditors; in either case, the conveyance cannot prejudice the right of foreclosure.[6]

The relative rights of the grantor and grantee, as to liability for the payment of the mortgage debt, will be discussed in a later section. But it may here be remarked that a purchaser of property from a mortgagor thereof, after the mortgage has been recorded, who assumes no liability to the mortgagor which the latter can enforce, is in no sense the surety of his vendor.[7] And it is to be remarked that the possession held by the grantee of the mortgagor is in subordination to the title of the mortgagee to the same extent as that of his grantor; and it cannot cease to be of that character, and become such an adverse possession as may ripen into a paramount title under the statute of limitations, until there is an open assertion of a distinct title, with the knowledge of the mortgagee, or until the mortgage is barred by limitations.[8]

§ 253. Same; Mortgage Not Recorded.—We have already seen that a mortgage is not effective against a subsequent pur-

on a bond for a deed, and the mortgagor subsequently reconveys the land to his vendor before any forfeiture is declared on the bond, his grantor will succeed to the rights of the mortgagor, and is entitled to pay off the mortgage and prevent a sale; and until the right of redemption has expired, he is entitled to retain the possession and enjoy the rents and profits. Baker v. Bishop Mill Colony, 45 Ill. 264.

[4] Kruse v. Scripps, 11 Ill. 98.

[5] Reed v. Jennings, 196 Ill. 472, 63 N. E. Rep. 1005.

[6] Fetrow v. Merriwether, 53 Ill. 275.

[7] Maher v. Lanfrom, 86 Ill. 513.

[8] Alsup v. Stewart, 194 Ill. 595,

chaser of the land, who has no actual notice of it, unless it is recorded;[9] and that a recorded mortgage gives constructive notice to subsequent purchasers only so far as the description of the property, in the mortgage and record, is correct or sufficient to identify the property with certainty.[10] In this connection it is said: "If one purchases land of the owner, knowing that the latter has already mortgaged it to another, although by a wrong description, the purchaser will take the land subject to the mortgage; and even if the purchaser has no actual notice of the mortgage having been made by such wrong description, yet if the circumstances attending the transaction are of a character to have put a reasonably prudent man on such inquiry as would, by the exercise of reasonable diligence, have led to a discovery of the existence of the mortgage, the purchaser will be bound in the same manner as if he had actual notice. On the other hand, if there is nothing in the attending circumstances calculated to put the purchaser on inquiry, further than the fact that the mortgage with such wrong description is upon the records of the county, and has been seen and read by the purchaser, he will hold the land discharged from the mortgage incumbrance."[11] Again, if, at the time the owner of land sells it to another, there is a mortgage on the land actually existing and unpaid, but which has been mistakenly or fraudulently discharged of record, the purchaser's rights will depend on his knowledge and good faith. If he had no actual notice that the mortgage really remained a lien on the land, nor knowledge which ought to have put him on inquiry, but honestly believed that the recorded discharge was valid and effectual, the land, in his hands, will be clear of the mortgage. But if, at the time the mortgagee's equities are brought to his knowledge, he has not paid all the purchase money, the mortgage may be foreclosed as to the balance of the purchase money remaining unpaid.[12]

§ 254. Same; Covenant Against Incumbrances.—If the grantee in a deed of land agrees, either in writing dehors the deed or by parol, to assume and pay a mortgage incumbrance resting on the premises, he will be held upon the agreement,

62 N. E. Rep. 795; Harding v. Durand, 36 Ill. App. 238.

[9] Supra, § 153.

[10] Supra, §§ 62, 153.

[11] Slattery v. Rafferty, 93 Ill. 277.

[12] Sheldon v. Holmes, 58 Mich. 138, 24 N. W. Rep. 795.

not only by his grantor but also by the mortgagee, notwithstanding the fact that his deed contains an express covenant
that the property is free from incumbrances.[13] On the other
hand, a vendor who conveys by a deed containing a covenant
against incumbrances, and takes the notes of the purchaser,
secured by trust deed on the property, for the unpaid purchase
money, is bound to protect the purchaser against any incumbrances which were on the land when he conveyed, before he
can properly demand payment of the notes given for the purchase money. It is the right of a purchaser of property under
a deed with covenants against incumbrances to have all liens
that may be on it removed before his vendor can sell it under
the purchase-money mortgage.[14]

§ 255. Sale of Land "Subject to" Existing Mortgage.—
When a mortgagor of land, in selling and conveying it to a
third person, inserts in the deed a clause to the effect that it is
made "subject to" the existing mortgage, this, and the acceptance of the deed by the grantee, will not create any personal
liability on the part of the latter to pay the outstanding incumbrance, unless he has specially agreed to do so, or unless
the amount of the mortgage debt is deducted from the purchase money. To create such a liability, there must be something in the nature of a contractual obligation amounting to
an agreement by the grantee to pay off the mortgage incumbrance.[15] But the land itself remains subject to the lien of
the mortgage. The effect of such a clause is to make the land
the primary fund, as between all the parties, for the satisfaction of the lien; it charges the land conveyed with the incumbrance of the mortgage debt as effectually as if the grantee
had expressly assumed the payment of the debt.[16] It is said

[13] Eggleston v. Morrison, 84 Ill.
App. 625.

[14] Coffman v. Scoville, 86 Ill. 300.
But where the grantee in a warranty deed conveying premises
subject to a prior mortgage remains in undisturbed possession,
no suit to collect the debt secured,
or to foreclose the mortgage, or to
evict him, having been brought, it
is no defense to foreclosure of his
purchase-money mortgage that the
prior mortgage is an outstanding

incumbrance. Gager v. Edwards,
26 Ill. App. 487.

[15] Comstock v. Hitt, 37 Ill. 542;
Fowler v. Fay, 62 Ill. 375; Nichols
v. Spremont, 111 Ill. 631; Crawford
v. Nimmons, 180 Ill. 143, 54 N. E.
Rep. 209; Richardson v. Venn, 84
Ill. App. 601; Elliott v. Sackett,
108 U. S. 132; Shepherd v. May,
115 U. S. 505; Middaugh v. Batchelder, 33 Fed. Rep. 706; Elser v.
Williams, 104 Ill. App. 238.

[16] Miller v. Robinson Bank, 34

that "the difference between the purchaser's assuming the payment of the mortgage, and simply buying subject to the mortgage, is simply that in the one case he makes himself personally liable for the payment of the debt, and in the other case he does not assume such liability. In both cases he takes the land charged with the payment of the debt, and is not allowed to set up any defense to its validity."[17] And further, the land being the primary fund for the discharge of the mortgage debt, as above stated, equity will not permit the purchaser to force his vendor into paying off the mortgage, on the ground that the vendor is personally liable for the debt while he is not. If the mortgagee collects the debt by personal action against the mortgagor, the latter may be subrogated to the rights of the mortgagee, or treated as an equitable assignee of the mortgage, so as to enable him to subject the property to sale for his reimbursement. If the purchaser, on the other hand, pays the amount of the mortgage debt to the mortgagee, and takes an assignment of the mortgage, the law will not permit him to hold it as a valid claim against his grantor, nor use it as a set-off in an action by the grantor for the purchase money; the assignment will be treated simply as a payment of the mortgage debt, freeing the land from its lien.[18]

§ 256. Assumption of Mortgage by Purchaser.—When a deed of mortgaged land contains a recital that the purchaser "assumes and agrees to pay" the mortgage, it imposes upon him a personal liability for the mortgage debt, provided he has assented to such provision of the deed, and estops him to deny the validity of the mortgage or that the particular land which he has bought is subject to its lien.[19] While the usual and full form of this clause is as above given, it is held that a recital that the grantee "assumes" a certain mortgage on the land conveyed is equivalent to a statement that he "assumes to

---

Ill. App. 460; Donk v. St. Louis Glucose Co., 17 Ill. App. 369; Monarch Coal & Mining Co. v. Hand, 99 Ill. App. 322. But a grantee of land need not pay a mortgage thereon which constituted no part of the consideration of his purchase, and which was not made in good faith for a real debt, notwithstanding his deed is expressed to be "subject to incumbrances." Robinson Bank v. Miller, 153 Ill. 244, 38 N. E. Rep. 1078.

[17] Hancock v. Fleming, 103 Ind. 533, 3 N. E. Rep. 254.

[18] Donk v. St. Louis Glucose Co., 17 Ill. App. 369.

[19] Sidwell v. Wheaton, 114 Ill. 267, 2 N. E. Rep. 123.

pay" it, and amounts to a personal covenant on his part to
discharge the mortgage debt.[20] Nor is it even necessary that
the assumption of a mortgage indebtedness should be incorporated in the deed; it may be by a separate written contract,
or even by a parol promise;[21] and when a part of the purchase
money is withheld for the purpose of paying the mortgage
debt, the agreement of the vendee to pay the same is not within the statute of frauds, as a parol promise to pay the debt of
another, because it is not his money, but the vendor's, which
is to be used for such payment.[22] But in order to make the
assumption clause in a deed binding and obligatory on the
purchaser, the law requires something more than the mere
insertion of such a clause in the deed by the grantor. In some
way the grantee's assent to the contract must be shown; as,
by his acceptance of the deed with full knowledge and understanding of its terms.[23] The fact that the deed contains such
a clause, will not fix a personal liability upon the purchaser,
for the benefit of a mortgagee who neither gave nor suffered
anything as a consideration for such assumption, when the
grantee did not in fact execute the deed, or when it appears
that his promise to assume the mortgage was obtained by fraud
or artifice or given under a mistake.[24] The undertaking of the
grantee will inure to the benefit of the mortgagee, and the
latter may, if he chooses, release the mortgagor from all
liability on the mortgage debt, and agree to look alone to the
purchaser for satisfaction. But the fact that the mortgagee
has not expressly consented to the substitution of the purchaser in place of the original mortgagor will not affect the
liability of such purchaser after he has assumed the mortgage.[25] If the purchaser has not expressly or virtually agreed
to assume the mortgage, he cannot be held personally liable
therefor, although the deed to him, by a mistake of the draftsman, is made to contain an assumption clause. In such a case,
a court of equity will reform the instrument, or will refuse to

[20] Eggleston v. Morrison, 84 Ill.
App. 625; Schley v. Fryer, 100 N.
Y. 71, 2 N. E. Rep. 280.

[21] Eggleston v. Morrison, 84 Ill.
App. 625; Lang v. Dietz, 191 Ill.
161, 60 N. E. Rep. 841.

[22] Tuttle v. Armstead, 53 Conn.
175, 22 Atl. Rep. 677.

[23] Thompson v. Dearborn, 107
Ill. 87; Boisot v. Chandler, 82 Ill.
App. 261; Baer v. Knewitz, 39 Ill.
App. 470.

[24] Schmitt v. Merriman, 101 Ill.
App. 443.

[25] Bay v. Williams, 112 Ill. 91,
1 N. E. Rep. 340.

enforce the clause of assumption.[26] But the purchaser cannot escape liability on such a clause, on the ground that he was ignorant of its insertion, unless he clearly proves that fact. If his testimony on that point is contradicted by the grantor, and the latter's evidence is corroborated by pertinent circumstances, the grantee must be held chargeable with the mortgage debt.[27]

The grantee of a mortgagor may also assume the payment of only a specified amount of mortgage indebtedness, expressly stated in his deed; and in this case, he cannot be held personally liable for the whole of a larger mortgage covering the land.[28] But one who contracts, as a consideration for a deed conveying certain lots to him, to pay "all notes" secured by a trust deed on the lots is liable for the entire debt evidenced by such notes, although the trust deed covers other lots not included in his purchase, and his liability in such a case is not restricted to so much of the debt as may be equitably chargeable to the lots purchased.[29] But on the other hand, a covenant in a mortgage that the premises are free from all incumbrances is not one which runs with the land; and a purchaser of the property from the mortgagor, who assumes and agrees to pay the mortgage debt, does not become responsible for a breach of such covenant. Hence if there were unpaid taxes against the land, which constituted a lien upon it at the time the mortgage was made, the mortgagee, having paid them, cannot recover the amount on foreclosure of the mortgage against the purchaser of the premises.[30] When a mortgagee, having the elder lien, buys the premises, and agrees, as a part of the consideration, to pay a mortgage debt which is junior to his, equity will require him to pay it, or will order a sale of the land for its payment.[31]

§ 257. Same; Deduction of Mortgage from Purchase Price. —On the sale of land incumbered by a mortgage, if the amount of the mortgage is included in and forms a part of the consideration which the grantee promises to pay for the property,

[26] Adams v. Wheeler, 122 Ind. 251, 23 N. E. Rep. 760; Drury v. Hayden, 111 U. S. 223.

[27] Moran v. Pellifant, 28 Ill. App. 273.

[28] Garrett v. Peirce, 74 Ill. App. 225

[29] Mead v. Peabody, 183 Ill. 126, 55 N. E. Rep. 719, affirming 83 Ill. App. 297.

[30] Fuller v. Jillett (U. S. Circt. Ct. N. D. Ill.) 2 Fed. Rep. 30.

[31] Huebsch v. Scheel, 81 Ill. 281.

and he retains that part of the purchase price, the law will
create a personal liability against him, upon the ground that
he has agreed to pay such indebtedness.[32] And where it is
doubtful whether a deed of mortgaged premises binds the
grantee to pay an existing incumbrance, evidence of the value
of the property, or of the agreed consideration for it, and as
to whether the grantee retained any of the consideration to pay
the debt, is admissible to aid in construing the deed.[33] But
the implied contract to pay to the holder of a mortgage money
retained for that purpose by the grantee arises only from the
presumed understanding of the parties, and cannot exist when
there was an express understanding to the contrary and a distinct refusal by the grantee to pay the debt.[34]

§ 258. Same; Estoppel to Dispute Mortgage.—Where the
purchaser of real estate assumes the payment of a mortgage
debt upon the property, as a part of the consideration for the
conveyance to him, he will be estopped to dispute the validity
of the mortgage (as, on the ground that there was no consideration for the mortgage debt), and this estoppel extends to
those claiming under him.[35] So, where one promises a mortgagee that, if the latter will let him buy the mortgaged premises, he will pay the mortgage debt, he cannot afterwards
repudiate his promise on the ground that, by reason of a mistake in the description, the mortgage does not cover the land.[36]

§ 259. Same; Personal Liability of Purchaser.—Where one
purchases real estate incumbered by a mortgage, and, as a part
of the consideration, assumes and agrees to pay the incumbrance, such an undertaking will create a personal liability
on the purchaser, in favor of the holder of the mortgage, which
may be enforced in an appropriate action.[37] The promise of

[32] Siegel v. Borland, 191 Ill. 107,
60 N. E. Rep. 863; Twitchell v.
Mears, 8 Biss. C. C. 211, Fed. Cas.
No. 14,286.

[33] Winans v. Wilkie, 41 Mich.
264, 1 N. W. Rep. 1049.

[34] Siegel v. Borland, 191 Ill. 107,
60 N. E. Rep. 863, reversing 93 Ill.
App. 320. And see Maher v. Lanfrom, 86 Ill. 513.

[35] Lang v. Dietz, 191 Ill. 161, 60
N. E. Rep. 841 (affirming 93 Ill.

App. 148); Hancock v. Fleming,
103 Ind. 533, 3 N. E. Rep. 254; Mill-
ington v. Hill, 47 Ark. 301, 1 S. W.
Rep. 547.

[36] Kellums v. Hawkins, 36 Ill.
App. 161.

[37] Rogers v. Herron, 92 Ill. 583;
Rapp v. Stoner, 104 Ill. 618;
Thompson v. Dearborn, 107 Ill. 87;
Wager v. Link, 134 N. Y. 122, 31 N.
E. Rep. 213.

the purchaser inures to the benefit of the mortgagee, and the latter, in proceedings to foreclose, is entitled to a decree against such purchaser for any deficiency that may arise on a sale of the mortgaged premises; and the bringing of the suit is a sufficient acceptance of the purchaser's promise by the mortgagee.[38] Further, when this personal liability on the part of the purchaser has once attached, it cannot be taken away by a release from liability given to him by his grantor, the original mortgagor, without the permission and consent of the mortgagee, even though such a release may be executed before any express acceptance by the mortgagee of the benefit of the arrangement.[39] Nor can the purchaser relieve himself from the liability which he has thus assumed by a voluntary reconveyance of the property to his grantor, the mortgagor.[40] And he will continue to be liable for the payment of the mortgage debt, even though the mortgage may be rendered void, after its execution and delivery, by an unauthorized alteration.[41]

§ 260. Same; Mortgagee's Right of Action against Purchaser.—When the grantee of the mortgagor assumes and agrees to pay the debt secured by the mortgage, the mortgagee is not restricted to a foreclosure of the mortgage, as a means of recovering his debt, but, in view of the personal liability assumed by such grantee, the creditor may bring assumpsit (or other proper action) in his own name directly against the purchaser to recover the amount of the note or other evidence of debt secured by the mortgage. This right of action rests on the principle of law that a third person, for whose benefit a contract is made, may sue thereon in his own name, whether the contract be simple or sealed.[42] This is considered in Illinois a sufficient ground on which to rest the right of action. But in some other states, the courts have preferred to support it on the ground that the covenant of the purchaser is a col-

[38] Bissell v. Bugbee, Fed. Cas. No. 1,445, 8 Cent. Law J. 272.

[39] Bay v. Williams, 112 Ill. 91, 54 Am. Rep. 209; Betts v. Drew, 12 Chicago Legal News, 65, Fed. Cas. No. 1,372; New York Life Ins. Co. v. Aitkin, 125 N. Y. 660, 26 N. E. Rep. 732.

[40] Ingram v. Ingram, 172 Ill. 287, 50 N. E. Rep. 198, affirming 71 Ill. App. 497.

[41] Daub v. Englebach, 109 Ill. 267.

[42] Webster v. Fleming, 178 Ill. 140, 52 N. E. Rep. 875, affirming 73 Ill. App. 234. And see Episcopal City Mission v. Brown (U. S. Circt. Ct. N. D. Ill.) 43 Fed. Rep. 834.

lateral security obtained by the mortgagor, which, by equitable subrogation, inures to the benefit of the mortgagee.[43]

§ 261. Same; Liability of Purchaser by Mesne Conveyances. —When the grantee of land assumes a mortgage on the same as a part of the consideration, and conveys the land to another, who likewise assumes the mortgage, the first grantee stands in the position of a surety for the second, and, if compelled to pay the debt, may recover from the latter.[44] And where any purchaser of mortgaged premises takes the same under a deed containing a covenant by which he assumes and agrees to pay the mortgage, as a part of the consideration of the conveyance, he will be liable for the amount of the mortgage, and may be sued by the mortgagee in assumpsit on the bond secured by the mortgage, although his grantor was not liable on it, the mortgage having been made by a prior owner of the land.[45] The fact that the notes secured by a deed of trust were

[43] Crowell v. Currier, 27 N. J. Eq. 154; Francisco v. Shelton, 85 Va. 779, 8 S. E. Rep. 789.

[44] Stover v. Tompkins, 34 Nebr. 465, 51 N. W. Rep. 1040. And see Episcopal City Mission v. Brown, 43 Fed. Rep. 834.

[45] Dean v. Walker, 107 Ill. 540, 47 Am. Rep. 467. In this case it was said by Judge Craig: "Deeds of lands made subject to a mortgage, and deeds containing an assumption clause purporting to bind the grantee to pay an existing incumbrance, have been the source of much discussion in the courts in regard to the rights and duties of the grantor, grantee, and the person holding the incumbrance on the property conveyed. A deed made subject to an outstanding mortgage creates no personal liability on the grantee to pay off the incumbrance, in the absence of a contract to pay, or unless the amount of the mortgage has been deducted from the purchase price and left in the hands of the grantee. Comstock v. Hitt, 37 Ill. 542; Fowler v. Fay, 62 Ill. 375. Thus far the law seems to be well settled. Where, however, a deed contains a clause in which the grantee assumes an incumbrance on the premises conveyed, and agrees to pay the same, and an action is brought to enforce such a contract, the questions growing out of such contract transaction have been attended with more difficulty. But we think the law may be regarded as well settled, where A. has given a mortgage on a tract of land to B., and subsequently conveys to C., the deed containing a contract that C. assumes the mortgage and agrees to pay the same, that B. may compel the grantee to pay the mortgage indebtedness, either by a suit at law or by a bill in equity foreclosing the mortgage, and a personal decree against the mortgagor and the purchaser of the mortgaged premises for any deficiency. * * * Whether this is the true relation of the parties or not, where the mortgagor, who is bound for the payment of a sum of money, secured by mortgage on land, conveys the same, and the

not signed by the maker of the deed, but by a third person, does not affect the validity of a contract of assumption by a purchaser of the mortgaged premises, by which he agrees to

grantee, by a clause in the deed, assumes the payment of the mortgage indebtedness, no reason is perceived which will prevent the mortgagee, for whose benefit the clause in the deed is inserted, from maintaining an action upon such a contract against the grantee. It is a familiar rule, and one well sustained by authority, that where one person for a valuable consideration makes a promise to another for the benefit of a third person, such third person may maintain an action upon it. It is not necessary, in such a case, that there should be any consideration moving from the third person for whose benefit the promise is made, or that there should be any privity between them. The conveyance of the land is the consideration for the promise, and the fact that the consideration moves from the mortgagor is a matter of no moment. The position is taken here that a grantee of mortgaged premises cannot be made liable to pay the mortgage indebtedness by an assumption clause in the deed, however strong the intent may be expressed by the language used, unless the grantor is himself, at the time of making the deed, liable for such indebtedness. We are aware of the fact that there are cases which sustain this view of the law (citing certain New York cases), but we are not inclined to follow them. The New York cases are predicated upon the principle that, where the grantor is liable for the mortgage indebtedness, and the deed under which he conveys contains an assumption clause, the grantee becomes the

principal debtor by virtue of the agreement, and the grantor occupies the situation of a mere surety for him as to the payment of the mortgage indebtedness. Such being the relative situation of the parties in equity, the creditor, who is the mortgagee, is entitled to the benefit of all collateral obligations for the payment of a debt which a person standing in the situation of a surety for others has received for his indemnity to release him or his property from liability for such payment. It is quite true that this principle of equity could not be invoked, and this remedy in equity made available, if the grantor of the mortgaged premises was not himself liable for the mortgage indebtedness, for the reason that the situation of principal debtor and surety would not exist between the grantor and grantee. But is there no other principle of law upon which the grantee may be rendered liable upon a contract which he has deliberately made upon a valid consideration? We think there is,— that it may be placed upon the broad and well-settled principle that where one person makes a promise to another based upon a valid consideration for the benefit of a third person, such third person may maintain an action upon it. Here it was not necessary that any consideration should pass from the owners of the mortgages to Walker (the grantee). It was enough that his contract was based upon a consideration which moved from Dean to him. A portion of the purchase price of the land was left in his hands, in consideration

pay specified portions of the indebtedness evidenced by the notes as part of the purchase price.[46]

§ 262. Release of Mortgagor's Liability.—An agreement by the grantee of mortgaged premises with his grantor to pay off the mortgage on the property will not release or cut off any rights or remedies of the mortgagee, unless with the latter's consent; on the contrary, it gives him an additional remedy, by way of an action at law, against the grantee; it does not affect his right to sue the mortgagor for the debt secured or to foreclose the mortgage against the land.[47] It is of course competent for the mortgagee, if he chooses, to release the mortgagor from liability for the debt, and to agree to look solely to the grantee for any deficiency which may arise on foreclosure of the mortgage. But unless the mortgagee has done this, both the mortgagor and his grantee (whatever may be their rights as against each other) will be liable to the holder of the debt secured, in the character of principal debtors.[48]

§ 263. Mortgagor's Liability as Surety.—When the purchaser of mortgaged lands assumes and agrees to pay the mortgage debt, by a clause in the deed, and the arrangement

of which he agreed with his grantor, Dean, to pay the mortgages. It was a matter of no consequence to him whether Dean was legally bound to pay those mortgages or not. Dean had the right to make such a disposition of the purchase money as he saw proper in selling the land. He might have decided that the purchase money should be paid by Walker to some public charity, to a church or a college, and if Walker, in making the purchase, agreed to pay the purchase money to any or either of these objects, no reason is perceived why he might not be compelled to perform his contract. It was no concern of his to whom the purchase money should be paid; Dean had the right to make such disposition of it as he saw proper, and when, for some reason known to himself, he saw proper to direct that the

mortgage on the land should be paid from the purchase money which Walker agreed to pay for the premises, and Walker expressly agreed to pay these mortgages, it is a matter in which he is in no manner concerned whether Dean was legally liable to pay such mortgage indebtedness or not; it was enough that he, for a valuable consideration, assumed the mortgage and agreed to pay the same."

[46] Harts v. Emery, 184 Ill. 560, 56 N. E. Rep. 865, affirming 84 Ill. App. 317.

[47] Hazle v. Bondy, 173 Ill. 302, 50 N. E. Rep. 671.

[48] Webster v. Fleming, 178 Ill. 140, 52 N. E. Rep. 975 (affirming 73 Ill. App. 234); Connecticut Mut. Life Ins. Co. v. Tyler, 8 Biss. C. C. 369, Fed. Cas. No. 3109.

is known and assented to by the mortgagee, the effect is to
make such purchaser the principal debtor, while his grantor,
the original mortgagor, occupies the position of a surety for
him.[49] Thus, if the mortgagor is compelled to pay the debt,
he will have the right, in the character of a surety, to be
subrogated to the rights of the mortgagee and to foreclose the
mortgage for his own benefit.[50] It follows also from this principle that if the mortgagee grants an extension of time for the
payment of the mortgage debt, to the purchaser of the property, without the knowledge or consent of the mortgagor, this
will discharge the latter from all personal liability.[51] But the
mortgagor is not entitled to have rents which accrued prior
to the filing of the bill for foreclosure, and which were not
subject to the lien of the mortgage, applied upon the deficiency
decree, where there is nothing to show that the grantee is not
able to discharge the obligation which he has assumed.[52]
Where each of several successive purchasers of a parcel of
land covenants to pay the mortgage thereon, each becomes an
original promisor, and the original mortgagor is virtually their
surety; and he may pay the mortgage debt when due, and
acquire the title, without cancelling the debt as to them or
releasing the lien.[53] At the same time it must be remarked
that the conveyance of mortgaged property to one who assumes
and agrees to pay the mortgage debt does not make the mortgagor a surety, as regards the mortgagee, in such sense that the
latter's failure to foreclose the mortgage, or bring suit after
notice under the statute, will release the mortgagor, unless the
mortgagee has accepted the mortgagor as surety only.[54]

§ 264. Sale of Part of Mortgaged Land; Order of Liability
on Foreclosure.—When the mortgagor of realty sells and conveys a portion of the land covered by the mortgage to a third
person, retaining a portion himself, it is the rule, as between
the mortgagor and his grantee, that the portion retained by the

[49] Union Mut. Life Ins. Co. v.
Hanford, 143 U. S. 187; Gandy v.
Coleman, 196 Ill. 189, 63 N. E. Rep.
625; Fairchild v. Lynch, 99 N. Y.
359, 2 N. E. Rep. 20.

[50] Kinney v. Wells, 59 Ill. App.
271.

[51] Union Mut. Life Ins. Co. v.
Hanford, 143 U. S. 187.

[52] Gandy v. Coleman, 196 Ill. 189,
63 N. E. Rep. 625.

[53] Flagg v. Geltmacher, 98 Ill.
293.

[54] Fish v. Glover, 154 Ill. 86, 39
N. E. Rep. 1081, affirming 51 Ill.
App. 566.

mortgagor shall be first applied to the payment of the mortgage debt.[55] This rule rests upon the reason that the mortgagor sells a part of the mortgaged premises relieved from the incumbrance and retains a portion for himself, and consequently, as between the parties to the conveyance, the part held by the mortgagor should, in equity and good conscience, be first subjected to the payment of the mortgage; and the same principle will apply as between a purchaser of the equity of redemption, taking subject to the mortgage, and a purchaser from him.[56] But this rule is never allowed to work hardship or injustice to third persons. The right of the purchaser to insist that the land retained by the mortgagor shall be first applied to the satisfaction of the mortgage is subject to the right of the mortgagee, acting in good faith, to collect his money in the way that is most to his interest.[57] And the rule does not apply to cases where a portion of the equity of redemption is sold on execution against the mortgagor, unless the execution is on a judgment for the debt secured by the mortgage.[58] Further, if a party is equitably entitled to have a part of the mortgaged premises, not alienated by the mortgagor, first sold under a power in the mortgage, he must apply to a court of equity before the sale, and if he does not, the sale cannot be set aside as against a bona fide purchaser.[59]

While the mortgagee, as above stated, should not be prejudiced by any such claim of the purchaser against the mortgagor, yet he may bind himself to accept it and act in subordination to it. Thus, if the mortgagee has full knowledge of the conveyance of a portion of the mortgaged land, and thereafter releases from his mortgage the part not sold, he will be held thereby, as between himself and the purchaser, to have released a share of the debt equal to the value of the property so released.[60] The rule stated in this section does not apply where the purchaser assumes the mortgage. When a deed to a portion of the land covered by a mortgage is expressly made subject to the mortgage, the grantee has no equity, as against

---

[55] Iglehart v. Crane, 42 Ill. 261; Boone v. Clark, 129 Ill. 466, 21 N. E. Rep. 850; Clark v. Wallick, 56 Ill. App. 30.

[56] Brown v. McKay, 151 Ill. 315, 37 N. E. Rep. 1037.

[57] Hawhe v. Snydaker, 86 Ill. 197.

[58] Erlinger v. Boul, 7 Ill. App. 40.

[59] St. Joseph Mfg. Co. v. Daggett, 84 Ill. 556.

[60] Warner v. De Witt County Nat. Bank, 4 Ill. App. 305.

the mortgagor, to require that the portion retained by the latter shall be first subject to sale in case of foreclosure.[61]

§ 265. Same; Land Sold Successively in Parcels.—Where there are several parcels of land, all subject to the lien of one mortgage, and the owner sells and conveys them at different times to different purchasers, they will be made to contribute to the redemption or satisfaction of the mortgage debt in the inverse order of their alienation, and the parcel last sold will be first chargeable, to its full value, and this must be exhausted before recourse is had to the next in order. In such a case, the equities between the several purchasers may be equal, but the first purchaser, having the prior equity, is preferred.[62] If the mortgagee subjects the several parcels to the satisfaction of his debt in a different order, a right to contribution will exist as between the successive purchasers, according to the rule of their liability.[63] But the operation of this rule may be waived, limited, or modified by the terms of the deed made to any of the grantees, which will bind those claiming under him.[64] And the rule does not apply at all where the deeds from the mortgagor expressly subject each tract to the incumbrance of the mortgage. In that case, the parcels are subjected to its payment pro rata.[65] And where part of the mortgaged land has been sold to one who assumed payment of the mortgage, and part of it to one who did not assume it, the latter cannot compel the mortgagee to exhaust his personal

[61] Monarch Coal & Mining Co. v. Hand, 197 Ill. 288, 64 N. E. Rep. 381. In this case it appeared that a coal company bought 3 acres of land out of a tract of 116 acres, with the right to mine coal under the entire tract, subject to a mortgage covering the whole property; and it was held proper, on foreclosure of the mortgage, for the decree to provide for the sale of the entire tract, or so much thereof as might be necessary to satisfy the debt, with the privilege to the coal company to pay the debt within 40 days, and in default thereof that it be enjoined from committing waste or further removing coal. Affirming 99 Ill. App. 322.

[62] Iglehart v. Crane, 42 Ill. 261; Matteson v. Thomas, 41 Ill. 110; Briscoe v. Power, 47 Ill. 447; Lock v. Fulford, 52 Ill. 166; Tompkins v. Wiltberger, 56 Ill. 385; Niles v. Harmon, 80 Ill. 396; Meacham v. Steele, 93 Ill. 135; Hosmer v. Campbell, 98 Ill. 572; Moore v. Shurtleff, 128 Ill. 370, 21 N. E. Rep. 775; Boone v. Clark, 129 Ill. 466, 21 N. E. Rep. 850; Alexander v. Welch, 10 Ill. App. 181.

[63] Matteson v. Thomas, 41 Ill. 110.

[64] Vogel v. Shurtliff, 28 Ill. App. 516.

[65] Briscoe v. Power, 47 Ill. 447.

remedy against the former before foreclosing. The mortgagee's right to a prompt foreclosure of his mortgage will not be impeded or delayed by compelling him to resort to a personal action against the purchaser who took subject to the lien. The most that the other can ask is to have the land sold in the inverse order of alienation.[66] Further, this rule is never applied to the injury of an innocent mortgagee. Before he can be required to shape his action in reference to the order of alienation of the several parcels, he must have actual notice of what that order was, and not merely the constructive notice derived from the registry of the deeds made by the mortgagor subsequent to the mortgage. He is under no obligation to search the record. The law makes it the duty of a subsequent purchaser of mortgaged property to give actual notice of his interest to the prior mortgagee if he intends to insist on the rule as to the order of liability of the parcels. He will not be permitted to remain silent until the sale has been made, and then invoke the aid of a court of equity to undo what he might have prevented by giving timely notice of his interest in the premises.[67]

The rule established by the statutes of a state, or by the decisions of its courts, as to the order in which real estate, covered by a mortgage and subsequently sold at different times to different purchasers, shall be subjected to the satisfaction of the mortgage, is a rule of property, which will be followed by the federal courts sitting within that state.[68]

§ 266. Judicial Sale of Mortgaged Land.—A debtor's equity of redemption in property on which he has given a mortgage may be levied on and sold under execution against him; as against all persons save the mortgagee, he is regarded as the absolute owner of the property.[69] But the purchaser of land at a judicial sale under a judgment or decree against the owner, where there is a valid mortgage or deed of trust of record from the owner prior to the time when the judgment became a lien, will take the same subject to the incumbrance, unless the party secured by the mortgage or trust deed has done some-

---

[66] Palmer v. Snell, 111 Ill. 161.

[67] Dates v. Winstanley, 53 Ill. App. 623; Hosmer v. Campbell, 98 Ill. 572; Matteson v. Thomas, 41 Ill. 110; Lausman v. Drahas, 8 Nebr. 457, 1 N. W. Rep. 445.

[68] Orvis v. Powell, 98 U. S. 176.

[69] Fitch v. Pinckard, 5 Ill. 69; Curtis v. Root, 20 Ill. 53; Vallette v. Bennett, 69 Ill. 632; Moffett v. Sheehey, 52 Ill. App, 376.

thing to make it inequitable to enforce his lien against the property.[70] As a general rule, the purchase on execution of the mortgagor's equity of redemption by a stranger to the mortgage (the judgment being for a debt other than the mortgage debt) will not affect the right of the mortgagee or his assignee to resort to any or all of the remedies he had before. Such a purchase will not render the buyer the debtor of the mortgagee, or release the mortgagor, either at law or in equity. Hence the mortgagor has no right, in equity, to compel such purchaser to redeem from the mortgage or lose his debt; though the mortgage creditor may do so, if he chooses, by foreclosure.[71] The execution purchaser will generally have no right to ask that some other fund be applied in discharge of the mortgage debt, in relief of his estate,[72] and if, after acquiring title, he pays off an existing mortgage, of which he had notice, he cannot keep the same alive by taking an assignment thereof to himself.[73] The equity of redemption may also be ordered sold in probate proceedings on the estate of the deceased mortgagor. But the mortgagee should be made a party to a proceeding by the administrator to sell the land for the payment of debts of the estate. If he is not joined, the lien of the mortgage will not be divested by the administrator's sale.[74] But it is said that, where a portion of mortgaged premises are sold under an order of the court, to pay the deceased mortgagor's debts, the residue of the premises remaining to the heirs of the mortgagor must be first resorted to for the satisfaction of the mortgage, that sold being only secondarily liable.[75]

§ 267. Partition of Mortgaged Estate.—A statute in Illinois provides that, when a petition is filed for the partition of land as between joint tenants or tenants in common thereof, "every person having any interest, whether in possession or otherwise, and who is not a petitioner, shall be made a defendant to such petition."[76] Accordingly it is held that a mortgagee, whose mortgage covers either the entire estate or the undivided

[70] Meacham v. Steele, 93 Ill. 135.

[71] Rogers v. Meyers, 68 Ill. 92; Funk v. McReynolds, 33 Ill. 481.

[72] Krueger v. Ferry, 41 N. J. Eq. 432, 5 Atl. Rep. 452.

[73] Bunch v. Grave, 111 Ind. 351, 12 N. E. Rep. 514.

[74] Holloway v. Stuart, 19 Ohio St. 472. And see Gibson v. Lyon, 115 U. S. 439.

[75] Moore v. Chandler, 59 Ill. 466.

[76] Rev. Stat. Ill. c. 106, § 6.

interest of one of the tenants in common, is a necessary party
to a proceeding for partition of the land.[77] And a decree of
partition will not be binding on the holder of a debt secured
by a deed of trust on a portion of the premises partitioned,
where he was not made a party to the suit, even though the
trustee in the deed was made a party.[78] The statute further
enacts that, on such a petition for partition, "the court shall
ascertain and declare the rights, titles, and interest of all the
parties to such suit, the petitioners as well as the defendants,
and shall give judgment according to the rights of the parties."[79] Under this provision, the court has power to ascertain
and declare that an existing mortgage constitutes a valid lien
on the property or upon the interest of one of the tenants in
common, and give judgment accordingly; but the court has
no power to enter a judgment for the amount of the mortgage
debt, or to enforce its payment by execution or otherwise.[80]

[77] Loomis v. Riley, 24 Ill. 307;
Vogle v. Brown, 120 Ill. 333, 11 N.
E. Rep. 327; Spencer v. Wiley, 149
Ill. 56, 36 N. E. Rep. 627; Cheney
v. Ricks, 168 Ill. 533, 48 N. E. Rep.
75.

[78] Vogle v. Brown, 120 Ill. 338,
11 N. E. Rep. 327. Where an entire tract of land covered by a
deed of trust is partitioned among
the joint tenants in a suit to
which the trustee, but not the
beneficiary, is made a party, and
one portion is set apart for the
payment of the deed of trust, and
is sold by the master in chancery
for that purpose, the lien on the
balance of the land is not released;
and if this parcel fails to satisfy
the trust deed, the lien may be
enforced against the rest of the
land. Brown v. Shurtleff, 24 Ill.
App. 569.

[79] Rev. Stat. Ill. c. 106, § 15.

[80] Spencer v. Wiley, 149 Ill. 56,
36 N. E. Rep. 627. In this case
it was said: "It seems too clear
for argument that section 15 (of
the Partition Act) does not give
the court power to enter a money

judgment or decree in favor of one
party to the suit against another;
that is to say, the court could not,
under that section, enter a judgment or decree against the maker
of the note described in the mortgage, and enforce its payment by
execution or otherwise. The action is for no such purpose. The
proceeding is for the purpose of
severing the interests in common,
and the power of the court to ascertain and declare the right, title
and interest of the mortgagee is in
no sense a power to enforce the
collection of his debt. The debt
may not be, and often is not, due
for years after the partition. The
jurisdiction over the parties to the
mortgage is for the purpose only
of enabling it to make partition of
the mortgaged property fairly and
equitably between the owners. Under that section it is not made the
duty of the court to ascertain the
amount due on a debt secured by
mortgage. It may ascertain and
declare that the mortgagee has a
valid mortgage upon the interest
of one of the tenants in common,

It is also provided by the statute that "a person having a mortgage, attachment, or other lien on the share of a part owner, shall be concluded by the judgment in partition, so far as it respects the partition and the assignment of the shares, but his lien shall remain in full force upon the part assigned to or left for such part owner."[81]   That is, the lien of the mortgage will be transferred to the part of the mortgaged premises assigned to the mortgagor, when the share of such mortgagor is assigned to him in severalty, but in that case only.[82]   In case the premises cannot be divided, but are ordered to be sold under the decree of the court, it is made the duty of the court to divide the proceeds of the sale according to the interests of the parties; and hence, in decreeing a partition of land, the court has the power, and it is its duty, to provide for the satisfaction of any valid mortgage upon the interest of any one of the tenants in common, in case a sale of the premises is ordered.   Moreover, the mortgagee of an undivided interest in the land may bring his bill for foreclosure, upon breach of condition, and have a decree, even during the pendency of a suit for partition of the premises; but the decree can only be enforced in conformity with the adjudication in the partition proceedings, —that is, in case of division, to sell the part allotted to the mortgagor, and in case of sale, to appropriate the proceeds which would otherwise go to the mortgagor, pro tanto, in satisfaction of the amount due upon the mortgage.[83]   A decree of sale in partition may properly provide for the satisfaction of a valid mortgage on the land without allowing redemption, as is allowed in decrees of foreclosure.[84]   It is also to be noted that the equitable claim of one tenant in common against his co-tenant, for rents and profits received in excess of his share,

and give judgment accordingly. By that judgment, whether it declares the amount then due on the debt or not, the relation of debtor and creditor between the parties to the mortgage is not changed, but, under the provisions of section 24, the mortgagee's lien remains in full force upon the part assigned or left for the mortgagor.   If, upon the coming in of the report of the commissioners, it is found necessary to sell the land, the court may ascertain the amount due on the mortgage debt, and order it paid out of the distributive share of the mortgagor in the proceeds of the sale.   But that may be done even after the sale."

[81] Rev. Stat. Ill. c. 106, § 24.

[82] Cheney v. Ricks, 168 Ill. 533, 48 N. E. Rep. 75.

[83] Thompson v. Frew, 107 Ill. 478.

[84] Davis v. Lang, 153 Ill. 175, 38 N. E. Rep. 635.

is not superior to the lien of a mortgage executed by one of the tenants prior to the institution of proceedings for partition; on the contrary, the lien of the mortgage will take precedence of the decree in such suit for rents and profits.[85]

As to voluntary partition among the co-tenants, it is held that an arrangement between two or more mortgagors, by which a partition of the mortgaged premises is made, and one of them assumes to pay off the mortgage, and to indemnify the others against the same, so far as it covers the property taken by him in the partition, may be binding between themselves, but cannot affect the right of the mortgagee to foreclose the mortgage against the entire estate. Nor will a person purchasing the mortgage debt, though after such arrangement was made, and with knowledge of the facts, be bound by it.[86]

§ 268. Condemnation of Mortgaged Land under Eminent Domain.—When property incumbered by a mortgage or deed of trust is condemned for public use under the power of eminent domain, the lien of the mortgage is lifted from the land and attaches to the money awarded as compensation for the property taken, which thereafter becomes the primary fund for its satisfaction.[87] The mortgagee, that is, will have a lien upon the fund derived from the condemnation proceedings equal to the lien of his mortgage, and his equity therein will be superior to that of a subsequent judgment creditor of the mortgagor.[88] It follows from this rule that it is proper, in such proceedings, to award to the owner of the property the full value of the land taken, without deducting the amount of the mortgage, since the damages awarded stand in the place of the land and can be subjected to the payment of the mortgage.[89] It is proper for the condemnation money to be paid into court, for distribution according to the rights of the parties. But if no award is made to the mortgagee, it seems that the person or corporation taking the land may tender to the owner the amount of the award, on condition of receiving a satisfaction of the mortgage.[90] But it is also held that if no

[85] McArthur v. Scott, 31 Fed. Rep. 521.

[86] Hards v. Burton, 79 Ill. 504.

[87] Union Mut. Life Ins. Co. v. Chicago & Western Indiana R. Co., 146 Ill. 320, 34 N. E. Rep. 948; Calumet River Ry. Co. v. Brown, 136 Ill. 322, 26 N. E. Rep. 501.

[88] Keller v. Bading, 169 Ill. 152, 48 N. E. Rep. 436.

[89] Thompson v. Chicago, S. F. & C. Ry. Co. (Mo.), 19 S. W. Rep. 77.

[90] Devlin v. City of New York, 131 N. Y. 123, 30 N. E. Rep. 45.

payment is made or tendered to the mortgagee, and if he is not made a party to the proceedings for the condemnation of the land, or notified thereof, he is not affected by such proceedings, and may foreclose his mortgage, by proper action, against the corporation taking the property.[91] If it appears that the compensation awarded to the owner is greater than the amount due on the mortgage, and has not yet been paid, it is not proper to order a sale, on bill to foreclose the mortgage, but the amount due should be ordered to be paid out of the condemnation money.[92] If the mortgagee is in possession of the premises, and a railroad company condemns and appropriates a right of way through the mortgaged lands, and pays the damages therefor to the mortgagee, the amount so received by him is to be deducted from the amount of the mortgage debt, when the mortgagor offers to redeem.[93] But a mortgagee cannot complain that the amount of the damages awarded for the condemnation of a part of the mortgaged premises is not paid to him, to be applied on the mortgage debt, when the court finds that the entire amount is necessary to restore improvements destroyed, and orders the money to be paid to the mortgagor to be used for that purpose alone.[94]

When the taking of the land needed by a corporation is managed by private agreement and grant between the parties, without resorting to judicial proceedings, the rights of a mortgagee of the premises are not so clear. In one state, it is held that, if the mortgagor of land grants a right of way to a railroad company without the consent of the mortgagee, and without any proceeding against the mortgagee to condemn the land, the mortgagee's interest is not affected, and the purchaser at foreclosure sale under the mortgage, or his grantee, may sue the company for compensation, though he cannot recover damages incident to the entry before he acquired title.[95] But in another state, it is said that a settlement by the mortgagor of damages occasioned to the property by the construction of a railroad, which does not enter upon the mort-

[91] Dodge v. Omaha & S. W. R. Co., 20 Nebr. 276, 29 N. W. Rep. 936.

[92] Colehour v. State Savings Inst., 90 Ill. 152.

[93] Heacock v. Swartwout, 28 Ill. 291.

[94] Stopp v. Wilt, 177 Ill. 620, 52 N. E. Rep. 1028, affirming 76 Ill. App. 531.

[95] Livermon v. Roanoke & T. R. R. Co., 109 N. Car. 52, 13 S. E. Rep. 734.

gaged land or take anything from it, but passes along an
adjoining highway, is conclusive upon the mortgagee, and he
cannot recover damages against the railroad company for the
depreciation in the value of his security caused by such construction.[96]

§ 269. **Dedication of Mortgaged Property to Public Use.**—
A dedication of property for public use is in the nature of a
conveyance for the purposes of such use; but a person can
convey or donate no more estate or greater title than he holds.
If he has no title, or if his title is conditional, and it fails, the
dedication fails. Consequently, a mortgagor cannot make a
dedication or donation of any part of the mortgaged premises,
to the public or otherwise, unless the mortgagee joins with
him.[97] But the mortgagee may be bound by his express assent
thereto, by acts equivalent to a positive donation, or by way of
estoppel, and his assent may be implied from his making no
objection and his subsequent acts done in reference thereto.
Thus, where the mortgage expressly provides for the making
of a subdivision of the mortgaged premises into lots, whenever
the mortgagor shall deem it advisable, the consent of the
mortgagee will be implied to laying out the usual and proper
streets and alleys, and their dedication to public use, and when
they are so laid out he will be bound by the act.[98]

[96] Knoll v. New York, C. & St.
L. Ry. Co., 121 Pa. St. 467, 15 Atl.
Rep. 571.

[97] City of Alton v. Fishback, 181
Ill. 396, 55 N. E. Rep. 150; Gridley
v. Hopkins, 84 Ill. 528; Elson v.
Comstock, 150 Ill. 303; Smith v.
Heath, 102 Ill. 130.

[98] Smith v. Heath, 102 Ill. 130;
Boone v. Clark, 129 Ill. 466, 21 N.
E. Rep. 850.

CHAPTER XXII.

RELEASE AND RENEWAL OF MORTGAGES.

§ 270. Release of Lien of Mortgage.—A release of the lien of a mortgage on realty, made by the mortgagee voluntarily and without any fraud, imposition, or undue influence exercised upon him, for the purpose of enabling the mortgagor to sell the land with a clear title, will be as valid and binding upon all parties, and will be treated in the same way, as a release given upon the payment of the debt.[1] But an agreement by a mortgagee to release his mortgage whenever it should appear that one personally liable on the mortgage debt would suffer loss unless the same was released, will not entitle the latter to a release merely because the mortgage is about to be foreclosed, since he could not be said to suffer loss by a foreclosure.[2]

§ 271. Consideration for Release.—A release of the lien of a mortgage on land, like any other contract, must be supported by a valid and sufficient consideration, and will be voidable (at least as between the immediate parties) if it is shown that it was executed without any consideration or that the consideration has failed.[3] The consideration need not

---

[1] McMillan v. McMillan, 184 Ill. 230, 56 N. E. Rep. 302.

[2] Irwin v. Brown, 145 Ill. 199, 34 N. E. Rep. 43.

[3] Hanlon v. Doherty, 109 Ind. 37, 9 N. E. Rep. 782; Hemstreet v. Burdick, 90 Ill. 444. Where three joint tenants agreed upon a partition of the joint estate, and the mortgagee of the land agreed to hold one of them (and the portion allotted to him) liable for only a certain proportion of the mortgage debt, the others being equally

necessarily move from the mortgagor; since it may be to the interest of other parties to have the lien of the mortgage lifted. Thus, a promise made to the mortgagee by a third person to pay a part of the mortgage debt, in consideration of the mortgagee's relinquishment of his lien, is a sufficient consideration and is not within the statute of frauds.[4] The agreement for a release is not required to be in writing. A verbal agreement being established, to the effect that the surrender of certain property should operate as the-consideration for the release of a mortgage, and the property having been surrendered in accordance therewith, equity will treat the mortgage as released.[5] But a mere verbal agreement, without consideration, between the mortgagor and the mortgagee, to release the lien of the mortgage, cannot bind third persons who are interested in the property and are not parties to the agreement.[6]

§ 272. Form of Release.—In regard to the form and manner of making a release, it is necessary to distinguish between the mortgage, considered as a conveyance of the estate, and the debt which the mortgage is given to secure. The mortgagee may deal with the debt secured in the same manner as if it were unsecured. He may forgive it or cancel it, release it or discharge it, either in writing or by mere parol agreement, and without any reference to the mortgage. But of course, when the debt is released or discharged, the mortgage falls with it, for the mortgage cannot stand unless it has a consideration to support it. But if it is intended to release the lien of the mortgage, either from the entire tract covered or from a part of it, without cancelling the debt, the release should be executed in writing, and should be under seal and placed on the

liable for the balance, it was held that the agreement was an entire one; and that, the consideration of each part entering into and forming a part of the consideration of every part, the restriction of the mortgage security was supported by an adequate consideration. Mutual Mill Ins. Co. v. Gordon, 121 Ill. 366, 12 N. E. Rep. 747. So, a release made on a promise by the mortgagor to raise money on the land, and to give an interest in cattle to be bought with it, is on a sufficient consideration, though the money is not raised; and if it has been ratified by the surrender of the note and mortgage, and the acceptance of a new note, the mortgage cannot be foreclosed. Seymour v. Mackay, 126 Ill. 341, 18 N. E. Rep. 552.

[4] Power v. Rankin, 114 Ill. 52, 29 N. E. Rep. 185.

[5] Ellis v. Sisson, 96 Ill. 105.

[6] Snell v. Palmer, 12 Ill. App. 337.

record.[7] But it need not be strictly in the form of a release, nor is the employment of the word "release" necessary to its efficacy. Since a mortgage is regarded as conveying the legal title to the mortgagee, it is held that the execution and delivery of a quitclaim deed, in the usual form, from the mortgagee to the mortgagor, will operate as a release of the mortgage.[8] When the question arises whether or not a particular transaction amounts to a release of the lien of a mortgage on real estate, it is to be determined in accordance with the intention of the party making the alleged release. In a doubtful case, an intention to release will not be implied against his interest; but when it is clear that a release was intended, equity will enforce the agreement as such.[9] And in general, where the holder of a mortgage, for a valuable consideration, agrees to cancel the mortgage as to a part of the property covered and release the same, but fails to do so, it will amount to an equitable release; for equity considers that as done which ought to have been done.[10] On the other hand, a mortgagee does not extinguish the mortgage or release its lien merely by making the mortgagor his executor.[11]

§ 273. **Authority to Make Release.**—The trustee in a deed of trust given to secure a debt, although he may be vested with the legal title to the land, has no authority to release the same from the lien of the deed without the consent of the creditor who owns the debt secured. But if the latter, when informed of the act of the trustee in executing a release, fails to repudiate it, and quiescently allows other persons to advance money on the faith of the release, he cannot afterwards deny the trustee's authority.[12] Where the mortgage was given jointly to two creditors as mortgagees, neither will have the right to release it without the concurrence or consent of the other, unless in a case where the party making the release is the survivor of the two creditors, having authority to control the collection of the debt.[13] But if one of two joint mortgagees assents to a release of the mortgage made by the other alone,

[7] Mutual Mill Ins. Co. v. Gordon, 20 Ill. App. 559. And see supra, § 157, and Rev. St. Ill. c. 95, § 9.

[8] Donlin v. Bradley, 119 Ill. 412, 10 N. E. Rep. 11.

[9] Stribling v. Splint Coal Co., 31 W. Va. 82, 5 S. E. Rep. 321.

[10] Huff v. Farwell, 67 Iowa, 298, 25 N. W. Rep. 252.

[11] Miller v. Donaldson, 17 Ohio, 264.

[12] Barbour v. Scottish-American Mortgage Co., 102 Ill. 121.

[13] Wall v. Bissell, 125 U. S. 382.

and especially if he receives a part of the money paid to obtain the release, with knowledge of the circumstances, he will be bound by the release.[14] Authority to release a mortgage may be conferred on an agent or attorney. But a creditor whose mortgage has been released of record by forgery, and without his knowledge, by a party to whom he had confided the notes merely for the purpose of collecting the interest thereon, is entitled to have the release declared void and to have the mortgage foreclosed to protect his rights.[15] And a release of a mortgage, signed by one as "attorney in fact," when there is nothing of record to show that he had any authority to release the mortgage, is insufficient.[16] But it is said that the cashier of a bank, acting in conformity with the rules and practice of the institution, may release a debt secured by mortgage in its favor.[17]

§ 274. Conditional Release.—A release of the lien of a mortgage may be restricted to a particular purpose, or conditioned upon the performance of some act by the mortgagor, and in either case it will not become effective beyond the intentions of the parties, or unless the condition is complied with.[18] Where a release of a mortgage was executed by the mortgagee and sent to an agent, to be delivered on the payment of the balance due on the mortgage, but it was delivered to a subsequent purchaser of the property on his promise to pay the sum due, in a few weeks, which he neglected to do, it was held that the release did not become operative until the mortgage debt was fully paid.[19] In another case, it appeared that the mortgagee executed a release to the mortgagor, and placed it in the hands of a third person, to be delivered upon the performance of certain things to be done by the mortgagor. The latter never performed his undertaking, and the release was never delivered to him, but by some accident or mistake, it was placed upon the record. It was held that a judgment creditor of the mortgagor acquired no rights or advantages by the recording of the release, and that, on a bill by the mortgagee, he should

---

[14] Hubbard v. Jasinski, 46 Ill. 160.

[15] Hait v. Ensign, 61 Iowa, 724, 17 N. W. Rep. 163.

[16] O'Neill v. Douthitt, 40 Kans. 689, 20 Pac. Rep. 493.

[17] Ryan v. Dunlap, 17 Ill. 40.

[18] See Gould v. Elgin City Banking Co., 136 Ill. 60, 26 N. E. Rep. 497; Piper v. Headlee, 39 Ill. App. 93.

[19] Hale v Morgan, 68 Ill. 244.

be restrained from selling, under his execution, anything more than the equity of redemption of the mortgagor.[20]

§ 275. Release of Part of Mortgaged Property.—A mortgagee may release part of the premises from the lien of his mortgage, and retain his lien for the whole indebtedness on the remainder, if no rights of third persons would be prejudiced, or in the absence of notice to the mortgagee that third persons have become interested in other parts of the property than that released.[21] But if the mortgagee has knowledge of the fact that two or more parcels of the land covered by his mortgage have been conveyed to different subsequent purchasers by the mortgagor, he cannot release one parcel without thereby also releasing the others pro tanto or altogether, according to the circumstances of the case.[22] "If the mortgagee, with actual notice of the facts, releases from the mortgage that portion of the premises primarily liable [that is, the portion of the estate still retained by the mortgagor, or that parcel which was last sold[23]], he thereby releases pro tanto the portion secondarily liable. When the mortgage is sought to be enforced against the owner of the latter, he can claim an abatement of his liability to the extent of the value of that portion which should have been made the primary fund."[24] But the mortgagee must have actual notice of the conveyance of the mortgaged premises subsequent to his mortgage, in order to make a release of one parcel a release pro tanto of those previously sold.[25] At least, it is said that, while he is not bound, before releasing a part of the mortgaged premises, to make an examination of the record for subsequent conveyances, still if he has notice of facts and circumstances sufficient to put a careful and prudent man upon inquiry as to matters which the record would disclose, he should, if he desires to act fairly, examine into them, and if necessary con-

[20] Stanley v. Valentine, 79 Ill. 544.

[21] Hazle v. Bondy, 173 Ill. 302, 50 N. E. Rep. 671. See Bush v. Sherman, 80 Ill. 160. Where a mortgagee releases part of the land, and it is agreed that the security shall remain in force as to the remainder, the mortgage as to such remainder is valid against subsequent judgments against the mortgagor. McAfee v. McAfee, 28 S. Car. 218, 5 S. E. Rep. 593.

[22] Ames v. Witbeck, 179 Ill. 458, 53 N. E. Rep. 969; Layman v. Willard, 7 Ill. App. 183; Boone v. Clark, 129 Ill. 466, 21 N. E. Rep. 850.

[23] Supra, §§ 264, 265.

[24] Iglehart v. Crane, 42 Ill. 261.

[25] Idem.

sult the record.[26] But where the mortgage was given to secure
the payment of several notes, and, upon the maturity of a part
of them, the mortgagor sells a portion of the land, and the
mortgagee releases his lien on the part sold, and receives the
purchase money in payment of the notes then due, he does not
thereby release his right to sue for and recover the amount of
the other notes when they fall due.[27] And it is said that, if
the mortgagee can secure a part payment on the mortgage
debt by releasing a portion of the land retained by the mortgagor (after the sale of another portion), so as to allow the
mortgagor to sell it, and by applying as a credit on the mortgage the full price of the property last sold, such release will
not charge the mortgagee with more than the amount actually
given as the price of the released portion, unless the price was
so inadequate as to show a want of good faith.[28] Again, where
a stranger bought one-half of the mortgaged land from the
mortgagor, on the strength of an agreement by the mortgagee,
which was duly recorded, that he would hold the stranger's
purchase liable for only one-half of the residue of the mortgage debt, provided certain installments thereof were paid,
and the purchaser paid the installments and half of the residue of the mortgage debt, it was adjudged that he thereupon
held his purchase free from the lien of the mortgage, so that
a sale thereof under a power in the mortgage would pass no
title.[29] Further, an agreement between the mortgagor and
mortgagee, that the latter will, on payment of a certain sum,
release part of the mortgaged land if the mortgagor finds an
opportunity to sell it, does not inure to the benefit of one who
has purchased the land at an execution sale, and who afterwards receives a deed therefor from the mortgagor without
consideration.[30]

§ 276. **Successive Partial Releases on Payment by Installments.**—A provision in a mortgage or deed of trust, covering
a tract of land divided into many lots, by which the mortgagee
agrees to release the various lots incumbered upon payment of
not less than a specified sum on each lot, in accordance with
which some of the lots are so released, does not constitute the
instrument, in legal effect, a separate mortgage on each lot,

[26] Dewey v. Ingersoll, 42 Mich.
17, 3 N. W. Rep. 235.

[27] Edgington v. Hefner, 81 Ill. 341.

[28] Hawhe v. Snydaker, 86 Ill. 197.

[29] Cowen v. Loomis, 91 Ill. 132.

[30] Palmer v. Snell, 111 Ill. 161.

securing separate and distinct sums of money; and on foreclosure it would not be proper to apportion the total amount
found due among the several lots. But it will be ordered that
the lots still owned by the mortgagor be first sold, and then the
others (not released) in the inverse order of their alienation.[31]
A stipulation in a mortgage that the tract of land covered by
the incumbrance may be subdivided, and that, on payment of
a certain sum or more at any time, a part or parts of the
premises shall be released from the mortgage, to be determined
at certain rates per front foot, does not require that the subdivision shall precede the payment, but a release may be had
for previous payments upon a subsequent subdivision of the
property.[32] But where the mortgage provides that the mortgaged premises shall be released as fast as the several debts
secured thereby shall be paid, a demand on the mortgagee to
release property under such provision should state some definite or particular part of the property sought to be released.[33]
Where one has the right to redeem lots by surrendering a
number of bonds, under the provision of a deed of trust that
the trustee, "on receiving the schedule price of any lot or
lots," shall release the same, and has tendered an amount of
bonds sufficient to procure the release of all the lots, he may
nevertheless elect to redeem a less number by the surrender of
the amount of bonds proportionally necessary.[34]

§ 277. Effect of Release on Junior Liens.—A mortgagee,
with notice of subsequent liens on the same property, has no
right to release his mortgage when it would operate to the
injury of the owners of such liens.[35] But on the other hand,
it is entirely competent for the holder of a first mortgage to
release the same of record, for the purpose of giving priority

[31] Domestic Building Ass'n v.
Nelson, 172 Ill. 386, 50 N. E. Rep.
194, affirming 66 Ill. App. 601.
Where the mortgage contains such
a provision, each purchaser from
the mortgagor takes subject to it;
and if he fails to procure a release
from the mortgagee of the part
purchased by him, according to the
terms of the mortgage, he cannot
have any part of the money paid
by the purchasers of other portions applied as a discharge of the
mortgage debt pro tanto as against
the part purchased by him. Hawhe
v. Snydaker, 86 Ill. 197.

[32] Lane v. Allen, 162 Ill. 426, 44
N. E. Rep. 831, reversing 60 Ill.
App. 457.

[33] Perry v. Pearson, 135 Ill. 218,
25 N. E. Rep. 636.

[34] Sanders v. Peck, 30 Ill. App.
238.

[35] McLean v. Lafayette Bank, 3
McLean, 587, Fed. Cas. No. 8888.

to a junior mortgage; and when this is the only object of the
release, the first mortgage will still continue in force as between the parties to it.[36] In one of the cases, it appeared that
a mortgagee, according to a stipulation to that effect in the
mortgage, executed a release in favor of the United States, to
enable the mortgagor to begin business as a distiller, providing
that the lien of the government for any taxes or penalties
should take precedence of the mortgage, and that, in case of a
forfeiture of the property to the United States, the title should
vest in the government free from the lien of the mortgage;
and the release was duly recorded. It was held, as against a
party claiming under a junior incumbrance, that the instrument did not operate as a general release of the premises from
the lien of the mortgage, but its only effect was to give the
government a priority of lien.[37] Where the holder of a second
mortgage gives a release, and afterwards acquires title to the
first mortgage, such release will not affect his rights under the
first mortgage.[38]

§ 278. **Renewal by Taking New Mortgage.**—When the
holder of a mortgage, at or before the time of the maturity of
the debt secured, desires to renew the security or to extend
the time for its payment, and for that purpose takes from the
mortgagor a new note or notes and a new mortgage, and surrenders the old notes and executes and records a release or
cancellation of the old mortgage, his lien is simply continued
in force without interruption, and the new mortgage does not
become subordinate or inferior to a second incumbrance,
created in favor of a third person after the recording of the
old mortgage and before the execution of the new one, at least
where the release of the old mortgage and the new mortgage
are recorded on the same day,[39] and the mortgagee has no
actual knowledge of the existence of the intervening lien;[40]
and especially where the new mortgage recites the fact that it
is given for the securing of the same debt which was secured
by the old mortgage,[41] or where the intervening junior mort-

---

[36] Wood v. Wood, 61 Iowa, 256,
16 N. W. Rep. 132. See Darst v.
Bates, 95 Ill. 493.

[37] Flower v. Elwood, 66 Ill. 438.

[38] Tarbell v. Page (Mass.), 29 N.
E. Rep. 585.

[39] Shaver v. Wil'iams, 87 Ill. 469;

McChesney v. Ernst, 89 Ill. App.
164.

[40] Campbell v. Trotter, 100 Ill.
281; Geib v. Reynolds, 35 Minn.
331, 28 N. W. Rep. 923.

[41] Roberts v. McNeal, 80 Ill.
App. 536.

gage expressly recognized the old mortgage as the prior lien on the property.[42] And the same rule applies as against an intervening judgment creditor of the mortgagor.[43] Of course there may be special equities which would give the junior incumbrancer the right to priority over the new mortgage. And this would appear to be the case if there is a substantial difference in the amount of the debt stated to be secured by the two mortgages, or a material variance in their terms, so that the later one does not show that it is a mere continuation or renewal of the former one. But it is said to be immaterial that, by a mere error in calculation, the new notes are made for a larger sum than the old ones, or that interest was calculated on interest;[44] and clearly a reduction of the rate of interest to be paid on the secured debt will give the junior mortgagee no claim to priority of lien.[45] In a case where the maker of certain notes secured by a mortgage gave a check for their payment, and the cashier of the bank assured the payee that the check was good (but the maker had deposited no funds in the bank), and the maker thereupon gave a new note and mortgage for the same amount at a lower rate of interest, and the check was returned to him, but the old notes and mortgage were left uncancelled, it was held that there was no payment of the first notes.[46]

§ 279. Change or Substitution of Securities.—Where it clearly appears that the giving of new security was intended as an absolute payment of a mortgage indebtedness, it will have that effect, but not otherwise. The presumption is always the other way. The mortgage is the incident, the debt the principal thing; and the incident follows its principal in the various changes of the latter, whether by renewal, judgment, or otherwise. Hence the general rule that no change in the evidence of the mortgage debt,—as by the renewal or extension of the note secured, or by the substitution for it of a new note or of some other form of security,—will operate as a discharge of the mortgage, or interrupt the continuity of its

[42] Roberts v. Doan, 180 Ill. 187, 54 N. E. Rep. 207.

[43] Piper v. Headlee, 39 Ill. App. 93.

[44] Campbell v. Trotter, 100 Ill. 281.

[45] Roberts v. Doan, 180 Ill. 187, 54 N. E. Rep. 207.

[46] Woodburn v. Woodburn, 115 Ill. 427, 5 N. E. Rep. 82.

lien.[47] Thus, where, by mutual agreement of the parties, new notes are given and accepted in lieu of and for the purpose of correcting a mistake in the notes originally given and secured by mortgage, the maker is entitled to have the old notes cancelled, but the mortgage securing them will stand as security for the new notes.[48] So, where a junior mortgage was given to secure the payment of certain promissory notes which were also partially secured by the indorsement of a third person, and the prior mortgagee released in favor of the junior mortgage, it was held that a subsequent change in the form of the debt, by taking up the original notes and giving new notes with no indorser, instead of them, did not affect the lien of the junior mortgage; nor could the rendering of a judgment on the substituted notes, as between the parties to the arrangement, release the premises from the lien of the mortgage.[49]

§ 280. **Extension of Time of Payment.**—An extension of the time of payment of a debt secured by mortgage, given to the mortgagor while he continues to hold the equity of redemption, will not release or discharge the lien of the mortgage.[50] Nor will such an extension release the lien in favor of an assignee of the equity of redemption. The latter is not a surety for the original mortgagor in any such sense that an extension given to the principal debtor will release him.[51]

---

[47] Bond v. Liverpool, London & G. Ins. Co., 106 Ill. 654; Rogers v. School Trustees, 46 Ill. 428; Salem Nat. Bank v. White, 159 Ill. 136, 42 N. E. Rep. 312; Citizens' Nat. Bank v. Dayton, 116 Ill. 257, 4 N. E. Rep. 492; Jones v. New York Guaranty Co., 101 U. S. 622. See Burt v. Batavia Paper Mfg. Co., 86 Ill. 66. And see infra, § 298.

[48] Granger v. Bissonnette, 68 Ill. App. 235.

[49] Darst v. Bates, 51 Ill. 439.

[50] Maher v. Lanfrom, 86 Ill. 513. Where a mortgage given to secure the debt of one who does not own the land, provides that the holder of the note may extend the time of payment on the maker's executing coupons for interest to accrue during such extension, the holder of the note may extend it, and fix the rate of interest which such coupons shall bear after maturity, without further consent of the mortgagor. Benneson v. Savage, 130 Ill. 352, 22 N. E. Rep. 838. Where, by the original condition in a mortgage, the debt secured by it was payable sixty days after demand, a new agreement, extending the time of payment to a day certain, when binding, has the effect, in equity, of modifying the original condition of the mortgage to the same extent as if the terms of the new agreement were incorporated into the condition. Union Central Life Ins. Co. v. Bonnell, 35 Ohio St. 365.

[51] Maher v. Lanfrom, 86 Ill. 513.

Without an extension actually indorsed on the note or mortgage, the agreement of the mortgagee to give further time for payment will be a good defense to a suit in equity to foreclose the mortgage; and a mere verbal promise is sufficient for this purpose.[52] Thus, where, after the maturity of the debt secured by a deed of trust, the creditor promises the debtor that he need not pay until a demand shall be made, and that he shall have personal notice, the creditor will not be allowed to foreclose the deed of trust without compliance with these conditions, or, if a sale has been made, it may be set aside. Thus, in the case supposed, a sale made by the trustee without any demand or notice, and after an advertisement published only in an obscure newspaper which was not seen by the debtor, will be vacated in equity.[53] So, where an arrangement existed between the parties to a mortgage that the time for payment of the principal sum thereby secured might be extended until those from whom it was due were notified that the holder of the note wanted it, and a foreclosure and sale were made without such notice, it was held that this was a fraud against which equity would relieve.[54] But if the mortgagor would have a foreclosure sale set aside on the ground that he was promised additional time within which to pay, he must clearly prove the facts relied on by him as showing the promise, the debt being overdue at the time of foreclosure.[55] Thus, a sale under a trust deed will not be declared void at the suit of one who purchased the property subject to the incumbrance, merely because he was assured that the property would not be sold so long as the interest on the debt secured should be promptly paid; for no promise to extend the time of payment could be inferred from such an assurance, and, if it could be inferred, the agreement would be without consideration, the holder of the note being entitled to prompt payment of interest in any event.[56]

An agreement for an extension must be supported by a consideration. The receipt by the creditor of a sum exceeding the

[52] Measurall v. Pearce (N. J. Eq.), 4 Atl. Rep. 678. And see Schoonhoven v. Pratt, 25 Ill. 457.

[53] Clevinger v. Ross, 109 Ill. 349; Webber v. Curtiss, 104 Ill. 309.

[54] Rounsavell v. Crofoot, 4 Ill. App. 671.

[55] Hairston v. Ward, 108 Ill. 87.

[56] Booth v. Wiley, 102 Ill. 84.

interest already due, will serve for this purpose.[57]   But in some states, it is held that a bonus which is in excess of the legal rate of interest, paid for the extension of a mortgage, is usurious, and should be applied towards the satisfaction of the mortgage on final settlement.[58]

[57] Schoonhoven v. Pratt, 25 Ill.   (N. Y.), 619, citing Trust Co. v. 457.   Kech, 69 N. Y. 248.
[58] Burhans v. Burhans, 48 Hun.

CHAPTER XXIII

RELEASE OF EQUITY OF REDEMPTION TO MORTGAGEE AND MERGER.

§ 281. **No Waiver of Equity of Redemption.**—The debtor's equity of redemption is a privilege of which he cannot divest himself by any agreement or stipulation in the mortgage itself. Whatever may be the form of the mortgage, the equity of redemption is a necessary part of it, or incident to it, and is regarded as fundamental to the very conception of a mortgage. Hence a court of equity will invariably refuse to enforce an agreement for the waiver of the equity of redemption. It will be conclusively presumed that such an agreement was wrung from the necessitous condition of the debtor, and hence made under a species of duress, and equity will treat it as entirely void and inoperative. Thus, even the mortgagor's solemn agreement incorporated in the mortgage, that, if prompt payment is not made, the estate shall be forfeited and the title shall vest absolutely in the mortgagee, cannot bar a redemption; that can be done only by a foreclosure.[1] So, the parties cannot make a conveyance of land, absolute in form, a security for the payment of money by a given day, and, if payment is not then made, have it treated as an absolute sale

---

[1] Willets v. Burgess, 34 Ill. 494; And see supra, § 8. Compare Essley v. Sloan, 16 Ill. App. 63; Strother v. Law, 54 Ill. 413. Tennery v. Nicholson, 87 Ill. 464.

and conveyance. Every deed takes effect from its delivery, and its character thereby becomes at once fixed. What is once a mortgage is always a mortgage; and if the instrument is a mortgage when delivered, it will so continue until the right of redemption is barred by some of the modes recognized by law.[2] The parties to a mortgage may indeed agree for a release of the equity of redemption. But this must be done by a separate contract, subsequent to the original contract of mortgage, and entirely disconnected from it, and it must be perfectly fair and not oppressive to the debtor, and for a valuable consideration.[3]

§ 282. **Mortgagor May Release Equity of Redemption to Mortgagee.**—A subsequent bona fide agreement for the extinguishment or purchase of an equity of redemption in mortgaged lands, if based on a good consideration, will be sustained. There is no rule of law to prevent a mortgagor from disposing of his equity to the mortgagee by private arrangement, though courts of equity will not permit the latter to take advantage of his position so as to wrest from the mortgagor his equity by an unconscionable bargain. But if the agreement is a fair one, under all the circumstances of the case, it will be upheld.[4] Thus, a release under seal, given by the mortgagor to the mortgagee in possession of the mortgaged premises, will pass all the mortgagor's rights to the land.[5] Also it is competent for the parties to agree that the mortgagee shall receive a conveyance in fee of a part of the mortgaged land, and in consideration thereof shall release and discharge the mortgage and the debt which it secures.[6] But where a mortgagor conveyed the mortgaged premises to the mortgagee in satisfaction of the debt, with an agreement that a certain portion of the land should be reconveyed to the mortgagor on the payment of a certain sum of money, it was held that the mortgagor's right to redeem from the mortgage continued as to the portion specified in the agreement, and a bill would lie to enforce such right.[7]

[2] Bearss v. Ford, 108 Ill. 16.
[3] Peagler v. Stabler, 91 Ala. 308, 9 South. Rep. 157.
[4] Wynkoop v. Cowing, 21 Ill. 570; Shaw v. Walbridge, 33 Ohio St. 1.
[5] Clark v. Clough, 65 N. H. 43, 23 Atl. Rep. 526.
[6] Tarleton v. Vietes, 1 Gilm. 470.
[7] Kirchoff v. Union Mut. Life Ins. Co., 33 Ill. App. 607.

§ 283. Degree of Fairness and Good Faith Required.—A

court of equity, having regard to the relative situation of the
parties to a mortgage, will subject any dealing between them
in the nature of a sale or release of the equity of redemption
to a careful and jealous scrutiny; and it will not sanction or
enforce such an agreement unless well satisfied of its entire
fairness, and that it is wholly independent of the original
contract of mortgage and disconnected from it.[8] Any arrangement between the parties under which the creditor secures the
property for himself at less than its value, through an advantage which his position as mortgagee enables him to take of
the necessities of the mortgagor, is liable to be set aside or
adjudged void.[9] Thus, if the mortgagee purchases the equity
of redemption for a grossly inadequate price, under circumstances which show that the mortgagor was induced to make
the sale by threats from the mortgagee, a court of equity will
allow a redemption.[10] At the same time, courts must avoid
the danger of applying this rule with too great strictness.
While "it is true that courts watch transactions between such
parties very closely in order to prevent oppression, yet it
would be folly to push this jealousy to such an extent as to
authorize the mortgagor to repudiate at his discretion every
contract he may make with the mortgagee. We are not aware
why a privilege should be given to him that is given to no
other person not standing in a fiduciary relation. It is said,
indeed, that a sale by a mortgagor to a mortgagee stands on
the same principle as a sale between parties having no connection with each other, and can only be impeached on the ground
of fraud. The authorities apply a more rigid rule than this;
but we understand the principle to be that the mortgagee must
have availed himself of his position to extort an unreasonable
advantage before a court will interfere to set aside the sale.
If the parties deal at arms' length with each other, without
threats, oppression, compulsion, or fraud, we do not know
why a sale by the mortgagor of his equitable estate to the mortgagee should be rescinded, on the ground of inadequacy of
consideration alone, any sooner than it would be if the sale
had been to a third person."[11] The Supreme Court of the

[8] Wynkoop v. Cowing, 21 Ill. 570; Brown v. Gaffney, 28 Ill. 149.

[9] Niggeler v. Maurin, 34 Minn. 118, 24 N. W. Rep. 369.

[10] Brown v. Gaffney, 28 Ill. 149.

[11] West v. Reed, 55 Ill. 242. And see, as following the same principles, Jones v. Foster, 175 Ill. 459,

United States also has said: "We are unwilling to lay down
a rule which would be likely to prevent any prudent mortgagee in possession, however fair his intentions may be, from
purchasing the property, by making the validity of the purchase depend on his ability afterwards to show that he paid
for the property all that anyone would have been willing to
give. We do not deem it for the benefit of mortgagors that
such a rule should exist."[12]

§ 284. **Intention of Parties as Qualifying Transaction.**—
An absolute and unconditional conveyance by a mortgagor to
his mortgagee, purporting to pass the equity of redemption
in the mortgaged premises, will not bar the right of redemption unless that is manifestly the intention of the parties. It
will be regarded as a mere change in the form of the security
unless the intention of the parties is clearly otherwise.[13]
Further, "in order to determine whether a conveyance made
by the mortgagor to the mortgagee operates as an extinguishment of the right of redemption, it must be made to appear
that the parties intended such conveyance to be a payment of
the debt. The intention to pay the debt by a deed of the property will not be inferred where the creditor retains the evidences of the indebtedness and the securities pledged for its
payment."[14] Accordingly, in the case cited, it was held that a
deed from the mortgagor to the mortgagee should be regarded
as an additional security for the debt, and not as a release of
the equity of redemption, the facts appearing as follows: That
the deed was without consideration; that the mortgage was
not under seal; that the mortgagee was defending a suit
brought by third persons to recover the property; that the
property was worth more than the mortgage debt; that the
mortgagee did not surrender the mortgage notes, and subsequently claimed the land in said suit as mortgagee; and that
the mortgagor had agreed to make such other transfers, assignments, and writings as might be necessary.

§ 285. **Consideration for Release of Equity.**—A release of

51 N. E. Rep. 362; Miller v. Green,
37 Ill. App. 631.

[13] Russell v. Southard, 12 How.
139. And see Walker's Adm'x v.
Farmers' Bank (Del.), 14 Atl. Rep.
819.

[13] Ennor v. Thompson, 46 Ill.
214; Goodell v. Dewey, 100 Ill. 309;

[14] Burton v. Perry, 146 Ill. 71, 34
N. E. Rep. 60.

the equity of redemption to the mortgagee will not be valid
unless supported by a consideration. Of the adequacy of such
a consideration the courts will judge, when appealed to. But,
as appears from the preceding sections, they are not very much
disposed to annul such a release on the mere ground that the
consideration was inadequate, if there are no circumstances to
show any fraud, oppression, or unconscionable conduct on the
part of the mortgagee. In other words, if the mortgagor was
a perfectly free agent in the transaction, the courts will not
be sedulous to give him relief simply because he made a poor
bargain. "It is sometimes said that a purchase of the equity
of redemption will be sustained only when it is based on an
adequate consideration. There is much reason, however, in
the rule that, in the absence of fraud, undue influence, or unconscionable advantage, the mortgagor may, at any time after
the execution of the mortgage, by a new and separate contract,
sell or release his equity of redemption to the mortgagee for
a consideration that is not grossly inadequate. This we incline
to hold to be the better rule."[15] Equity might be disposed to
look with disfavor upon a release founded on no other consideration than the exoneration of the mortgagor from personal
liability for the mortgage debt. But it is held that the mortgagee's release to the mortgagor of a part of the premises
covered by the incumbrance will be a valid consideration for
the mortgagor's conveyance in fee of the residue to the mortgagee.[16] However, a court of equity will set aside such a sale
where the only apparent consideration was an undertaking
on the part of the mortgagee to correct a mistake in the statement of the amount due, which the mortgagee was in any case
bound in equity to correct.[17]

§ 286. Form of Conveyance to Mortgagee.—The usual
method of releasing to a mortgagee the mortgagor's equity of
redemption in the premises is by a deed in fee. And where,
in addition to such a conveyance, the mortgagor takes a lease
from his grantee, and also receives from him a contract giving
him the privilege of re-purchasing the land within a certain
time on certain terms, the original mortgage is extinguished

---

[15] Stouts v. Rouse, 84 Ala. 309, 4
South. Rep. 170. And see West v.
Reed, 55 Ill. 242; Jones v. Foster,
175 Ill. 459, 51 N. E. Rep. 862.

[16] McCagg v. Heacock, 42 Ill. 153.
[17] Russell v. Southard, 12 How.
139.

and cannot be invoked by the mortgagor on a bill to enforce specific performance of the contract to sell.[18] A parol surrender of the equity of redemption, by the mortgagor to the mortgagee, may be repudiated by the former, if there are no circumstances which would make it inequitable to rescind the agreement, and the mortgagor may recover the possession on paying the mortgage debt. But such a parol surrender, admitted by the mortgagor, and followed by a deed from him to the mortgagee, will pass a good title as against one who, with notice and without consideration, has obtained a deed from the mortgagor after the parol surrender, though before the deed to the mortgagee.[19]

When the mortgage is in the form of an absolute deed, with a written or parol defeasance, a formal deed of conveyance is not necessary to release the grantor's equity of redemption. A bona fide agreement between the parties to vest the entire estate in the mortgagee will be sustained; and such a release may be shown by subsequent transactions between them. If those transactions would make it inequitable to allow a redemption, equity will treat the mortgagee as the absolute owner of the estate, and will refuse its aid to the mortgagor.[20] Where the defeasance takes the form of a contract by which the mortgagee binds himself to reconvey the land on payment of the debt by a certain time, the relation of mortgagor and mortgagee will be terminated by the act of the mortgagor in surrendering such contract and accepting a lease of the land, if he acts voluntarily and without oppression.[21] And if the original conveyance was accompanied by a formal instrument of defeasance, which the mortgagor afterwards voluntarily cancels, this will give to the deed which it was intended to defeat the effect of an original absolute conveyance as between the parties.[22]

§ 287. General Doctrine of Merger.—It is a general rule of real property law that when a greater and a less estate, or a legal and an equitable estate, coincide and meet in one and the

---

[18] Longfellow v. Moore, 102 Ill. 289.

[19] Duff v. McDonough, 155 Pa. St. 10, 25 Atl. Rep. 608.

[20] Scanlan v. Scanlan, 134 Ill. 630, 25 N. E. Rep. 652, affirming 33 Ill. App. 202.

[21] Seymour v. Mackay, 126 Ill. 341, 18 N. E. Rep. 552.

[22] Shaw v. Walbridge, 33 Ohio St. 1. Compare Howe v. Carpenter, 49 Wis. 697, 6 N. W. Rep. 357.

same person, without any intermediate estate, the less or inferior estate is immediately absorbed or merged in the greater estate, and ceases thereafter to have any separate existence. Hence, at law, when the owner of a mortgage acquires the equity of redemption also, the two titles unite to form one perfect and absolute title to the mortgaged property, and the result is to extinguish the mortgage, which thereafter has no separate existence or validity.[23]   In equity, however, as will be more fully shown in a later section, this rule is not invariably applied, but will be disregarded if inconsistent in the particular case with those principles which the courts of chancery are accustomed to enforce. It must also be remarked that, when a merger takes place, it always consists in the absorption of the lesser estate into the greater, not vice versa. Thus, where one person acquires in his own right (1) the legal title to the equitable estate arising under a resulting trust, (2) the equitable interest created therein by a deed of trust based thereon, and (3) the equity of redemption from such trust deed, this will not cause the merger of the legal title and equity under the trust deed in the equity of redemption, but the other interests are merged in the legal title, which is the greatest of the three.[24]

§ 288. Merger of Estates in Mortgagee.—When an estate in land created by a mortgage thereon and the equity of redemption from such mortgage become united in the same person, the rule at law is that the former title is merged in the latter, the mortgage is discharged, its lien obliterated, and the mortgage debt extinguished; and this rule will be applied unless there are sufficient equitable reasons for keeping the mortgage alive.[25] This result follows not only in cases where the mortgagor conveys his equity of redemption to the mortgagee, but also where the acquisition of the fee by the latter is in some other mode than by direct transfer from the mortgagor. Thus, where the mortgagee is one of the heirs of the mortgagor, and the other heirs, after the death of the mortgagor, convey their interests in the mortgaged premises to the mortgagee, the mortgage becomes merged and extinguished.[26] After such a

[23] Fowler v. Fay, 62 Ill. 375.

[24] Coryell v. Klehm, 157 Ill. 462, 41 N. E. Rep. 864.

[25] Shinn v. Fredericks, 56 Ill. 439; Weiner v. Heintz, 17 Ill. 259;

Lyman v. Gedney, 114 Ill. 388, 29 N. E. Rep. 282; Lynch v. Pfeiffer, 110 N. Y. 33, 17 N. E. Rep. 402.

[26] Clark v. Clark, 76 Wis. 306, 45 N. W. Rep. 121.

merger has taken place, an assignment of the note and mortgage by the mortgagee, even though for a valuable consideration, will not so far revive and give renewed vitality to the lien as to enable the assignee to enforce it by foreclosure.[27] But a conveyance of the mortgagor's equity of redemption to the mortgagee, after the latter has parted with the notes and mortgage to a bona fide purchaser cannot, in equity, be treated as a merger of the mortgage estate in the fee.[28] Again, there is no merger when the conveyance of the equity of redemption is made to the mortgagee jointly with one or more other persons, so that he becomes the owner of only an undivided interest in the fee.[29] When the mortgagor has already sold a portion of the mortgaged premises to a third person, the rights of the latter must be considered in determining the effect of a transfer of the equity of redemption to the mortgagee. Here the rule is that the residue of the mortgaged estate, remaining in the mortgagor, is in equity the primary fund out of which to discharge the debt. Hence if the mortgagee, with notice of the purchaser's rights, buys from the mortgagor the unsold portion, and accepts a deed therefor, by which the equitable estate is merged in the legal title, this will operate as a discharge of the mortgage debt in the ratio the value of the purchased portion bears to the total value of the mortgaged estate.[30]

§ 289. **Mortgagee Buying at Judicial Sale.**—When a mortgagor's equity of redemption in the mortgaged land is sold on execution under a judgment against him, and the holder of the mortgage becomes the purchaser, the mortgage will be merged in the legal title thus acquired, the lien of the mortgage will be extinguished, and the mortgagee will also lose his remedy on the note secured, provided that the land is worth more than the mortgage and the amount paid at the execution sale,[31] or if the officer conducting the sale announced

[27] Gage v. McDermid, 150 Ill. 598, 37 N. E. Rep. 1026.

[28] Cole v. Beale, 89 Ill. App. 426; Buchanan v. International Bank, 78 Ill. 500.

[29] Cole v. Beale, 89 Ill. App. 426.

[30] Meacham v. Steele, 93 Ill. 135. And see supra, § 264.

[31] McClain v. Weise, 22 Ill. App. 272. Equity will not permit the mortgagee to hold the land and also collect the mortgage debt from the mortgagor. As remarked in this case, "the rule that the intention is the controlling consideration would not have application as being necessarily paramount to all other considerations,

that it was made subject to the prior lien of the mortgage, and
the bidders so understood it,[32] so that, in either case, the price
paid at the sale would only be the value of the equity of redemption. The same rule applies where a single mortgage is
given to secure the payment of several promissory notes falling due at different dates (or for the payment of one debt in
installments), and the mortgagee files a bill to foreclose for the
non-payment of a portion of the notes, or of the debt, then
due, and it is decreed that the mortgaged premises shall be
sold to satisfy the amount then due, and that the remainder
of the debt, not yet matured, shall constitute a lien on the
premises. In such a case, if the mortgagee becomes the purchaser at the foreclosure sale, the mortgage estate will be
merged in the fee, the notes not yet due will be discharged and
he cannot collect the remainder of the debt against the mortgagor.[33] But if a redemption from the foreclosure sale is effected by the mortgagor, or by a judgment creditor of the
mortgagor, then the debt not due at the time of the sale, as
well as the lien of the mortgage for its security, will remain
in force, and the mortgagee may again foreclose as to it.[34]
When a deed of trust has been foreclosed by a sale under its
provisions, and the fee vested in the beneficiary as purchaser,
a party buying from him afterwards cannot be considered as
having purchased the deed of trust to be held as security for
the money expended in such purchase, although he may have
made a verbal promise to the grantor that he would buy the
land and convey it to him upon repayment to him of all money

when such intention was not clearly expressed at the very time of
the transaction involved; and even
when so   expressed, a court of
equity would not permit it to be
used by the party who gave utter-
ance to the expression as a sword
for the accomplishment of fraud,
or of wrong and injustice to others."

[32] Biggins v. Brockman, 63 Ill.
316.

[33] Weiner v. Heintz, 17 Ill. 259;
Mines v. Moore, 41 Ill. 273; Hughes
v. Frisby, 81 Ill. 188. When a
mortgage upon land is given to secure the payment of several notes

maturing at different times, and a
foreclosure and sale is had for a
part of the notes, leaving one note
unpaid, and the holder of that note
becomes the purchaser of the
mortgaged premises and receives a
master's deed, the legal and equitable titles to the premises will be
merged, and it will operate as a
satisfaction of the mortgage and
the remaining indebtedness, for
the reason that the purchaser in
such a case is presumed to have
bought the land at its value less
the unpaid note. Robins v. Swain,
68 Ill. 197.

[34] Hughes v. Frisby, 81 Ill. 188.

expended; nor can the purchaser be treated as the agent of the grantor in the deed of trust, in making such purchase, and as holding the title as a trustee.[35] So where, on the foreclosure of a second mortgage, the mortgagee thereunder, who was also the owner of the first mortgage, bought in the property, and the sale was confirmed by the court and not redeemed from, it was held that this amounted to a satisfaction of the first mortgage lien, notwithstanding the fact that a deed was not taken out on the certificate of sale, and that the time therefor had expired.[36]

§ 290. **Purchase of Mortgage by Owner of Equity of Redemption.**—Where a mortgagor of land, still remaining the owner of the equity of redemption, acquires by purchase the rights of the mortgagee, this will ordinarily operate as an extinguishment of the mortgage lien and a discharge of the debt. This is not so much on the theory of a merger of estates, as on the ground that the transaction amounts simply to a payment of the mortgage debt.[37] And the same rule applies when the mortgage interest is bought in by one who has acquired the equity of redemption by purchase from the mortgagor,[38] at least if there are no equitable reasons why he should be permitted to keep the mortgage alive. But the mortgagor, after he has sold his equity of redemption, may take an assignment of the mortgage,[39] and so may the purchaser of the equity of redemption if it is to his interest to hold it as a subsisting lien, instead of allowing it to merge in the fee. In effect, the question whether or not the acquiring of a note and mortgage by the owner of the fee of the incumbered property operates in equity as a merger, depends upon the intention of the parties and the surrounding circumstances, and any act by the owner of the fee showing that he regards the incumbrance as still subsisting is strong evidence that there is no merger.[40] A person owning the title of real estate in fee has the right to buy a mortgage lien thereon, created by a predecessor in title, to keep such lien alive for certain pur-

[35] Wilson v. McDowell, 78 Ill. 514.

[36] Belleville Savings Bank v. Reis, 34 Ill. App. 495, affirmed in 136 Ill. 242, 26 N. E. Rep. 646.

[37] Drury v. Holden, 121 Ill. 130, 13 N. E. Rep. 547.

[38] Lilly v. Palmer, 51 Ill. 331.

[39] Supra, § 180.

[40] Security Title & Trust Co. v. Schlender, 190 Ill. 609, 60 N. E. Rep. 854, affirming 93 Ill. App. 617.

poses, and to prevent a merger of the mortgage lien in the fee. This he may do to protect his title by cutting off intervening claims which are liable to come in between the mortgage and the conveyance in fee; but in such cases there must be an intention to prevent a merger, and in the absence of such an intention, the merger will be presumed.[41] Thus, where a mechanic's lien is barred by limitation as to a mortgage on property against which it is sought to be enforced, it may be held to be barred also as to the owner of the equity of redemption and his grantees, who, for the protection of the title, have paid off the mortgage.[42]

§ 291. **Equitable Rule as to Merger.**—In equity, notwithstanding the rule of law in this regard, a merger of estates will be permitted or prevented according to the application of equitable principles to the particular case. Whether the less estate is to be absorbed in the greater, or is to continue its individual existence, will depend, in equity, upon the actual and lawful intention of the parties, the requirements of justice, the effect of such merger upon the rights of third persons, or the furtherance of the parties' own interests.[43] If a party acquires an estate upon which he holds an incumbrance, the incumbrance is, in equity, considered as subsisting or extinguished, according to his intention expressed or implied. The intention is the first and controlling consideration. But if no intention has been manifested, equity will consider the incumbrance as subsisting or extinguished according as may be most conducive to the interests of the parties. If there is no agreement between the parties as to keeping the lien alive, and no intention in that regard made out, and if it is a matter of indifference to the party in whom the two estates meet, and there are no rights of third persons to be protected, then equity will follow the rule of law and the merger will take place.[44]

§ 292. **Same; Intention of Parties.**—As stated in the preceding section, the intention of the parties is first to be looked to in determining the question of merger. Where a party acquires a deed of land upon which he already holds a mortgage,

[41] Hester v. Frary, 99 Ill. App. 51.

[42] Watson v. Gardner, 119 Ill. 312, 10 N. E. Rep. 192.

[43] Fowler v. Fay, 62 Ill. 375.

[44] Campbell v. Carter, 14 Ill. 286; Jarvis v. Frink, Id. 396; Fowler v. Fay, 62 Ill. 375.

and the question arises whether the incumbrance is discharged by the conveyance, the intention of the party at the time the deed was obtained will, in equity, be regarded as the controlling consideration.[45] Thus, a deed by a mortgagor to a mortgagee, intended as additional security only, and not as a satisfaction of the mortgage, will not merge the mortgage in the greater estate, so as to give priority to another mortgage which is a second lien.[46] And a mortgage lien is not merged in the fee under a deed to the mortgagee from one of the mortgagors after the death of the other, when the deed was intended merely as a change in the form of the mortgagee's security, and was executed in the mistaken belief that the grantor was the sole owner of the premises, the fact being that the deceased mortgagor was the owner of an undivided half.[47] And so, a mortgage on land is kept alive, on assigning a judgment for the debt secured thereby against an administrator, reserving the real estate security with all rights therein, but releasing all claims against the estate for anything due upon the judgment, although the mortgagee, as a part of the same transaction, receives a conveyance of the land from a person claiming title under the heirs.[48] Where the holder of a mortgage takes a conveyance from the mortgagor, but retains the note and mortgage, the mortgage will not be considered to have been merged or extinguished, unless there be proof of an intention to that effect.[49]

§ 293. Same; Interests of Parties.—When the holder of a mortgage receives a conveyance of the premises from the mortgagor or his grantee, the mortgage will not be held to merge in the fee if it is for the interest of the mortgagee that the lien should be kept alive, or if this is necessary for the protection of his rights or his title. The intention of the parties is, as stated, the controlling consideration. But in the case supposed, if no intention has been manifested or expressed, but is left to be made out from the circumstances, equity will infer or presume an intention in accordance with the real interest of the party.[50] Even though the mortgage has been formally dis-

[45] Shaver v. Williams, 87 Ill. 469; Aetna Life Ins. Co. v. Corn, 89 Ill. 170; Cole v. Beale, 89 Ill. App. 426.

[46] Huebsch v. Scheel, 81 Ill. 281.

[47] Farrand v. Long, 184 Ill. 100, 56 N. E. Rep. 313.

[48] Robertson v. Wheeler, 162 Ill. 566, 44 N. E. Rep. 870.

[49] Dunphy v. Riddle, 86 Ill. 22.

[50] Edgerton v. Young, 43 Ill. 464; Dunphy v. Riddle, 86 Ill. 22; Worcester Bank v. Cheeney, 87 Ill. 602;

charged of record, on the acquisition of the fee by the mortgagee, it will be considered in equity as still subsisting where,
by reason of an intervening mortgage, the mortgagee's interest
so requires.[51] And a mortgage of the equitable interest of the
beneficiary in a resulting trust in land, and the equity of redemption of such beneficiary, do not merge upon the acquire-
ment of the latter interest by the mortgagee, when such a
merger would not be for the mortgagee's interest.[52] This principle finds its most usual and important application in the rule
that, where a mortgagee becomes the owner of the fee, the
mortgage will be kept alive and not allowed to merge, in case
such a result is necessary to protect the mortgagee against an
intervening title or incumbrance.[53] Thus, where the mortgage
is the oldest lien on the property, and its amount equals or exceeds the value of the mortgaged premises, and the mortgagee,
to avoid the expense of a foreclosure, takes a conveyance from
the mortgagor, a court of equity will not permit the mortgaged
premises to be swept away from him by a junior judgment
creditor, without payment of the mortgage, under the pre-
tense that its lien has been lost by merger, but will enjoin the
sale at law, or restrict the judgment creditor's lien to the equity
of redemption.[54] So, when it is necessary to prevent the holder
of a purchase-money mortgage from losing his lien because of
an intervening mortgage, equity will not permit a merger to
take place, although the holder of the purchase-money mortgage may have acquired the title to the land, and although the
parties may have undertaken to discharge the mortgage.[55]

Meacham v. Steele, 93 Ill. 137; In-
ternational Bank v. Wilshire, 108
Ill. 143; Sprague v. Beamer, 45 Ill.
App. 17; Mann v. Mann, 49 Ill.
App. 472; Shippen v. Whittier, 117
Ill. 282, 7 N. E. Rep. 642.

[51] Lowman v. Lowman, 118 Ill.
582, 9 N. E. Rep. 245.

[52] Coryell v. Klehm, 157 Ill. 462,
41 N. E. Rep. 864.

[53] Lowman v. Lowman, 118 Ill.
582, 9 N. E. Rep. 245; Woodward
v. Davis, 53 Iowa, 694, 6 N. W.
Rep. 74; Colby v. McOmber, 71
Iowa, 469, 32 N. W. Rep. 459.

[54] Richardson v. Hockenhull, 85
Ill. 124; Lowman v. Lowman, 19
Ill. App. 481.

[55] Hanlon v. Doherty, 109 Ind. 37,
9 N. E. Rep. 782.

CHAPTER XXIV.

PAYMENT AND SATISFACTION OF MORTGAGES.

§ 294. Who May Pay Mortgage Debt.—The right to pay or tender the amount of a mortgage debt to the holder thereof, at its maturity, with all the legal consequences of a valid tender, appertains not alone to the original mortgagor, or to the person primarily responsible for the discharge of the debt, but also to certain other persons who have rights or interests in the property which can be adequately protected only by the extinguishment of the lien of the mortgage. Thus, the holder of a second or junior mortgage on the same premises may pay off the elder incumbrance, when such a course is necessary for the protection of his own security.[1] And the same is true of a grantee of the mortgaged premises, who is compelled to pay off the incumbrance in order to protect himself or to perfect his own title, provided, of course, that he did not assume the mortgage in taking his own conveyance.[2] A similar rule ob-

---

[1] Tyrrell v. Ward, 102 Ill. 29; Ball v. Collahan, 95 Ill. App. 615; supra, § 172.

[2] Hazle v. Bondy, 173 Ill. 302, 50 N. E. Rep. 671; Smith v. Dinsmore, 16 Ill. App. 115.

tains in the case of a surety or guarantor of the mortgage
debt, when the principal debtor makes default,[3] and in the
case of the widow of a deceased mortgagor,[4] as also in the case
of one of two joint mortgagors of the same property.[5] Again,
a stranger to the mortgage may pay it off, when he advances
the money for that purpose upon an agreement with the debtor
that the security shall be assigned to him or that a new mortgage upon the same premises shall be given to him.[6] But, except in cases such as that just mentioned, a stranger or mere
volunteer cannot claim any right to pay off a mortgage, or compel the mortgagee to accept his tender of the amount due, or
found any claims to the benefit of the mortgage security on
the mortgagee's acceptance of the debt at his hands.[7] Thus,
the claimant of land under a tax title, which is not subject to
the mortgage, and who has no right of redemption, cannot
make a valid tender of the amount due on the mortgage.[8]

As to the right of persons acting in fiduciary capacities for
others, it is said that "a guardian may, without the direction
of the court, pay a deed of trust or mortgage which is a direct
and immediate charge upon the land [of the ward] and which,
if left unredeemed, would probably destroy the ward's interest. It is advisable that the guardian should, when it is practicable, and especially in cases of doubtful propriety, act under the direction of the court in discharging incumbrances on
the land of the minor; but where he has acted in good faith,
and advisedly, and his acts have been beneficial to the interests
of the ward, and have probably had the effect of preventing a
foreclosure and the loss of the estate, justice requires the approval of such acts."[9] As to the authority of an executor to
discharge such an incumbrance on the estate, the question will
depend upon the extent of the powers given to him by the will,
and upon the terms of that instrument in regard to the charging of debts upon the estate.[10]

[3] Richeson v. Crawford, 94 Ill.
165.

[4] Stinson v. Anderson, 96 Ill. 373.

[5] Simpson v. Gardiner, 97 Ill.
237.

[6] Home Savings Bank v. Bierstadt, 168 Ill. 618, 48 N. E. Rep.
161, affirming 68 Ill. App. 656.

[7] Hough v. Aetna Life Ins. Co.,

57 Ill. 318; Young v. Morgan, 89
Ill. 199; Bennett v. Chandler, 199
Ill. 97, 64 N. E. Rep. 1052.

[8] Sinclair v. Learned, 51 Mich.
335, 16 N. W. Rep. 672.

[9] Cheney v. Roodhouse, 135 Ill.
257, 25 N. E. Rep. 1019.

[10] Under a will requesting the
payment of debts and expenses,

§ 295. To Whom Payment to be Made.—A mortgagor may
pay the debt or settle with the person having apparent authority to receive satisfaction of the mortgage; and a discharge of
the mortgage thus obtained will prevail against any person
having a secret, concealed, or reserved interest in the mortgage.[11] But if the mortgagor pays the amount of the debt to
one who (as he knows) has not the possession of the papers,
and who merely undertakes to procure a release from the mortgagee, the mortgagor makes the payment at his peril and assumes the risk of the release not being given.[12] Thus, payment
of the mortgage debt to the broker who negotiated the loan,
but after he had parted with the possession of the notes and
mortgage, does not relieve the mortgagor from liability; and
it is wholly immaterial that the mortgagee has other transactions with the same broker and has money on deposit with
him.[13] But the acceptance of a conveyance of the mortgaged
property by the holder of the mortgage, as a satisfaction
thereof, will be regarded as complete and binding, although
the mortgagee was absent when the deed was made, when the
business was done by his brother and business partner, pursuant to previous negotiations, and where the deed was recorded after the mortgagee's return and he did not repudiate
it for more than three months thereafter.[14] On the other hand,
the fact that a person is made the trustee in a deed of trust
gives him no right or authority to receive payment of the debt
secured by such deed.[15] And one who pays the debt to the
trustee, the latter not being specially authorized to receive the
payment, and takes from him a release, but does not obtain the
surrender of the notes, which remain all the time in the possession of the payee, is chargeable with notice of the trustee's
want of power to accept the payment; and the payee, having no

though not expressly charging the
estate with their payment, making
numerous pecuniary bequests and
some devises, and requesting the
executors "to use their best judgment about selling the property,"
it is the duty of the executors to
pay a mortgage on the real estate,
exhausting the personal assets before resorting to the land. Wood
v. Hammond, 16 R. I. 98, 18 Atl.
Rep. 198.

[11] Sheldon v. McNall, 89 Ill. App.
138; Mason v. Beach, 55 Wis. 607,
13 N. W. Rep. 884.

[12] Lane v. Duchac, 73 Wis. 646,
41 N. W. Rep. 962.

[13] Viskocil v. Doktor, 27 Ill. App.
232.

[14] Ernst v. McChesney, 186 Ill.
617, 58 N. E. Rep. 399, affirming
86 Ill. App. 164.

[15] Leon v. McIntyre, 86 Ill. App.
349; supra, § 47.

knowledge of the payment to the trustee, is not bound by it, nor affected by the release given by the trustee.[16] Where the mortgage was made to two mortgagees jointly, a release thereof given by either of them, which acknowledges the full payment of the mortgage debt, will be sufficient to protect the mortgagor.[17] It is also said that, if there is no person in existence competent to receive payment of the debt to secure which a trust deed was given, the court, after the lapse of a long term of years (for instance, sixteen years), will decree a conveyance by the trustee to the heirs of the debtor.[18]

§ 296. Same; Agent of Mortgagee.—When a mortgagor pays the debt, at its maturity, to an agent of the mortgagee, instead of to the latter personally, the validity of the payment will depend upon the authority of the agent to receive it; and on this question, his possession of the papers evidencing the debt (or the fact that they are not in his possession, as the case may be) will be an important, but not the controlling, consideration. It is said generally that if the mortgagor tenders payment of the debt to the mortgagee's agent, who has the note in his hands at the time, and the agent refuses to accept it, the mortgagor may then maintain a bill in equity to redeem.[19] And if it is a fact that the agent has full authority from a non-resident principal to make loans on real estate, to use his own judgment, collect the principal at maturity or extend the time of payment, determine the length of loans, pass on titles, pay taxes, make repairs, procure insurance, look after tenants, and in general to care for the principal's entire interests, without limitation by any writing, this will warrant the implication that the agent has authority to receive payment of a loan even before its maturity; so that if he so receives payment of a loan not yet due, and satisfies the mortgage securing it, a subsequent purchaser of the property is justified in relying on the satisfaction, without more particular inquiries into the extent of the agent's authority.[20] On the

[16] Fortune v. Stockton, 182 Ill. 454, 55 N. E. Rep. 367, affirming Stockton v. Fortune, 82 Ill. App. 272.

[17] Lyman v. Gedney, 114 Ill. 388, 29 N. E. Rep. 282.

[18] Saunders v. Mason, 5 Cranch C. C. 470, Fed. Cas. No. 12,376.

[19] Willemin v. Dunn, 93 Ill. 511.

[20] Thornton v. Lawther, 169 Ill. 228, reversing Lawther v. Thornton, 67 Ill. App. 214. So, in Kent v. Congdon, 83 Fed. Rep. 228, it is said that, where the entire negotiation and collection of mortgage loans is intrusted to an agent, the

other hand, authority given to an agent to collect the interest
on a mortgage does not authorize him to receive the principal;
and it is incumbent on a debtor who makes a payment on such
a debt to an agent to see that the securities are in the agent's
possession on each occasion when payments are made.[21]   In
one case, where an agent received payment of a mortgage to
his principal after the latter's death, and with knowledge of
that fact, and executed a release of the mortgage, and the
debtor neglected to make any inquiries concerning the principal or the authority of the agent, it was held that, the agent's
authority having been revoked by his principal's death, the
attempted release of the mortgage was void.[22]   And where a
grantee of the mortgagor, who has assumed the mortgage debt,
pays the amount thereof to an agent who was originally authorized to receive the payment, but whose authority has been
revoked, and the mortgagor has actual knowledge of the revo-
cation of the agent's authority, but, being present at the payment, omits to disclose his knowledge on this point, he will be
liable, at the suit of the mortgagee, for the amount of the
debt.[23]

§ 297. **Medium of Payment.**—Payment of a debt secured by
a mortgage may be made otherwise than in money, if the parties so agree. Thus, the debt may be discharged by the delivery of articles of merchandise, notes of a third person, or any
other species of personal property, if tendered and received
for that purpose.[24]   When the promise to pay principal or
interest on a mortgage or the bond secured is in the alternative,
that is, a promise to pay in money or in some other medium
of payment (such as scrip, corporate stock, or good paper),
the promisor has an election to pay either in money or in the
equivalent; but after the day of payment has elapsed without
payment, the right of election on the part of the promisor
is gone, and the promisee is entitled to payment in money.[25]

---

mortgagors having no intercourse
with his principal, payment on demand to the agent discharges the
mortgage, though the bond was, by
its terms, payable elsewhere, and,
at the time of payment, the agent
had not in his possession the
bond and mortgage.

[21] Brewster v. Carnes, 108 N. Y.
556, 9 N. E. Rep. 323.

[22] Weber v. Bridgman, 113 N. Y.
600, 21 N. E. Rep. 985.

[23] Green y. Rick, 121 Pa. St. 130,
15 Atl. Rep. 497.

[24] Ryan v. Dunlap, 17 Ill. 40;
Ketchem v. Gulick (N. J. Eq.), 20
Atl. Rep. 487; Burke v. Grant, 116
Ill. 124, 4 N. E. Rep. 655.

[25] Marlor v. Texas & P. R. Co.,
21 Fed. Rep. 383.

A contract expressly made payable in gold coin is enforceable as made, and cannot, at the option of the debtor, be discharged in any other legal tender currency.[26] Thus, a clause in a mortgage stipulating for payment of the debt secured thereby in gold coin of the United States of the existing standard of weight and fineness, is valid, and may be enforced in the courts, by a judgment or decree directing payment to be made in such coin, without violating any principle of law or public policy, although legal tender notes and silver may be in circulation at the time.[27]

A mortgagee may of course accept a check on a bank in payment of the mortgage debt, if he is willing to do so. But an agent having authority to collect the mortgage debt when due, will generally have no right to accept anything but money in payment. However, if the agent accepts an uncertified check, and places the same in his bank to his credit, and the check is actually paid by the bank on which it is drawn, this will operate as a payment of the mortgage.[28]

§ 298. Substitution of Securities.—Where the holder of a mortgage surrenders the evidences of the debt secured, and accepts in lieu thereof new notes or different obligations of any kind, intending merely a substitution of securities, and not to release the lien of the mortgage, this will not be equivalent to a payment of the mortgage debt, nor be attended by any of the legal consequences of a payment.[29] "As a general rule, a mere change in the form of the debt does not satisfy a mortgage given to secure it, unless it is intended so to operate. The lien of the debt attaches to the mortgaged property,

[26] Belford v. Woodward, 158 Ill. 122; Rae v. Homestead Loan & Guaranty Co., 76 Ill. App. 548, affirmed in 178 Ill. 369, 53 N. E. Rep. 220.

[27] Dorr v. Hunter, 183 Ill. 432, 56 N. E. Rep. 159, affirming 83 Ill. App. 334.

[28] Harbach v. Colvin, 73 Iowa, 638, 35 N. W. Rep. 663.

[29] Flower v. Elwood, 66 Ill. 438; Hugunin v. Starkweather, 10 Ill. 492; Bond v. Liverpool, London & G. Ins. Co., 106 Ill. 654; Salem Nat. Bank v. White, 159 Ill. 136, 42 N. E. Rep. 312; Irwin v. West, 50 Fed. Rep. 362; supra, § 279. "A mortgage secures a debt, and not the evidence of it. Hence no change in the form of the evidence of the debt, or in the mode or time of payment,—in fact, nothing short of actual payment of the debt or an express release,—will operate to discharge the mortgage. The mortgage remains a lien until expressly released or until the debt it was given to secure is paid." Gelb v. Reynolds, 36 Minn. 331, 28 N. W. Rep. 923.

23

and the lien can, as between the parties, only be destroyed by
the payment or discharge of the debt, or by a release of the
mortgage. Mere change of the form of the evidence of the debt
in no wise affects the lien. A renewal of the note, its reduction to
judgment, or other change, not intended to operate as a discharge of the lien, still leaves it, as between the parties, in full
vigor. This is a rule in equity that is sanctioned by many adjudged cases. In that forum, mere form is disregarded, and
the substance only is considered."[30]   Thus, the assignment of
a lease as additional security does not operate as a payment of
a note of the assignor, nor prevent the foreclosure of a mortgage given to secure the note.[31]   Nor will the mortgage debt
be cancelled by the mortgagor's giving a new note for the balance found due on a settlement, and the mortgagee's taking
judgment thereon by confession, which is not collected.[32]   The
delivery to a first mortgagee of bonds secured by a second
mortgage does not amount to satisfaction of his mortgage,
where the bonds are merely delivered to him for sale, and he is
unable to sell them and returns them to the mortgagor.[33]   But
on the other hand, the acceptance of a new note for the indebtedness covered by a trust deed, with full knowledge of a release of the deed, will be held to be a ratification of such release.[34]   And so, where a party who had taken notes secured
by a mortgage on land sold, takes other notes from a subsequent purchaser, secured by mortgage on the same land for the
same amounts and falling due at the same time, this will be
regarded as a payment of the prior notes and a discharge of
the mortgage given to secure them.[35]   And so also, a mortgage
will be held to be released by the mortgagee's acceptance of
new notes, payable in two years, under a composition agreement made after he had instituted proceedings in bankruptcy
against the mortgagor.[36]

§ 299. **Application of Payments.**—In applying partial payments on a debt secured by mortgage, the rule is that interest
is first to be satisfied, and if the payment exceeds the interest
due, the balance is to be applied in reduction of the principal

[30] Flower v. Elwood, 66 Ill. 438.
[31] Maloney v. Lafayette Building
& Loan Ass'n, 69 Ill. App. 35.
[32] Darst v. Bates, 95 Ill. 493.
[33] Mullanphy Bank v. Schott, 135
Ill. 655, 26 N. E. Rep. 640.

[34] Seymour v. Mackay, 21 Ill.
App. 449.
[35] Tucker v. Conwell, 67 Ill. 552.
[36] Jarnagan v. Gaines, 84 Ill. 203.

debt. If the payment falls short of the interest then due, the balance of interest is not to be added to the principal, but remains as interest, to be satisfied by the next adequate payment.[37] Where the mortgage secures several different notes which are in part due, partial payments are to be applied on the notes in the order of their maturity, both interest and principal of the first note being paid before anything is applied on the next note.[38] But if the creditor holds two separate mortgages on the same property, and the debtor sends him money. merely stating that it is to pay "interest due on mortgage," the creditor may apply it to either mortgage as he chooses.[39] But where the creditor holds several claims against the debtor, some of which are secured by the mortgage and others not, the debtor, in making a payment, has the right to direct how it shall be applied; and a direction, given at the time of the payment, that the money shall be applied on the mortgage debt is binding on the creditor. Moreover, if the payment is made from the proceeds of a sale of the mortgaged property, then it must be applied to the mortgage without any special direction to that effect.[40] Where a partial payment has been made on a mortgage debt, and credit therefor indorsed on the note, it is competent for the parties to agree that such payment shall be applied on a different debt, not secured by the mortgage, and to cancel the original mortgage note and substitute for it another note of like tenor and amount; and if no further payments are made, the mortgage may be foreclosed for the whole amount which it originally secured. But as against the wife of the mortgagor, who joined in the mortgage, releasing her rights of dower and homestead, this cannot be done; she is entitled to have the amount of the payment credited on the mortgage debt, and, as against her, the mortgage can be foreclosed only for the balance remaining due after deducting the payment.[41] It is also a rule that money derived from rents conveyed by a mortgage must, in the absence of any contrary agreement, be applied by the mort-

[37] McFadden v. Fortier, 20 Ill. 509.

[38] Trimble v. McCormick (Ky.), 15 S. W. Rep. 358.

[39] Blair v. Harris, 75 Mich. 167, 42 N. W. Rep. 790.

[40] Ellis v. Mason, 32 S. Car. 277, 10 S. E. Rep. 1069.

[41] Brockschmidt v. Hagebusch, 72 Ill. 562.

gagee towards the payment of the mortgage, rather than to the satisfaction of any other indebtedness of the mortgagor.[42]

§ 300. **Evidence of Payment.**—It is the part of prudence for a mortgagor, on paying off the incumbrance, to insist that the note, or other evidence of the mortgage debt, shall be cancelled and returned to him, and also to have satisfaction of the mortgage duly entered of record. But still the question of payment is always a matter of evidence. His possession of the mortgage notes, surrendered to him by the mortgagee, and of the mortgage itself with an indorsement of satisfaction thereon, will be prima facie evidence of the payment of the debt. But such evidence is not conclusive; the presumption arising from the mortgagor's possession of the papers may be rebutted by parol evidence, as, by proof that the mortgage and notes had been sent for collection, but were not to be delivered to the mortgagor except on full payment.[43] So, the cancellation of the mortgage on the record is prima facie a satisfaction and discharge of it, but it may be shown to have been made by accident, fraud, or mistake, and the mortgage will remain in force against the mortgagor, if not against innocent purchasers and incumbrancers.[44] Parol testimony is also admissible to establish the fact of payment where there is no written evidence of it.[45] Thus, where the evidence is conflicting as to whether a mortgage debt had been paid, and whether the mortgage was simply held by the assignee as security for advances made to a subsequent purchaser of the land, the mortgagor may testify to admissions by the mortgagee to the effect that

[42] See Roberts v. Pierce, 79 Ill. 378; Darden v. Gerson, 91 Ala. 323, 9 South. Rep. 278; Bryant v. Charter Oak Life Ins. Co., 24 Fed. Rep. 771.

[43] Allen v. Sawyer, 88 Ill. 414; Flower v. Elwood, 66 Ill. 438.

[44] Flower v. Elwood, 66 Ill. 438. An entry of satisfaction by the owner of a mortgage, after his assignment for the benefit of creditors, is competent to show payment of the mortgage debt before the assignment, the jury being instructed that he had no right to make the entry unless he had re-ceived payment before his assignment. Cox v. Ledward, 124 Pa. St. 435, 16 Atl. Rep. 826.

[45] In New Jersey, it is held that a debt on bond and mortgage cannot be extinguished by a mere voluntary statement by the creditor that he will forgive it, but the purpose voluntarily to extinguish such a debt must be executed by an instrument as solemn as the instrument by which the debt is created. Tulane v. Clifton, 47 N. J. Eq. 351, 20 Atl. Rep. 1086, citing Irwin v. Johnson, 36 N. J. Eq. 347.

the mortgage debt had been paid by such purchaser.[46] So also, as between the original parties, parol evidence is admissible to prove that other payments have been made on certain notes than those mentioned in a deed of trust afterwards made to secure them.[47] Per contra, a certificate, under seal, reciting the payment of a mortgage and the note accompanying it, and authorizing the register of deeds to satisfy the mortgage on the record, may be contradicted by parol, in an action on the note; so far as the rules of evidence are concerned, such a certificate is like any other written receipt.[48]

§ 301. **Presumption of Payment from Lapse of Time.**— Where twenty years have elapsed since a mortgage fell due, without any proceedings to foreclose it, and with no evidence of any intervening acknowledgment or recognition of the mortgage, or any part payment or promise to pay it, on the part of the mortgagor, the latter or his heirs having remained in the possession of the premises, there is a presumption of law that the mortgage has been paid and satisfied, although it may remain uncancelled on the record.[49] But there is no such presumption from mere lapse of time if an attempt has been made to foreclose the mortgage, or if the mortgagor or his heirs have not resided within the state.[50] And in any case, this presumption is not conclusive; it may be rebutted by evidence, and will not stand against clear and satisfactory proof that there has been no payment of the mortgage.[51] And a payment of interest upon the mortgage debt, or any portion of the principal, by any person interested in the equity of redemption, and having actual or constructive notice of the mortgage, will repel the presumption that the mortgage has been paid, and will take the case out of the statute of limitations, not only as to the person making the payment, but as to all the owners of the equity.[52] It is also said that, while the presumption of

[46] Blake v. Broughton, 107 N. Car. 220, 12 S. E. Rep. 127.

[47] Estes v. Fry, 94 Mo. 266, 6 S. W. Rep. 660.

[48] Thompson v. Layman, 41 Minn. 295, 42 N. W. Rep. 1061.

[49] Blaisdell v. Smith, 3 Ill. App. 150; Lammer v. Stoddard, 103 N. Y. 672, 9 N. E. Rep. 328; Kellogg v. Dickinson, 147 Mass. 432, 18 N. E.

Rep. 223; Agnew v. Renwick, 27 S. Car. 562, 4 S. E. Rep. 223.

[50] Brobst v. Brock, 10 Wall. 519; Kibbe v. Thompson, 5 Biss. C. C. 226, Fed. Cas. No. 7,754.

[51] Michener v. Michener (Pa.), 2 Atl. Rep. 508; Delano v. Smith, 142 Mass. 490, 8 N. E. Rep. 644.

[52] Hollister v. York, 59 Vt. 1, 9 Atl. Rep. 2.

payment arising from the lapse of twenty years' time is available as a shield for the protection of the mortgagor or those who have succeeded to his rights, it is not available as a weapon of attack by a party invoking affirmative relief based on the alleged or presumed payment of the debt.[53]

§ 302. **Effect of Payment.**—It was the doctrine of the common law that if payment of the debt secured by a mortgage was made on or before the day appointed, the mortgage would become inoperative and void, the legal title would revest in the mortgagor, and there would be no necessity for any release or reconveyance by the mortgagee. But the payment of the mortgage money after the law-day had expired would not revest the title in the mortgagor, by the mere acceptance of the money, but would merely give him a right to redeem, or rather, a right to go into chancery to compel a reconveyance.[54] And of course a mortgagor is still entitled to require a reconveyance of the mortgaged premises, upon fully reimbursing the mortgagee, if the form of the security, or the subsequent dealings of the parties with it, were such as to make a conveyance from the mortgagee necessary to clear the mortgagor's title.[55] But the modern doctrine is that the debt is the principal thing, and the mortgage only an incident of it, and that when the debt is paid or extinguished, the mortgage necessarily falls with it; so that the payment of the debt at any time before a foreclosure will terminate the life of the mortgage, and nothing is required to restore the legal title to the mortgagor except an entry of satisfaction of the mortgage on the record in the usual form. Payment of the debt will also terminate any power of sale contained in the mortgage; so that a sale made under such power, after the payment of the debt, will be void, even as against a bona fide purchaser.[56] On similar principles, the performance of the stipulated conditions will fully discharge and extinguish an indemnity mortgage.[57] Again, the payment and release of a mortgage will terminate the right of possession by a lessee under the mortgagee.[58] But

[53] Allen v. Everly, 24 Ohio St. 97.
[54] Munson v. Munson, 30 Conn. 425; Griswold v. Mather, 5 Conn. 435; Perkins' Lessee v. Dibble, 10 Ohio, 433.
[55] Heacock v. Swartwout, 28 Ill.

291; Smith v. Orton, 21 How. (U. S.) 241.
[56] Redmond v. Packenham, 66 Ill. 434.
[57] See McConnel v. Dickson, 43 Ill. 99.
[58] Holt v. Rees, 44 Ill. 30.

where the mortgage is given to secure a debt, and the debt
becomes merged in a judgment, the mortgage stands as security for the judgment, and a surety's right of subrogation is not
affected. If he pays the judgment, he will be entitled to an
action on the mortgage.[59] But when the demand of a creditor
is paid by the money of a third person, not himself a creditor, without any agreement that the security shall be assigned
or kept alive for the benefit of such third person, the demand
is absolutely extinguished.[60] However, the parties to a note
secured by a mortgage or deed of trust have the right, in their
dealings with each other, to treat the note as unpaid and as
standing as security for future advances, and the note will be
good for such advances as between the parties and as to all
others not prejudiced thereby.[61] If the mortgagor himself remains the debtor principally and primarily liable for the mortgage debt, and pays the amount of it to the creditor, he necessarily discharges and extinguishes it, and he cannot keep the
mortgage in existence by any agreement with the creditor or
by any other form of conveyance. That is, he cannot, owning the equity of redemption, also hold a satisfied mortgage
as a living lien on the land, to the prejudice of other incumbrancers or parties otherwise interested. But if the mortgagor
has sold and conveyed his interest in the property to a third
person, who has assumed the mortgage debt and agreed to pay
the same, as a part of the consideration for the purchase, thus
becoming the principal debtor to the mortgagee, the mortgagor, on paying off the mortgage debt, may keep the mortgage alive, and have the benefit of the lien of the mortgage to
secure his reimbursement.[62]

§ 303. Tender.—A party who has placed an incumbrance
on his property, by a mortgage or deed of trust, may come into
a court of equity to obtain the removal of the incumbrance,
by compelling the creditor to accept payment of the debt upon
the terms and in the manner in which the debtor is entitled to
discharge the same, according to the proper legal construction
of their contract.[63] So, where the mortgagee is in possession

[59] Peirce v. Garrett, 65 Ill. App.
682.

[60] Poole v. Kelsey, 95 Ill. App.
233. See Loewenthal v. McCormick. 101 Ill. 143.

[61] Darst v. Gale, 83 Ill. 136.

[62] See Funk v. McReynolds, 33
Ill. 481.

[63] McGoon v. Shirk, 54 Ill. 408.

after breach of condition, and the mortgagor brings ejectment, proof that the latter tendered what he claimed was the balance due on the mortgage debt is not enough to show that the mortgagee's right of possession has terminated, unless it is also made to appear that the sum so tendered was the full amount remaining due.[64] The holder of a note secured by mortgage may, before sale under a power therein contained, make a valid tender of payment of another note secured by the same mortgage, whether the latter be a prior, equal, or subsequent lien.[65] But where the defendant in a foreclosure suit desires to make payment of the amount due, in order to avoid further costs and expenses, he should offer to pay all sums due under the conditions of the mortgage, with the costs already accrued, and also (if so provided in the mortgage) a reasonable attorney's fee for services already performed.[66] A tender in such a proceeding which does not include the costs nor a solicitor's fee is insufficient.[67] But a tender of a sum suggested by the attorney who filed the bill to foreclose, by way of a solicitor's fee in addition to the other sums due, will be sufficient.[68] The tender of a check, not certified, and which would not be honored unless the note and mortgage were first surrendered to the drawer, is not a good tender.[69]

§ 304. Form of Satisfaction or Discharge.—It is provided by statute in Illinois that "a mortgage or trust deed of real or personal property may be released by an instrument in writing executed by the mortgagee, trustee, or his executor, administrator, heirs, or assignee of record, and such instrument may be acknowledged or proved in the same manner as deeds for the conveyance of land."[70] But while a formal release of a mortgage should be in writing and under seal, it is also held that a verbal or written discharge of the debt by its payment in money, property, or other securities, will discharge the mortgage; and to this end it is not necessary that there should be a release or satisfaction entered upon the mortgage itself or upon the margin of the record, as provided by statute. That

[64] Fountain v. Bookstaver, 141 Ill. 461, 31 N. E. Rep. 17.

[65] Flower v. Elwood, 66 Ill. 438.

[66] Brand v. Kleinecke, 77 Ill. App. 269.

[67] Neiman v. Wheeler, 87 Ill. App. 670.

[68] Smith v. Jackson, 153 Ill. 399, 39 N. E. Rep. 130.

[69] Harding v. Commercial Loan Co., 84 Ill. 251.

[70] Rev. Stat. Ill. c. 95, § 9.

provision is made for the protection of mortgagors and others, by the recording and preservation of evidence of satisfaction of the mortgage on the same public record, but not as prescribing a rule of evidence.[71] It is also competent to discharge a mortgage by the execution of a quitclaim deed, from the mortgagee to the mortgagor, conveying the premises covered by the mortgage.[72]

§ 305. **Entry of Satisfaction on Margin of Record.**—Another clause of the same statute in Illinois provides a simple and effective manner of obtaining the formal discharge of a mortgage which has been paid, by making it the duty of the mortgagee, or his successor in interest, upon full payment of the debt secured, and at the request of the mortgagor, to enter a release or satisfaction on the margin of the record of the mortgage, the same to be attested by the recorder, and providing that such an entry, so attested, shall forever discharge the mortgage and bar all actions which may be brought thereon.[73] In a neighboring state, having a similar statutory provision, it is held that a discharge on the record is not an absolute bar to a foreclosure of the mortgage, unless there has been actual satisfaction. Such a discharge is evidence sufficient to sustain the rights of all persons interested, unless the party setting up the discharged mortgage shall show some accident, mistake,

[71] Ryan v. Dunlap, 17 Ill. 40; Lucas v. Harris, 20 Ill. 165; Vansant v. Allmon, 23 Ill. 30.

[72] Woodbury v. Aikin, 13 Ill. 639.

[73] "Every mortgagee of real or personal property, his assignee of record, or other legal representative, having received full satisfaction and payment of all such sum or sums of money as are really due to him from the mortgagor, and every trustee, or his successor in trust, in a deed of trust in the nature of a mortgage, the notes, bonds, or other indebtedness secured thereby having been fully paid, shall, at the request of the mortgagor, or grantor in a deed of trust in the nature of a mortgage, his heirs, legal representatives, or assigns, enter a release or satisfaction upon the margin of the record of such mortgage or deed of trust in the recorder's office, which release or satisfaction shall be attested upon the margin of said record by the recorder of said county, and when so attested shall forever thereafter discharge and release the same, and shall bar all actions or suits brought or to be brought thereon. All releases of mortgages and deeds of trust which have heretofore been made on the margin of record, in accordance with the provisions of this section, shall be held legal and valid, and shall have the same force and effect as if made under the provisions of this section as amended." Rev. Stat. Ill. c. 95, § 8.

or fraud; and unless this be shown satisfactorily, the discharge is conclusive proof of payment in favor of third persons who have a right to look to the record for protection.[74] And this doctrine is in accordance with the general weight of authority.[75]

§ 306.   Penalty for Failure to Enter Satisfaction.—The statute of Illinois provides that "if any mortgagee, or trustee in a deed of trust in the nature of a mortgage, of real or personal property, or his executor or administrator, heirs or assigns, knowing the same to be paid, shall not, within one month after the payment of the debt secured by such mortgage or trust deed, and request and tender of his reasonable charges, release the same, he shall, for every such offense, forfeit and pay to the party aggrieved the sum of fifty dollars, to be recovered in an action of debt before a justice of the peace."[76] This statute applies only in cases where the mortgage debt is paid without foreclosure; when it is necessary to foreclose, and a decree is rendered for that purpose, the mortgage becomes merged in the decree, and a satisfaction of the decree is all that is required.[77] As to the parties who are subject to the operation of the statute, it is held that an assignee of the mortgage is not liable to the penalties of the statute unless his assignment is on the record. The reason is that the purpose of the law is to clear the record, and the defaulting party must have some recorded connection with the mortgage or trust deed, or else his entry of satisfaction would only appear to be an impertinent interference by a stranger.[78]

An action of debt to recover the statutory penalty is not a criminal or quasi-criminal proceeding. But still the statute is a penal one, and therefore, according to well-known rules of construction, must be interpreted strictly.[79] The mortgagee,

[74] Ferguson v. Glassford, 68 Mich. 36, 35 N. W. Rep. 820.

[75] See Henschel v. Mamero, 120 Ill. 660, 12 N. E. Rep. 203; Bruce v. Bonney, 12 Gray (Mass.) 111; Heyder v. Excelsior Building Loan Ass'n, 42 N. J. Eq. 403, 8 Atl. Rep. 310; Seiple v. Seiple, 133 Pa. St. 460, 19 Atl. Rep. 406; Smith v. Lowry, 113 Ind. 37, 15 N. E. Rep. 17; Fidelity Ins. Co. v. Shenandoah Val. R. Co., 32 W. Va. 244, 9 S.

E. Rep. 180. Compare Ivinson v. Hutton, 3 Wyom. 61, 2 Pac. Rep. 238.

[76] Rev. Stat. Ill. c. 95, § 10.

[77] Murray v. Brokaw, 67 Ill. App. 402.

[78] Thomas v. Reynolds, 29 Kans. 804; Low v. Fox, 56 Iowa, 221, 9 N. W. Rep. 131.

[79] Lane v. Frake, 70 Ill. App. 303.

when called upon to enter satisfaction of a mortgage alleged
to have been paid, is only required to act in good faith and in
a reasonable manner. He must not raise captious or frivolous
objections. But on the other hand, the law will not punish
him for an honest, though mistaken, reliance upon his supposed
legal rights. He is not bound to determine unsettled or disputed questions, and he is not liable, under the statute, for a
failure or refusal to enter satisfaction when the right of the
person making the demand upon him to have such action taken
is a disputed matter of fact or an unsettled question of law.[80]
He will not be compelled to pay the statutory penalty, where
there was a reasonable and substantial doubt, in law or fact, as
to the relative rights of the parties, although it should turn
out, on foreclosure proceedings, that the mortgagor was really
entitled to a discharge.[81] So, if the mortgagee honestly believes that he has not received all that he is entitled to under
the mortgage, or that, if he owes the mortgagor money, it is
not enough to discharge the balance on the mortgage, he will
not be liable for the penalty.[82] And where the superior court
is applied to for an injunction to stay the prosecution of an
action for the statutory penalty, that court has jurisdiction
to hear and determine the question whether the party demanding an entry of satisfaction is entitled to it.[83]

§ 307. **Fraudulent or Forged Satisfaction.**—An entry of release or satisfaction of a mortgage obtained through fraud or
mistake may be cancelled on a bill in equity for that purpose,
or, as between the parties, it will be held inoperative and null,
and will constitute no defense to a bill for the foreclosure of
the mortgage.[84] But it must be remembered that a proper and
formal release or satisfaction is prima facie valid, and can be
impeached only by clear and satisfactory evidence; and the
mere fact that the debt remained outstanding and unpaid when

[80] Lane v. Frake, 70 Ill. App.
303; Parkes v. Parker, 57 Mich.
57, 23 N. W. Rep. 458.

[81] Huxford v. Eslow, 53 Mich.
179, 18 N. W. Rep. 630.

[82] Wilber v. Pierce, 56 Mich. 169,
22 N. W. Rep. 316; Canfield v.
Conkling, 41 Mich. 371, 2 N. W.
Rep. 191.

[83] Lane v. Frake, 57 Ill. App. 616.

[84] Henschel v. Mamero, 120 Ill.
660, 12 N. E. Rep. 203; Remann v.
Buckmaster, 85 Ill. 403; McLean v.
Lafayette Bank, 3 McLean, 587,
Fed. Cas. No. 8,888; Independent
Building & Loan Ass'n v. Real-
Estate Title Ins. Co., 156 Pa. St.
181, 27 Atl. Rep. 62. Thus, a re-
lease of a mortgage given by a
borrower to a building and loan

the release was executed, is not sufficient to raise a presumption of fraud or mistake.[85]

As to the effect of such an entry upon the rights of third persons, it is said that, if the cancellation of the mortgage was the result of negligence on the part of the mortgagee (as, if he carelessly permitted the mortgagor to have the custody of the mortgage), he will not be permitted to establish his lien against subsequent bona fide purchasers or mortgagees acting upon the faith of the entry of satisfaction on the record.[86] If a person by mistake enters on the record a satisfaction of a mortgage which he does not own, this will not affect the rights of the true owner of the mortgage, even as against persons subsequently dealing with the property. The person who made the mistaken entry may be liable for the resulting loss to a subsequent purchaser of the property affected, who buys on the faith of a clear title as shown by the record. But if the entry of satisfaction contains a reference by which any one looking the matter up would ascertain that it was the actual intention

association, executed by its officers fraudulently and without authority to do so, is not binding upon the association. Olney Loan & Bldg. Ass'n v. Rush, 97 Ill. App. 349.

[85] Battenhausen v. Bullock, 8 Ill. App. 312.

[86] Heyder v. Excelsior Building Loan Ass'n, 42 N. J. Eq. 403, 8 Atl. Rep. 310. In this case it was said: "Between a mortgagee whose mortgage has been discharged of record solely through the unauthorized act of another party, and a purchaser who buys the title in the belief, induced by such cancellation, that the mortgage is satisfied and discharged, the equities are balanced, and the rights in the order of time must prevail. The lien of the mortgage must remain despite the apparent discharge. But this is apart from any default attributable to the holder of the lien. If through his negligence, the record is permitted to give notice to the world that his claim is satisfied, he cannot, in the face

of his own carelessness, have his mortgage enforced against a bona fide purchaser taking his title on the faith that the registry is discharged. Where one gives to another the power to practice a fraud upon innocent parties, the court will not interfere in his protection at the expense of those who have been deceived and misled by such fraud. What circumstances shall be sufficient to establish negligence, such as shall preclude a mortgagee from a decree establishing his cancelled paper must be determined as a question of fact in each particular case, tested by those rules of conduct which men of common prudence usually observe in the care and management of such securities. That it is negligence in the owner of a mortgage to permit it to be in the custody and control of the mortgagor or owner of the mortgaged premises, in view of the provisions of our statute of registry, will not admit of denial."

not to satisfy that mortgage, but to satisfy one which the person did own, he will not be so liable.[87]

A forged entry of satisfaction has no effect on the rights of the mortgagee. It is the duty of both the trustee in a trust deed and the cestui que trust, when a forged release of their deed is recorded, to inform all persons who may apply to them for information that such release is a forgery; but the law does not require them to execute and record any instrument to counteract the forgery. "The law requires the execution and recording, by the person holding the title, of no instrument in addition to that which evidences his title, that we are aware of, to counteract the forgery by which he is sought to be robbed of his property; nor does it require that the owner of the title shall, within any particular period, commence proceedings at law or in equity against the forger, to vindicate his good title against the fraudulent claim of the forger or one claiming under him. He may bide his time and trust to the strength of his title."[88] And the good faith of a second mortgagee, in taking his mortgage on the strength of a forged discharge of the prior mortgage, will not avail him in a suit to foreclose the elder lien, if the holder of it had nothing to do with deceiving him.[89] And so, where a fraudulent and forged satisfaction of a mortgage is entered on the record, whereby a subsequent purchaser of the land is misled to his detriment, he cannot maintain an action for damages against the recorder, unless he can show that the latter knew of the character of the instrument and recorded it with a corrupt intent.[90]

§ 308. Cancelling Entry of Satisfaction.—A mortgage discharged from the record through fraud, accident, or mistake, may be restored in equity, and given its original priority as a lien, when the rights of innocent third parties will not be affected.[91] Nothing but the actual payment of a debt secured by a mortgage will release the lien of the mortgage; and where a mortgage is released in ignorance of an intervening lien,

[87] Binney's Appeal, 116 Pa. St. 169, 9 Atl. Rep. 186.

[88] Chandler v. White, 84 Ill. 435.

[89] Keller v. Hannah, 52 Mich. 535, 18 N. W. Rep. 346.

[90] Ramsey v. Riley, 13 Ohio, 157.

[91] Ferguson v. Glassford, 68 Mich. 36, 35 N. W. Rep. 820.

"There is no virtue in the satisfaction of a mortgage, except, perhaps, as to purchasers or other mortgagees without notice, that prevents either a fraud or mistake in the satisfaction from being corrected." Appeal of Callahan, 124 Pa. St. 138, 16 Atl. Rep. 638.

though of record, equity will relieve against the mistake.[92] But in a proceeding to cancel a release of a mortgage on the ground of fraudulent representation and mistake, in the absence of evidence of such fraud or mistake, the release cannot be avoided on the mere ground of a want of consideration.[93] When the mortgagee makes the mistake of entering on the record a release or satisfaction of one mortgage, actually intending to release an entirely different mortgage, equity will grant him relief, by restoring him to his original rights; and this action cannot be objected to by a second mortgagee who took subject to the prior incumbrance.[94]

§ 309. **Release of Deed of Trust.**—When the debt secured by a deed of trust has been fully paid, it is the statutory duty of the trustee therein to enter satisfaction on the margin of the record.[95] But the trustee cannot lawfully release or satisfy the deed of trust unless the debt which it secures has been in fact paid; and the fact that the note evidencing the debt, not yet matured and not cancelled, remains in the possession of the payee, is sufficient to put mortgage creditors upon inquiry as to whether the note has been paid.[96] The legal title to the property being vested in the trustee, his release of the deed of trust will restore the title to the grantor, although it may constitute a breach of trust, the debt being actually unsatisfied. But a release or entry of satisfaction made by the trustee when the secured debt has not been paid, and the act is not authorized by the holder of the obligation, will not discharge the lien of the trust deed as between the original parties, nor as to any subsequent purchasers or incumbrancers who are chargeable with notice of the nonpayment of the debt. But as to one who had no notice, and relied on the title as shown by the record, whether as a purchaser from the mortgagor or as a subsequent incumbrancer, the trustee's release would be effective both at law and in equity.[97] In a suit to foreclose a trust

---

[92] Liggett v. Himle, 38 Minn. 421, 38 N. W. Rep. 201; following Geib v. Reynolds, 35 Minn. 331, 28 N. W. Rep. 923.

[93] Stephenson v. Hawkins, 67 Cal. 106, 7 Pac. Rep. 198.

[94] Bond v. Dorsey, 65 Md. 310, 4 Atl. Rep. 279.

[95] Rev. Stat. Ill. c. 95, § 8.

[96] Lang v. Metzger, 86 Ill. App. 117.

[97] Lennartz v. Quilty, 191 Ill. 174, 60 N. E. Rep. 913 (affirming 92 Ill. App. 182); Stiger v. Bent, 111 Ill. 328; Williams v. Jackson, 107 U. S. 478; Connecticut Gen. Life Ins. Co. v. Eldredge, 102 U. S. 545; supra, § 43.

deed, an entry of satisfaction made by the trustee without authority from the holder of the note secured may be disregarded without formally setting it aside.[98]

§ 310. **General Doctrine of Subrogation.**—As applied in the law of mortgages, subrogation is a device of equity by which a person who is not primarily responsible for the payment of the mortgage debt, but who has paid it as a measure necessary for the protection of his own rights or interests, or who has paid it under an agreement with the debtor that he shall have the protection of the security, is substituted in the place of the original creditor, so far as to entitle him to control the mortgage and to enforce it against the debtor, as the original mortgagee could have done if there had been no payment, without receiving any assignment or other formal transfer of the mortgage to himself. This equitable principle is enforced solely for the accomplishment of substantial justice, where one has an equity to invoke which cannot injure an innocent person. The right of subrogation which springs from the mere fact of the payment of the debt by one who was forced to discharge it for his own protection, without any contract or understanding with the debtor, is termed "legal" subrogation. There is also a so-called "conventional" subrogation, "which results from an equitable right springing from an express agreement with the debtor, by one who advances money to pay a claim for the security of which there exists a lien, by which agreement he is to have an equal lien to that paid off, whereupon he is entitled to the benefit of the security which he has satisfied with the expectation of receiving an equal lien. It is the agreement that the security shall be kept alive for the benefit of the person making the payment which gives the right of subrogation, because it takes away the character of a mere volunteer. Where a payment is made at the request of the debtor, the person so paying is never a volunteer."[1] The right of subrogation is not lost by the fact that the party asserting the right takes or holds collateral security.[2] Thus, the fact that one has taken a deed of trust on property to secure advances made to discharge prior liens thereon will not prevent his being subrogated to the rights of the lien holders.[3]

[98] Stiger v. Bent, 111 Ill. 328.

[1] Home Savings Bank v. Bierstadt, 168 Ill. 618, 48 N. E. Rep. 161.

[2] Smith v. Dinsmoor, 119 Ill. 656, 4 N. E. Rep. 648.

[3] Worcester Bank v. Cheeney, 87 Ill. 602.

§ 311. **Subrogation on Partial Payment.**—So far as regards what is called "legal" subrogation, no person can claim this right until he has paid the mortgage debt in full. Payment of an installment of interest, or of a portion of the principal, will give him no right to be substituted in the place of the mortgage creditor, even pro tanto. Until the original creditor has been wholly satisfied, there ought to be, and can be in law, no interference with his rights or his securities which might hinder him in the collection of the residue of his claim.[4] But in the case of a "conventional" subrogation, resulting from an express agreement with the creditor to the effect that the security held by him shall be assigned to the person paying, or kept on foot for his benefit, it is no objection that it extends only to a part of the mortgage debt or security.[5]

§ 312. **Who Entitled to Subrogation.**—The right of subrogation can be accorded only to a person who was not primarily responsible for the payment of the debt. No one is entitled to hold a mortgage security by way of subrogation when he paid the debt which the mortgage secured because he was bound and obliged to pay it.[6] But the case is different if, without direct liability for the mortgage debt, he discharged it because such a course was necessary for the protection or saving of his own interest in the property affected. Thus, a junior mortgagee who pays off the senior mortgage to prevent the sacrifice of his own security on the property, will be en-

---

[4] Appeal of Allegheny Nat. Bank (Pa.), 7 Atl. Rep. 788; Loeb v. Fleming, 15 Ill. App. 503. In the case last cited it was said: "In order to be entitled to subrogation, or substitution by operation of law, to the rights and interests of the senior mortgagee in lands by redemption, the party redeeming must pay the entire amount of an incumbrance which is senior to his own estate. A junior mortgagee who claims to be an equitable assignee, or an assignee by operation of law, stands in the same position, in respect to a partial payment of the senior mortgage, as a surety does in respect to a partial payment of the claim against his principal. It is well settled that a surety can neither at law nor equity call for an assignment of the claim of the creditor against his principal, or be clothed, by the mere operation of law and upon principles of equity, with the rights of an assignee of such claim, unless he has paid the entire debt of the creditor. A pro tanto assignment will not be allowed."

[5] Loeb v. Fleming, 15 Ill. App. 503.

[6] Richardson v. Traver, 112 U. S. 423. And see Pearce v. Bryant Coal Co., 121 Ill. 590, 13 N. E. Rep. 561.

titled to subrogation to the rights of the elder lienor as against the common debtor.[7] So also, when the debt is paid by one who occupies the position of a surety for the mortgagor, or a guarantor of the mortgage debt, he will be entitled to subrogation for his own indemnity, not only to the creditor's rights under the mortgage, but also to rights accruing under any and all securities held as collateral to the debt secured by the original mortgage; and hence he will be entitled to the control of a subsequent mortgage obtained by the mortgagee. as additional security.[8] So again, where a widow pays off a debt secured by a mortgage given by her deceased husband, the same being a valid lien, and thereby preserves the property, she will have the right to foreclose the mortgage for her own benefit.[9] On similar principles, an officer of a corporation who, to preserve the property for the parties whom he represents, pays the interest due on a mortgage of such property, out of his private funds, is entitled to be subrogated to their rights.[10] Again, where a mortgage rests upon land owned by two joint tenants or tenants in common, and one of them pays off the entire incumbrance, in order to save the property from foreclosure and sale, he will be subrogated to the rights of the mortgagee, in order to enable him to enforce contribution of his proportionate share from his co-tenant.[11] And where two partners purchase lands in trust for the firm, giving a mortgage back to secure the purchase money, which the whole firm is to pay, but neglects to pay, and one of the partners is compelled to pay the whole debt to protect his own interest and save the property from sale under a power in the mortgage, he will have a clear right to be subrogated to the position of the mortgagee.[12]

[7] Tyrrell v. Ward, 102 Ill. 29; Ball v. Callahan, 95 Ill. App. 615; supra, §§ 172, 294.

[8] Richeson v. Crawford, 94 Ill. 165; Conwell v. McCowan, 53 Ill. 363; Havens v. Willis, 100 N. Y. 482, 3 N. E. Rep. 313.

[9] Stinson v. Anderson, 96 Ill. 373.

[10] Bush v. Wadsworth, 60 Mich. 255, 27 N. W. Rep. 532.

[11] Simpson v. Gardiner, 97 Ill. 237. See infra, § 338.

[12] McMillan v. James, 105 Ill. 194.

So where, on the dissolution of a partnership, one partner assumes the payment of a partnership note, and executes a mortgage to the payee of the note to secure its payment, and also to indemnify his co-partner against the payment thereof, such co-partner will be entitled to be subrogated to the rights of the mortgagee, to the extent of any payment he may have to make on such note. Conwell v. McCowan, 81 Ill. 285.

24

§ 312. Same; Purchaser of Mortgaged Premises.—When a purchaser of property which is subject to an existing mortgage assumes and agrees to pay the mortgage debt, the same forming a part of the purchase price, neither he nor his grantee can claim the right to be subrogated to the rights of the mortgagee on paying off the incumbrance.[13] But if such a purchaser has not assumed the mortgage debt, nor otherwise become responsible for it, the primary obligation still resting upon the mortgagor, he may discharge the incumbrance to prevent a sale, or to perfect his own title, and thereupon claim the right to succeed to the position of the mortgagee; and in this case it makes no difference that the mortgage was not assigned to him, or even that it was released of record.[14] So, where the grantee of mortgaged land pays off the incumbrance, and thereafter the deed under which he claims is set aside as having been made with intent to defraud the creditors of the grantor, the grantee will have the right to be subrogated, as to the sum so paid by him, to the rights of the holder of the incumbrance.[15] Conversely, when a mortgagor sells the premises to one who assumes and agrees to pay the mortgage debt (the same forming a part of the consideration of the purchase, even though the purchaser did not enter into any written agreement to pay it), the grantor becomes, as between the parties, the surety of the grantee, and hence if the grantor is compelled to pay the mortgage debt he may be subrogated to all the rights of the mortgagee.[16] So where a mortgagee obtains a judgment of foreclosure by scire facias, and one of several subsequent purchasers from the mortgagor pays the judgment, equity will thereupon work a subrogation of such purchaser to the rights of the mortgagee, so far as may be necessary to enable the former to compel contribution from persons liable thereto, and this right of subrogation will accrue

[13] Goodyear v. Goodyear, 72 Iowa, 329, 33 N. W. Rep. 142.

[14] Young v. Morgan, 89 Ill. 199; Hough v. Aetna Life Ins. Co., 57 Ill. 318; Smith v. Dinsmore, 16 Ill. App. 115; Hazle v. Bondy, 173 Ill. 302, 50 N. E. Rep. 671.

[15] Young v. Ward, 115 Ill. 264, 3 N. E. Rep. 512. But where one claiming title to land voluntarily discharges a mortgage thereon given by his grantor, and a third party is subsequently adjudged to be the owner in fee, the former is not entitled to have the amount so paid adjudged a charge upon the land as against the latter. Wadsworth v. Blake, 43 Minn. 509, 45 N. W. Rep. 1131.

[16] Wood v. Smith, 51 Iowa, 156,

immediately upon payment of the judgment, independently of
any assignment thereof.[17] It also appears that the right of
subrogation may be exercised in favor of a purchaser of the
debtor's equity of redemption at a sale thereof under execution, if he has been compelled to pay the mortgage debt or to
deposit the amount in court for the benefit of the mortgagee.[18]
But the mortgagor, whose equity has been sold on execution,
cannot be subrogated to the rights of the mortgagee, thus compelling the purchaser of the equity of redemption to pay the
mortgage debt or lose his purchase. On the contrary, the mortgagor, being both legally and equitably bound to pay the debt,
must redeem from the execution sale or lose the property.[19]
Where the equity of redemption in mortgaged land is sold by
the administrator of the deceased mortgagor, a purchaser, who
discharges the mortgage, will not be entitled to be subrogated
to the rights of the mortgagee, so as to cut off by foreclosure
the widow's right of dower.[20]

§ 314. Same; Purchaser at Void Foreclosure Sale.—The purchaser of property at a sale on foreclosure of a mortgage
thereon, or his assignee, will be entitled to be subrogated to
the rights of the mortgagee in the event that the sale proves
void or ineffectual to convey the title, and he may thereupon
demand a valid foreclosure of the mortgage for his own benefit.[21] So a bona fide purchaser at a sale made under a power
contained in the mortgage is entitled, the sale proving invalid,
to be subrogated to the rights of the mortgagee, although the
conveyance to him contains no language amounting to a legal

50 N. W. Rep. 581. And see supra,
§ 263.

[17] Matteson v. Thomas, 41 Ill.
110.

[18] Magill v. De Witt County Nat.
Bank, 26 Ill. App. 381.

[19] Rogers v. Meyers, 68 Ill. 92.

[20] Cox v. Garst, 105 Ill. 342.
Where a purchaser of land at a
guardian's sale pays off a mortgage on the premises as a part of
the price, but was guilty of fraud
in acquiring his title, having made
a corrupt agreement by which he
prevented competition at the sale
and secured the land at a price
below its real value, there will be

no error in allowing him interest
only at the rate of six per cent. on
the money paid by him, although
the mortgage bore interest at the
rate of ten per cent.; for his payment was one made in wrong and
in the carrying out of an unlawful
bargain, and therefore presents no
case for the application of the
equitable doctrine of subrogation.
Devine v. Harkness, 117 Ill. 145,
7 N. E. Rep. 52.

[21] Bruschke v. Wright, 166 Ill.
183, 46 N. E. Rep. 813; Dutcher v.
Hobby, 86 Ga. 198, 12 S. E. Rep.
356; Jordan v. Sayre, 29 Fla. 100,
10 South. Rep. 823.

assignment of the security, and although the mortgage was discharged of record after the sale.[22]

§ 315. **Same; Stranger Advancing Money to Pay Mortgage.**—Where a third person pays a debt which is secured by a mortgage, at the instance and request of the mortgagor, or furnishes the latter with the money necessary to pay the mortgage debt, under an agreement with the debtor that he shall receive an assignment of the security, or that a new mortgage shall be made to him upon the same property to secure his advance, such person will be entitled to be subrogated to all the rights of the original creditor, if the debtor fails to procure the assignment of the old mortgage, or refuses to make a new mortgage as agreed, or if the new mortgage, when executed, proves to be invalid or defective.[23] This equitable right of subrogation may indeed be defeated by the existence of equal or superior equities in other persons,[24] but one advancing money for such a purpose, at the solicitation of the mortgagor, cannot be regarded as a mere stranger or volunteer intermeddling between the debtor and creditor.[25] And although the original mortgage was released or discharged on the payment of the money, and the debt may be considered at law as extinguished, yet it will not be so regarded in equity if it would be contrary to equity so to consider it.[26] On similar principles, it is held that, where a creditor of a mortgagor of chattels is compelled, by an order of court in which he has filed a bill, to bring into court the amount secured by the mortgage, and the mortgagee, by leave of the court, withdraws the same, then, even though such order was erroneously made, the creditor will have the right in equity to be subrogated to the rights of the mortgagee under the mortgage.[27] But the mere fact that money raised by a second mortgage is used in paying off a prior mortgage does

[22] Brewer v. Nash, 16 R. I. 458, 17 Atl. Rep. 857.

[23] Caudle v. Murphy, 89 Ill. 352; Home Savings Bank v. Bierstadt, 168 Ill. 618, 48 N. E. Rep. 161; Robertson v. Mowell, 66 Md. 530, 8 Atl. Rep. 273; Baker v. Baker (S. Dak.), 49 N. W. Rep. 1064; Crippen v. Chappel, 35 Kans. 495, 11 Pac. Rep. 453; Yaple v. Stephens, 36 Kans. 680, 14 Pac. Rep. 222.

[24] Home Savings Bank v. Bierstadt, 168 Ill. 618, 48 N. E. Rep. 161.

[25] Robertson v. Mowell, 66 Md. 530, 8 Atl. Rep. 273.

[26] Milholland v. Tiffany, 64 Md. 455, 2 Atl. Rep. 831.

[27] Magill v. De Witt County Savings Bank, 126 Ill. 244, 19 N. E. Rep. 295.

not entitle the second mortgagee to be subrogated to the rights
of the prior mortgagee, where there is nothing to show that it
was his understanding that his money should be thus used,
or that the prior mortgage should be assigned to him, or that
it should be kept alive for his benefit.[28]

§ 316. Volunteer Not Entitled to Subrogation.—A mere
stranger or volunteer cannot, by paying a debt for which
another is bound, acquire a right to be subrogated to the
creditor's rights in respect to the security given by the original
debtor.[29] "It is only where the payment of incumbrances is
necessary to protect rights of the payer, or where they are paid
pursuant to an agreement with the debtor that the payer shall
hold them as security for the money advanced, that the payer
will be subrogated to the rights of the holders of such liens,
and the liens will be kept alive for his benefit. Where the
demand of a creditor is paid with the money of a third person,
not himself a creditor, without any agreement that the security
shall be assigned or kept on foot for the benefit of such third
person, the demand is absolutely extinguished.''[30] Thus, where
an agent who had been employed to invest money for the mortgagee, on failure of the mortgagor to pay the interest coupons,
which had been sent to him by the mortgagee for collection,
remitted the amount of such coupons to the mortgagee, but
the mortgagor had no knowledge of his having done so, and
the mortgagee did not know that the remittance was from the
individual funds of the agent, it was held that the latter was
a mere volunteer and was not entitled to be subrogated to the
rights of the mortgagee.[31]

[28] Jeffries v. Allen, 29 S. Car. 501, 7 S. E. Rep. 828.

[29] Hough v. Aetna Life Ins. Co., 57 Ill. 318; Young v. Morgan, 89 Ill. 199; Bouton v. Cameron, 99 Ill. App. 600; Nicholls v. Creditors, 9 Rob. (La.) 476; Weil v. Enterprise Ginnery Co., 42 La. Ann. 492, 7 South. Rep. 622.

[30] White v. Cannon, 125 Ill. 412, 17 N. E. Rep. 753.

[31] Bennett v. Chandler, 199 Ill. 97, 64 N. E. Rep. 1052.

CHAPTER XXV.

REDEMPTION FROM MORTGAGES.

§ 317. The Right of Redemption.—Redemption is the right of a mortgagor to save his estate from sale on foreclosure of the mortgage, liberate the same from the lien of the mortgage, and recover the absolute title for himself, by paying all that is justly due to the mortgagee, after there has been a breach of the condition of the mortgage, whereby, at law, the defeasible title of the mortgagee would become fixed and absolute. If the claims of the creditor are satisfied on or before the day fixed for the discharge of the debt, it is a payment, not a redemption. The right to redeem does not come into existence until default has been made in the payment of the debt or performance of the other conditions of the mortgage, for until breach of condition there is no forfeiture of the estate. The estate remaining in the mortgagor after he has executed a valid mortgage on his property is commonly called an "equity of redemption;" but it is more properly an equitable title, which is not reduced to a mere privilege of redeeming until breach of condition. This right of redemption, primarily belonging to the mortgagor, may also be exercised by his successors in interest and by various other parties having an interest in the

mortgaged premises, as will be shown in a later section; and
it may be claimed and exercised not only against the original
mortgagee, but also against any assignee or holder of the mortgage debt. It is a necessary element of every contract in the
nature of a mortgage. "Wherever there is a mortgage, there
is a right in the mortgagor or grantor to redeem the thing
mortgaged. It need not be expressed, for the right to redeem
will be implied wherever it is shown that property is transferred or pledged as security, unless the nature of the agreement forbids such implication."[1] It cannot be waived in advance. No court of equity will give effect to a stipulation or
agreement contained in the mortgage itself to the effect that
the mortgagor's right of redemption shall be absolutely cut
off and forfeited upon failure to perform the condition by a
particular time.[2] But the equity of redemption may be released to the mortgagee, thus vesting him with the absolute
title, when the agreement therefor is subsequent to the mortgage and entirely disconnected from it, and is founded upon
an adequate consideration, and is perfectly fair and free from
all oppression and undue influence.[3] The right to redeem is a
favorite equity, and will not be taken away except by a strict
compliance with the steps necessary to divest it.[4] At the same
time, it is a privilege of the debtor, in the sense that he is not
legally compelled to avail himself of it if he does not choose
to do so. "No mortgagor is under any legal obligation to
redeem the mortgaged premises. It is his right, which he can
elect to exercise or omit."[5]

The right of redemption is of three kinds, or rather, presents
itself under three aspects, viz., as a common-law right, a statutory right, and an equitable right. The common-law right of
redemption is the right of paying off the debt and redeeming
the estate, at any time after breach of condition, and before
the mortgagor's privilege in this behalf is cut off by a fore-

[1] Cadman v. Peter. 12 Fed. Rep.
363.

[2] Supra, §§ 3, 281. And see Quartermous v. Kennedy, 29 Ark. 544.

[3] Supra, §§ 281-286.

[4] Chicago, D. & V. R. Co. v. Fosdick, 106 U. S. 47.

[5] Morgan v. Clayton, 61 Ill. 35.
A mortgagee, whose debt is secured on two lots, on one of which
there is a prior mortgage for a
much larger sum, will not be compelled to redeem on a foreclosure
of such prior mortgage, so as to
give a subsequent mortgagee on
the other lot the benefit of the security. Lewis v. Hinman, 56 Conn.
55, 13 Atl. Rep. 143.

closure or barred in some other of the modes recognized by the law. In this aspect, the right of redemption cannot be limited to any particular time by stipulations embodied in the mortgage. On the principle that "what is once a mortgage is always a mortgage," it is not essential to the right of the mortgagor to redeem that he should do so within the time limited in the defeasance. There is no rule of law which requires a redemption to be made within the time fixed by the mortgage itself. Until foreclosed, it is a subsisting right, unless barred by the lapse of time.[6] But this common-law right of redemption is absolutely cut off and extinguished by a valid decree of foreclosure and a sale thereunder. After such proceedings, the mortgagor can claim no further right to redeem the premises, in the absence of a statutory provision on the subject.[7] In most of the states, however, the statutes now give to the mortgagor, and to those claiming under him, and to certain other classes of persons interested in the property, a privilege of redeeming from the foreclosure sale within a limited time thereafter. In Illinois, so far as concerns the mortgagor, this time is fixed at twelve months from the sale. This statutory right is entirely distinct from the common-law right of redemption. It does not come into existence until the other has been foreclosed; but neither can it be cut off by judicial proceedings. No judgment or decree can take away the statutory right of redemption.[8] But it is not equivalent to a title or equity in the land affected. The mortgagor's legal estate is divested by the decree of foreclosure. After the rendition of such a decree, and a sale of the mortgaged premises thereunder, the mortgagor's statutory right of redemption is not such an ownership of the property, for instance, as will support a mechanic's lien.[9] The third species or aspect of the right of redemption is that which is available only in equity. It arises in cases where the form of the mortgage security was abnormal,—as where the debtor gave a deed absolute in form, with a parol agreement for a defeasance, which the grantee now refuses to recognize,—where foreclosure proceedings had on the mortgage were invalid or were nugatory as to the party

[6] Preschbaker v. Feaman, 32 Ill. 475; Stover v. Bounds, 1 Ohio St. 107.

[7] Parker v. Dacres, 130 U. S. 43; Weiner v. Heintz, 17 Ill. 259.

[8] De Wolf v. Haydn, 24 Ill. 525.

[9] Stone v. Tyler, 173 Ill. 147, 50 N. E. Rep. 688, reversing 67 Ill. App. 17.

seeking to redeem, and where the parties made special terms as to the redemption, which cannot be enforced at law. This right of redemption is made effective by means of a bill in equity.

§ 318. Laches Barring Right to Redeem.—A right of redemption from a mortgage, claimable at common law or in equity, may be lost by the laches of the mortgagor. That is, it may be forfeited if not asserted within a reasonable time and before the situation of the parties has changed or the rights of third persons have intervened.[10] Thus, it is said that when the right to foreclose a mortgage is barred by limitations, the right to redeem is also barred, the two rights being reciprocal.[11] And it is a general rule of equity that, by analogy to the ordinary limitation of rights of entry and actions of ejectment, a mortgagor's right of redemption in equity will be barred in twenty years from the time the mortgagee enters into possession after breach of condition.[12] But this must not be regarded as a rigid and invariable rule. It must be allowed sufficient elasticity to meet the facts of particular cases. A much greater delay than twenty years in asserting the right of redemption may be excused by circumstances; and on the other hand, a much less delay may be held inexcusable in the particular situation of the parties. It is said: "In the absence of the existence of a statute of limitations, the time in which a party will be barred from relief in a court of equity must necessarily depend, to a certain extent, upon the facts of each case as it may arise; but when the statute has fixed the period of limitations, under which the claim, if interposed in a court of law, would be barred, courts of equity, by analogy, follow the limitation provided by law. A court of equity will, however, often treat a lapse of a less period than that provided in actions at law as a presumptive bar, on the ground of discouraging stale claims or gross laches, or unexplained acquiescence in the assertion of an adverse right."[13] But in order that lapse of time should bar the right

[10] Walker v. Warner, 179 Ill. 16, 53 N. E. Rep. 594.

[11] Fitch v. Miller, 200 Ill. 170, 65 N. E. Rep. 650.

[12] Hallesy v. Jackson, 66 Ill. 139. The same rule is recognized and applied by the courts of the United States. Hughes v. Edwards, 9 Wheat. 489; Slicer v. Bank of Pittsburg, 16 How. 571; Amory v. Lawrence, 3 Cliff. 523, Fed. Cas. No. 336.

[13] Castner v. Walrod, 83 Ill. 171; Walker v. Warner, 179 Ill. 16, 53

to redeem, there must be continued actual possession of the premises on the part of the mortgagee, and not merely constructive possession. In one case, it was held that, even after the lapse of thirty-five years from the time of condition broken, a mortgagor might be allowed to redeem, where the land had remained wild and unoccupied until a year before his bill was filed.[14] And where land is conveyed by a deed absolute in form, though intended only as a mortgage, and the grantee takes possession, he exercises a trust in respect to the land, and the grantor has a right to rely upon his performing the trust, until the doing of some act unequivocally disavowing it, which is brought to his actual knowledge. Hence the grantor cannot be charged with laches merely because he delays, without such knowledge, to bring a suit to redeem.[15] Further, the rule that equity will treat the right of redemption as lost after twenty years' delay is subject to an important qualification, which has been expressed as follows: "If a mortgagee in possession shall, after the equity of the mortgagor has become barred by lapse of time, admit, either by word or act, that his mortgage is still a subsisting lien, the bar previously existing will be considered to have been waived, and the equity of the mortgagor revived. And an admission having this effect will be considered to have been made if the mortgagee institutes proceedings, either by suit or otherwise, to foreclose his mortgage; the reason assigned being that such act is entirely inconsistent with any pretension on his part that his possession had ripened into a title."[16] It is also to be observed that laches will not bar a bill filed by the United States to redeem from a mortgage property purchased by it at a sale under execution in its favor; as it holds the title to such property, as it does to all other property, for public and not private purposes.[17] There

---

N. E. Rep. 594. Thus, a delay for 14 years by one having a right to redeem from a foreclosure sale, meantime permitting interest and taxes to accumulate in a large amount, although he has no written evidence of his right to redeem, and nothing but a verbal agreement resting within the knowledge of witnesses already aged, constitutes such laches as will bar any right of action. Mc-Dearmon v. Burnham, 158 Ill. 55, 41 N. E. Rep. 1094. And see Lynch v. Jackson, 28 Ill. App. 160, affirmed in 129 Ill. 72, 21 N. E. Rep. 580.

[14] Locke v. Caldwell, 91 Ill. 417.

[15] Jackson v. Lynch, 129 Ill. 72, 21 N. E. Rep. 580.

[16] Chapin v. Wright, 41 N. J. Eq. 438, 5 Atl. Rep. 574.

[17] United States v. Insley, 130 U. S. 263.

is also a rule converse to that discussed in this section, to wit, where twenty years have elapsed since a sale on foreclosure, and no conveyance has been made to the purchaser, it will be presumed that the land has been redeemed from the sale.[18]

§ 319. Constitutionality of Statutes Regarding Redemption. —The time for redemption from a mortgage, and the conditions on which it may be made, whether fixed by the parties or regulated by statute, enter into the mortgage contract and form a part of it, so far as to be immune from change by the legislature. The terms of sale and redemption under a power in the mortgage, for example, are governed by the law in force when the mortgage was executed, and cannot be affected by a subsequent act extending the time for redemption or making it run from the filing of a notice of the sale.[19] So, the statute of Illinois of 1841, giving to mortgagors a right to redeem within twelve months after the sale of the property on foreclosure, was adjudged by the Supreme Court of the United States to be unconstitutional and void, in so far as it applied to mortgages executed before its enactment and which carried no such right of redemption, because, as to such mortgages, it impaired the obligation of contracts.[20]

§ 320. Construction of Statutes Allowing Redemption.— Statutes allowing redemption from foreclosure sales should not be subjected to a strict construction. On the contrary, as remarked by the Supreme Court of Illinois, "redemptions are looked upon with favor, and when no injury is to follow, a liberal construction should be given our redemption laws, to the end that the property of the debtor may pay as many of the debtor's liabilities as possible."[21] But, "while the law authorizing redemptions from judicial and execution sales is remedial in its character, and should not, therefore, be defeated on merely technical grounds in cases fairly brought within its provisions, yet the right of redemption from such sales is purely statutory, and courts are not warranted in extending such right to a class of cases which the legislature, in its wisdom, has not seen proper to provide for."[22]

[18] Reynolds v. Dishon, 3 Ill. App. 173.

[19] Smith v. Green, 41 Fed. Rep. 455.

[20] Bronson v. Kinzie, 1 How. (U. S.) 311. And see Barnitz v. Beverly, 163 U. S. 118.

[21] Schuck v. Gerlach, 101 Ill. 338; Whitehead v. Hall, 148 Ill. 253, 35 N. E. Rep. 871.

[22] Thornley v. Moore, 106 Ill. 156.

§ 321. **What Constitutes Redemption.**—The difference between a redemption, properly so called, and a payment of the
mortgage debt, was explained in the beginning of this chapter.
But the question sometimes arises as to whether a party paying
money to a mortgage creditor has effected a redemption of the
mortgaged premises, which would discharge the mortgage and
extinguish its lien, or an assignment of the mortgage security
to himself, which would keep it alive for his benefit. This is
largely a question of intention. But it is held that, when the
owner of the equity of redemption pays to the purchaser at
foreclosure sale the amount of his bid with interest, and takes
an assignment of the certificate of purchase, this is not a
redemption as required by the statute, and will not prevent a
judgment creditor from redeeming under the statute.[23] And
on similar principles, where a junior mortgagee buys the certificate of purchase under foreclosure proceedings on the elder
mortgage, this is not a statutory redemption from the sale.
He simply steps into the place of the original purchaser, and
succeeds to his rights as such, and to no different or greater
rights. Consequently, he cannot set up such a purchase to
prevent a judgment creditor from redeeming in conformity
with the terms of the statute.[24]

§ 322. **Parties Entitled to Redeem.**—Not only the original
maker of the mortgage may redeem, but also any person who
has succeeded to his rights or interests, or who holds a title
or estate in the premises subordinate to his. Thus, the owner
of an easement in the land covered by the mortgage may
redeem it,[25] as also a tenant for life,[26] a tenant for years or
holder of a leasehold estate,[27] a tenant in tail,[28] a remainder-
man or reversioner,[29] and one of two or more tenants in common.[30] So also, the grantee of the mortgagor's interest in the
premises has a right to redeem, though not mentioned in the

---

[23] Boynton v. Peirce, 49 Ill. App.
497, affirmed in 151 Ill. 197.

[24] Schroeder v. Bauer, 41 Ill.
App. 484; Lloyd v. Karnes, 45 Ill.
62; Schroeder v. Bauer, 140 Ill.
135, 29 N. E. Rep. 560.

[25] Bacon v. Bowdoin, 22 Pick.
(Mass.) 401.

[26] Lamson v. Drake, 105 Mass.
564.

[27] Arnold v. Green, 116 N. Y. 572;
Hamilton v. Dobbs, 19 N. J. Eq.
227.

[28] Playford v. Playford, 4 Hare,
546.

[29] Davies v. Wetherell, 13 Allen
(Mass.), 60; Rafferty v. King, 1
Keen, 601.

[30] Brown v. McKay, 151 Ill. 315,
37 N. E. Rep. 1037; Titsworth v.
Stout, 49 Ill. 78.

decree of foreclosure.[31]   And the same is true of a purchaser
who had only an executory contract for the sale of the land,
coupled with possession, at the time of the foreclosure sale,
but who afterwards acquired a deed from the mortgagor.[32]
And where the owner of the land, after conveying it by a
deed of trust to secure debts, conveys it to another in fee, subject to the deed of trust, expressly reserving a lien for the
purchase money, he has the right, by reason of such lien interest, to redeem from foreclosure of the deed of trust.[33]
Again, a purchaser of the equity of redemption, at a sale thereof on execution on a judgment junior to the mortgage, has a
right to redeem from the mortgage, if he was not made a party
to the proceedings to foreclose the same.[34]   And so, one who,
after the entry of the decree of foreclosure, but before the sale
thereunder, purchases the land on a sale on execution against
the mortgagor, acquires the right of redemption.[35]   But the
purchaser at an invalid sale on execution has no right to
redeem from a mortgage foreclosure sale, and an attempted
redemption by him will not divest the title acquired under the
foreclosure.[36]

As to the right of a surety for the mortgagor, it appears to
be the doctrine of the cases that such a surety may pay off the
mortgage debt, before any foreclosure, and thereupon be subrogated to the rights of the creditor.[37]   But the right of any
person to redeem after a sale on foreclosure depends entirely
upon the statute, and the case of a surety does not appear to
be embraced within the terms of the law.[38]   Neither does the
right of redemption appertain to the holder of a tax title on
the mortgaged premises.   He does not derive his title from
or through the mortgagor.   It comes from an independent
source.   If invalid, it confers no sort of right upon him; but
if valid, it vests in him all the titles belonging to every person
interested in the property.   He is not a necessary or proper
party to foreclosure proceedings, and is under no obligation
to redeem from the mortgage to protect his own title, and
consequently has no right to do so.[39]   And although the owner

31 Farrell v. Parlier, 50 Ill. 274.

32 Noyes v. Hall, 97 U. S. 34.

33 Pearcy v. Tate, 91 Tenn. 473,
19 S. W. Rep. 323.

34 Grob v. Cushman, 60 Ill. 201.

35 Willis v. Smith, 66 Tex. 31, 17
S. W. Rep. 247.

36 Wooters v. Joseph, 137 Ill. 113,
27 N. E. Rep. 80.

37 Supra, §§ 294, 312.

38 See Miller v. Ayres, 59 Iowa,
424, 13 N. W. Rep. 436.

39 Witt v. Mewhirter, 57 Iowa,
545, 10 N. W. Rep. 890.

of the mortgaged property contests the validity of a tax levied on it, and so estops himself from questioning the tax in another suit, this estoppel does not constitute the holder of the tax title the owner of the equity of redemption as against the mortgagee, nor entitle him to redeem.[40]

A judgment creditor of the mortgagor has the right to redeem the estate from the lien of the mortgage,[41] provided his judgment constitutes an existing lien on the premises; after its lien has been lost by lapse of time, he has no longer a right to redeem.[42] And the wife of the mortgagor (provided she has not joined with him in conveying away the equity of redemption) has a right of redemption, in virtue of her actual or possible rights of dower and homestead.[43] But this rule does not apply to a mortgage on the land made by the mortgagor before his marriage.[44] The widow of a deceased mortgagor, by right of her dower estate, has the privilege of redeeming from the mortgage and can compel contribution from the heirs,[45] and if she pays the debt, and takes a deed to herself, the mortgagor's heirs may redeem.[46] Generally speaking, and without particular reference to the rights of a dowress, the heirs of a deceased mortgagor are entitled to redeem, if the equity of redemption remained in the mortgagor at the time of his death, that is, if he had not sold or assigned it and did not devise it.[47] If he devised it by his will, then, upon his death, the devisee is the proper person to effect the redemption.[48] And it is said that a legatee of the mortgagor, whose legacy is made a charge on the estate, has also such an interest as will entitle him to redeem.[49]

A mortgagee, who is also a creditor of the mortgagor under another and separate claim, may, on the allowance of his claim

---

[40] Miller v. Cook, 135 Ill. 190, 25 N. E. Rep. 756.

[41] Lamb v. Richards, 43 Ill. 312; Grob v. Cushman, 45 Ill. 119; Fitch v. Wetherbee, 110 Ill. 475.

[42] Ewing v. Ainsworth, 53 Ill. 464.

[43] Whitcomb v. Sutherland, 18 Ill. 578; Sanford v. Kane, 24 Ill. App. 504. The latter case was reversed in 127 Ill. 591, 20 N. E. Rep. 810, but solely on the ground

of a want of jurisdiction in the appellate court.

[44] Burson v. Dow, 65 Ill. 146.

[45] Supra, § 239.

[46] Hunter v. Dennis, 112 Ill. 568.

[47] Hunter v. Dennis, 112 Ill. 568; Stover v. Bounds, 1 Ohio St. 108; Chew v. Hyman, 10 Biss. C. C. 240.

[48] Denton v. Nanney, 8 Barb. (N. Y.) 618; Stokes v. Solomans, 9 Hare, 75.

[49] Batcheller v. Middleton, 6 Hare, 75.

against the deceased mortgagor's estate, redeem the premises from his own foreclosure sale, the same as any other creditor.[50] Generally speaking, no one has any right to redeem from a mortgage unless he has an existing interest in the land; yet a tender of the redemption money is construed as the claim of such an interest, and if the mortgagee accepts and retains the money tendered, he cannot repudiate the claim.[51]

§ 323. Same; Junior Mortgages.—A junior incumbrancer, or holder of a second mortgage on the land, may redeem from the senior mortgage, although he is not bound to do so.[52] If the senior mortgage was foreclosed by suit, and the junior lienor was not made a party to the proceedings, he will have a right to redeem from the purchaser at the foreclosure sale, and as against any one else redeeming from the sale.[53] This right the junior mortgagee may also assign, by a sale and conveyance of all his interest in the mortgaged premises.[54] But though junior incumbrancers are not absolutely barred by foreclosure proceedings on the elder mortgage, to which they were not made parties, yet they cannot be permitted to assert their equity of redemption against an equity still stronger.[55] It is also held that the right of the successive holders of a series of notes, maturing at different times and all secured by the same mortgage, to redeem from a foreclosure and sale in favor of the holder of the note first maturing, is the same as that of separate junior incumbrancers to redeem from the foreclosure of a prior mortgage.[56]

Where, on the foreclosure of a senior mortgage, the mortgaged property is bid in by the senior mortgagee for less than the mortgage debt, a statutory redemption by a junior mortgagee gives the latter a first lien on the land, without regard to the balance still due on the senior mortgage; since, by the foreclosure, the lien of the elder mortgage is absolutely extinguished.[57] Still, if equity requires it, the junior mortgagee, effecting a redemption, may be regarded as subrogated to the

[50] Tewalt v. Irwin, 164 Ill. 592, 46 N. E. Rep. 13.

[51] Millard v. Truax, 50 Mich. 343, 15 N. W. Rep. 501.

[52] Rogers v. Herron, 92 Ill. 583; supra, § 174.

[53] Strang v. Allen, 44 Ill. 428; Hodgen v. Guttery, 58 Ill. 431.

[54] Roberts v. Fleming, 53 Ill. 196.

[55] Kenyon v. Schreck, 52 Ill. 382.

[56] Preston v. Hodgen, 50 Ill. 56.

[57] Seligman v. Laubheimer, 58 Ill. 124; Ogle v. Koerner, 140 Ill. 170, 29 N. E. Rep. 563.

rights of the senior mortgagee, and to that extent the lien of
the elder mortgage may be kept alive. Thus, if the second
mortgagee redeems from the sale on foreclosure of the first
mortgage, and afterwards forecloses under his own mortgage,
and buys in the property at the sale, a judgment creditor,
whose lien is junior to both mortgages, cannot redeem from
the sale under the second mortgage by paying the amount of
that mortgage alone; he must redeem from both mortgages.[58]
If the junior mortgagee is made a party to foreclosure proceedings on the senior mortgage, his rights will be adequately
protected by the decree in such proceedings. If, while the proceedings are pending, the senior mortgagee sells the property
under a power of sale contained in his mortgage, the junior
mortgagee may have relief against the sale on a cross-bill filed
for that purpose; but he must not omit to join as a party the
purchaser at the sale made by the senior mortgagee.[59] When
the senior mortgagee forecloses and sells and buys in the property, thereby acquiring the equity of redemption, the privilege
belongs to him, in turn, of redeeming the junior mortgage, by
paying to the holder the amount that is due to him.[60]

§ 324. Same; Volunteer.—In accordance with a well-settled
general principle, it is held that a mere volunteer has no right
or equity to redeem an estate from the lien of a mortgage.[61]
A stranger, not claiming any title to the premises, nor any lien
thereon or interest therein, and not acting as the agent of the
mortgagor, cannot successfully make any pretension to redeem
from the mortgage or from a sale on foreclosure thereof. If
he offers to do so, the mortgage creditor may with perfect
propriety decline to receive the money tendered. Yet the mere
act of redemption may be performed by one having no right
to redeem, as well as by one having that right, if the creditor
is willing to accept it. If the latter sees fit to accept the
amount of the debt, when offered to him by a stranger, this
will work an actual redemption and have the effect to divest
all rights acquired under the mortgage or the sale, and no
one else can question the validity of the redemption so
effected.[62]

[58] Flachs v. Kelly, 30 Ill. 462.
[59] Hurd v. Case, 32 Ill. 45.
[60] Smith v. Shay, 62 Iowa, 119,
17 N. W. Rep. 444.

[61] Beach v. Shaw, 57 Ill. 17; Rogers v. Meyers, 68 Ill. 92.
[62] Meyer v. Mintonye, 106 Ill.
414; Pearson v. Pearson, 131 Ill.

§ 325. Redemption by Stranger for Mortgagor's Benefit.—
An agreement to hold the title to property for the benefit of
one for whom it is redeemed from foreclosure sale is not within
the statute of frauds. A stranger may effect a redemption,
with the consent of the mortgagee or the foreclosure purchaser,
as stated in the preceding section. And if he does this as a
matter of favor or accommodation to the owner, advancing the
money necessary for the purpose, and taking the title to himself, a trust will result for the benefit of the owner, and though
the agreement rests in parol, it is not for that reason invalid.[63]
So, a contract by which the assignee of a certificate of purchase on foreclosure agrees to re-convey the property to the
mortgagor on repayment of the sum advanced by the assignee,
with interest, within a specified time, may be enforced in
equity, by bill for specific performance, upon the mortgagor's
compliance with the conditions, though the assignee has obtained a master's deed to the property.[64]

It is doubtful whether a stranger can make a valid tender
of the redemption money, when he acts in the interest and
behalf of the mortgagor, but without any agreement with the
latter, and without express authority from him. There may
be exceptional circumstances in which the courts would be
justified in holding a redemption to have been effected by such
a tender. For instance, if the person having the right of
redemption was insane, with no conservator, or an infant without a guardian, or absent from home, no one knowing where
to find him, there is some ground for holding that a third
person might tender the redemption money in his behalf,
agency and authority to act for him being presumed because
the very necessities of the case would warrant such an inference. These principles were discussed in an interesting case in
Michigan,[65] in which it appeared that the mortgagor of certain land had left his home and none of his relatives knew
where he was. The mortgage was foreclosed in his absence,

464, 28 N. E. Rep. 418; Smith v.
Jackson, 153 Ill. 399, 39 N. E. Rep.
130.

[63] O'Connor v. Mahoney, 159 Ill.
69, 42 N. E. Rep. 378.

[64] Joiner v. Duncan, 174 Ill. 252,
51 N. E. Rep. 323.

[65] Squire v. Wright, 85 Mich. 76,

48 N. W. Rep. 286. In the Roman
law, a transaction of this kind was
legally binding, and not of infre-
quent occurrence. Such unauthorized action on behalf of another
came under the description of
"negotiorum gestio." See Mack-
eldey, Roman Law, § 492 et seq.

and just before the expiration of the time for redemption, his father, who was his natural heir, made a deed of the land to another son, so that the latter might have an apparent right to redeem it. This son paid the amount of the redemption money to the register, stating that, if his brother was living, he made the redemption for his benefit, but if not, then for his own benefit. It was held that the redemption was valid and effectual.

§ 326. **Amount Required for Redemption.**—On redemption of a mortgage before foreclosure sale, the mortgagee is entitled to receive all that is actually due to him under the mortgage, or the obligations which it secured. This may not correspond with the face of the mortgage. If the amount really advanced to the mortgagor was less than the consideration stated in the mortgage, it is only the smaller sum which can be demanded on redemption.[66] And from the payment is to be deducted any portion of the debt which the mortgagee may have already realized on collateral securities.[67] Interest should be charged at the rate contracted for in the mortgage (not being usurious) up to the day when the money is paid to the mortgagee or brought into court and tendered.[68] The mortgagee is also entitled to receive, as part of the redemption money, all sums paid by him for the discharge of prior incumbrances for the protection of his own title,[69] and also sums advanced for the payment of taxes or assessments on the property.[70] And where the purchaser of land at foreclosure sale pays taxes which become a lien during the time allowed for redemption, and the property is redeemed, such taxes so paid,

[66] Walker v. Carleton, 97 Ill. 582.

[67] Hardin v. Eames, 5 Ill. App. 153.

[68] Joiner v. Enos, 23 Ill. App. 224. In a suit to redeem from a mortgage given to secure a debt evidenced by notes, which were destroyed when the mortgage was given, the mortgagee, after unsuccessfully resisting the suit on the ground that the mortgage was an absolute deed, is entitled to interest on his debt up to the destruction of the notes at the rate specified therein, and after that at only six per cent. Conant v. Riseborough, 139 Ill. 383, 28 N. E. Rep. 789, affirming 30 Ill. App. 498. Where the right to redeem from a trust deed is predicated upon a tender of certain bonds, the interest coupons attached to the bonds at the time of the tender which fall due between that date and the final decree must be delivered with the bonds, in order to keep the tender good. Sanders v. Peck, 131 Ill. 407, 25 N. E. Rep. 503.

[69] Harper v. Ely, 70 Ill. 581.

[70] Supra, § 229.

with interest, are by statute to be included in and paid as part
of the money required for redemption. This is for the reason
that the payment inures to the benefit of the mortgagor and
to the preservation of his estate.[71]

When the holder of the equity of redemption seeks to redeem
the property, under the statute, after the sale on foreclosure, he
must not only pay the sum for which the property was sold,
but the whole sum actually due on the mortgage if that be
greater.[72] But where a purchaser under a decree of foreclosure
bids more than the amount actually due on the decree and costs,
for the purpose of defrauding a judgment creditor having a
junior lien, the latter, upon showing the fraud, will be entitled
to redeem by paying the same sum as if the mortgaged premises had been sold for the amount of the decree with the
costs.[73]

As to allowance for improvements, it is said that one who
has acquired possession of mortgaged premises in the belief
that he holds the title under foreclosure proceedings, is entitled
to claim, upon redemption being made under the mortgage, the
value of improvements made by him.[74] At any rate, if the
holder of the equity of redemption (who acquired the same
from the original mortgagor, and who still has a right to redeem because he was not made a party to the foreclosure proceedings) stands by in silence and allows the purchaser at
foreclosure sale to expend his money and labor in making
improvements, in the belief that he has a good title, the holder
of the equity, thereafter undertaking to redeem, must pay for
the improvements, less amounts received by the purchaser in
the way of rents and profits.[75] But the person having the right
to redeem is not bound to pay for any improvements made by
the foreclosure purchaser after the filing of a bill to redeem.[76]
If a junior incumbrancer conceives that a decree, to which he
was not a party, foreclosing the senior mortgage, is too large,
he may allege that fact in his bill to redeem; and if a mistake
has occurred, it may thus be corrected.[77]

§ 327. Partial or Proportionate Redemption.—The general
rule is that a mortgagor, or one claiming under him, seeking

[71] Davis v. Dale, 150 Ill. 239, 37
N. E. Rep. 215, affirming Dale v.
Davis, 51 Ill. App. 328.

[72] Bradley v. Snyder, 14 Ill. 263.

[73] Grob v. Cushman, 45 Ill. 119.

[74] Poole v. Johnson, 62 Iowa,
611, 17 N. W. Rep. 900.

[75] Bradley v. Snyder, 14 Ill. 263.

[76] Smith v. Sinclair, 10 Ill. 108.

[77] Strang v. Allen, 44 Ill. 428.

to redeem the mortgaged premises, must redeem the whole
and pay the whole of the mortgage debt. He cannot require
the mortgagee to accept a partial payment and release a corresponding portion of the land. This rule is made for the benefit of the mortgagee, and the reason of it is that the latter
should not be compelled, to the detriment of his own interests,
or even where it would merely cause him inconvenience, to
apportion his claim and divide his security.[78] It follows also
that one who, since the execution of the mortgage, has become
the owner of a part of the mortgaged premises, whether by
purchase from the mortgagor or otherwise, cannot redeem the
part acquired by him by paying a proportion of the mortgage
debt. The mortgagee is entitled to retain his lien upon every
part of the mortgaged property until the whole of the mortgage
debt is paid. He will not be obliged in equity to release a
portion of the estate upon the payment of a proportionate part
of the incumbrance on the whole.[79] And the same rule applies
to one whose right of redemption is based on his having a lien
on a part of the premises; he must redeem the whole.[80] Where
two lots covered by the same mortgage are sold to different
persons, and thereafter the mortgage is foreclosed and the
property is sold en masse under the decree, a creditor by
judgment against one of such persons only, who makes redemption under the statute of both lots en masse, acquires title only
to the lot owned by his judgment debtor,[81] though, as to the
other, he may be subrogated to the rights of the foreclosure
purchaser. But if the mortgagee has extinguished the right
of redemption as to a part of the mortgaged premises, and has
become the absolute owner thereof, there may be a redemption of the other part; for in such a case the reason of the
rule no longer exists.[82]

It is entirely competent for the parties to agree that the
mortgage debt shall be apportioned, and a part of it made the
sole burden upon a part of the incumbered property; and in

[78] Union Mut. Life Ins. Co. v.
Kirchoff, 133 Ill. 368, 27 N. E. Rep.
91; Robinson v. Fife, 3 Ohio St.
551.

[79] Brown v. McKay, 151 Ill. 315,
37 N. E. Rep. 1037; Meacham v.
Steele, 93 Ill. 135; Coffin v. Parker,
127 N. Y. 117, 27 N. E. Rep. 814.

[80] O'Brien v. Kreuz, 36 Minn. 136,
30 N. W. Rep. 458.

[81] Huber v. Hess, 191 Ill. 305, 61
N. E. Rep. 61.

[82] Robinson v. Fife, 3 Ohio St.
551.

this case, a part of the property may be redeemed by the payment of that part of the debt apportioned to it. The doctrine which forbids partial redemptions "has no application whatever to a case where the mortgagor and mortgagee have entered into an agreement under which a redemption may be made. The mortgagee may by contract extend the period allowed by law for redemption, and a court of equity will enforce such an agreement; and we perceive no reason why the mortgagee may not accept money or land in satisfaction of a part of the mortgage debt, and enter into a valid agreement to give the mortgagor an extension of time to pay a specified sum of money to redeem a part of the premises. No reason is perceived why an agreement to apportion the mortgage debt may not be made and enforced as made."[83]

It is also a general rule that a joint tenant or co-tenant of the equity of redemption has no right to compel the mortgagee, or a purchaser of the property at the foreclosure sale, whose rights are the same as those of the mortgagee, to release such part of the mortgage title as is proportionate to his share in the equity of redemption on being paid a corresponding part of the mortgage debt. The mortgagee is not obliged to accept payment of anything less than the whole debt, nor is the purchaser at the foreclosure sale obliged to accept less than the whole of the purchase money, and become a co-tenant in the property with the redemptioner.[84] But in Illinois, it is provided by statute that "any joint owner, his executors, administrators, or assigns, or a decree or judgment creditor of such joint owner, may redeem the interest of such joint owner in the premises sold on execution or decree, in the manner and upon the conditions hereinbefore provided, upon the payment of his proportion of the amount which would be necessary to redeem the whole."[85] Thus, where a foreclosure is made after the death of the mortgagor, judgment creditors of the heirs of

---

[83] Union Mut. Life Ins. Co. v. Kirchoff, 133 Ill. 368, 27 N. E. Rep. 91, affirming Kirchoff v. Union Mut. Life Ins. Co., 33 Ill. App. 607.

[84] Paige v. Smith, 2 McCrary, 457, 5 Fed. Rep. 340; Buettel v. Harmount, 46 Minn. 481, 49 N. W. Rep. 250. Where partnership land has been sold under a power in a mortgage, one partner, after the dissolution of the firm, has the right to redeem the whole, after which his rights and those of the other partner in the land must be adjudicated in a separate action. Lehman v. Moore, 93 Ala. 186, 9 South. Rep. 590.

[85] Rev. Stat. Ill. c. 77, § 26.

the mortgagor may redeem, the creditor of any particular heir paying that proportion of the sum for which the land was sold which such heir's interest in the land bears to the whole.[86] And where land owned by two persons as tenants in common is sold on foreclosure of a mortgage given by them, a sale under a redemption made by a judgment creditor of one of them will pass the title of that one only.[87] But it will be noted that this statute applies only to the statutory right of redemption from a sale on foreclosure. As to the right of redemption existing at common law or in equity, before a foreclosure, the general rule remains that a joint owner or co-tenant must redeem the whole.

§ 328. **Agreement to Extend Time for Redemption.**—A contract between the parties to a mortgage, extending the time for the redemption of the property sold on foreclosure, beyond the time limited by the statute, is valid and will be enforced in equity, and a redemption allowed, within the time designated in the contract.[88] The statutory right of redemption after sale being a mere option to redeem or not on the part of the owner, it appears that, if a further consideration passes for an extension of that option for a longer period, it is a valid contract without any absolute agreement or promise that the owner will redeem within the extended time.[89] Where the time within which the mortgagor himself has a legal right to redeem has already expired, but not the time within which his judgment creditors may redeem, and some of them are willing to do so, it is held that there is a sufficient consideration for an agreement to extend the time of redemption in the mortgagor's

[86] Schuck v. Gerlach, 101 Ill. 338. And the holder of a judgment against the original mortgagor may redeem and subject to his claim three-fifths of the land, after creditors of the mortgagor's heirs have acted similarly with regard to two-fifths thereof, the time limited for such redemption not having expired. Id.

[87] Fischer v. Eslaman, 68 Ill. 78.

[88] Schoonhoven v. Pratt, 25 Ill. 457; Pensoneau v. Pulliam, 47 Ill. 58; Davis v. Dresback, 81 Ill. 393. An oral promise by the president of a corporation holding a trust deed that the debtor shall have time, after foreclosure, to pay the debt thereby secured, if acted on by the debtor, renders the corporation, on thus acquiring the legal title for much less than its value, a trustee holding the title as a mortgagee for payment of the debt; and the debtor may yet redeem by paying the sum due with expenses. Union Mut. Life Ins. Co. v. White, 106 Ill. 67.

[89] Honnihan v. Friedman, 13 Ill. App. 226.

promise to pay the amount necessary for a legal redemption by a judgment creditor.[90] It is also competent for the purchaser at the foreclosure sale, or an assignee of the certificate of purchase, to agree with the mortgagor to allow him a longer time for the redemption of the property than the statutory period; and if the holder of the certificate of purchase afterwards repudiates his contract, and applies for a deed, the mortgagor may maintain a bill in equity to enforce his right of redemption.[91] But such a bill is not sustained by proof that, after the sale, the purchaser offered to resell the property to the mortgagor at a price which the latter refused to give.[92] It is also to be noted that where property has been sold under a mortgage, and the mortgagor has also sold and conveyed the equity of redemption, and the grantee of the equity applies to the holder of the certificate of purchase at the sale for leave to redeem the property, after the expiration of the statutory time for such redemption, and the holder of the certificate, as a matter of favor, and for the purpose of allowing a redemption and for no other purpose, accepts the money due on the certificate, and indorses and delivers the same to the owner of the equity of redemption, this is a redemption, and not an assignment or sale, and the certificate is null and void, and cannot be used as the basis of a title.[93]

§ 329. **Redemption After Foreclosure Sale.**—It is provided by statute in Illinois that "any defendant, his heirs, administrators, or assigns, or any person interested in the premises, through or under the defendant, may, within twelve months from said sale [i. e., any judicial sale of realty, including the sale on foreclosure of a mortgage] redeem the real estate so sold, by paying to the purchaser thereof, his executors, administrators, or assigns, or to the sheriff or master in chancery or other officer who sold the same, or his successor in office, for the benefit of such purchaser, his executors, administrators, or assigns, the sum of money for which the premises were sold or bid off, with interest thereon at the rate of six per cent. per annum from the time of such sale, whereupon such sale and certificate shall be null and void."[94] The effect of this section

[90] Chytraus v. Smith, 141 Ill. 231, 30 N. E. Rep. 450.

[91] Taylor v. Dillenburg, 168 Ill. 235, 48 N. E. Rep. 41.

[92] Ryan v. Sanford, 133 Ill. 291, 24 N. E. Rep. 428.

[93] Frederick v. Ewrig, 82 Ill. 363.

[94] Rev. Stat. Ill. c. 77, § 18.

of the statute is that, "in all cases of the sale of mortgaged
lands, under a decree in equity, the same right of redemption
is given as in cases of the sale of lands under an execution at
law. This section was intended to, and does, prohibit sales of
mortgaged lands, under a decree of foreclosure, without redemption."[95] Prior to 1843, when the law was enacted, the
property was sold without redemption, or a strict foreclosure
was had. But under the statute, the right of redemption must
in all cases be allowed; and the decree of foreclosure requires
the master to give to the purchaser a certificate of purchase,
to hold during the time allowed for redemption, and usually
requires him to execute a deed if the property is not redeemed.[96] In proper cases, a strict foreclosure may still be
decreed, that is, a foreclosure which vests the mortgaged property in the mortgagee without any sale. But if the decree
orders a sale of the premises, then the statutory right of
redemption must always be allowed; the court could not rightfully ignore or cut off this privilege; and it makes no difference whether the security under which the sale is ordered
is a mortgage or a deed of trust.[97] But when the twelve
months allowed to the mortgagor by the statute have expired
without redemption, or without any agreement for an extension of time, then all his rights and equities in the property
are absolutely lost and gone, and he has no interest in a subsequent redemption by a judgment creditor.[98]

The statute giving this right of redemption, not only to the
mortgagor and his heirs and personal representatives, but also
to any person who is interested in the premises through or
under the mortgagor, it will clearly include a purchaser of
the equity of redemption from the mortgagor,[1] as well as the
heirs, devisees, or assignees of such purchaser.[2] In regard to

[95] Farrell v. Parlier, 50 Ill. 274.

[96] Walker v. Schum, 42 Ill. 462.

[97] Levy v. Burkle (Cal.), 14 Pac.
Rep. 564. A decree ordering an
absolute deed to be made to the
purchaser twelve months after the
sale, is bad, since the statute allows judgment creditors fifteen
months in which to redeem.
Rhinehart v. Stevenson, 23 Ill. 524.

[98] Bozarth v. Largent, 128 Ill. 95,
21 N. E. Rep. 218.

[1] A purchaser of the equity of redemption, who is made a party to
the proceedings on foreclosure,
will not be allowed a longer period
in which to redeem than the
twelve months prescribed for the
mortgagor; he will not have the
longer time allowed to a judgment creditor. Dunn v. Rodgers,
43 Ill. 260.

[2] Chew v. Hyman, 10 Biss. C. C.
240, 7 Fed. Rep. 7.

the right of a junior mortgagee, it has been held in another state, under a similar statute, and with excellent reason, that the equity of redemption of a junior incumbrancer is independent of the statutory right to redeem from the foreclosure sale; and that if the junior mortgagee was not made a party to the proceedings for foreclosure, he may still redeem, after the sale, standing on his equitable rights, and without regard to the expiration of the time limited by the statute for redemption.[8]

§ 330. Same; In the Federal Courts.—The laws of the state in which land is situated control exclusively its descent, alienation, and transfer from one person to another, and the effect and construction of instruments intended to convey it. All such laws in existence at the time when a contract in regard to real estate is made, including the contract of mortgage, enter into and become a part of such contract. Hence a state statute (like that of Illinois) which allows to a mortgagor a limited period within which to redeem after a sale of the premises on foreclosure of the mortgage, and a certain time thereafter for redemption by his judgment creditors, governs to that extent the mode of transferring the title, and confers a substantial right, and thereby becomes a rule of property. It follows that

*

[8] Spurgin v. Adamson, 62 Iowa, 661, 18 N. W. Rep. 293. In this case it was said: "Defendants insist that the equitable right of redemption is merged in the statutory right, and limited as to the time of its exercise by the provisions of the statute. There is nothing to be found in the statute taking away the equity of redemption and substituting therefor the statutory redemption. Code § 3321 provides that sales of land under foreclosure of mortgages are subject to redemption as in cases of sales upon general executions. Under this statute, an incumbrancer, or one holding an interest in the land, which, under the statute, would give him the right to redeem, may exercise that right within the time prescribed by the statute, although he was a party to the foreclosure action and his equity of redemption was cut off by the decree of foreclosure. The equity of redemption ceases to exist after the expiration of the time fixed by the decree of foreclosure or the rules of chancery applicable thereto. The statute, under our view, confers a right upon the junior incumbrancer not given by chancery. By its terms it does not limit the right of redemption before existing under the rules of equity. That right is therefore not taken away by it. It was not the purpose of the statute, in conferring this right of redemption, to take away another and different right recognized by equity. The equity of redemption exists independent of statute, and will be enforced by the court of chancery until it is taken away by express legislative enactment."

this right of redemption after sale is obligatory on the courts of the United States sitting in equity, as it is on the courts of the state; and if proceedings to foreclose a mortgage upon lands within the state are taken in a federal court, that court must permit a redemption to be made in accordance with the provisions of the state statute.[4] Whether or not provision is made for it in the decree of foreclosure rendered by the federal court, the defendant will still have the right to redeem from the sale at any time within the period allowed by the state statute.[5] This right cannot be cut off by a clause in the decree forever barring the right of redemption.[6] But after the decree has been entered, an objection that it does not give the time allowed for redemption by the statutes of the state cannot be urged by creditors of the mortgagor except in connection with an offer to redeem.[7]

§ 331. Same; By Judgment Creditor.—The statute of Illinois provides that if redemption from a mortgage foreclosure sale is not made by the debtor, or other persons primarily entitled, within twelve months after the sale, "any decree or judgment creditor, his executors, administrators, or assigns, may, after the expiration of twelve months and within fifteen months after the sale, redeem the premises in the following manner: Such creditor, his executors, administrators, or assigns, may sue out an execution upon his judgment or decree, and place the same in the hands of the sheriff or other proper officer to execute the same, who shall endorse upon the back thereof a levy on the premises desired to be redeemed, and the person desiring to make such redemption shall pay to such officer the amount for which the premises to be redeemed were sold, with interest thereon at the rate of six per cent. per annum from the date of the sale, for the use of the purchaser of such premises, his executors, administrators, or assigns,

---

[4] Brine v. Hartford Fire Ins. Co., 96 U. S. 627; Orvis v. Powell, 98 U. S. 176; Swift v. Smith, 102 U. S. 442; Mason v. Northwestern Mut. Life Ins. Co., 106 U. S. 164; Parker v. Dacres, 130 U. S. 43; Blair v. Chicago & Pac. R. Co., 12 Fed. Rep. 750; Singer Mfg. Co. v. McCollock, 24 Fed. Rep. 667; Jackson & Sharp Co. v. Burlington & L. R. Co., 29 Fed. Rep. 474. And see, infra, § 492.

[5] Burley v. Flint, 9 Biss. C. C. 204, Fed. Cas. No. 2, 168.

[6] Mason v. Northwestern Mut. Life Ins. Co., 106 U. S. 163.

[7] Hards v. Connecticut Mut. Life Ins. Co., 8 Biss. C. C. 234, Fed. Cas. No. 6,055.

whereupon such officer shall make and file in the office of the recorder of the county in which the premises are situated a certificate of such redemption, and shall advertise and offer the premises for sale under said execution as in other cases of sale on execution.'' At the sale thereon, the redeeming creditor shall be considered as having bid the amount of the redemption money paid by him, with interest, and if no greater amount is bid, the premises shall be struck off to such creditor, and the officer shall forthwith convey the premises to him by deed, and no other redemption shall be allowed. If more than the amount of the redemption money is bid, the excess shall be applied on the execution under which the redemption was made; and a certificate shall be given to the new purchaser, entitling him to a deed in sixty days, unless the premises are. redeemed by some other judgment creditor. Where there are several judgment creditors, the one having the oldest judgment shall have the preferential right to redeem during the first two days after the expiration of the twelve months, and then the other creditors in their order, each having the preference for two days. If two judgments are of the same date, the creditor first paying the redemption money has the preference.[8]

The benefits of this statute can be claimed only by creditors holding judgments or decrees original in courts of record.[9] But to entitle such a judgment creditor to redeem, it is not necessary that his judgment should be a lien on the land sold; though such land be the debtor's homestead, for instance, and therefore free from the lien of the judgment, this will not affect the creditor's right to redeem.[10] But the judgment must be alive, and so far active as that the creditor is still entitled to take out an execution upon it.[11] Nevertheless, as we stated in an earlier section, the person entitled to receive the redemption money is at perfect liberty, if he chooses, to accept a tender of it when made by a person who has no right at all to redeem.[12] And although the offer is made by a judgment

---

[8] Rev. Stat. Ill. c. 77, §§ 20-24.

[9] Thornley v. Moore, 106 Ill. 496. The owner of the equity of redemption may confess judgment for the express purpose of enabling the judgment creditor to redeem, provided there is a bona fide existing indebtedness from him to such creditor. Strauss v. Tuckhorn, 200 Ill. 75.

[10] Schroeder v. Bauer, 41 Ill. App. 484.

[11] See Albee v. Curtis, 77 Iowa, 644, 42 N. W. Rep. 508.

[12] Supra, § 324.

creditor whose execution is void, and who has no right to levy and sell under the same, still if the money is accepted and the redemption acted upon as valid by the mortgagee or foreclosure purchaser, the foreclosure sale will be annulled and the rights of the parties will be the same as if the redemption had been properly made.[13] In any case, however, the taking out of an execution is a prerequisite to the creditor's right to redeem. Whether his judgment was recovered in the lifetime of the debtor or arose by allowance against his estate after his death, it is essential, if the creditor desires to redeem from a foreclosure sale, that he should take out execution on .the judgment. The special execution provided by statute, to enable owners of claims allowed against the estates of decedents to redeem lands sold at judicial sale, must be taken out within seven years from the time such claims are allowed; if issued after that time, the execution is void.[14] This statutory right of redemption in judgment creditors cannot be taken away by the decree of foreclosure. It is important to join them as parties in the foreclosure proceedings, in order to cut off their common-law right of redemption; but this does not affect the privilege given to them by the statute. "Where a party files a bill to foreclose a mortgage, and there are judgment creditors who have liens against the mortgaged premises subsequent to the mortgage, the judgment creditors are necessary parties to the bill to foreclose; but it has never been understood, because they may be made parties defendant to a bill to foreclose the mortgage, they lose their right to redeem as judgment creditors."[15]

As to the time within which the redemption by a judgment creditor may be made, it is to be observed that the additional three months, after the debtor's year for redemption, are given to them only in the capacity of judgment creditors. Hence, if such a creditor sells the land on execution, and buys it in, and takes a sheriff's deed, thereby acquiring the debtor's equity of redemption, he must redeem from the foreclosure sale in the character of an owner, and therefore within the twelve months. If he fails to do this, other judgment creditors will have the

---

[13] Clingman v. Hopkie, 78 Ill. 152.

[14] McIlwain v. Karstens, 152 Ill. 135, 38 N. E. Rep. 555.

[15] Boynton v. Peirce, 151 Ill. 197, 37 N. E. Rep. 1024; People v. Bowman, 181 Ill. 421, 55 N. E. Rep. 148.

right to redeem within the ensuing three months.[16] But when
the right to redeem in the character of a judgment creditor has
accrued and become fixed by the expiration of the first twelve
months, it makes no difference that the creditor thereafter obtains a deed of the premises from the mortgagor.[17] Where the
foreclosure and sale were in favor of a senior mortgagee, the
junior mortgagee will have the right to redeem from that sale
at any time within twelve months. But if the junior mortgagee has obtained a personal judgment or decree for the debt
secured by his mortgage, and a sale of the mortgaged premises, he will have the right to redeem from the sale under the
elder mortgage after the expiration of the twelve months
and within the next three months, as a judgment creditor.[18]

When a judgment creditor redeems in good faith and before
the expiration of the statutory period, he succeeds to all the
rights of the purchaser under the foreclosure sale.[19] Hence
a junior mortgagee, who is made a party to a suit to foreclose
the senior mortgage, and who afterwards purchases the certificate of sale issued in such proceedings, cannot assert the
lien of his junior mortgage as against a judgment creditor who
redeems from the sale after the junior mortgagee's time for
redemption has expired.[20] For the same reason, where the
sale was made on foreclosure of a mortgage which duly released the homestead estate, and the mortgagor does not redeem within the time allowed him, a judgment creditor who
afterwards redeems and buys in the property at the execution
sale under his judgment, takes the title free from the estate
of homestead.[21] In one of the cases dealing with this statutory right of redemption, it appeared that the mortgage, when
made, covered only a wife's separate property, but her husband joined in the mortgage, and, before foreclosure, acquired
a life estate in the premises as tenant by the curtesy, in consequence of the death of the wife leaving issue. It was held
that this estate inured to the benefit of the mortgagee, under
the covenants of the mortgage, and passed on sale under fore-

[16] McRoberts v. Conover, 71 Ill.
524.
[17] People v. Bowman, 181 Ill.
421, 55 N. E. Rep. 148.
[18] Whitehead v. Hall, 148 Ill. 253,
35 N. E. Rep. 871.
[19] Lamb v. Richards, 43 Ill. 312.

[20] Schroeder v. Bauer, 140 Ill.
135, 29 N. E. Rep. 560.
[21] Herdman v. Cooper, 138 Ill.
583, 28 N. E. Rep. 1094; Smith v.
Mace, 137 Ill. 68, 26 N. E. Rep.
1092.

closure so as to entitle a subsequent judgment creditor of the husband to redeem.[22]

When the premises are struck off to the redeeming creditor at the sale on his execution, no one bidding a greater amount than the redemption money paid by him, the provision of the statute requiring the officer making the sale to convey the property to him by deed "forthwith" is only directory; and the failure of the officer to make the deed immediately after the sale will not render the redemption and sale invalid.[23]

§ 332. Same; Railroad Mortgages.—Where proceedings are taken for the foreclosure of a mortgage given by a railroad company, which covers its franchises, as well as its property, both real and personal, the sale on foreclosure may be ordered to be made without any right of redemption; and this, notwithstanding the statute providing for redemptions from judicial sales, including mortgage foreclosure sales. For the statute cannot be deemed to apply to a case where the mortgage covers personal property as well as real estate. To the former it has no application. And the effect of applying it to such railroad mortgages would be to compel a separate sale of the franchise, the personalty, and the realty, whereby the value of each might be lost,—a result which the legislature cannot be presumed to have intended.[24] This is also the doctrine of the federal courts in Illinois.[25]

§ 333. Same; Mode of Effecting Redemption.—A person to whom the statute gives the privilege of redeeming from a mortgage foreclosure sale has an absolute right to effect such a redemption, of which he cannot be deprived against his will. Nor is it necessary that any person should consent to the redemption or accept the money tendered. If the redemption is made by a judgment creditor, he is to pay the redemption money to the sheriff holding his execution; if by the mortgagor or any one claiming under him, the money may be paid either to the foreclosure purchaser or to the officer who made the sale. The refusal of the foreclosure purchaser to accept the money or consent to the redemption does not affect the

[22] Bozarth v. Largent, 128 Ill. 95, 21 N. E. Rep. 218.

[23] Idem.

[24] Peoria & Springfield R. Co. v. Thompson, 103 Ill. 187.

[25] Hammock v. Farmers' Loan & Trust Co., 105 U. S. 77; Turner v. Indianapolis, B. & W. Ry. Co., 8 Biss. C. C. 380.

rights of the redemptioner. He may then deposit the proper amount with the officer, and when he has done so, the redemption is effected, provided such deposit is made within the time limited by the statute.[26] If the sheriff or other officer refuses to receive the money when tendered to him for the purpose of a redemption, it is thought that this will not cancel the lien of the foreclosure purchaser. In such a case, the sheriff is not the agent of either party, and the rights of the foreclosure purchaser can neither be waived nor prejudiced by his acts. The only office of such a tender and refusal is to preserve and protect the right of the redemptioner (if seasonably and properly asserted) to have the redemption perfected by application to the holder of the certificate of purchase, or by proceedings against the sheriff to compel him to perform his official duty.[27] On the other hand, if the money paid to the sheriff is accepted from him by the foreclosure purchaser, under the mistaken belief that the person attempting to redeem had the right to do so, such purchaser may save his rights by returning the money immediately on discovering his mistake. When this is done, the mere handling of the money by the purchaser will not work an equitable assignment of the certificate of purchase, even in the case of a grantee of the person who attempted to redeem, provided such grantee had notice, actual or constructive, of the grantor's want of legal right to redeem.[28]

The payment by the redemptioner should of course be made in money; but it is said that a redemption made by means of a bank check drawn by a responsible party upon a solvent bank, and accepted by the officer as money, is not invalid for that reason if the money is promptly realized thereon, and ready for the proper party when required, and within the time allowed by statute.[29]

When a redemption is effected in accordance with the provisions of the statute, "it shall be the duty of the purchaser, sheriff, master in chancery, or other officer or person from whom said redemption takes place, to make out an instrument in writing, under his hand and seal, evidencing such redemption, which shall be recorded in the recorder's office of the

[26] Traeger v. Mutual Building & Loan Ass'n, 63 Ill. App. 286.

[27] Schroeder v. Lahrman, 28 Minn. 75, 9 N. W. Rep. 173.

[28] Byer v. Healey (Iowa), 50 N. W. Rep. 70.

[29] Sardeson v. Menage, 41 Minn. 314, 43 N. W. Rep. 66.

proper county, in like manner as other writings affecting the title to real estate are filed and recorded, which recording shall be paid for by the party redeeming."[30] An officer's certificate of redemption under this provision is not so far conclusive upon the redemptioner that he may not contradict it when necessary to show that his redemption was valid and effectual. He will be at liberty to prove that he paid the full amount of the redemption money within the time fixed by the statute for the making of a valid redemption, though the certificate may recite a different state of facts, either as to the time or the amount paid.[31]

§ 334. Same; Paying Redemption Money to Clerk of U. S. Court.—While the local statute law giving the right of redemption from foreclosure sales, first to the mortgagor and then to his judgment creditors, is a rule of property and obligatory on the federal courts sitting within the state, yet it is competent for those courts, by rule, to prescribe the mode in which redemption from sales under their own decrees may be effected. And although the state statute requires the redemptioner to pay the money to the officer who made the sale or who holds the execution, yet the federal court may make a rule requiring such payment to be made to the clerk of the court; for such a rule comes within the domain of practice, and does not affect the substantial right to redeem within the time fixed by the local statute.[32] Also a rule of the federal court requiring the party redeeming to pay a commission of one per cent. to the clerk, on the amount paid into court for the redemption of the property, in addition to the amount going to the purchaser, is in accordance with U. S. Rev. Stat. § 828, and is not in derogation of the right of redemption given by the state law. That right must be permitted in the federal court subject to the Act of Congress fixing the amount to be paid to the clerk on all moneys received, kept, and paid out by him in pursuance of any statute or under any order of court.[33]

§ 335. Suit in Equity to Redeem.—Where the privilege of redeeming from a mortgage, claimed by the mortgagor, is

[30] Rev. Stat. Ill. c. 77, § 19.
[31] Paige v. Smith, 2 McCrary, 457, 5 Fed. Rep. 340.
[32] Connecticut Mut. Life Ins. Co. v. Cushman, 108 U. S. 51; Connecticut Mut. Life Ins. Co. v. Crawford, 21 Fed. Rep. 281.
[33] Blair v. Chicago & P. R. Co., 12 Fed. Rep. 750; Connecticut Mut. Life Ins. Co. v. Crawford, 21 Fed. Rep. 281.

unlawfully denied by the mortgagee, the latter may be compelled to do justice, by means of a bill in equity. For instance, where the security took the form of an absolute deed, defeasible upon conditions which have been performed by the grantor, or which he is ready to perform, but the grantee repudiates the agreement and claims to be the absolute owner of the property; or where proceedings for the foreclosure of the mortgage have been taken, but were invalid and ineffective as against the party seeking to redeem; or where the owner of the mortgage refuses to abide by a contract which he made, by which the debtor was to have an extension of the time for paying the mortgage debt;—in such cases, and similar cases, a court of equity will entertain a bill for redemption.[34] A bill to redeem mortgaged lands, after foreclosure of the mortgage, will also lie at the suit of one holding a certificate of purchase under an execution sale, who was not made a party to the foreclosure proceedings; and it need not be brought in the court in which the decree foreclosing the mortgage was rendered.[35]

Where a complainant files his bill in equity to redeem from a mortgage, and states in the bill that he is the owner of the equity of redemption, and alleges the existence and terms of the mortgage, these facts are all that are required to give him a prima facie right to redeem. He is not required to offer to pay the money due before filing his bill, nor to make any allegation of such an offer. Nor need he offer in and by his bill to pay the amount due on the mortgage. He may entitle himself to costs and to a suspension of interest by a proper tender of the amount due before the commencement of the suit; and under such circumstances, to show his right to relief in those respects, the allegation of an offer to pay the money due before filing the bill would be a material one, but not otherwise.[36]

[34] See Sanders v. Peck, 131 Ill. 407, 25 N. E. Rep. 508; Stinson v. Pepper, 10 Biss. C. C. 107, 47 Fed. Rep. 676; Adair v. Adair, 22 Oreg. 115, 29 Pac. Rep. 193; Taylor v. Dillenburg, 168 Ill. 235, 48 N. E. Rep. 41. In Ware v. Cratty, 66 Ill. 197, a bill by a mortgagor to open a decree of foreclosure and charge the mortgagee with rents and profits, and offering to pay any deficiency necessary to redeem, was dismissed for want of equity, in seeking to treat the debt as still subsisting.

[35] Grob v. Cushman, 45 Ill. 119.

[36] Barnard v. Cushman, 35 Ill. 451; Dwen v. Blake, 44 Ill. 135; Taylor v. Dillenburg, 168 Ill. 235, 48 N. E. Rep. 41.

All the mortgagees or assignees of the mortgage, in whom the legal title is vested, are necessary parties to a bill in equity to redeem from it.[37] And a purchaser of the mortgaged premises from the mortgagee, pending a suit to redeem, will hold subject to the equities of the parties seeking the redemption.[38] But a mortgagor who has transferred his entire interest in the mortgaged property to the complainant is not a necessary or proper party to the bill to redeem.[39]

§ 336. **Same; Decree; Terms; Costs.**—On a bill in equity to redeem from a mortgage, when the court finds in favor of the complainant, the proper decree to be entered is one allowing him to redeem the mortgaged premises upon the payment of the amount found to be due, within a reasonable time to be fixed by the decree, together with the costs if they are charged against the complainant, and directing the defendant to discharge the mortgage on the payment of the money, or, in default of such payment, that the bill be dismissed; it is not necessary or proper to order a sale of the property on the failure of the complainant to comply with the terms of the decree; the dismissal of his bill is a sufficient provision for that contingency.[40] The decree should state the precise amount found to be due to the defendant, so as to leave nothing to computation.[41] But a decree which declares that, upon redemption being made, the mortgagor shall hold the premises discharged from the mortgage, and free from all right, title, and estate under the mortgagee, gives no additional rights to the mortgagor, as against tenants of the mortgagee, which he would not otherwise have upon redemption.[42] As to the time to be allowed to the mortgagor to make the payment ordered by the decree, it is said that "the time within which the redemption is to take place rests within the sound discretion of the court, in view of all the circumstances; but the time which seems to have been usually adopted by the courts is six months."[43] But this is not an invariable rule. The matter

[37] Essley v. Sloan, 16 Ill. App. 63.

[38] Roberts v. Fleming, 53 Ill. 196.

[39] Thomas v. Jones, 84 Ala. 302, 4 South. Rep. 270.

[40] Decker v. Patton, 120 Ill. 464, 11 N. E. Rep. 897 (affirming 20 Ill. App. 210); Massachusetts Mut. Life Ins. Co. v. Boggs, 121 Ill. 119, 13 N. E. Rep. 550; Chicago & Calu-met Rolling-Mill Co. v. Scully, 141 Ill. 408, 30 N. E. Rep. 1062 (affirming 43 Ill. App. 622). Compare Hollingsworth v. Koon, 117 Ill. 511, 6 N. E. Rep. 148.

[41] Stevens v. Coffeen, 39 Ill. 148.

[42] Holt v. Rees, 46 Ill. 181.

[43] Decker v. Patton, 20 Ill. App. 210.

depends a good deal upon the amount of the payment, and some other circumstances. In one case, where the amount to be paid was over $6,000, and the court, on according the mortgagor the right to redeem, allowed him only thirty days in which to do it, it was held that this was an unreasonably short time, and that ninety days should be allowed.[44]

The suit being in equity, to enforce an equitable right, it is within the power of the court to impose such terms upon both the parties as may be necessary to accomplish a perfectly just result. There may be circumstances in which the mortgagee should be allowed the cost of valuable improvements put upon the land by him before the filing of the bill, and also it may be proper to charge him with the rents and profits received from the premises, or which might have been received by reasonable effort and proper management of the property.[45] Again, the complainant may be required to do equity by paying any prior mortgage debt on the premises before he can obtain relief. As pointed out in the case cited, the equity of redemption established by the courts is entirely different from the statutory right of redemption; in the enforcement of the one, the complainant must pay all that is equitably due, in the other he need only comply with the statute.[46]

Ordinarily, upon a bill to redeem, the complainant does not recover costs, and most frequently he has to pay costs to the defendant, as a consequence of the wrong position in which he has put himself by breach of the condition of the mortgage. But if the mortgagor is forced to a suit for redemption, in consequence of the mortgagee's denying his right to redeem, he is entitled to costs in case of victory.[47] And also it is said that, where other relief is sought in the bill, such as to establish the complainant's right to rents and profits, and to have them set off against the amount due on the mortgage, he will be treated with more leniency than in the ordinary case.[48]

[44] Taylor v. Dillenburg, 168 Ill. 235, 48 N. E. Rep. 41.

[45] Roberts v. Fleming, 53 Ill. 196.

[46] Ogle v. Koerner, 41 Ill. App. 452.

[47] Mowry v. First Nat. Bank, 66 Wis. 539, 29 N. W. Rep. 559.

[48] McConnel v. Holobush, 11 Ill. 61. And see Sanders v. Peck, 131 Ill. 407, 25 N. E. Rep. 508.

CHAPTER XXVI.

CONTRIBUTION TO REDEMPTION.

§ 337. **General Doctrine of Contribution.**—Contribution is the doctrine of equity which provides for the ratable reimbursement of a person who has paid off an incumbrance which was chargeable, not alone upon his own estate, but upon the estates of other persons jointly and equally with his own. In such case, he is entitled to require from each of such other persons a contribution of his proportionate share of the total expense. This right he may enforce by bill in equity. And he may hold the whole estate thus freed from incumbrance subject to his lien for reimbursement and until he is paid. In relation to mortgages, the rule assumes the following form: Where a mortgage is a lien upon several estates held by different persons, and one of these persons pays off the whole incumbrance, thus redeeming all the estates, all the other persons must contribute to the cost, each in proportion to his interest, and the one who has paid the debt has the rights and remedies above mentioned to secure reimbursement.

§ 338. **As Between Joint Tenants.**—Where the title to land is held by several persons as joint tenants or tenants in common, and the property is incumbered by a mortgage, either given by the co-tenants as joint mortgagors or created by their common predecessor in title, and one of them pays the mortgage debt, or redeems from a sale on foreclosure of the mortgage, the others will be entitled to have the benefit of the payment or redemption, but they must contribute to the extent of their respective interests; and, to secure such contribution, an equitable lien upon their interests, of the same character as that which has been removed, will be enforced by a court of chancery. The tenant effecting the redemption, in order to secure contribution, is substituted to the same lien which he

404

has redeemed.[1] As remarked by a learned court in another state: "When several persons are interested in land which is incumbered by a mortgage, whether that interest be as owners of distinct parcels of the land, or as tenants in common of the whole, the mortgagee is not in general obliged to take notice of their separate and distinct interests, but on the non-payment of the mortgage money is entitled (unless perhaps under very peculiar circumstances) to a decree of foreclosure against all of them jointly. If the amount of the decree be not paid, the mortgagee takes the whole land, and the rights of the claimants to the equity are extinguished. None of the several owners of the equity is obliged to redeem; but each of them is at liberty to do so, for the protection of his own interest; and when one of several owners does so redeem, he becomes substituted, in equity, in the place of the mortgagee, and is entitled to hold the land as if the mortgage existed, until the other owners pay him their shares of the incumbrance, their shares being the pro rata value of their respective interests. The party redeeming becomes in effect the assignee of the mortgagee, for the purpose of enabling him to obtain the whole title to the land, if the other owners decline to contribute their respective shares towards the removal of the incumbrance."[2] In one of the cases, it appeared that the several tenants in common of the land claimed under a deed made by a minor. A mortgage on the property had been given by the minor's guardian to raise money for his ward's use, and this was paid off by one of the tenants. After the death of the minor, the deed was avoided by his heir, who thereupon sought a partition. It was held proper to require the heir to pay his proportion of the incumbrance, as a condition to relief, as well as his proportion of taxes and assessments paid by his co-tenants, and that the amount so payable should be decreed to be a lien on the land set off to such heir.[3]

It will be observed that the rule in question is made for the benefit of the tenant or joint owner who lifts the incumbrance, but is not a limitation upon the rights of the mortgagee. The latter is not to be hampered in the collection of his

[1] Titsworth v. Stout, 49 Ill. 78; Fischer v. Eslaman, 68 Ill. 78; Baird v. Jackson, 98 Ill. 78; Oliver v. Hedderly, 32 Minn. 455, 21 N. W. Rep. 478.

[2] Hubbard v. Ascutney Mill-Dam Co., 20 Vt. 402, 50 Am. Dec. 41.

[3] Illinois Land & Loan Co. v. Bonner, 91 Ill. 114.

debt by equities claimable as between the co-tenants. For example, where three persons, being tenants in common of land, make a joint and several obligation for the payment of money and secure the same by their joint mortgage on the land, and one of them pays to the mortgagee one-third of the amount due on the mortgage, and thereafter the mortgagee brings his bill to foreclose as to the remainder, the mortgagor who made the payment has no equity to compel the mortgagee to resort first to the undivided two-thirds interest of his co-tenants for satisfaction of the balance of the debt, but the mortgagee may proceed to subject the entire estate covered by the mortgage to its payment. The proper rule in such cases is to require payment from all or either of the mortgagors, according to their undertakings, and if, as between themselves, either is compelled to pay more than his equitable share, he may be subrogated to the rights of the mortgagee to enforce contribution from those jointly liable with him.[4] But this equitable right of contribution cannot be claimed, nor tho rights or titles of the co-tenants embarrassed by such a claim, until there has been an actual payment of the mortgage in whole or in part, or one tenant has been compelled to do or suffer something on account of it in excess of his ratable proportion of the burden.[5]

§ 339. **As Between Grantees of Different Parcels.**—Where different parcels of land, all covered by the same mortgage, are owned by different persons, not as co-tenants but in severalty, a similar rule of contribution applies. That is, if the owner of one lot pays the whole amount necessary to redeem from a foreclosure of the mortgage, he can compel the other owners to contribute their proportionate shares, in the absence of countervailing equities.[6] And if the owner of a piece of land, after placing a mortgage upon it, divides it into parcels, which he sells and conveys at different times to different purchasers, the parcels will be made to contribute to the redemption of the mortgage debt in the inverse order of their alienation, the parcel last sold being first chargeable to its full value, and this must be exhausted before recourse is had to the next in order.[7] This rule is based on the theory

[4] Schoenewald v. Dieden, 8 Ill. App. 389.

[5] In re Estate of Labauve, 39 La. Ann. 388, 1 South. Rep. 830.

[6] Coffin v. Parker, 127 N. Y. 117, 27 N. E. Rep. 814.

[7] Meacham v. Steele, 93 Ill. 135; Vogle v. Brown, 120 Ill. 338, 11 N.

that the equities of the several purchasers are equal, and
therefore the first in time is preferred. But, to entitle the
owner of one lot to contribution from the owner of another lot
for redemption from a mortgage·covering both properties, it
is essential that the equities of the parties should be equal,
since if there was any obligation resting upon the person who
made redemption to discharge the debt as his own, he can
claim nothing from the other, even though the latter is benefited by the redemption.[8] Thus, where mortgaged land was
sold in two parcels, and the purchaser of one agreed, in his
deed, to protect the grantor from the payment of the mortgage debt except as to the sum of $200, and that parcel was
sold on foreclosure of the mortgage, it was held that the
owner thereof could call upon the owner of the other parcel
for contribution only in the sum of $200, with interest from
the time of commencing the suit for contribution, not for a
proportionate share of the whole amount.[9] In another case,
the grantee of one of the two parcels of land covered by the
mortgage made a parol agreement with the grantor, at the
time of the conveyance, by which he retained a portion of
the purchase money with which to discharge the incumbrance,
and afterwards paid the mortgage debt. In his action against
the grantee of the other parcel, to recover the proportion which
equitably attached to the latter's land, it was held that there
could be no recovery, for the reason that the plaintiff had discharged the mortgage, not with his own money, but with the
funds of the common grantor, which he had retained out of
the purchase money for that purpose.[10]

§ 340. As Between Life-Tenant and Reversioner.—Where a
party holding an estate for life in lands devised pays off a
mortgage executed by the testator in his life-time, in order
to save the lands to himself and the owners of the reversion,
a court of equity has full power to compel the owners of the
reversion to pay a proportionate share of the amount so ex-

E. Rep. 327; Beard v. Fitzgerald,
105 Mass. 134; Hopkins v. Wolly,
81 N. Y. 77; supra, §§ 264, 265. In
Erlinger v. Boul, 7 Ill. App. 40, it
is held that the general rule does
not apply where the equity of redemption has been sold on execution, under a judgment other than
for the mortgage debt.

[8] Huber v. Hess, 191 Ill. 305, 61
N. E. Rep. 61.

[9] Moore v. Shurtleff, 128 Ill. 370,
21 N. E. Rep. 775.

[10] Pool v. Marshall, 48 Ill. 440.

pended.[11]   And since the reversioner has equally a right to redeem, it appears logical to accord to him also the right of contribution from the tenant for life. As we have seen in an earlier chapter,[12] if the widow of the mortgagor redeems from the mortgage, in order to save her dower, she can require the heirs to contribute; and conversely if the heirs redeem, the widow cannot have dower in the land except upon making just contribution.

§ 341. As Between Junior Mortgagees.—There is in general no contribution between junior mortgagees for the redemption of the property from the paramount lien. But the rule is otherwise where such redemption inures equally to the benefit of all creditors of the same class. Thus, it appeared that a trustee held property in trust for six creditors, who were all liable for such advances as might be necessary to remove prior incumbrances. Two of the creditors requested the trustee to sell the property at a sum sufficient to cover all advances then made by him, but he refused in consequence of the opposition of the other creditors, and it did not appear that there was any abuse of his discretion in the matter. It was held that this would not have the effect of releasing the two creditors from contribution for the advances made to remove incumbrances and protect the property.[13] In another case, it was ruled that a bill cannot be maintained in equity to enforce from innocent holders of first mortgage bonds of a railroad company, transferred to them by a construction company to secure a bona fide indebtedness, contribution to parties who purchased the right of way after the execution of the mortgage (which covered after-acquired property) for loss occasioned by breach of the construction company's contract to deliver to such parties first mortgage bonds sufficient to cover the expense of purchasing the right of way.[14]

[11] Boue v. Kelsey, 53 Ill. App. 295, citing Jones v. Gilbert, 135 Ill. 27.

[12] Supra, §§ 239, 240.

[13] Condict v. Flower, 106 Ill. 105.

[14] Frost v. Galesburg, E. & E. R. Co., 167 Ill. 161, 47 N. E. Rep. 357.

CHAPTER XXVII.

ACCOUNTING BY MORTGAGEE.

§ 342. Rights and Duties of Mortgagee in Possession.—
When the mortgagee of real property has obtained the possession of the same after breach of the condition of the mortgage, he will have the right to retain the possession until his
debt is fully paid.[1] But this does not make him the absolute
owner of the estate; that cannot be the case until the equity
of redemption is foreclosed. Consequently, the mortgagee in
possession holds the estate in the character of a trustee—
primarily for his own benefit, but also, in a measure, for the
benefit of the owner of the equity of redemption. "A mortgagee in possession is deemed by a court of equity a trustee,
but there is no other than a constructive trust, raised by implication, for the purpose of a remedy, to prevent injustice."[2]
First of all it is the duty of the mortgagee in this situation
to apply the rents and profits which he may receive from the
land in reduction of the mortgage debt. As his occupation is
not for any other purpose than to make his security effective,
the income of the property does not belong to him otherwise
than as it helps to pay the mortgage debt. It is also his duty
to manage the estate in the character of a prudent administrator; that is, with such a degree of care, diligence, and provi-
dence as may reasonably be expected from a careful and con-
scientious trustee. For instance, in regard to letting the property to tenants and the collection of the rents, the mortgagee's
responsibility will not be limited to the rents actually received
by him, if it is shown that a greater sum could have been realized by reasonable diligence; he will be answerable for any

[1] Harper v. Ely, 70 Ill. 581.   [2] Russell v. Southard, 12 How.
(U. S.) 139.

gross neglect or wilful default resulting in loss to the mortgagor.[3] Again, the mortgagee in possession cannot with impunity commit waste upon the premises. If, for instance, he cuts and removes timber which constituted a substantial part of the value of the property, he will be charged with the consequent loss to the owner of the equity.[4] But he is entitled to crops raised and harvested by him, during the period of his occupancy, at least if his operations have been conducted in accordance with good husbandry, and not to the injury of the soil.[5] It is also his duty to prevent dilapidation and keep the property in a state of proper and ordinary repair. He may recover all money expended by him for this purpose, and he is liable for all damages caused by his failure to maintain the premises in proper condition, without regard to the good faith with which he acted.[6] Moreover, the mortgagee in possession is bound to keep down the taxes on the property, so as to prevent its sacrifice by a tax sale; and to keep up insurance on the buildings, if his contract binds him so to do, though otherwise this is a measure which he may or may not take for his own protection. If the mortgagee sells the property to a purchaser who takes with notice of the mortgagor's right to redeem, the mortgagee should account for the purchase money, on redemption, with interest from the date of sale.[7] In a case where, by agreement with the mortgagor, the mortgagee sold the premises, taking the purchaser's promissory notes in payment, and refused to collect the last of the notes, which represented the surplus due to the mortgagor, it was held that equity would interfere in favor of the latter, although he might have a remedy at law.[8] But a prior mortgagee, under a mortgage upon an estate for a term of years, who takes possession under a purchase of the fee from the mortgagor, who had acquired the fee after he made the mortgage, is not to be regarded as a mortgagee in possession, and accountable as such for the rents and profits to a junior mortgagee of the same term, but as a purchaser.[9]

[3] Moshier v. Norton, 100 Ill. 63.

[4] See Perdue v. Brooks, 85 Ala. 459, 5 South. Rep. 126; Harrell v. Stapleton, 55 Ark. 1, 16 S. W. Rep. 474.

[5] Holton v. Bowman, 32 Minn. 191, 19 N. W. Rep. 734.

[6] Barnett v. Nelson, 54 Iowa, 41, 37 Am. Rep. 183, 6 N. W. Rep. 49.

[7] Union Mut. Life Ins. Co. v. Slee, 123 Ill. 57, 12 N. E. Rep. 543.

[8] Gillett v. Hickling, 16 Ill. App. 392.

[9] Rogers v. Herron, 92 Ill. 583.

§ 343. Principles of Accounting.—Upon redemption from a mortgagee in possession, it is proper and usual to take an account between the parties, for the purpose of ascertaining to what extent the income derived from the premises during the mortgagee's occupation of them exceeds the amount he has been obliged to expend upon the property, and applying the balance, if any, in reduction of the mortgage debt. It is not, however, an inseparable incident to a bill to redeem. The right to an account may be extinguished by a release or an accord and satisfaction, or it may be barred by such neglect of the mortgagor to assert his claim as would render it unfair for him to insist upon an account extending over the whole period of possession, and unjust towards the mortgagee to order such an account.[10]

When an account is taken, the mortgagee should be allowed credit for all that is due to him under the mortgage, whether as principal or interest, including all advances made by him to the mortgagor and intended to be covered by the mortgage, whether or not embraced in the written contract between the parties.[11] He must also be credited, as will appear from later sections of this chapter, with moneys expended by him in the payment of taxes on the property, and with the cost of keeping it in repair, and, in some cases, with the value of improvements put upon the estate. On the other hand, the income from the property is to be applied in defraying these necessary expenses, and then in the payment of current interest on the mortgage debt. And if, in any given year, there is a surplus of receipts above the interest and disbursements, the balance should be applied in reduction of the principal of the mortgage debt; and this, irrespective of whether or not there was interest in arrear when the mortgagee took possession.[12] If there is a surplus of receipts over disbursements, but not enough to pay the year's interest in full, the balance of interest is not to be added to the principal, but remains as interest, to be satisfied by the next adequate payment.[13] It is also a rule that the mortgagee must devote the entire net amount of the rents and profits to the payment of the debt secured by the mortgage, and he cannot divert any part thereof to the

---

[10] Russell v. Southard, 12 How. (U. S.) 139.

[11] Brown v. Gaffney, 32 Ill. 251.

[12] Moshier v. Norton, 100 Ill. 63; McConnel v. Holobush, 11 Ill. 61.

[13] McFadden v. Fortier, 20 Ill. 509.

satisfaction of other and unsecured claims due to him from the mortgagor, unless with the latter's express assent.[14] If there are several claims, or classes of claims, all equally secured by the mortgage, it appears to be the doctrine of the courts that the mortgagee in possession should apply the net income of the property so as to reduce the more onerous undertakings of the debtor, if this can be done consistently with the mortgagee's receipt of all the debtor has contracted to pay him. Thus, if one of the obligations secured by the mortgage bears compound interest, and the other simple interest, the net income must be applied so as first to extinguish the one bearing the heavier interest.[15]

On taking such an account, the proper practice is for the court first to declare, by interlocutory decree, the rights of the parties and the rule to be adopted in stating the account, and then to refer the cause to a master in chancery. Counsel cannot, by stipulation or otherwise, impose upon the court the necessity of performing labors which properly belong to the office of the master.[16] An equitable assignee of the mortgage is an indispensable party to an accounting, before the master, between the mortgagor and the mortgagee.[17]

§ 344.   Charge for Rents and Profits.—If a mortgagee, having taken possession of the mortgaged property upon default, has himself remained in the occupation and enjoyment of the premises, he is chargeable, upon an accounting, with the reasonable value of such occupation and use, that is, with a fair rent for the property.[18] If he has leased the premises to a tenant or tenants, the mortgagor may show the actual amount of rent received by the mortgagee, and this amount (less proper credits) is to be applied on the mortgage debt, first to interest, as above stated, and then to principal.[19] Ordinarily, the mortgagee in possession is only required to account for the actual receipts, less such sums as he may have paid out for taxes and necessary repairs, unless it is shown that a larger income from the property could have been realized by the exercise of reasonable diligence.[20] The mortgagee will indeed

[14] Caldwell v. Hall, 49 Ark. 508, 1 S. W. Rep. 62.

[15] Murdock v. Clarke, 88 Cal. 384, 26 Pac. Rep. 601.

[16] Moshier v. Norton, 83 Ill. 519.

[17] Union Mut. Life Ins. Co. v. Slee, 123 Ill. 57, 12 N. E. Rep. 543.

[18] Dyer v. Brown, 82 Ill. App. 17.

[19] Rooney v. Crary, 11 Ill. App. 213; Connelly v. Connelly, 36 Ill. App. 210.

[20] Harper v. Ely, 70 Ill. 581;

be responsible for losses occasioned by his gross negligence or wilful default, in the letting of the property or the collection of the rents, but if no such default or negligence on his part is shown, he will be held to have exercised the reasonable diligence required of him.[21] Moreover, the mortgagor cannot sit idly by and watch his property go to ruin, and hold the mortgagee responsible for the loss, when he could have aided in preventing its deterioration. If, for instance, the mortgagor resides near the mortgaged property, with opportunities of knowing how the property is rented or managed, he should take an interest in it, and afford his aid and advice, and communicate any cause of dissatisfaction to the mortgagee.[22] Nor can the mortgagee be convicted of a lack of reasonable care and diligence merely upon a showing that a higher rent could have been obtained from the premises under certain conditions. A certain measure of discretion must be allowed him, in respect to the character of the tenants whom he admits and the uses to which he permits the property to be devoted. For example, in a case where there was a hotel upon the mortgaged premises, it was adjudged that the mortgagee, on taking possession and leasing the property to a third person, was not obliged to allow the keeping of a bar for the sale of liquors in the hotel; and the fact that a higher rent could have been obtained, if such privilege had been allowed, was not sufficient to render him accountable for the higher rent.[23]

Some of the decisions hold that due care and diligence on the part of the mortgagee in possession require him to keep accounts of the income of the property, and that if he fails to do this, he is properly chargeable with what he may be presumed to have received.[24] In any case, however, he is not entitled to compensation for his personal care and trouble in taking care of the estate and renting it, and cannot be allowed any sum as commissions for collecting the rents and looking after the property. It will be enough if he is allowed what he

Moshier v. Norton, 83 Ill. 519; Clark v. Finlon, 90 Ill. 245; Pinneo v. Goodspeed, 120 Ill. 524, 12 N. E. Rep. 196; Jackson v. Lynch, 129 Ill. 72, 21 N. E. Rep. 580; Magnusson v. Charleson, 9 Ill. App. 194; Pinneo v. Goodspeed, 22 Ill. App. 50.

[21] Stevens v. Payne, 42 Ill. App. 202; Moshier v. Norton, 83 Ill. 519.

[22] Stevens v. Payne, 42 Ill. App. 202.

[23] Curtiss v. Sheldon, 91 Mich. 390, 51 N. W. Rep. 1057.

[24] Dexter v. Arnold, 2 Sumn. 108, Fed. Cas. No. 3,858; Gordon v.

may actually have paid out, to agents, in fees or commissions for managing the tenants and collecting the rents.[25]

§ 345. Allowance for Taxes and Insurance.—Upon an accounting by a mortgagee who has been in possession of the premises, he should be allowed credit for all sums which he has expended in paying taxes or assessments on the property, which the mortgagor should have paid, but failed or neglected to discharge.[26] And it is also said that money paid by the mortgagee for water rates due, to prevent the supply of water from being cut off from the premises, is properly chargeable to the mortgagor.[27] If the mortgage contained a covenant that the mortgagor would keep the buildings on the mortgaged premises insured for the benefit of the mortgagee, and if he fails or refuses to comply with such undertaking, it is the right of the mortgagee, being in possession, to effect and maintain a suitable insurance; and the amount which he pays as the cost of such insurance, will be credited to him on his accounting, if not unreasonably great.[28]

§ 346. Allowance for Repairs and Improvements.—Unless the condition of the premises would render repairs injudicious, a mortgagee in possession of the mortgaged property is bound to make all reasonable and necessary repairs, to keep the estate in good condition and prevent waste; and the cost of such repairs will be credited to him on his accounting.[29] He will be responsible for damage occasioned by any wilful default or gross neglect on his part, in the matter of repairs; but he is not bound to make good dilapidations caused by the natural effects of waste and decay from lapse of time.[30]

But a mortgagee in possession has no right, unless by the consent of the mortgagor, to put new improvements upon the property, even though they may be of permanent value to the

Lewis, 2 Sumn. 143, Fed. Cas. No. 5,613; Frey v. Campbell (Ky.), 3 S. W. Rep. 368.

[25] Harper v. Ely, 70 Ill. 581; Snow v. Warwick Institution for Savings, 17 R. I. 66, 20 Atl. Rep. 94.

[26] McCumber v. Gilman, 15 Ill. 381; supra, § 229. And see Moshier v. Norton, 83 Ill. 519; Clark v. Finlon, 90 Ill. 245; Magnusson v. Charleson, 9 Ill. App. 194.

[27] Donohue v. Chase, 139 Mass. 407, 2 N. E. Rep. 84.

[28] Supra, § 210. And see McCumber v. Gilman, 15 Ill. 381.

[29] McCumber v. Gilman, 15 Ill. 381; Moshier v. Norton, 83 Ill. 519; Clark v. Finlon, 90 Ill. 245; Magnusson v. Charleson, 9 Ill. App. 194.

[30] Dexter v. Arnold, 2 Sumn. 108, Fed. Cas. No. 3,858.

estate; and he will not be allowed credit, on his accounting, for the cost of such improvements, unless he can show that they were proper and necessary to keep the premises in good condition, and hence are rather repairs than improvements. "A mortgagee in possession is authorized, and even bound, to lay out money to keep the estate in necessary repair and to preserve it; but he is not authorized to make new improvements and tack the expense to the amount due upon the mortgage or pay it out of the rents and profits, except under very extraordinary circumstances."[31] "The law will not allow one person to make another his debtor in this way. New improvements made by a mortgagee in possession have sometimes been allowed and sometimes not. When allowed, the allowance is made to depend upon the particular circumstances of the case, and is considered rather as an exception to the general rule than the rule itself."[32] But where improvements are made in good faith by a party who believed that he had made a valid purchase of the premises, and the expenditure was a judicious one for the benefit of the estate, such party may be allowed the cost.[33] So, where one made an absolute deed of land to another to secure a general indebtedness, and neither party supposed that the land would be redeemed, but a bill for redemption is brought by a judgment creditor of the grantor, the grantee may be allowed the value of the improvements made by him on the premises.[34] Improvements may of course be made and charged for with the consent of the mortgagor. But one entitled to redeem from the mortgage is not rendered liable for unreasonable improvements made by the mortgagee in possession by the mere fact that he knew they were being made and did not object thereto.[35] If the improvements are properly to be allowed, on the accounting, as having been made with the consent and approval of the mortgagor, it is said that the latter should be charged with their actual cost, rather than with the amount by which they may have enhanced the value of the land.[36] It also appears that a mortgagee in possession

[31] McConnel v. Holobush, 11 Ill. 61.

[32] Smith v. Sinclair, 10 Ill. 108. And see McCumber v. Gilman, 15 Ill. 381.

[33] McConnel v. Holobush, 11 Ill. 61.

[34] Blair v. Chamblin, 39 Ill. 521.

[35] Merriam v. Goss, 139 Mass. 77, 28 N. E. Rep. 449.

[36] Gleiser v. McGregor, (Iowa), 52 N. W. Rep. 366.

may lawfully take down and carry away buildings erected by him on the mortgaged land, the materials of which were his own, and not so connected with the soil that they cannot be removed without injury to it.[37]

§ 347. **Discharge of Prior Incumbrances.**—If a mortgagee in possession finds it necessary to pay off a prior incumbrance on the estate, in order to protect his own security, he may do so, and the amount which he thus expends will be allowed him as a part of the debt secured by his mortgage, on his accounting with the mortgagor; and he may be allowed interest on the money so expended in removing a prior lien at the same rate which would have been payable to the holder thereof.[38]

---

[37] Cook v. Cooper, 18 Oreg. 142, 22 Pac. Rep. 945.   [38] Harper v. Ely, 70 Ill. 581.

CHAPTER XXVIII

REMEDIES OF MORTGAGEE ON BREACH OF CONDITION.

§ **348.** **Concurrent Remedies of Mortgagee.**—In the ordinary case of a mortgage securing a debt which is evidenced by a note or bond, or other written obligation, the mortgagee has his choice of various remedies upon breach of condition. ''He may bring his action upon the note, or put himself in possession of the rents and profits by an ejectment after condition broken, or, if the mortgage be recorded, proceed by scire facias on the record and obtain a judgment to sell the land, or he may file his bill in chancery for a strict foreclosure of the equity of redemption, which the courts will allow under a proper state of circumstances, or file a bill for foreclosure and sale, which is the usual practice in this state.''[1] And the mortgagee may not only choose, from among these various remedies, that which seems most likely to be successful, but he may pursue any or all of them successively or concurrently, until he obtains satisfaction of his debt.[2] With the choice of remedies the debtor has ordinarily nothing to do. It appears that a creditor might be precluded from enforcing a mortgage by seeking other relief, if his action has tended to throw the mortgagor off his guard or lull him into a false security.[3] But generally, a creditor by note or bond and mortgage cannot, without some special equity in favor of the debtor, be restrained from proceeding, at his election, upon any or all of his remedies, provided only that he does not take a double satisfaction of the debt.[4] In the case of railroad mortgages

---

[1] Vansant v. Allmon, 23 Ill. 30.

[2] Delahay v. Clement, 4 Ill. 201; Vansant v. Allmon, 23 Ill. 30; Karnes v. Lloyd, 52 Ill. 113; Erickson v. Rafferty, 79 Ill. 209; Bar-chard v. Kohn, 157 Ill. 579, 41 N. E. Rep. 902.

[3] Tartt v. Clayton, 109 Ill. 579.

[4] Newbold v. Newbold, 1 Del. Ch. 310.

containing a provision which authorizes the trustee, on default of the company to pay principal or interest, to take possession of the road and operate it and receive its income, and, upon notice, to sell it, it is held that this is a cumulative remedy, and does not affect the right of foreclosure by bill in equity.[5]

§ 349. **Recovery of Possession.**—After breach of the condition of the mortgage, the mortgagee is entitled to possession of the mortgaged premises. If the mortgagor remains in possession, the mortgagee may consider him as his tenant for some purposes; and if he elects so to consider him, it is as a tenant at sufferance, and he is not entitled to notice to quit.[6] If the mortgagee wishes to obtain control of the rents and profits of the land, so as to apply them on the debt, he may take possession of the land by the consent of the mortgagor, or by any other legal means which will save the necessity of an action of ejectment, and once in, the law will protect him, and he may defend his possession against either the mortgagor or any other person attacking it, unless it be a claimant by a superior lien.[7] But this action must be taken in due season. Where possession is taken under a mortgage before the right of entry has expired by lapse of time, the party may defend under the mortgage in ejectment brought by the mortgagor, even after the mortgage debt is barred by the statute; but after the debt is barred, the right of entry is gone, and an entry made under a dead mortgage will not restore its vitality, but on the contrary is wrongful.[8] If the mortgagor refuses to surrender possession on demand, the mortgagee may enforce his right thereto by appropriate action. While, in equity, the mortgage is only an incident of the debt which it secures, yet at law, it so far passes title as to confer the right to reduce the premises to possession as a means of obtaining satisfaction of the debt, and to render the right effective ejectment may be maintained against the mortgagor at any time that a recovery

[5] Alexander v. Central Railroad of Iowa, 3 Dill. 487, Fed. Cas. No. 166.

[6] Jackson v. Warren, 32 Ill. 331.

[7] Peterson v. Lindskoog, 93 Ill. App. 276; Fitzgerald v. Beebe, 7 Ark. 310; Gilchrist v. Patterson, 18 Ark. 575. The status of a mortgagee in possession under an informal foreclosure is not that of a trespasser, but of a mortgagee in possession. Blain v. Rivard, 19 Ill. App. 477.

[8] Emory v. Keighan, 88 Ill. 482. And see Banning v. Sabin, 45 Minn. 431, 48 N. W. Rep. 8.

may be had on the debt, that is, at any time after default in the payment of the debt, and until the right to sue thereon has become barred by the statute of limitations; and previous notice to the mortgagor, or notice to quit, is not necessary.[9] But possession is accorded to the mortgagee only as a means of collecting his debt. "There is no such thing, under our statute, as a foreclosure of a mortgage by the mortgagee taking possession of the premises. His possession as mortgagee will not ripen into a title in fee to the premises or bar the equity of redemption. As mortgagee in possession, he may unquestionably retain the same until his debt is satisfied out of the rents and profits, or by payment, but when so satisfied he is no longer entitled to the possession and has acquired no title to the property."[10]

§ 350. **Rights as Against Lessee in Possession.**—"It is in the power of the mortgagee, on entry for condition broken, where the property has been leased subsequent to the making of the mortgage, to treat the tenant as a trespasser, and bring ejectment, even without notice, or the mortgagee may elect to recognize the lessee as his tenant. The authorities all agree in holding, where the mortgagee has entered for condition broken, and received rents of the tenant, that the relation of landlord and tenant will be created between the parties. The single act of demanding rent has been held not to be sufficient for that purpose. There must be some distinct act on the part of the mortgagee that manifests the intention to recognize the lessee as his tenant. The question of the time for which it will be considered that the tenancy is created by the fact that the mortgagee received rents from the lessee—whether for the entire period of the unexpired lease, or for only a shorter

[9] Pollock v. Maison, 41 Ill. 516; Carroll v. Ballance, 26 Ill. 9; Johnson v. Watson, 87 Ill. 535. Ejectment to recover possession of the mortgaged property and a bill in equity for the foreclosure of the mortgage may be maintained at the same time. "It has never been regarded as an objection to the prosecution of ejectment at law and of foreclosure in equity at the same time against the mortgagor of realty, that the one proceeds upon the theory of title in the mortgagee and the other upon the theory of title in the mortgagor. Notwithstanding their apparent inconsistency, they may proceed concurrently until the debt secured is satisfied, it being always understood that there can be but one satisfaction." Barchard v. Kohn, 157 Ill. 579, 41 N. E. Rep. 902.

[10] French v. Goodman, 167 Ill. 345, 47 N. E. Rep. 737.

period—is a question of more difficulty of solution. The generally received doctrine seems to be that the receipt of rents by the mortgagee will only create a tenancy from year to year, in analogy to the rule where the tenant holds over after the expiration of the lease. The doctrine proceeds upon the ground that the lease is inoperative as to the mortgagee, and is terminated by the act of entry. The rule of the common law is well established, that the mortgagor cannot, without the consent of the mortgagee, execute a lease that will prevail against the rights of the mortgagee, and it has been uniformly held that the entry of the mortgagee puts an end to the lease.''[11]

§ 351. **Action at Law to Recover Debt.**—The remedy by a suit at law upon the note secured by a mortgage, against the maker thereof, or the taking of a judgment thereon by confession, may be pursued concurrently with a proceeding to foreclose the mortgage against the property.[12] And the fact that the mortgagor's equity of redemption has been sold on execution for other indebtedness does not deprive the holder of the mortgage of his right to sue on the note.[13] Further, the recovery of a judgment at law, unsatisfied, on the note or other obligation secured by a mortgage or deed of trust, will not operate as a release of the security so as to prevent a foreclosure and sale of the land. The mortgage simply stands as security for the judgment, the change in the form of the debt having no effect on the mortgage.[14] And when a mortgagee has thus recovered judgment on the debt secured, he may proceed on his judgment by execution, and subject to its payment other property of the debtor than that covered by the mortgage, and still the mortgage will not be released or affected unless such execution yields full satisfaction.[15] But of course,

[11] Gartside v. Outley, 58 Ill. 210.

[12] Hazle v. Bondy, 173 Ill. 302, 50 N. E. Rep. 671.

[13] Rogers v. Meyers, 68 Ill. 92.

[14] Hamilton v. Quimby, 46 Ill. 90. "In such cases, reducing the debt to judgment does not release the mortgage; it merely changes the form of the debt, so that the mortgage becomes a security for the payment of the judgment. The judgment on the note without satisfaction is no bar to a proceeding in equity to foreclose, and the two suits may be pending at the same time. The lien of the debt, secured by the mortgage, attaches to the mortgaged property, and, as between the parties, can only be defeated by the payment or discharge of the debt or by the release of the mortgage." Barchard v. Kohn, 157 Ill. 579, 41 N. E. Rep. 902.

[15] Karnes v. Lloyd, 52 Ill. 113. Thus, one holding a judgment-

when proceedings on the judgment, whether against the mortgaged property or other property, produce enough to satisfy
the creditor in full, then there can be no proceedings on the
mortgage; for, its only office being to secure the debt, when
the debt is paid, however the funds may be raised, the mortgage is functus officio.[16]

If proceedings for the foreclosure of the mortgage are first
taken, but the sale does not realize enough to pay the creditor
in full, he may then proceed by an action at law against the
debtor to recover the balance.[17] And the right to do this is
not taken away by the statute in Illinois authorizing a personal decree on the foreclosure of a mortgage for any balance
remaining due after the sale of the premises, and the award
of an execution therefor. It simply gives the mortgagee his
option to sue at law for any deficiency remaining after the
foreclosure sale, or to pray for and obtain the deficiency decree and execution provided by the statute; or he may in the
first instance sue at law on the note and proceed to foreclose
the mortgage in equity at the same time.[18] And even the fact
that there has been a decree of foreclosure and a sale of the
mortgaged property for a sum sufficient to pay the debt, will
not preclude the mortgagee from suing at law, so long as the
equity court retains its jurisdiction over the foreclosure suit,
with power to set the sale aside, the exercise of which power
would leave the debt precisely as if no sale had taken place.
If the sale under the foreclosure is consummated, the satisfaction of the debt becomes absolute, and relates back to the day
of the sale; but until it is consummated, the sale will operate
only as a conditional satisfaction; it is a proceeding in fieri,
which may or may not extinguish the debt; and while the proceedings under the foreclosure are in that condition, the holder
of the debt may properly commence an action at law thereon,
subject to be defeated if the foreclosure sale is afterwards
consummated, but which may be prosecuted to judgment if

note of a merchant in failing
circumstances, which is secured by
a mortgage on real estate, may obtain judgment by confession and
levy on the stock of goods, and
the court, upon subsequent voluntary assignment proceedings, may
protect his rights, without requiring him to resort first to the fore-

closure of his mortgage. Fried-
lander v. Fenton, 180 Ill. 312, 54 N.
E. Rep. 329, affirming Heidelbach
v. Fenton, 79 Ill. App. 357.

[16] Yourt v. Hopkins, 24 Ill. 326.

[17] Esty v. Brooks, 54 Ill. 379.
And see Gordon v. Gilfoil, 99 U. S.
168.

[18] Palmer v. Harris, 100 Ill. 276.

the sale should be set aside.[19] Hence, in an action on a promissory note, a plea that the plaintiff had already obtained judgment on a mortgage executed to secure the payment of the same debt for which the note was given, is bad if it does not aver that such judgment has been paid.[20] On similar principles it is held that proof of a debt against the estate of a deceased mortgagor, and the receipt of a dividend from the assets of the estate, less than the whole debt, will not extinguish the mortgage given to secure the debt nor prevent its foreclosure, the only effect being that the dividend received must be credited on the mortgage.[21]

An election to sue at law upon a note secured by a mortgage does not make it necessary for the holder to exhaust his remedies at law before he can go into equity to enforce the mortgage,[22] unless there has been an agreement of the parties to that effect. And even where the mortgage stipulates that it is not to be foreclosed until the property of the maker of the mortgage note is exhausted, this condition is complied with when, after judgment against him on the note, it is found that he has no property subject to execution; and thereupon the creditor may foreclose at once.[23]

§ 352. **Choice of Methods of Foreclosure.**—The fact that a mortgagee has obtained a judgment on a scire facias issued on the record of his mortgage, and that there is a special execution issued thereon, still in the hands of the sheriff, is no defense to a bill filed to foreclose the same mortgage. The mortgagee can pursue his several distinct remedies at the same time, although he can have but one satisfaction.[24] And as a general rule, one holding a mortgage on real property should not be prevented from foreclosing because, by delay, other property may be sold simultaneously, to the probable advantage of the mortgagor and others.[25] Also it is said that the holder of an invalid tax title cannot compel a mortgagee to exhaust his remedy against other property on which he holds another mortgage securing the same debt, before bringing suit to set

[19] Morgan v. Sherwood, 53 Ill. 171.

[20] Russell v. Hamilton, 3 Ill. 56.

[21] Schuelenberg v. Martin, 1 McCrary, 348, 2 Fed. Rep. 747.

[22] Ober v. Gallagher, 93 U. S. 199.

[23] Riblet v. Davis, 24 Ohio St. 114.

[24] Erickson v. Rafferty, 79 Ill. 209. Compare State Bank v. Wilson, 9 Ill. 57.

[25] Olyphant v. St. Louis Ore & Steel Co., 23 Fed. Rep. 465.

aside the tax title, since equity will not aid the holder of a tax title.[26] In the case of a deed absolute in form, it is held that the delivery of such an instrument invests the grantee with the legal title, even though the transaction is converted into an equitable mortgage by the subsequent execution of an unsealed agreement to re-convey, and no affirmative action to divest the mortgagor of his right of redemption is necessary to invest the mortgagee with the full legal title.[27]

[26] Miller v. Cook, 135 Ill. 190, 25 N. E. Rep. 756.

[27] Fitch v. Miller, 200 Ill. 170, 65 N. E. Rep. 650.

CHAPTER XXIX.

FORECLOSURE BY SCIRE FACIAS.

§ 353. Statutory Provisions.—The statute of Illinois provides a method for the foreclosure of mortgages of real estate, duly executed and recorded, and securing the payment of a debt in money, when the whole of such debt shall be due and unpaid, or the last installment, if the debt is payable in that manner, by the suing out of a writ of scire facias from the office of the clerk of the circuit court in the county in which the mortgaged land is situated, or any part of it. This writ is directed to, and served by, the sheriff or other proper officer of the county or counties where the defendants, or any of them, may reside or be found, and requires them to show cause why judgment should not be rendered for such sum of money as may be due under the mortgage. Upon sufficient service of process, or the appearance of the defendant, the court may proceed to judgment as in other cases, and the judgment is to be satisfied by a sale of the mortgaged premises under a special writ of fieri facias awarded for that purpose.[1] It will be observed that this statute applies only to mortgages "duly executed and recorded." For this purpose, the acknowledgment is an essential part of the execution, and scire facias does not lie to foreclose a mortgage which is not duly acknowledged. "A scire facias is a proceeding or writ founded on some matter of record, and the rule is, without exception, that the record must be complete in itself, and no testimony is admissible aliunde for the purpose of making out a case."[2] Again, this statutory remedy applies only to mortgages made to secure the payment of money. It does not extend to mortgages made to

[1] Rev. Stat. Ill. c. 95, §§ 17-20.
[2] Kenosha & P. R. Co. v. Sperry,

[3] Biss. C. C. 309, Fed. Cas. No. 7,712.

424

secure the delivery of specific articles of property or the performance of other acts. In such cases the mortgagee may bring ejectment to recover the possession of the mortgaged premises, or a bill in equity to foreclose the mortgage, but cannot have scire facias.[3]

§ 354. **Process and Service.**—A scire facias to foreclose a mortgage should, like other process, run in the name of the People of the State of Illinois; if it does not, it is void on its face, and may be reached by general demurrer, though a motion to quash would be more proper. But it is amendable in this particular.[4] The return of the officer serving the writ should show clearly and affirmatively that it was regularly served upon the defendant; if it is defective in this particular, it will be irregular to render a judgment by default on the scire facias.[5] But a sufficient service may be shown by the defendant's written indorsement upon the writ, acknowledging service of it and praying the court to enter his appearance accordingly; and a recital in the judgment that it appeared to the court that the defendant had been duly served with process is satisfactory proof that he made the indorsement in question.[6]

If the defendant is not found, or if the writ is returned "nihil," the proper practice is to issue an alias writ of scire facias. And it is held, in accordance with the ancient rule of the common law, that two returns of "nihil" on a scire facias to foreclose a mortgage are equivalent to an actual service on the defendant,[7] so that a judgment of foreclosure may be entered without personal service, upon two returns of "nihil" on writs issued and returnable to two different terms of the court, notwithstanding that each writ was returned on the same day it was issued.[8]

§ 355. **Non-Resident Defendant.**—It is provided that "if the defendant is a non-resident, or hath gone out of the State, or on due inquiry cannot be found, or is concealed within the State, or evades the service of process, the plaintiff or his attorney

[3] McCumber v. Gilman, 13 Ill. 542.

[4] McFadden v. Fortier, 20 Ill. 509.

[5] Belingall v. Gear, 4 Ill. 575; Montgomery v. Brown, 7 Ill. 581.

[6] Russell v. Brown, 41 Ill. 183.

[7] Cox v. McFerron, Breese, 28; McCourtie v. Davis, 2 Gilm. 298. See 1 Black, Judgm. § 487.

[8] Williams v. Ives, 49 Ill. 512.

may file affidavit in the same form as in like cases in chancery, and notice may be given as in such case.'"[9]

§ 356. Plaintiff's Right of Action.—In the case of a debt payable by installments, as will be seen by reference to the statute, the mortgagee cannot have a scire facias to foreclose until the last and all are due. Upon default in the payment of earlier installments, he has other remedies against the mortgagor—such as an action at law on the debt due or an action of ejectment to obtain possession of the mortgaged premises—but not the remedy by this writ.[10] But a mortgage given to secure the payment of money may be foreclosed in this manner although the mortgagor was primarily liable for only a part of the debt so secured, his liability as to the residue being merely secondary, and accruing only in the event of non-payment by other parties and notice thereof.[11] When the mortgagor is dead, the writ is to be served upon his heirs, executors, or administrators. In this case, the mortgagee is not required to wait for the expiration of a year from the time of the mortgagor's decease, before suing out scire facias to foreclose. This writ is the initiation of a proceeding in rem, and not an action in the ordinary meaning of that term; the mortgage lien binds the specific property, and is not affected by the solvency or insolvency of the mortgagor's estate.[12]

§ 357. Parties.—When a mortgage has been assigned, scire facias to foreclose it is properly brought in the name of the mortgagee for the use of the assignee.[13] This proceeding being at law, and being governed by the practice of courts of law, and not of courts of equity, no persons but the mortgagor need be made defendants to such an action, or in case of his death, his personal representatives. The mortgagor's assignee or trustee in bankruptcy is not a necessary party, although he would be in case of a bill in chancery to foreclose. Assignees in bankruptcy, as well as subsequent purchasers and incumbrancers, are required to take notice of proceedings by scire facias and to protect their own rights.[14] The heirs of a deceased mortgagor need not be made parties, for the statute

---

[9] Rev. Stat. Ill. c. 95, § 18. For the practice in chancery in similar cases see Rev. Stat. Ill. c. 22, §§ 12-14.

[10] Osgood v. Stevens, 25 Ill. 89; Carroll v. Ballance, 26 Ill. 9.

[11] Russell v. Brown, 41 Ill. 183.

[12] Menard v. Marks, 2 Ill. 25.

[13] Winchell v. Edwards, 57 Ill. 41; supra, § 192.

[14] Chickering v. Failes, 26 Ill. 507.

authorizes the proceeding by making either the heirs, executors, or administrators parties.[15] But the wife of the mortgagor, if she signed the mortgage, is a proper and necessary party in order to bar her equity of redemption and right of dower.[16]

§ 358. Pleading.—A proceeding by scire facias to foreclose a mortgage is a proceeding in rem, and the writ performs the office of both process and declaration. It must contain every material averment required in a declaration; and defects in it are properly objected to by demurrer.[17] An objection, for instance, that the scire facias does not set out the mortgage in full cannot be taken on a plea in abatement.[18] The writ must contain an allegation of a breach of the condition of the mortgage by non-payment of the debt secured thereby.[19] But it is not fatally defective for failing to allege that default had been made in the payment of the money secured by the mortgage, if it appears from the mortgage itself, as set out in the scire facias, that the money should have been paid at a date before the issuing of the writ.[20] If the writ sets out a mortgage not under seal, a mortgage under seal is not admissible in evidence under it; the variance is fatal.[21] Where the plaintiffs in a proceeding to foreclose a mortgage are partners, it is not sufficient to describe them in the scire facias by the firm name only; the writ is fatally defective if it does not disclose the persons composing the firm and give their Christian names as well as surnames.[22] But any mere clerical errors or omissions in the scire facias, not calculated to mislead or surprise the defendant, may be corrected by amendment.[23]

§ 359. Defenses.—At common law, the only defenses which can be interposed to a scire facias on a record are payment and "nul tiel record." Now a mortgage, being recorded, was treated as a record in a proceeding by scire facias to foreclose it. In that character, it imported absolute verity, and nothing could be averred against it except that it was void ab initio,

[15] Rockwell v. Jones, 21 Ill. 279.
[16] Camp v. Small, 44 Ill. 37; Gilbert v. Maggord, 2 Ill. 471.
[17] Osgood v. Stevens, 25 Ill. 89; McFadden v. Fortier, 20 Ill. 509; Marshall v. Maury, 2 Ill. 231.
[18] Menard v. Marks, 2 Ill. 25.
[19] Osgood v. Stevens, 25 Ill. 89.

[20] Mitcheltree v. Stewart, 3 Ill. 17.
[21] McFadden v. Fortier, 20 Ill. 509.
[22] Day v. Cushman, 2 Ill. 475.
[23] State Bank v. Buckmaster, 1 Ill. 176; Marshall v. Maury, 2 Ill. 231; McFadden v. Fortier, 20 Ill. 509.

and never a valid lien, or that it had been paid, discharged, or released. No defense could be set up unless of such a character as to attack the existence or validity of the mortgage or to show it to have been paid or satisfied. Hence the defendant was not allowed to plead usury,[24] or fraud,[25] or want or failure of consideration,[26] nor could he plead "non est factum,"[27] nor set off a demand against the plaintiff.[28] But now the statute provides that "the defendant may plead or set off [set up?] any defense, and be allowed to set off a demand in his favor, in the same manner, and the same rules shall apply thereto, as if the suit were in any other form of action."[29] Thus, in the case of a purchase-money mortgage, want of title in the vendor is a good defense to a scire facias to foreclose it. But a plea which alleges that the vendor represented himself to be the owner of the land in fee simple, which he was not, and that the vendee has since acquired the legal title from the real owner, is defective unless it also avers that the vendee relied on such representations and was thereby induced to take the conveyance.[30]

§ 360. Judgment.—The statute provides that "if the defendant appear and plead or set up any defense, or make default after having been served with scire facias or notified as aforesaid, the court may proceed to give judgment, with costs, for such sum as may be due by said mortgage, or appear to be due by the pleadings, or after the defense, if any be made."[31] It will be observed that judgment on a scire facias to foreclose a mortgage must be in rem, and not general against the person of the defendant.[32] But if the judgment directs, first, that the plaintiff recover of and from the defendant the sum so found to be due, and then awards a special execution for a sale of the mortgaged premises, this is not a judgment in personam, which would be erroneous, but one in rem.[33] But it must direct a sale of the mortgaged property; a direction merely to the effect that "a special execution issue according to the statute,"

[24] Carpenter v. Mooers, 26 Ill. 162; Camp v. Small, 44 Ill. 37.

[25] White v. Watkins, 23 Ill. 480.

[26] Woodbury v. Manlove, 14 Ill. 213; Fitzgerald v. Forristal, 48 Ill. 228.

[27] Camp v. Small, 44 Ill. 37.

[28] Woodbury v. Manlove, 14 Ill. 213.

[29] Rev. Stat. Ill. c. 95, § 20.

[30] McFadden v. Fortier, 20 Ill. 509.

[31] Rev. Stat. Ill. c. 95, § 19.

[32] Osgood v. Stevens, 25 Ill. 89.

[33] Williams v. Ives, 49 Ill. 512.

is not sufficient.[34] The mere recovery of a judgment on scire facias to foreclose a mortgage will not extinguish the relation of mortgagor and mortgagee, nor discharge either the note or mortgage; the right of redemption will still remain.[35]

§ 361. **Execution.**—The statutory provision as to the enforcement of the judgment is that "the mortgaged premises may be sold to satisfy any judgment the plaintiff in such an action may recover, and the court may award a special writ of fieri facias for that purpose, to the county or counties in which said mortgaged premises may be situated, and on which the like proceedings may be had as in other cases of execution levied upon real estate; provided, however, that the judgment aforesaid shall create no lien on any other lands or tenements than the mortgaged premises, nor shall any other real or personal property of the mortgagor be liable to satisfy the same; but nothing herein contained shall be so construed as to affect any collateral security given by the mortgagor for the payment of the same sum of money, or any part thereof, secured by the mortgage deed."[36] Since the proceeding by scire facias is purely an action at law, and appertains in no respect to the jurisdiction of equity, it is held that the execution must be directed to the sheriff of the county, and not to a master in chancery. The court has no power to appoint a master to sell the property, and a sale so made would be void.[37]

[34] Marshall v. Maury, 2 Ill. 231.
[35] Rockwell v. Servant, 63 Ill. 424.
[36] Rev. Stat. Ill. c. 95, § 21.
[37] Tucker v. Conwell, 67 Ill. 552.

CHAPTER XXX.

FORECLOSURE BY SUIT IN EQUITY.

PART I. JURISDICTION.

§ 362. Jurisdiction in General.—Jurisdiction to hear and determine suits for the foreclosure of mortgages on real estate is inherent in courts of equity. It is not derived from, nor dependent upon, the statutes. Neither does it depend in any degree upon the consent or agreement of the parties. It is not necessary to such jurisdiction that the mortgage itself should make any provision for the foreclosure of the equity of redemption. On the contrary, it is not in the power of the parties to prevent the courts of equity from taking jurisdiction in a proper case, and enforcing their decree in the usual manner, by providing a mode of enforcing the security upon default and declaring that it shall be exclusive of all others.[1] Jurisdiction of the parties being acquired in some proper manner, the only other requisite to the action of the court is that the land to be affected should lie within its territorial jurisdiction. Real estate is governed only by the law of its situs, and only the courts of the state or country within which it lies can have any jurisdiction over it; it cannot be directly affected by the judgment or decree of any foreign court. Hence, although a court of equity in one state may make a valid and binding decree as between parties who are properly before it, it has no power to order the foreclosure of a mortgage on lands situated in another state; and an attempted sale of such lands would pass no title. Outside the boundaries of its own state, the decree has no effect, except that it may be made the basis of another suit in the state where the property lies, and that it will have the ordinary conclusive effect of a judgment in such second suit.[2]

[1] Guaranty Trust Co. v. Green Cove Springs & M. R. Co., 139 U. S. 137.

[2] 2 Black, Judgm. § 872; Farmers' Loan & Trust Co. v. Postal Tel. Co., 55 Conn. 334, 11 Atl. Rep.

§ 363. Service of Process.—It is necessary to the validity of a decree of foreclosure that the defendant, if within the jurisdiction of the court, should have been duly served with process. But if the sheriff's return shows that he was personally served with the summons, and his appearance was entered by the attorney who filed the answer, he cannot, in a subsequent proceeding to enforce the foreclosure decree, deny jurisdiction of his person in that suit.[3] And the same result follows if the defendant acknowledges service on the back of the summons, and in the same writing authorizes the complainant's solicitor to enter his appearance, which is done on proof of the execution of the acknowledgment.[4] Further, a recital in a decree of foreclosure that the defendant had been duly served with process is conclusive, especially after the lapse of a considerable time, unless there is something in the record itself showing that such recital is not or could not be true. Proof from outside the record is not admissible to contradict it, where such contradiction would affect the rights of third persons acquired under the decree.[5] And an objection that the service on a tenant, whose term had substantially expired, was insufficient, and that a decree pro confesso as to him was erroneous, is not available to the mortgagor.[6]

If the mortgage to be foreclosed was executed jointly by a husband and wife, process must be served on both. If there is service on the husband alone, it is error to decree foreclosure against both the defendants, although it did not appear what was the nature of the wife's interest in the mortgaged premises. It was indeed the rule at common law that a summons issued against husband and wife might be served on the husband alone, with the effect of binding both. But this rule is so far changed by the legislation in Illinois in respect to the property rights of married women that, whenever it is sought, by

184; Appeal of Pittsburgh & St. L. R. Co. (Pa.) 4 Atl. Rep. 385; Lynde v. Columbus, C. & I. C. Ry. Co., 57 Fed. Rep. 993; Brown v. Todd (Ky.), 29 S. W. Rep. 621; Frank v. Snow, 6 Wyom. 42, 42 Pac. Rep. 484.

3 Lancaster v. Snow, 184 Ill. 534, 56 N. E. Rep. 813. The fact that the foreclosure summons was served by a person specially appointed by a deputy sheriff pro hac vice could not be relied on as a defense to an action to enforce payment of the bid made by the purchaser at the foreclosure sale. Thrift v. Frittz, 7 Ill. App. 55.

4 Snell v. Stanley, 63 Ill. 391.

5 Riggs v. Collins (U. S. Circt. Ct. N. D. Ill.), 2 Biss. 268.

6 Brown v. Miner, 128 Ill. 148, 21 N. E. Rep. 223.

a judicial proceeding, to affect the rights of property of a feme covert, she must be served with process. And even at common law, it was held necessary, when the plaintiff was seeking satisfaction out of the separate property of a wife, that process should be served on her.[7]

§ 364. Non-Resident Defendant.—A suit in equity to foreclose a mortgage and satisfy the creditor by a sale of the premises is in the nature of a proceeding in rem, so that service of process on absent parties is not essential to give the court jurisdiction, a reasonable constructive notice of the action being all that is necessary.[8] If the mortgagor or his successor in interest is a non-resident, or is not found, so that he cannot be served personally with process within the state, the court may decree a sale of the property on such substituted or constructive service of process as the legislature may provide; but in such case there is no presumption in favor of the jurisdiction of the court, and unless the record shows a compliance in all essential particulars with the statute authorizing such service, the decree is not valid.[9] But a decree of foreclosure rendered on service by publication is not void on collateral attack, merely because the affidavit for publication was defective, when the decree recites due notice by publication, and that the defendant could not be found for the purpose of serving him with process.[10] And where several parties are joined as defendants in the suit, and all are personally served except one non-resident, as to whom service by publication is attempted, he alone can object that the publication was insufficient or irregular; that objection cannot be raised by the other defendants.[11] In a case where the complainant caused service by publication to be made upon the mortgagor, who was a non-

[7] Piggott v. Snell, 59 Ill. 106.

[8] 2 Black, Judgm. § 810; Russell v. Brown, 41 Ill. 184; Williams v. Ives, 49 Ill. 512. The provisions of the Illinois statute regulating service of process by publication, on defendants in proceedings in chancery who are non-residents or who cannot be found, may be seen at large in Rev. Stat. Ill. c. 22, §§ 12-17. On the application of this statute, see Hamas v. Hamas, 110 Ill. 53; Schaefer v. Kienzel, 123 Ill.

430; Thornmeyer v. Sisson, 83 Ill. 188; Wallahan v. Ingersoll, 117 Ill. 123; Millett v. Pease, 31 Ill. 377; Tompkins v. Wiltberger, 56 Ill. 385; Connely v. Rue, 148 Ill. 207; Burke v. Donnovan, 60 Ill. App. 241.

[9] Swift v. Meyers, 37 Fed. Rep. 37.

[10] Reedy v. Canfield, 159 Ill. 254, 42 N. E. Rep. 833.

[11] Fergus v. Tinkham, 38 Ill. 407.

resident, obtained a decree of strict foreclosure, and then sold the property to purchasers who made valuable improvements upon it, and afterwards the mortgagor entered an appearance and obtained leave to answer, it was held to be proper practice for him to file a cross bill, making the purchasers defendants. Thereupon it was adjudged that the land should be valued, and if its value was found to be less than the mortgage debt, a strict foreclosure might be decreed, but with leave to the mortgagor to redeem. On the other hand, if the land, apart from the improvements, was found to be of greater value than the debt, then the mortgagor should be allowed to redeem, as in the other case, but if no redemption was made, then a sale should be ordered, and the proceeds distributed as follows: first, the costs; then to the mortgagee the amount due on the mortgage, with any taxes paid by him before he sold the land; then to the mortgagor the excess of the value of the land unimproved over the amount of the costs, debt, and taxes; and to the purchasers the value of the improvements independently of the land.[12]

§ 365. **Property in Possession of Receiver.**—When the mortgaged property is in the possession of a receiver appointed in another suit, in the same or a different court, the mortgagee should properly first obtain leave of the court which appointed the receiver to bring a bill for foreclosure against him. It is a contempt of that court if he proceeds against the receiver without asking and obtaining leave, and the foreclosure suit may in that case be dismissed on motion of the receiver. But still the failure of the complainant to obtain such permission will not deprive the court in which his bill is filed of jurisdiction over the suit for foreclosure, nor invalidate the proceedings had therein, especially when the receiver waives the objection by his acquiescence in the proceedings.[13] And the objection that the receiver was sued without leave cannot be raised by the mortgagor, after the latter has entered his appearance, filed an answer, and taken part in the examination of the complainant's witnesses.[14] When a decree of foreclosure is rendered, and a sale ordered and made, the court may order the

[12] Scott v. Milliken, 60 Ill. 108.

[13] Mulcahey v. Strauss, 151 Ill. 70, 37 N. E. Rep. 702; Muncie Nat.

Bank v. Brown, 112 Ind. 474, 14 N. E. Rep. 358.

[14] Jerome v. McCarter, 94 U. S. 734.

receiver to deliver possession of the property to the purchaser.[15]

§ 366. Conflicting Jurisdiction.—Questions of conflicting jurisdiction in foreclosure suits most frequently arise between the courts of the state and the federal courts. These questions will be more fully discussed in the chapter relating to mortgage foreclosures in the courts of the United States. But here it may be remarked that, while a final adjudication in either of such courts will generally constitute a bar to any similar proceedings on the same cause of action in the other court, yet the mere pendency of an action for foreclosure in a federal court will not prevent a state court from taking cognizance of a bill for the foreclosure of the same mortgage, if it has jurisdiction of the parties and the subject-matter, and vice versa.[16] Also it should be noted that a suit by the receiver of an insolvent national bank to foreclose a mortgage given to it is not within any of the classes of cases in which the federal courts have exclusive jurisdiction, and consequently such an action may be instituted and maintained in any state court having jurisdiction in other respects.[17]

§ 367. Appellate Jurisdiction.—Ordinarily, a proceeding in equity to foreclose a mortgage is not an action "involving a freehold," within the meaning of the Act of June 2, 1877 (Rev. Stat. Ill. c. 110, § 91), and therefore an appeal from a decree of foreclosure should be taken to the Appellate Court, and not in the first instance to the Supreme Court.[18] But a late decision holds that a freehold is involved if, by the defense in the case, the homestead is put directly in issue, and the decree awards it, and the assignment of errors in the Appellate Court also puts it directly in issue.[19]

§ 368. Termination of Jurisdiction.—The rights of the parties to a suit to foreclose a mortgage are at an end when the time allowed for redemption from the sale expires without any redemption being effected. Up to that point the court re-

[15] Heffron v. Knickerbocker, 57 Ill. App. 336.

[16] See Seymour v. Bailey, 66 Ill. 288; Atkins v. Wabash, St. L. & P. Ry. Co., 29 Fed. Rep. 161.

[17] Witters v. Sowles, 61 Vt. 366, 18 Atl. Rep. 191.

[18] Akin v. Cassiday, 105 Ill. 22; Grand Tower Mfg. Co. v. Hall, 94 Ill. 152; Pinneo v. Knox, 100 Ill. 471; McIntyre v. Yates, Id. 475; Beach v. Peabody, 188 Ill. 75, 58 N. E. Rep. 679.

[19] Kellogg Newspaper Co. v. Corn Belt Nat. B. & L. Ass'n, 105 Ill. App. 62.

tains jurisdiction over the case for proper purposes. But when this stage of the proceedings is reached, the title of the purchaser at the foreclosure sale becomes fixed and absolute, and the jurisdiction of the court whose aid was invoked for the purposes of the foreclosure suit terminates and ceases.[20]

PART II. COMPLAINANT'S RIGHT OF ACTION.

§ 369. **The Right to Foreclose.**—A mortgagee's right to enforce his security by the process of foreclosure and sale is a valuable right, which must be considered as forming a part of the mortgage contract, and which cannot be divested by retroactive legislation. "The remedy thus provided when the mortgage is executed enters into the convention of the parties, in so far that any change by legislative authority which affects it substantially, to the injury of the mortgagee, is held to be a law impairing the obligation of contracts within the meaning of the provision of the Constitution upon the subject."[21] But the mortgagee's right of action depends upon the continued existence of the debt secured. The existence of the debt which the mortgage was given to secure is essential to the life of the mortgage; and when the debt is paid, discharged, released, or barred by the statute of limitations, or by the judgment of a court, the mortgage is functus officio and has no longer any validity or effect.[22] But the conditional surrender of notes secured by a mortgage does not cut off the right to foreclose the mortgage for their satisfaction in a case where the condition is not fulfilled.[23] On the same principle, after the execution, delivery, and recording of a quit-claim deed, the legal

---

[20] Stoddard v. Walker, 90 Ill. App. 422.

[21] Clark v. Reyburn, 8 Wall. 318.

[22] Emory v. Keighan, 88 Ill. 482. A sale of land under a mortgage will be enjoined where it is clear from the evidence that the mortgage debt has been paid. Long v. Pomeroy, 119 Ill. 600, 8 N. E. Rep. 194.

[23] Pugh v. Fairmount G. & S. Min. Co., 112 U. S. 238.

effect of which is to release and discharge a mortgage of record, a foreclosure by sale under a power in the mortgage is void.[24] Moreover, it is essential to the complainant's right of action that he should be the present owner of the debt secured by the mortgage. His right to maintain the bill may not indeed be affected by an equitable assignment of a portion of the indebtedness, when he has retained the legal title, as well as a large equitable interest,[25] but if it appears that the complainant is not the owner of the note secured, and has no legal title to it, but obtained possession of it tortiously, the bill will be dismissed.[26] There may also be cases where the mortgagee should be held estopped to enforce his rights by foreclosure of the mortgage, particularly where his conduct has been such as to mislead or deceive innocent third persons whose rights have attached to the property in question, and who would be seriously prejudiced by the enforcement of the lien.[27] On the other hand, third persons, whatever may be their rights and interests in the premises, have generally no legal right to compel a mortgagee to foreclose his mortgage, if he does not choose to exercise the privilege which a breach of the condition gives to him.[28]

An action at law will lie for suing for the foreclosure of a mortgage maliciously and without right. But it must be averred and shown, in a manner sufficient to satisfy a reasonable man, that the defendant had no other ground for proceeding but his desire to injure the plaintiff, and also that the attempted foreclosure proceedings terminated favorably to the mortgagor; and want of probable cause cannot be inferred from the existence of malice.[29]

§ 370. **Breach of Condition.**—The condition of a mortgage is the clause reciting the circumstances under which the defeasance is to become operative and the mortgage itself void. A breach of the condition is the failure of the mortgagor to discharge the obligation imposed upon him by the terms of the instrument, and which the mortgage is given to secure, at the

[24] Benson v. Markoe, 41 Minn. 112, 42 N. W. Rep. 787.

[25] Boone v. Clark, 129 Ill. 466, 21 N. E. Rep. 850.

[26] Weaver v. Field, 114 U. S. 244.

[27] But see Powell v. Rogers, 105 Ill. 318.

[28] Hannah v. Hannah (Mo.), 19 S. W. Rep. 87.

[29] Tanton v. Boomgarden, 79 Ill. App. 551; Marable v. Mayer, 78 Ga. 710, 3 S. E. Rep. 429.

time and in the manner therein stipulated, whether that obligation be the payment of a sum of money or the performance of some other act. Upon breach of condition, the estate is forfeited at law, but in equity the mortgagor retains a right to redeem. The object of a suit for foreclosure is to cut off this equity of redemption and apply the property to the satisfaction of the debt or claim secured. Breach of the condition is an essential prerequisite to the mortgagee's right to maintain a suit for foreclosure.[30] A demand by the mortgagee for the payment of the money due under the mortgage is not generally necessary to enable him to begin foreclosure proceedings; it is enough if the day of payment has passed without payment or a sufficient tender.[31] But such demand may of course be included in the agreement of the parties. Thus, where the provision is that the mortgage shall be void if the note secured shall be paid "within sixty days after demand," a demand of payment of the note is necessary to work a breach of condition.[32] But where the mortgagee, before the maturity of the debt, declares that he will not accept in satisfaction the amount actually due, a forfeiture should not be declared for want of a tender.[33] Where the mortgage secures several different notes falling due at different times, and the provision is that it shall become void if the mortgagor shall pay all the notes as they become due, a suit for foreclosure may be maintained upon the non-payment of the first note.[34]

The payment of the obligations secured by the mortgage may also be conditioned upon the performance of other acts, such as the acquisition of an outstanding title, or the tender of a conveyance from third parties claiming interest in the property; and the due performance of such conditions will be essential to the right to foreclose.[35] In the case of a purchase-money mortgage, there is often a condition inserted requiring a defect in the title to the premises, or a portion thereof, to

[30] A conveyance of the fee by the mortgagor with full covenants, or a failure to apply the purchase money in paying off the mortgage debt, is not such a breach of trust as to work a forfeiture of the credit due on that debt, so as to give an immediate right of foreclosure. Coffing v. Taylor, 16 Ill. 457.

[31] Norton v. Ohrns, 67 Mich. 612, 35 N. W. Rep. 175.

[32] Union Cent. Life Ins. Co. v. Curtis, 35 Ohio St. 343.

[33] Gorham v. Farson, 119 Ill. 425, 10 N. E. Rep. 1.

[34] Fisher v. Milmine, 94 Ill. 328.

[35] See Gibbons v. Hoag, 95 Ill. 45.

be cured or the title perfected by the vendor before the debt secured shall be deemed due and payable; and here the mortgagee (vendor) must fulfill this condition before he can be permitted to foreclose the mortgage.[36] So, where a party who owes a debt secured by a mortgage enters into a contract with another, by which the latter is to assume the debt, and he in turn makes a contract with the mortgagee by which the mortgage is to be transferred to him upon the performance of certain conditions, so long as the mortgagee remains bound by this agreement he cannot foreclose the mortgage against the original debtor.[37]

In the case of indemnity mortgages, a breach of condition occurs when the mortgagee suffers loss or damage on the claim against which he was to be secured. Thus, a mortgage to secure the mortgagee on a debt of the mortgagor's on which he was surety, cannot be foreclosed until the mortgagee has paid the debt or some part of it.[38] But where the mortgagor covenants to pay, within a fixed time, all debts contracted by him for labor and material for the construction of a building, and not merely that he would indemnify the mortgagee against liens on it, it is not necessary to constitute a default that the debts shall have been adjudged liens, or even that claims for liens shall have been filed.[39] When the mortgage, given to secure the payment of certain promissory notes, is conditioned "that if any of the notes prove to be insolvent or worthless, the mortgage is to be good and valid, otherwise to be null and void," it is necessary, to constitute a breach of the condition, that the notes or some of them should prove worthless; the mere non-payment of the notes does not constitute a breach.[40]

§ 371. Partial and Successive Foreclosures.—Where a mortgage is given to secure the payment of a debt in installments, or sums of money falling due at different periods, the creditor

[36] Weaver v. Wilson, 48 Ill. 125. Where a mortgage is given to secure notes made payable whenever the plaintiff shall perfect a certain title to the satisfaction of certain attorneys named in the notes, the mortgage cannot be foreclosed if the attorneys named, in good faith and from no improper motive, withhold their approval of the title, even though the title may be good in the opinion of the court. Church v. Shanklin (Cal.), 30 Pac. Rep. 789.

[37] Crabtree v. Levings, 53 Ill. 526.

[38] Forbes v. McCoy, 15 Nebr. 632, 20 N. W. Rep. 17.

[39] Houston v. Nord, 39 Minn. 490, 40 N. W. Rep. 568.

[40] Fetrow v. Merriwether, 53 Ill. 275.

may foreclose by bill in equity as they severally fall due. He
is not obliged to wait for the whole indebtedness to ripen before he can proceed to collect what is already payable.[41] And
where interest is stipulated to be paid annually, each year's
interest constitutes an installment, default in the payment of
which will give the creditor the right to foreclose.[42] But the
creditor must include in his foreclosure all the several installments or separate obligations which are due at the time of filing
the bill. The sale on foreclosure will release the land from
the lien of the mortgage as to any portions of the debt which
were then due but were not included in the bill and decree.[43]
Whatever amount is due under the mortgage at the time of the
foreclosure, including taxes paid by the mortgagee for the protection of his security, constitutes but a single and indivisible
demand; it cannot be split up and collected by several actions.[44] On the other hand, the mortgagee can foreclose and
sell only for the amount which is then due according to the
terms of the mortgage; when one or more installments are due,
it is error to render a decree for those which are not yet due.[45]
Where a suit in foreclosure is prosecuted for the non-payment
of one or more of a series of notes, or of interest coupons, it is
proper for the decree to direct that the sale of the premises
shall be made subject to the continuing lien of the mortgage as
security for the remaining notes and for any further disbursements made by the mortgagee under its provisions.[46] It is also
the settled doctrine of the courts that the legal holder of a
matured interest coupon is not required to wait until the principal note secured by the mortgage or deed of trust (or the
other interest coupons) shall fall due before he can enforce
his security by foreclosure, notwithstanding that the right to

[41] Morgenstern v. Klees, 30 Ill.
422; Vansant v. Allmon, 23 Ill. 30;
Bressler v. Martin, 133 Ill. 278, 24
N. E. Rep. 518. The dismissal of
a bill to foreclose a trust deed to
satisfy that part of the indebtedness which is due, is no bar to a
second suit to foreclose for the
interest on the notes not included
in the former suit. Telford v.
Garrels, 132 Ill. 550, 24 N. E. Rep.
573.

[42] Morgenstern v. Klees, 30 Ill.
422.

[43] Rains v. Mann, 68 Ill. 264;
Smith v. Smith, 32 Ill. 198.

[44] Johnson v. Payne, 11 Nebr.
269, 9 N. W. Rep. 81.

[45] Boston v. Nichols, 47 Ill. 353;
Smith v. Smith, 32 Ill. 198.

[46] Boyer v. Chandler, 160 Ill. 394,
43 N. E. Rep. 803; Schlatt v.
Johnson, 85 Ill. App. 445. Compare Hards v. Burton, 79 Ill. 504.

foreclose upon non-payment of such coupons is not expressly given by the mortgage or trust deed.[47]

§ 372. **Right to Anticipate Maturity of Debt.**—Mortgages and deeds of trust frequently contain a provision that the creditor may, at his option, declare the entire debt due and payable if default shall be made in the payment of any portion or installment of the sum secured, or of any installment of interest. A stipulation of this kind is not regarded as enforcing a penalty or forfeiture of the kind which is odious to equity. It merely authorizes an acceleration or anticipation of the time of payment, and will be enforced in equity as well as at law. Equity may indeed relieve against an oppressive or vexatious exercise of the power thus given to the mortgagee, but will not otherwise prevent him from enforcing his just rights under such a provision.[48] Therefore, when the mortgage contains a stipulation of this kind, and the contemplated default has been made, and the mortgagee has exercised his option to call in the entire debt secured, he may bring and maintain his suit in equity for a foreclosure of the mortgage for the whole amount of the debt.[49] And when the mortgage covenants that all the notes secured shall become due upon default in the payment of any of them, the fact that the pay-

[47] Silverman v. Silverman, 189 Ill. 394, 59 N. E. Rep. 949 (affirming Silverman v. McCormick, 90 Ill. App. 120); Boyer v. Chandler, 160 Ill. 394, 43 N. E. Rep. 803; Schlatt v. Johnson, 85 Ill. App. 445.

[48] Magnusson v. Williams, 111 Ill. 450; Houston v. Curran, 101 Ill. App. 203; Hoodless v. Reed, 112 Ill. 105, 1 N. E. Rep. 118; Ottawa Plank Road Co. v. Murray, 15 Ill. 336; Holland v. Sampson, (Pa.) 6 Atl. Rep. 772; supra, § 64. Compare Tiernan v. Hinman, 16 Ill. 400. In Condon v. Maynard, 71 Md. 601, 18 Atl. Rep. 957, it was said: "As the appellant expressly covenanted that a failure to pay the taxes would authorize an exercise of the power of sale contained in the mortgage, his objection that there has been no breach justifying the sale cannot be sustained. Such a covenant was lawful, and there is nothing in the record to indicate that its enforcement was designed for the mere purpose of oppression. Had these taxes been but a few days in arrear when Maynard [the mortgagee] advertised the property for sale, a different question might perhaps have been presented; because a court of equity is always reluctant to lend any aid towards consummating oppressive contracts, especially when its intervention would, in effect, result in the enforcement of a forfeiture. But no such difficulty arises here."

[49] Terry v. Trustees of Eureka College, 70 Ill. 236; Ottawa Plank Road Co. v. Murray, 15 Ill. 336; Hoodless v. Reid, 112 Ill. 105.

ment of one of them depends on an outstanding title being procured by the mortgagee, does not prevent a foreclosure in case of default in the payment of another of the notes.[50] And where several notes are secured by the same mortgage and passed to different holders, and it is provided that if default is made in the payment of either or any part of them, the whole principal sum secured by the various notes shall immediately become due "at the option of the legal holder or holders, or any or either thereof," a creditor may foreclose on default in the payment of any of the notes, although such default does not affect him directly, the note which he himself holds not being yet due.[51]

A similar right may be given to the mortgagee upon the breach of other conditions than that for the payment of the debt. Thus, if the mortgage contains a clause giving the mortgagee the right to declare the debt due and payable upon the breach by the mortgagor of any of his covenants or agreements, and one of the covenants binds the mortgagor to keep down taxes on the property, the mortgagee will have the right to declare the principal due and to begin foreclosure proceedings upon the mortgagor's failure to pay taxes, without regard to the terms of the note evidencing the debt.[52] But this power will not be inferred from ambiguous provisions, and close attention must be paid to the terms of the mortgage in this regard. Thus, a provision that, on default in the payment of any installment of interest, it shall be lawful to sell the mortgaged premises, does not make the entire debt due on such default.[53] In examining the question of this power on the part of the mortgagee, the mortgage or trust deed and the note which it secures, being contemporaneous instruments, must be considered and construed together.[54] Where the provision is that, upon default in the payment of either of the notes secured, all shall become "immediately due at the option of the holder," the words "immediately due" are construed as meaning "due immediately upon or after the holder's election," and he is not bound to elect immediately after default.[55]

[50] Wisner v. Chamberlin, 117 Ill. 568, 7 N. E. Rep. 68.

[51] Hennessy v. Gore, 35 Ill. App. 594.

[52] Gray v. Robertson, 174 Ill. 242, 51 N. E. Rep. 248.

[53] Brokaw v. Field, 33 Ill. App. 138.

[54] Gregory v. Marks, 8 Biss. C. C. 44, Fed. Cas. No. 5, 802.

[55] Wheeler & Wilson Mfg. Co. v. Howard, 28 Fed. Rep. 741.

Upon suit to foreclose the mortgage, under a power of this kind, an assignee of the equity of redemption, who has assumed the mortgage debt, has such an interest as will entitle him to object to any provisions in the decree not warranted by the actual terms of the mortgage.[56]

§ 373. Same; Notice of Mortgagee's Election.—When a mortgage or trust deed provides that, in case of default in the payment of any installment of principal or interest, the entire debt shall become at once due and payable at the option of the mortgagee, it is not necessary that any particular act or form of expression should be used for the purpose of declaring such option.[57] The formation of an intention in the mind of the person who has the option to declare the debt due, accompanied by any affirmative act or declaration evincing such determination, will be sufficient. The preparation of a bill to foreclose, and authorizing the same to be filed, is sufficient evidence of the intention to exercise the option.[58] Thus, in one of the cases it was said: "When the first series of notes became due and payment was not made, three of the holders of the notes called on the trustee and informed him that they wanted their money. They then prepared a notice in writing, addressed to him as trustee, in which they called upon him to foreclose the deed of trust because of default in the payment of the principal debt. They did not declare in so many words that, on account of a default in the payment of a part of the debt, they elected to declare the whole debt due, but such was the import of what was said and done;" and this was held a sufficient declaration of election.[59] Moreover, if the mortgage or deed makes no provision for notice of the exercise of such an option, neither the mortgagor nor those claiming under him can be permitted to insist upon notice of the exercise of the option as a condition precedent to the right of the mortgagee to file a bill to foreclose for the whole debt.[60] If the bill for foreclosure contains a declaration that the mortgagee elects

[56] Jones v. Ramsey, 3 Ill. App. 303.

[57] Harper v. Ely, 56 Ill. 179; Owen v. Occidental Building & Loan Ass'n, 55 Ill. App. 347.

[58] Brown v. McKay, 151 Ill. 315, 37 N. E. Rep. 1037.

[59] Heffron v. Gage, 149 Ill. 182, 36 N. E. Rep. 569.

[60] Brown v. McKay, 151 Ill. 315, 37 N. E. Rep. 1037; Hoodless v. Reed, 112 Ill. 105, 1 N. E. Rep. 118; Princeton Loan & T. Co. v. Munson, 60 Ill. 371; Cundiff v. Brokaw, 7 Ill. App. 147.

to consider the whole debt due, according to the terms of the mortgage, that will be sufficient in itself.[61] And the mortgagor receives all the notice to which he is entitled by the mere filing of the bill.[62] So, where the mortgage stipulates that it may be foreclosed upon failure to pay the taxes on the premises when the same are by law due and payable, the mortgagee, as soon as the taxes are delinquent, may pay them and then at once foreclose. It is not necessary for him to notify the mortgagor that the taxes are due (the mortgagor being bound to know that fact for himself), nor to warn him that he is about to pay the same, or that he has paid them.[63] Of course the mortgage or deed of trust may provide not only for a declaration of the creditor's option upon default, but also for notice to the mortgagor; and in this case, its terms must be fully complied with. Thus, where, by the terms of the mortgage, the principal debt does not become absolutely due upon the failure to pay interest, except at the election of the trustees, as declared and notified by them to the mortgagor, the right to foreclose for the whole debt must be established by such declaration and notice; failure to pay interest alone is not enough.[64]

§ 374. Same; Waiver of Forfeiture.—A clause in a mortgage permitting the mortgagee to declare the whole debt due and payable upon default in the payment of any installment of principal or interest, is for the benefit of the mortgagee, and he is not bound to take advantage of it unless he chooses. And even after he has elected to declare the principal sum due, for default in the prompt payment of interest, he may, upon the payment of the interest or for any other reason satisfactory to himself, waive his election and permit the contract as to the time and terms of payment to continue as it was originally. But the mere acceptance, after a default, of the amount of the interest then due is not in itself a waiver of a prior notice of election to declare the principal due, though where such interest is accepted as the entire amount then due, it becomes a question of fact whether the acceptance was intended

[61] Johnson v. Van Velsor, 43 Mich. 208, 5 N. W. Rep. 265.

[62] Sweeney v. Kaufman, 168 Ill. 233, 48 N. E. Rep. 144, affirming 64 Ill. App. 151; Heffron v. Gage, 149 Ill. 182, 36 N. E. Rep. 569;

Owen v. Occidental Building & Loan Ass'n, 55 Ill. App. 347.

[63] Ellwood v. Walcott, 32 Kans. 526, 4 Pac. Rep. 1056.

[64] Chicago, D. & V. R. Co. v. Fosdick, 106 U. S. 47.

as a waiver of the election or not.[65] So, a foreclosure as to
one note on default of its payment, is no bar to a subsequent
suit for foreclosure as to the other notes secured by the same
mortgage, which the mortgagee might have declared due at
that time, if he had chosen to exercise his option.[66] Where the
mortgagor is declared to be in default in the payment of one
of several coupon notes secured by the mortgage, the mortgagee, by accepting payment of a subsequent coupon note, or
of interest, after his declaration of forfeiture, does not, as
against the mortgagor, waive the effect of such declaration.[67]

§ 375. **Proceedings against Estate of Deceased Mortgagor.**—
The right to foreclose a mortgage or deed of trust against
lands of a deceased person is not barred by a failure to exhibit
the claim to the probate court for allowance within two years
after letters are granted, under the statute providing that all
demands not so exhibited shall be forever barred unless the
creditor shall find other estate not inventoried or accounted
for.[68] Hence a mortgagee, relying entirely on his security,
need not probate his claim, but may foreclose on default against
the property covered by the mortgage; and his rights in this
respect are not affected by the fact that the executor includes
the mortgaged property in his inventory of the estate as
assets. But if the mortgagee desires to have recourse to the
inventoried assets, in the event of a deficiency after the sale
of the mortgaged premises, he must present his claim for allowance by the probate court.[69] Also it is held that a mortgagee
is not estopped from foreclosing by appearing and allowing a
default in proceedings to sell the land and pay the debts of
the deceased mortgagor, where his rights were set out in the
petition to sell and the decree protects his interests.[70]

[65] Van Vlissingen v. Lenz, 171
Ill. 162, 49 N. E. Rep. 422. And
see Moore v. Sargent, 112 Ind. 484,
14 N. E. Rep. 466.

[66] Bressler v. Martin, 34 Ill. App.
122.

[67] Houston v. Curran, 101 Ill.
App. 263.

[68] Kittredge v. Nicholes, 162 Ill.

410, 44 N. E. Rep. 742, affirming
60 Ill. App. 604.

[69] Waughop v. Bartlett, 165 Ill.
124, 46 N. E. Rep. 197, affirming
61 Ill. App. 252. And see McClure
v. Owens, 32 Ark. 443.

[70] Kittredge v. Nicholes, 162 Ill.
410, 44 N. E. Rep. 742, affirming
60 Ill. App. 604.

§ 376. Statutory Limitation as to Foreclosures.—It is provided by statute in Illinois that "no person shall commence an action or make a sale to foreclose any mortgage or deed of trust in the nature of a mortgage, unless within ten years after the right of action or right to make such sale accrues."[71] When notes secured by mortgage are reduced to judgment after their maturity, the statute of limitations begins to run against the right to foreclose at the date of such judgment.[72] Ordinarily, it is said, a plea of the statute of limitations is a personal right, and if the mortgagor does not plead it in an action to foreclose, a junior mortgagee cannot have the sale set aside on the ground that the proceedings were barred, at least where he never had the legal title or the possession, was not a party to the foreclosure proceedings, and merely stands upon such rights as his mortgage gives him.[73] But in an action for foreclosure against the heirs of the mortgagor, he being dead, the defendants may plead the bar of the statute just as their ancestor might have done if he were alive and a party.[74]

§ 377. Action after Debt is Barred.—The mortgage being regarded in equity as a mere incident to the debt which it secures, and depending for its vitality upon the continued existence of the debt as an enforceable claim, there can be no foreclosure of the mortgage after the time at which an action at law upon the mortgage debt would be barred by the statute of limitations. The rule is that, where there is a legal remedy and an equitable remedy in respect to the same subject-matter, the latter is under the control of the same statutory bar as the

---

[71] Rev. Stat. Ill. c. 83, § 11. As to the application of this statute to mortgages made before its enactment, see Von Campe v. City of Chicago, 140 Ill. 361, 29 N. E. Rep. 892; Drury v. Henderson, 143 Ill. 315, 32 N. E. Rep. 186.

[72] Litch v. Clinch, 136 Ill. 410, 26 N. E. Rep. 579.

[73] Sanger v. Nightingale, 122 U. S. 176.

[74] Fraser v. Bean, 96 N. Car. 327, 2 S. E. Rep. 159.

former. Consequently, when the statute has run at law against the mortgage debt, equity will not entertain a bill for foreclosure of the mortgage, unless, perhaps, in cases where the complainant shows his delay to have been justifiable.[75] So, there can be no foreclosure of a mortgage where original proceedings to that end were dismissed for want of prosecution, and the mortgage note is barred by the statute when the new bill is filed.[76]

Conversely, it is held that, so long as the mortgage indebtedness exists as a binding obligation upon the mortgagor, the mortgage may be foreclosed upon the mortgaged premises against him or his grantee; and the rule that the mortgage, as a mere incident of the debt secured, is barred only when the debt is barred and not before, is not changed or affected by section 11 of the limitation law, cited in the preceding section.[77] Thus, if the debt secured by a recorded deed of trust has been kept alive by a purchaser of the property, who assumed the debt and for a sufficient consideration agreed to pay it, a grantee of such purchaser takes subject to the incumbrance, and cannot plead the statute of limitations to defeat foreclosure while the debt remains alive.[78]

§ 378. **Circumstances Arresting the Statute.**—The statute of limitations, in respect to actions on bonds, promissory notes, and other evidences of debt, provides that if any payment or new promise to pay shall have been made in writing within or after the period of ten years originally allowed for the commencement of such actions, then the right of action shall continue until ten years after the time of such payment or promise to pay.[79] This section is to be read and construed in connection with the section relating to the limitation of actions for

[75] Harding v. Durand, 138 Ill. 515, 28 N. E. Rep. 948; Quayle v. Guild, 91 Ill. 378; Hancock v. Harper, 86 Ill. 445; Carter v. Tice, 120 Ill. 277, 11 N. E. Rep. 529; Pollock v. Maison, 41 Ill. 516; March v. Mayers, 85 Ill. 177; Emory v. Keighan, 88 Ill. 482; McMillan v. McCormick, 117 Ill. 79, 7 N. E. Rep. 132; Boone v. Colehour, 165 Ill. 305, 46 N. E. Rep. 253.

[76] Merritt v. Merritt, 33 Ill. App. 63.

[77] Hibernian Banking Ass'n v. Commercial Nat. Bank, 157 Ill. 524, 41 N. E. Rep. 919; Richey v. Sinclair, 167 Ill. 184, 47 N. E. Rep. 364; Murray v. Emery, 187 Ill. 408, 58 N. E. Rep. 327; Jones v. Lander, 21 Ill. App. 510.

[78] Murray v. Emery, 187 Ill. 408, 58 N. E. Rep. 327, affirming 85 Ill. App. 348.

[79] Rev. Stat. Ill. c. 83, § 16.

the foreclosure of mortgages, above adverted to, and consequently an action to foreclose a mortgage is not barred when payments on the note or bond secured thereby have been made within ten years before filing the bill.[80] But an unauthorized payment by the widow of the mortgagor, on a mortgage indebtedness on property in which she has but a homestead and dower interest, will not operate to remove the bar of the statute of limitations from the indebtedness as against the heirs, who own the fee.[81] In accordance with the statute, the recognition of the debt by the mortgagor as a subsisting obligation, with his written promise to pay it, will take it out of the bar of the statute, although the time of limitation may have already expired.[82] But an acknowledgment made by the mortgagor to a stranger of the existence of the debt secured by the mortgage, without any express promise made to the mortgagee to pay such debt, will not prevent the bar of the statute from applying in a suit to foreclose the mortgage.[83]

It is also to be observed that where the mortgagee, after condition broken, and before the debt becomes barred by the statute of limitation, takes possession of the mortgaged property, the statute will not run against the mortgage debt while he retains such possession. In a case where a mortgagee had taken possession under these circumstances, it was said that "by so doing she pursued one of the recognized modes, under the law, for the collection of the mortgage debt. She occupied the same position in that regard as an original mortgagee in possession, and became liable to account for the rents and profits actually received, or which by proper diligence she might have received, to be credited upon the indebtedness from year to year. Manifestly, while she was thus proceeding to collect the debt, in a lawful manner, no statute of limitations could run against her. She had the right to remain in possession until the debt was fully satisfied."[84] It is also a rule that the statute of limitations will not run while the mortgagor resides outside the limits of the state; and the fact that

[80] Schifferstein v. Allison, 123 Ill. 662, 15 N. E. Rep. 275; Aetna Life. Ins. Co. v. McNeely, 166 Ill. 540, 46 N. E. Rep. 1130.

[81] Aetna Life Ins. Co. v. McNeely, 166 Ill. 540, 46 N. E. Rep. 1130, affirming 65 Ill. App. 222.

[82] Harding v. Durand, 36 Ill. App. 238; Kreits v. Hamilton, 28 Ill. App. 566.

[83] Biddel v. Brizzolara, 64 Cal. 354, 30 Pac. Rep. 609.

[84] Fountain v. Bookstaver, 141 Ill. 461, 31 N. E. Rep. 17.

a mortgagor of real estate situated in Illinois removed to and resided in another state for such a length of time as would defeat an action at law upon the note secured by the mortgage will not affect the creditor's right to proceed in chancery for the foreclosure of the mortgage.[85]

§ 379. **Adverse Possession.**—Under the general limitation law, possession of real property for seven years, with the payment of taxes thereon, gives a title by adverse possession. But this statute cannot be invoked by a grantee of the mortgagor to bar a foreclosure proceeding against him. From the peculiar relation of a mortgagor and mortgagee, and the fact that a purchaser from the former succeeds only to his rights, with notice of the incumbrance, and the consequent privity between the parties, it is held that the possession of such a purchaser must be considered as in subordination to the mortgage, and not hostile or adverse to the mortgagee; and it cannot cease to be of that character until there is an open disclaimer of holding under it, and the assertion of a distinct title, with the knowledge of the mortgagee.[86] But on the other hand, it is a general rule that if the mortgagor, after breach of condition, has been permitted for twenty years to retain the possession of the mortgaged premises, the mortgage will be presumed to have been discharged, unless circumstances can be shown sufficiently strong to rebut the presumption, such as payment of interest, or a promise to pay the debt, or an acknowledgment by the mortgagor that the mortgage is still a subsisting incumbrance, or the like.[87] And while this is not an act of limitations, nor indeed founded on any statute at all, yet the presumption thus raised, if not successfully rebutted, will defeat the action of foreclosure as effectually as would the bar of the statute.

§ 380. **Limitation in Case of Absolute Deed.**—Where the grantor in a deed, which is absolute in form but intended merely as a security for the payment of a debt, in the nature of a mortgage, remains in the possession of the premises after failure to perform the condition on which he was to receive a re-conveyance of the land, he holds as a tenant at will; and the only statute of limitations which he can set up as a bar

[85] Wooley v. Yarnell, 39 Ill. App. 595; Harding v. Durand, 36 Ill. App. 238.

[86] Medley v. Elliott, 62 Ill. 532;

Brown v. Devine, 61 Ill. 260; Palmer v. Snell, 111 Ill. 161.

[87] Locke v. Caldwell, 91 Ill. 417; Hughes v. Edwards, 9 Wheat. 489.

to a foreclosure by the grantee is that of twenty years' adverse possession.[88]

§ 381. **General Rule as to Parties.**—It is the duty of the complainant, in an action for the foreclosure of a mortgage, to join, as parties, all persons who have rights or interests in the mortgaged premises such as may be affected by the decree. "It is one of the cherished objects of a court of equity to avoid a multiplicity of actions concerning the same subject-matter, by bringing all of the parties interested before it, and making a full and complete settlement between them of their respective rights. Hence the general rule that all persons ought to be made parties whose rights or interests may be affected by the decree. This rule is especially applicable to the case of a foreclosure, where a sale of the mortgaged premises is sought. All persons having an interest in the equity of redemption, and in the distribution of the surplus, are highly proper if not indispensable parties. Such are subsequent purchasers and incumbrancers."[89] A distinction must of course be made between proper parties and necessary parties. But as to the latter, it is said that if any such persons cannot be reached by process and do not voluntarily appear, the bill must be dismissed; when a decree can be made as to those

---

[88] Reed v. Kidder, 70 Ill. App. 498, citing Locke v. Caldwell, 91 Ill. 417.

[89] Montgomery v. Brown, 7 Ill. 581. And see Robbins v. Arnold, 11 Ill. App. 434.

present without affecting the rights of those who are absent, the court may proceed; but if the interests of those present and those absent are inseparable, the obstacle is insuperable.[90] A party may be brought in under a general allegation that he has or claims to have some interest in the equity of redemption; and if he does not disclaim all such interest, he is properly retained as a defendant, and cannot claim immunity from liability for costs.[91] But although one who was a party to the transaction out of which the mortgage originated might properly enough have been made a party to the foreclosure suit, yet the omission to join him will not be fatal; he will simply not be bound by the proceedings taken in the suit.[92] Unless there is some special ground of equitable jurisdiction, a third person who is liable for the mortgage debt in the character of a guarantor, surety, or indorser for the mortgagor, cannot be made a party defendant, with the purpose of recovering a judgment against him for the deficiency; the remedy against him is at law.[93] And so, on bill to foreclose a mortgage, a receiver of one of the mortgagors, appointed on a bill by that mortgagor against another to wind up and settle a partnership, where no conveyance of the mortgagor's property has been made to the receiver, will not be a necessary party.[94]

§ 382. Joint Mortgagees and Holders of Separate Notes.— The holders of two notes may join in a bill for foreclosure, where the notes are for the same amount, and the same land is pledged in one mortgage for their security, on the principle that where several persons have distinct rights against a common fund, they are allowed to file a bill for the purpose of promoting their right against the common fund liable to their demand.[95] And where the mortgage was given as security for the payment of several different notes, which have become the property of as many different holders, the assignee of any one of the notes, the same having matured and remaining unpaid, may institute foreclosure proceedings in his own name. But in such case the holders of all the other notes must be joined as parties, in order that the court may do complete equity by determining the amount and priority of their respective

[90] Ribon v. Chicago, R. I. & P. R. Co., 16 Wall. 446.

[91] Botsford v. Botsford, 49 Mich. 29, 12 N. W. Rep. 897.

[92] Dow v. Seely, 29 Ill. 495.

[93] Walsh v. Van Horn, 22 Ill. App. 170.

[94] Heffron v. Gage, 149 Ill. 182, 36 N. E. Rep. 569.

[95] Pogue v. Clark, 25 Ill. 351.

claims.[96] Even where the owners of some of the notes secured
by a mortgage or deed of trust are unknown to the complainant
in a bill for foreclosure, they are necessary parties if the proceeding may affect their rights, and must be joined.[97] But it
is now ruled that if some of the notes secured by the mortgage
have not yet matured, the holders thereof are not necessary
parties to a suit for foreclosure brought by the owner of one or
more of the notes which have matured, provided the bill does
not seek for any relief which may injuriously affect the holders
of the unmatured notes, but only asks for a sale of the premises
subject to the balance due or to become due under the mortgage.[98]

§ 383. **Mortgagee's Successor in Interest.**—If the owner
of a mortgage has been adjudged a bankrupt, an action for the
foreclosure of the mortgage may be maintained by his assignee
in bankruptcy or by a receiver appointed in that proceeding.[1]
So it is held that a receiver appointed in a suit against an
insolvent corporation, and "authorized and directed to institute such suits at law and in equity as in his judgment may be
necessary against all persons who are indebted to said corporation, or against whom debts are claimed by said corporation,
and who fail or refuse to pay without suit," has authority to
file a bill as sole complainant for the foreclosure of a mortgage
given to the corporation.[2] And a mortgage taken by a
guardian of a minor, as security for a loan of money of his
ward, may be foreclosed, after his death, by the person
appointed as his successor in the guardianship.[3]

§ 384. **Representatives of Deceased Mortgagee.**—The rule of
the common law required the heirs of a deceased mortgagee to
be joined with the administrator in proceedings to foreclose
the mortgage. This rule rested on the ground that the heir
was the only person who could reconvey the estate to the mortgagor. But the statute of Illinois having now provided that a
mortgage may be released or satisfied of record by the executor

[96] Myers v. Wright, 33 Ill. 284;
Funk v. McReynolds, Id. 481;
Koester v. Burke, 81 Ill. 486;
Flower v. Elwood, 66 Ill. 438;
Preston v. Hodgen, 50 Ill. 56;
Lietze v. Clabaugh, 59 Ill. 136.

[97] St. Louis Brewing Ass'n v.
Geppart, 95 Ill. App. 187.

[98] Boyer v. Chandler, 160 Ill.
394, 43 N. E. Rep. 803.

[1] Iglehart v. Bierce, 36 Ill. 133.

[2] Comer v. Bray, 83 Ala. 217, 3
South. Rep. 554.

[3] Norton v. Ohrns, 67 Mich. 612,
35 N. W. Rep. 175.

or administrator of a deceased mortgagee, the reason for the common-law rule no longer exists in that state. Moreover, notes and mortgages have now come to be regarded as mere personal assets, which pass to the personal representatives of the mortgagee upon the latter's death. So that the modern doctrine is that the executor or administrator is the proper complainant in a bill to foreclose the mortgage, and the heirs are not necessary parties.[4] And a husband whose wife has died intestate cannot sue on a note and mortgage executed to her, without first taking out letters of administration on her estate.[5]

§ 385. Assignee of Mortgage as Plaintiff.—It was shown in earlier sections of this work that a suit to foreclose a mortgage which has been assigned, if begun by scire facias, should be brought in the name of the mortgagee for the use of the assignee; but if by bill in equity, it should be in the name of the real owner of the debt secured. In the latter case, the name of the original mortgagee should not be used as complainant, but an error in this respect is amendable. The assignor is not even a necessary party to the assignee's bill for foreclosure.[6] So, the holder of a bond and mortgage, claiming to own the same by gift from the mortgagee, though he may have pledged the same to secure a loan, is a proper party to a bill by another, claiming adversely, to foreclose the mortgage; and if he is not made a party to the bill, he will not be concluded by the decree, and his assignee may maintain a bill to impeach the decree on the ground that the party so foreclosing the mortgage did not own the securities and had no equitable title to the same.[7]

§ 386. Trustee and Beneficiaries.—A bill to foreclose a deed of trust in the nature of a mortgage is properly brought in the name of the trustee, joining with him as complainants the present owners of the notes or other obligations secured. But if the beneficiaries are very numerous, they need not be made parties to the bill, being sufficiently represented by the trustee.[8] If the holders of some of the notes or bonds secured apply to

[4] Citizens' Nat. Bank v. Dayton, 116 Ill. 257, 4 N. E. Rep. 492; Dayton v. Dayton, 7 Ill. App. 136; Marsh v. Wells, 89 Ill. App. 485.

[5] Clark v. Clark, 76 Wis. 306, 45 N. W. Rep. 121.

[6] Supra, §§ 192, 357.

[7] Wellington v. Heermans, 110 Ill. 564.

[8] Chicago & Great Western R. R. Land Co. v. Peck, 112 Ill. 408.

the trustee to whom the deed of trust was executed, to take
steps for its foreclosure, upon default, and he refuses to do so,
they may bring a suit for that purpose, making the trustee
and any other holders of the notes or bonds, who refuse to join
them in the suit, defendants therein.[9] The trustee, however,
is in all cases a necessary party, and a bill which fails to make
him a party is demurrable.[10] Where the deed of trust gives
the trustee the right to declare the bonds due upon default in
the payment of interest, and a suit is brought under that provision at the request of one of the bondholders, the decree may
include all the other holders of the bonds, whether they formally pray for a foreclosure or not.[11] A bill filed by the
beneficiary in the trust deed and the trustee therein sufficiently
indicates the representative character of the latter, though the
word "as" does not precede the word "trustee," when such
trustee has no other relation to the suit.[12] And when the complainant in a foreclosure proceeding is the owner and holder of
the note secured, and is the same person named as trustee in
the deed of trust, and is known to the defendant as such, it is
not necessary that he should also be joined in the suit in his
capacity as trustee.[18]

§ 387. Corporation and Stockholders.—Where a bill for
foreclosure is brought against a corporation as mortgagor, the
stockholders are not necessary parties defendant. In making
this decision the court said: "The corporation represents the
stockholders in bringing and defending suits to which the
corporation is a party." But the court added: "It is not
intended to intimate that, in a case where the stockholders
have a right upon well-defined grounds to defend their own
interests in a suit against the corporation, they may not, as
stockholders, be permitted, in the discretion of the trial court,

---

[9] Omaha Hotel Co. v. Wade, 97
U. S. 13.

[10] Harlow v. Mister, 64 Miss. 25,
8 South. Rep. 164. In a suit in
equity to foreclose a trust deed,
the trustee is a necessary party
defendant, and the controversy is
not severable, as between such
trustee, the owner of the equity
of redemption, and subsequent incumbrancers, so as to be removable

to a federal court on the ground
of a separate controversy between
citizens of different states. Maher
v. Tower Hotel Co., 94 Fed. Rep.
225.

[11] Chillicothe Paper Co. v.
Wheeler, 68 Ill. App. 343.

[12] Kinsella v. Cahn, 185 Ill. 208,
56 N. E. Rep. 1119, affirming 85
Ill. App. 382.

[18] Dearlove v. Hatterman, 102
Ill. App. 329.

to intervene. But upon the mere ground that they are stockholders, and therefore per se necessary parties defendant, we hold that no right to intervene exists."[14]

§ 388. **Subsequent Purchaser from Mortgagor.**—A purchaser or grantee of the mortgagor's equity of redemption in the mortgaged premises, taking title after the execution of the mortgage and before the institution of proceedings for the foreclosure of the same, should be made a party defendant. If he is not joined, the court has no jurisdiction over him, and cannot bind him by its decree. As to him the decree is a mere nullity. His rights cannot be changed, enlarged, diminished, or cut off by the decree. As to other parties properly joined, the decree is not invalid merely for the failure to join such purchaser, and the legal title to the property will be sold at the foreclosure sale and will pass by the master's deed. The purchaser, not joined, simply retains the right which he had before the suit, to wit, the right to redeem the property. This right he may still exercise without abridgment by the foreclosure proceedings. If a strict foreclosure was decreed, still the purchaser, in the case supposed, may assert in equity his right to redeem. If the sale of the property was ordered and made under the usual terms, such purchaser may claim his right of redemption as against the foreclosure purchaser; and it should be carefully noted that this right of redemption is the equitable right to redeem, and not the right of redemption from the sale given by the statute. And further, not being a party to the decree, such purchaser will be at full liberty in a subsequent proceeding to contest the validity of the mortgage, and assert rights adversely thereto.[15] On similar principles, one who is in possession of the land under a contract for its purchase from the mortgagor should be made a party to the suit for foreclosure.[16] But one who merely holds an unre-

---

[14] Gunderson v. Illinois T. & S. Bank, 100 Ill. App. 461, affirmed in 199 Ill. 422.

[15] The various propositions stated in the text will be found to be fully sustained by the following authorities: Bradley v. Snyder, 14 Ill. 263; Cutter v. Jones, 52 Ill. 84; Kelgour v. Wood, 64 Ill. 345; Jeneson v. Jeneson, 66 Ill. 259; Scates v. King, 110 Ill. 456; Patton v. Smith, 113 Ill. 499; Taylor v. Adam, 115 Ill. 570, 4 N. E. Rep. 837; Walker v. Warner, 179 Ill. 16, 53 N. E. Rep. 594; Alsup v. Stewart, 194 Ill. 595, 62 N. E. Rep. 795.

[16] Martin v. Morris, 62 Wis. 418, 22 N. W. Rep. 525.

corded deed for the land from the mortgagor, and who is not
in possession, and of whose interests the mortgagee has no
notice, is not a necessary party to the foreclosure suit.[17] Where
the owner of the equity of redemption acquired his title by
purchase at a sale on execution against the mortgagor, on a
judgment the lien of which was subsequent to the mortgage,
he is not only a proper but a necessary party defendant, the
same as if he held under a direct conveyance from the mortgagor.[18] And the same is true of a purchaser at an invalid
sale under a deed of trust on the same premises.[19] And where
a purchaser of the equity of redemption, taking subsequently
to the mortgage and with notice thereof, has conveyed the
premises to a trustee for the benefit of his creditors, the trustee
is affected with the notice to his grantor, but the creditors
for whose benefit he holds the title need not be made parties
to the bill for foreclosure.[20] A purchaser from the mortgagor,
who takes his deed after the filing of the bill for foreclosure
is to all intents and purposes a party to the decree of foreclosure. The same proceedings can be taken against him which
can be taken against the mortgagor, and he is as conclusively
bound by the result of the litigation as if he had been a party
thereto from the outset.[21]

§ 389. When Mortgagor not a Necessary Party.—When the
mortgagor of realty has sold and conveyed the land before the
filing of a bill for foreclosure of the mortgage, the purchaser
assuming the mortgage, and under such an arrangement among
the parties that the mortgagor no longer remains personally
liable for the debt (or when no personal decree is sought
against him), he is not a necessary party to the foreclosure
suit,[22] and other defendants properly joined cannot urge that ✓
a decree of foreclosure was void because the mortgagor was
not joined or was not served with process,[23] and there is no
error in refusing to allow him to be made a party, at the
request of the defendant, merely for the purpose of settling

[17] Oakford v. Robinson, 48 Ill.
App. 270; Connely v. Rue, 148 Ill.
207, 35 N. E. Rep. 824.

[18] Kepley v. Jansen, 107 Ill. 79.

[19] Wolff v. Ward, 104 Mo. 127, 16
S. W. Rep. 161.

[20] Willis v. Henderson, 5 Ill. 13.

[21] Norris v. Ile, 152 Ill. 190, 38

N. E. Rep. 762; Chickering v.
Fullerton, 90 Ill. 520.

[22] Stiger v. Bent, 111 Ill. 328;
Boutwell v. Steiner, 84 Ala. 307, 4
South. Rep. 184. Compare Sick-
mon v. Wood, 69 Ill. 329.

[23] Watts v. Creighton (Iowa), 52
N. W. Rep. 12.

matters between them in which the complainant has no interest.[24]

§ 390. **Tenants in Possession.**—A party who was in possession of the mortgaged premises at or before the time of the commencement of a suit to foreclose, as a tenant of the mortgagor, must be joined as a defendant; if he is not, his interest will not be affected by the decree, and the writ of possession cannot be issued against him.[25] But the mortgagor himself, when made a defendant and properly brought before the court, cannot complain because tenants in possession of the mortgaged premises are not made parties to the decree, if his own rights are not injuriously affected by the omission to join them.[26]

§ 391. **Same; The State as Tenant.**—When the owner of the equity of redemption in mortgaged lands, or the tenant in possession, is a state, it is held that no proceedings for foreclosure and sale can be maintained, because the state would be a necessary party to such a proceeding and it cannot be sued. But in some cases where the state, not having the title in fee or the possession of the property, has some lien upon it or claim against it, the foreclosure and sale of the property will not be prevented by the interest which the state has in it; but the state's right of redemption will remain.[27] In New York, however, it is said that after the land of a mortgagor has escheated to the state at his death, for want of heirs capable of taking, a foreclosure sale in a suit in which the state is not made a party will pass no title.[28]

§ 392. **Adverse Claimants.**—Persons who claim title to the property in suit adversely to the mortgagor and mortgagee, and independently of the mortgage, and who do not derive their interests in any manner from or through the parties to the instrument, are not proper parties to a bill for foreclosure. Being strangers to the mortgage, their interests are not affected by it, nor by any proceedings for its enforcement, and could not rightfully be adjudicated upon in such proceedings. Hence

[24] Bennett v. Mattingly, 110 Ind. 197, 10 N. E. Rep. 299.

[25] Richardson v. Hadsall, 106 Ill. 476; Brush v. Fowler, 36 Ill. 53.

[26] Rhodes v. Missouri Sav. & Loan Co., 63 Ill. App. 77.

[27] Christian v. Atlantic & N. C. R. Co., 133 U. S. 233.

[28] McCabe v. Kenney, 52 Hun, 514, 5 N. Y. Supp. 678.

the mortgagee has no right to join such claimants as defendants, for the purpose of litigating their claims; and if the pleadings and evidence disclose the fact that any of the defendants are adverse claimants, in this sense, they should be dismissed from the suit.[29] On this principle, the holder of a tax title to the mortgaged premises should not be brought into a suit for foreclosure of the mortgage, and the validity of his title cannot be tried in such proceedings.[30]

§ 393. **Assignee in Bankruptcy of Mortgagor.**—If the mortgagor has been adjudged a bankrupt, after the execution of the mortgage, the suit to foreclose must be brought against the assignee or trustee in bankruptcy. If the latter is not made a party, the decree will not extinguish the equity of redemption, but the assignee will be entitled to redeem.[31] This rule, however, applies only where the proceeding to foreclose is by bill in equity; in the case of a foreclosure by scire facias, only the mortgagor need be made a defendant, not his trustee in bankruptcy.[32] If the bankrupt mortgagor, in his schedule in bankruptcy, has set down the mortgaged premises as his homestead, he must be made a defendant in the foreclosure proceedings, and he cannot be made to appear by his assignee,

---

[29] Frye v. Bank of Illinois, 11 Ill. 367; Gage v. Perry, 93 Ill. 177; Runner v. White, 60 Ill. App. 247; Carbine v. Sebastian, 6 Ill. App. 564; Kinsley v. Scott, 58 Vt. 470, 5 Atl. Rep. 390; Davis v. Hamilton, 53 Ill. App. 94; Smith v. Kenney, 89 Ill. App. 293. A court of equity will not assume to determine the validity of an adverse and independent title in a suit for the foreclosure of a mortgage, neither will it assume the existence of such a title without some competent evidence tending to show the fact. Where a party joined as a defendant in a foreclosure proceeding claims such a title, adverse to the mortgagor and not in any manner derived from or through him, the burden of proof is upon him to establish the fact that his claim is under an adverse title, and when this is made to appear, the court will, as to such defendant, proceed no further. Such controversies are to be settled in courts of law. Runner v. White, supra. And conversely, a party cannot, by a cross-bill on a mere bill to foreclose a mortgage, compel the complainant to litigate an adverse title. Parlin & Orendorff Co. v. Galloway, 95 Ill. App. 60.

[30] Carbine v. Sebastian, 6 Ill. App. 564; Gage v. Directors of Chicago Theological Seminary, 8 Ill. App. 410; Whittemore v. Shiell, 14 Ill. App. 414; Zitzer v. Polk, 19 Ill. App. 61.

[31] Barron v. Newberry, 1 Biss. C. C. 149, Fed. Cas. No. 1,056; Cole v. Duncan, 58 Ill. 176.

[32] Chickering v. Failes, 26 Ill. 507.

unless the mortgage of the homestead was acknowledged according to the provisions of the state statute regulating the acknowledgment of such mortgages.[33] If the mortgagor was adjudged bankrupt, and his assignee appointed, after the filing of the bill for foreclosure, and pending the proceedings thereon, the assignee may intervene if he chooses, but he must have himself made formally a party to the suit, otherwise he stands in the position which would be occupied by any other purchaser on whom the title had fallen pending the suit. If he does not come into the proceedings, his non-intervention will raise an implication either that he has no defense to the foreclosure or that he has elected to waive any defense he may have. If he fails to intervene, a decree for the sale of the premises will conclude him, and a sale made in execution of the decree will bar his rights as effectually as it does those of the bankrupt.[34]

§ 394. Wife of Mortgagor.—When the wife of a mortgagor of realty has joined in the execution of the mortgage, she must be made a defendant to a bill in equity to foreclose it.[35] If not joined as a party, she will not be in any way affected by the decree. If she has any rights in the premises, she may at any time institute proceedings to establish them; and if she executed the mortgage, the holder of the security may foreclose the same against such title when she does assert her claim.[36] But generally the only reason for joining the wife of the mortgagor is to bar the equity of redemption in her right of dower, or to give her the opportunity before foreclosure to redeem and prevent the sale of the property; and a decree issued against both defendants is not a personal decree, but a decree for the sale of the premises subject to redemption according to law.[37] It will be observed that this rule does not apply in the case of a mortgage given to secure the purchase money of the land. As against a purchase-money mortgage, no claim for dower can be asserted. And therefore, the wife of the mortgagor, having no interest in the premises, is not a necessary or proper party to a suit for its foreclosure.[38]

[33] Dendel v. Sutton, 20 Fed. Rep. 787.

[34] Eyster v. Gaff, 91 U. S. 521; Mount v. Manhattan Co., 43 N. J. Eq. 25, 9 Atl. Rep. 114.

[35] Gilbert v. Maggord, 2 Ill. 471;

Leonard v. Villars, 23 Ill. 377; Camp v. Small, 44 Ill. 37; Orvis v. Cole, 14 Ill. App. 283.

[36] McIntire v. Yates, 104 Ill. 491.

[37] Wright v. Langley, 36 Ill. 381.

[38] Baker v. Scott, 62 Ill. 86;

Again, if it appears that the acknowledgment of the mortgagor's wife was not such as is required by law, it is not proper to make her a party to the suit.[39] And where the mortgaged land has been sold to a purchaser, who assumed the mortgage debt and became responsible for it, as part of the purchase price, the wife of the original mortgagor, having no longer any interest in the property, is not a necessary party to a bill to foreclose brought after the sale of the land.[40]

§ 395. **Personal Representatives of Deceased Mortgagor.**— An administrator is not a necessary party defendant to a bill to foreclose his intestate's mortgage, where the bill seeks a foreclosure only, and not to charge him or the personal estate in his hands.[41] "It is not necessary to make the administrator of the mortgagor a party to a bill of foreclosure, except where he has an interest in the equity of redemption, as where the mortgage is upon a chattel interest, or where the bill seeks not only a foreclosure but a decree for any deficiency against the personal estate; and though by our statute an administrator may redeem from a sale of mortgaged premises under a decree of a court of equity, it does not follow that he is a necessary party to a bill of foreclosure."[42] On similar principles, the administrator of one who has purchased land subject to a mortgage, but without personally assuming the payment of the mortgage debt, is not a necessary party to a suit for the foreclosure of the mortgage.[43] Where the bill makes a certain person defendant as executor and as guardian, and the return of the process shows that he was served as executor and guardian, and the bill states that he has an individual interest in the mortgaged land, a decree of foreclosure binds him as well in his individual as in his representative capacity.[44]

§ 396. **Heirs of Mortgagor.**—If the mortgagor of realty is dead at the time of commencing a suit in equity for the foreclosure of the mortgage, the proper defendants in the action

Short v. Raub, 81 Ill. 509; Stephens v. Bicknell, 27 Ill. 444; supra, § 235.

[39] Sheldon v. Patterson, 55 Ill. 507.

[40] Stiger v. Bent, 111 Ill. 328; Koerner v. Gauss, 57 Ill. App. 668.

[41] Roberts v. Tunnell, 165 Ill.

631, 46 N. E. Rep. 713 (affirming 65 Ill. App. 191); Bissell v. Marine Co., 55 Ill. 165.

[42] Roberts v. Flatt, 42 Ill. App. 608, affirmed in 142 Ill. 485.

[43] Stiger v. Bent, 111 Ill. 328.

[44] Cornell v. Green, 43 Fed. Rep. 105.

are his heirs,[45] except in cases where the particular parcel of land affected by the mortgage has been devised by the will of the deceased mortgagor, in which case the devisee (or a purchaser of the property from him) is the proper defendant,[46] and the heirs need not be joined unless they dispute the title of the devisee. Where the mortgage was made by a husband and his second wife, it was held that children of the husband by his former marriage were not necessary parties to a suit to foreclose it.[47] Also it is ruled that the supposed heirs of a person who is presumed to be alive, although it is not known where he is, are not necessary parties to a proceeding to foreclose a mortgage given by him.[48] And where the mortgagor, in his life-time has sold and conveyed the mortgaged premises, his heirs are not necessary parties to a bill to foreclose the mortgage, as they have no interest in the land to be affected.[49]

§ 397. Junior Incumbrancers.—Where the same property is incumbered by two or more successive mortgages, and a suit in equity is brought for the foreclosure of the senior lien, the junior mortgagees should be made parties defendant, the object being to cut off their right of redemption; if they are not joined, they will not be affected by the decree, and may redeem on the same conditions as before the suit.[50] And in a case where the elder lien was a mortgage, and the junior lien a deed of trust, it was held, on foreclosure of the mortgage, that both the trustee in the deed and the beneficiary therein should be made defendants to the bill.[51] The same rules apply where the junior incumbrancers liable to be affected by the foreclosure of the senior lien are judgment creditors of the mortgagor whose judgments were recovered subsequent to the execution of the mortgage,[52] or attachment creditors levying their

[45] Harvey v. Thornton, 14 Ill. 217; Lane v. Erskine, 13 Ill. 501; Fraser v. Bean, 96 N. Car. 327, 2 S. E. Rep. 159.

[46] Ohling v. Luitjens, 32 Ill. 23.

[47] Douglas v. Soutter, 52 Ill. 154.

[48] Reedy v. Camfield, 159 Ill. 254, 42 N. E. Rep. 833.

[49] Medley v. Elliott, 62 Ill. 532.

[50] Jeneson v. Jeneson, 66 Ill. 259; Augustine v. Doud, 1 Ill. App. 588; Brooks v. Vermont Central R. Co., 14 Blatchf. 463, Fed. Cas. No. 1,964. The filing of a cross-bill is not necessary to the preservation of the rights of a junior mortgagee of the same premises, as against the prior mortgagee. Boone v. Clark, 129 Ill. 466, 21 N. E. Rep. 850.

[51] Woolner v. Wilson, 5 Ill. App. 439.

[52] Boynton v. Pierce, 151 Ill. 197, 37 N. E. Rep. 1024.

attachments before the commencement of the foreclosure proceedings,[53] or the holder or assignee of a mechanic's lien on the mortgaged premises.[54]

§ 398. Senior Incumbrancers.—In proceedings to foreclose a junior mortgage, the senior mortgagee is not a necessary party, for the reason that his rights cannot be affected by the decree in such a suit.[55] If he is joined as a defendant, the proper decree to be entered is for a sale of the premises subject to the lien of the senior mortgage.[56] If, however, there is any dispute between the senior and junior incumbrancers as to their relative rights, or as to the rank or priority of the two liens, or if the validity of the elder incumbrance is to be attacked, it is entirely proper for the junior mortgagee to make the senior mortgagee a defendant to his suit for foreclosure, and the court may then determine and settle the questions arising between them.[57]

PART V. PLEADINGS AND EVIDENCE.

§ 399. Requisites of Bill.—The complainant in a suit in equity for the foreclosure of a mortgage should set out in his bill such allegations as will clearly show the identity and relation of the parties, the nature and terms of the debt or other obligation secured, the terms and conditions of the mortgage. and the default or breach of condition on which his right of action accrues. Thus, the bill must allege a debt as the founda-

[53] Dickinson v. Lamoille County Nat. Bank, 12 Fed. Rep. 747.

[54] Atkins v. Volmer, 21 Fed Rep. 697.

[55] Crawford v. Munford, 29 Ill. App. 445; Galford v. Gillett, 55 Ill. App. 576; Chandler v. O'Neil, 62 Ill. App. 418. See Shinn v. Shinn, 91 Ill. 477; Warner v. De Witt County Nat. Bank, 4 Ill. App. 305;

Jerome v. McCarter, 94 U. S. 734; Hague v. Jackson, 71 Tex. 761, 12 S. W. Rep. 63.

[56] Hibernian Banking Ass'n v. Law, 88 Ill. App. 18.

[57] Foster v. Trowbridge, 44 Minn. 290, 46 N. W. Rep. 350; First Nat. Bank v. Salem Capital Flour-Mills Co., 31 Fed. Rep. 580.

tion of the mortgage.[58] And it must be described in such substantial conformity to the terms of the mortgage as to avoid a variance.[59] But an averment that the defendant made his note to the complainant for a designated sum is sufficient to show that he borrowed and received that amount.[60] It is also necessary to allege such facts as will show the mortgage to be valid and effectual as a conveyance. But an allegation that the defendant "made, executed, acknowledged, and delivered a certain deed of mortgage" is held to be sufficient, since it can only be construed as meaning that the mortgage was properly made and valid in its operation.[61] And in a bill to foreclose a mortgage claimed to have been executed by husband and wife, upon land owned by the latter in fee, the mortgage may be stated according to its legal effect, without averring in detail the various matters which are necessary to the transfer of a married woman's title.[62] There should also be a description of the premises affected by the mortgage, sufficient to identify the land clearly. But a bill is sufficient without any description of the mortgaged property if it has annexed to it a copy of the mortgage, wherein the land is fully and correctly described.[63] And no ground of complaint arises to the mortgagor if the mortgagee, either purposely or by inadvertence, omits from the description a parcel of the land mortgaged, thereby in effect releasing that parcel from the foreclosure.[64] If the mortgage, as executed and delivered, was imperfect or contained mistaken descriptions, the complainant may include in his bill a prayer for its reformation. That is, a bill which asks for the reformation of the mortgage and then for its foreclosure as reformed is not bad for multifariousness.[65]

[58] Nye v. Gribble, 70 Tex. 453, 8 S. W. Rep. 608. On a bill to foreclose a mortgage given for the purchase price of an interest in a mill, the controversy being as to the existence of a partnership between the mortgagor and mortgagee in running the mill, it is error to decree a foreclosure when the pleadings are in a state which prevents the investigation of the question as to the existence or settlement of the partnership. Gammon v. Wright, 31 Ill. App. 353.

[59] Benneson v. Savage, 130 Ill. 352, 22 N. E. Rep. 838.

[60] Snyder v. State Bank of Illinois, 1 Ill. 161.

[61] Moore v. Titman, 33 Ill. 358; Prieto v. Duncan, 22 Ill. 26.

[62] Williams v. Soutter, 55 Ill. 130.

[63] Whitby v. Rowell, 82 Cal. 635, 23 Pac. Rep. 40.

[64] Coffeen v. Thomas, 65 Ill. App. 117.

[65] Hutchinson v. Ainsworth, 73 Cal. 452, 15 Pac. Rep. 82.

§ 400. Allegations as to Claims of Third Persons.—A general allegation in a bill for foreclosure that a party joined as a defendant, but who is not a party to the mortgage, claims some interest in the mortgaged premises, or some lien thereon, which is inferior to the mortgage, is sufficient, without undertaking to describe more particularly the nature of the interest or lien claimed; and it will put such defendant under the duty of setting up his interest by way of answer and establishing it by proof; if he merely denies the allegations of the bill, it is an admission that he has no interest in the property, or lien thereon, and will estop him from afterwards claiming any such interest.[66] But where a senior mortgagee is made a party to a suit for foreclosure by the junior mortgagee, the latter should distinctly allege in his bill the purpose for which the former is brought in. If it is intended to assert that the elder mortgage is invalid or that it should, for any reason, be postponed to the junior incumbrance, the facts relied on in that behalf should be pleaded. Under the general allegation that defendant has or claims some interest in the mortgaged premises, as purchaser, mortgagee, or otherwise, which interest, if any, accrued subsequent to the lien of complainant's mortgage, the senior mortgagee is not bound to set up his rights, and is not affected by a decree taken pro confesso against him.[67] When a stranger thus joined, in answer to the general allegation that he claims some interest in or lien upon the premises, sets up a judgment against the mortgagor and alleges that it is the first lien on the premises, the complainant may show that the property in suit was the mortgagor's homestead, and therefore not subject to the lien of a judgment.[68]

§ 401. Defendant's Plea and Answer.—Where the defendant in a suit to foreclose a mortgage chooses to demur to the bill, and his demurrer is overruled and it appears that he has no

[66] Kehm v. Mott, 187 Ill. 519, 58 N. E. Rep. 467, affirming 86 Ill. App. 549. So also, in other states, it is held to be a sufficient allegation in regard to a stranger thus brought in that he "has or claims some interest in or lien upon said real property, but the same, whatever it may be, is subject to the lien of said mortgage." (Dexter v. Long, 2 Wash. 435, 27 Pac. Rep.

271), or that he "has or claims to have some interest or claim upon said premises, which interest is subsequent to and subject to the lien of plaintiff's mortgage." Sichler v. Look, 93 Cal. 600, 29 Pac. Rep. 220.

[67] Foval v. Benton, 48 Ill. App. 638.

[68] German Ins. Co. v. Nichols, 41 Kans. 133, 21 Pac. Rep. 111.

defense, he may be required to answer instanter, and on his failure to do so, the bill may be taken as confessed and a decree of sale entered.[69] But the statute in Illinois imperatively requires that, if an answer in chancery is adjudged insufficient, on exceptions filed, the defendant must be ruled to answer further before the cause can be set down for hearing. So where, in a suit to foreclose a mortgage, on allowing exceptions filed by the complainant to defendant's answer, the court at once entered a decree of foreclosure, it was held that the decree was premature, as the defendant should first have been ruled to put in a sufficient answer.[70] Where the defendant answers generally and also pleads in bar a prior adjudication, the trial should be upon the merits, and should not be confined to the plea in bar alone.[71] Where the bill alleges that the defendant made, executed, acknowledged, and delivered the mortgage or deed of trust, the default of the defendant admits these several facts and concludes him as to them.[72] A tender by the defendant in the progress of foreclosure proceedings is a confession that the complainant has a good cause of action to the amount tendered, and that it is correctly set forth in the bill, and that the defendant has broken the contract in the manner and to the extent declared; and after such a tender, it is error in the court to find that the evidence does not sustain the allegations of the bill and to dismiss it for want of equity.[73]

§ 402. Cross-Bills.—A defendant in equity who seeks affirmative relief generally proceeds by the filing of a cross-bill, and this is the proper form of pleading when the relief sought is asked as against another defendant in the same suit. Thus, on a bill to foreclose a mortgage, to which a subsequent purchaser of the premises is made a defendant, a cross-bill by the mortgagor, seeking to have his conveyance of the property to that defendant set aside on the ground of fraud and failure of consideration is proper, for the purpose of determining who has the right of redemption.[74] But a defendant who does not

[69] Snell v. Stanley, 63 Ill. 391.

[70] Holly v. Powell, 63 Ill. 139; Rev. Stat. Ill. c. 22, § 24.

[71] Coleman v. Hunt, 77 Wis. 263, 45 N. W. Rep. 1085.

[72] Terry v. Trustees of Eureka College, 70 Ill. 236; Williams v. Soutter, 55 Ill. 130; Moore v. Titman, 33 Ill. 358.

[73] Mason v. Uedelhofen, 102 Ill. App. 116.

[74] Dawson v. Vickery, 150 Ill. 398, 37 N. E. Rep. 910.

ask affirmative relief, but simply that a piece of property received by the complainant on his debt should be applied in payment pro tanto, need not file a cross-bill.[75] In a case where several defendants are brought in under the general allegation that they claim some interest in or lien upon the premises in suit, and their answers severally claim liens on the property, the court has power, without the filing of a cross-bill, to determine the existence and priority of the various liens, and to order the premises sold and the proceeds distributed in discharge of such liens according to their priority.[76] So also, "it is a well-established rule that where junior incumbrancers are made parties defendant to a foreclosure suit, a cross-bill is not necessary to enable them to participate in the distribution of a surplus. A defendant in such case can prove his claim, and if there is a surplus above the superior incumbrance, he may have satisfaction out of it." It is sufficient if his right to participate is claimed in his answer and made out by proof.[77] But where the defendants in a foreclosure suit set up a title derived from a sheriff's sale, except as to the part of the land set out as a homestead, it was held that a decree that the part so set out should be first sold could not properly be rendered without the filing of a cross-bill therefor.[78]

§ 403. **Evidence in General.**—The complainant in a foreclosure suit must sustain the burden of proving all the facts which are essential to the relief which he asks, except in so far as the same may have been admitted by the defendant. Thus, he must prove the due execution of the mortgage, unless that fact is admitted,[79] and that he is the owner of the note or other obligation secured by the mortgage, having a present right to maintain the suit,[80] and also that there has been a breach of the condition of the mortgage, and the existence of any fact which the mortgage itself makes a prerequisite to the right of foreclosure.[81] Again, in foreclosure suits, as in all

[75] Edgerton v. Young, 43 Ill. 464.

[76] Gardner v. Cohn, 191 Ill. 553, 61 N. E. Rep. 492 (affirming 95 Ill. App. 26); Rock Island Nat. Bank v. Thompson, 173 Ill. 593, 50 N. E. Rep. 1089, affirming 74 Ill. App. 54.

[77] Wallen v. Moore, 187 Ill. 190, 58 N. E. Rep. 392 (affirming 88 Ill. App. 287); Romberg v. McCormick, 194 Ill. 205, 62 N. E. Rep. 537; Armstrong v. Warrington, 111 Ill. 430.

[78] Erlinger v. Boul, 7 Ill. App. 40.

[79] Fergus v. Tinkham, 38 Ill. 407.

[80] Ross v. Utter, 15 Ill. 402.

[81] Carr v. Fielden, 18 Ill. 77.

other proceedings in equity, the allegations, the proof, and the decree must correspond; and where the evidence fails to sustain the allegations of the bill, the complainant cannot be given a decree upon other grounds disclosed by the evidence, and which, if pleaded, would have warranted it, unless where he is permitted to amend his bill to conform to the case disclosed by the testimony.[82] In a case where the bill made a subsequent purchaser a defendant, but there was no averment of notice, it was held that evidence relating to the question of notice was not irrelevant merely for the want of such averment in the bill, when both parties had proceeded as though that were in issue, introducing testimony on the question.[83]

§ 404. Proof of Debt.—The complainant in a bill for foreclosure is bound to prove the indebtedness secured by his mortgage, and the defendant may disprove it, even though he did not specifically set up the defense that the mortgage debt had been paid.[84] Where there is no denial of the execution of the notes secured by the mortgage, on a bill to foreclose, the production of the notes on the hearing is sufficient evidence of their execution.[85] And the introduction in evidence of the note and mortgage, the same being lawfully and properly in the possession of the complainant, makes a prima facie case for foreclosure; and the burden is then upon the defendant to prove the defenses set up in his answer.[86] That is, notes introduced in evidence on foreclosure of a mortgage or deed of trust are evidence prima facie sufficient to authorize the master to find and report whether they are the ones secured, and, if so, the amount due thereunder for which he recommends a decree.[87] And where the execution of the mortgage is duly proven and the notes or bonds offered correspond with those described in the mortgage, it is prima facie evidence that they are the same as those mentioned in the mortgage as having been executed by the mortgagor.[88] But it is erroneous for the court

[82] Dorn v. Gueder, 171 Ill. 362, 49 N. E. Rep. 492.

[83] Moshier v. Knox College, 32 Ill. 155.

[84] Fridley v. Bowen, 5 Ill. App. 191.

[85] Dean v. Ford, 180 Ill. 309, 54 N. E. Rep. 417; Brown v. McKay, 151 Ill. 315, 37 N. E. Rep. 1037, affirming 51 Ill. App. 295.

[86] Boudinot v. Winter, 190 Ill. 394, 60 N. E. Rep. 553, affirming 91 Ill. App. 106.

[87] Ording v. Burnet, 178 Ill. 28, 52 N. E. Rep. 851, affirming 77 Ill. App. 220.

[88] Wolcott v. Lake View Building & Loan Ass'n, 59 Ill. App. 415.

to render a decree for the foreclosure of a mortgage, unless the mortgage and the note which it secures are produced in evidence, or their non-production duly accounted for; and secondary evidence of the contents of the note and mortgage would not be admissible without first making proof of the loss or destruction of the originals.[89] And although the answer of the defendant may admit the execution of the note and mortgage, this will not relieve the complainant of the necessity of producing them. For, as the court observed, "a promissory note is a negotiable instrument; the ownership and title could be changed by indorsement. The fact that the defendants admitted in their answer that they executed the notes and mortgage did not show that the complainant, at the time of the trial, owned them and had the right to a judgment thereon.'"[90] But in the federal courts in Illinois, it is said that, in a suit to foreclose a trust deed, the bonds secured need not be produced before the master nor until a decree of foreclosure is rendered.[91] And in a case where the mortgage and certified copies of the notes were, without objection, referred to a special master to state an account in the foreclosure suit, it was held that the court properly refused to set aside a decree based upon the master's report.[92] Where the mortgage purports to secure a note therein described, but the petition in foreclosure alleges that there was no such note, but that the mortgage was intended to secure future advances, it is competent for the court to decree foreclosure for the amount of such advances, without requiring the production of the mythical note or proper excuses for its non-production.[93] So, where the mortgage recites an indebtedness of the mortgagor on book account, without any reference to any bond or note as evidence of the debt, it will be inferred, in the absence of sufficient evidence to the contrary, that no bond or note was given; and a foreclosure may be decreed without an order for the production of a bond or note.[94] Again, on a bill to foreclose a mortgage, a prior settlement between the debtor and creditor as to the

[89] Dowden v. Wilson, 71 Ill. 485; Moore v. Titman, 35 Ill. 310; Lucas v. Harris, 20 Ill. 165.

[90] Dowden v. Wilson, 71 Ill. 485.

[91] Northern Trust Co. v. Columbia Straw-Paper Co., 75 Fed. Rep. 936.

[92] Pogue v. Clark, 25 Ill. 351.

[93] Moses v. Hatfield, 27 S. Car. 324, 3 S. E. Rep. 538.

[94] Field v. Brokaw, 148 Ill. 654, 37 N. E. Rep. 80.

amount of principal and interest then due, will be held to be conclusive and to furnish a proper basis on which to compute the interest thereafter accruing.[95]

PART VI. DEFENSES.

§ 405. Defenses Available to De-   § 406. Defect or Failure of Title.
fendant.   407. Set-Off.

§ 405. **Defenses Available to Defendant.**—It is stated to be a general principle that "the same defenses may be interposed against a suit upon the mortgage as against the notes for which the mortgage is security. The mortgage must share the fate of the notes, and whatever will defeat the notes should defeat the mortgage."[96] Among the defenses which are commonly available to a mortgagor, and which may be set up in opposition to the mortgagee's suit in equity for foreclosure, we may specify the following:

(a) Want of capacity in the complainant to sue; that is, the defendant may show that the complainant is not the present owner of the debt secured by the mortgage, or is, for any other reason, disabled to maintain a suit for its foreclosure. It is said, indeed, that the mortgagor is estopped by the terms of the mortgage from asserting that the money secured thereby belonged to a person other than the mortgagee, by whom the loan is recited to have been made, or to contest the beneficial interest of the mortgagee.[97] But clearly he may show that the complainant has parted with the note or bond secured, by assignment to a third person. And also, the defendant being a purchaser of the equity of redemption, he may show that the complainant, being the owner of the mortgage in suit, a junior lien, had agreed to sell it to him for a certain price, and afterwards refused to transfer it.[98]

(b) A mortgage will be invalidated by fraud, deception, or

[95] Haworth v. Huling, 87 Ill. 23.
[96] Miller v. Marckle, 21 Ill. 152.
[97] Stevens v. Shannahan, 160 Ill. 330, 43 N. E. Rep. 350.
[98] Cavanaugh v. McWilliams, 22 Ill. App. 197. The right of a party who is a director of a bank to foreclose a mortgage will not be affected by the fact that he and another director thereof had acted improperly towards the bank in procuring the money loaned. That was merely a matter between the directors and the stockholders of the bank. Darst v. Bates, 95 Ill. 493.

undue influence practised upon the mortgagor in its procurement; and its invalidity on these grounds may be pleaded in defense to a suit to foreclose it.[99]

(c) Want or failure of consideration may be set up as a defense to a foreclosure suit.[1] The maker of a mortgage will be estopped to deny an indebtedness recited and set forth in the mortgage;[2] but where the note and mortgage were executed in consideration of the mortgagee's agreement to transfer property to the mortgagor, or to perform some other act for his benefit, a foreclosure can be prevented by showing failure of performance on the part of the mortgagee.[3] So where a purchaser of land, who has been deceived and defrauded as to the character or value of the land, has paid down all the land is worth, and given notes and a mortgage for the balance of the purchase price, he may wait until proceedings to foreclose the mortgage are begun, and set up the fraud in his answer, showing that the notes and mortgage were without consideration, and maintain a cross-bill for their cancellation.[4]

(d) Illegality of the consideration upon which a mortgage is based will invalidate it and may be pleaded in defense to a suit for foreclosure.[5]

(e) Usury, while not a defense to the foreclosure of the mortgage as a lien on the premises affected, will cause a forfeiture of all interest if duly pleaded and proven.[6]

(f) Payment of the mortgage debt before suit, since it extinguishes the claim secured by the mortgage, terminates the life of the security and of course prevents any foreclosure.[7] The defendant setting up this plea must assume the burden of proving the payment by a preponderance of the evidence.[8]

[99] See, supra, §§ 142, 143.

[1] Supra, §§ 122, 123.

[2] Brokaw v. Field, 33 Ill. App. 138. See Palmer v. Sanger, 28 N. E. Rep. 930.

[3] Gammon v. Wright, 31 Ill. App. 353.

[4] Allen v. Henn, 197 Ill. 486, 64 N. E. Rep. 250, affirming 97 Ill. App. 378.

[5] Supra, §§ 145-147.

[6] Supra, §§ 128, 135, 136.

[7] Supra, § 302. It is a good defense to a suit to foreclose a mortgage that the note secured was actually paid in full, at a time prior to its maturity, the mortgagee consenting to receive payment then; but the mortgagor must assume the burden of proving this fact. Kelly v. Butterworth, 103 Ill. App. 87. In a foreclosure proceeding, when it appears that the mortgagee has been overpaid, the defendant, under an answer, is not entitled to affirmative relief; but the cause will be remanded that defendant may file a cross-bill. Hathaway v. Hagan, 59 Vt. 75, 8 Atl. Rep. 678.

[8] Curtis v. Perry (Nebr.) 50 N. W. Rep. 426.

(g) A valid agreement on the part of the mortgagee to give the debtor further time for payment, after the maturity of the mortgage debt, will prevent him from foreclosing the mortgage until the time so extended has expired.[9] Also in cases where the mortgagee, at the time of executing the papers, and as a part of the agreement, indorses on the mortgage a stipulation that he will not call in the loan except upon two years' written notice of his intention to do so, the want of such notice may be pleaded in defense to a suit to foreclose the mortgage, either by the original mortgagor or by his grantee.[10]

(h) A release or conveyance of the equity of redemption in the mortgaged premises to the mortgagee will generally cause a merger of estates in him, extinguish the lien of the mortgage, and so take away the right to sue for its foreclosure.[11]

(i) The statute of limitations may be pleaded in defense to a foreclosure suit. This defense has been fully considered in earlier sections of this chapter.[12]

(j) A former adjudication of the matter in controversy may be pleaded in a foreclosure suit, with conclusive effect, either as a bar to the action or as conclusive of particular points in issue, according to the circumstances. Thus, a judgment for the defendant in a prior action to foreclose the same mortgage, at the suit of a third person claiming to be the assignee of the mortgage, will be a good defense if it is shown that the present complainant was connected with the former proceeding or was in privity with the plaintiff therein, and that the former judgment was on the merits.[13] But an abortive attempt to foreclose a mortgage or deed of trust by the exercise of a power of sale contained therein, will be no bar to the right to foreclose by suit in equity, if the mortgage still remains unpaid and enforceable.[14] In another case, it appeared that the debtor gave a bond with warrant of attorney to confess judgment, and

[9] Supra, § 280. Where no definite time for payment was fixed, circumstances may justify the creditor in beginning a suit for foreclosure, after waiting a reasonable time, without previous demand or notice. See Seymour v. Bailey, 66 Ill. 288.

[10] Belmont County Bank v. Price, 8 Ohio St. 299.

[11] Supra, §§ 281-286.

[12] Supra, §§ 376-380. See McCormick v. Bauer, 122 Ill. 573, 13 N. E. Rep. 852. As to who may plead the statute of limitations, see Houston v. Workman, 28 Ill. App. 626.

[13] Cheney v. Patton, 134 Ill. 422, 25 N. E. Rep. 792.

[14] Rogers v. Benton, 39 Minn. 39, 38 N. W. Rep. 765.

a mortgage as collateral security to such bond. Judgment was entered on the bond, and the debtor filed a petition to have the judgment opened on the ground of fraud and want of consideration for the bond. The petition was denied, and it was held that this made the question of fraud and want of consideration res judicata, so that it could not afterwards be pleaded in defense to a suit to foreclose the mortgage.[15] So, where a claim against a decedent's estate is presented to the probate court, contested, and disallowed, a mortgage given to secure it falls with it, and cannot afterwards be enforced as a separate claim.[16] But the fact that mortgaged property is subject to be administered in bankruptcy proceedings against the mortgagor will not entitle him to resist the administration of it by foreclosure and sale under proceedings for that purpose in the proper court of the state.[17]

§ 406. Defect or Failure of Title.—A mortgagor cannot be permitted to set up, as a defense to a bill of foreclosure, that he had no title to the property which he has himself mortgaged. In such a proceeding, the mortgagor is estopped to deny his own title.[18] But the case is different where the mortgage is given for purchase money and the question is as to the title of the vendor. It is sometimes said that it is no defense to a bill to foreclose such a mortgage that the title has failed or is defective, but that such defects can be relieved against only on the vendor's covenants.[19] But where both the note given for the purchase money and the mortgage securing it stipulated that the money should not become payable until the title to the land should be perfected in the grantor, the mortgagor, in resisting foreclosure of the mortgage, may rely on the condition precedent, instead of the covenants of warranty in the deed.[20] And where a mortgage is given upon one tract of land to secure the purchase money of another tract, which the mortgagee covenants to convey, with warranty, but to which he has no title, such failure of title in the vendor is a good defense to a bill in equity to foreclose the mortgage.[21] So,

[15] Heilman v. Kroh, 155 Pa. St. 1, 25 Atl. Rep. 751.

[16] Sanger v. Palmer, 36 Ill. App. 485. See Palmer v. Sanger, 143 Ill. 34, 32 N. E. Rep. 390.

[17] Broach v. Powell, 79 Ga. 79, 3 S. E. Rep. 763.

[18] Racine & Miss. R. Co. v. Farmers' Loan & Trust Co., 49 Ill. 331.

[19] Barry v. Guild, 28 Ill. App. 39. And see same case, 126 Ill. 439, 18 N. E. Rep. 759.

[20] Weaver v. Wilson, 48 Ill. 125.

[21] Smith v. Newton, 38 Ill. 230.

where land is conveyed with full covenants of warranty, and a purchase-money mortgage given for half the price, the balance being paid in cash, and the grantor had title only to an undivided three-fourths interest in the land, the grantee, in a suit in equity by the assignee of the mortgage to foreclose the same, is entitled to a rebate of one-fourth of the purchase price.[22] In another case, the owner of land granted and conveyed by deed the right to flow water upon the land, and afterwards sold the land to a third person, conveying to him the title in fee, by deed with the usual covenants, and taking back a mortgage to secure the notes given for deferred payments of the purchase money. On default in the payment of certain of the notes, he brought his bill for foreclosure, and it was held that the defendant (the grantee of the land) might have the amount of damages sustained by him in consequence of the flowage of the land applied in reduction of the notes due and of those subsequently maturing, such an outstanding easement in another being a breach of the covenant against incumbrances and a proper defense to the notes.[23] So also, in a suit to foreclose a purchase-money mortgage, the defendant may set up in his answer a breach of the covenant against incumbrances, in that a private way existed over the premises in question.[24]

§ 407. **Set-Off.**—Where the defendant in a foreclosure proceeding has a fixed and liquidated claim or demand against the complainant, although it is not connected with the transaction out of which the mortgage debt arose, he may be permitted to plead it as a set-off against the complainant's demand, if it would be pleadable in a similar manner at law. If, for example, defendant's claim is such as could be presented as a set-off in an action at law upon the note or bond secured by the mortgage, it may be so presented in a suit to foreclose. It is also true that a court of equity will sometimes allow a set-off when the same would not be permitted at law. But the circumstances calling for such action must be special; that is, special grounds demanding such action must be shown, as, the insolvency of the complainant, which is perhaps the reason that has most frequently moved courts of equity to

---

[22] Burton v. Perry, 146 Ill. 71, 34 N. E. Rep. 60. And see Comegys v. Davidson, 154 Pa. St. 534, 26 Atl. Rep. 618.

[23] Patterson v. Sweet, 3 Ill. App. 550.

[24] Schmisseur v. Penn, 47 Ill. App. 278.

allow a set-off when not permissible at law. But an unliqui-
dated demand, in no way connected with the mortgage debt,
which demand is not a proper subject of set-off at law, cannot
be set off in the foreclosure suit, unless there is some peculiar
equity to take it out of the general rule. And where the defendant in foreclosure, by his answer, showed that he had
several suits pending against the complainant, and sought, by
a cross-bill, to have the claims involved in such suits set off
against the complainant's demand, it was held that his claim
of set-off was properly denied because of the pendency of such
suits.[25] So, the defendant in foreclosure cannot set off the
value of stock in a loan association, purchased by him from the
mortgagee, when the transaction by which he acquired the
stock has no connection whatever with the notes secured by the
mortgage, and is consequently not a subject of set-off, unless
there is some equitable circumstance which would make it
so.[26]

PART VII. APPOINTMENT OF RECEIVER.

§ 408. Grounds for Appointing Receiver.—A court of equity,
having jurisdiction of a pending action for the foreclosure of
a mortgage, has authority to appoint a receiver to take charge
of the mortgaged premises and collect the rents and profits,
for the purpose of preserving not only the corpus of the estate
but also its income for the satisfaction of the debt secured
by the mortgage.[27] But the creditor cannot demand, as a
matter of legal right, that this action be taken, and the courts
will not be willing unnecessarily to interfere with the possession of the mortgagor. Hence the rule that, to obtain the
appointment of a receiver, the complainant must show that the
mortgaged property is inadequate as a security for the debt,

---

[25] Smith v. Billings, 62 Ill. App.
77, affirmed in 170 Ill. 543, 49 N.
E. Rep. 212.

[26] Alderton v. Conger, 78 Ill.
App. 533.

[27] Grant v. Phoenix Mut. Life
Ins. Co., 121 U. S. 105.

or is in danger of becoming insufficient for that purpose, in consequence of waste, deterioration, or fraudulent mismanagement on the part of the possessor, and also that the mortgagor (or other person individually liable for the debt) is insolvent, or of very questionable ability to pay it.[28] The whole object to be attained by the appointment of a receiver is to divest the rents and profits from the mortgagor and to vest them in the mortgagee. By the appointment of a receiver, the mortgagee obtains a specific lien upon the rents and profits to pay the deficiency or anticipated deficiency. Such an order is merely a collateral remedy against a fund which, in equity, is secondarily liable for the payment of the deficiency. Hence the appointment of a receiver in such a case is not a legal right of the creditor, but an equitable remedy, which will not be granted except upon equitable grounds and for substantial reasons, such as those mentioned above.[29]

Further, on the question of appointing a receiver in a foreclosure case, very much must be left to the discretion of the court of first instance; and an appellate court should not interfere unless it is shown that this discretion has been exercised unwisely and to the injury of the party complaining.[30] And if the court has jurisdiction of the parties and the subject-matter, its order appointing a receiver and directing the application of the rents and profits, cannot be collaterally attacked upon the ground that it erroneously directed the rents collected during the period of redemption to be paid to the holder of the certificate of purchase.[31]

These rules may be relaxed by the agreement of the parties. Thus, where the mortgagor expressly waives all right to the possession and income of the premises pending foreclosure proceedings, and agrees to the appointment of a receiver, it is not necessary for the court, when applied to in that behalf, to consider any question of the adequacy of the security or the solvency of the mortgagor, as these considerations do not limit the rights of the mortgagee in the circumstances sup-

28 Cross v. Will County Nat. Bank, 177 Ill. 33, 52 N. E. Rep. 322; Silverman v. Northwestern Mut. Life Ins. Co., 5 Ill. App. 124; White v. Mackey, 85 Ill. App. 282; Richey v. Guild, 99 Ill. App. 451.

29 Ortengren v. Rice, 104 Ill. App.

428; Lechner v. Green, Id. 442; McLester v. Rose, Id. 433.

30 Jacobs v. Gibson, 9 Nebr. 386, 2 N. W. Rep. 893.

31 Equitable Trust Co. v. Wilson, 200 Ill. 23, reversing 98 Ill. App. 81.

posed.[32] In that case, the court will appoint a receiver unless good reasons are shown why it should not.[33]

Substantially the same principles apply to the foreclosure of deeds of trust. When such a deed authorizes the trustee to take possession of the mortgaged premises upon default and do such things as may be necessary for the proper protection of the property, a court of equity will have power, in case the trustee refuses to act, to appoint a receiver to take charge of the estate, without reference to any question of depreciation of the property, and independently of any consideration as to the solvency or insolvency of the grantor or person primarily liable for the debt. But in ordinary circumstances, a receiver will not be appointed unless the property mortgaged is insufficient security for the debt, and the party personally liable for the debt is either insolvent or of very questionable responsibility.[34]

§ 409. Where Mortgage Covers Rents and Profits.—It is entirely competent for the parties to a mortgage to stipulate that the rents and income of the mortgaged property shall be pledged for the payment of the debt secured, as well as the land itself. When this is done, the income of the property constitutes a fund which is primarily liable for the satisfaction of the mortgage debt, in the same sense and to the same extent as the corpus of the estate; and therefore a receiver may be appointed, in the discretion of the court, on the application of the mortgagee, without his showing that the land alone is not adequate security, and without any question as to the mortgagor's solvency in view of a possible deficiency.[35] Still, even in this case, the appointment of a receiver cannot be demanded as an absolute right, and simply because it is stipulated for in the mortgage. The court retains its discretion, and is not bound to enforce such a provision where it is not necessary to enforce the lien on the rents and profits. It is held that such an agreement in the mortgage is entitled to weight in deter-

[32] Loughridge v. Haughran, 79 Ill. App. 644.

[33] Clark v. Logan Mut. Loan & Bldg. Ass'n, 58 Ill. App. 311.

[34] Gooden v. Vinke, 87 Ill. App. 562.

[35] Oakford v. Robinson, 48 Ill. App. 270; Niccolls v. Peninsular Stove Co., Id. 317; Fountain v. Walther, 66 Ill. App. 529; Ball v. Marske, 100 Ill. App. 389; Clark v. Logan Mut. Loan & Bldg. Ass'n, 58 Ill. App. 311; Ortengren v. Rice, 104 Ill. App. 428; Lechner v. Green, Id. 442; McLester v. Rose, Id. 433.

mining whether the power of the court to make the appointment should be exercised or not, but it is not controlling.[36]

§ 410. Appointing Receiver After Foreclosure Sale.—The inadequacy of the mortgaged property as security for the debt, and the consequent necessity of sequestrating the rents and profits to supply the deficiency, frequently does not appear until after the rendition of the decree of foreclosure and the sale had thereunder. Ordinarily, the owner of the equity of redemption is entitled to retain the possession of the property and to collect the income thereof during the running of the period allowed for redemption. But where the decree includes a judgment for the deficiency, and the sale of the property under the foreclosure does not bring enough to satisfy the mortgage debt, and it appears that the person liable on the deficiency decree is insolvent or of doubtful responsibility, then the court has power to appoint a receiver to take charge of the property during the time allowed for redemption, and to collect the rents and profits and apply them on the deficiency. This power should not be exercised improvidently, and the appointment is not proper when it appears that injustice would be done thereby, or when reasons exist justifying the expectation that the deficiency can be otherwise made up; but still it is a power which the court is fully competent to exercise in a proper case, and it exists even when there are no express words in the mortgage giving a lien upon the rents and profits.[37] So also, if it appears that the rights of the purchaser at the foreclosure sale are impaired or placed in jeopardy by reason of the mortgagor's retaining possession, the court may appoint a receiver of the rents and profits, after the sale, and before the time for redemption has expired.[38] And where the terms of the mortgage expressly give to the mortgagee the right to have a receiver appointed to collect the rents after a sale is had and a deficiency judicially ascertained, it is error to refuse to appoint a receiver when the conditions stated have arisen. The contract of the parties as to remedies should be

[36] Bagley v. Illinois Trust & Sav. Bank, 199 Ill. 76, 64 N. E. Rep. 1085, affirming 100 Ill. App. 251.

[37] First Nat. Bank v. Illinois Steel Co., 174 Ill. 140, 51 N. E. Rep. 200 (affirming 72 Ill. App. 640); Christie v. Burns, 83 Ill.

App. 514; Haas v. Chicago Building Society, 89 Ill. 498; Boruff v. Hinkley, 66 Ill. App. 274.

[38] Lapham v. Ives, 11 Chicago Legal News, 297, Fed. Cas. No. 8,082.

followed.[39] But after the term of court at which the foreclosure decree was entered, where no deficiency decree was
sought or obtained by any one, the court has no power, in the
same proceeding, to reach the rents and profits during the
period of redemption, for the purpose of applying them on a
second mortgage on which no relief had been sought or obtained.[40]

§ 411. **Appointment on Application of Junior Mortgagee.**—
When a second mortgagee brings suit for foreclosure and procures the appointment of a receiver, he is entitled to have the
rents and profits collected by the receiver applied upon his
mortgage to the exclusion of the senior mortgagee, provided it
appears that the first mortgagee was not a party to the suit,
or that the receiver was appointed for the benefit of the junior
mortgagee alone, and not for the benefit of all the parties to the
suit. In such a case, the senior mortgagee will not be entitled
to payment out of the rents unless he files a bill to foreclose
his own mortgage and procures the receivership to be extended
to his security.[41] So, in a proceeding for the foreclosure of a
first mortgage, where the second mortgagee files a cross-bill
asking for the foreclosure of his mortgage, the court may, when
the circumstances warrant it, appoint a receiver upon the
application of the second mortgagee, even though it denies an
application for the same relief on the part of the first mortgagee.[42] And again, "when a receiver is appointed in a suit
to foreclose a first mortgage, the second mortgagee being a
party, and the first mortgage is satisfied out of the proceeds of
the foreclosure sale, leaving the second mortgage unpaid, either
altogether or in part, resort may be had, for the deficiency
upon the second mortgage, to the rents collected by the receiver. In such case, if the first mortgagee, who has procured
the receiver and has the right to satisfy his debt either out of
the proceeds of the sale or out of the rents collected by the
receiver, elects to take the proceeds of sale, the second mortgagee is entitled to be subrogated to the rents." And in such
a case if it appears that the mortgagor is insolvent and the

[39] Wright v. Case, 69 Ill. App.
535.

[40] Burleigh v. Keck, 84 Ill. App.
607.

[41] Cross v. Will County Nat.
Bank, 177 Ill. 33, 52 N. E. Rep.

322 (affirming 71 Ill. App. 404);
Miltenberger v. Logansport Ry.
Co., 106 U. S. 286.

[42] Clark v. Logan Mut. Loan &
Bldg Ass'n, 58 Ill. App. 311.

security insufficient to protect the second mortgagee, he will be entitled to have the receivership continued for his benefit and to receive the rents and profits during the period of redemption, as against the owner of the equity of redemption.[48] But in a suit to foreclose the elder mortgage, if neither the bill nor a cross-bill filed by the junior mortgagee prays for the appointment of a receiver, the court should not appoint one, even though the junior mortgage may provide for such an appointment.[44] And where the suit is to foreclose the junior mortgage, if the complainant obtains enough from the proceeds of the sale of the premises to satisfy his incumbrance, the entire object of his suit will be accomplished, and his bill will furnish no warrant for continuing a receivership before granted, and directing the receiver to retain possession during the period allowed for redemption and apply the rents collected to the payment of interest on the first mortgage, paying the balance to the purchaser at the foreclosure sale.[45]

§ 412. Rights and Duties of Receiver.—By procuring the appointment of a receiver to collect the rents and profits of mortgaged property, in connection with proceedings for the foreclosure of the mortgage, the mortgagee obtains an equitable claim upon the rents due and to accrue, and such claim is superior to any other (arising subsequent to the mortgage) of any person claiming under the mortgagor. It is the duty of the receiver to exercise a proper degree of care and diligence in managing the property and collecting the income, and tenants in possession may be compelled to attorn to him.[46] He is required to account for the income of the property, and it is his duty, out of such income, to keep the property insured, not only against fire,[47] but also, in proper cases, against damage to plate glass on the premises.[48] The receiver may also be directed by the court to pay accruing taxes on the property out of current income.[49] But after the payment of such proper charges as may be allowed by the court, including payments on

[43] Roach v. Glos, 181 Ill. 440, 54 N. E. Rep. 1022, affirming Glos v. Roach, 80 Ill. App. 283.

[44] Gillespie v. Greene County Sav. & Loan Ass'n, 95 Ill. App. 543.

[45] Evans v. Eastman, 60 Ill. App. 332.

[46] Woodyatt v. Connell, 38 Ill. App. 475.

[47] Robinson Bank v. Miller, 47 Ill. App. 310.

[48] Stevens v. Hadfield, 196 Ill. 253, 63 N. E. Rep. 633.

[49] Elliott v. Magnus, 74 Ill. App. 436.

the mortgage debt as well as the proper expenses of the
receivership, he holds the balance for the owner of the equity
of redemption, and not for the benefit of the purchaser at the
sale.[50]   And so, a judgment creditor of the mortgagor is not
entitled to payment from rents and profits in the hands of the
receiver, and has no right to complain of an order directing
their application to the payment of taxes.[51]   But if the purchaser at the foreclosure sale takes the title subject to a prior
mortgage which he covenants to pay, the receiver in foreclosure
has no right to pay the interest on such prior mortgage during
the period of redemption nor to pay taxes on the mortgaged
premises.[52]   The receiver has of course no power to expend the
funds in improving the property, nor even in making repairs,
without the order of the court.   In a case in New York, it was
held that he would have no right, without such an order, to
expend the money in his hands in protecting a wall made dangerous by an excavation; and it was said to be immaterial that
a statute authorized a municipal department to make such walls
secure at the expense of the owners.[53]

   § 413.   Discharge of Receiver.—When a receiver of the rents
and profits of mortgaged property has been appointed pending
proceedings for the foreclosure of the mortgage, and, at the
sale made under the decree of foreclosure, the property is bid
off for the full amount of the debt, interest, and costs, there
is no necessity for continuing the receivership further, and
accordingly he should then be discharged and the possession of
the property should be restored to the owner of the equity of
redemption, to hold during the period allowed for redemption.[54]
Also it is said that when the amount due on the mortgage debt
is definitely fixed by the court, the defendant has a right to
pay that sum and have a restoration of his property and a
discharge of the receiver.[55]   And so, when the period allowed
for redemption under a foreclosure decree and sale expires,

[50] Stevens v. Hadfield, 196 Ill.
253, 63 N. E. Rep. 633.
   [51] Elliott v. Magnus, 74 Ill. App.
436.
   [52] Stevens v. Hadfield, 196 Ill.
253, 63 N. E. Rep. 633, affirming
90 Ill. App. 405.
   [53] Wyckoff v. Scofield, 103 N. Y.
630, 9 N. E. Rep. 498.

   [54] Roach v. Glos, 181 Ill. 440, 54
N. E. Rep. 1022; Bogardus v.
Moses, 181 Ill. 554, 54 N. E. Rep.
984 (affirming 78 Ill. App. 223);
Davis v. Dale, 150 Ill. 239, 37 N. E.
Rep. 215, affirming Dale v. Davis,
51 Ill. App. 328.
   [55] Milwaukee & M. R. Co. v.
Soutter, 2 Wall. 510.

no redemption having been made, the purchaser becomes the absolute owner of the property, and thereupon the rights and duties of a receiver appointed in the foreclosure proceedings come to an end, and thereafter he has no right to collect rents from tenants on the property or otherwise to deal with them.[56]

PART VIII. DECREE OF FORECLOSURE.

§ 414. Decree of Strict Foreclosure.—A decree of strict foreclosure of a mortgage finds the amount due under the mortgage, orders its payment within a certain limited time, and provides that, in default of such payment, the debtor's right and equity of redemption shall be forever barred and foreclosed. Its effect is to vest the title of the property absolutely in the mortgagee, on default of payment, without any sale of the property. The debtor's legal title having been forfeited by his failure to pay the mortgage debt at its maturity, and his equity of redemption being cut off by the decree, the title of the creditor, which before was conditional and defeasible, becomes absolute and unconditional without a sale or conveyance of the estate.[57] This method of foreclosure is occasionally in

[56] Stoddard v. Walker, 90 Ill. App. 422.

[57] "In a strict foreclosure at common law, the decree simply cut off the equity of redemption, and foreclosed the mortgagor from redeeming his estate by payment of the mortgage debt, and the estate of the mortgagee, which, in its inception, was conditional and defeasible, became thereby absolute. Thereafter the mortgagee was in as of the estate granted and conveyed by the mortgage, discharged from the condition of defeasance, and he held the estate as if the original conveyance had been absolute." Champion v. Hinkle, 45 N. J. Eq. 162, 16 Atl. Rep. 701.

use in Illinois. The statute which regulates the time and terms of redemption of mortgaged lands, when sold under a decree of foreclosure, does not in terms prohibit strict foreclosures.[58] Still, such decrees are not very much in accord with the policy of the statute; and the remedy of a strict foreclosure is regarded as a harsh and severe one, and not to be resorted to except in cases where a statutory foreclosure and sale would be inappropriate or an unnecessary formality.[59] As far back as 1855 it was judicially declared that, although equity may grant relief by a strict foreclosure, the practice should not be encouraged.[60] But a mortgagor has not in every case a right to insist that the court shall order a sale of the premises; and where the interests of the parties plainly require that the foreclosure should be strict, it may be so ordered.[61] So the courts have now established the general rule that a decree of strict foreclosure may be entered when the four following facts are made to appear: (1) That the mortgagor is insolvent; (2) that the mortgaged land is not worth the amount due upon the mortgage; (3) that the mortgagee is willing to take the property in satisfaction of his debt; (4) that there are no junior incumbrancers, purchasers of the equity of redemption, or other creditors of the mortgagor who might be interested in having the property put up for sale.[62] So also, when the bill shows that the mortgage was given for the entire purchase money of the mortgaged premises, and that the value of the premises does not exceed the amount due on the mortgage, and where no appearance has been entered for the mortgagor, the case is one where a strict foreclosure may properly be decreed.[63] Again, where all the persons who derive title through the mortgagor disclaim any interest in the land, and tender it to the mortgagee, it is proper to decree that he shall receive the land in full satisfaction of the mortgage debt, although the time during which he might have demanded a master's deed

[58] Johnson v. Donnell, 15 Ill. 97.
[59] Jefferson v. Coleman, 110 Ind. 515, 11 N. E. Rep. 465.
[60] Weiner v. Heintz, 17 Ill. 259.
[61] Johnson v. Donnell, 15 Ill. 97; Brahm v. Dietsch, 15 Ill. App. 331; Flagg v. Walker, 113 U. S. 659.
[62] Stephens v. Bichnell, 27 Ill. 444; Horner v. Zimmerman, 45 Ill. 14; Farrell v. Parlier, 50 Ill. 274; Sheldon v. Patterson, 55 Ill. 507; Carpenter v. Plagge, 192 Ill. 82, 61 N. E. Rep. 530; Greenemeyer v. Deppe, 6 Ill. App. 490; Miller v. Davis, 5 Ill. App. 474; Hollis v. Smith, 9 Ill. App. 109; Griesbaum v. Baum, 18 Ill. App. 614.
[63] Wilson v. Geisler, 19 Ill. 49.

has expired.[64] And the parties to a bill in equity for the foreclosure of a mortgage may stipulate and agree that the court shall enter a decree of strict foreclosure against the premises.[65]

§ 415. Same; When Not Proper.—If the estate mortgaged is claimed as a homestead, or materially exceeds in value the amount for which it was incumbered, a strict foreclosure should not be allowed; and unless the homestead right has been waived, the sale should be made subject to it.[66] And it may be stated as a general rule that a decree of strict foreclosure is not proper, and should not be allowed, when the equity of redemption is in the hands of a purchaser from the mortgagor, or when there are liens upon the property subsequent to the mortgage, or other creditors of the mortgagor.[67] The reason of this rule is that it is for the interest of such persons that an attempt at least should be made, by a public sale, to make the property bring more than the amount of the mortgage debt, and further that it is the policy and intention of the statute allowing redemptions from judicial sales to make the property pay as much of the mortgagor's debts as it is worth. And so also, in cases where the mortgagor is dead, and his estate is insolvent, and the equity of redemption has descended to infant heirs, the proper course is to order a sale of the property, and not to decree a strict foreclosure.[68] But circumstances may arise in which a decree of strict foreclosure would be proper, on a showing that the mortgagor is insolvent, and the property worth less than the amount of the mortgage debt, and that the mortgagee is willing to take it in satisfaction, notwithstanding that there may be a judgment creditor of the mortgagor whose lien is junior to the mortgage. The general rule that no strict foreclosure can be decreed when there are other incumbrancers or creditors or purchasers of the equity of redemption is not inflexible. It is subject to exceptions,

[64] Belleville Savings Bank v. Reis, 136 Ill. 242, 26 N. E. Rep. 646.

[65] Bissell v. Marine Co., 55 Ill. 165.

[66] Young v. Graff, 28 Ill. 20.

[67] Edwards v. Helm, 5 Ill. 142; Warner v. Helm, 6 Ill. 220; Horner v. Zimmerman, 45 Ill. 14; Farrell v. Parlier, 50 Ill. 274; Boyer v. Boyer, 89 Ill. 447; Illinois Starch Co. v. Ottawa Hydraulic Co., 125 Ill. 237, 17 N. E. Rep. 486; Rourke v. Coulton, 4 Ill. App. 257; Miller v. Davis, 5 Ill. App. 474; Greenemeyer v. Deppe, 6 Ill. App. 490; Hollis v. Smith, 9 Ill. App. 109; Griesbaum v. Baum, 18 Ill. App. 614; Flagg v. Walker, 113 U. S. 659.

[68] Boyer v. Boyer, 89 Ill. 447.

growing out of the facts of particular cases, where justice and
sound reason require that such exceptions should be made.
"The court of conscience will not sacrifice or endanger the
rights of a complainant, who comes within her portals with a
just cause, and holding the oldest and preferred lien and best
equity, for a bare possibility of a wholly improbable benefit
to one having a second lien and subordinate equity."[69]

§ 416. Same; Cases Excepted by Statute.—In Illinois, under
the provisions of the statutes, there can be no strict foreclosure
of a mortgage given by a guardian upon the property of his
ward, but such mortgages must be foreclosed by petition in the
county court, and redemption shall be allowed as is provided
by law in cases of sales on execution upon common-law judgments.[70] The laws likewise forbid strict foreclosure of mortgages given by executors under authority of the court,[71] and of
mortgages made by the conservator of a lunatic, idiot, or spendthrift.[72]

§ 417. Frame of Decree of Strict Foreclosure.—In proceedings for a strict foreclosure, the settled practice in England
is to decree that the amount due be ascertained and the costs
taxed, and that upon the payment of both within a fixed time,
the complainant shall reconvey to the defendant, but in default
of payment within the time limited, it is ordered that the defendant shall "stand absolutely debarred and foreclosed of
and from all equity of redemption of and in the said mortgaged premises." It is essentially necessary that the defendant
should be allowed some time in which to redeem by paying the
amount due with the taxed costs. The length of time rests
very much in the discretion of the chancellor, and is to be regulated by the circumstances of the particular case, but the right
of redemption cannot be entirely withheld. In England, the
settled practice is to allow six months. And a decree of strict
foreclosure which does not find the amount due, which allows
no time for the payment of the debt and the redemption of
the estate, and which is final and conclusive in the first instance, cannot be sustained.[73] In Illinois, the practice in cases

[69] Illinois Starch Co. v. Ottawa
Hydraulic Co., 23 Ill. App. 272,
affirmed in 125 Ill. 237, 17 N. E.
Rep. 486.

[70] Rev. Stat. Ill. c. 64, § 27;

United States Mortgage Co. v.
Sperry, 138 U. S. 313.

[71] Rev. Stat. Ill. c. 3, § 122.

[72] Rev. Stat. Ill. c. 86, §§ 20-22.

[73] Clark v. Reyburn, 8 Wall. 318;

of this kind differs from the English practice in this respect—
that it is not considered necessary to enter first an interlocutory decree for foreclosure if the debt be not paid within the
time limited, and then a final order on proof that the money
has not been paid; but the final decree may be made in the
first instance. A decree which finds the amount due on the
mortgage, and orders the same to be paid to the complainant
within a certain fixed time, and decrees that, in default of such
payment, the defendant shall be forever barred and foreclosed
of all right and equity of redemption in the premises, and
that all the right, title, and interest, both legal and equitable,
of the defendant therein shall be vested absolutely and uncon-
ditionally in the complainant, is a final decree, in the usual and
approved form, and vests in the mortgagee, on default of payment, all the title conveyed by the mortgage, without any
further decree of the court.[74] It has even been held, in this
state, that a decree of strict foreclosure need not specify in
whom the legal title to the lands shall be vested; for, by
barring the equity of redemption, it confirms the title in the
mortgagee.[75] It should also be remarked that a strict foreclosure of a mortgage does not extinguish the debt secured by the
mortgage, unless the value of the land is equivalent to the
debt.[76]

§ 418. **Decree of Foreclosure and Sale.**—A decree of foreclosure in the ordinary form fixes the amount due under the
mortgage, orders the defendant to pay the same within a limited time, and provides that, if such payment is not made, the
land shall be sold and the proceeds applied in satisfaction
of the mortgage debt. In the provision directing the sale there
should be a clear and accurate description of the premises affected, although it is said that the decree is sufficient in this
respect if it describes the property substantially in the terms
of the mortgage.[77] And if the mortgage is made part of the
bill of complaint, the decree need only direct a sale by reference to the bill without a formal description of the property
to be sold.[78] It is also said that "a decree of foreclosure should
direct a sale of the particular estate or interest of the mort-

Chicago, D. & V. R. Co. v. Fosdick, 106 U. S. 47.
[74] Ellis v. Leek, 127 Ill. 60, 20 N.
E. Rep. 213.
[75] Johnson v. Donnell, 15 Ill. 97.

[76] Vansant v. Allmon, 23 Ill. 30.
[77] Cook v. Shorthill, 82 Iowa,
277, 48 N. W. Rep. 84.
[78] Logan v. Williams, 76 Ill. 175.

gagor in the mortgaged premises, as the same has been described in the mortgage, because it is that and only that which has been mortgaged as security for the payment of the mortgage debt. If such a decree directs the sale of any greater or less estate or interest than that described in the complaint and mortgage, it is erroneous, and should be corrected on motion."[79] But in a case where the decree ordered a sale of the premises and "all the right and interest of the respondents therein," it was held to include their homestead right, although the same was not specified; the statutory requirement that a deed shall contain an express release of the homestead relates to the evidence, and not to the averments in the pleadings and the findings.[80]

It is probably not necessary for the decree to specify the steps to be taken after the sale; for the right of redemption is granted and regulated by the statute, and the foreclosure purchaser can secure his rights, if no redemption is made, by further application to the court. But a decree which provides that, if the premises are not redeemed within the time fixed by the statute, the master shall execute a deed to the holder of the certificate of purchase, and that thereupon possession of the property shall be delivered up to him, is entirely proper.[81] The decree may also settle incidental or collateral rights of the parties, or equities arising out of their situation with reference to the mortgage. For example, in a proceeding to foreclose a mortgage given to a building and loan association, it is proper to provide by the decree for the cancellation of the stock of the mortgagor where he has been credited with the full withdrawal value of the same in reduction of his indebtedness.[82] So, a decree foreclosing a mortgage upon leased land should make provision for the payment of ground-rent due; and this, even if the forfeiture of the lease has been obtained in fraud of the rights of the mortgagee.[83] But where the mortgage does not provide for repairs to be made by the mortgagee, the right to a lien for such repairs, if any exists, must rest on the mechanic's lien statute; and such lien cannot

[79] Schwartz v. Palm, 65 Cal. 54, 2 Pac. Rep. 735.

[80] West v. Krebaum, 88 Ill. 263.

[81] Baker v. Scott, 62 Ill. 87; Bird v. Belz, 33 Kans. 391, 6 Pac. Rep. 627.

[82] Rhodes v. Missouri Sav. & Loan Co., 63 Ill. App. 77.

[83] Johnston v. Worthington, 8 Ill. App. 322.

be sustained on a bill to foreclose the mortgage which does not aver the facts on which the lien could be predicated under the statute.[84] Again, while suits to foreclose trust deeds executed by the same parties may be consolidated, a decree which consolidates the debts by ordering that the property covered by the deeds be sold for the payment of the whole amount is erroneous when the deeds cover separate tracts.[85] And in a case where the bill sought the foreclosure of two mortgages, one of which embraced land not included in the other, and where the whole debt was not due, and the decree found that the mortgagor was insolvent, and that the premises could not be sold in parcels without prejudice to the parties, where there was no allegation in the bill to admit such proof, and authorized a sale en masse for the whole debt due and to become due, it was held that the decree was erroneous.[86]

§ 419. **Adjudication as to Amount Due.**—It is essential that a decree of foreclosure should determine and state the amount due to the complainant, in order that persons interested may be able to redeem before sale without taking risks as to the correctness of the amount tendered. A decree which simply orders the payment of the sum due on the debt secured by the mortgage, without finding the amount, is erroneous.[87] And when several mortgages upon separate parcels of land are foreclosed together in one action, the decree must find the amount due on each, and not the aggregate amount secured by all.[88] The computation of the amount due is properly left to the master in chancery, except in so far as judicial questions may be involved; these can be settled only by the court.[89] But in a case where the mortgage was given to secure the payment of certain bills of exchange on which the mortgagor was indorser,

[84] Seiler v. Schaefer, 40 Ill. App. 74.

[85] Brown v. Kennicott, 30 Ill. App. 89.

[86] Blazey v. Delius, 74 Ill. 299.

[87] Tompkins v. Wiltberger, 56 Ill. 385.

[88] Knight v. Heafer, 79 Ill. App. 374. Where a master, to whom the court had referred the question of the amount due under a mortgage which was sought to be foreclosed, reported the amount due on the note described in the mortgage, and also the amount due on another note given by the mortgagor, and held by the complainant, as to which there was no evidence that the mortgagor intended to secure it by the mortgage, it was held to be error to decree a foreclosure for the amount of both notes. Wiley v. Eccles, 4 Ill. App. 126.

[89] De Leuw v. Neely, 71 Ill. 473.

as well as a promissory note of which he was the maker, it was said to be proper, since the damages rested in computation, for the court to direct the clerk to compute them, the court instructing him at what rate to compute them, both as to the interest and the legal damages for protest.[90] And where the master has reported the several items of credit and their dates, the case need not be again referred to him to calculate the sum due.[91]

The decree cannot properly adjudge to the complainant a greater sum than that claimed in his bill; to do so is error, though it is not sufficient to make the decree absolutely void and open to collateral impeachment.[92] And when the decree is for too large an amount, the error cannot be cured on appeal by filing in the appellate court evidence that the mortgage has been satisfied.[93] But while the appellate court will reverse a decree and send the case back, when the amount adjudged is materially and substantially in excess of the proper sum, it will not consider such a course necessary when the error in this respect amounts to no more than a mere trifle.[94] Thus, a decree of foreclosure will not be reversed at the instance of a subsequent incumbrancer, merely because it is excessive to the amount of one day's interest (amounting to $56), where the value of the entire property is less than the sum actually due and there is a decree for deficiency, especially when the party against whom the decree was entered does not complain.[95] If, in drawing the mortgage, a larger amount was inserted than the debt actually due, the recovery must be confined to the correct sum and the decree framed accordingly.[96] But in Pennsylvania, it is said that the fact that a judgment on a mortgage is entered for the penal sum named in the bond, without any suggestion as to the real debt, is not ground for opening the judgment and letting the mortgagor in to defend, although no more than the real debt can be collected.[97]

We must also remark that, where the bill for foreclosure

---

[90] Russell v. Brown, 41 Ill. 183.

[91] Haworth v. Huling, 87 Ill. 23.

[92] Ketchum v. White, 72 Iowa, 193, 33 N. W. Rep. 627.

[93] Crosby v. Kiest, 135 Ill. 458, 26 N. E. Rep. 589.

[94] McNutt v. Dickson, 42 Ill. 498.

[95] Primley v. Shirk, 163 Ill. 389, 45 N. E. Rep. 247, affirming 60 Ill. App. 312.

[96] Laylin v. Knox, 41 Mich. 40, 1 N. W. Rep. 913.

[97] Citizens' Savings & Loan Ass'n v. Heiser, 150 Pa. St. 514, 24 Atl. Rep. 733.

states the amount due at the time it is filed, it is not error to
include in the decree a greater amount, when the increase is
the result of the accumulation during the interval between
the filing of the bill and the hearing.[98] Thus, it is proper to
allow the complainant for money advanced for the payment of
taxes after the filing of the bill, under the prayer for general
relief, the contingencies which would justify such payment
having been set forth in the bill.[99] And the mortgagee is
entitled to interest on the mortgage note, at the contract rate,
from the date of the note until the rendition of the decree of
foreclosure.[1] And generally, the court may include in its decree amounts expended by the mortgagee for taxes, insurance,
and extension of an abstract of title, when such items are authorized by the mortgage and the payments are shown by the
evidence.[2] Upon the foreclosure of a mortgage for non-payment of interest, when the principal is not due, and is not,
by the terms of the mortgage, to become due upon default in
payment of interest, it is both proper and necessary for the
court to find the amount of principal unpaid, and decree its
payment out of the proceeds when the property is to be sold
as an entirety; but the decree should permit the mortgagor to
redeem, before sale, on payment of the overdue interest and
costs only.[3] Where the mortgage is one given to a building
and loan association, it is proper to set off against the amount
due under the mortgage any sum that may be due the defendant on matured stock in the association held by him.[4] And
it should be noted that a mortgagee, by selling under the foreclosure decree, waives any objection to the amount therein
decreed to him.[5]

§ 420. **Terms as to Payment and Redemption.**—A proper decree of foreclosure gives the debtor a last opportunity to effect
the redemption of the premises before a sale, by decreeing

[98] Rhodes v. Missouri Sav. &
Loan Co., 63 Ill. App. 77; Wolcott
v. Lake View Bldg. & Loan Ass'n,
59 Ill. App. 415.

[99] Loewenstein v. Rapp, 67 Ill.
App. 678; supra § 229.

[1] Arneson v. Haldane, 105 Ill.
App. 589.

[2] Loughridge v. Northwestern
Mut. Life Ins. Co., 180 Ill. 267, 54

N. E. Rep. 153, affirming 79 Ill.
App. 223.

[3] Grape Creek Coal Co. v. Farm-
ers' Loan & Trust Co. (U. S. Circ.
Ct. of App., 7th Circuit) 12 C. C.
A. 350, 63 Fed. Rep. 891.

[4] Novak v. Vypomocny Spolek
Bldg. & Loan Ass'n, 68 Ill. App.
682, affirmed in 167 Ill. 264.

[5] Trogden v. Safford, 21 Ill. App.
240.

that he may pay the amount adjudged to be due within a certain limited time, and that, in default of such payment, the property shall be sold. There is no statute fixing the time which should be thus allowed to the debtor for payment. It must be a reasonable time, having regard to the amount of the debt and other pertinent circumstances; but what is a reasonable time is to be determined by the court itself in the exercise of a sound judicial discretion.[6] As to the statutory right of redemption after the foreclosure sale, that is entirely independent of the decree. No action of the court is necessary to confer it on parties entitled, and no action of the court can take it away. The more formal mode of decreeing the foreclosure of a mortgage is to direct that the mortgagor pay the amount found to be due, and, in default of payment, that the master sell the land, and if it is not redeemed, then that all the rights of the defendant be foreclosed and barred. But the right of redemption provided by the statute will not be considered as denied by a decree, although it may declare a foreclosure without any reference to the subject of redemption.[7]

§ 421. **Personal Judgment not Proper.**—In Illinois, the courts of equity have no jurisdiction to render a personal judgment or decree for the payment of the mortgage indebtedness against the defendant in a foreclosure proceeding. The action is in rem, for the foreclosure of the lien, and a judgment in personam against the mortgagor would not be proper. Under the statute, the court can only render a decree for the balance of the amount that may be found to be remaining unpaid after the mortgaged premises have been sold and the proceeds applied under the decree.[8] Thus, a decree which provides that the defendant pay the complainant the amount of the mortgage debt and costs, and that the complainant have execution

---

[6] Wright v. Neely, 100 Ill. App. 310. And see Gochenour v. Mowry, 33 Ill. 331.

[7] Boester v. Byrne, 72 Ill. 466.

[8] Phelan v. Iona Savings Bank, 48 Ill. 171. "A court is without power in a foreclosure suit to render a personal judgment in the first instance against a mortgagor, where there is no statute that authorizes it; and except for the statute, there is no power to render a personal decree for a deficiency after sale, but the mortgagee would be left to resort to law. It is only for the deficiency, if any, that exists after the foreclosure sale, that our statute authorizes a personal decree." Cook v. Moulton, 64 Ill. App. 429. It is error to enter a personal judgment against a nominal defendant in a foreclosure proceeding. Idem.

therefor, is erroneous; the statute authorizes an execution only for the deficiency after the sale.[9] And the mortgagor cannot be heard to complain that the foreclosure decree did not direct him to pay the amount found due, but merely ordered the premises to be sold in default of payment, as the latter is the proper form of a decree in rem.[10] So, a personal decree against the wife of the mortgagor, or owner of the equity of redemption, or against others who are merely tenants on the mortgaged premises, for the payment of the mortgage debt, cannot be sustained.[11] But a decree which finds the amount due from the mortgagor, and requires a subsequent purchaser to pay the same by a day named, and if he does not, that the mortgaged premises be sold, is not a personal decree against the mortgagor, but is in effect an alternative one, and is not erroneous.[12] It is also to be noted that an ordinary decree in foreclosure is not a decree "for the payment of money," within the meaning of the statute (Rev. Stat. Ill. c. 77, § 39) providing that when the person against whom such a decree or judgment is rendered shall die after its rendition, no sale thereunder shall be made until after the expiration of twelve months from his death and after three months notice of the existence of such judgment or decree to be given to the personal representatives or heirs of the decedent.[13]

§ 422. **Validity and Effect of Decree.**—A decree of foreclosure must correspond with the mortgage, and with the allegations of the bill and the evidence, or it will be reversible for error. Thus, it is erroneous to enter a decree of foreclosure on premises not mentioned in the mortgage.[14] A total want of jurisdiction of the parties will render the decree, as also a sale made thereunder, absolutely void; yet even in this case, if no redemption has been made or attempted, the mortgagor or his heirs cannot maintain ejectment against the mortgagee or his grantee in possession.[15] If there was jurisdiction, the decree will be supported by the presumptions of regularity and validity which ordinarily attend judicial sentences, and if

[9] Rooney v. Moulton, 60 Ill. App. 306.

[10] Shaffner v. Appleman, 170 Ill. 281, 48 N. E. Rep. 978.

[11] Snell v. Stanley, 58 Ill. 31; O'Brian v. Fry, 82 Ill. 274.

[12] Glover v. Benjamin, 73 Ill. 42.

And see Winkelman v. Kiser, 27 Ill. 21.

[13] Kronenberger v. Heinemann, 104 Ill. App. 156.

[14] Troutman v. Schaeffer, 31 Ill. 82.

[15] Oldham v. Pfleger, 84 Ill. 102.

it is not void, although it may be erroneous or irregular, it will not be open to collateral attack or impeachment.[16] And it is said that a foreclosure decree and sale constitute color of title in good faith, although the decree is erroneous or even void, if not attended with any fraud.[17] The failure of the judge to sign a decree of foreclosure or the record does not affect the validity of the decree actually rendered.[18] A decree of foreclosure is assignable, and the assignee occupies the same position as the original mortgagee, and hence may maintain a bill to enjoin the commission of waste by the mortgagor.[19] Such a decree also draws interest from the date of its rendition.[20]

§ 423. Review and Vacation of Decree.—The court which rendered a decree of foreclosure has power to vacate and set it aside on proper cause shown and on seasonable application. This action is proper, for example, on a bill alleging that the complainant is the real owner of the note secured by the mortgage and always has been; that the bill for foreclosure was filed in the name of a fictitious person and without the complainant's knowledge or consent, and that he has never adopted such proceeding or derived any benefit from it.[21] And so, where no rights of third persons have intervened, a bill lies to review a decree of foreclosure entered by default, which, by mistake not apparent from the face of the record, provides for the foreclosure of the interests of heirs not parties to the mortgage.[22] But a decree which is erroneous in such a particular as this (as, for instance, where it directs the purchaser of the equity of redemption, instead of the mortgagor, to pay the mortgage debt) cannot, if otherwise regular, be impeached by a bill of review, if it appears that the premises have been sold in satisfaction of the debt, and the decree satisfied.[23]

[16] Martina v. Muhlke, 88 Ill. App. 12; Kibbe v. Dunn, 5 Biss. C. C. 233, Fed. Cas. No. 7,753; Hughes v. Frisby, 81 Ill. 188; Gibson v. Lyon, 115 U. S. 439; 1 Black on Judgm. § 246.

[17] Reedy v. Camfield, 159 Ill. 254, 42 N. E. Rep. 833. And see Horner v. Zimmerman, 45 Ill. 14.

[18] Fouts v. Mann, 15 Nebr. 172, 18 N. W. Rep. 64. And see 1 Black on Judgm. § 109.

[19] Williams v. Chicago Exhibition Co., 188 Ill. 19, 58 N. E. Rep. 611.

[20] Connecticut Mut. Life Ins. Co. v. Stinson, 86 Ill. App. 668.

[21] Monarch Brewing Co. v. Wolford, 179 Ill. 252, 53 N. E. Rep. 583.

[22] Karr v. Freeman, 166 Ill. 299, 46 N. E. Rep. 717.

[23] Dunn v. Rodgers, 43 Ill. 260; Burley v. Flint, 105 U. S. 247.

Again, a decree of foreclosure, entered in default of an answer after appearance of the defendant by counsel, will not be set aside on the ground of accident or mistake, where the only accident or mistake relied on was the neglect of the attorney to file the answer and make the defense.[24] On the other hand, where a decree for foreclosure has been entered, and is afterwards assigned, and before execution a hostile and fraudulent title springs up, and stands in the way of execution, the assignee may have the decree revived on a bill setting forth the facts proving the fraud.[25]

§ 424. **Conclusiveness of Decree.**—The rules governing the conclusive effect of decrees in equity apply with full force to decrees of foreclosure. Thus, if such a decree is of such force, character, and effect that it would estop the mortgagee from disputing the title of the mortgagor, on an offer by the latter to redeem from the sale, then, in the converse case, where the mortgagor does not choose to redeem, the decree will be equally conclusive upon him on the question of title.[26] The question of the validity of the mortgage is one which is necessarily involved in the foreclosure proceedings; it is a fact which must have been either admitted or proved as a necessary condition to the rendition of the decree. Hence it is conclusively settled by the decree, and cannot be again drawn in question between the same parties or those in privity with them.[27] On an even stronger reason this is the case where the point was actually litigated. Thus, where the mortgagor pleaded insanity, and, after the joinder of issue on the plea, he died, and his administrator was substituted as a party, and the issue was then determined in favor of the mortgagee, it was held that a decree of foreclosure of the mortgage was an adjudication determining its validity, and was binding on the heirs of the mortgagor.[28] So, where the bill alleged the conveyance of the premises in fee simple, subject to a condition of defeasance, and the answer set up an unreleased estate of homestead, and the decree found for the complainant according to the allegations of his bill, ordered a sale as prayed

---

[24] Butler v. Morse (N. H.), 23 Atl. Rep. 90.

[25] Cunningham v. Doran, 18 Ill. 385.

[26] Bostwick v. Skinner, 30 Ill. 147.

[27] Finley v. Houser, 22 Oreg. 562, 30 Pac. Rep. 494; Woolery v. Grayson, 110 Ind. 149, 10 N. E. Rep. 935.

[28] Harsh v. Griffin, 71 Iowa, 608, 34 N. W. Rep. 441.

for, and declared the equity of redemption barred, it was held that the defendant was precluded by the decree from asserting the defense of homestead to an ejectment suit brought by the purchaser at the foreclosure sale.[29] It is also stated in some of the cases, in general terms, that a final decree of foreclosure is conclusive as to all matters and points which might have been urged in defense, whether or not they were actually pleaded, at least in so far as that they cannot be re-litigated except on a bill of review.[30] But the decree is clearly not res judicata as to any matter which the defendant was not entitled, as a matter of right, to have litigated in the foreclosure proceedings.[31] And it is not conclusive as against persons who were not parties to the litigation nor in privity with the parties of record. Thus, a decree foreclosing a mortgage, in a suit in which the question whether or not the mortgage was executed to defraud the mortgagor's creditors was not in issue, does not preclude a creditor of the mortgagor, who was not a party to the foreclosure suit, from attacking the mortgage on that ground.[32] And so, where no issue is raised in the foreclosure proceedings as to the rights of subsequent lienors, the decree for foreclosure and sale is not conclusive as to the priority of liens of the subsequent mortgagees.[33] After a mortgage has been duly foreclosed in a federal court having jurisdiction of parties and subject-matter, and the statutory period for redemption has expired, a state court will not decree redemption on the ground of an agreement extending the time of payment of the mortgage debt.[34]

§ 425. **Lien of Decree.**—A statute of Illinois provides that all decrees in equity shall be a lien upon all real estate respecting which such decrees shall be made, and whenever, by any decree, any party shall be required to perform any act other than the payment of money, or to refrain from performing any act, the court may order that the same shall be a lien upon the real or personal property of such party, and such lien shall have the effect and be subject to the same limitations as

[29] Goltra v. Green, 98 Ill. 317.

[30] Burt v. Thomas, 49 Mich. 462, 12 N. W. Rep. 911; Ludeling v. Chaffe, 40 La. Ann. 645, 4 South. Rep. 586.

[31] Oliver v. Cunningham, 7 Fed. Rep. 689

[32] Brookes v. Munoz, 125 N. Y. 256, 26 N. E. Rep. 258.

[33] Burchell v. Osborne, 119 N. Y. 486, 23 N. E. Rep. 896.

[34] Windett v. Connecticut Mut. Life Ins. Co., 130 Ill. 621, 22 N. E. Rep. 474.

judgments at law.[35] But it is held that the lien created by a
decree of foreclosure is not subject to the limitations governing judgments at law, and consequently the right to proceed
with the sale of the mortgaged premises on a decree of foreclosure and sale is not barred by the lapse of seven years.[36]
And a decree of foreclosure fixes a lien on realty as specifically
as a levy and sale.[37]

§ 426. Decree for Deficiency.—A statute in Illinois provides
that, "in all decrees hereafter to be made in suits in equity
directing foreclosure of mortgages, a decree may be rendered
for any balance of money that may be found due to the complainant over and above the proceeds of the sale or sales, and
execution may issue for the collection of such balance, the same
as when the decree is solely for the payment of money. And
such decree may be rendered conditionally, at the time of decreeing the foreclosure, or it may be rendered after the sale
and the ascertainment of the balance due."[38] The conditional
deficiency decree thus authorized to be entered in advance of
the foreclosure sale simply establishes the complainant's right
to a money decree after the amount of the deficiency is determined, prior to which time it is not a money decree in such
sense as to give the mortgagee the right to maintain a creditor's bill.[39] But such a decree, when entered, merges the
mortgagee's cause of action. Thereafter he must rely on the
foreclosure and on the deficiency decree for satisfaction of his
claims, and he cannot proceed to sue at law on the note or
bond secured by the mortgage.[40]

Though the decree on foreclosure does not specifically find

[35] Rev. Stat. Ill. c. 22, § 45.

[36] Kirby v. Runals, 140 Ill. 289, 29 N. E. Rep. 697, affirming 37 Ill. App. 186.

[37] Sues v. Leinour, 16 Ill. App. 603.

[38] Rev. Stat. Ill. c. 95, § 16. It is doubtful whether such a decree can be rendered in the absence of some distinct obligation on the part of the mortgagor to pay the mortgage debt. In a case in Iowa, where the mortgage provided that the instrument should be void on the payment of certain sums at certain times, but contained no

promise to pay such sums, nor was there any such promise in any instrument outside the mortgage, it was held that there could be no personal judgment against the mortgagor for any deficiency after sale on foreclosure. Weil v. Churchman, 52 Iowa, 253, 3 N. W. Rep. 38.

[39] Cotes v. Bennett, 183 Ill. 82, 55 N. E. Rep. 661, affirming 84 Ill. App. 33.

[40] Mutual Life Ins. Co. v. Newton, 50 N. J. Law, 571, 14 Atl. Rep. 756.

the amount due from the defendant, or provide, in the first instance, for a possible deficiency, yet if it orders the master to
sell the mortgaged premises and to specify in his report of such
sale the amount of the deficiency, if any, the court may properly enter a decree against the defendant for the amount of
the deficiency as shown by the report.[41]   And the following
has been held to be a good and sufficient formula for this part
of the decree: "And it is further ordered, adjudged, and decreed that if the moneys arising from such sale [of the mortgaged premises] shall be insufficient to pay the amount so due,
with the interest, costs, and expenses of sale, said master shall
specify the amount of such deficiency in his report of sale, and
on the coming in and confirmation of the report, the defendant
B., who is personally liable for the payment of the debt secured
by said mortgage, shall pay to the complainant the amount of
such deficiency, with interest thereon from the date of said
last-mentioned report, and that said complainant have execution therefor."[42]   A deficiency decree is not erroneous, although
the mortgage debtor may be released from the debt by a decree in another case, which the parties afterwards abrogate on
a settlement of their differences.[43]   And error in a deficiency
decree, consisting in its being rendered for too great a sum,
may be cured by a remittitur.[44]   But the court, in allowing
a decree for the deficiency, with interest, should see to it that
interest is not compounded on interest.[45]

   § 427. Same; Jurisdiction.—A proviso to the statute quoted
in the preceding section declares that execution for the deficiency "shall issue only in cases where personal service shall
have been had upon the defendant or defendants personally
liable for the mortgage debt, unless their appearance shall be
entered in such suits."[46]   Where a decree of foreclosure against
two defendants, one of whom was brought into court by publication, provided that the master appointed to sell should
report any deficiency after the sale, and that an execution
should issue against the defendants personally liable to pay
the debt for such sufficiency, and, more than three years after

---

41 Springer v. Law, 84 Ill. App.
623, affirmed in 185 Ill. 542.

42 See Baker v. Scott, 62 Ill. 86.

43 Mulcahey v. Strauss, 151 Ill.
70, 37 N. E. Rep. 702, affirming 52
Ill. App. 252.

44 Mosely v. Schoonhoven, 12 Ill.
App. 113.

45 Baker v. Scott, 62 Ill. 86.

46 Rev. Stat. Ill. c. 95, § 16.

such report, the court ascertained the deficiency and awarded
an execution against one of the defendants, without any new
notice of the intended action, under which land was sold, it
was held that the court had no jurisdiction to make the supplemental order awarding the execution, and that the sale
thereon was a nullity.[47] On similar principles, after the confirmation of a report of sale, the filing of a substituted report
and the entry of a personal decree for a deficiency should not
be allowed except on notice to parties interested.[48]

§ 428. Same; What Persons Liable.—In the case where several defendants are jointly and severally liable for the payment of a mortgage debt, the mortgagee, on obtaining a decree
of foreclosure against them, may have a decree for the deficiency against all; but if he takes a deficiency judgment
against one defendant only, no disposition being made of the
case as to the others, the cause of action merges in the decree
and the other defendants will be released.[49] And where one
of the defendants held the legal title to the property in trust
for the other, and the deficiency decree provided for the issue
of an execution against "the defendants who are personally
liable," it was held that the decree was indefinite and uncertain as to which was personally liable, but as it was joint
against the "defendants" an execution could not be issued
against one of them only.[50] If a purchaser of the mortgaged
premises from the mortgagor, taking title before the suit, assumed the mortgage debt and agreed to pay it, a decree for
the deficiency may be rendered against him, provided he was
joined as a defendant in the foreclosure proceeding and was
personally served with process,[51] but not where he merely
bought the property subject to the mortgage, without assuming it or agreeing to pay it, so that the debt remained the
debt of the original mortgagor.[52] Where the wife of a mortgagor joins in the mortgage merely for the purpose of releasing her dower, the debt being the husband's debt and not hers,
she is of course not to be held liable for a deficiency. And

[47] Mulvey v. Carpenter, 78 Ill.
580.

[48] Chicago & Great Western R.
R. Land Co. v. Peck, 112 Ill. 408.

[49] Travelers' Ins. Co. v. Mayo,
170 Ill. 498, 48 N. E. Rep. 917, affirming 70 Ill. App. 627.

[50] Mulvey v. Carpenter, 78 Ill.
580.

[51] Palmeter v. Carey, 63 Wis.
426, 21 N. W. Rep. 793.

[52] Rourke v. Coulton, 4 Ill. App.
257; Cundiff v. Brokaw, 7 Ill. App.
147.

even where the circumstances are such as to impose a personal liability upon her, and the evidence shows this to be the case, a personal decree against her for the deficiency is not proper unless the bill contained proper allegations to show her personal responsibility.[53] Where the mortgagor is dead, but would have been personally liable for a deficiency after the sale, a decree for such deficiency may be rendered against his executor or administrator (being a party to the suit) in his representative capacity.[54] And it is said, in another state, that the legatees of the mortgagor, to the extent of their legacies, are liable for the full amount of the deficiency judgment rendered on foreclosure of the mortgage, and this, though a portion of the proceeds of the sale was applied to the costs of foreclosure, instead of to the reduction of the debt.[55] But the statute does not authorize the joinder in a foreclosure suit of a third person, who is liable for the mortgage debt only in the capacity of a surety, guarantor, or indorser, and the rendition of a decree against him for a deficiency.[56]

PART IX. SALE ON FORECLOSURE.

§ 429. **Formalities of Sale.**—In theory, a mortgage foreclosure sale is made by the court of equity as vendor. Although the sale is to be conducted, and the deed made to the purchaser, by an officer of the court, the transfer of title is not complete and binding until the sale has been reported to the court and judicially confirmed. It is the common practice to appoint

[53] Brown v. Kennicott, 30 Ill. App. 89; Pawtucket Inst. for Savings v. Bowen, 7 Biss. C. C. 358, Fed. Cas. No. 10,852.

[54] Hodgdon v. Heidman, 66 Iowa, 645, 24 N. W. Rep. 257; Weir v. Field, 67 Miss. 292, 7 South. Rep. 355.

[55] Colgan v. Dunne, 50 Hun. (N. Y.), 443, 3 N. Y. Supp. 309.

[56] Walsh v. Van Horn, 22 Ill. App. 170.

a master in chancery to make the sale, though the court is
not strictly bound to this course, as appears from the statutory
provision that the deed shall be executed "by the sheriff, master in chancery, or other officer who made the sale, or by his
successor in office."[57] When the sale is made under a special
execution, it is necessary that the writ should run in the name
of the people of the State of Illinois, as required by the Constitution; if not, the sale is void and may be impeached collaterally.[58] The master or other officer appointed to make the
sale cannot appoint an agent or deputy to take his place. He
may of course employ an auctioneer to cry the sale, but it must
be made in the presence of the officer and under his personal
supervision and direction.[59] It is not necessary to the validity
of a sale under a decree of foreclosure of a mortgage that it
should be made within one year after the rendition of the decree, as the lien of the decree is not terminated by the expiration of that period.[60]

§ 430. Notice of Sale.—The law does not require that notice
of a sale under a decree of foreclosure should be given to the
parties personally, nor that it should be actually brought home
to the knowledge of parties interested.[61] And though the master in chancery may have made a promise to give to a party
interested in a decree of foreclosure actual personal notice of
the day of sale, his neglect to do so is not such an official de-
linquency as would justify a court in setting aside a sale
otherwise regularly made.[62] The only notice required is a
published notice, prescribed by the court making the decree;
and its terms, as to the manner of publication and the length
of time it is to be published, rest very much in the discretion
of the court. The statutory provision prescribing the notice
which shall be given of execution sales of land does not apply
to sales made by a master under such a decree. And it is said
that, "while it would be good practice to require by decree
the master to give the same notice that a sheriff is required
to give, still a failure to prescribe such notice in the decree,
in the absence of a statute, is not erroneous. Where a court

[57] Rev. Stat. Ill. c. 77, § 30.

[58] Sidwell v. Schumacher, 99 Ill.
426.

[59] Heyer v. Deaves, 2 Johns. Ch.
(N. Y.) 154.

[60] Karnes v. Harper, 48 Ill. 527.

[61] Springer v. Law, 84 Ill. App.
623, affirmed in 185 Ill. 542; Sanford v. Haines, 71 Mich. 116, 38 N.
W. Rep. 777.

[62] Crumpton v. Baldwin, 42 Ill.
165.

of chancery decrees the sale of lands for the payment of money, it may, under its general chancery powers, prescribe such notice to be given of the time of sale as may be reasonable." And in the same case it was held that a provision for publication of the notice of sale for three weeks was reasonable.[63] The due publication of the notice may be proved by the certificate of the publisher of the paper printing such notice, with a copy of the notice annexed, stating the number of times the same has been published, and giving the dates of the first and last papers containing such notice; the certificate need not show the dates of other intervening publications.[64] As to the contents of the notice, it must contain such a description of the premises affected as will suffice to convey accurate and reliable information both to the owner of the equity of redemption and to intending bidders. Minor errors of description will not vitiate the notice, provided it contains enough to identify the property clearly.[65] It is also necessary that the notice should state the time of the sale; and in this respect, it is not sufficient merely to state the day on which the sale will take place, but the notice must also give the hour of the sale, or state that the sale will be made between certain named hours of the business portion of the day; and further the sale itself must take place at a convenient or public place, accessible to bidders, and during the ordinary business hours of the day.[66]

§ 431. Adjournment of Sale.—The court has power to order the foreclosure sale adjourned from the day originally fixed, if it shall appear necessary. Thus, where the sale of the property on the day appointed would be ultimately detrimental to the interests of all concerned, and good cause is shown therefor, a petition for the postponement of the sale to a future day fixed should be granted.[67] It is also within the discretion of

---

[63] Crosby v. Kiest, 135 Ill. 458, 26 N. E. Rep. 589. Where notice of sale under a decree was ordered to be published "for three successive weeks," and in fact notice was published in three successive weeks, but the first publication was only 19 days before the sale, and the last publication 5 days before, it was held, after 10 years' delay, and in the absence of proof that injury had accrued to any one from want of notice, that the sale should not be set aside. Garrett v. Moss, 20 Ill. 549.

[64] Clarke v. Chamberlin, 70 Ill. App. 262.

[65] Lindsey v. Delano, 78 Iowa, 350, 43 N. W. Rep. 218.

[66] Trustees of Schools v. Snell, 19 Ill. 156.

[67] Farmers' Loan & Trust Co. v. Oxford Iron Co., 13 Fed. Rep. 169.

the master in chancery, subject to the controlling power of the court, to adjourn the sale, when he finds that such a course is necessary in order to prevent a sacrifice of the property. If, for example, no bidders appear at the sale, it will be proper to postpone it. But the master cannot be required to adjourn the sale merely because the mortgagee himself is the only bidder.[68] On the other hand, he cannot be prevented from adjourning the sale, if good reason therefor exists, at the instance of the person making the highest bid. That is, a bidder, whose bid has not been accepted, although it may have been the highest and best bid, cannot insist on leave to pay in the amount of his bid and have a confirmation of the sale to him, when the officer conducting the sale has announced its adjournment for good and sufficient cause.[69] But while the officer has thus a right to postpone a foreclosure sale to a future day, yet, after declaring the sale postponed, with the consent of the bidder to whom the property was knocked down, and giving to the printers the notice of the adjourned day of sale for publication, he has no right to change his mind and execute a deed as though a valid and complete sale had been made.[70] A notice of the adjournment of the sale should be published; and in some jurisdictions it is required by law to be published in the same paper in which the original notice was given; but the omission to comply with this direction is a mere irregularity which may be waived by the parties, and which cannot be set up to impeach the title to the property after the sale has been duly confirmed.[71]

§ 432. **Order of Sale.**—Where the land covered by a mortgage has been divided into parcels and sold by the mortgagor, before foreclosure, the rule established with reference to the order of its sale is that the portion retained by the mortgagor (if any) shall be first put up for sale, being first liable for the satisfaction of the mortgage debt, and that, as between different purchasers of separate parcels of the mortgaged premises, taking title thereto at different times, their holdings are to be subjected to the foreclosure sale in the inverse order of their alienation, that which was last conveyed by the mort-

---

[68] Equitable Trust Co. v. Shrope, 73 Iowa, 297, 34 N. W. Rep. 867.

[69] Blossom v. Milwaukee & C. R. Co., 3 Wall. 196.

[70] Miller v. Miller, 48 Mich. 311, 12 N. W. Rep. 209.

[71] Bechstein v. Schultz, 120 N. Y. 168, 24 N. E. Rep. 388.

gagor being first liable.[72] It is also to be remarked that, where two mortgages on different tracts of land are foreclosed in the same action, each tract should be sold to satisfy the debt for which it was separately mortgaged; it is improper to sell both together for the aggregate amount of the decree.[73]

§ 433. Sale in Separate Parcels.—When the mortgage covers two or more separate and distinct tracts or parcels of land, separately described, and especially when these are owned by different persons, the decree of foreclosure should order them to be sold separately and not as an aggregate, and the master making the sale should offer the tracts separately and in succession, and stop the sale when enough has been sold to satisfy the mortgage debt, with the costs and expenses.[74] But on the other hand, the master is authorized to sell mortgaged property en masse, or as a single tract, where it is so described in the mortgage and in the decree of sale, and there is nothing in the evidence to show that it is susceptible of advantageous division into parcels.[75] And further, if the master making the sale under a decree of foreclosure first offers the land to be sold in separate lots, tracts, or parcels, and does not succeed in obtaining any bid, he may then offer and sell the

---

[72] Supra, §§ 264, 265. And see National Sav. Bank v. Creswell, 100 U. S. 630; Stephens v. Clay, 17 Colo. 489, 30 Pac. Rep. 43; Sternberger v. Hanna, 42 Ohio St. 305.

[73] Home Loan Ass'n v. Wilkins, 66 Cal. 9, 4 Pac. Rep. 697.

[74] Waldo v. Williams, 3 Ill. 470; Ohling v. Luitjens, 32 Ill. 23. "Ordinarily a decree of foreclosure may be wholly silent as to the order in which the premises shall be offered for sale, but when the mortgaged land consists of separate government subdivisions, belonging to different persons, the decree should so direct the order of sale of the lots or tracts as to preserve the rights and equities of the separate owners. A decree absolutely requiring such premises to be sold in one body, in the absence of imperative reasons for such a course, cannot be upheld. The decree under consideration forbids a sale of the tracts separately, and this we regard as a fatal objection to it. The clause in the trust deed authorizing the trustee, in his discretion, to sell the property en masse cannot avail to support the decree. An abuse of such discretion would not have been permitted in a sale made by the trustee." Skaggs v. Kincaid, 48 Ill. App. 608.

[75] Field v. Brokaw, 159 Ill. 560, 42 N. E. Rep. 877 (affirming 59 Ill. App. 442); Patton v. Smith, 113 Ill. 499. "Where several distinct tracts of land are ordered sold by a master in chancery, by decree, it would, no doubt, be the duty of the officer to offer for sale each tract separately; but where a mortgage is given on a certain

whole property as one aggregate.[76] It must also be remembered that it is the duty of the master to sell the property so as to procure the most money with the least injury to the mortgagor, and hence the rule that, if this cannot be done by a sale in separate parcels, the property may be sold en masse.[77] Thus, upon the foreclosure of a mortgage upon the property of a manufacturing corporation, it is proper to direct that the property be sold as an entirety, where it appears that a division of it into parcels would lessen its selling value.[78] So, a mortgage given to secure the bonds of a railroad company, and covering the entire road, must, on breach of condition, be foreclosed as to the whole, and not merely as to the portion graded by the mortgagor company.[79]

Where the property has been sold as an entirety, when such action was not necessary, or when it would have been more proper to sell it in parcels, the sale is not absolutely void for that reason. At most it is irregular; and the court may refuse to confirm it, if objection is made on the coming in of the report, or may set it aside on proper application in due time.[80] The parties affected by such an irregular sale may move to have the same set aside before the period for redemption expires.[81] And where the sale of the property as an entirety produced such an inadequacy in the price as to amount to great wrong and oppression, the court may well entertain jurisdiction even two or three years after the sale, and afford relief against the purchaser, if he has not parted with the title, upon a reasonable excuse being shown for the delay.[82] But generally speaking, a sale of property en masse will not be set aside where it does not appear that there was any fraud or injury or any violation of the conditions of sale imposed by the

quarter section, or a tract of land described by metes and bounds as one tract, and a decree of sale is rendered in which the land is described as in the mortgage, we are aware of no rule that requires the master in chancery to offer the land for sale in subdivisions." Davis v. Dresback, 81 Ill. 393.

[76] Bozarth v. Largent, 128 Ill. 95, 21 N. E. Rep. 218; Malaer v. Damron, 31 Ill. App. 572.

[77] Stone v. Missouri Guarantee Sav. & Bldg. Ass'n, 58 Ill. App. 78.

[78] Central Trust Co. v. United States Rolling-Stock Co., 56 Fed. Rep. 5.

[79] Chicago, D. & V. R. Co. v. Loewenthal, 93 Ill. 433.

[80] Bozarth v. Largent, 128 Ill. 95, 21 N. E. Rep. 218; Waldo v. Williams, 3 Ill. 470; Stone v. Missouri Guarantee Sav. & Bldg. Ass'n, 58 Ill. App. 78.

[81] Flynn v. Wilkinson, 56 Ill. App. 239.

[82] Fergus v. Woodworth, 44 Ill. 374.

decree. Thus, when the master's report shows that the premises were in different tracts or parcels and were sold en masse, but no objections were made to it in the court below, and there was nothing in the record to show that any fraud was practised or any of the parties injured, or that the property was susceptible of division, and salable as divided, the question of the irregularity of the sale cannot be raised for the first time on appeal.[83]

§ 434. Setting Off Homestead.—The statute not having in terms pointed out the particular manner in which a court of chancery shall proceed to set off a homestead, when it becomes necessary to enforce a lien in equity on the premises, it is proper to adopt the mode prescribed by the statute when an officer holds an execution. Hence, in a decree of sale upon foreclosure of a mortgage, it is proper to direct the master in chancery "to proceed according to law to summon three householders as commissioners, who shall, upon oath, administered to them by such master, appraise the value of the premises in which homestead is claimed, and if the premises can, in their opinion, be divided without injury to the interests of the parties, to set off so much thereof, including the dwelling house, as shall be worth $1,000, and that the master sell the residue of said premises." In summoning such commissioners, the master acts as an officer of the court, for and on behalf of all the parties to the proceeding, and he need not consult the owner of the premises in selecting the commissioners.[84]

§ 435. Who May Purchase.—The creditor whose debt is secured by a mortgage, or a holder of bonds secured by a deed of trust, may bid, either for himself alone or for himself and other bondholders jointly, at a sale on foreclosure of the mortgage or deed of trust.[85] And so may the heirs and administrator of a deceased mortgagee.[86] And where a wife loans money to her husband, and he gives a mortgage on his land to a third person as security for the wife's benefit as to such loan, and the land is sold on foreclosure of the mortgage after the husband's death, the widow may become the purchaser at the sale, or may buy the certificate of purchase, and take the

---

[83] Dates v. Winstanley, 53 Ill. App. 623.

[84] Cummings v. Burleson, 78 Ill. 281.

[85] Chillicothe Paper Co. v. Wheeler, 68 Ill. App. 343.

[86] Briant v. Jackson, 99 Mo. 585, 13 S. W. Rep. 91.

absolute title to herself.[87] Again, the relation of the life-tenant
to the remainder-man is not of such a fiduciary nature that
the former cannot purchase the property at a foreclosure sale;
and his vendee for a valuable consideration, and without
knowledge of any fraud, takes a good title in fee simple.[88]
The rule also permits the purchase to be made by a third person to whom the mortgagor had sold and conveyed an undivided interest in the mortgaged premises after the execution
of the mortgage.[89] But where the mortgagor himself becomes
the purchaser at the foreclosure sale (or where a stranger
buys with money advanced by the mortgagor) and this is done
with a fraudulent purpose to cut out a junior mortgagee or
creditor, equity will have the right and power to treat the
payment as a redemption from the sale, or to hold the ostensi-
ble purchaser as a trustee for the mortgagor, and subject the
title in his hands to the rights of subsequent incumbrancers
or creditors.[90] As to purchases at such sales by married
women, it is said that where the statutes give them the same
right to acquire and hold property as a feme sole, a married
woman has the same right as any other person to purchase her
husband's real estate at a mortgage foreclosure sale thereof,
and to hold it free from any liability on account of her husband's debts, provided she makes the purchase in good faith
and with her own money. But if she makes the purchase with
her husband's money, or with money furnished by him, then,
as to his creditors and as to subsequent incumbrancers, she
would merely be a trustee for him, and her purchase would, as
to them, amount to a payment of the mortgage or a redemption
from the sale.[91]

§ 436. Combinations Among Bidders.—It was at one time
generally held that any agreement or arrangement among the
prospective bidders at a judicial sale, having a tendency to
prevent or suppress competition, was absolutely void as against
public policy. But the modern doctrine is that "agreements
between two or more persons, that all but one shall refrain
from bidding and permitting that one to become the purchaser,

[87] Kyle v. Wills, 166 Ill. 501, 46
N. E. Rep. 1121.

[88] German-American Title Co. v.
Fidelity Ins. Co., 132 Pa. St. 36,
18 Atl. Rep. 1090.

[89] Burr v. Mueller, 65 Ill. 258.

[90] Shinn v. Shinn, 15 Ill. App.
141; Campbell v. Benjamin, 69 Ill.
244.

[91] Houston v. Nord, 39 Minn. 490,
40 N. W. Rep. 568.

are not necessarily and under all circumstances void. They may be entered into for a lawful purpose, and from honest motives, and in such cases will be upheld; and they will not vitiate the purchase, or necessarily destroy the completed contracts to which they refer and in respect to which they were made.''[92] And so, several persons interested may form a combination for the purchase of the property. Thus, the fact that creditors of the mortgagor have fairly combined to buy in the property of the debtor at the foreclosure sale will afford no ground for the interposition of a court of equity at the instance of other creditors, when nothing was done to deprive the latter of their right to bid at the sale.[93] So, on a foreclosure sale, two mortgagees, who have separate liens on the mortgaged lands, which each claims to be superior to the other, may purchase the premises for their joint benefit, and are not obliged to bid against each other.[94]

§ 437. **Rights and Liabilities of Bidders.**—In one of the earlier cases in Illinois, it was declared that a master in chancery, conducting a foreclosure sale, should report to the court, for its approval, the largest bid received, and that a bid, although accepted by the master, did not become an absolute contract until approved by the court.[95] But afterwards this decision was overruled, and it was said that it was ''not in harmony with previous decisions of this court or with the practice in this State. The practice is, if the decree of the court does not otherwise direct, to strike the property off to the highest bidder, and it has not been usual to report bids to the court. If the bidder complies with all the terms of the sale, it is not usual for the court to refuse to confirm the sale, unless fraud, accident, mistake, or some great irregularity, calculated to do injury, has occurred.''[96] Hence a valid and binding contract of sale is made when the hammer falls. This must indeed be confirmed by the court; but in the absence of some sufficient cause for refusing confirmation or for setting aside the sale, the purchaser becomes entitled to receive a certificate of purchase on complying with the terms of the sale.[97]

[92] Hopkins v. Ensign, 122 N. Y. 144, 25 N. E. Rep. 306. And see Ritchie v. Judd, 137 Ill. 453, 27 N. E. Rep. 682.

[93] Kropholler v. St. Paul, M. & M. R. Co., 1 McCrary, 299, 2 Fed. Rep. 302.

[94] Huber v. Crosland, 140 Pa. St. 575, 21 Atl. Rep. 404.

[95] Dills v. Jasper, 33 Ill. 262.

[96] Comstock v. Purple, 49 Ill. 158.

[97] Jackson v. Warren, 32 Ill. 331.

A bidder may of course retract his bid before it has been accepted by the master; and even after the property has been struck off to him, the master may consent to the withdrawal of the bid, and renew the sale or adjourn it. If the bidder announces that he retracts his bid, and the master then adjourns the sale, this releases the bidder, and the master cannot afterwards tender him a certificate of purchase.[98] Ordinarily, however, a bidder who wishes to recede from his bid, after the sale, should apply to the court to be released. Where he.had full knowledge of the facts, but parted with his money under a mistaken conception of the law (as, where he erroneously supposed that it would be necessary for him to bid on the property in order to protect his own claims against it), his application for release will ordinarily be granted if made within a reasonable time; but if he does not avail himself of the privilege allowed by a court of equity to inform himself of the law and the facts, so as to secure in the same suit a release from his bid or a return of the money he has paid, the delay will be considered unreasonable.[99] Where the purchaser at a foreclosure sale fails to comply with the terms of his bid, the property will be sold again; but there should be some action of the court disposing of the sale to the defaulting purchaser before the property is again put up. But although it is not the proper practice for the master to re-sell without such an order of the court, yet if he does re-sell on his own responsibility, it will not necessarily be sufficient ground for holding the second sale to be void.[1]

§ 438. Report and Confirmation of Sale.—The master in chancery is a public officer, an agent of the court, engaged in discharging an official duty; and he is required to make a report to the court of a foreclosure sale made by him under its decree, in order that the same may be confirmed by the court. Either party to the proceeding can compel the performance of such duty at any time. But the failure of the master to report the sale to the court is not of itself sufficient reason to warrant the court in setting aside the sale.[2] The report of the master

[98] Miller v. Miller, 48 Mich. 311, 12 N. W. Rep. 209.

[99] Barnard v. Wilson, 66 Cal. 251, 5 Pac. Rep. 237; Sullivan v. Jennings, 44 N. J. Eq. 11, 14 Atl. Rep. 104.

[1] Augustine v. Doud, 1 Ill. App. 588.

[2] McPherson v. Wood, 52 Ill. App. 170.

should be sufficiently extended to show that the sale was conducted in accordance with the requirements of the decree. It
is not necessary to set out the notice of sale; it will be enough
if the master reports that he gave the notice required by the
decree.[3] Objections to the sale as made may now be filed by
parties in interest, and will be heard on the application for
confirmation. If such objections are sustained, a re-sale will
be ordered; if they are overruled, the proper course is to enter
an order confirming the sale. But where it is ordered that the
master's report be confirmed unless objections are filed, and
objections are filed for the sole purpose of determining who
is entitled to the surplus money, an order disposing of the surplus amounts to a confirmation of the sale as against the ob-
jectors.[4] The confirmation of a mortgage foreclosure sale cures
all irregularities in the proceedings; but such sale may afterwards be set aside in a proper case for fraud, if application is
made within a reasonable time.[5]

§ 439. Setting Aside Sale.—A foreclosure sale may be vacated and set aside by the court when it is voidable on account
of errors or irregularities, such, for example, as a failure to
give proper notice, or any improper or irregular conduct at the
sale. But an application for this relief must be made with reasonable promptness. Long delay, unjustified and unexplained,
amounting to laches, will prevent the court from granting relief on an application to set aside a foreclosure sale on such
grounds.[6] Thus, where the owner of the equity of redemption
does not invoke the aid of the court to set aside the sale for
two years after he has full knowledge of his rights, he will
have lost his right to insist upon having such sale vacated for
mere irregularities, especially when the property has passed
to an innocent purchaser.[7] And in other cases, it has been held
that a delay of about four years, before filing a bill to set aside
a foreclosure sale, even though the sale was voidable, when
the land has advanced in value, constitutes such laches as to
bar the relief sought.[8] But in a case where it appeared that

[3] Moore v. Titman, 33 Ill. 358.

[4] Lambert v. Livingston, 131 Ill.
161, 23 N. E. Rep. 352.

[5] McKeighan v. Hopkins, 19
Nebr. 33, 26 N. W. Rep. 614.

[6] Vail v. Arkell. 146 Ill. 363, 34
N. E. Rep. 937; Quinn v. Perkins,
159 Ill. 572, 43 N. E. Rep. 759; Cornell v. Newkirk, 44 Ill. App. 487,
affirmed in 144 Ill. 241.

[7] Racine & Miss. R. Co. v. Farmers' Loan & Trust Co., 86 Ill. 187.

[8] Connely v. Rue, 148 Ill. 207, 35
N. E. Rep. 824; Cornell v. New-

the purchaser had made no payment, that no duplicate of the certificate of purchase had been filed for record, and it was doubtful whether such certificate had been delivered to the purchaser except for examination, and no report of the sale had been made to the court, it was held proper to vacate the sale fifteen months after it was made, at the time when the purchaser applied for a deed.[9]

When the application to set aside the sale is based on the ground of fraud or oppression, resulting in substantial injury to the party complaining, the line is not so strictly drawn as against delay. But, on general principles, a party who seeks the aid of the courts must show that he has not been slothful or negligent. And even in this case, the courts will expect some reasonable excuse to be offered if there has been any considerable delay in the assertion of a right to impeach the sale.[10] Fraud, peculiarly odious to equity, is always ground for granting such relief. But it must be fraud which has actually injured some one. An agreement, for instance, by a senior mortgagee with junior mortgagees, that, if they would make no objection to his recovering judgment in a suit instituted by him on his mortgage, he would foreclose and sell only a part of the land, and bid the amount of his mortgage for that part, is not fraudulent nor against justice or equity.[11] A mortgagor who wishes to present the question whether, under the power contained in the mortgage, a sale can be made for the whole amount secured, must do so in his pleadings, and not seek to enjoin the sale or have it set aside.[12]

When the sale is vacated and set aside, it will be ordered that the property be again offered for sale. But when a resale of the property is thus ordered to be made, it must be made subject to the right of redemption.[13]

§ 440. Same; Inadequacy of Price.—The mere inadequacy of the price realized at a sale of property on foreclosure of a mortgage will not be considered sufficient ground for setting the sale aside, unless so gross as to raise a presumption of fraud.[14]

kirk, 144 Ill. 241, 33 N. E. Rep. 37.

[9] Harwood v. Cox, 26 Ill. App. 374.

[10] Fergus v. Woodworth, 44 Ill. 374; Walker v. Schum, 42 Ill. 462.

[11] Garrett v. Moss, 20 Ill. 549.

[12] Conlin v. Carter, 93 Ill. 536.

[13] Bruschke v. Wright, 166 Ill. 183, 46 N. E. Rep. 813.

[14] Comstock v. Purple, 49 Ill. 158; Duncan v. Sanders, 50 Ill. 475; Mixer v. Sibley, 53 Ill. 61; Heberer v. Heberer, 67 Ill. 253; Connely v. Rue, 148 Ill. 207, 35 N.

To this rule, however, there are statutory exceptions in the case of the foreclosure of mortgages made by executors and by guardians. As to sales made on the foreclosure of such mortgages, it is provided that the court may, at any time before confirmation, set them aside for inadequacy of price or for other good cause, and that they shall not be binding on the mortgagor until confirmed by the court.[15]

§ 441. Certificate of Purchase.—The statutes of Illinois provide that the master in chancery or other officer making a foreclosure sale shall give to the purchaser a certificate describing the premises purchased by him, showing the amount paid therefor (or the amount of his bid if the purchaser was the mortgagee), and the time when the purchaser will be entitled to a deed unless the premises are redeemed. The officer is also required to file a duplicate of this certificate in the office of the recorder of the county in which the property is situated, and such duplicate shall be recorded by the recorder, and the certificate, or duplicate, or the record thereof, or a certified copy of the record, shall be evidence of the facts therein stated.[16] The statutory requirement for the filing of a duplicate of the certificate, to be recorded, is not for the purpose of notifying the parties to the foreclosure proceeding that the master has executed the decree, but to notify persons who, as judgment creditors or subsequent purchasers, or otherwise, are interested in but not connected with the proceedings as parties.[17] This statutory provision, so far as it relates to filing the duplicate, is merely directory, and a failure to comply with it will not invalidate the sale.[18] The certificate of purchase does not represent such an interest in real estate as is subject to the levy of an execution, especially before the time for redemption has expired. The holder cannot exercise acts of ownership over the premises, simply because he owns the certificate, when his right to a deed has not matured.[19] But the statute provides that the certificate "shall be assignable by indorsement thereon, under the hand of such purchaser or his heirs, executors, administrators, or assigns, and every person to whom the same

B. Rep. 824; Springer v. Law, 84 Ill. App. 623, affirmed in 185 Ill. 542.

[15] Rev. Stat. Ill. c. 3, § 121; Id. c. 64, § 26.

[16] Rev. Stat. Ill. c. 77, §§ 16, 17.

[17] McPherson v. Wood, 52 Ill. App. 170.

[18] Johnson v. Day, 2 N. Dak. 295, 50 N. W. Rep. 701.

[19] Shobe v. Luff, 66 Ill. App. 414.

shall be so assigned shall be entitled to the same benefits therefrom in every respect that the person therein named would have been [entitled to] if the same had not been assigned."[20] The assignment and delivery of a certificate of purchase, as collateral security for an indebtedness, is in the nature of an equitable mortgage of the holder's contingent interest in the land, and not a mere pledge of personal property. This being so, the owner of such certificate has an unquestionable right to maintain a bill to redeem from such a pledge or assignment of the certificate, even after a waiver of the right to redeem contained in the agreement by which the pledge was made.[21] But the assignee of a certificate of purchase takes only an equitable title, and is chargeable with notice of all irregularities which may invalidate the sale, and with notice of all defenses which could be interposed against his assignor.[22]

PART X. RIGHTS OF FORECLOSURE PURCHASER.

§ 442. **Title Acquired by Purchaser.**—The purchaser of real estate at a master's sale in foreclosure proceedings acquires no title, legal or equitable, to the property, until he receives his deed. Pending the period allowed by law for redemption, he has only a lien upon the property, and is not entitled to possession. It is not the master's sale which passes the title. The purchaser acquires thereby the right to a conveyance of the title only in case the premises are not redeemed, and no new title vests until the period of redemption has expired.[23] Hence

---

[20] Rev. Stat. Ill. c. 77, § 29.

[21] Shobe v. Luff, 66 Ill. App. 414.

[22] Bruschke v. Wright, 166 Ill. 183, 46 N. E. Rep. 813, reversing Wright v. Bruschke, 62 Ill. App. 358.

[23] Strauss v. Tuckhorn, 200 Ill.

75; Bartlett v. Amberg, 92 Ill. App. 377. Although no deed is made to the purchaser, a decree entered by the court declaring the title to the property to be vested in him will give such an equitable estate as will preclude the heirs of the

the purchaser cannot maintain ejectment or any other possessory action merely on his certificate of purchase.[24] In a sense it may be said that he succeeds to the rights of the mortgagee; he occupies the same position as the mortgagee in respect to the priority of claims or liens on the property.[25] But when the time for redemption expires and the purchaser receives a deed, the title thereby acquired relates back to the execution of the mortgage, and the purchaser takes the title as then existing in the mortgagor, divested of sales, liens, or leases subsequently made by the mortgagor or by persons claiming under him.[26] He "acquires all the right in the mortgaged premises which the mortgagor had at the time of the execution of the mortgage, entirely unaffected by the title or lien of purchasers or incumbrancers subsequent to the recording of the mortgage, or with notice, who, in order to save themselves, must redeem as in cases of an ordinary sale on execution at law."[27] Tenants in possession under subsequent leases may be treated as trespassers by the foreclosure purchaser, and ejected without notice. Or the purchaser may accept an occupying tenant as his tenant; but the single act of demanding rent will not be sufficient to establish the relation of landlord and tenant between them, when such demand has not been acted on.[28] But it also follows from this doctrine that the foreclosure purchaser acquires no greater or stronger title than the mortgagor had at the time of executing the mortgage.[29] But he is entitled to all the mortgagor's interest. The purchaser cannot be compelled to accept anything not amount-

mortgagor from asserting title by bill in equity for partition of the land. Barlow v. Standford, 82 Ill. 298.

[24] Rockwell v. Servant, 63 Ill. 424.

[25] Davis v. Connecticut Mut. Life Ins. Co., 84 Ill. 508.

[26] Bartlett v. Hitchcock, 10 Ill. App. 87. "In a suit by the mortgagor to enforce his mortgage, whether by scire facias or by bill for foreclosure and sale, a purchaser at the sale of the mortgaged premises takes the place of the mortgagee in proceedings in strict foreclosure at common law.

His title relates back to the time of the execution of the mortgage. He succeeds as well to the title and estate acquired by the mortgagee by the delivery of the mortgage deed, as to the estate the mortgagor had at the time of the execution of the mortgage." Champion v. Hinkle, 45 N. J. Eq. 162, 16 Atl. Rep. 701.

[27] State Bank v. Wilson, 9 Ill. 57.

[28] Bartlett v. Hitchcock, 10 Ill. App. 87.

[29] McMahill v. Torrence, 163 Ill. 277, 45 N. E. Rep. 269.

ing to a complete transfer of the mortgagor's entire interest. "The purchaser at a judicial sale is always entitled to such interest as the defendant actually has. If a sale, for any defect in the proceedings, is so void that it cannot transfer such title and interest as the defendant has, then the purchaser is not bound by his bid, but may successfully resist any action seeking its enforcement. This is not upon the ground that the title is worthless, but because the title bought cannot be transferred to him by the sale."[30] The purchaser, however, cannot acquire or take title to any other property than that coming within the description of the mortgage.[31]

Since the purchaser does not acquire title by the master's sale, and since the mortgagor is entitled to remain in possession and enjoyment of the premises during the period allowed for redemption, it is held that crops raised on the land during this period or which have fully matured and are ready to be harvested at the time the purchaser takes out his deed, belong to the mortgagor and cannot be claimed by the foreclosure purchaser.[32]

§ 443. How Affected by Errors or Reversal of Decree.— Purchasers under a decree of a court of equity, while it is in full force and before any writ of error has been prosecuted, and without any notice whatever of claims and equities of the parties thereto, will be protected notwithstanding the decree is afterwards reversed.[33] "Where there is no lack of jurisdiction, the title of a bona fide purchaser who is not a party or chargeable as such, obtained by judicial sale, cannot be affected by mere errors in the proceedings in the suit, even though the judgment or decree may afterwards be reversed on account of such errors. The same principle extends to the assignee of such a purchaser."[34] Thus, where a decree of foreclosure recites that one of the defendants, who was not served with process, was dead, and the decree is afterwards reversed be-

[30] Thrift v. Frittz, 7 Ill. App. 55.

[31] Jones v. Lake, 43 La. Ann. 1024, 10 South. Rep. 204.

[32] Johnson v. Camp, 51 Ill. 219. And see Dobbins v. Lusch, 53 Iowa, 304, 5 N. W. Rep. 205; Hecht v. Dittman, 56 Iowa, 679, 7 N. W. Rep. 495; Everingham v. Braden, 58 Iowa, 133, 12 N. W. Rep. 142; Richards v. Knight, 78 Iowa, 69, 42 N. W. Rep. 584; Woehler v. Endter, 46 Wis. 301, 1 N. W. Rep. 329; Allen v. Enderkin, 62 Wis. 627, 22 N. W. Rep. 824. Compare Parker v. Storts, 15 Ohio St. 351.

[33] Barlow v. Standford, 82 Ill. 298.

[34] Tormohlen v. Walter, 175 Ill. 442, 51 N. E. Rep. 706; Lambert v. Hyers, 83 Ill. App. 48.

cause the fact of the death was not proved, such reversal does not affect the title of a purchaser at the foreclosure sale, when such party was in fact dead, and the purchaser was not a party to the suit.[35] Also, the fact that the foreclosure purchaser asks the appellate court to modify as to him the supersedeas issued on appeal from the decree does not make him a party to the suit so as to affect him with notice of errors.[36]

§ 444. Rights of Purchaser Under Invalid Sale.—If the sale on foreclosure of a mortgage was entirely void, or is vacated by the court, the purchaser does not lose his money. He is to be regarded in that case as an equitable assignee of the mortgage.[37] Or he will be entitled to be subrogated to the rights of the mortgagee.[38] That is, he will take the mortgage with all the rights of the original mortgagee to enforce it for the satisfaction of the debt secured. And where the holder of the mortgage, or of the debt secured, himself becomes the purchaser at the foreclosure sale, and takes possession, but afterwards the mortgagor procures the sale to be set aside in equity for fraud or irregularities, the mortgagee will not be regarded as a trespasser upon the premises, but he will be considered as a mortgagee in possession for breach of condition, and will have the rights attaching to that character.[39] It is also held that remote purchasers are not chargeable with notice of defects in a mortgage foreclosure sale; and even in case they have actual notice thereof, the sale is only voidable.[40]

§ 445. Rule of Caveat Emptor.—"It is a general rule, subject to few if any exceptions, unless it be where a fraud is practised upon a purchaser at a judicial sale, that the doctrine of caveat emptor applies. In our researches, no case has been found where a bill has been sustained to enable such a purchaser to recover back the money paid by him for a defective title, or where, by his purchase, he acquired no title. The officer of the law can only sell such title as the debtor has, and he has no power to warrant the title, or impose terms or conditions on the sale beyond those that are imposed by the law. In all judicial sales, the presumption is that, as the rule of caveat

[35] Lambert v. Livingston, 131 Ill. 161, 23 N. E. Rep. 352.
[36] Lambert v. Livingston, supra.
[37] Muir v. Berkshire, 52 Ind. 149;

Johnson v. Robertson, 34 Md. 165; supra, ¶ 185.
[38] Supra, ¶ 314.
[39] Harper v. Ely, 70 Ill. 581.
[40] Johnson v. Watson, 87 Ill. 535.

33

emptor applies, the purchaser will examine the title with the
same care that a person does who receives a conveyance of land
by a simple quit-claim deed. When he knows there are no
covenants to resort to in case he acquires no title, the most
careless, saying nothing of the prudent, would look to the
title and see that it was good before becoming a purchaser at
such a sale. Or if not, he must expect to procure it on such
terms as he might sell the claim for a profit. As well might a
person purchasing a quit-claim deed file a bill to be reimbursed
on the failure of the title, as where the purchase is made at a
sale by an administrator. Both kinds of purchase depend upon
the same rule. It is the policy of the law to only invest a
sheriff, master in chancery, or administrator, in making sales
of real estate, with a mere naked power to sell such title as the
debtor or deceased had, without warranty or any terms except
those imposed by the law. They are the mere instruments of
the law to pass such, and only such, title as was held by the
debtor or intestate."[41]

§ 446. **Possession Pending Redemption.**—The defendant in
a foreclosure proceeding is entitled to retain the possession
of the mortgaged premises, after the decree and sale, until the
time allowed by statute for redemption expires and the master's deed is executed to the purchaser; and it is error to enter
a decree giving the purchaser the right to possession upon the
giving of the master's certificate of purchase.[42] "The form of
mortgage giving a lien on the real estate only [that is, not
including the rents and profits] simply authorizes the mortgagee, upon default in payment, to sell the premises and apply
the proceeds of such sale to the payment of the debt. If that
be all the court decrees, the possession of the premises remains
in, and the rents and profits continue to be the property of,
the mortgagor until the master's certificate has ripened into a
deed."[43] As explained in another connection, the possession
may be vested in a receiver appointed in a proper case. But
a stipulation for an early hearing on condition that no receiver

[41] Bishop v. O'Conner, 69 Ill.
431. The rule of caveat emptor
applies to a sheriff's sale of land
under foreclosure of a mortgage
by scire facias. Walbridge v. Day,
31 Ill. 379. And to a sale under a
deed of trust in the nature of a
mortgage. Brewer v. Christian, 9
Ill. App. 57.

[42] Kihlholz v. Wolff, 8 Ill. App.
371; Bennett v. Matson, 41 Ill. 332;
Myers v. Manny, 63 Ill. 211.

[43] Ortengren v. Rice, 104 Ill.
App. 428.

shall be appointed, and that the possession of the mortgagor shall not be disturbed until the time for redemption expires, is a proper one for counsel to make and should be enforced.[44]

§ 447. Deed to Purchaser.—If property sold on foreclosure of a mortgage is not redeemed in pursuance of law, the legal holder of the certificate of purchase becomes entitled to take out a deed therefor at any time within five years after the expiration of the time of redemption. This deed is to be executed by the sheriff, master in chancery, or other officer who made the sale, or by his successor in office, or by some person specially appointed by the court for the purpose.[45] A master in chancery who has conducted a foreclosure sale under a decree of the court and issued a certificate of purchase, is before the court at all times, on notice, and may be compelled, in a summary proceeding before the chancellor, to execute a deed in accordance with the rights of the holder. There is no necessity for resorting to a writ of mandamus to enforce this action on his part, and it is not the proper practice.[46] Where a sheriff made the sale, his deed to the purchaser is not invalid because made after the expiration of his term of office.[47]

It is also provided by the statute that if the deed is not taken out within the five years limited by the act, the certificate of purchase shall be null and void, "but if such deed is wrongfully withheld by the officer whose duty it is to execute the same, or if the execution of such deed is restrained by injunction or order of a court or judge, the time during which the deed is so withheld or the execution thereof restrained shall not be taken as any part of the five years within which said holder shall take a deed."[48] The consequence of neglecting to obtain the deed within the five years thus allowed to the foreclosure purchaser, is to render his certificate of purchase null and void, and to forfeit all his rights under the sale or certificate; and if no sufficient excuse for his negligence is shown, equity will not interfere to relieve him from the legal effect of such negligence by ordering a re-sale.[49] And further, if the certificate of purchase thus becomes void, the mortgagor be-

[44] Evans v. Heaton, 26 Ill. App. 412.

[45] Rev. Stat. Ill. c. 77, § 30.

[46] People v. Bowman, 181 Ill. 421, 55 N. E. Rep. 148.

[47] Bozarth v. Largent, 128 Ill. 95, 21 N. E. Rep. 218.

[48] Rev. Stat. Ill. c. 77, § 30.

[49] Trustees of Schools v. Love, 34 Ill. App. 418.

comes the absolute owner of the premises, and if the mortgagee became the purchaser at the foreclosure sale, he will lose all his rights as against the mortgagor or his alienees.[50]

A statute also provides that, in deeds made by masters in chancery or sheriffs, under and by virtue of a judgment or decree of a court, it shall not be necessary to copy the judgment or decree in the deed; but it is sufficient to refer to the same by the title of the cause, the name of the court, and the date or term of court at which the proceedings were had or the judgment or decree obtained.[51] And the master's deed to the foreclosure purchaser "shall convey to the grantee therein named all the title, estate, and interest of the person against whom the execution was issued, of every nature and kind, in and to the premises thereby conveyed, but such deed shall not be construed to contain any covenant on the part of the officer executing the same."[52] Such a deed, it is said, is prima facie evidence of the regularity of the sale, but not of the decree under which it was made.[53] If the deed, by mistake, omits a portion of the land actually sold on the foreclosure, the purchaser may have the mistake corrected by due application to the court. This cannot, however, be done on mere motion; it is necessary for the purchaser to file a bill in equity for that purpose.[54]

§ 448. **Recovery of Possession Under Deed.**—The purchaser at a foreclosure sale cannot be considered as in actual or constructive possession of the premises merely in consequence of his purchase. He obtains only a right of possession. And where a possession adverse to his rights is persisted in, after he has obtained a deed, he must resort to legal proceedings to acquire the possession.[55] But the court of equity which decreed the foreclosure and sale of the property has power to put the purchaser in possession, without compelling him to resort to an action at law.[56] It is usual to incorporate in

<hr/>

[50] Lightcap v. Bradley, 186 Ill. 510, 58 N. E. Rep. 221. Where nearly twenty years have elapsed after a foreclosure sale, and no conveyance has been executed to the purchaser, it will be presumed that the land has been redeemed from the sale. Reynolds v. Dishon, 3 Ill. App. 173.

[51] Rev. Stat. Ill. c. 30, § 12 (Starr & C. § 13).

[52] Rev. Stat. Ill. c. 77, § 32.

[53] Reed v. Ohio & M. Ry. Co., 126 Ill. 48, 17 N. E. Rep. 807.

[54] Foster v. Clark, 79 Ill. 225.

[55] Beggs v. Thompson, 2 Ohio, 95.

[56] Aldrich v. Sharp, 4 Ill. 261.

the decree of foreclosure an order requiring the surrender of the premises to the foreclosure purchaser, after the expiration of the period for redemption and the issue of a deed to him; but if this is omitted, the purchaser may move the court for an order on the mortgagor to yield possession to the purchaser, and after due notice of the application, such order may issue.[57] If the order is not obeyed, the purchaser may obtain a writ of assistance. Or it is equally open to him to proceed by an action of forcible detainer against the party in possession; and these are concurrent remedies, so that the purchaser may resort to both of them at the same time and may prosecute both proceedings until he obtains possession through the one or the other.[58]

The theory has also been advanced that the court of equity, on making its order for the surrender of possession to the purchaser, may enforce the mortgagor's obedience thereto by the threat to punish him for contempt if he refuses to yield, and thus indirectly get possession for the purchaser. The point is doubtful. In this connection it has been said: "While it may be considered settled that the court will, by its writ of assistance or other proper process, put the purchaser in actual possession, it does not seem so clear from the authorities that it will resort to the more indirect mode of enforcing a surrender by attachment for contempt. But if proceedings through the medium of attachments for contempt are admissible, they must be carried on stricti juris, and the party resorting to them must show a full compliance with all the required conditions preliminary thereto."[59]

It has been held, in another jurisdiction, that, where the mortgagor or his grantee remains in possession after the title to an undivided interest in the land has passed by a foreclosure sale to a purchaser thereof, the former's possession is presumed amicable and in subordination to the title of the purchaser until the contrary appears. The parties so jointly owning the land become tenants in common, the possession of one being deemed the possession of both; and the statute of limitations does not begin to run against such purchaser until an ouster or the

---

[57] Freeman v. Freeman, 66 Ill. 53.

[58] Vahle v. Braeckensick, 48 Ill. App. 190 (affirmed in 145 Ill. 231);

Kessinger v. Whittaker, 82 Ill. 22.

[59] Murphy v. Abbott, 13 Ill. App. 68.

assertion of some hostile claim by the tenant in possession denoting an intention to hold adversely to his co-tenant.[60]

§ 449. **Same; Action of Forcible Detainer.**—It is provided by statute in Illinois that the purchaser at a foreclosure sale may recover possession of the premises, when they remain in the possession of the mortgagor or of any other person who was a party to the foreclosure proceeding, after the expiration of the time for redemption, by an action of forcible entry and detainer, when the occupant neglects or refuses to surrender possession after demand in writing by the person entitled thereto or his agent.[61] And it is held that such an action will also lie against a party in possession of land under the grantor in a deed of trust, by the purchaser at the trustee's sale, and a demand of possession upon such occupant will be sufficient.[62] When the foreclosure purchaser proceeds at law, in this form of action, for the recovery of possession, he is not required, before commencing his suit, to serve upon the person in possession a copy of the decree and produce and exhibit his deed, as he must do when he chooses the remedy afforded by means of the writ of assistance. In such cases, the person entitled to possession is required only to comply with the statute, that is, to make a demand in writing before bringing suit.[63] In such an action, the mortgagor is not permitted, by way of defense, to dispute the title acquired by the purchaser under the foreclosure proceedings and sale.[64] Nor can the mortgagor defend on the ground that the legal title is now in a third person, who acquired the same at a tax sale, and under whom the mortgagor claims as lessee, when it appears that the land was sold for the taxes of the very year in which the mortgage was given, and that the tax purchaser was enabled to get his deed by collusion with the mortgagor, who gave no notice to the mortgagee of the tax proceedings or of the tax purchaser's action of ejectment, in which the latter gained the possession.[65]

§ 450. **Same; Writ of Assistance.**—"The practice in this state, conforming to the general chancery practice, is, where the decree orders the defendant, on the execution of the deed

---

[60] Lowry v. Tilleny, 31 Minn. 500, 18 N. W. Rep. 452.

[61] Rev. Stat. Ill. c. 57, § 2.

[62] Rice v. Brown, 77 Ill. 549.

[63] Braeckensieck v. Vahle, 48 Ill. App. 312.

[64] Woods v. Soucy, 184 Ill. 568, 56 N. E. Rep. 1015.

[65] Frazier v. Gates, 61 Ill. 180.

by the master in chancery, to surrender the possession to the purchaser, to serve a copy of the decree on the defendant in possession, or, if others are in under him, as purchasers, tenants, or otherwise, then upon them, and upon possession being refused, the court will, on filing an affidavit of the facts, award a writ of possession. But where the original decree ordering the sale fails to order possession to be thus surrendered, and the person in possession refuses to surrender it, the court will, on proper notice and motion, make such an order, and upon like service of a copy and demand of possession, will, on motion and without notice, order an injunction against the party to deliver possession, and then, on affidavit of the service of the injunction and a refusal to deliver possession, a writ of assistance directed to the sheriff to put the purchaser into possession issues, of course, on motion and without notice."[66] But the only persons who can be put out of possession on a writ of assistance are those who were parties to the foreclosure suit or those who have come in, pending the proceedings, under parties to that suit.[67] Thus, one who entered under a person who was neither party nor privy to the foreclosure proceedings, claiming an independent title to the premises, as, under

[66] Oglesby v. Pearce, 68 Ill. 220. And see Higgins v. Peterson, 64 Ill. App. 256; Kessinger v. Whittaker, 82 Ill. 22; O'Bryan v. Fay, Id. 87.

[67] Heffron v. Gage, 44 Ill. App. 147, affirmed in 149 Ill. 182. The writ of assistance can go only against the parties to the suit, or against those who have come into possession under them since the commencement of the suit. Hence such a writ, issued out of chancery upon the foreclosure of a mortgage, will not justify the officer to whom it is directed in executing it upon a party who was in possession of the premises before and at the time of the commencement of the foreclosure suit, but who was not made a party to that suit nor named in the writ. Where the officer finds such a person in possession, it is his duty to return the writ with a statement of the facts as he finds them, and a return that he was unable to execute the writ for the reasons given. If an attempt or threat is made to disturb the possession of such party by means of such a writ, he may obtain an injunction to restrain all persons concerned from dispossessing him. Or if he is actually deprived of the possession under the writ of assistance, he may maintain an action of forcible entry and detainer against the officer and so regain the possession. The foreclosure purchaser, in such circumstances, must resort to an action at law against the possessor of the property, in order to gain possession of it for himself, and it appears that forcible entry and detainer is the proper form of action. Brush v. Fowler, 36 Ill. 53.

a tax deed, which, if valid, is paramount to the mortgage and to all rights derived therefrom, cannot be disturbed in his possession under a writ of assistance issued to the foreclosure purchaser.[68] But when property in the possession of a receiver has been legally sold to satisfy an existing mortgage, it is proper for the court to order the receiver to deliver possession of the property to the purchaser.[69]

An application by the foreclosure purchaser for the writ of assistance to put him in possession of the premises is not the institution of a new suit, but is auxiliary or incidental to the decree previously rendered, whereby the rights of the parties have become fixed and determined.[70] The purchaser may apply for such a writ pending an appeal from the decree.[71] And the court has power to re-docket the foreclosure suit, as against the parties thereto, and enter such order as may be necessary to execute its decree by the delivery of possession to the purchaser, where no new rights have been acquired by the defendant since the entry of the original decree.[72] And under the statute, a judge of the circuit court has power, in vacation, to order the issuing of a writ of possession to carry into effect a decree of foreclosure.[73]

The right of the foreclosure purchaser to apply to the court for a writ of assistance to put him in possession is not barred by the fact that he has already been defeated in an action of forcible detainer against the party in possession. The application for the writ, as just stated, is not a new suit, but an incident of the original foreclosure proceeding; and the judgment in the forcible detainer proceeding may have resulted from a want of demand or the insufficiency of the notice, and in such case it cannot preclude the right to possession adjudicated on a direct proceeding.[74]

[68] Ricketts v. Chicago Permanent Bldg. & Loan Ass'n, 67 Ill. App. 71.

[69] Heffron v. Knickerbocker, 57 Ill. App. 336.

[70] Vahle v. Brackenseik, 145 Ill. 231, 34 N. E. Rep. 524; Kessinger v. Whittaker, 82 Ill. 22.

[71] Lambert v. Livingston, 131 Ill. 161, 23 N. E. Rep. 352.

[72] Vahle v. Brackenseik, 145 Ill. 231, 34 N. E. Rep. 524.

[73] Kessinger v. Whittaker, 82 Ill. 22; Rev. Stat. Ill. c. 37, § 67.

[74] Lancaster v. Snow, 184 Ill. 534, 56 N. E. Rep. 813; Vahle v. Brackenseik, 145 Ill. 231, 34 N. E. Rep. 524; Cochran v. Fogler, 116 Ill. 194, 5 N. E. Rep. 383.

§ 451. Taxation of Costs.—A party brought into a foreclosure proceeding as a defendant, and who succeeds in establishing the contention that his claim against the property constitutes a lien paramount to that of the mortgage, will be entitled to his costs.[75] Where a decree is rendered, in a suit in equity for the foreclosure of a mortgage, which settles the rights of the parties and directs a sale of the premises, but leaves the question of costs undisposed of, and the whole case stands over to await the report of the master, the parties being retained in court in view of further probable action in the case, it is competent for the court to require the costs to be taxed at a term subsequent to that at which the decree was rendered.[76]

§ 452. Allowance of Attorney's Fee.—The statutes do not authorize the courts to include a fee for the complainant's solicitor in the taxable costs of a proceeding for the foreclosure of a mortgage. Hence, in the absence of a statutory provision, the entire matter of decreeing an allowance of any sum as solicitors' fees in foreclosure, to be paid out of the proceeds of the sale, rests solely upon contract, and in the absence of a contract, no such allowance can be made.[77] It should be remarked, however, that this rule is not observed by the United States courts. Since their procedure in equity is not controlled by state laws, it is considered that they may, in accordance with the general principles of equity, allow a reasonable attorney's fee in a foreclosure case, even though the parties have not stipulated therefor, or though their agreement in that regard is void.[78] In any case, however, it is against public policy

[75] First Nat. Bank v. Adam, 138 Ill. 483, 25 N. E. Rep. 576.

[76] Northern Illinois R. Co. v. Racine & Miss. R. Co., 49 Ill. 356.

[77] Atwood v. Whittemore, 94 Ill.

App. 294; Conwell v. McCowan, 53 Ill. 363.

[78] Dodge v. Tulleys, 144 U. S. 451.

and improper to allow an attorney fees for his own professional services in his own case.[79]

§ 453. **Stipulation in Mortgage for Attorney's Fee.**—In Illinois, it is considered entirely proper and permissible for the parties to a mortgage or deed of trust to incorporate in the instrument a stipulation for the allowance of a fee to the mortgagee's solicitor in case of foreclosure by suit, and to give a lien upon the mortgaged premises for the same. The agreement may be for a fixed sum, to be allowed as such fee, or for a percentage of the mortgage debt, or it may provide that the court shall allow, in addition to the taxable costs and disbursements, whatever sum the creditor may have reasonably and necessarily paid or become liable to pay on account of the services of an attorney or solicitor in the suit. In either case, there is no statute or rule of law or equity which forbids such an agreement of the parties; and upon the foreclosure of a mortgage or deed of trust containing a provision of this kind, it is proper for the court to include in its decree the allowance of a solicitor's fee, and to direct its payment out of the proceeds of the sale of the mortgaged land.[80] But such fee must be clearly included within the provisions of the mortgage. Thus, a clause in a trust deed providing for the payment out of the proceeds of sale of all costs, charges, and expenses, including commissions to the trustee, gives no right to a solicitor's fee upon foreclosure by suit, though the suit was made necessary by the refusal of the trustee to act.[81] And nothing can be taxed as an attorney's fee where it does not appear that the attorney did anything within the terms of the stipulation.[82] But though the mortgagee signs the bill for foreclosure in his own name and behalf, still he may be allowed a solicitor's fee, the mortgage providing for it, where he is represented in the litigation by other solicitors.[83] And a

[79] Garrett v. Peirce, 74 Ill. App. 225.

[80] Wright v. Jacksonville Benefit Bldg. Ass'n, 48 Ill. 505; McIntire v. Yates, 104 Ill. 491; Mulcahey v. Strauss, 151 Ill. 70, 37 N. E. Rep. 702; Haldeman v. Massachusetts Mut. Life Ins. Co., 21 Ill. App. 146; Barnett v. Davenport, 40 Ill. App. 57; Buckley v. Jones, 58 Ill. App. 357; Burke v. Tutt, 59 Ill. App. 678; Piasa Bluffs Improvement Co. v. Evers, 65 Ill. App. 205.

[81] Fowler v. Equitable Trust Co., 141 U. S. 384.

[82] Soles v. Sheppard, 99 Ill. 616.

[83] Barry v. Guild, 126 Ill. 439, 18 N. E. Rep. 759, affirming 28 Ill. App. 39.

tender by a mortgagor, after the beginning of a suit to foreclose, in order to be effective, must include an offer to pay
a reasonable attorney's fee for services already rendered,
where the mortgage provides for the payment of such a fee .
on foreclosure.[84] Where the note secured by the mortgage
contained an agreement for the payment of an attorney's fee
by the mortgagor "in case of collection by suit," a bill in
equity to foreclose the mortgage is a suit for the collection of
the note, within the meaning of this clause.[85]

Where the parties name and agree upon the amount to be
allowed as a solicitor's fee, in the mortgage or trust deed itself,
there is no reason why they should not be concluded by the
amount so agreed upon, unless it should appear that the
amount was inserted as a cover for usury or that it is unreasonable or excessive; and in the absence of a showing of these
facts, the court may properly allow the sum fixed by the parties.[86] If the debtor objects to the amount or percentage he
has agreed to pay, on the ground that it is unreasonably great,
he must prove that it is excessive; the burden is not on the
creditor to show its reasonableness. It is not error for the
court to allow the sum stipulated for in the mortgage without
evidence that such amount is reasonable, when there is no
offer to show the contrary.[87] But if the mortgage provides for
a certain sum for solicitors' fees in foreclosure, such amount
cannot be increased by the court, although it may be reduced
if unreasonably great.[88] And when the mortgage provides for
the allowance of a reasonable attorney's fee, without fixing
its amount, and the note secured by the mortgage provides
for a specific sum as such fee, only the amount named in the
note can be allowed.[89]

§ 454. **What is a Reasonable Fee.**—Although the mortgage,
in stipulating for the allowance of a solicitor's fee in case of

[84] Fuller v. Brown, 167 Ill. 293, 47 N. E. Rep. 202.

[85] Hand v. Simpson, 99 Ill. App. 269.

[86] Heffron v. Gage, 149 Ill. 182, 36 N. E. Rep. 569; Baker v. Jacob-son, 183 Ill. 171, 55 N. E. Rep. 724; Sweeney v. Kaufman, 168 Ill. 233, 48 N. E. Rep. 144.

[87] Dorn v. Ross, 177 Ill. 225, 52 N. E. Rep. 321 (affirming 77 Ill. App. 223); Thornton v. Common-wealth Loan & Bldg. Ass'n, 181 Ill. 456, 54 N. E. Rep. 1037, affirming 79 Ill. App. 657.

[88] Henke v. Gunzenhauser, 195 Ill. 130, 62 N. E. Rep. 896, affirming Gunzenhauser v. Henke, 97 Ill. App. 485.

[89] Sawyer v. Perry, 62 Iowa, 238, 17 N. W. Rep. 497; Hamlin v. Rog-ers, 79 Ga. 581, 5 S. E. Rep. 125.

foreclosure, fixes a sum which is exorbitantly large in view of all the circumstances of the case, still this will not preclude the right to a reasonable fee for complainant's solicitor, to be fixed by the court.[90] And the question of what is a reasonable and proper amount to be allowed as an attorney's fee in a mortgage foreclosure case is a question of fact, on which evidence is proper, and which must be determined according to the weight of evidence. The amount is not controlled by the percentage alone, nor simply by the amount involved, nor by the locality, but by all the facts and circumstances in the case.[91] The proportion which the proposed fee may bear to the amount of the mortgage debt furnishes no just basis, in itself alone, for determining what is a reasonable fee; the question to be considered is rather what is reasonable considering the services rendered in the case.[92] Or, according to another line of cases, to aid in deciding what would be a reasonable solicitor's fee in a particular case, evidence may be introduced to show what is the usual and customary fee charged by solicitors for similar services; and in fact, an agreement to pay a "reasonable" fee is considered equivalent to an agreement to pay the "usual and customary" charge.[93] And on this point the evidence of practising attorneys is competent. Thus, where the mortgage provides for a solicitor's fee of five per cent. of the amount found due, and an attorney testifies that this would be a customary and reasonable fee, it may be allowed.[94] So, the supreme court refused to set aside an allowance of $781 for solicitors' fees in a suit for the foreclosure of a mortgage securing a debt exceeding $15,000, where the defendant offered no proof to rebut the evidence of three witnesses for the complainant, who testified that the amount allowed was reasonable, usual, and customary.[95] In another case, it was held proper to allow $250 as an attorney's fee in a suit to foreclose a deed of trust securing a debt of $9,000, the

[90] Neiman v. Wheeler, 87 Ill. App. 670.

[91] Follansbee v. Northwestern Mut. Life Ins. Co., 87 Ill. App. 609.

[92] Wattson v. Jones, 101 Ill. App. 572. In this case the amount of the mortgage debt was $700, and a solicitor's fee of $150 was allowed.

[93] Nathan v. Brand, 167 Ill. 607, 47 N. E. Rep. 771 (affirming 67 Ill. App. 540); Wright v. Neely, 100 Ill. App. 310.

[94] Hough v. Wells, 86 Ill. App. 186; Goodwin v. Bishop, 145 Ill. 421, 34 N. E. Rep. 47.

[95] Cohn v. Northwestern Mut. Life Ins. Co., 185 Ill. 340, 57 N. E. Rep. 38.

deed providing for the payment of a "reasonable" fee.[96] And
again, where the amount of the mortgage debt as found by the
decree was $42,000, the allowance of a solicitor's fee of $1,000,
supported by testimony that the amount is reasonable, will not
be disturbed on appeal.[97] And so, an attorney's fee of $100
in a litigated foreclosure suit, being but little more than five
per cent. of the amount involved, is not unreasonable.[98] As
much as ten per cent. of the debt may be reasonable and proper
in some cases. This amount was allowed, and sustained on
appeal, in a case where the mortgage debt amounted to $5,000,
where a change of venue was taken to another county, eight
days were occupied in taking depositions, the suit was stub-
bornly contested, and two practising lawyers testified that $500
would be a reasonable fee.[99] While much will be left to the
discretion of the court of first instance, in this particular, the
appellate court will see to it that there is no abuse of such discretion. The allowance of a large and apparently excessive
amount will be carefully investigated on appeal, and cannot
be sanctioned unless it appears that there was full and satisfactory proof that such amount was no more than the usual
and customary charge.[1]

§ 455. Bill Must Pray Allowance of Fees.—If the complainant in a suit for foreclosure intends to claim the allowance of
a fee to his attorney, a prayer therefor must be inserted in the
bill. No such allowance can be made in the decree, even upon
a default, when no claim is made in the bill, notwithstanding
the mortgage itself contains a provision for the payment of
attorney's fees in case of foreclosure. A default admits only
what is properly pleaded; and a defendant may choose to
suffer a default rather than incur the expense of a defense,
but the complainant cannot be permitted, after a default, to
prove against the defendant a claim which the latter might
have chosen to defend if informed of it by the bill.[2] But if
the mortgage makes provision for an attorney's fee in case
of foreclosure, and the mortgage or a copy of it is made a part

[96] Telford v. Garrels, 132 Ill.
550, 24 N. E. Rep. 573.

[97] Burke v. Donnovan, 60 Ill.
App. 241.

[98] Magloughlin v. Clark, 35 Ill.
App. 251.

[99] Casler v. Beyers, 28 Ill. App.

128, affirmed in 129 Ill. 657, 22 N.
E. Rep. 507.

[1] Stone v. Billings, 167 Ill. 170,
47 N. E. Rep. 372, affirming 63 Ill.
App. 371.

[2] Augustine v. Doud, 1 Ill. App.
588.

of the bill, then the prayer for an accounting, to ascertain the amount due, will justify the taking of proof as to such fee and the allowance of it in the decree.[3]

§ 456. Allowance of Fees to Other Incumbrancers Made Parties.—Where the holder of a mortgage files a bill for foreclosure, claiming priority over another mortgage, and the holder of the latter answers, setting up the priority of his mortgage, and files a cross-bill for foreclosure, it is proper, on granting relief on the cross-bill and foreclosing the mortgage therein set up, as the first lien, to allow solicitors' fees.[4] So, where a second mortgagee seeks foreclosure subject to a prior mortgage, without making the prior mortgagee a party to his bill or seeking to affect his rights, and the prior mortgagee is permitted to answer the bill and file a cross-bill to foreclose his mortgage, and foreclosure is decreed, a solicitor's fee may be allowed him pursuant to a provision in the elder mortgage, and included in the amount found due thereunder.[5] And where the senior mortgagee is made a defendant in the foreclosure suit of the junior mortgagee, and his mortgage unsuccessfully attacked for fraud, all the costs should be paid from the fund, and if this is not sufficient, the first mortgagee should be protected as far as possible.[6] But when a bill to foreclose a senior mortgage makes the junior mortgagee a party, so that it is not necessary for him to file a cross-bill to protect his interest, an attorney's fee should not be allowed to him.[7]

§ 457. Attorney's Fee on Foreclosure of Trust Deed.—Attorneys' fees may be allowed to the holder of notes secured by a trust deed, on his bill for foreclosure of the deed, where the deed provides for the payment of such fees to the trustee in case of foreclosure, since it makes no difference to the grantor whether he pays to the trustee or to the holder of the notes.[8] But the trustee in a trust deed, who is also an attorney

---

[3] Knight v. Heafer, 79 Ill. App. 374.

[4] Schaeppi v. Glade, 195 Ill. 62, 62 N. E. Rep. 874; Lego v. Medley, 79 Wis. 211, 48 N. W. Rep. 375.

[5] Town v. Alexander, 185 Ill. 254, 56 N. E. Rep. 1111, affirming 85 Ill. App. 512.

[6] Scattergood v. Keeley, 40 N. J. Eq. 491, 4 Atl. Rep. 440.

[7] Gillespie v. Greene County Sav. & Loan Ass'n, 95 Ill. App. 543.

[8] Abbott v. Stone, 70 Ill. App. 671, affirmed in 172 Ill. 634. Compare Payette v. Free Home Bldg. Ass'n, 27 Ill. App. 307; Cheltenham Imp. Co. v. Whitehead, 26 Ill. App. 609. See Fuller v. Brown, 167 Ill. 293, 47 N. E. Rep. 202.

at law, is not entitled to an allowance for professional services rendered in foreclosing the deed in his own behalf and for his co-complainant, the holder of the note, although the deed provides for the allowance of a reasonable sum as a fee for complainant's solicitor.[9] But a person named in a trust deed as a successor in the trust is not thereby precluded from acting as an attorney in foreclosure proceedings, and a decree allowing him the stipulated solicitor's fee is proper.[10] Finally, where the trust deed of which foreclosure is prayed does not contain any provision authorizing the creditor to charge and collect against the debtor the cost of an abstract of title, such a charge cannot properly be allowed by the court.[11]

§ 458. Application of Proceeds to Mortgage Debt.—A payment to the mortgage creditor from the proceeds of the sale of the mortgaged premises must be applied upon the debt secured by the mortgage, at least in the absence of an agreement of the parties for a different application thereof.[12] And it has been said that the rule that a creditor who holds several claims or obligations against his debtor has the right to apply a payment made to him by the debtor, in the absence of any application by the latter, is confined to cases of voluntary payments. The proceeds of a sale under foreclosure of a mortgage given by the debtor to secure various debts are paid over to the creditor, not as a voluntary payment, but by operation of law, and, in the absence of directions given in the security, their application is to be made by the court in accordance with equitable principles. And the rule established by the courts of equity in some of the states, in such cases, where the pro-

---

[9] Gray v. Robertson, 174 Ill. 242, 51 N. E. Rep. 248 (reversing 74 Ill. App. 201); Heffron v. Gage, 44 Ill. App. 147, affirmed in 149 Ill. 182.

[10] Durham v. Behrer, 54 Ill. App. 564.

[11] Iglehart v. Miller, 41 Ill. App. 439.

[12] Snider v. Stone, 78 Ill. App. 17.

ceeds are not sufficient to satisfy all of the debts secured, is
that they should be applied pro rata, each debt sharing in the
fund without regard to priority of date or to the fact that for
some of the debts the creditor holds other security.[18] But in
Illinois, it is said that equity requires a debtor to pay all his
obligations, and will apply payments so as to give the creditor
the best security for the debts remaining unpaid. Hence,
where the defendant in foreclosure appealed, and gave a bond
to secure the payment, in case of affirmance, of such interest
as might accrue and remain otherwise unpaid upon the decree
from the date thereof, it was held proper, upon affirming the
decree, to apply the proceeds of the sale to satisfy the fees
and costs and the principal of the debt, before satisfying interest on the decree, because the deficiency, if any, would thereby
embrace the interest secured by the appeal bond. Nor, it was
said, can the debtor take exceptions to such a course, for his
right to direct the application of a payment exists only in the
case of voluntary payments, not where the payment is made
under compulsory process of law.[14]

§ 459. Same; Mortgage Notes Held by Different Persons.—
In the foreclosure of a mortgage or trust deed securing several
different notes which are held by different persons, it is proper
for the master to find the amount due on each and to whom
due, and for the court to decree a foreclosure for the aggregate
amount so found due. The court will afterwards see to it that
payments made, or the amount realized on foreclosure, are distributed properly, and it has ample power in this regard.[15]
We have already seen that, in distributing the proceeds of the
foreclosure of a mortgage given to secure the payment of
several different notes which have been assigned to, and are
held by, as many different owners, it is the established rule
that the holders of the several obligations are entitled to a

---

[18] Orleans County Nat. Bank v.
Moore, 112 N. Y. 543, 20 N. E. Rep.
357. And see Farmers' Bank v.
Woodford, 34 W. Va. 480, 12 S. E.
Rep. 544; Chaplin v. Sullivan, 128
Ind. 50, 27 N. E. Rep. 425.

[14] Monson v. Meyer, 190 Ill. 105,
60 N. E. Rep. 63. Where the proceeds of mortgages executed to secure an individual note and a

joint note were not sufficient to
pay both, it was held that the
holder of the notes was not
obliged to apply the sum pro rata
upon both notes, but that he might
apply it wholly to the individual
note. Small v. Older, 57 Iowa,
326, 10 N. W. Rep. 734.

[15] Shaffner v. Healy, 57 Ill. App.
90.

priority of payment according to the order of the maturity of the notes.[16]

§ 460. **Right to Surplus.**—If the mortgagor remains the owner of the equity of redemption at the time of the foreclosure sale, he will be entitled to any surplus of the proceeds of the sale after satisfying the mortgage debt with the interest and costs. But if he has parted with his interest in the premises, it is error to order that the surplus be paid over to him. The surplus should be ordered to be brought into court, in order that its proper distribution may be settled and decreed.[17] If, at the time of the foreclosure sale, the legal title has passed from the grantor or mortgagor, either by his own deed of conveyance of the premises, or by a sheriff's deed given to the purchaser of the equity of redemption on a sale thereof under execution against the mortgagor, the grantee will be entitled to the whole of the surplus. But in the case of a sale on execution, if the judgment creditor is not entitled to a deed at the time of the foreclosure sale, by reason of the fact that the time allowed for redemption from the execution sale has not yet expired, such creditor will be entitled to share in the surplus to the extent of the amount of his bid, with ten per cent. interest, and will have a lien on the surplus for that amount; and the mortgagor will be entitled to the balance, if any, although his right to redeem from the sheriff's sale may have expired at the time of the foreclosure sale.[18] As between the mortgagor and a sheriff holding a valid execution against him, the surplus arising on a sale under foreclosure of the mortgage may be paid to the sheriff in satisfaction of the execution.[19] And where, after foreclosure and payment of the mortgage debt, a fund remains in the hands of a receiver who had been appointed to collect the rents and profits, which does not belong to either party, any person claiming such fund may file a petition that it be paid over to him, and the court must determine his right thereto.[20]

§ 461. **Application of Surplus to Junior Liens.**—A lien on land, junior to that of a mortgage, will be defeated by a foreclosure of the mortgage, if the property does not bring a

[16] Supra, § 188.

[17] Buck v. Delafield, 55 Ill. 31.

[18] Hart v. Wingart, 83 Ill. 282.

[19] Field v. Brokaw, 159 Ill. 560,

42 N. E. Rep. 877, affirming 59 Ill. App. 442.

[20] Illinois Trust & Sav. Bank v. Robbins, 38 Ill. App. 575.

greater sum than will satisfy the debt secured by it; but if any surplus is left, the junior lien will attach to it in equity.[21] Such surplus may be applied for the benefit of a subsequent incumbrancer who was not a party to the foreclosure suit, but, to entitle himself thereto, he must either intervene and file a cross-bill, or he must establish his claim by proof at the trial or before the master.[22] On the other hand, where the bill for foreclosure makes junior mortgagees or judgment creditors of the mortgagor parties defendant, and their rights are shown by answer and proof, it will be proper, in decreeing a foreclosure and sale, to direct the payment of any surplus, after satisfying the first mortgage, among the other creditors according to their respective rights and equities; and no cross-bill is necessary for this purpose.[23] In effect, as remarked by the court in another state, "the fund realized from the sale of the land represents the land itself, and is subject to the same liens and rights. It stands in the place of the land, and those having an interest in the latter have the same measure of interest in the former."[24] It appears also that a judgment creditor, who was properly made a party to the foreclosure suit while his judgment was alive, will not lose his right to share in the distribution of the money arising from the sale by the fact that his judgment became dormant pending the action.[25] When the mortgagee himself becomes the purchaser at the foreclosure sale, having bid a sum greater than the amount of his debt, he is bound to pay over the surplus, to be disposed of according to law, and he cannot himself apply it in paying off other incumbrances on the land.[26]

[21] Hart v. Wingart, 83 Ill. 282.

[22] Ellis v. Southwell, 29 Ill. 549.

[23] Crocker v. Lowenthal, 83 Ill. 579; Walker v. Abt, Id. 226; Dillman v. Will County Nat. Bank, 138 Ill. 282, 27 N. E. Rep. 1090; Shaver v. Williams, 87 Ill. 469.

[24] White v. Fulghum, 87 Tenn. 281, 10 S. W. Rep. 501.

[25] Dempsey v. Bush, 18 Ohio St. 376.

[26] Hopkins v. Hemm, 159 Ill. 416, 42 N. E. Rep. 848, affirming Hemm v. Small, 56 Ill. App. 480.

CHAPTER XXXI

FORECLOSURE OF TRUST DEEDS AND MORTGAGES WITH
POWER OF SALE.

§ 462. **Statutory Provisions.**—A statute of Illinois, enacted in 1874, provided that, in case of the death of the grantor in any mortgage or trust deed in the nature of a mortgage, having been the owner of the equity of redemption at the time of his decease, or in case of the death of any person owning the equity of redemption of any premises mortgaged or conveyed in trust as security for money, no sale should be made by virtue of any power of sale contained in the mortgage or trust deed, or given in relation thereto, but the same should be foreclosed in the same manner as mortgages not containing any power of sale might then be foreclosed at law or in chancery.[1] Five years later this statute was broadened so as to apply to all cases, without reference to the death of the mortgagor; and

_____

[1] Stat. Ill. 1874, July 1, § 13; Rev. Stat. Ill. c. 95, § 13. This statute was not retroactive, and therefore did not nullify the provisions of a deed of trust which were legal at the time the deed was executed and delivered. Fisher v. Green, 142 Ill. 80, 31 N. E. Rep. 172, affirming 43 Ill. App. 595. Indeed, the right to foreclose, pursuant to the statute in force at the time of the execution of a mortgage or deed of trust, under the power of sale contained in it, could not constitutionally be taken away by subsequent legislation. O'Brien v. Kreutz, 36 Minn. 136, 30 N. W. Rep. 458.

it is now the law that "no real estate within this State shall be sold by virtue of any power of sale contained in any mortgage, trust deed, or other conveyance in the nature of a mortgage, executed after the taking effect of this act; but all such mortgages, trust deeds, and other conveyances in the nature of a mortgage, shall only be foreclosed in the manner provided for foreclosing mortgages containing no power of sale; and no real estate shall be sold to satisfy any such mortgage, trust deed, or other conveyance in the nature of a mortgage, except in pursuance of a judgment or decree of a court of competent jurisdiction."[2] At present, therefore, a security of this kind cannot be enforced by the parties, by a trustee's sale, without resort to the courts. But since these statutes were not retroactive, and since the validity of titles may still depend upon the regularity of sales made under powers prior to the enactment of the laws in question, it will be important to review the decisions in regard to the execution of such powers of sale, made while that method of enforcing trust deeds was still legal and permitted. First, however, some decisions must be noted as to the practice on foreclosing a trust deed or power-of-sale mortgage by bill in chancery.

§ 463. By Suit in Equity.—A bill for the foreclosure of a deed of trust may be filed by the legal owner and holder of the note secured. Even though the deed itself merely provides that the trustee or his successor in the trust may enter on default and file a bill in his own name and obtain a decree of sale, yet the holder of the indebtedness may sue as plaintiff, making the trustee a defendant.[3] The trustee, however, is an indispensable party, and the omission to join him will be fatal to the validity of the decree.[4] Where he is named as a party, but not served with process, and the bill is dismissed as to him without any reason being assigned, or any evidence in the record of his death, removal, or resignation, the decree of foreclosure must be reversed.[5] But if the original trustee has been replaced by a successor, in accordance with the provisions of

[2] Ill. Act May 7, 1879; Myers' Rev. Stat. Ill. c. 95, § 22; 2 Starr & C. Stat. c. 95, § 17.

[3] Dorn v. Colt, 180 Ill. 397, 54 N. E. Rep. 167, affirming 79 Ill. App. 656; Frink v. Neal, 37 Ill. App. 621.

[4] Walsh v. Truesdell, 1 Ill. App. 126; Chandler v. O'Neil, 62 Ill. App. 418; Hayes v. Owen, 69 Ill. App. 553.

[5] Lambert v. Hyers, 22 Ill. App. 616.

the deed, upon the former's removal from the state, or his disability or refusal to act, it is sufficient if the successor in interest is made a party.[6]

The decree of the court, on a bill to foreclose a mortgage with power of sale, or a trust deed, must allow a redemption, just as in the case of an ordinary mortgage. A complainant who seeks the foreclosure in equity of such a conveyance, according to the usual practice of the court, cannot resort to the powers contained in the deed or mortgage, but will be considered as having abandoned them.[7] And in a case where a decree was rendered specifying the notice to be given, the manner of the sale, and the distribution of the proceeds, and requiring the trustee appointed to make the sale to report his acts to the court for approval, it was held that the sale was not under the power in the deed, but under the decree of the court, and that the same right of redemption existed as in the case of a mortgage without power of sale.[8] Where property covered by a deed of trust is also incumbered by various other liens, and it is necessary to resort to a court of equity for the enforcement of the liens, the court will fix the terms of sale according to the rules of equity, without regard to the terms of sale prescribed in the trust deed.[9]

§ 464. Who May Execute the Trust.—A power in a deed of trust authorizing the trustee to sell the property on default in the payment of the note secured thereby, upon application of the legal holder of the same, can be exercised only by the trustee himself or by some person who has legally succeeded to his title. It cannot be executed by the holder of the note, even if the note was in the first place delivered to the trustee indorsed in blank, and by him transferred to another by delivery.[10] If the deed, as is commonly the case, provides that the power shall be exercised by the trustee or his "legal representative," it will be held to mean that the assignee or grantee of the trustee, having the legal title that was in the trustee, shall make the sale, and not that a mere stranger, having no legal title, such as the administrator of the trustee,

[6] Fisher v. Stiefel, 62 Ill. App. 580. And see Wilson v. Spring, 64 Ill. 14.

[7] Warner v. DeWitt County Nat. Bank, 4 Ill. App. 305.

[8] Fitch v. Wetherbee, 110 Ill. 475.

[9] Barbour v. Tompkins, 31 W. Va. 410, 7 S. E. Rep. 1.

[10] Cushman v. Stone, 69 Ill. 516.

may do so.[11] It is also customary to make provision for the devolution of the trust upon a successor to the original trustee, in the case of the trustee's death, removal from the state, resignation, or legal disability or refusal to act; and in that event, the sale may legally be made by one duly succeeding to the trust.[12] If no such provision is made, or if there is a vacancy in the office of trustee not provided for in the deed, a court of equity, on due application, may appoint a trustee to execute the power of sale.[13] And the interference of equity may be invoked when there is any good and sufficient reason why the nominal trustee should not be permitted to act. But where a bill filed to obtain an injunction against the sale of property under a trust deed alleged, among other reasons, that the trustee was insolvent, but failed to show that he became so after he was appointed, or that there was danger that he would misapply the money arising from a sale, it was held that this afforded no ground for the relief sought.[14]

§ 465. Same; Delegation of Authority.—A person authorized or appointed to conduct a judicial sale cannot delegate his authority to an agent; and a sale made by such agent may be set aside, if no rights of innocent purchasers have intervened.[15] On this principle, the trustee appointed in a deed of

---

[11] Warnecke v. Lembca, 71 Ill. 91.

[12] Where the grantor in a deed of trust with power of sale appointed a successor to the trustee, to act on certain conditions, and the deed did not require that a notice of sale by the successor should recite the condition, the happening of which had devolved the trust upon him, the sale is not invalidated by a recital in the notice and in the deed that the cause of his acting was the absence of the first trustee, although the only valid reason for his acting was in fact the refusal of the former to act. Irish v. Antioch College, 126 Ill. 474, 18 N. E. Rep. 768.

[13] Rice v. Brown, 77 Ill. 549.

[14] Tooke v. Newman, 75 Ill. 215.

[15] Chambers v. Jones, 72 Ill. 275; Fuller v. O'Neal, 69 Tex. 349, 6 S. W. Rep. 181. In the latter case it was remarked: "The office of trustee is one of personal confidence and cannot be delegated, unless authority to do so is expressly granted in the instrument from which he derives his powers. The course marked out for the trustee to pursue must be strictly followed by him; for the method of enforcing the collection by such deeds is a harsh one. The grantor of the power is entitled to have his directions obeyed; to have the proper notice of sale given; to have it take place at the time and place and by the person appointed by him. He gives these directions because he thinks that a sale made by the person se-

trust cannot lawfully delegate to another the powers granted to him by the deed. He is selected and confidence is reposed in him by the parties, and he must execute the trust. He may indeed employ an agent to perform the merely mechanical parts of the sale, or to act as an auctioneer,[16] but he must be present in person, and supervise and control the sale for the best interests of the parties, and should, so far as he may be able, prevent the sacrifice of the interests of either party.[17]

§ 466. Same; Power of Sale in Mortgage.—Similar principles prevail in the case of a mortgage with power of sale. The power to sell the property conferred by such an instrument must be strictly pursued and cannot be delegated to an-

lected, and under the circumstances stated, will be to his interest and make his property produce the largest amount of money. Of the prescribed conditions none is more important than that which requires that the trustee shall in person make the sale. He is chosen because of the confidence the grantor has in his integrity and discretion. The trustee, in making the sale, and during the time the property is under the hammer, is expected to protect the interests of the grantor, to see that no fraud is practised detrimental to his interests, and that no improper bid is accepted, and that the property is not knocked off without giving a fair opportunity for it to bring its reasonable value. Perhaps the agent selected by the trustee to attend to this important matter is not one to whom the grantor himself would have intrusted it. He has reposed confidence in the party selected by him, and that confidence cannot be transferred without his consent. The trustee can no more absent himself while the sale is going on than he can make it at a time or place, or for a character of consideration, different from that authorized in the deed. These views are so well supported by authority that it is unnecessary to elaborate them further. The act thus performed is not merely ministerial, such as is performed by a crier when the trustee is present, directing and superintending the sale, but it requires an exercise of judgment and discretion in the matters mentioned, as well as in others. The failure to perform it is not such a defect in the execution of the power as will be aided by a court of equity. A court of equity will hardly interpose in case of a trust created for the purpose of securing a debt, to assist the trustee in executing the powers conferred upon him, in a manner substantially and materially different from the mode prescribed by the grantor, and when his failure to obey the wishes of the grantor might have resulted in injury to the latter. The power was not in this respect directory, but of the strictest character, and can be exercised only under the circumstances prescribed in the instrument by which it is created."

[16] Taylor v. Hopkins, 40 Ill. 442; McPherson v. Sanborn, 88 Ill. 150; Gillespie v. Smith, 29 Ill. 473.

[17] Taylor v. Hopkins, 40 Ill. 442.

other, unless by express authority in the mortgage itself.[18]
At the same time, it is held that a mortgage sale made by an
agent or attorney of the person intrusted with the execution
of the power therein given is not absolutely void, but is only
voidable at the instance of the mortgagor; his creditors cannot
question the regularity of the sale; and an unreasonable delay
for several years on the part of the mortgagor in filing a bill
to avoid a sale so made, if not justified or explained, will be
fatal to relief in equity; and an innocent purchaser, without
notice of such irregularity in the sale to his grantor, will be
protected.[19] So, where the sale is made by an attorney of
the mortgagee, in his absence, and the mortgagee, in whom the
legal title as well as a power of sale, coupled with an interest,
is vested by the mortgage, subsequently ratifies the sale by
making the necessary deed for the property, the mere fact that
the sale was conducted by the attorney in the absence of the
mortgagee will not render the title derived therefrom absolutely void.[20] The mortgagee may of course employ an auctioneer to cry the sale; and the sale is not invalidated by the
fact that it was made by an auctioneer whose license had expired, where the mortgagor is not injured, and the mortgagee
was ignorant of the neglect of the auctioneer to renew his
license.[21] By statute in Illinois, it is also lawful for the mortgagor to insert in the mortgage a clause authorizing the sheriff
of the county where the land lies to execute the power of sale;
and when this is done, the sheriff is to advertise and sell the
property and make the deed to the purchaser as attorney in
fact of the mortgagor.[22]

Such mortgages commonly vest the power of sale in the
mortgagee or his assigns or legal representatives. In this case,
a person nominated in the mortgagee's will as his executor,
and who qualifies as such after the mortgagee's death, may
execute the power, the provision of the mortgage being a sufficiently certain designation of the person.[23] And under such
a provision, the power of sale may properly be exercised by
the administrator of the mortgagee.[24] But, to show the right
of one to exercise the power of sale contained in the mortgage,

[18] Flower v. Elwood, 66 Ill. 438.

[19] McHany v. Schenk, 88 Ill. 357.

[20] Munn v. Burges, 70 Ill. 604.

[21] Learned v. Geer, 139 Mass. 31,
29 N. E. Rep. 215.

[22] Rev. Stat. Ill. c. 95, § 11.

[23] Yount v. Morrison, 109 N.
Car. 520, 13 S. E. Rep. 892.

[24] Merrin v. Lewis, 90 Ill. 505.

as the administrator of the mortgagee, some evidence of the death of the latter and of the appointment of the person making the sale as his administrator is necessary, beyond the mere recital of these facts in the administrator's deed.[25] A power of sale in a mortgage to a non-resident of the state in which the mortgaged premises are situated may be exercised by the administrator appointed in the state of his residence, as the legal title to the mortgage vests in such administrator, and the power is not one dependent upon the laws of either state relating to the administration of decedents' estates.[26]

§ 467. **The Power to Sell.**—Where a deed of trust confers upon the trustee power to sell the premises upon default in the payment of the debt secured, the power does not become operative until there has been a default. If the debt is not yet due at the time of a sale, or if it has been already paid, there is no proper ground for the exercise of the trustee's power, and a sale made under such circumstances, if not absolutely void, is at least voidable at the instance of the grantor against any purchaser having notice that there was no default, or who is constructively chargeable with such notice, or against the grantee of such purchaser with like notice.[27] "If there is no default, and the trustee assumes to sell, all persons purchase at their peril. Bidders must see to it that at least a portion of the debt thus secured remains due and unpaid, and that it is in default according to the terms and conditions imposed by the power."[28] If any title passes to the purchaser by a sale made under such conditions, he will merely hold it as a trustee for the debtor,[29] being of course entitled to a return of his money on the cancellation of the sale. Again, although the

[25] Taylor v. Lawrence, 148 Ill. 388, 36 N. E. Rep. 74.

[26] Stevens v. Shannahan, 160 Ill. 330, 43 N. E. Rep. 350; Hayes v. Frey, 54 Wis. 503, 11 N. W. Rep. 695.

[27] Chicago, R. I. & P. R. Co. v. Kennedy, 70 Ill. 350; Lycoming Fire Ins. Co. v. Jackson, 83 Ill. 302, 25 Am. Rep. 386. And generally, the purchaser at a sale under a power takes with the peril of the sale's proving void if a material condition for the exercise of

the power does not exist. Where the validity of the sale and of the deed depends on some fact, or the absence of some fact, in pais, such as the non-payment of the note, it is the purchaser's duty to ascertain whether that fact exists. Shippen v. Whittier, 117 Ill. 282, 7 N. E. Rep. 642.

[28] Ventres v. Cobb, 105 Ill. 33.

[29] Chicago, R. I. & P. R. Co. v. Kennedy, 70 Ill. 350; Chapin v. Billings, 91 Ill. 539.

debt may be overdue, it may not be the wish of the creditor
to have a sale of the property; and it has been ruled that a
sale made by the trustee without the consent of the owner
of the debt is void.[30]   But the bankruptcy of a subsequent
mortgagee is no objection to the execution of a power of sale
contained in the prior mortgage.   That is, although the sale
will cut off the junior mortgagee's right of redemption, it is
not necessary to obtain leave of the bankruptcy court before
making the sale.[31]   Where the note secured by a trust deed
is pledged as collateral security for a loan, a sale by the trustee under the power in the deed is not rendered invalid by the
fact that it is made pending a suit to foreclose the pledge.[32]
And where the description in a trust deed of lots in a subdivision of a block is a matter of record, the trustee's power
to sell upon default of payment is not defeated by a re-sub-
division of the block.[33]   And where the deed provides that it
shall be lawful for the grantee, in case of default, to enter in
and upon the premises conveyed, and to sell and dispose of the
same at auction, after giving notice, etc., it is not necessary,
in order that a legal sale of the premises may be had by the
trustee, that an entry or demand for possession should first be
made by him.   Entry in such case is not a condition precedent
to the making of the sale.[34]   But a provision in a mortgage
of realty for a public sale by the mortgagee at a specified
place and after advertising for a given time, will cut off the
right to private sale by the mortgagee.[35]

§ 468.   Notice of Sale.—Personal notice of the intention to
foreclose a deed of trust or power-of-sale mortgage, by a sale
of the property thereunder, need not be given to the grantor
or mortgagor, unless the deed itself requires it.   He is supposed
to know when he is in default and what are the remedies of
the mortgagee.   It is sufficient if the published notice or advertisement is given in accordance with the terms of the instrument.[36]   And the same rule applies where the mortgagor or

---

[30] Magee v. Burch, 108 Mo. 336,
18 S. W. Rep. 1073.

[31] Long v. Rogers, 6 Biss. C. C.
416, Fed. Cas. No. 8,482.

[32] Jenkins v. International Bank,
111 Ill. 462.

[33] Meacham v. Steele, 93 Ill. 135.

[34] Kiley v. Brewster, 44 Ill. 186;

Hamilton v. Halpin, 68 Miss. 99,
8 South. Rep. 739; Jones v. Hagler,
95 Ala. 529, 10 South. Rep. 345.

[35] Griffin v. Marine Co., 52 Ill.
130.

[36] Marston v. Brittenham, 76 Ill.
611; Cleaver v. Green, 107 Ill. 67;
Princeton Loan & Trust Co. v.

grantor has sold his equity of redemption to a third person.[37] It is true a sale under such a conveyance might be adjudged invalid if it were shown that the mortgagee had purposely and effectually concealed from the mortgagor his intention to sell the property; but not as against a purchaser who had no knowledge of such concealment.[38]

In regard to the contents of the notice, it is first of all requisite that it should show the amount of the debt for which the sale is to be made. But a notice which states the date and amount of the note secured, and the rate of interest thereon, and sets forth that the holder has elected to declare the note due and payable "with all interest thereon," sufficiently discloses the amount of the indebtedness.[39] Where the notice describes a different and other or larger indebtedness than that described in or secured by the mortgage, the rule is that the sale had thereunder will not be vitiated, so as to entitle the mortgagor to have it set aside or to redeem, unless it is shown that the selling value of the property was injuriously affected by the overstatement of the debt, or that it deterred bidders from attending the sale, or that it was so published for a fraudulent purpose.[40] And where the deed of trust does not require the notice of sale to state the amount due and for which the property is to be sold, a failure to give such amount in the notice is no ground for vacating the sale, unless fraud is established.[41] The notice should also describe the property to be sold with such particularity as will serve clearly to identify it. But a sale under three deeds of trust on different tracts of land, to secure separate notes, may be made under one notice, and if the sales are made separately, they will not be set aside for the want of separate notices.[42] It is also required, having regard to the protection of the interests of the debtor, and to the importance of encouraging bidders to attend, that the

Munson, 60 Ill. 371; Carver v. Brady, 104 N. Car. 219, 10 S. E. Rep. 565.

[37] Robbins v. Arnold, 11 Ill. App. 434.

[38] Ritchie v. Judd, 137 Ill. 453, 27 N. E. Rep. 682.

[39] Reedy v. Millizen, 155 Ill. 636, 40 N. E. Rep. 1028. And see Hoyt v. Pawtucket Savings Institution, 110 Ill. 390.

[40] Hamilton v. Lubukee, 51 Ill. 415, 99 Am. Dec. 562; Fairman v. Peck, 87 Ill. 156; Kerfoot v. Billings, 160 Ill. 563, 43 N. E. Rep. 804; Bowman v. Ash, 36 Ill. App. 115.

[41] Jenkins v. Pierce, 98 Ill. 646.

[42] Tyler v. Massachusetts Mut. Life Ins. Co., 108 Ill. 58.

notice of sale should give reasonable publicity to the time, the place, and the terms of the sale.[43] As to this point, it has been held that, where a mortgage sale is announced to take place on a certain day between the hours of 9 A. M. and 4 P. M., the advertisement is sufficient, the hours named belonging to the ordinary business portion of the day.[44] But any misstatement in the notice which has a tendency to discourage prospective bidders from attending the sale, or to lessen the amount they are willing to bid, will be ground for vacating the sale. Thus, such a sale will be set aside where the notice erroneously stated that other persons than the parties to the trust deed claimed some interest in the land, in consequence of which the property was sold at a heavy sacrifice.[45] But it has been held that a notice is sufficient which sets out correctly the place of record of the mortgage, although it does not give the name of either the mortgagor or mortgagee, or of any one connected with the mortgagor; for any person desiring to know the names can learn them from the record.[46]

The length of time during which the notice shall be published, or the number of times it shall be published, is generally prescribed by the deed or mortgage. And "in the computation of time, as to such notices, the rule is, when an act is to be performed within a particular period, or on a particular day, from and after a certain day, to exclude the day named and include the day on which the act is to be done. Or more concisely stated, it is, to count one day in and the other out."[47] Where the deed requires that thirty days' previous notice of the sale shall be given by publication once each week for four weeks, it is not essential that the notice shall be published precisely thirty days before the sale.[48] And in a case where the deed required a prior notice of five consecutive days, the last of which should be ten days before that fixed for the sale,

---

[43] Meacham v. Steele, 93 Ill. 135.

[44] Burr v. Borden, 61 Ill. 389.

[45] Equitable Trust Co. v. Fisher, 106 Ill. 189.

[46] Cogan v. McNamara, 16 R. I. 554, 18 Atl. Rep. 157.

[47] Harper v. Ely, 56 Ill. 179. Where a trust deed requires a notice of sale to be published for thirty days, a publication on August 23d of notice for a sale on September 22d is sufficient, the last day named not being a Sunday. Such an instrument does not require that there shall be thirty secular or working days between the publication and the sale. Magnusson v. Williams, 111 Ill. 450.

[48] Taylor v. Reid, 103 Ill. 349.

it was held that making the last publication a few days more than was required could not invalidate the sale, although making it less would not be a sufficient compliance with the deed, as it would lessen the chance of securing bidders.[49] Where the notice of sale is required to be published in a newspaper, it is not essential to select the one of the most general character or the largest circulation; if reasonable care and good faith are exercised, it is sufficient to publish the notice in a law periodical, though its circulation may be limited.[50] But on the other hand, although the trustee, in choosing the newspaper in which to advertise the notice of sale, complies literally with the terms of the power, yet if the paper chosen is a small and obscure sheet published in a remote part of the county, and it is apparent that it was selected for that reason, and that, in consequence of the premises, the mortgagor's interests may have suffered, he will be permitted to redeem notwithstanding the sale.[51] Where the deed required notice of sale to be posted in four of the most public places in the county, and two of the notices were posted at different places in the same town, which it was insisted vitiated the sale, it was held that, even if the objection was well taken, it could only be availed of in a proceeding to set aside the sale in a court of equity, and could not be set up in an action at law.[52]

While a total want of the prescribed notice, or material defects or misstatements in the notice, may be ground for vacating the sale, it must always be remembered that an application in that behalf is addressed to equity, and will be determined on equitable principles. Long delay in attacking the validity of the sale, especially when the land has passed into the hands of remote purchasers, will strongly incline a court of equity to refuse such an application.[53] The burden of showing that a notice of sale under the power in a mortgage or trust deed was defective is on the party objecting to the notice.[54] And a sale will not be disturbed for an alleged defect in the notice of sale, where the bill contains no allegation to that effect, but seeks to set aside the sale as a fraud on creditors.[55] And further, if relief is granted on this ground, it

[49] Tooke v. Newman, 75 Ill. 215.
[50] Taylor v. Reid, 103 Ill. 349.
[51] Webber v. Curtiss, 104 Ill. 309.
[52] Rice v. Brown, 77 Ill. 549.
[53] Farrar v. Payne, 73 Ill. 82.
[54] Tartt v. Clayton, 109 Ill. 579.
[55] Sawyer v. Bradshaw, 125 Ill. 440, 17 N. E. Rep. 812.

will be granted only on condition that the complainant shall do the equity of paying that portion of the debt secured by the trust deed which was discharged by the sale of the land.[56]   A sale under a power in a mortgage is not rendered defective by the fact that it is twice advertised, where the second advertisement was rendered necessary by a defect in the first notice, and no sale took place under the first notice, and it is not shown that any one was misled thereby.[57]   It remains to be noted that the statute concerning the giving of notice of sales under powers contained in mortgages and deeds of trust in the county in which the mortgaged property is situated, does not apply to a sale under a mortgage of a line of railroad extending through several counties.[58]

§ 469.   Time and Place of Sale.—The power of sale contained in a mortgage or deed of trust must be strictly pursued as to the time and place stipulated in the instrument, otherwise a sale under it will be void.[59]   But a sale advertised to take place at eleven o'clock in the morning is properly made at any time before twelve o'clock noon, in the absence of any showing that any intending bidders left on account of the delay; that is, the hour of eleven will be considered as lasting until twelve, if the attendance continues.[60]   And in a case where the sale was advertised for ten o'clock, and the trustee appeared at the place of sale at that hour and opened the sale by reading the notice, and remained on the ground until the sale was completed, which was some time after eleven o'clock, but delayed in order to enable parties in interest to apply for an injunction to restrain the sale, it was held that the delay did not affect the validity of the sale.[61]

Where the place of sale named in a deed of trust is at the "north door of the court house," this does not require that a sale made under it should be in or at the north door of the court house as it was constructed at the time of executing the deed.   If the court house then standing is destroyed by fire, and a new one erected in the same location, the sale may be

---

[56] Phoenix Ins. Co. v. Rink, 110 Ill. 538.

[57] Ritchie v. Judd, 137 Ill. 453, 27 N. E. Rep. 682.

[58] Craft v. Indiana, Decatur & W. Ry. Co., 166 Ill. 580, 46 N. E. Rep. 1132.

[59] Hall v. Towne, 45 Ill. 493.

[60] McGovern v. Union Mut. Life Ins. Co., 109 Ill. 151; Lester v. Citizens' Sav. Bank (R. I.), 20 Atl. Rep. 231.

[61] Erwin v. Hall, 18 Ill. App. 315.

made at the north door of the new court house; or, before the
new one is built, the sale can properly be made at the ruins at
the north door. The essential element in the power is that the
place of sale is rendered certain by the description, and
whether the same door, or a new one, or none at all, is at the
place at the time of the sale, is not material.[62] And it has
been said that an objection to a trustee's sale on the ground
that it was made at the door of the court house, whereas the
deed required that the property should be sold "on the premises," cannot be raised by a party who is a stranger to the
deed, and not one for whose benefit the direction as to the
mode of sale was inserted.[63]

§ 470. Presence of Trustee at Sale.—A trustee in a deed of
trust fails in his duty, exposes the interests of the grantor to
injury, and invalidates the effect of a sale under the power in
the deed, if he is not personally present at the sale. As was
stated in a preceding section, he cannot lawfully delegate to
another the powers conferred upon him by the deed, nor depute
to a third person the confidence reposed in him by the parties.
Though he may employ an auctioneer to conduct the sale, yet
his personal supervision and control of the sale for the best
interests of the parties concerned are essential to its validity.[64]
Hence the rule that a sale under a deed of trust not personally
conducted by the trustee, and at which the trustee was not
present, is voidable and may be set aside in equity.[65] But
where the deed of trust is executed to two trustees jointly, and
authorizes them jointly (or authorizes either of them severally)
to sell the property upon default in the payment of the debt,
and both join in the giving of the notice and in the execution
of a deed to the purchaser, the power is well executed if only
one of them attends in person and conducts the sale, at least
where there is no well-founded suspicion of fraud or unfairness, or of the absence of the one trustee being caused or
procured by sinister motives.[66]

§ 471. Conduct of the Sale.—Where by the terms of a deed
of trust the trustee is directed to sell the property at public

[62] Waller v. Arnold, 71 Ill. 350;
Chandler v. White, 84 Ill. 435; Al-
den v. Goldie, 82 Ill. 581. And see
Davis v. Hess, 103 Mo. 31, 15 S.
W. Rep. 324.

[63] Nixon v. Cobleigh, 52 Ill. 387.

[64] Supra, § 465.

[65] Taylor v. Hopkins, 40 Ill. 442;
Grover v. Hale, 107 Ill. 638.

[66] Weld v. Rees, 49 Ill. 428;
Smith v. Black, 115 U. S. 308.

auction, he is bound to conform to that mode of sale, and cannot sell privately under any circumstances, even though he might be able to obtain a better price at private sale.[67]   And where, under a deed so providing, the trustee fixed the price at which the property should be sold, and procured his own attorney to bid in the property at the sum decided on, in behalf of the beneficiary in the deed, and no other bidders were present, it was held to be a mere private sale, and the grantor was given the right to redeem.[68]   The trustee is also bound to see that the sale is fairly made; and some of the authorities go to the length of holding that he must see to it that there is a real competition, and that if he finds there are only sham competitors, he ought not to proceed with the sale at that time, but adjourn it and give a new notice.[69]   This, however, is probably too severe a rule.   To require an actual competition in all cases would frequently defeat the very object of giving the power of sale.   On the one hand, the property should not be sacrificed, and courts will not sanction any attempt to prevent or stifle competition, or to keep bidders away from the sale, or to discourage them in bidding.   And there may be other circumstances, not attributable to the parties,—such as severe inclemency of the weather on the day of the sale,—having a tendency to deter purchasers from attending, which ought to be considered in connection with a lack of competition and the inadequacy of the selling price, as ground for setting aside the sale.   But on the other hand, the rights of the creditor are to be considered, no less than those of the debtor; and if the sale was fair, free, and open, with nothing to prevent possible purchasers from attending and bidding, it should not be undone in the courts merely because there was only one person who bid.[70]   And in such circumstances it will not be presumed, in the absence of evidence, that the purchaser exercised any undue control over the person selling.[71]   But any unfair dealing or attempt to shut out competition will be fatal to the sale.   Thus, in one case, it appeared that the mortgage creditor

[67] Greenleaf v. Queen, 1 Pet. (U. S.) 138.

[68] Williamson v. Stone, 128 Ill. 129, 22 N. E. Rep. 1005.

[69] Fairfax v. Hopkins, 2 Cranch C. C. 134, Fed. Cas. No. 4,614.

[70] On this point see Learned v. Geer, 139 Mass. 31; Chilton v. Brooks, 69 Md. 584; Campbell v. Swan, 48 Barb. 109; Bonnett v. Brown, 59 Hun. 619, 13 N. Y. Supp. 395; Roberts v. Roberts, 13 Gratt. 639.

[71] Dempster v. West, 69 Ill. 613.

attended the sale, and, in the hearing of the various persons
who were present at the sale, he declared that he had a deed
for the property and that any person purchasing would be
subject to a lawsuit, and that the sale under the trust deed was
a mere legal form to perfect his title. No one else bid and he
bought in the property at a considerable sacrifice. It was held
that the sale should be set aside and a re-sale ordered.[72] But
an agreement between the mortgagee and a prospective buyer,
by which the former agrees to foreclose and the latter agrees
to bid at the sale the full amount due on the mortgage, and to
buy up certain conflicting claims to the land, but which contains no provision that the land shall be sold to him unless he
is the highest bidder therefor, is not fraudulent as against the
mortgagor.[73] Where a party bids at a sale under a deed of
trust, under a misapprehension as to the terms of the sale, not
knowing that the price would have to be paid in gold, he may
be permitted by the trustee to withdraw his bid, without thereby affecting the validity of the sale, although upon a further
offering of the property it does not bring as much as the
amount of the bid withdrawn.[74]

§ 472. **Order of Sale.**—Whether land covered by a trust
deed should be divided into parcels, for the purposes of a
foreclosure sale, or sold as an entirety, will depend upon the
terms of the trust deed, upon the character of the property
with reference to its susceptibility to advantageous division,
and upon the probability of its bringing a higher price in the
one form than in the other. If the deed gives the trustee
authority to sell the property either entire or in parcels, as he
shall think best, it is said that his discretion is not an arbitrary
one, but must be governed by a regard to the best interests of
the mortgagor, so that a sale in gross will be set aside if it is
apparent that a better price could have been obtained by selling the land in parcels.[75] But the mere fact that the property
was sold in the one form or the other is not alone sufficient to
vitiate the sale; fraud or prejudice to some one must be shown
as a result of the failure of the trustee to sell the land in

---

[72] McGuire v. Briscoe, 2 Hawy.
& H. 54, Fed. Cas. No. 8,813a.

[73] Ritchie v. Judd, 137 Ill. 453, 27
N. E. Rep. 682.

[74] Waterman v. Spaulding, 51
Ill. 425.

[75] Cassidy v. Cook, 99 Ill. 385;
Loveland v. Clark, 11 Colo. 265, 18
Pac. Rep. 544.

separate parcels, before equity will vacate the sale on that ground.[76] Frequently the character and extent of the land will have a determinative influence on this question. Thus, where the land was a tract about two hundred feet square, lying outside the limits of a city, and no larger than many private residence sites near it, it was held that the trustee was not bound to divide it into lots for the purposes of his sale.[77] And where the title to the tract of land is vested in the trustee by two deeds of trust, executed by the same grantor and for the benefit of the same creditor, each deed being for an undivided half of the land, the whole property should be sold together, and not half at one time and half at another.[78] On the other hand, where several distinct parcels of land are included in one mortgage, there is no legal objection to their being sold, at one sale, to separate purchasers.[79]

Where the trustee is authorized to sell the land and pay the particular debt secured, and also all costs, commissions, and liens on the property, and the holder of the secured debt has also become the owner of a judgment against the grantor, which is a lien upon the land, the authority of the trustee is not exhausted when he has sold enough of the land to pay the mortgage debt, but he may proceed to sell enough to pay the judgment also.[80]

§ 473. **Terms of Sale.**—When a deed of trust or mortgage which confers a power of sale upon the trustee or mortgagee requires such sale to be made for cash, the requirement is mandatory and must be complied with, and the sale cannot properly be made upon credit, or for anything else than cash.[81] A promissory note of the party who will be entitled to the proceeds of the sale is not cash, and a tender of such a note is not a compliance with the terms of sale.[82] And strictly speaking the trustee would have no authority to accept a check of the bidder; but it seems that the sale is not vitiated by the receipt of a check in payment of the successful bid, where it is shown that the check would have been paid if presented.[83]

Although the trust deed forbids the sale to be made upon

[76] Kerfoot v. Billings, 160 Ill. 563, 43 N. E. Rep. 804; Fairman v. Peck, 87 Ill. 156.

[77] Cleaver v. Green, 107 Ill. 67.

[78] Coffman v. Scoville, 86 Ill. 300.

[79] Holmes v. Turner's Falls Lumber Co., 150 Mass. 535, 23 N. E. Rep. 305.

[80] Hall v. Gould, 79 Ill. 16.

[81] Strother v. Law, 54 Ill. 413.

[82] Pursley v. Forth, 82 Ill. 327.

[83] McConneaughey v. Bogardus,

credit, this will not prevent the secured creditor from lending
to the purchaser a portion of the money required to pay his
bid; and it is also held that the creditor may properly authorize the trustee to sell on credit to the extent of the debt due to
him, leaving the surplus, if any, which will be payable to the
mortgagor, to be paid as required by the terms of the trust
deed.[84]   And where the holder of the note secured by the deed
of trust himself becomes the purchaser of the property at the
trustee's sale, a mere indorsement of the amount of his bid on
the notes will be a sufficient compliance with the requirement
of the trust deed that the sale shall be for cash.[85]

§ 474. Adjournment of Sale.—A trustee having authority
to sell the property covered by a deed of trust also has power
to adjourn the sale whenever it shall seem to him necessary or
proper to do so. And it is his duty to adjourn the sale whenever, for any cause, a reasonably fair price cannot be obtained.
But it is held, in Illinois, that in case of such an adjournment,
the same notice must be given as was originally required.
Hence if the trust deed requires thirty days' notice of sale to
be given, an adjournment cannot be had for any less number
of days, for thirty days' notice of the time and place where
the sale will be resumed must be given.[86] Under these decisions, it would clearly be incompetent for the trustee to change
the day fixed for the sale, before it arrives, unless by a new
notice published for the whole length of time required; and
clearly, also, he would have no power to appear at the time
and place appointed for the sale in the published notice, and
by a mere public announcement adjourn the sale to a future
day, and make a valid sale at such future day, without other
notice than such an announcement.[87]

106 Ill. 321. Where the holder of
notes secured by a trust deed attended at the trustee's sale of the
land, made under decree, and held
late on a Saturday afternoon, and
bid $10,070, and exhibited his cer-
tified check on a bank for $10,000,
and paid the amount of his bid on
the following Monday, it was held,
on a contest with the next lowest
bidder, that the terms of sale, announced to be for cash, were substantially complied with. Jacobs
v. Turpin, 83 Ill. 424.

[84] Waterman v. Spaulding, 51
Ill. 425; Strother v. Law, 54 Ill.
413; Burr v. Borden, 61 Ill. 389;
Sawyer v. Campbell, 130 Ill. 186,
22 N. E. Rep. 458.
[85] Jacobs v. Turpin, 83 Ill. 424.
[86] Thornton v. Boyden, 31 Ill.
200; Griffin v. Marine Co., 52 Ill.
130. And see Richards v. Holmes,
18 How. (U. S.) 143.
[87] Wolff v. Ward, 104 Mo. 127,
16 S. W. Rep. 161.

The circumstances of the particular case must determine when it is the duty of the trustee to adjourn the sale, or when to proceed with it. In this particular, he must exercise a sound discretion; and the sale will not be set aside unless it is shown that he acted unfairly or maliciously, or committed a grave error of judgment. For instance, where the sale was attended by about a dozen purchasers, several of whom made bids, the successful competitor bidding twice, and the property brought more than the mortgage debt and costs, the court will not say that the circumstances demanded an adjournment.[88] On the other hand, where the trustee agreed with the owner of the equity of redemption to postpone the sale for one hour, to enable the latter to obtain a certified check with which to pay the whole amount of the incumbrance, but instead of waiting, sold the land within the hour for less than that amount, it was held that the sale should be set aside as fraudulent.[89]

§ 475. **Who May Purchase.**—A trustee under a deed of trust or mortgage containing a power of sale cannot become a purchaser at his own sale, either directly, or by procuring another person to buy for his benefit; if he does so, the sale is voidable at the instance of the grantor or mortgagor.[90] But the latter may estop himself from questioning the validity of the sale, by his subsequent dealings with the trustee so purchasing,[91] and while the sale may be set aside for this cause so long as the property remains in the hands of the trustee, this action cannot be taken after its transfer to a bona fide purchaser without notice of the breach of trust.[92] It is also to be observed that, after the trustee has made the sale, under his power as trustee, in good faith, and has fully discharged his trust, so that he no longer occupies confidential relations to any one claiming the property, he is not forbidden by law to deal with what was the trust property, the same as a stranger might, and, acting in good faith, he may then buy it.[93]

When the sale is made by a trustee, under a deed of trust, the creditor owning the debt secured may become the purchaser. And he may make the purchase through the inter-

[88] Stevenson v. Hano, 148 Mass. 616, 20 N. E. Rep. 200.

[89] Ventres v. Cobb, 105 Ill. 33.

[90] Roberts v. Fleming, 53 Ill. 196; Jenkins v. Pierce, 98 Ill. 646;

Watson v. Sherman, 84 Ill. 263.

[91] Jenkins v. Pierce, 98 Ill. 646.

[92] Farrar v. Payne, 73 Ill. 82.

[93] Bush v. Sherman, 80 Ill. 160; Watson v. Sherman, 84 Ill. 263.

vention of an agent. Thus, where his agent bid off the property in his own name, but paid no money on his bid, received a deed and conveyed the premises to his principal, it was held that this was not irregular, as it would have been an idle ceremony to pay his principal's money to the trustee and then for the trustee to pay it back to the creditor.[94] But where the creditor secured by the deed of trust directs the trustee to sell for the entire debt due, but sends no bid nor authorizes any to be made for him, a bid by the trustee in the creditor's name is without authority, and the making of a deed for the property to the creditor and recording the same will not affect his rights if he does not accept the deed, and no title will pass.[95] A receiver of a corporation, holding notes given to the company and secured by deed of trust, has the right to bid in the property to save it from sacrifice. He succeeds to the rights of the corporation in this respect.[96] But generally speaking, no person occupying fiduciary or confidential relations to the mortgagor is a proper purchaser at the trustee's sale. Still, where the relations sustained to the grantor in the trust deed by one who purchases the land at the sale are such that he is not a proper purchaser, the sale, while irregular, is merely voidable, and not absolutely void, and it may be ratified by the grantor.[97] The purchase by an attorney, at a sale under a deed of trust, of property of his client, who had employed him to secure a loan to protect the property from sale, is valid against the latter, if open, fair, and honest.[98] And so, where the grantor in a trust deed dies, leaving heirs, some of whom are adults and others minors, and the property is sold under the trust deed for default in payment of the debt, there is no reason why the adult heirs may not purchase the same at such sale, and acquire title thereby, unless prevented by occupying a fiduciary relation to the other heirs.[99] And a stepfather does not stand in such a relation of trust to his minor children that he is bound to extinguish a mortgage on their real estate, and he can purchase at a sale under the mortgage, the same as a stranger.[1]

[94] Weld v. Rees, 48 Ill. 429.

[95] Ellsworth v. Harmon, 101 Ill. 274.

[96] Jacobs v. Turpin, 83 Ill. 424.

[97] Eastman v. Littlefield, 164 Ill. 124, 45 N. E. Rep. 137. And see Coffman v. Scoville, 86 Ill. 300.

[98] Herr v. Payson, 157 Ill. 244, 41 N. E. Rep. 732.

[99] Chicago, R. I. & P. R. Co. v. Kennedy, 70 Ill. 350.

[1] Otto v. Schlapkahl, 57 Iowa, 226, 10 N. W. Rep. 651.

§ 476. Purchase by Mortgagee at His Own Sale.—When the sale of property is made by the mortgagee himself, without the intervention of a trustee, under a power contained in the mortgage, public policy forbids the mortgagee to become the purchaser. He cannot act both as buyer and seller. In that case, the sale will be voidable; and it is not necessary to show that wrong or injury has resulted to the mortgagor; equity will set the sale aside without that.[1] But such a sale is not absolutely void. It may be vacated at the instance of the mortgagor, if he takes reasonably prompt action,[2] but it cannot be impeached by third persons in a collateral proceeding,[3] and cannot be vacated after the title has been transferred to a purchaser in good faith.[4] The rule forbidding the mortgagee to purchase also extends to partnerships in which he has an interest; so that, when the note secured by the mortgage has been transferred by the payee to a firm of which he has become a member, all the partners are equally prohibited from purchasing at a sale made by virtue of the power given in the mortgage.[5] Neither can the mortgagee make the purchase indirectly, through the medium of a third person. If such a person,—whether it be an agent or attorney of the mortgagee, or a member of his family, or a stranger,—bids in the property at the foreclosure sale, at the request and for the benefit of the mortgagee, and under an agreement to convey it to him,

---

[1] Mapps v. Sharpe, 32 Ill. 13; Moore v. Titman, 44 Ill. 367; Waite v. Dennison, 51 Ill. 319; Griffin v. Marine Co., 52 Ill. 130; Mulvey v. Gibbons, 87 Ill. 367; Gibbons v. Hoag, 95 Ill. 45; People v. Wiltshire, 9 Ill. App. 374. In the case first cited it was said: "This presents the question whether a mortgagee may become a purchaser at a sale made in pursuance of a power contained in the mortgage. It only needs a statement of the proposition to determine that he cannot, as the law will not authorize him to act as both the vendor and vendee. In such a sale there is every temptation to promote his own interest at the sacrifice of that of the owner. The law will neither subject nor suffer him to be so tempted to act unjustly. It is believed to be a rule of universal application that the officer or person charged with the sale of property at auction, whether by authority of law or under a power derived from the owner, is prohibited from becoming the purchaser. If sanctioned, it would lead to oppression, wrong, and fraud, highly injurious to the owner."

[2] Mulvey v. Gibbons, 87 Ill. 367.

[3] People v. Wiltshire, 9 Ill. App. 374.

[4] Gibbons v. Hoag, 95 Ill. 45.

[5] Mapps v. Sharpe, 32 Ill. 13; Lockett v. Hill, 1 Woods, 552, Fed. Cas. No. 8,443.

the sale will be voidable to the same extent and on the same conditions as if the purchase had been made directly by the mortgagee.[7] And it has even been held that an agent of the mortgagee cannot act as the agent of a third person in making a bid. "It can make no difference in the result that the same agent employed to make the sale is employed to make the bid for an independent purchaser. There is a legal incompatibility in one man's occupying such adverse relations, and representing antagonistic interests in the transaction; and a court of equity will not tolerate the attempt and give efficacy to what is done, when opposed by competent parties in interest."[8] But the mere fact that the notices of sale were prepared by the prospective buyer is no proof that he was the owner of the mortgage.[9]

The rule here stated may be obviated by an agreement inserted in the mortgage expressly allowing the mortgagee to buy at the sale.[10] But where it is claimed that the mortgage itself confers upon the mortgagee the right to purchase at his own sale, the instrument will be strictly construed in that regard. Such a privilege the law does not give to the mortgagee, and does not favor; and if it is claimed under a clause in the mortgage, he must show that it has been given in clear and unmistakable terms. Such a clause would be analogous to one providing that the mortgagee might purchase the equity of redemption at a fixed price, and would place the mortgagor substantially at the mercy of the mortgagee. Whether it would be void, as being extorted from the necessities of the mortgagor, or whether the mortgagee, acting under it, would be required to show, as against a claim of the mortgagor to redeem, that the sale had been fair and the property had brought a reasonable price, was not decided in the case cited, but it was said that, upon the question whether the language used did confer the right, it must receive a strict construction, being regarded with disfavor by the courts.[11]

But when the mortgagee makes a fair and proper sale of the

---

[7] Harper v. Ely, 56 Ill. 179; Nichols v. Otto, 132 Ill. 91, 23 N. E. Rep. 411; Ross v. Demoss, 45 Ill. 447. And see Burr v. Borden, '61 Ill. 389.

[8] Gibson v. Barber, 100 N. Car. 192, 6 S. E. Rep. 766.

[9] Ritchie v. Judd, 137 Ill. 453, 27 N. E. Rep. 682.

[10] Hall v. Towne, 45 Ill. 493.

[11] Griffin v. Marine Co., 52 Ill. 130.

premises to a stranger, under the power of sale contained in the mortgage, and conveys the premises to the purchaser in good faith, and without any previous arrangement or agreement for a reconveyance, his duties as trustee, in regard to the mortgaged property, are at an end, and he is at liberty thereafter to deal with the purchaser in relation to the property the same as if such purchaser had derived the title through some other source.[12]

It is also to be noted that, by statute in Illinois, when a power-of-sale mortgage authorizes the sheriff of the county to execute the power, and the sale is accordingly made by that officer, the mortgagee, or his assigns or legal representatives, may fairly and in good faith purchase the property or any part of the same.[13]

§ 477. **Effect of Sale Under Power.**—Where a mortgage or deed of trust contains a power of sale on default, and an express covenant that a sale made in pursuance thereof shall bar the equity of redemption, neither legal nor equitable proceedings were necessary (before the statute forbidding the execution of such powers by sale) to enforce the security; but after a sale and conveyance made in accordance with the provisions of the instrument, the equity of the mortgagor was extinguished, the same as it would be by a strict foreclosure in a court of equity.[14] And where the property sold for only a portion of the debt, and the creditor recovered a judgment for the remainder and collected it, this does not open the sale and authorize the debtor to redeem.[15] Moreover, a trustee's sale under powers contained in a deed of trust will have the effect of cutting out or extinguishing all junior liens as effectually as an equitable decree of foreclosure could do.[16] Where a party, in his deed of trust, covenanted with the trustees to give immediate possession to the purchaser in case of a default and sale under the power therein, an action of forcible detainer may be employed to dispossess him upon his refusal to deliver possession after the sale, although the law in force at the time of the execution of the deed did not extend that remedy to

[12] Munn v. Burges, 70 Ill. 604.

[13] Rev. Stat. Ill. c. 95, § 11.

[14] Bloom v. Van Rensselaer, 15 Ill. 503; Ryan v. Sanford, 133 Ill. 291, 24 N. E. Rep. 428, affirming 25 Ill. App. 571; Aiken v. Bridge-ford, 84 Ala. 295, 4 South. Rep. 266.

[15] Weld v. Rees, 48 Ill. 428.

[16] Plum v. Studebaker, 89 Mo. 162, 1 S. W. Rep. 217.

deeds of trust, but was afterwards amended so as to cover the case of sales under such deeds; for a change in the law, giving a more speedy remedy to enforce a party's contract or covenant to surrender possession, does not impair the obligation of the contract, and therefore may constitutionally be made retroactive.[17]

§ 478. **Effect of Defects or Irregularities.**—A purchaser under a deed of trust containing a power of sale is chargeable with notice of defects and irregularities attending the sale, and their effect cannot be evaded by him. He is bound to know whether proper notice was given by the trustee of the sale, and whether the sale was made at a time and in the manner required by the power contained in the deed of trust. As to him, the rule of caveat emptor applies. But the rule is different as to subsequent and remote purchasers. If there is nothing on the face of the deed given by the trustee to the purchaser, to show that the sale was not made in full compliance with the terms and directions of the trust deed, a subsequent purchaser, who has no notice in fact of any defect or irregularity in the sale by the trustee, is not bound to go behind the deed to learn whether or not its recitals are true, but he will be protected as an innocent purchaser.[18] Even as against the original purchaser, if the mortgagor receives the surplus proceeds of a sale made under the power in the mortgage or trust deed, in ignorance of defects which would be sufficient to invalidate the sale, but afterwards acquires knowledge of such defects and continues to retain the proceeds, he will be estopped to deny the purchaser's title.[19]

§ 479. **Deed to Purchaser.**—When property is sold under a power contained in a deed of trust, it is the duty of the trustee to execute and deliver a deed therefor to the purchaser. This deed relates back to the execution of the deed of trust, and the law does not require that it shall be recorded when the trust deed is recorded, in order to protect the grantee against attaching creditors of the original owner, and those claiming under them. The notice of sale is all that is required. The record of the trust deed is sufficient to put all persons on

[17] Chapin v. Billings, 91 Ill. 539.
[18] Gunnell v. Cockerill, 79 Ill. 79; Wilson v. South Park Commissioners, 70 Ill. 46; Hamilton v. Lubukee, 51 Ill. 415; Stephens v. Clay, 17 Colo. 489, 30 Pac. Rep. 43.
[19] Brewer v. Nash, 16 R. I. 458, 17 Atl. Rep. 857.

inquiry as to whether a sale has been made under the same.[20] Though the trustee should properly be named as the grantor in his deed to the purchaser, yet it is held that, even though his name is not mentioned in the body of the deed, yet it is sufficient if it recites the date of the trust deed, names the beneficiary therein, describes the property, and refers to the volume and page of the record of the trust deed, which record, on inspection, will show who was the trustee.[21] And in the case cited it was also held that, where the sale was made in pursuance of the power in the deed of trust, it was not essential for the trustee to recite in his deed the exact date of the sale.[22] And although the trustee's deed does not recite the fact that the sale was advertised as required by the deed of trust under which it was executed, the fact may be proved by extraneous evidence.[23] A covenant of warranty contained in a trustee's deed, made in pursuance of a trust deed given to secure the payment of money, and empowering the trustee, in case of sale thereunder, to convey by deed with full covenants of warranty, binds the grantor in the trust deed.[24]

When the sale is made by the mortgagee, instead of by a trustee, he is the person to make a deed to the purchaser; and mortgages with power of sale commonly provide that the mortgagee shall execute such deed in the name of the mortgagor and as his attorney in fact. When the mortgagee, instead of complying with such a direction, makes the deed in his own name, the sale is not invalidated, but an equitable title will pass, and a court of equity will aid to establish the legal title in the grantee.[25] But it seems that an assignee of the mortgage can only convey the title as the attorney of the mortgagor, and by using the name of his principal, and that a deed made by the assignee in his own name as grantor would not pass the title.[26] On similar principles, it is ruled that a deed made in the name of the auctioneer at a sale under a power in the mortgage, instead of in the name of the donee of the power, does not convey the legal title.[27]

§ 480. **Trustee's Deed as Evidence.**—The deed given by the

[20] Farrar v. Payne, 73 Ill. 82.
[21] Jones v. Hagler, 95 Ala. 529, 10 South. Rep. 345.
[22] Idem.
[23] Allen v. De Groodt, 105 Mo. 442, 16 S. W. Rep. 494.
[24] Thurmond v. Brownson, 69 Tex. 597, 6 S. W. Rep. 778.
[25] Gibbons v. Hoag, 95 Ill. 45.
[26] Speer v. Hadduck, 31 Ill. 439.
[27] Sanders v. Cassady, 86 Ala. 246, 5 South. Rep. 503.

trustee to a purchaser at a sale made by the former in pursuance of the power contained in the trust deed under which he acts, is prima facie evidence of the facts which it recites regarding the provisions of the deed of trust, the default, notice, and circumstances of the sale.[28] For instance, in an action of forcible detainer for land sold under a power in a deed of trust, where the sale was made before the principal sum was due, for default in the payment of interest notes, under a provision that, in case of such default, the payee might treat the entire debt as due and require the trustee to sell, the plaintiff, being the purchaser at the sale, is not required to prove, independently of the recitals in the trustee's deed to him, that there had been a default in the payment of interest, or that the holder of the notes had elected to treat the principal as due.[29] Moreover, in a court of law, a trustee's deed under a power of sale contained in the deed of trust is conclusive evidence of a sale under the power; if it is intended to impeach it for fraud preceding its execution, this must be attempted in equity, not at law.[30] And when the trustee's deed shows the sale to have been made in strict conformity with the power contained in the trust deed, a subsequent purchaser (that is, a purchaser from the foreclosure purchaser) who has had no actual notice of any irregularities in the sale, will be protected, as against any such irregularities, in the character of an innocent purchaser.[31] But to show the right of one to execute the power of sale contained in a mortgage, as the administrator of the mortgagee, some evidence of the death of the latter and of the appointment of the person making the sale as his administrator is necessary, beyond the mere recital of these facts in the administrator's deed.[32]

§ 481. **Setting Aside Sale.**—It is the settled doctrine of equity, in Illinois, that sales of land by a mortgagee or trustee under a power of sale, without recourse to legal proceedings, will be jealously scrutinized by the courts of equity, and upon proof of the slightest fraud or unfair conduct, or a departure

[28] Miller v. Shaw, 103 Ill. 277; Savings & Loan Society v. Deering, 66 Cal. 281, 5 Pac. Rep. 353.

[29] Chapin v. Billings, 91 Ill. 539.

[30] Windett v. Hurlbut, 115 Ill. 403, 5 N. E. Rep. 589.

[31] Hosmer v. Campbell, 98 Ill. 572; Jenkins v. Pierce, Id. 646; Gunnell v. Cockerill, 84 Ill. 319.

[32] Taylor v. Lawrence, 148 Ill. 388, 36 N. E. Rep. 74.

from the power, they will be instantly set aside.[33] The trustee, in particular, is bound to act with the utmost fairness and impartiality; and the sale will not be allowed to stand if there is evidence of any unfairness on his part resulting in injury to the debtor.[34] "A trustee's duties are not merely formal. It is his duty, in the faithful discharge of his trust, to inform himself as to the condition of the property which he is about to sell, and to adopt that course which, in his judgment, will bring the highest price."[35] Hence a sale by a trustee may be set aside by a court of chancery where it appears to have been wrongful or fraudulent, not authorized by the deed to be made except upon conditions which were not fulfilled, or otherwise a breach of trust.[36] Thus, where the trustee sells only a part of the premises, but makes a conveyance to the purchaser purporting to pass more land than was sold, this will be regarded as such misconduct on the part of the trustee as will compel the setting aside of the sale.[37] Misconduct on the part of the creditor in procuring the sale to be made will also furnish ground for the same action. Thus, where a senior mortgagee, whose mortgage contained a power of sale, brought a formal bill in equity to foreclose, making the junior incumbrancers parties thereto, but while this suit was pending he exercised his power of sale and sold the property, it was

[33] Stone v. Williamson, 17 Ill. App. 175; Longwith v. Butler, 8 Ill. 32.

[34] Williamson v. Stone, 128 Ill. 129, 22 N. E. Rep. 1005. In this case it was said: "Where a trust deed is made to secure the payment of a debt, the trustee named therein is the representative, not only of the owner of the indebtedness, but also of the maker of the trust deed. He is the agent of both the creditor and the debtor. His duty is to act fairly towards both, and not exclusively in the interest of either. The law requires the conduct of such a trustee to be absolutely impartial as between the two parties whom he represents. Hence his relations with one of them ought not to be of such a character as to tempt him to neglect the interests of the other. A court of equity will always examine with the closest scrutiny a sale that is made under the power contained in a trust deed, and where the rights of third persons have not intervened, redemption from such a sale, conditioned upon the full payment, to the holder of the indebtedness, of all that is due to him, will be allowed where there is evidence of any such unfairness on the part of the trustee, whether intentional or unintentional, as has resulted in injury to the debtor."

[35] Cassidy v. Cook, 99 Ill. 385.

[36] Stone v. Fargo, 55 Ill. 71; Weld v. Rees, 48 Ill. 428; Flint v. Lewis, 61 Ill. 299.

[37] Wallwork v. Derby, 40 Ill. 527.

considered that this had a tendency to lull the parties into a false security, and so furnished ground for vacating the sale.[38] And the same result will follow from a secret bargain between the mortgagee and the foreclosure purchaser, which has a tendency to prevent competition in the bidding.[39] But the fact that one joint maker of a note secured by mortgage, upon the refusal of the other maker to pay his part of an installment due, refuses to pay his part and suggests a sale under the power, is not evidence of his fraudulently procuring a foreclosure of the mortgage.[40] And so, the existence of a prior incumbrance is no ground for setting aside a sale under a trust deed given to secure the unpaid purchase money on a conveyance with warranty.[41] And a mortgagee's or trustee's sale fairly made, under a power of attorney not under seal, will give the purchaser such an equitable title as will bar a suit in equity to have the sale set aside.[42] On a bill to impeach a sale of land under a power in a deed of trust, on the ground that there is no legal evidence of a decree appointing a successor in the trust to make the sale, the burden of showing the invalidity of the sale is upon the complainant.[43]

When a sale under a power is set aside, for fraud or irregularities, but the mortgage debt is due and unpaid, the relief asked by the debtor will be granted only on condition of his doing equity by paying the debt. Or, in other words, the court will give him the privilege of redeeming. The proper form of decree in such cases grants the debtor a certain time within which to redeem by paying the amount due under the mortgage or deed of trust, and provides that, on his failure to pay as required, his bill shall be dismissed and the sale under the mortgage or trust deed shall be allowed to stand confirmed and unimpeached.[44] On a bill to redeem from a fraudulent or unfair sale under a trust deed, it is not error to charge the party in possession with the reasonable rents and profits of the land until the possession is restored; and he will not be

[38] Hurd v. Case, 32 Ill. 45.

[39] Mapps v. Sharpe, 32 Ill. 13.

[40] St. Joseph Manuf'g Co. v. Daggett, 84 Ill. 556.

[41] Fairman v. Peck, 87 Ill. 156.

[42] Watson v. Sherman, 84 Ill. 263.

[43] Bowman v. Ash, 143 Ill. 649, 32 N. E. Rep. 486.

[44] Burgess v. Ruggles, 146 Ill. 506, 34 N. E. Rep. 1036. And see Bremer v. Calumet & C. Canal Co., 127 Ill. 464, 18 N. E. Rep. 321.

allowed to receive compensation for his alleged improvements in cutting away timber.[45]

§ 482. **Inadequacy of Price.**—When an application is made to a court of equity to set aside a sale under a power contained in a mortgage or deed of trust, the fact that the property brought a price materially less than its fair market value is a circumstance proper to be considered in connection with any other facts which tend to show that the sale was irregular, fraudulent, or unfair to the debtor, and should have its due weight in influencing the decision of the court.[46] It has been said that inadequacy of the price realized at the sale "has significance only when taken in connection with other facts tending to show bad faith, mistake, an undue advantage taken of the ignorance or weakness of the person whose property rights will be affected by the sale, or some other of the grounds of equitable relief."[47] Probably this statement of the rule is too severe; but at any rate it is firmly settled that inadequacy of price, considered as the sole ground of an application to set aside such a sale, will not justify the court in taking such action, unless so gross as to shock the conscience and to raise a presumption of fraud.[48] It must not be forgotten that the debtor agrees, by the mortgage or trust deed, that the property shall be sold to the highest bidder. And as this is a legal contract, a court of equity will not make a different contract for him. If he is not willing to take the risk, he can insert other conditions in the mortgage or deed. In one of the cases, where it appeared that the property sold at the trustee's sale for two-thirds of its fair value, and no fraud or unfairness attended the sale, it was held that this was not such an inadequacy of price as amounted to fraud, requiring the sale to be set aside.[49] And in another case it was adjudged that a trustee's sale was not invalid because the property was sold for about $6,000, although a loan of $10,000 had been raised on

[45] Equitable Trust Co. v. Fisher, 106 Ill. 189.

[46] See Kerfoot v. Billings, 160 Ill. 563, 43 N. E. Rep. 804.

[47] Hudgens v. Morrow, 47 Ark. 515, 2 S. W. Rep. 104.

[48] Booker v. Anderson, 35 Ill. 66; Waterman v. Spaulding, 51 Ill. 425; Jenkins v. Pierce, 98 Ill. 646;

Burns v. Middleton, 104 Ill. 411; Laclede Bank v. Keeler, 109 Ill. 385; Magnusson v. Williams, 111 Ill. 450; Hoodless v. Reid, 112 Ill. 105; Kerfoot v. Billings, 160 Ill. 563, 43 N. E. Rep. 804; Bowman v. Ash, 36 Ill. App. 115; Clark v. Trust Co., 100 U. S. 149.

[49] Weld v. Rees, 48 Ill. 428.

it a few years before, and although the property was actually sold for $18,000 a few years after the sale under the trust deed.[50]

§ 483. Same; Laches Barring Relief.—When a mortgagor or grantor in a trust deed, under which a sale of the property has been made, believes himself entitled to have the sale set aside, on account of defects or irregularities which render it voidable, he is required to act with reasonable promptness. Acquiescence, unexplained, for any considerable length of time, in a sale which is voidable, but not void, will be deemed a waiver of all mere irregularities which may have intervened. A party, to avoid a sale of the land covered by his mortgage, for such causes, must take early measures to have it vacated, and he cannot wait to speculate on the chance of a rise in the value of the property.[51] For example, a bill filed nearly ten years after the foreclosure, and seeking to avoid the sale on the sole ground that the mortgagee purchased at his own sale, comes too late unless the delay is satisfactorily explained.[52] If the property has meanwhile passed into the hands of subsequent purchasers, a much less delay than this will be considered too great. Thus, laches will be imputed to a mortgagor who delays for five years,[53] or even for four years,[54] to take the proper steps for setting aside a sale under the mortgage or deed of trust, when a third person has in the meantime bought the property, relying on the validity of the sale, and where the ground of the application is an irregularity or defect in the execution of the power of sale, or an alleged defect in the notice, or the inadequacy of the price realized at the sale, or a combination of these circumstances, not sufficient to render the sale absolutely void. On the other hand, it has been ruled that a delay of only about eight months in bringing suit to set aside a sale under a deed of trust is not unreasonable, and will not bar the suit.[55]

[50] Parmly v. Walker, 102 Ill. 617.

[51] Bush v. Sherman, 80 Ill. 160; Hoyt v. Pawtucket Savings Inst., 110 Ill. 390.

[52] Askew v. Sanders, 84 Ala. 356, 4 South. Rep. 167. In Dempster v. West, 69 Ill. 613, under somewhat similar circumstances, it was held that a delay of seven years in seeking relief was so great as to amount to laches.

[53] Gibbons v. Hoag, 95 Ill. 45; Eastman v. Littlefield, 164 Ill. 124, 45 N. E. Rep. 137.

[54] Hoyt v. Pawtucket Savings Inst., 110 Ill. 390; Hamilton v. Lubukee, 51 Ill. 415.

[55] Walker v. Carleton, 97 Ill. 582.

§ 484. **Costs and Expenses.**—Trust deeds and power-of-sale mortgages usually provide for the payment out of the proceeds of the sale of the costs and expenses of executing the power, together with a fee or commission to the trustee. A clause providing for the payment, out of the proceeds of sale, of the "costs and charges" of the trust, applies only to such costs and expenses as would necessarily be made by the trustee if he should sell the property under the power in the deed.[56] But where the deed provides that the trustee shall be entitled to a reasonable compensation for all services, to be paid by the grantor, he may, on foreclosure, be allowed a reasonable compensation for his services out of the proceeds of the sale.[57] And if the trust deed provides for the payment of all the fees and charges of the trustee in executing the trust, he may be allowed reasonable counsel fees for foreclosing the deed.[58] But a deed which authorizes the trustee, in case of foreclosure, to pay certain specified claims, and "also all other expenses of the trust," does not warrant the payment of the cost of an abstract of title.[59] On the other hand, where the trustee and the creditor conspire to make a fraudulent sale of the property, for the purpose of defeating the title of a subsequent purchaser, they will be charged with the costs and expenses of making such sale.[60]

§ 485. **Disposition of Surplus.**—The maker of a deed of trust in the nature of a mortgage may provide for any disposition of the surplus of the proceeds of a sale under it, after satisfying the debt secured, that he chooses, provided only that there is no fraud on creditors.[61] And where, on a sale under such a deed, the trustee refuses to pay over the surplus to the party entitled thereto, he may be compelled by an action at

---

[56] Cooper v. McNeil, 9 Ill. App. 97.

[57] Guignon v. Union Trust Co., 156 Ill. 135, 40 N. E. Rep. 556, affirming 53 Ill. App. 581.

[58] Cheltenham Imp. Co. v. Whitehead, 128 Ill. 279, 21 N. E. Rep. 569; Guignon v. Union Trust Co., 156 Ill. 135, 40 N. E. Rep. 556. Where the sum of $50,000 was secured by nine different notes and trust deeds on different lots, it

was held that $150 as trustee's fees allowed as damages on dissolving an injunction restraining the sale, was not an unreasonable charge. Marsh v. Morton, 75 Ill. 621.

[59] Cheltenham Imp. Co. v. Whitehead, 128 Ill. 279, 21 N. E. Rep. 569.

[60] Hopkins v. Granger, 52 Ill. 504.

[61] Hall v. Gould, 79 Ill. 16.

law.[62]   Where the trust deed foreclosed by sale was a first lien on the property, and a surplus remains after satisfying the creditor secured thereby, such surplus belongs to the second incumbrancer rather than to the grantor in the deed of trust.[63] And if, in such a case, the senior lienor becomes the purchaser, bidding more for the land than is sufficient to satisfy his own debt, he becomes liable to the junior mortgagee for the excess.[64] On similar principles, where the deed of trust authorizes the trustee, on default, to sell the land and pay the costs, commissions, and other liens on the land, as well as the particular debt secured, he is authorized to pay, out of the proceeds of the sale, any judgment which may be a lien on the land at the time of the sale, whether it existed at the time the deed was executed or not; and the owner of such judgment can subject any surplus in the hands of the trustee to its payment, after the particular debt secured by the deed of trust is paid.[65]

[62] Ballinger v. Bourland, 87 Ill. 513.

[63] Ballinger v. Bourland, 87 Ill. 513. Where property subject to mortgage and other liens, is sold by the first mortgagee, he becomes a trustee for the benefit of all concerned. If he regards the interests of others as well as his own, seeks to promote the common welfare, and keeps within the scope of his authority, a court of equity will not hold him responsible for mere errors of judgment or results, however unfortunate, which he could not reasonably have anticipated. Upon the sale of such property, the liens attach to the proceeds thereof in the same manner, order, and effect as they bound the premises before the sale, the new securities standing in substitution for the old. Markey v. Langley, 92 U. S. 142.

[64] Laughlin v. Heer, 89 Ill. 119.

[65] Hall v. Gould, 79 Ill. 16.

CHAPTER XXXII.

MORTGAGE FORECLOSURE IN THE FEDERAL COURTS.

§ 486. **Lis Pendens in State Court No Bar.**—It is a general rule that the pendency of another suit, upon the same subject-matter or cause of action and between the same parties, in a state court, cannot be successfully pleaded in bar or abatement of an action in a court of the United States.[1] The two courts, though not foreign to each other, belong to different jurisdictions in such a sense that the doctrine of lis pendens is not applicable as between them. Hence the mere fact of the pendency of a suit in a state court for the foreclosure of a mortgage will not bar a suit in the proper federal court between the same parties for the foreclosure of the same mortgage, the only question being as to the jurisdiction of the federal court.[2] And although proceedings for the foreclosure of a mortgage are pending in a state court, the debt itself may be prosecuted by action in the United States court.[3] And although the mortgagor or grantor in a deed of trust has brought a suit in a state court, against the trustee in the deed of trust and other defendants, to restrain and enjoin the trustee from selling the mortgaged property under the power of sale in the deed, which action remains pending and unde-

---

[1] Stanton v. Embrey, 93 U. S. 548; Gordon v. Gilfoil, 99 U. S. 168; Insurance Co. v. Brune's Assignee, 96 U. S. 588.

[2] Weaver v. Field, 16 Fed. Rep. 22. The pendency in the state courts of a suit by the trustees of a railroad mortgage to foreclose is not a bar to a similar suit in the federal court by a bondholder secured thereby. Beekman v. Hudson River West Shore Ry. Co., 35 Fed. Rep. 3.

[3] Gordon v. Gilfoil, 99 U. S. 168.

termined, this will be no defense to a suit for the foreclosure of the deed of trust in the proper federal court.[4] For similar reasons, where a mortgagee sues to foreclose in a federal court, and makes judgment creditors of the mortgagor's grantor parties defendant, the suit will not be postponed until the termination of proceedings instituted by those creditors in a state court to establish their liens on the land, to which proceedings the mortgagee is not a party.[5]

§ 487. Same; Assignment for Creditors Under State Law.— When an assignee for the benefit of creditors has been judicially appointed in proceedings had under the insolvency laws of a state, and has been accepted and qualified, so that all the insolvent's property and rights of property are vested in him under the trust, such property is thereby placed in gremio legis, and cannot be seized on process issuing from another court.[6] But the filing of a voluntary assignment for the benefit of creditors, and of the assignee's bond, in a probate court having jurisdiction, under the statutes of the state, does not prevent a creditor, who is a citizen of another state, and has not become a party to the proceedings in the state court, from suing in equity in a federal court to set aside a mortgage made by the debtor contemporaneously with the assignment.[7] And it is held that although a mortgagor of realty has made a statutory general assignment for the benefit of his creditors, this does not affect the right of the mortgagee, being a citizen of another state, to sue in the federal court for the foreclosure of the mortgage; nor is it necessary for him to obtain the permission of the state court having jurisdiction.[8]

§ 488. Jurisdiction Depending on Diverse Citizenship.—A mortgagee of realty, being a citizen of a state other than that of the mortgagor, may maintain a bill in equity for the foreclosure of the mortgage in the proper circuit court of the United States, and such court will have jurisdiction of the action in consequence of the diverse citizenship of the parties.[9]

---

[4] Pierce v. Feagans, 39 Fed. Rep. 587. And see Woodbury v. Allegheny & K. R. Co., 72 Fed. Rep. 371.

[5] Converse v. Michigan Dairy Co., 45 Fed. Rep. 18.

[6] Geilinger v. Philippi, 133 U. S. 246. And see The J. G. Chapman, 62 Fed. Rep. 939.

[7] Smith Middlings Purifier Co. v. McGroarty, 136 U. S. 237; Morris v. Landaer, 4 C. C. A. 162, 54 Fed. Rep. 23.

[8] Edwards v. Hill, 8 C. C. A. 233, 59 Fed. Rep. 723.

[9] McDonald v. Smalley, 1 Pet. (U. S.) 620; Connecticut Mut. Life Ins. Co. v. Crawford, 21 Fed. Rep.

But it is the universal rule of those courts that, when jurisdiction of an action or suit is alleged to attach by reason of diversity of citizenship, it must appear that all the parties on one side of the controversy are citizens of a different state, or of different states, from all the parties on the other side. Hence in a suit for the foreclosure of a mortgage, in which it is sought to charge the mortgage debtor with any balance of the mortgage debt which may remain due after the security is exhausted, the debtor is a necessary party, and if his citizenship stands in the way of the assumption of jurisdiction by the federal court, the suit cannot be maintained therein, even though, if he were not a party, the person with whom he is joined as a defendant, to whom he had sold the equity of redemption after the execution of the mortgage, would be entitled to invoke the federal jurisdiction.[10]

"Questions concerning diverse citizenship, where trustees are concerned, most frequently arise in actions brought to foreclose deeds of trust in the nature of mortgages. Such an action is properly brought in the name of the trustee, and his citizenship, as compared with that of the defendant, will govern the question of jurisdiction. The fact that the beneficiary is a citizen of the same state with the grantor in the deed will not defeat the jurisdiction of the federal court, if the trustee is a citizen of a different state.[11] But if the trustee refuses to take such action, it is permissible for any one of the beneficiaries (as, in cases where the trust deed is given to secure the payment of a series of bonds distributed among a number of holders) to bring the suit in his own name, making the trustee a defendant, and also any of the other beneficiaries who refuse to join as plaintiffs. In this event, the citizenship of the trustee is not less material than before, and the action will not be removable to a federal court (or originally maintainable therein) if there is community of citizenship between any of the plaintiffs and any of the defendants. But the question then arises on which side of the controversy the trustee is to be arrayed, when he is thus formally made a defendant. Some of the cases hold that the trustee, when thus joined, is to be counted among the defendants, since the action

281; Pooley v. Luco, 76 Fed. Rep. 146.

[10] Ayres v. Wiswall, 112 U. S.

187; Coney v. Winchell, 116 U. S. 227.

[11] Dodge v. Tulleys, 144 U. S. 451.

of the plaintiff is in hostility to him; and therefore the suit
will be removable if all the defendants of record are citizens of
different states from the plaintiff, although the trustee may
be a citizen of the same state with some one or more of the
other defendants.[12] On the other hand, there are cases holding
that, although the trustee is nominally a defendant, he is really
to be counted on the same side with the beneficiary suing, and
hence the federal jurisdiction cannot attach if the trustee and
any of his co-defendants are citizens of the same state.[13] A
very reasonable solution of this question is found in a recent
decision of one of the Circuit Courts of Appeals, where it is
held that, if the bill shows no conflict between the complainant
and the trustee, and where the bill is such a one as the trustee
should himself have filed, the trustee will, for purposes of
jurisdiction, be ranged on the same side of the controversy
with the complainant; but where the object of the bill is to
procure a decree excluding all other beneficiaries than the
complainant from the equal benefits of the security, the trustee
is properly an opposite party to the subject-matter of that
controversy, and should, for purposes of jurisdiction, be
ranged with the other defendants to the suit."[14] In a suit to
foreclose a mortgage brought in a federal court in one state
against a corporation of that state by bondholders, citizens of
another state, other bondholders who are citizens of the state
where the suit is brought cannot be made parties plaintiff, as
the jurisdiction is dependent upon citizenship; but, under such
circumstances, the plaintiffs can foreclose the mortgage separately, and the proceeds of sale, if a sale is made, will be
distributed according to the rights of all.[15]

It should be noted that where a federal court already has
possession, through its receiver, of the property covered by a
mortgage, its jurisdiction over the res will give it jurisdiction

[12] Omaha Hotel Co. v. Wade, 97
U. S. 13; Reinach v. Atlantic &
G. W. R. Co., 58 Fed. Rep. 33.

[13] Shipp v. Williams, 10 C. C. A.
247, 62 Fed. Rep. 4.

[14] Black's Dillon on Removal of
Causes, § 93; First Nat. Bank v.
Radford Trust Co., 26 C. C. A. 1,
80 Fed. Rep. 569. Where a mortgagor and the trustee of the mortgage are citizens of the same

state, the holders of bonds secured
by the mortgage cannot bring suit
in a federal court to foreclose the
mortgage in their own names,
without showing reason why the
suit is not brought by the trustee.
Needham v. Wilson, 47 Fed. Rep.
97.

[15] Jackson & Sharp Co. v. Burlington & L. R. Co., 29 Fed. Rep.
474.

of a suit to foreclose the mortgage, without regard to the citizenship of the parties.[16] And under the Act of Congress which provides that "when, in any suit commenced in any circuit court of the United States to enforce any legal or equitable lien upon real or personal property within the district where such suit is begun, one or more of the defendants therein shall not be an inhabitant of, or found within, the said district, it shall be lawful for the court to make an order directing such absent defendant or defendants to appear," the court has jurisdiction of a suit by a resident of another district to foreclose a mortgage on land situated within the district, though some of the defendants are, and others are not, residents of the district in which the suit is brought.[17] Where corporations of several states are consolidated into one, a federal court of equity, in foreclosing a consolidated mortgage upon the entire property, has jurisdiction to order the sale of all the property in all the states; and separate suits are not necessary.[18]

A suit for the foreclosure of a mortgage, originally begun in a state court, may be thence removed by the defendant to the United States circuit court, under the provisions of the Act of Congress regulating the removal of causes, if the prescribed conditions are met and all the parties on one side of the controversy are citizens of different states from those on the other.[19] But where the jurisdiction of the federal court, in a foreclosure proceeding, is based on the diverse citizenship of the parties, or on the fact that one of them is an alien, it must appear on the face of the record.[20]

§ 489. Same; Suit by Assignee.—The Act of Congress regulating the jurisdiction of the circuit and district courts of the United States provides that no such court "shall have cognizance of any suit, except upon foreign bills of exchange, to recover the contents of any promissory note or other chose in action in favor of any assignee, or of any subsequent holder

---

[16] Fish v. Ogdensburgh & L. C. R. Co., 79 Fed. Rep. 131; Park v. New York, L. E. & W. R. Co., 70 Fed. Rep. 641.

[17] Ames v. Holderbaum, 42 Fed. Rep. 341. And see Detweiler v. Holderbaum, 42 Fed. Rep. 337.

[18] Blackburn v. Selma, M. & M. R. Co., 2 Flip. 525, Fed. Cas. No. 1,467.

[19] Ayres v. Wiswall, 112 U. S. 187; Connecticut Mut. Life Ins. Co. v. Crawford, 21 Fed. Rep. 281.

[20] Mossman v. Higginson, 4 Dall. (U. S.) 12.

if such instrument be payable to bearer and be not made by
any corporation, unless such suit might have been prosecuted
in such court to recover the said contents if no assignment or
transfer had been made.''[21] In other words, if the action is
by an assignee of a promissory note or other chose in action
(except in the case of the negotiable bonds or other securities
of a corporation), it cannot be instituted in a federal court,
nor removed thereto from a state court, unless the plaintiff's
assignor would have been entitled to sue in the federal court if
no assignment had been made; that is, the federal court will
have no jurisdiction unless the plaintiff's assignor and the
defendant are citizens of different states.[22] Now an action to
foreclose a mortgage, as a means of realizing the debt which it
secures, whether that debt be evidenced by a note or bond or
otherwise, is a suit to ''recover the contents of a promissory
note or other chose in action,'' within the meaning of the
statute, the debt being considered as the principal thing and
the mortgage as a mere incident. Hence, when the mortgagor
and mortgagee are citizens of the same state, an assignee of
the mortgage, though a citizen of another state, cannot maintain a bill for foreclosure in the federal courts, nor, if he
brings the suit in a state court, can the defendant remove it to
a federal court.[23]

If the assignment of the mortgage was merely fictitious and
collusive, and for no other purpose than to make a case which
would be cognizable in the federal court, the statute requires
that court to dismiss or remand it. But when notes and
mortgages are transferred to a non-resident for a valuable
consideration, and the assignor's interest thereupon entirely
determines, the mere fact that one of the purposes of the
transfer was to establish the diversity of citizenship necessary
to bring the case within the jurisdiction of the federal court
will not render the transaction collusive within the meaning of
the law.[24] To that end it is necessary to bring home to the
assignee a knowledge of such motive and purpose for the
transfer; till then, he must be considered an innocent pur-

[21] Act of Congress, August 13,
1888; 25 U. S. Stat. 433, § 1.

[22] Mexican Nat. R. Co. v. Davidson, 157 U. S. 201.

[23] Sheldon v. Sill, 8 How. (U.

S.) 441; Shoecraft v. Bloxham, 124
U. S. 730; Blacklock v. Small, 127
U. S. 96; Hill v. Wynne, 1 Biss.
C. C. 275, Fed. Cas. No. 6,503.

[24] Cross v. Allen, 141 U. S. 528.

chaser without notice.[25] And indeed the Supreme Court has said that the transfer of a note and mortgage, though made for the purpose of making a case cognizable in the federal court, will not be treated as collusive, so as to require the action to be dismissed, if it was made without any agreement or understanding as to a return of the consideration.[26]

§ 490. Jurisdiction Independent of State Statutes.—The equity jurisdiction of the courts of the United States is not subject to either limitation or restraint by the authorities of the states, and is uniform throughout the different states of the Union.[27] The fact that a state statute may provide that all actions of a particular character arising within its limits shall be brought in a certain state court will not affect the jurisdiction of the federal courts in such actions, if otherwise competent to take cognizance thereof. Hence where a state statute provides that guardians may be licensed to mortgage the estates of their wards, but that foreclosure of such mortgages shall be made only by petition to the county court (as is the case in Illinois), this will not preclude the mortgagee from bringing a suit for the foreclosure of such a mortgage in a federal court, if the citizenship of the parties and the amount involved are sufficient to confer jurisdiction.[28] On the same principle, a federal circuit court has jurisdiction in equity of a proceeding to foreclose a mortgage, the necessary elements of jurisdiction being present, notwithstanding a statute of the state where it sits provides that mortgages shall be foreclosed by actions in courts of law only.[29] And although the state statute may provide a special remedy at law for the enforcement of a deed absolute in form, when intended as a security for the payment of money, this will not prevent the grantee, in a proper case from maintaining a bill in equity in a federal court for the foreclosure of the conveyance as a mortgage.[30]

§ 491. Procedure Conforming to State Practice.—Proceedings for the foreclosure of a mortgage in a federal court should

---

[25] Smith v. Kernochen, 7 How. (U. S.) 198.

[26] Lanier v. Nash, 121 U. S. 404.

[27] Gamewell Fire-Alarm Tel. Co. v. Mayor, 31 Fed. Rep. 312; Woodbury v. Allegheny & K. R. Co., 72 Fed. Rep. 371.

[28] United States Mortgage Co. v. Sperry, 138 U. S. 313; Davis v. James, 10 Biss. C. C. 51, 2 Fed. Rep. 618; supra, § 93.

[29] Keith & Perry Coal Co. v. Bingham, 97 Mo. 196, 10 S. W. Rep. 32.

[30] Ray v. Tatum, 18 C. C. A. 464, 72 Fed Rep. 112.

proceed upon the ordinary lines of foreclosure proceedings in the courts of the state where the mortgaged property is situated.[81] And the federal court may adopt and use the particular form of action prescribed by the state law as proper for a foreclosure, such, for example, as an action by scire facias or a real action for possession on breach of condition.[82] When the proceeding is by a bill in equity, the requirements of the state law should be complied with, and the forms of proceeding pursued, as nearly as may be practicable.[83] Thus, where the statute law of the state wherein the mortgaged land lies, or the decisions of its courts, have established the rule that land covered by a mortgage and afterwards sold in parcels to different purchasers at different times must be sold, on foreclosure of the mortgage, in parcels and in the inverse order of its alienation, this constitutes a rule of property which must be followed by the federal courts sitting within that state.[84] And so, where the statute of the state requires the whole recovery on the mortgage debt to be had in one action of foreclosure, and forbids the maintenance of a separate personal action for judgment on the debt secured by the mortgage, the federal courts will follow this rule.[85] Sales of mortgaged premises, under a decree of foreclosure, are usually made in the federal courts by the marshal of the district where the decree was entered, or by a master appointed by the court as directed in the decree.[86] But though the state law may make no provision for a confirmation of a judicial sale by the court which decreed it, yet where the proceeding is in a United States court, it is proper for the officer making the sale to make a report or return to the court for confirmation.[87]

§ 492. **Allowing Redemption.**—A state statute, together with any rules of practice of the state courts framed for the enforcement of it, declaring a right of redemption of mortgaged property on foreclosure, is a rule of property and obligatory on the federal courts, in actions for the foreclosure of

[81] Knickerbocker Trust Co. v. Penacook Mfg. Co., 100 Fed. Rep. 814.

[82] Black v. Black, 74 Fed. Rep. 978; Whiting v. Wellington, 10 Fed. Rep. 810.

[83] Nalle v. Young, 160 U. S. 624.

Compare Dow v. Chamberlin, 5 McLean, 281, Fed. Cas. No. 4,037.

[84] Orvis v. Powell, 98 U. S. 176.

[85] Winters v. Hub Min. Co., 57 Fed. Rep. 287.

[86] Blossom v. Milwaukee & C. R. Co., 3 Wall. 196.

[87] Nalle v. Young, 160 U. S. 624.

mortgages on real property within the state, no less than upon the courts of the state.[38] But if the federal courts give substantial effect to the right of redemption secured by a state statute, they are at liberty, in so doing, to adhere to their own modes of proceeding. Thus, in a case where it appeared that the statute gave the debtor twelve months from the confirmation of the sale in which to redeem, and the practice of the state courts was to report the sale at once for confirmation, but the federal court gave the debtor twelve months from the day of sale, in which to redeem, it being its practice to make the final confirmation and the deed at the same time, that is, after the expiration of the year, it was held that this was a substantial recognition of the right to redeem within twelve months and the decree of the federal court should not be disturbed on appeal.[39] So, where the decree is good in other respects, but the deed is made at the time of the sale, and is thereby inoperative until after the expiration of the statutory period of redemption, it will be held operative from and after that time, where no attempt has been made to assert the right of redemption during that period.[40] And a rule of the federal court, requiring a judgment creditor redeeming from a foreclosure sale to pay the redemption money to the clerk of the court, instead of to the officer holding the execution (as prescribed by the state statute), is proper, as it belongs within the domain of practice and does not affect the substantial right of redemption.[41] The same remark applies to a rule of the federal court requiring a person redeeming from a foreclosure sale under decree of such court to pay, in addition to the amount required to effect the redemption, a commission of one per cent. to the clerk of the court, this being in accordance with the federal statute regulating the fees and commissions of the clerks.[42] But a state statute requiring a person seeking to redeem from a mortgage, in certain cases, to tender the amount due on the mortgage, has regard solely to suits in the courts of the state, and does not impose a limitation upon the jurisdiction of the federal courts in equity.[43]

[38] Orvis v. Powell, 98 U. S. 176; Brine v. Insurance Co., 96 U. S. 627; supra, § 330.

[39] Allis v. Northwestern Mut. Life Ins. Co., 97 U. S. 144.

[40] Suitterlin v. Connecticut Mut. Life Ins. Co., 90 Ill. 483.

[41] Connecticut Mut. Life Ins. Co. v. Cushman, 108 U. S. 51.

[42] Blair v. Chicago & Pac. R. Co., 11 Biss. C. C. 320, 12 Fed. Rep. 750.

[43] Gordon v. Hobart, 2 Sumn. 401, Fed. Cas. No. 5,609.

§ 493. Decree for Deficiency.—In the absence of a rule of the Supreme Court authorizing it to be done, it was not competent for an inferior federal court to make a decree that the mortgagor should pay the balance that might remain unsatisfied after exhausting the proceeds of the mortgaged property.[44] But this case has been covered by Equity Rule No. 92, which provides that "in suits in equity for the foreclosure of mortgages in the circuit courts of the United States, a decree may be rendered for any balance that may be found due to the complainant over and above the proceeds of the sale or sales, and execution may issue for the collection of the same as is provided in the eighth rule of this court regulating equity practice where the decree is solely for the payment of money." Under this rule, it is held that, when the proceeds of the foreclosure sale are less than the amount due on the mortgage, the complainant is entitled to a deficiency judgment as a matter of right.[45] But the rule does not authorize a deficiency decree unless the bill shows that the amount is actually due.[46] It is also said that a vendor's lien expressly reserved on the face of the deed, has, in equity, the same effect as a mortgage, and therefore comes within the provision of the rule under consideration.[47]

§ 494. Attorneys' Fees.—In regard to the validity and effect of a stipulation in a mortgage, providing for the allowance of a solicitor's fee to the complainant, in case of foreclosure, and for its payment out of the proceeds of the sale, and in respect to the authority of the court decreeing foreclosure to include in its judgment a fee so stipulated for, the federal courts will be governed by the statutes and judicial decisions of the courts of the state wherein the proceeding for foreclosure is brought. If, by the law of the state, such a stipulation is unlawful and void, it cannot be enforced in a federal court upon the foreclosure of a mortgage on land in that state.[48] And conversely, if the laws of the state recognize an agreement of that kind as valid, the complainant in a federal court will have

[44] Noonan v. Lee, 2 Black (U. S.) 499; Orchard v. Hughes, 1 Wall. 73.

[45] Northwestern Mut. Life Ins. Co. v. Keith, 23 C. C. A. 196, 77 Fed. Rep. 374. Compare Phelps v. Loyhead, 1 Dill. 512.

[46] Ohio Cent. R. Co. v. Central Trust Co., 133 U. S. 83.

[47] White v. Ewing, 16 C. C. A. 296, 69 Fed. Rep. 451.

[48] Bendey v. Townsend, 109 U. S. 665; Gray v. Havemeyer, 10 U. S. App. 456, 3 C. C. A. 497, 53 Fed. Rep. 174.

the same right, in regard to recovering attorneys' fees, as in a court of the state.

§ 495. **Writ of Assistance to Purchaser.**—A court of the United States which has decreed the foreclosure of a mortgage and the sale of the property, may employ the writ of assistance to put the purchaser in possession. In one of the decisions of the Supreme Court it was remarked by Mr. Justice Field: "A writ of assistance is undoubtedly an appropriate process to issue from a court of equity to place a purchaser of mortgaged premises under its decree in possession after he has received the commissioner's or master's deed, as against parties who are bound by the decree and who refuse to surrender possession pursuant to its direction or other order of the court. The power to issue the writ results from the principle that the jurisdiction of the court to enforce its decree is co-extensive with its jurisdiction to determine the rights of the parties and to subject to sale the property mortgaged. It is a rule of that court to do complete justice when that is practicable, not merely declaring the right, but by affording a remedy for its enjoyment. It does not turn the party to another forum to enforce a right which it has itself established. When, therefore, it decrees the sale of property, it perfects the transaction by giving with the deed possession to the purchaser. But the writ of assistance can only issue against parties bound by the decree, which is only saying that the execution cannot exceed the decree which it enforces."[49]

§ 496. **Decree Not Reviewed or Vacated by State Courts.**—A decree of a federal circuit court for the foreclosure of a mortgage cannot be vacated or set aside by the state courts, on the ground of any error or irregularity in the proceedings not affecting the jurisdiction, and a redemption allowed from the mortgage. An error in allowing a sale without redemption will not divest the federal court of jurisdiction. If there are any equitable grounds for relief against such a decree, they must be presented to the federal court. So, where a decree of strict foreclosure has been rendered in the federal court against a person under disability (as, a lunatic), that court is the only proper forum in which to apply for relief against the decree. The state courts have no power or authority to review, revise,

[49] Terrell v. Allison, 21 Wall. 289.

or correct the decree.[50] So, where the federal court had jurisdiction of the parties and the subject-matter, and the statutory time for redemption has expired, a state court will not decree a redemption on the ground that, pending the foreclosure suit, an agreement was made to reduce the rate of interest and extend the time of payment of the mortgage debt.[51] Similarly, a state court has no jurisdiction or power to interfere, by injunction, with a decree of foreclosure made by a United States circuit court in any case where the latter court had full jurisdiction of the parties and of the subject-matter of the action.[52]

[50] Maloney v. Dewey, 127 Ill. 395, 19 N. E. Rep. 848.

[51] Windett v. Connecticut Mut. Life Ins. Co., 130 Ill. 621, 22 N. E. Rep. 474, affirming 27 Ill. App. 68.

[52] Gernsheim v. Olcott, 7 N. Y. Supp. 872.

INDEX.

[THE NUMBERS REFER TO SECTIONS.]

A.

JUDGMENT CREDITORS,
    of mortgagor, redemption by, 322.
        rights under statute, 329.
    sharing in surplus on foreclosure, 460.

JUDICIAL SALE,
    purchase at, when treated as a mortgage, 20.
    purchase at, for benefit of another, when an equitable mort-
      gage, 37.
    of mortgaged lands, 266.
        purchase by mortgagee, 289.
        subrogation of purchaser paying off mortgage, 312.

JUNIOR MORTGAGEE,
    rights of, as against senior mortgage for future advances, 125.
    right of, to plead usury in senior mortgage, 137.
    impeaching senior mortgage as given for gambling debt, 147.
    rights of, as against unrecorded senior mortgage, 153.
    record of senior mortgage as notice to, 154.
    when entitled to priority over senior mortgage, 166, 169.
    duty of senior mortgagee to protect security, 170.
    right to attack validity of senior mortgage, 171.
    rights of, on paying off senior mortgage, 172.
    doctrine of tacking, 173.
    redemption from elder mortgage, 174.
    cannot compel foreclosure of senior mortgage, 175.
    effect of foreclosure of senior mortgage, 176.
    doctrine of marshalling securities, 177.
    foreclosure of junior mortgage, 178.
    how affected by release of elder lien, 277.
    right to pay off senior mortgage, 294, 347.
    subrogation to rights of senior mortgagee, 312.
    redemption by, from senior mortgage, 323.
    contribution as between junior mortgagees, 341.
    allowance to, for senior mortgage paid off, 347.
    as party to foreclosure of senior mortgage, 397.
    foreclosing, joinder of senior mortgagee, 398.
    cross-bill by, on foreclosure of senior mortgage, 402.
    appointment of receiver on application of, 411.
    allowance of attorney's fee to, 456.
    right to surplus on foreclosure, 461.
    surplus on trustee's sale under power, 485.

JURISDICTION,
    of scire facias for foreclosure of mortgage, 354, 355.
    of suit in equity for foreclosure, 362-368.
        jurisdiction in general, 362.
        service of process, 363.
        non-resident defendant, 364.
        property in possession of receiver, 365.
        conflicting jurisdiction, 366.

612   INDEX.

[THE NUMBERS REFER TO SECTIONS.]

616 INDEX.

V.

VACATING,

decree of foreclosure, 423.
sale on foreclosure, 439.
sale under deed of trust, 481-483.

VALIDITY,

of corporate mortgages to directors or stockholders, 54.
of mortgage, as affected by fraud, 138-142.
    by undue influence, 143.
    by duress, 144.
    by illegality of consideration, 145-147.
what law governs, 148.
of senior mortgage, impeachable by junior mortgagee, 171.
of decree of foreclosure, 422.

VENDEE,

under executory contract for purchase of land, may mortgage his interest, 107.
cannot claim homestead as against purchase-money mortgage, 113.
of mortgaged land, right to plead usury, 136.
rights of, as against unrecorded mortgage, 153, 253.
record of mortgage as constructive notice to, 154.
of mortgaged lands, liability of, to mortgagee, 252
    purchase "subject to" mortgage, 255.
    assumption of mortgage by, 256.
    estoppel to deny validity of mortgage, 258.
    personal liability of, 259.
    mortgagee's right of action against, 260.
    liability of purchaser by mesne conveyances, 261.
    right to pay off mortgage, 294.
    subrogation to rights of mortgagee, 313.
at foreclosure sale, see "Purchaser."
of mortgaged land, redemption by, 322.
contribution between successive vendees, 339.
of mortgagor, adverse possession by, 379.
    as party to foreclosure suit, 388.
    deficiency decree against, 428.

VENDOR,

title of, under executory contract of sale of land, is mortgageable, 107.
of mortgaged lands, liability of, to mortgagee, 262, 263.

VENDOR'S LIEN,

implied, not assignable, 38.
express, enforceable as a mortgage, 38.
holder of, entitled to redeem from mortgage, 322.

VOLUNTARY ASSIGNMENT,

for creditors, distinguished from mortgage, 10.